Uncle John's MONUMENTAL BATHROOM READER®

Including

*Uncle John's All-Purpose Extra Strength
Bathroom Reader*

and

*Uncle John's Supremely Satisfying
Bathroom Reader*

By the Bathroom Readers' Institute

iv

Uncle John's Monumental Bathroom Reader
is a compilation of the following previously
published Bathroom Reader titles:
Uncle John's All-Purpose Extra Strength Bathroom Reader
ISBN: 1-57145-494-2 (first printing 2000)
Uncle John's Supremely Satisfying Bathroom Reader
ISBN 1-57145-698-8 (first printing 2001)

For information, write: The Bathroom Readers' Institute,
P.O. Box 1117, Ashland, OR 97520
www.bathroomreader.com
888-488-4642

Library of Congress Cataloging-in-Publication Data
Uncle John's monumental bathroom reader : including Uncle John's
all-purpose extra strength bathroom reader and Uncle John's
supremely satisfying bathroom reader / by the Bathroom Readers'
Institute.
p. cm
ISBN-13: 978-1-59223-839-2 (hardcover)
ISBN-10: 1-59223-839-4 (harcover)
1. American wit and humore. 2. Curiosities and wonder. I. Bathroom
Readers' Institute (Ashland, Or.) II. Uncle John's All-Purpose Extra
Strength Bathroom Reader. III. Uncle John's Supremely Satisfying
Bathroom Reader. IV. Title: Monumental bathroom reader. V.
Title: Bathroom reader.
PN6165.U5375 2007
081.2'07--dc22
007004573

Printed and bound in Canada
08 09 10 11   9 8 7 6 5 4 3

THANK YOU!

The Bathroom Readers' Institute sincerely thanks the following people whose advice and assistance made this book possible:

Gordon Javna	Howard Richler
John Dollison	Matt Marchesy
JoAnn Padgett	Bill Zurynetz
Melinda Allman	Claudia Bauer
Amy Miller	Eric Kennan
Sandy Ursic	Dan Mansfield
Jeff Altemus	Gideon Javna
Jay Newman	Rebecca Kaiser
Julia Papps	Marley & Catie Pratt
Brian Boone	Spectrum Books
Jennifer Payne	Sydney Stanley
Connie Vazquez	Maggie Javna
John Javna	Kim Weimer
Michael Brunsfeld	Laurie Larson
Sharilyn Hovind	Sam & Dave Hartstein
Jennifer Massey	Mana Monzavi
Jennifer Strange	Liz Stahlman
John Darling	Dee & Keller
Jeff Cheek	Eric Stahlman
Elizabeth McNulty	Sam Javna
Taylor Clark	Paula Leith
Selene Foster	Raincoast Books
Janet Spencer	Shobha Grace
Dylan Drake	Porter the Wonderdog
Sharon Freed	Thomas Crapper

* * *

"Truth is stranger than fiction—fiction has to make sense."
—**Leo Rosten**

Hiya, Sophie! Hiya, Jesse!

CONTENTS

Because the BRI understands your reading needs, we've divided the
contents by subject, as well as by length:

Short—a quick read

Medium—2 to 3 pages

Long—for those extended visits, when something a little more
involved is required

*Extended—for those leg-numbing experiences

INTRODUCTION

Greetings from the Bathroom Readers' Institute! Here it is, in the palm of your hands: *Uncle John's Monumental Bathroom Reader.*

Why "monumental"? Well, we at the BRI can't get enough of monuments—the Great Wall of China, Mount Rushmore, the World's Largest Ball of Twine—all those awe-inspiring creations that are bigger than life and built to last. And that's exactly what we wanted to bring you—a huge book that will stand the test of time, full of the most fascinating facts and the strangest stories we could find. It's built for all occasions—everything from a quick pit stop to a long, long reading voyage.

How did we build a book so *Monumental*? First, we searched through two of our most popular titles, *Uncle John's All-Purpose Extra Strength Bathroom Reader* and *Uncle John's Supremely Satisfying Bathroom Reader.* Then we chose the best bits of bathroom reading from each, carefully rearranged them for maximum impact, and bound them up in this hardcover, road-ready package.

If you're new to *Bathroom Readers*, we're glad you're here. And we hope this first taste of what we're all about will capture your curiosity and lead you to our other *Bathroom Readers*—more than 30 and still counting!

And for you long-time fans, let us say again how much we appreciate your enthusiastic support and your love letters. In these pages you'll find an extra-large smorgasbord of the kinds of stories, articles, and trivia that you've come to expect in a *Bathroom Reader*, and maybe even a few classics that you recall. But do you *really* recall them? Okay, think fast: In what American war was the submarine first used? And Teddy Roosevelt was a big fan of those cuddly bears named after him, right?

What else have we got? Well, just look here:

• The *real* story behind those IQ tests you had to take in school (starting on page 406).

• Multi-part stories on: the history of Tarzan (page 510); Dracula and other creepy vampires (throughout the book); the bloody, bone-crunching history of football (page 55); the invention of the submarine (page 420); the fascinating story of photography (throughout the book); and even the dope on soap operas (page 213).

• *Hogan's Heroes*: harmless sitcom, or tasteless exploitation? (Page 455.)

• Mount Pelée, Mount Saint Helens, and other volcanoes that will scare the lava out of you (pages 45, 188, 237, and 303).

• Then there's a section on Canadiana. To our loyal readers from the Great White North—think you know the origin of the Royal Canadian Mounted Police? Turn to page 195 to find out.

• And a first: "Unkle John's Greatest Bloopers," a few of the—gasp!—mistakes we've made over the past 19 years. (Hey, we love bloopers, even our own.)

Our thanks go out to the cast of thousands who made this *Monumental* edition possible: John J, John D, Thom, Jay, Brian, Gideon, Janet Spencer, Cheeky Jeff Cheek, Taylor Clark, and all the other fabulous writers; our crack editorial team, Sharilyn, JoAnn, and Melinda; and the production staff who put the bricks in place and made them stay there—Sandy, Jennifer P, Amy, Michael, Jennifer M, Julia, and Jeff.

To all of them, we say, "If you build it, they will read."

And to all of you, we say,

Go with the Flow!

Uncle John and the BRI Staff

(Answers to trivia questions on previous page:) 1) The submarine was first used in the Revolutionary War. 2) Teddy Roosevelt hated Teddy Bears, and believed they interfered with the maternal instincts of little girls.

YOU'RE MY INSPIRATION

It's fascinating to see that some of our favorite songs were inspired by real people. Here are a few examples.

THE GIRL FROM IPANEMA. In 1962 two Brazilian songwriters named Antonio Carlos Jobim and Vinicius de Moraes were sitting in a bar near Ipanema beach. When a particularly striking woman named Heloisa Pinheiro sashayed past on her way to the beach, both men let out an "Ahhhhhh." They did that every day when she walked by. And they wrote a song about her—"The Girl From Ipanema." It became a huge hit that put the bossa nova style of Brazillian music on the map.

WONDERFUL TONIGHT. Clapton wrote this song about his wife, Patti Boyd Harrison. Don't let the title fool you—he intended the song "as an ironic and slightly exasperated comment on the amount of time she took getting ready to go out."

PEGGY SUE. The song by Buddy Holly and the Crickets was originally called "Cindy Lou" . . . until Crickets drummer Jerry Allison asked Holly to rename it so that he could impress his girlfriend Peggy Sue Rackham. It worked—Peggy Sue and Jerry eloped a year later, prompting Holly to follow up with "Peggy Sue Got Married." She recently appeared in a *Hot Rod* magazine layout alongside Buddy Holly's Chevy Impala.

MY SHARONA. In 1978 Doug Fieger met a 17-year-old high school senior named Sharona Alperin. He fell in love; she didn't. He pursued her for more than a year, writing "My Sharona," an ode to his sexual frustration. Four months after the song was written, Sharona finally came around. She and Fieger got engaged . . . but never married. Feiger's group, The Knack, made the song a #1 hit in 1979. Today Sharona sells Beverly Hills real estate—and isn't above letting her upscale customers know she is the inspiration for the song.

Martin Van Buren was the first U.S. president actually born in the United States.

COURT TRANSQUIPS

We're back with one of our regular features. Check out this real-life exchange—it was actually said in court and recorded word for word.

Clerk: "Please repeat after me: 'I swear by Almighty God…'"

Witness: "I swear by Almighty God."

Clerk: "That the evidence that I give…"

Witness: "That's right."

Clerk: "Repeat it."

Witness: "Repeat it."

Clerk: "No! Repeat what I said."

Witness: "What you said when?"

Clerk: "That the evidence that I give…"

Witness: "That the evidence that I give."

Clerk: "Shall be the truth and…"

Witness: "It will, and nothing but the truth!"

Clerk: "Please, just repeat after me: 'Shall be the truth and…'"

Witness: "I'm not a scholar, you know."

Clerk: "We can appreciate that. Just repeat after me: 'Shall be the truth and . . .'"

Witness: "Shall be the truth and."

Clerk: "Say: 'Nothing….'"

Witness: "Okay." (Witness remains silent.)

Clerk: "No! Don't say nothing. Say: 'Nothing but the truth…'"

Witness: "Yes."

Clerk: "Can't you say: 'Nothing but the truth?'"

Witness: "Yes."

Clerk: "Well? Do so."

Witness: "You're confusing me."

Clerk: "Just say: 'Nothing but the truth.'"

Witness: "Is that all?"

Clerk: "Yes."

Witness: "Okay. I understand."

Clerk: "Then say it."

Witness: "What?"

Clerk: "Nothing but the truth…"

Witness: "But I do! That's just it."

Clerk: "You must say: 'Nothing but the truth.'"

Witness: "I WILL say nothing but the truth!"

Clerk: "Please, just repeat these four words: 'Nothing.' 'But.' 'The.' 'Truth.'"

Witness: "What? You mean, like, now?"

Clerk: "Yes! Now. Please. Just say those four words."

Witness: "Nothing. But. The. Truth."

Clerk: "Thank you."

Witness: "I'm just not a scholar."

When the ground temperature is below freezing, it can't hail.

FOUNDING FATHERS

You already know the names. Here's who they belong to.

JOYCE C. HALL

Background: Hall started out selling picture postcards from a shoe box, but soon realized that greeting cards with envelopes would be more profitable.

Famous Name: He started a new company, Hallmark Cards, a play on his name and the word for quality and, in 1916, produced his first card. But the innovation that made Hallmark so successful had little to do with the cards themselves—it was their display cases. Previously, cards were purchased by asking a clerk to choose an appropriate one. Hall introduced display cases featuring rows of cards that the customer could browse through. When he died in 1982, the company he founded in a shoe box was worth $1.5 billion.

ORVILLE GIBSON

Background: In 1881 Gibson got a job working in a shoe store in Kalamazoo, Michigan, but in his spare time, he built musical instruments from wood.

Famous Name: The instruments were so popular that he quit the shoe store, and in 1902 he incorporated the Gibson Mandolin and Guitar Company. Gibson died in 1918, two years before a Gibson employee invented a microphone that would fit inside the guitar, creating a prototype of the electric guitar.

BENJAMIN FRANKLIN GOODRICH

Background: Goodrich was a surgeon in the Union Army, but when the bloody Civil War ended, he gave up medicine. In 1870 he bought the failing Hudson River Rubber Company and moved it from New York to Akron, Ohio, where it thrived.

Famous Name: In Akron, he produced his first actual product, a fire hose. The company went on to invent vinyl, synthetic rubber, and the first tubeless automobile tire, but not before changing its name to the B. F. Goodrich Company.

Alexander Graham Bell refused to have a phone in his study—the ringing drove him nuts.

DAVID PACKARD

Background: David Packard was an engineer with the General Electric Company. In 1938 he moved to California, where he renewed a friendship with William Hewlett. The two went into the electronics business, making oscillators that were smaller, cheaper, and better than anything else on the market.

Famous Name: Working from a small garage in Palo Alto, the Hewlett-Packard company earned $1,000 that first year. Today, the garage is a state landmark: "The Birthplace of Silicon Valley." Packard died in 1996 leaving an estate worth billions.

RICHARD WARREN SEARS

Background: In 1886 Richard Sears managed a railroad office in rural Minnesota. As station agent, he had the opportunity to buy an unclaimed shipment of gold watches. He quickly sold them all . . . then ordered more. He sold those, too, then took his $5,000 in profits and moved to Chicago.

Famous Name: Sears advertised for a watchmaker; the ad was answered by Alva Curtis Roebuck. Within two years they were partners, selling their wares via a mail-order catalog under the name . . . Sears, Roebuck & Co.

PAUL ORFALEA

Background: After graduating from the University of California at Santa Barbara, Orfalea opened a small copy shop next to a taco stand in nearby Isla Vista, starting with a single copy machine.

Famous Name: Business was brisk. He soon expanded the store, then branched out to the rest of California, and then all over the country. And all the stores bore his name, the nickname he got in college because of his curly red hair . . . Kinko's.

JAMES BEAUREGARD BEAM

Background: Beam was running the distillery founded by his great-grandfather, Jacob Beam, until 1920, when the Volstead Act made the sale of alcoholic beverages illegal and he had to close the place down.

Famous Name: When Prohibition was repealed in 1933, he celebrated by building a new distillery and introducing a new bourbon, which he named for himself . . . Jim Beam.

A bird's eyes, unlike human eyes, keep everything in focus at all times.

OOPS!

Everyone enjoys reading about someone else's blunders.
So go ahead and feel superior for a few minutes.

CHUTE!

"Twenty-year-old Mie Larsen was enjoying a Sunday tennis match with her boyfriend in Guildford, Surrey, when a British Army parachutist accidentally landed on her and knocked out her teeth. Parachutist Sgt. Gary Bird of the Royal Artillery display team was supposed to land a quarter of a mile away. 'I was in the middle of a game when I suddenly heard somebody shout, "Watch out!"' said Larsen. 'I saw this man coming straight at me, feet first, at high speed.' She tried to run out of the way but became trapped in the net, and Sergeant Bird landed on her back. Larsen, who suffered a fractured wrist, cuts, and bruises in addition to the broken teeth, plans to sue the Ministry of Defense."

—"The Edge," *The Oregonian*

PU-U-USH

BIRCHINGTON, England—"A 31-year-old woman had to be rescued by firemen after getting stuck in a dog flap. She and a friend were coming back from a late-night party and stopped at a friend's house where the pair were supposed to be dog-sitting. After discovering that the house keys were lost, she attempted to get in the house via the doggie door. She managed to squeeze the top half of her body through the opening, but her bottom half proved to be more tricky.

According to Officer Dave Coker, 'We tried pushing on her backside and pulling her by the thighs but we couldn't budge her. In the end we had to take out the complete plastic frame and cut her free.' After the rescue, the woman explained she was desperate to get into the house because the dogs inside were barking loudly."

—*Bizarre News*

DRIVE, HE SAID

LITTLETON, Colo.—"Mamileti Lakshmihart put himself in 'double jeopardy' after he backed his truck into the same patrol

---

The average car has 15,000 parts.

car that had pulled him over. After being given a warning, the 36-year-old became confused when he went to pull away and put his truck into reverse. The vehicle jerked backward and smashed the front of the patrol car, doing more than $1,000 in damage. Lakshmihart received a summons for careless driving."

—*Bizarre News*

FINDERS KEEPERS

NEW YORK—"The money came from all over—Italy, France, Turkey—intended for a United Nations environmental fund. But the $700,000 ended up in the account of a Brooklyn woman, who quit her job and spent much of the extra money before the bank noticed the error and froze the account.

Now Susan Madakor, 40, a single mother who lives in public housing, is fighting to get the money back. She went to court last week to ask a judge to grant her the money instead of the U.N.

The windfall showed up as 13 wire transfers from various countries between February and October 1998. Chase Manhattan Bank said the foreign governments used an account number with one incorrect digit. Madakor quit her $23,000-a-year job at a textile company and bought a laundry business for $100,000, set up a college fund for her 10-year-old son, paid off $30,000 in credit card debt, furnished a new apartment, and leased a van. She was negotiating to buy a liquor store when Chase discovered the mistake."

—*Anchorage Daily News*

"BUT I HAVE A LICENSE"

KALAMAZOO, Mich.—"Frank S. is the proud owner of a 1958 Edsel Corsair. However, this automobile's most unique feature, the push-button transmission, is also its most dangerous. Frank was about to take his dog, Buddy, to the store with him when he got out of the car to get something from the house. As he walked around the car, the dog stood up against the dashboard and hit the push button, putting the car in drive and pinning Frank's legs between the bumper and garage door. He was trapped for 20 minutes until his wife came home and heard him yelling for help. Amazingly, Frank suffered only bruising on both legs. The dog is no longer allowed in the car."

—*Bizarre News*

A stack of one trillion new dollar bills would be 69,000 miles high.

REVENGE!

*Revenge, Uncle John is fond of saying, is a dish best
served cold . . . with a side salad and French rolls.*

ALL SHOOK UP

Victims: Red and Sonny West, members of Elvis Presley's
"Memphis Mafia," and Dave Hebler, his bodyguard

What Happened: In July 1976, Vernon Presley fired all three men,
possibly to cut costs, possibly because Elvis was growing paranoid.

Revenge: They wrote *Elvis: What Happened?* a devastating exposé
that shattered the King's public image by revealing for the first
time the lurid and bizarre details of his private life, including his
temper tantrums, drug habit, and sex life. Two weeks after it was
published in 1977, Elvis died, leaving conspiracy theorists to speculate that the book drove him to suicide.

HELLO?

Victim: Almon Brown Strowger, a Kansas City undertaker

What Happened: In the late 1880s, a friend of Strowger's passed
away. He expected to get the funeral business, but the call never
came. He blamed the local switchboard operator, whom he suspected of steering calls to her husband—a rival undertaker.

Revenge: Strowger invented the world's first automatic telephone
exchange (and later the first dial telephone), making it possible for
people to dial directly, without the help of an operator.

WHERE THE STREETS HAVE *HIS* NAME

Victim: Cripple Creek, Colorado

What Happened: *Collier's* magazine commissioned writer and gourmet Julian Street to write a travel article about Cripple Creek,
Colorado. When he arrived in town, Street happened to stroll
down Myers Avenue and strike up a conversation with a red-
headed woman named Madame Leo, who informed him that he
was in the heart of the town's red-light district. Street described his
conversation with the bawdy lady at length in his article. Cripple
Creek's town fathers were humiliated.

Revenge: They changed the name of Myers Ave. to Julian Street.

An average dairy cow produces four times her body weight in manure each year.

BOX-OFFICE BLOOPERS

*We all love bloopers. Here are a bunch of movie
mistakes to look for in popular films.*

MOVIE: *Terminator 2: Judgment Day* (1991)
Scene: As Arnold Schwarzenegger's cyborg character
heads toward a bar, he passes a parked car.
Blooper: Arnie's cranial read-out says the car he's scanning is a
Plymouth sedan. It's actually a Ford.

Movie: *Forrest Gump* (1994)
Scene: In a sequence set around 1970, someone is shown reading a
copy of *USA Today*.
Blooper: The newspaper wasn't created until 1982.

Movie: *Camelot* (1967)
Scene: King Arthur (Richard Harris) expounds on the joys of his
mythical kingdom.
Blooper: The 6th-century king has a 20th-century Band-Aid on
the back of his neck.

Movie: *Wayne's World* (1992)
Scene: Wayne and Garth are filming their cable access show.
Blooper: The exterior shot of the house shows it's night. Look out
the window of the interior shot: it's daytime.

Movie: *The Invisible Man* (1933)
Scene: Claude Rains, in the title role, strips completely naked and
uses his invisibility to elude police.
Blooper: The police track his footprints in the snow. But check
out the footprints—they're made by feet wearing shoes.

Movie: *Field of Dreams* (1989)
Scene: Shoeless Joe Jackson is shown batting right-handed.
Blooper: The real Shoeless Joe was left-handed.

What do Mr. Rogers and Paul Newman have in common? They're both color blind.

Movie: *The Wizard of Oz* (1939)
Scene: Before the Wicked Witch of the West sends her flying monkeys to capture Dorothy and friends in the Haunted Forest, she tells the head monkey that she has "sent a little insect on ahead to take the fight out of them." What does she mean by that? She's referring to a song-and-dance sequence featuring "The Jitterbug," a bug that causes its victims to dance wildly until they are exhausted.
Blooper: The sequence was cut from the film before its release.

Movie: *Face-Off* (1997)
Scene: The hero (John Travolta) learns that a bomb is about to go off somewhere. But where? He's got six days to pry the information from the villain. We then see the bomb—it shows 216 hours.
Blooper: Do the math: 216 hours equals *nine* days. Did someone forget to tell us we've gone to 36-hour days?

Movie: *Entrapment* (1999)
Scene: Catherine Zeta-Jones's character says she needs 10 seconds to download computer files that will steal billions of dollars from an international bank. She states further that after 11:00 p.m. her computer will steal 1/10th of a second every minute, totaling ten seconds by midnight.
Blooper: More Hollywood math: One-tenth of a second per minute for 60 minutes equals only six seconds . . . four shy of the required ten.

Movie: *The Story of Robin Hood* (1952)
Scene: In one scene, Maid Marian (played by Joan Rice) wears a dress with a zipper in the back.
Blooper: Did they have zippers in the 12th century?

Movie: *Wild Wild West* (1999)
Scene: After thwarting the plans of the evil Loveless (Kenneth Branagh), Jim West (Will Smith) and Artemus Gordon (Kevin Kline) ride off into the sunset heading back to Washington, D.C.
Blooper: A romantic notion, but impossible: Washington is in the east and the sun sets in the west

---

A New Yorker could eat out every night of his life and never eat at the same restaurant twice.

LET ME WRITE SIGN— I SPEAK ENGLISH GOOD

When signs in a foreign country are in English, any combination of words is possible. Here are some real-life examples.

On the grass in a Paris park: "Please do not be a dog."

Outside a Hong Kong dress shop: "Ladies have fits upstairs."

A sign posted in Germany's Black Forest: "It is strictly forbidden on our Black Forest camping site that people of different gender, for instance men and women, live together in one tent unless they are married with each other for that purpose."

At a Belgrade hotel: "Restauroom open daily."

Outside an Athens shop: "Park one hour. Later dick dock goes the money clock."

In a Rome hotel room: "Please dial 7 to retrieve your auto from the garbage."

On a menu in Nepal: "Complimentary glass wine or bear."

In a Paris guidebook: "To call a broad from France, first dial 00, then the country's code and then your number."

In a Tokyo rental car: "When passenger of foot heave in sight, tootle the horn. Trumpet him melodiously at first, but if he still obstacles your passage then tootle him with vigor."

Detour sign in Japan: "Stop: Drive Sideways"

At a Seoul hotel desk: "Choose twin bed or marriage size; we regret no King Kong size."

In a Chinese menu: "Cold Shredded Children and Sea Blubber in Spicy Sauce"

On packaging for a kitchen knife in Korea: "Warning: Keep out of children."

On an Italian train: "Water not potatoble."

Good start: A one-day-old antelope can run 23 mph.

WORD ORIGINS

Ever wonder where these words come from?
Here are the interesting stories behind them.

MAYDAY
Meaning: A distress signal
Origin: "Mayday!—the international radio distress signal—has nothing to do with the first of May. It represents the pronunciation of the French *m'aider*, 'help me,' or the latter part of the phrase *venez m'aider*, 'come help me.'" (From *Word Mysteries & Histories*, by the editors of The American Heritage Dictionaries)

CASTLE
Meaning: A large building, usually of the medieval period, fortified as a stronghold
Origin: "*Castle* was one of the earliest words adopted by the British from their Norman conquerors. Originally hailing from the Latin *castellum* (diminutive of *castrum*, 'fort'), it reminds us that Old English also acquired *castrum*, still present in such place-names as Doncaster and Winchester. From Old French's *chastel* (a version of *castel*) came the word *château* (circumflex accent marking the lost 's')." (From *The Secret Lives of Words*, by Paul West)

CARTEL
Meaning: A combination of businesses formed to regulate prices, or of political interest groups in order to promote a particular cause or legislation
Origin: "The word comes from the Italian *cartello*. In the 16th century it meant a written challenge to a duel. In the 17th century it came to mean an agreement between warring nations concerning the exchange of prisoners of war. In the 20th century it acquired its meaning of an association of producers who seek to obtain monopoly advantages for their members.

Today the term refers chiefly to international associations seeking to control a world market by setting prices, restricting production, or allocating sales territories among their members." (From *Fighting Words*, by Christine Ammer)

Men of few words: 20 of the first 30 U.S. presidents did not have middle names.

GARGANTUAN

Meaning: Gigantic, colossal

Origin: "The legend of a giant named *Gargantua* had existed in French folklore for at least a century before François Rabelais wrote his masterpiece, *Gargantua and Pantagruel*, in 1532. Just before the giantess Gargamelle gave birth to Gargantua she consumed sixteen large casks, two barrels, and six jugs full of tripe. Emerging from his mother's left ear, he proceeded to cry, 'Give me a drink! a drink! a drink!' Given the enormous size of Gargantua and everything that surrounds him, it is no wonder that from his name the adjective was formed." (From Inventing English: *The Imaginative Origins of Everyday Expressions*, by Dale Corey)

SLOGAN

Meaning: A short, memorable phrase

Origin: "All slogans, whether they be catchy advertising phrases or the rallying cries of political parties, are direct descendants of Gaelic battle cries. The word itself derives from the *sluagh-ghairm* (the battle cry of the Gaels). Gaelic soldiers repeated these cries, usually the name of their clan or clan leader, in unison as they advanced against an enemy. Over the years the word came to describe any catchy phrase inducing people to support a cause or a commercial product." (From *The Facts on File Encyclopedia of Word and Phrase Origins*, by Robert Hendrickson)

MIGRAINE

Meaning: A severe recurring headache

Origin: "Migraine had its beginning as a word in the Greco-Latin parts *hemi-*, 'half,' and *cranium*, 'skull,' which is descriptive of the violent headache that attacks one-half of the head." (From *Word Origins*, by Wilfred Funk)

PALACE

Meaning: An official residence of royalty or a high dignitary

Origin: "The word comes through Old French from the Latin *Palatium*, the name of the Palatine hill in Rome, where the house of the emperor (Augustus) was situated." (From *The Oxford Dictionary of Phrase and Fable*)

FAMOUS FOR
15 MINUTES

Here's proof that Andy Warhol was right when he said that "in the future, everyone will be famous for 15 minutes."

THE STAR: Steven Thoburn, a greengrocer in Sunderland, England

THE HEADLINE: *In for a Penny, In for a Pound: Brits Chip in to Help Greengrocer Fight the System—The Metric System*

WHAT HAPPENED: In July 2001, a woman walked into Thoburn's market stall and asked for a pound of bananas, so Thoburn sold her a pound of bananas. Not long afterward, his stall was raided by agents of the Sunderland city council, who charged him with refusing to convert from pounds and ounces to the metric system as required by the European Union. He was later convicted of two counts of violating the Weights and Measures Act of 1985 and sentenced to six months' probation.

By that point, the court costs had climbed to more than £75,000. The Sunderland council promised not to sue for court costs unless Thoburn appealed his conviction and lost. Fearing bankruptcy, he agreed to give up the fight.

THE AFTERMATH: Thoburn's case resonated with British citizens who feared losing their autonomy—not to mention their their traditional pints of ale, pints of milk, and even the country mile—to unelected bureaucrats in the European Union. Supporters raised more than £100,000 for a defense fund, prompting Thoburn to resume his appeal. At last report, he's still fighting his conviction. "All I did was sell a pound of bananas to a woman who asked for a pound of bananas," he says. "What's wrong with that?"

THE STAR: Lisa Gebhart, a 25-year-old fundraiser for the Democratic Party

THE HEADLINE: *Pushy White House Intern Proves a Picture is Worth a Thousand Words and Then Some*

WHAT HAPPENED: In 1996 Gebhart went to a fundraiser for

then-President Bill Clinton. She wanted to shake hands with the president, so she made her way up to the front of the rope line just as he was approaching. "I was all beaming," she says, "just ten feet away from him. Then someone pushed me from behind, trying to get in there, very rude. . . . I had seen Monica Lewinsky around, but I didn't know her. She couldn't wait to get to Clinton." Lewinsky got a hug; all Gebhart got was a handshake.

When news of Clinton's affair with Lewinsky broke in 1998, footage of the 1996 hug, with a smiling Gebhart standing next to Lewinsky, became one of the most famous images of the Clinton presidency.

THE AFTERMATH: By the time the scandal broke, Gebhart had met a Welshman named Dean Longhurst over the Internet and was communicating with him by e-mail. Longhurst asked what Gebhart looked like. "I e-mailed him, 'Watch the news.'"

"When I saw her in real life," Longhurst told reporters in April 2001, "I thought she was even more beautiful." The two eventually met, fell in love, and got married.

THE STAR: Clint Hallam, a 48-year-old New Zealand man who lost his right hand in an "industrial accident"

THE HEADLINE: *Man Takes Hands-Off Approach to Hands-On Surgery; Still, You've Got to Hand It to Doctors for Trying*

WHAT HAPPENED: Hallam made medical history in September 1998 when a team of microsurgeons in Lyon, France, successfully attached the right forearm of a dead Frenchman to Hallam's right arm, replacing the forearm he claimed to have lost in an industrial accident a few years earlier. It was the world's first successful hand transplant. Bonus: Because the surgery was so experimental, the surgery and a lifetime supply of anti-rejection drugs were provided free.

Hallam qualified for the groundbreaking surgery following months of interviews and psychological testing. He was evaluated to determine not just whether he was emotionally capable of living with another man's hand attached to his body, but also whether he was likely to stick to the rigorous physical and drug regimens necessary to prevent his body from rejecting the forearm.

But the battery of tests failed to reveal that Hallam was lying about his "industrial job accident"—he was actually an ex-con and

---

The diamond is the only gem composed of a single element (carbon).

lost the limb in a chainsaw accident he suffered while serving time for fraud. He also turned out to be spectacularly unsuited for the surgery.

Hallam's new hand progressed to the point that he could write with it, hold a fork, and feel temperatures and pain. But then he went off his anti-rejection drugs and stopped coming in for checkups.

THE AFTERMATH: Hallam's body rejected his hand, and on February 2, 2001, he had to have it surgically removed. (The second surgery wasn't free: Hallum had to pay $4,000.) Says Dr. Nadey Hakim, "We gave him the chance of a lifetime and he ruined it."

THE STAR: "Two-Ton" Tony Galento, a saloon bouncer and professional boxer who lived in Orange, New Jersey, in the late 1930s

THE HEADLINE: *Two-Ton Tony Flattens the Champ*

WHAT HAPPENED: Two-Ton Tony wasn't much of a boxer; at 5'9", 240 pounds with a shape like a beer barrel, about all he was good at was throwing clumsy—but powerful—left hooks. His training technique consisted of sitting in the bar of New York's Plaza Hotel with his girlfriend and consuming huge quantities of beer, pasta, and cigars while his sparring partners jogged the footpaths of Central Park without him. "Why should I pay dem punks all dat money," he explained, "and then go out and run in the rain myself?"

His brush with the big time came in 1939, when he was inexplicably signed to fight Joe Louis in a championship bout at Yankee Stadium. "I'll moider da bum," Two-Ton Tony predicted. Needless to say, Louis was as shocked as everybody else when Two-Ton Tony clocked him with a haymaker early in the fight and laid him out flat on the canvas. The blow turned out to be little more than a wakeup call, however: Louis quickly made it back to his feet and proceeded to beat Two-Ton Tony so savagely that frightened ringsiders begged the referee to stop the fight, which he finally did in the fourth round. It took 23 stitches to close the cuts on Galento's face and healing his wounded pride took even more effort. For years afterward he blamed the referee for ending the fight "just when tings was goin' my way."

THE AFTERMATH: Two-Ton Tony fought 114 fights between 1929 and 1944 and won 82 of them. In 1947, by then up to 275 pounds, he turned to professional wrestling. His fans had not forgotten him—he sold out his first wrestling fight, and more than 2,000 people had to be turned away. He died in 1979.

The first person to wear silk stockings: England's Queen Elizabeth I. They were a gift.

FLUBBED HEADLINES

These are 100 percent honest-to-goodness headlines.
Can you figure out what they were trying to say?

Raleigh, N.C., Lays Down Law: Two Pigs Per Household

DR. TACKETT GIVES TALK ON MOON

CHOU REMAINS CREMATED

Mauling by Bear Leaves Woman Grateful for Life

PLO INVITED TO RAID DEBATES

Louisiana Governor Defends His Wife, Gift from Korean

ROBBER HOLDS UP ALBERT'S HOSIERY

New housing for elderly not yet dead

SILENT TEAMSTER GETS CRUEL PUNISHMENT: LAWYER

Greeks Fine Hookers

Council spits on shade tree appointment

FEDERAL AGENTS RAID GUN SHOP, FIND WEAPONS

TUNA BITING OFF WASHINGTON COAST

Connie Tied, Nude Policeman Testifies

Shouting match ends teacher's hearing

DEATH ROW INMATE SEEKS DIVORCE

MAN GOES BERSERK IN CAR SALESROOM, MANY VOLVOS HURT

TOXIC DIAPERS FOUND IN WASH.

Policeman Shot in Basque Area

CITY OUTLAWS GIVING OUT PHONE NUMBERS, ADDRESSES OF POLICE

MEN PICKY ABOUT NOSES

Yellow snow studied to test nutrition

Hand Waves Goodbye to County Board

Body search reveals $4,000 in crack

County Wants Money for Taking Dump

April Slated as Child Abuse Month

Lady luck? One in four compulsive gamblers is a woman.

LUCKY FINDS

*Ever found something really valuable? It's one of the
best feelings in the world. Here's an installment
of a regular* Bathroom Reader *feature.*

THE TRIP OF A LIFETIME

The Find: Taxi driver

Where He Was Found: In his taxicab, near Brighton in
Southern England

The Story: In August 2001, Colin Bagshaw, 39, and his girlfriend
hailed a cab and climbed in for a ride across town. In the cab,
Bagshaw's girlfriend happened to look at the driver's identification
badge and saw that his name was Barry Bagshaw—the driver was
Colin's father, whom he hadn't seen since 1966. His parents' marriage had broken up while his father was serving in the army in
Hong Kong; since then, Colin had always assumed that his father
was dead. He wasn't dead—in fact, in recent years he had been living just a few blocks from his son without realizing it. It's a good
thing they found each other when they did, because Colin was
about to move away. "The blood just drained out of me when he
said 'I'm your son,'" Barry Bagshaw, 61, told the BBC. "I didn't
recognize him."

FOWL PLAY

The Find: A piece of paper stuffed into a leather-bound datebook
from 1964

Where It Was Found: In a box of old books in Shelbyville,
Kentucky

The Story: Homeowners Tommy and Cherry Settle found the
datebook while looking through boxes in their basement. Inside
the datebook, they found a recipe for fried chicken, one that called
for 11 herbs and spices—a number that immediately clicked with
the Settles, because their home was once owned by Kentucky
Fried Chicken founder Colonel Harland Sanders. The Settles
believe the recipe may be a copy of Colonel Sanders's "Original
Recipe," a carefully guarded trade secret and the foundation on
which the $20 billion fast-food chain is built. Only a handful of

KFC employees know the recipe, and each of them is sworn to secrecy. When the company subcontracts out the recipe to other manufacturers, they always use at least two companies, so that no one else knows the complete recipe.

So is the Settles' find the genuine article? The Settles think so, because when they asked KFC about it, the chain filed a lawsuit to force them to hand the recipe over. "They didn't say anything," Cherry Settle says, "they just sent this court document." Estimated "value": priceless. If the recipe ever gets out, KFC is powerless to stop anyone else from using it.

LOST AND FOUND

The Find: A gold and sapphire ring

Where It Was Found: Stuck to the bottom of a shoe

The Story: In 1999 Katie Smith of Harrow, England, lost the ring, which was valued at $45, somewhere in her apartment. She looked for it and then gave it up for lost when she couldn't find it. Then in September 1999, she and her boyfriend Dave Gould went on a 10,000-mile trip around the world. They hiked along the banks of the Nile; they hiked across a desert; they hiked up a mountain in Costa Rica. Then they went back home to England. While Dave was cleaning off the mud that had accumulated during the trip, he found the ring . . . stuck to the sole of his hiking shoe. "It's a miracle it stayed in one piece after the pounding it took," Smith told reporters. "I never thought I'd see it again."

SUNKEN TREASURE

The Find: Bottles of beer—lots of bottles of beer

Where It Was Found: At the bottom of a river in Australia

The Story: On Easter weekend 2001, the driver of a beer truck lost control of his rig when a tire blew out as he was driving along the Tweed River in New South Wales. When the truck crashed, an estimated 24,000 bottles of beer ended up in the river. But they didn't stay there long. According to news reports, "several hundred people, some fully clad in scuba gear, spent the Easter weekend diving for the beer and loading up their cars, with one person reported to have recovered 400 bottles alone."

There's an oil well beneath the Oklahoma State capitol building.

IT'S ABOUT TIME

*It flows like a river, it flies when you're having fun,
and it waits for no man . . . but what do we really
know about time? Read on to find out.*

WHO INVENTED DAYLIGHT SAVING TIME?
Ben Franklin did. In 1784 he wrote an essay suggesting
that setting clocks ahead in the spring and behind in the
fall would be a wise idea because it would save expensive candles.
But the idea wasn't taken seriously until 1907 when a British
builder named William Willett was riding through the countryside
early one morning and noticed that in spite of the full daylight, all
the cottages' curtains were still drawn. It was a waste of daylight, he
thought, and he wrote a pamphlet advocating that the nation set its
clocks ahead by 20-minute increments on each of the four Sundays
in April, and set them back on the four Sundays in October. A bill
introduced in Parliament in 1909 was roundly ridiculed, but the
advent of World War I brought a dire need to conserve coal, so the
British Summer Time Act was passed in 1916. It set the time ahead
one hour in the spring and back one hour in the fall.

The United States followed suit and enacted Daylight Saving
Time in 1918 to conserve fuel for the war effort, but the measure
was so unpopular that it was repealed in 1919. It was reinstated
during World War II, again to conserve fuel, but when the war
ended, some localities opted to continue observing it and some
didn't. And those that did couldn't agree on when to set their
clocks forward and back. On a single 35-mile stretch of highway
between West Virginia and Ohio, for example, a traveler could
pass through no less than seven time changes. Confusion reigned.

BUS STOP

The transportation industry, led by the Greyhound Bus Company,
lobbied hard to remedy the situation, and finally in 1966 Congress
passed the Uniform Time Act. The law didn't make Daylight
Saving Time mandatory, but said that individual states needed to
observe it or not on a uniform basis.

Daylight Saving Time is now observed in about 70 countries
around the world.

In 1992 Barbie came out with her own exercise video.

Note: It's singular, not plural—it's Daylight Saving, not Daylight Savings. Why? We're saving daylight. According to the Department of Transportation, the United States saves about 1% of its energy every day DST is in effect. Maybe that makes it worth the effort for Americans to change three billion timepieces twice a year.

WHY ARE THERE 24 HOURS IN A DAY?

The standard started with the ancient Sumerians, who also invented the first known system of writing. Their mathematical system was based on the number 12, just as ours is based on the number 10. The Sumerians, it is surmised, counted not the 10 digits of the hands, but the 12 segments of the 4 fingers on each hand. Twelve was considered a magical number because it is the lowest number with the greatest number of divisors—it is easily split into half or thirds or quarters or sixths, whereas 10 can only be cut in half or into fifths.

Their systems of weights, measures, and money were all based on 12, and so was their system of time. It was the Sumerians who first divided the day into 12 parts, with each segment equal to 2 of our hours. Later, the Egyptians modified the system by dividing the day into 24 segments. And in case you were wondering, the Babylonians are responsible for our current system of having 60 minutes in an hour and 60 seconds in a minute.

WHY ARE THERE TIME ZONES?

You can thank the railroads for this one. Before the transcontinental railroads, there were no time zones. Noon in any city was whenever the sun reached the meridian of that particular place. Time actually varied by one minute for every 13 miles traveled, and cities only a few hundred miles apart had times that were different, which made scheduling trains very difficult. For example, when it was noon in Chicago, it was 12:31 in Pittsburgh, 12:17 in Toledo, 11:50 in St. Louis, and 11:27 in Omaha. At one time, U.S. railroads had nearly 300 different time zones.

This lack of consistency wasn't just inconvenient, it was dangerous. The possibility of train wrecks increased dramatically by the conflicting schedules. Something had to be done—not locally—but on a global basis.

By 1847 Great Britain had a unified time system, which meant

Versatility Ltd. of Dorset, England, manufactures bulletproof vests for dogs.

they had a single time zone across the entire country. That was fine for the small island nation. But it wasn't as easy in North America—the United States and Canada cover some 60 degrees of longitude.

In 1872 the Time-Table Convention was founded in St. Louis to look for a solution. Charles Dowd, a school principal from New York, recommended that the U.S. set up standard time zones, and brought his idea to Congress. Most lawmakers agreed with the idea, but were afraid it would upset their constituents, so the bill was stalled on the House floor for more than a decade.

STANDARD SANFORD

It wasn't until Sir Sanford Fleming, a well-respected Canadian Railroad engineer, brought a specific solution to Washington that the idea began to take hold. His idea: because there are 24 hours in a day, divide the Earth's 360 degrees by 24, which will create 24 equal time zones separated by 15 degrees.

In 1882 the Standard Time system was finally adopted, officially dividing the United States into four time zones—Eastern, Central, Mountain, and Pacific. At noon on Sunday, November 18, 1883—a day that became known as "the day with two noons"—the railroads set their clocks to this system.

On October 13, 1884, leaders from 25 nations gathered at the International Meridian Conference in Washington, D.C., divided the world into 24 time zones, with Greenwich, England, chosen to be the "prime meridian." The day would begin there, and time would change by one hour for each 15 degrees traveled from that point.

Slowly but surely the rest of the world adapted to the new time zones. Some applauded it, others rejected it—but because the railroads were the primary means of transportation and shipping at the time, people had little choice.

Still, it wasn't until 1918 that Congress got around to making the Standard Time Act a matter of law—a law made, coincidentally, in conjunction with passing the first Daylight Saving Time Act.

* * *

"We must not allow the clock and the calendar to blind us to the fact that each moment of life is a miracle and mystery."

Twenty-five percent of American men are six feet or taller.

FIRST LADY FIRSTS

Mrs. Uncle John insists that women don't read in the bathroom—and we might believe her . . . if we didn't get so many letters from women who do. In their honor, here's a bit of forgotten political history.

First Lady: Lucy Ware Webb Hayes, wife of Rutherford B. Hayes
Notable First: The first First Lady to be called a First Lady
   Background: From Martha Washington through Julie Grant, presidential wives did not have a title. In 1876, newspaper writer Mary Clemmer Ames first referred to Mrs. Hayes, wife of the 19th president, as "the First Lady" in her column, "Woman's Letter from Washington."

First Lady: Frances Folsom Cleveland, wife of Grover Cleveland

Notable First: The first First Lady to be married in the White House

Background: Frances Folsom was only 21 when she married 49-year-old President Cleveland on June 2, 1886. It was the first nuptial ceremony held in the White House for a presidential couple. Mrs. Cleveland was the nation's youngest First Lady. She was also the first First Lady to give birth to a child in the White House, when her daughter Esther was born in 1893.

First Lady: Letitia Christian Tyler, first wife of John Tyler

Notable First: The first First Lady to die in the White House

Background: John Tyler became president when President William Henry Harrison died 30 days after being sworn in. Letitia Tyler had suffered a paralytic stroke several years earlier, so her duties as First Lady were actually assigned to her daughter-in-law, Priscilla Cooper Tyler. After a lengthy illness, probably tuberculosis, Letitia died in September 1842.

First Lady: Jacqueline Bouvier Kennedy, wife of John F. Kennedy

Notable First: The first (and only) First Lady to receive an Emmy Award

---

Marlene Dietrich's beauty secret: to emphasize her high cheekbones, . . .

Background: To prod Congress into passing a bill giving permanent museum status to the White House, she conducted a tour of the mansion for television, which earned her a Special Emmy.

First Lady: Helen Herron Taft, wife of William H. Taft

Notable First: The first First Lady to decree that no bald-headed waiter or butler could serve in the White House

Background: Feeling the previous occupants of the White House were too informal and lacked dignity, Helen Taft, wife of the 27th president, thought this rule would create a favorable impression for guests. (Not to be confused with Lou Henry Hoover, wife of the 31st president, who insisted that all butlers, waiters, and footmen must be exactly five feet, eight inches tall.)

First Lady: Eliza McCardle Johnson, wife of Andrew Johnson

Notable First: The first First Lady to teach her husband to read and write (before he was president)

Background: President Andrew Johnson was born into poverty. Apprenticed to a tailor at a young age, he never spent a single day in school in his entire life. In 1827, the 19-year-old tailor married 16-year-old Eliza McCardle. Every night, after supper, Mrs. Johnson taught her husband how to read and write.

First Lady: Patricia Ryan Nixon, wife of Richard M. Nixon

Notable First: The first First Lady to visit an overseas combat zone

Background: "Visit" may be a slight overstatement. During the Nixons' 1969 trip to South Vietnam, Pat Nixon flew over the troops in an open helicopter.

First Lady: Florence Kling Harding, wife of Warren G. Harding

Notable First: The first First Lady to vote

Background: Women were granted the right to vote in August of 1920—perfect timing for Florence Harding, a strong supporter of Women's Suffrage. A couple of months later she cast her first ballot (presumably) for her husband Warren, who won the election by a landslide.

... she had her upper molars removed.

MOW 'EM DOWN

*You'd be surprised how many times lawnmowers find their way
into the news for one reason or another. Here are just a few
of the "clippings" that we've collected over the years.*

OBI-LAWN KENOBI

In 2000 the German garden equipment maker Wolf-Garten introduced a prototype of the first mower in the world that cuts grass using lasers instead of blades. Called the Zero, the mower uses a computer-guided array of four powerful lasers capable of cutting grass to an accuracy of one millimeter. And that's only the beginning—a stream of air then mixes the zapped blades with fertilizer before dumping them back on the lawn. The mower comes complete with a leather seat, CD player, and even Internet access. Estimated retail price when the commercial model hit the market in 2002: $30,000.

A MORE NATURAL APPROACH

Scientists at Australian National University prefer a more low-tech approach: They've introduced the Rolling Rabbit Run, the world's first lawnmower powered entirely by rabbits. Constructed from bicycle wheels, chicken wire, and buckets, the device is basically a cylindrical rabbit cage that rolls around on the lawn as the rabbits eat the grass and fertilize it "naturally." Perfecting the mower took a little longer than expected because scientists couldn't get the rabbits to roll the cage on their own. They finally solved the problem by replacing the original pair of rabbits—one male, one female—with two males, after discovering that the male and the female kept stopping to mate.

LAWN JOCKEY

In 1997, 12-year-old Ryan Tripp of Beaver, Utah, hopped onto his dad's riding lawnmower and set out for Washington, D.C., more than 3,000 miles away. He made the trip (with his parents' permission) to raise money for a four-month-old girl in his town who needed a liver transplant. Ryan arrived in Washington 42 days later, shattering the record for the world's longest trip on a lawnmower. Still, not everything went according to plan: Tripp had

---

Why isn't iron added to milk? Iron-fortified milk turns coffee green.

hoped to mow the White House lawn when he arrived, but he couldn't get permission and had to settle for mowing a patch of grass at the U.S. Capitol. Bonus: He got to skip five weeks of school.

THE LAWN ARM OF THE LAW

- In 1992 author Stephen King sued to have his name removed from Stephen King's *Lawnmower Man*, a film based on his short story by the same name. King's suit alleged that the movie bore no resemblance to his original story—the tale of a man who "cuts his lawn by eating it, and is ultimately swallowed by a lawnmower."

- In December 1999 Sacramento, California, police were called to the residence of one Francis Karnes, 39, after neighbors reported hearing shots fired. They arrived several minutes later. Sure enough, Karnes had indeed fired off a few shots—at his lawnmower, after it refused to start. He was arrested and charged with reckless endangerment; no word on whether the mower survived the assault.

- In March 1995, an unidentified 54-year-old Norwegian man was convicted of drunken driving—on a lawnmower—near the town of Haugesund. According to newspaper reports, police did not notice anything erratic about the man's driving, they just administered an alcohol test as part of a random spot-check of "motorists." The test revealed that the man had consumed the equivalent of three beers, well over the legal limit in Norway. He was convicted of driving under the influence, fined $795, and sentenced to 24 days in jail. But a court later suspended the sentence after concluding that "the lawnmower's top speed of 6 mph was too slow to be dangerous."

- On a Saturday morning in July 1996, Rickey Worthley of Belton, Missouri, woke up his 17-year-old son Michael at 6 a.m. and told him to mow the lawn. When Michael told his father that 6 a.m. was too early to mow the lawn and that he wanted to sleep a few hours longer, Worthley dragged the mower into Michael's room, fired it up, and started mowing the carpet. Michael called the cops on pop; they arrested Worthley and charged him with assault. Injured party: the carpet.

Armadillos can walk underwater in order to cross rivers.

CAMERA OBSCURA

Uncle John has an interesting chicken-and-egg question for you: What came first, the camera or the film? If you think they were invented at about the same time, this story will surprise you.

PICTURE THIS

The ancient principle of the camera is child's play. Hard to believe? Here's a simple experiment you can try at home: Cover the windows of a room with black construction paper or aluminum foil until absolutely no light is let in. Turn out the lights. Then poke a tiny hole in the paper or foil, so that a single pinprick of light enters the room and strikes the wall opposite the windows. What do you see?

If you do it just right, when the light enters the "dark room" (*camera obscura* in Latin) and hits the wall, it will form a faint upside-down image of the view outside the window. This simple phenomenon is the basis upon which the science of photography is built.

One of the first people to make note of such an image was a Chinese scholar Mo Ti, who lived in the fifth century B.C. In the 10th century A.D., Arab physicist Alhazen discovered that the smaller he made the hole, the sharper the image came into focus. If the hole was tiny enough, the image became very clear.

THROUGH THE LOOKING GLASS

Reproducing the image created by a camera obscura was easy: you simply held a piece of paper up against the wall, so that the image landed on the paper, then traced it. The camera obscura became a useful scientific tool. Scientists built special "dark rooms" for the sole purpose of studying the sky, eclipses, changes in the seasons, and other natural events. The tracings made with the aid of the camera obscuras were so detailed and accurate that by the 1500s, people were using them to paint portraits, landscapes, and other scenes.

In 1568 a professor at the University of Padua named Daniello Barbaro discovered that replacing the primitive pinhole with a glass lens brought the camera obscura image into a brighter and sharper focus.

Ice covers about 15 percent of the Earth's land mass.

In the 17th century, scientists and artists developed portable camera obscuras that allowed them to study objects in the field. Early versions were essentially lightproof tents with lenses sewn into the walls. Later versions were two-foot-long wooden boxes that projected an image onto a piece of frosted glass built into the lid. The user could then trace the image by placing a piece of paper over the glass.

PUTTING THINGS IN PERSPECTIVE

The images created by these early single-lens camera obscuras were circular in shape, with distortion along the edges. In the 1700s, a complex multilens system was introduced that corrected the distortion, and the camera obscura became as common a part of the painter's art as brushes and paint.

Artists weren't the only ones putting the camera to use— explorers took them on expeditions all over the world so that they could record the wonders they encountered. In the process, the boxes changed the way people saw the world.

IMAGE PROBLEMS

For all of these improvements, there was still no way to capture the camera obscura's image other than by manually tracing it. There it was, tantalizingly projected onto a wall or a pane of frosted glass. You could look at it, you could reach out and touch it. But capturing the actual image was as impossible as capturing one's own shadow. It would remain so for another 75 years . . . until the invention of film.

So which came first, the camera or the film? The camera—by centuries.

For "The History of Photography," turn to page 76.

* * *

THE TIMES THEY ARE A-CHANGIN'

The state of Arizona does not follow Daylight Saving Time, with the exception of the Navajo Reservation, which does—except for the Hopi Partitioned Land which lies inside the Navajo Reservation, which doesn't.

Actress Tuesday Weld was born on a Friday.

CLASSIC HOAXES

*The BRI library is full of books on hoaxes. We love them. It's
amazing how many times people have pulled off clever scams . . .
and gotten away with it. Here are a few of our favorites.*

THE MYSTERIOUS CHICKEN OF THE APOCALYPSE

Background: In a small village near Leeds, England, in
1806, a hen laid an egg that had the words "Christ is Coming,"
inscribed in black on its surface. The hen's owner, a woman named
Mary Bateman, explained that God had come to her in a vision
and told her that the hen would lay a total of 14 such eggs, at
which point the world would be destroyed in the apocalypse. Only
the holy would survive to live with Christ in heaven; everyone else
was condemned to burn in hell.

But there was some good news: God had given Bateman
special slips of paper sealed with the inscription "J.C." Anyone
possessing one of these slips would be automatically admitted into
heaven . . . and Mary Bateman was willing to part with the papers
for a shilling apiece.

"Great numbers visited the spot, and examined these wondrous
eggs, convinced that the day of judgement was near at hand,"
Charles Mackay writes in *Extraordinary Popular Delusions and the
Madness of Crowds.* "The believers suddenly became religious,
prayed violently, and flattered themselves that they repented them
of their evil courses." By the time the 14th and final egg was about
to be laid, more than 1,000 people had coughed up a shilling to be
admitted into heaven.

Exposed: A doctor who was skeptical of the story traveled to Leeds
to investigate the eggs in person. When he discovered that the
messages had been written on them with corrosive ink, he
informed the local authorities, who raided the tavern where the
chicken was being kept . . . just as Mary Bateman was cruelly shov-
ing an inscribed egg into the hen to "lay" later that day.

Batemen was sent to jail but was soon released. No longer
able to make a living in the prophecy business, she became an
abortionist, which was illegal, and for which she was later hanged.

Q: What was wrestler Bobo Brazil's signature move? A: The "Coco Butt."

THE AMITYVILLE HORROR

Background: In 1974 a man named Ronald DeFeo murdered his parents and four siblings as they slept in their home in Amityville, New York. He was convicted of the crimes and sentenced to six consecutive life sentences in prison.

The "murder house" was later sold for a song to a struggling couple named George and Kathy Lutz, who moved in a week before Christmas in 1975. Twenty-eight days later, they moved out, claiming the house was haunted—and that the evil spirits that had driven them away probably also caused DeFeo to murder his entire family. Their story inspired the 1977 bestselling book *The Amityville Horror*, and the hit film that premiered in 1979.

Exposed: In 1979 Ronald DeFeo's defense attorney William Weber filed a lawsuit against the Lutzes, accusing them of fraud and breach of contract, claiming that they reneged on an agreement to collaborate with Weber on the book. So where did the haunted house story come from? In an interview with the Associated Press, Weber admitted that he and the Lutzes had "concocted the horror story scam over many bottles of wine."

SOBER SUE

Background: One afternoon in 1908, the managers of Hammerstein's Victoria Theater on Broadway marched a woman onstage during intermission and offered $1,000 to anyone in the audience who could make the woman—introduced as "Sober Sue"—laugh. When no one in the audience succeeded in getting Sober Sue to even crack a smile, the theater managers upped the ante by inviting New York's top comedians to try.

Over the next several weeks, just about every headlining comedian in New York City performed their best material in front of Sober Sue, hoping to benefit from the publicity if they were first to get her to laugh. Everyone failed, but Sober Sue became one of Broadway's top theater attractions.

Exposed: It wasn't until after she left town that Sober Sue's secret finally leaked out: Her facial muscles were paralyzed—she couldn't have laughed even if she had wanted to. The Victoria Theater had cooked up the "contest" to trick New York's most famous—and most expensive—comedians into performing their routines for free.

Rod Stewart once worked as a gravedigger.

RANDOM SCIENCE TRIVIA

Some fascinating facts about the world around us.

If you could tap the energy released by an average-sized hurricane, it would be enough to satisfy all U.S. energy needs for six months.

In any given year, about 26,000 meteorites land on the Earth's surface, the vast majority dropping into the oceans. Only seven people in recorded history have been hit by one.

When glass breaks, the cracks travel faster than 3,000 mph.

Gold is so rare that all of the pure gold produced in the last 500 years would fit inside a 50-foot cube.

At least 100,000 separate chemical reactions occur in the human brain every second.

About 70 percent of Earth is covered with water, yet just one percent of it is drinkable.

Sound travels through steel 15 times faster than it travels through air.

To escape the Earth's gravitational pull, a spacecraft has to move faster than seven miles per second—a speed that would take you from New York to Philadelphia in under 20 seconds.

Rain contains vitamin B_{12}.

According to a University of Michigan study, men are six times more likely to be struck by lightning than women are.

If you could capture a comet's entire 10,000-mile vapor trail in a container, the condensed vapor would occupy less than one cubic inch of space.

Earth travels through space at 66,600 miles per hour—eight times faster than the speed of a bullet.

Goodyear once made a tire entirely out of corn.

THE BIRTH OF
THE DISHWASHER

We mentioned Josephine Cochrane briefly in our Fourth Bathroom
Reader, *but we've wanted to tell the whole story for years. Thanks
to her, most of us don't have to suffer through "dishpan hands."*

DISH-RESPECT

What really is the mother of invention? When it comes to
the invention of the dishwasher, necessity had nothing to
do with it. It was chipped china.

Josephine Cochrane was a wealthy socialite from Shelbyville,
Illinois. She gave a lot of dinner parties and was very proud of her
china, which had been in the family since the 17th century. But her
servants weren't particularly careful with the priceless dishes as they
washed them after each party. Pieces were chipped; pieces were
cracked; pieces were broken. Cochrane felt that the only way to protect her treasures was to wash them herself . . . but she hated the job.

Why should a rich 44-year-old woman be doing this menial job?
Why wasn't there a machine that would wash the dishes for her?
Well, there was—sort of. The first dishwasher was patented in
1850 by Joel Houghton. It was a wooden machine that splashed
water on dishes when a hand-turned wheel was rotated. It didn't
work very well, so Cochrane decided to invent a better one.

TO THE DRAWING BOARD

First, she set up a workshop in her woodshed. She measured her
dishes, and designed wire racks to hold them. She placed the racks
inside a wheel, then laid the wheel inside a tub. The wheel turned
while hot soapy water squirted up from the bottom of the tub,
falling down on the dishes. Then clean hot water squirted up to
rinse them. And finally, the dishes air-dried. It worked.

But while she was busy working on the dishwasher, her ailing
husband died. Mrs. Cochrane was left with little money and a lot
of debt. Now she needed to follow through on this invention not
for convenience, but out of necessity. She needed to earn a living.

Cochrane patented her design in 1886. A Chicago machine

In 1950, only seven percent of American women dyed their hair. Today, 75 percent do.

firm manufactured them for her while she managed the company and marketed the product.

Although Cochrane's wealthy friends immediately ordered the "Cochrane Dishwasher" for their own kitchens, the home model did not sell well. Few homes had electricity in those days. Water heaters were rare. Most available water was hard and did not create suds well. And the price tag of $150 was huge—equivalent to about $4,500 today. Furthermore, many housewives felt that there was nothing wrong with washing dishes by hand—it was a relaxing way to end the day.

Cochrane tried changing her sales pitch to point out that the water in her dishwashing machines was hotter than human hands could stand, resulting in germ-free dishes. But it didn't matter: her strongest potential market was not private homes, it was industry.

SUCCESS!

Cochrane got her big break when she exhibited her dishwasher at the World's Columbian Expo of 1893 in Chicago. Against heavy competition from around the world, her dishwasher received first prize for "best mechanical construction for durability and adaptation to a particular line of work." And she sold dishwashers to many of the restaurants and other establishments catering to the large crowds at the Expo. Hotels, restaurants, boardinghouses, and hospitals immediately saw the advantage of being able to wash, scald, rinse, and dry dozens of dishes of all shapes and sizes in minutes. One of the concessionaires sent her this glowing tribute: "Your machine washed without delay soiled dishes left by eight relays of a thousand soldiers each, completing each lot within 30 minutes."

Cochrane continued to improve her product, designing models with revolving washing systems, a centrifugal pump, and a hose for draining into a sink. She ignored the clergy (who claimed the dishwasher was immoral because it denied women the labor to which God had called them) and the servants (who claimed it would put them out of business). The company kept growing, pushed by Josephine Cochrane's energy and ambition until her death at age 74 in 1913. By the 1950s, the world finally caught up with Cochrane. Dishwashers became commonplace in ordinary homes . . . using the same design principles she had invented 70 years before.

Kiwis are the only birds that hunt by smell.

HOY, HOY

*Professor Howard Richler, etymologist and BRI
member, sent us this explanation of why we say
what we say every time the phone rings . . . Hello?*

BACKGROUND
The common English word of greeting dates back to the
14th century. Some sources say hello descends from the Old
German hala, a form of "to fetch." Others believe the word to be a
derivative of the Middle French hola, meaning "hey there." Still
another theory claims hello is a derivative of the cry *au loup* used
by Norman English hunters when they spotted a wolf.

Today, "*Hello*" is the most common telephone greeting in the
United States. But Alexander Graham Bell, inventor of the telephone, actually preferred the term "*Ahoy.*" In fact, the first telephone operators in New Haven, Connecticut, greeted callers with
"Ahoy! Ahoy!" The problem was that "*Ahoy*" didn't resonate with
landlubbers in Peoria.

WHO IS SPEAKING?
Expressions such as "Are you there?"—one of the first telephone
salutations—were too long, and "Good day" and "Good morning"
could be confusing in a continent with so many time zones.
American phone companies hunted for a new word to politely
and neutrally initiate telephone conversations. Enter "Hello."

By the late 1890s, only 10 years after Bell's invention went into
commercial use, Hello was a clear victor over "Ahoy." It was in
such common use that telephone operators were called "hello
girls." But Bell didn't like it. On January 12, 1914, he wrote in a
letter that he had "never used the exclamation hello in connection
with the telephone. My call is, and always has been "hoy, hoy." He
spent the rest of his life lobbying for the adoption of "Hoy" or
"Ahoy."

Why did Bell disdain the use of "Hello"? Because he didn't
think of it. Who did? Bell's rival, Thomas Edison. Edison thought
"Hoy, hoy" was silly and is generally credited with introducing
"Hello" as an alternative telephone greeting.

America's most popular candy bar? Snickers.

Q & A:
ASK THE EXPERTS

Kids always ask their parents questions like "Why is the sky blue?"
Uncle John asks the experts. Here are some of their answers.

JUST BLOW IT OFF

Q: *How does blowing on food cool it off?*

A: "When you see steam rising from hot food, it's because heat is coming out. The steam acts like a blanket that helps keep the heat in. The faster you blow the blanket of steam away, the faster the heat can leave the food, and the faster the food cools down." (From *Why Does Popcorn Pop?*, by Catherine Ripley)

PERCHANCE TO DREAM

Q: *Do insects sleep?*

A: "Let's put it this way. They get quiet and curl up and look like they're sleeping. But what's really going on inside those molecule-sized brains nobody knows.

The one sure way to know if an animal is sleeping is to hook it up to a machine that measures electrical patterns in the brain. That's how we know that birds and mammals—animals like dogs, cats, cows, and pigs—actually sleep. The problem with bugs is they don't have enough brains to hook the wires to. So we don't really know what they're doing." (From *Know It All!*, by Ed Zotti)

GOOD HORSE SENSE

Q: *How much is one horsepower?*

A: "Although it was originally intended to be measured as the average rate at which a horse does work, one horsepower has now been standardized to equal exactly 550 foot-pounds of work per second, or 746 watts of power.

Speaking of watts, they're named after James Watt, the Scottish engineer who invented an improved steam engine and then created the term *horsepower*. He needed some way to convince potential customers that his engine could outperform the horse. By devising a system of measurement based on the power of a horse,

---

Mozart was five years old when he wrote the melody "Twinkle, Twinkle Little Star."

customers could easily compare the work potential of his engine versus that of the beast." (From *Everything You Pretend to Know and Are Afraid Someone Will Ask*, by Lynette Padwa)

SKY WRITING

Q: *Why do migrating ducks and geese fly in V formation?*

A: "Scientists aren't really sure why this behavior occurs. Some believe that each bird in the V receives lift from the bird in front of it. (Lift, an upward draft created by air currents rushing over and under the wing, is also what gets airplanes off the ground.) By staying in close V formation, each bird, except the leader, may get enough of a lift that it can fly longer with less effort.

It may also be that the V formation helps birds avoid midair collisions, because each bird knows its position and can see the other members of the flock." (From *101 Questions and Answers About Backyard Wildlife*, by Ann Squire)

EYE DON'T THINK SO

Q: *Will TV cause eye damage?*

A: "Although the contrast between a bright screen and a dark room will temporarily tire the eyes, there is no long-term eye damage. According to Dr. Theodore Lawwill, of the American Academy of Ophthalmology, 'children like to be as close to the action as possible and would climb into the TV if they could.' Nevertheless, young children are able to focus sharply on objects as close as a few centimeters away from their eyes.'

Dr. William Beckner, of the National Council on Radiation Protection, also dispels the notion that TV causes radiation damage: 'No matter how close you sit to the set, X-rays just aren't a problem.'" (From *The Odd Body: Mysteries of Our Weird and Wonderful Bodies Explained*, by Dr. Stephen Juan)

TREASURE TROVE

Q: *How much gold does the United States store in Fort Knox?*

A: "The U.S. Bullion Depository at Fort Knox contains approximately 315 million troy ounces of gold. At the official government price of $42.222 per troy ounce, the gold in the vault is worth $13 billion. At a market price of $300 an ounce, the gold would be worth $94.5 billion." (From *Do Fish Drink Water?*, by Bill McLain)

Queen Elizabeth II was *Time* magazine's "Man of the Year" for 1952.

TEST YOUR EGG I.Q.

How well do you know your yolks from your whites? Are you an egghead . . . or an empty shell? Take our quiz and find out.

1. Without breaking it open, how can you tell if an egg is fresh?
   a) Carefully feel the shell—if it has soft spots, the egg is rotten.
   b) Hold the egg up your ear and shake it. If you hear the yolk sloshing around inside, the egg is still fresh. A silent egg is a rotten egg.
   c) Drop the egg in a glass of water. If it sinks to the bottom and lies on its side, it's fresh. If it sinks to the bottom and "stands" on one end, it's old but probably still edible. If it floats, it's rotten.

2. Which part of the egg is known as the "chalazae"?
   a) The protective coating on the outside of the shell.
   b) The membrane separating the yolk from the white.
   c) The thin strands of egg white that connect the yolk to the shell.

3. What's the difference between Grade A and Grade AA eggs?
   a) Grade AA eggs contain twice as much vitamin A, because the hens get a diet of fortified chicken feed.
   b) Grade AA eggs have plumper yolks and thicker whites.
   c) Grade AA hens, also known as "yearlings" or "freshmen" hens, are younger and healthier than the hens that lay Grade A eggs.

4. What's the best way to store an egg in the refrigerator?
   a) With the tapered end pointing up.
   b) With the tapered end pointing down.
   c) Neither—eggs keep best when they're lying on their side.

5. Without breaking it open, how can you tell if an egg is cooked?
   a) Spin it on a flat surface—raw eggs wobble; cooked ones don't.
   b) Hold it up to a bright light—eggshells that have been cooked for seven minutes or longer are slightly transparent.
   c) Carefully examine the shell—it's physically impossible to boil an egg without cracking the shell in at least one place.

Answers on page 742.

Monkey see, monkey do: Americans eat 12 billion bananas a year.

CHI MARKS THE SPOT

Ever heard of a chiasmus? Here's a clue:
Never let a fool kiss you or a kiss fool you.

GRAMMAR LESSON

Chiasmus is one of those parts of speech you didn't know even had a name. What is it? It's a figure of speech in which the order of the words in the first of two parallel clauses is reversed in the second, which gives it extra power or wit. Here are some examples:

"Ask not what your country can do for you; ask what you can do for your country."   —John F. Kennedy

"It's not the men in my life; it's the life in my men."—Mae West

Get the idea? Chiasmus (pronounced kye-AZ-muss) is named after the Greek letter chi (x), and indicates a crisscross arrangement of phrases. Here are some more examples:

"Pleasure's a sin, and sometimes sin's a pleasure."   —Lord Byron

"The value of marriage is not that adults produce children, but that children produce adults."   —Peter De Vries

CHIASMUS CLASSICS

Certain chiasmuses, such as "All for one and one for all," and the shortened Cicero quote "Eat to live, not live to eat" are also word palindromes—where the words, when repeated in reverse order, read identically.

Chiasmuses appear to reveal hidden truths and are popular in Biblical writing:

"Whoever sheds the blood of man; by man shall his blood be shed."   —Genesis 9:6

"There is no fear in love; but perfect love casteth out fear."   —1 John 4:18

"Many that are first shall be last; and the last shall be first."   —Matthew 19:30

Red blood cells live four months. In that time they make 75,000 trips to the lungs and back.

The two lines can express contradictory sentiments, as in the French proverb "Love makes time pass; time makes love pass"—the first line is romantic, the second line strips away this romance. Ernest Hemingway was fond of asking people which of these two statements they preferred: "Man can be destroyed but not defeated," or "Man can be defeated but not destroyed."

MODERN WORDPLAY

A chiasmus can also be implied. Oscar Wilde was a master at this type of ironic wordplay. Some of his classics: "Work is the curse of the drinking class" and "The English have a miraculous power of turning wine into water."

Other implied chiasmus quips include Mae West's lines "A hard man is good to find" and "A waist is a terrible thing to mind," Groucho Marx's "Time wounds all heels," and Kermit the Frog's observation that "Time's fun when you're having flies." A hangover has been described as "the wrath of grapes," and a critic who provided a harsh opening night review was said to have "stoned the first cast."

Had enough? The elements need not even be whole words; parts of words will suffice. There's Randy Hanzlick's song lyric, "I'd rather have a bottle in front of me than have a *front*al lo*bot*omy," and the Edwardian toast "Here's *champagne* for our *real* friends and *real pain* for our *sham* friends."

Finally, consider the chiasmus contest held by *The Washington Post* some years ago. The winning entry read:

> Bill Clinton before: "I don't know how I can make this any clearer."
>
> Bill Clinton after: "I don't know how I can clear this with my Maker."

* * *

GETTING THE LEAD OUT

Plumbing pipe was originally made from wood or earthenware. Eventually lead was used. The Latin word for "lead" is *plumbum* from which we get the word "plumber."

Marlon Brando owns a remote controlled whoopie cushion.

A (BAD) NIGHT AT THE OPERA

One of Uncle John's favorite movies is the Marx Brothers'
classic A Night at the Opera. *The Marx Brothers perform some*
unbelievable—and hilarious—antics on opening night . . . but
are they so far-fetched? Here are some real-life examples
of what can happen at the opera. Honk-honk!

CARMEN GET IT

A performance of *Carmen* was being staged in a bull ring in Mexico City. The singer playing the part of Don José had a long wait between acts three and four, so he decided to dash out for a beer in a local tavern. No sooner had he entered than he was arrested by a couple of cops who saw his scruffy costume, thought he was a bum, and dragged him off to jail. When he insisted he was a tenor singing in the opera, they accused him of being drunk. He could only convince them . . . by singing. (They let him go.)

DUMB GIOVANNI

In 1958 Cesare Siepi was playing the part of Don Giovanni in the Vienna State Opera. The script called for him to descend into Hell using a stagelift. So Cesare said good-bye to the world and stepped into the netherworld. But the lift got stuck halfway down, leaving his head and shoulders visible to the audience. Stage technicians brought the lift back up and tried to lower it again, but it got stuck a second time and was raised back to stage level. Cesare sang in Italian, "Oh my God, how wonderful—Hell is full!"

NOISE POLLUTION

When *The Wreckers* opened in England in 1901, King Edward VII came to the opening. Conductor Sir Thomas Beecham later asked the king's private secretary if the king had liked the music. "I don't know," was the reply. "But you were sitting right next to him—surely he must have said something!" "Oh, yes—he did. He woke up three-quarters of the way through and said, 'That's the fourth time that infernal noise has roused me!'"

In 1915 someone made a silent movie version of the opera *Carmen.*

JUST LIKE LEMMINGS

In the opera *Tosca*, two soldiers are to execute the character Cavaradossi while the heroine, Tosca, watches in horror. Prior to the performance in San Francisco in 1961, the director had too little time to instruct the firing squad. He told them, "When I cue you, march on stage, wait until the officer lowers his sword, then shoot." When they asked how to exit the stage, he said, "Exit with the principal characters." The soldiers marched on stage and were amazed to see two people against the execution wall: Tosca and Cavaradossi. They hadn't been told which one to shoot—so when the officer dropped his sword, they had to choose—and they shot Tosca. Wrong. Cavaradossi dropped dead 20 yards away, while the person they had just shot ran over to him weeping and wailing in Italian. Tosca then climbed to the top of the castle battlement to commit suicide. The firing squad, having been instructed to exit with the principal characters, followed her, leaping to their deaths as the curtains closed.

DEADPAN PERFORMANCE

In 1849 *Charles VI* premiered in Paris. At the beginning of the aria called "Oh God, Kill Him!" a member of the opera company fell dead. The next night at the same point in the production, a member of the audience died. When the orchestra leader fell dead at the third performance, Napoléon III banned the opera for good.

SLAPSTICK OOPERA

In 1960 the diva playing the role of Donna Elvira in *Don Giovanni* in New York was to make her entrance in a sedan chair carried by two porters, then step out and begin singing. Unfortunately, she weighed a lot and the two porters struggled with the sedan chair. The porter in front set his burden down to get a better grip, which threw all the weight on the porter in the rear, who in turn threw the chair forward. The violent rocking of the chair caused the soprano inside to fall forward into a somersault, where she promptly got stuck. The porters couldn't see inside the sedan chair, had no idea what had happened, and carried her onstage like that. There was nothing for her to do except sing upside down from the chair. When they carried her offstage at the end of the song, an axe was needed to extricate her from the chair. Her first act upon regaining her freedom was to slap the two porters.

The saguaro cactus can grow four stories tall, weigh 10 tons, and live 200 years.

UNCLE JOHN'S LIST OF SIXES

Uncle John's sixth sense tells him you're going to like this page.

Nobel Prize Categories
Peace, Chemistry, Physics, Physiology & Medicine, Literature, Economics

Wives of Henry VIII
Katherine of Aragon, Ann Boleyn, Jane Seymour, Anne of Cleves, Catherine Howard, Catherine Parr

Rodeo Contests
Saddle bronco riding, Bareback riding, Calf roping, Bull riding, Steer wrestling, Team roping

Parts of the Circulatory System
Heart, Arteries, Arterioles, Capillaries, Venules, Veins

Enemies of Mankind (Hinduism)
Lust, Angst, Envy, Avarice, Spiritual ignorance, Pride

Categories of Dog Breeds
Working, Sporting, Hounds, Terriers, Nonsporting, Toy

Layers of the Earth
Crust, Upper mantle, Lower mantle, Outer core, Transition region, Inner core

Foreign Places Named for U.S. Presidents
Cape Washington, Antarctica; Monrovia, Liberia; Lincoln Island, South China Sea; Cleveland, Brazil; Mount Eisenhower, Alberta, Canada; Avenue de President Kennedy, Paris

Branches of the U.S. Armed Forces
Army, Navy, Air Force, Marines, National Guard, Coast Guard

Elements (Buddhism)
Earth, Water, Fire, Wind, Space, Consciousness

Grades of Meat
Prime, Choice, Good, Standard, Commercial, Utility

Sinister Six (Spider-Man's Arch Enemies)
Kraven the Hunter, Dr. Octopus, Mysterio, Vulture, Electro, Sandman

Hockey Positions
Center, Left wing, Right wing, Left defense, Right defense, Goalie

STRANGE LAWSUITS

These days, it seems that people will sue each other over practically anything. Here are a few real-life examples of unusual legal battles.

THE PLAINTIFF: Teri Smith Tyler
THE DEFENDANTS: Jimmy Carter, Bill Clinton, Ross Perot, IBM, American Cyanamid, BCCI, David Rockefeller, and NASA
THE LAWSUIT: Tyler claimed to be a cyborg (part human, part robot) receiving telepathic instructions from "Proteus." According to the $5.6 billion lawsuit, she claimed the defendants had a secret plan to breed and enslave millions of black women.
THE VERDICT: Not guilty. Said the judge, "If this Court cannot order dismissal of *this* complaint . . . no district court can ever dismiss *any* complaint."

THE PLAINTIFF: Oreste Lodi
THE DEFENDANT: Oreste Lodi
THE LAWSUIT: Lodi, the defendant, was beneficiary to a trust fund. Lodi, the plaintiff, claimed he was tired of the defendant controlling his estate. So Lodi sued himself, asking the court to revoke his birth certificate so that he, Lodi, the plaintiff, could take control of his money away from Lodi, the defendant, and get sole possession of the trust.
THE VERDICT: Case dismissed. The decision, the court said, was eminently fair: "Although it is true that, as plaintiff, he loses, it is equally true that, as defendant, he wins!"

THE PLAINTIFF: Freshman Jason Wilkins
THE DEFENDANT: University of Idaho
THE LAWSUIT: Wilkins "mooned" some friends from his third-floor dorm window. But as he leaned his naked butt against the glass, he fell through and plummeted to the ground below, suffering a broken vertebra and severe cuts and bruises over his entire body. Humiliated, Wilkins sued the university for failing to warn students about "the dangerous nature of windows."
THE VERDICT: Not guilty. Wilkins suffered additional injury—

An astronaut can reach the moon in less time than it took a . . .

to his ego—when the local newspaper revealed the fact that he "was not intoxicated" at the time of the accident.

THE PLAINTIFFS: Ivan Jordan, Kaziah Hancock, and Cindy Stewart, three former members of The True and Living Church of Jesus Christ of Saints of the Last Days
THE DEFENDANT: Jim Harmston, self-proclaimed prophet
THE LAWSUIT: The three claimed that they had turned over all of their money and possessions to Harmston. Value: $264,390. In return, Harmston promised them a face-to-face meeting with Jesus Christ and did not deliver. Papers filed with the court said that Harmston took advantage of their "deepest spiritual needs."
THE VERDICT: Unknown.

THE PLAINTIFF: Robert Kropinski
THE DEFENDANT: Maharishi International University
THE LAWSUIT: Kropinski sued because, after 11 years at MIU, he still had not achieved "the perfect state of life" that was promised. Nor had he learned how to reverse the aging process or how to fly, which were also promised. He had only learned to "hop with his legs folded."
THE VERDICT: The jury agreed that the university had misled Kropinski and awarded him $137,890.

* * *

IN HOT PURSUIT

Selma Troyanoski, 53, an elected member of the board of supervisors of Portage County, Wisconsin, was charged with attempting to obstruct an officer in Lake Geneva, Wisconsin. The incident began when Troyanoski pulled into a rest stop for a nap. When an investigating officer saw her slumped over and tried to investigate, she suddenly sped off, leading police on a chase at speeds of up to 110 mph.

Officers finally cornered Troyanoski in a residential neighborhood. When she refused to exit the vehicle, they smashed her car window and opened the door to pull her out. That was when they discovered she wasn't wearing pants or underwear. She had fled the cops out of embarrassment. Troyanoski explained that she prefers to drive without pants or underwear on long trips because she "gets very sweaty." She faces up to three years in prison.

. . . stagecoach to travel the length of Great Britain in the 19th century.

THE BIRTH OF SCOTCHGARD

We mentioned the accidental discovery of Scotchgard in an earlier Bathroom Reader, but we've wanted to include a longer version for years. Here's the story.

SLICK DISCOVERY

After graduating from college in 1952, Patsy Sherman took a part-time job as a chemist with 3M. One day, while working on a new kind of synthetic rubber, an accident occurred: a bottle of a synthetic latex compound fell on the floor, splattering her assistant's tennis shoes with a milky, saplike substance.

They tried to wipe it off with soap, water, alcohol, and other solvents, but nothing worked—everything they tried just rolled off. Then she noticed that although the compound didn't alter the look or feel of the canvas shoe, as the shoe got dirtier, the spots where the chemical had landed remained white and clean.

Sherman found that fabric dipped in the compound prevented anything from penetrating it. The compound seemed to surround each fiber with a chemical shield that was impervious to water, oil, and dirt. It took three years to refine it, but when she was done she had invented a revolutionary new product that made fabrics stain-proof. 3M named it Scotchgard.

Eventually, dozens of Scotchgard products were developed for use on raincoats, carpets, upholstery, clothing, paper packaging, and even motion-picture film. It was one of 3M's most profitable products ever and funded their growth into a global industry.

Update: Scientists recently discovered that Scotchgard molecules pervade the world environment and are present in the bodies of most Americans. It's not necessarily a dangerous contamination, but because the molecules are inert, they will never deteriorate. 3M has been unable to find a more environmentally friendly formula, so in the year 2000, they announced they were phasing out the product. That's bad news for the La-Z-Boy company: 90 percent of their fabrics were once treated with Scotchgard.

Ten books on a bookshelf can be arranged in 3,628,800 different ways.

MOUNT PELÉE

What's worse than a volcanic eruption in your town?
A volcanic eruption in your town on Election Day. Here's one
of the strangest events in the history of Western democracy.

ELECTION DAY POLITICS

One of the worst volcanic disasters in history was caused not by the eruption . . . but by politics.

Mount Pelée, on the island of Martinique in the Caribbean Sea, began smoking and shaking in late April 1902. The people of St. Pierre, the town at the base of the volcano, remembered that the volcano had rumbled years earlier, but since it had quieted down and was seemingly dormant, they weren't too concerned . . . at first.

When scalding mud flows began pouring down the mountain and ashes fell faster than they could be swept away, many changed their minds and thought the town should be evacuated. As it happened, the city's elections were only a few days away. The mayor and the governor of the island were concerned about the growing popularity of a radical political party that stood for equal rights for all races and threatened the white supremacy of the island.

Mayor Fouche and Governor Mouttet refused to allow anything to delay the election even a single day. The editor of the paper was on their side and published articles by fictional "volcano experts" who had supposedly examined the situation and said there was no danger.

BLOWBACK

Soon the volcano became more violent. A giant mudslide wiped out the sugar mill on the edge of town, taking the factory workers with it, and a huge seismic wave spawned by undersea earthquakes wiped out the entire seafront district. People began packing to leave, but found the roads out of town blocked by soldiers sent by the governor. He was determined to prevent anyone from leaving before the election.

The people went to the local church and begged the bishop to

The Incas measured time by how long it took a potato to cook.

intervene on their behalf, but he refused to go against the wishes of the state. At dawn on election day, Mount Pelée exploded. A colossal cloud of super-heated gasses, ash, and rock blew out of a notch in the crater, directly at the town four miles away, at a rate of 100 mph. Within three minutes, the entire population—including the mayor, governor, bishop, and newspaper editor—was dead. Even ships anchored offshore were set ablaze, killing crew members and passengers.

Only two people in the town survived. A black prisoner condemned to death for murdering a white man was to have been hanged that day, but the governor had granted him clemency in the hopes that it would give him some of the black vote. The prisoner was being held in an underground cell with one small window facing away from the volcano. He was horribly burned, but survived and later toured with the Barnum and Bailey Circus as a sideshow attraction.

The only other survivor was the town cobbler, a religious fanatic who had been hiding in his cellar, praying, when the mountain erupted. He, too, was terribly burned, and some reports say that he never regained his sanity after coming out of his cellar to find every single one of the townfolk—30,000 people in all—dead.

* * *

RIDICULOUS POLITICAL WORDS

- **Flugie:** A rule that helps only the rule maker.
- **Bloviate:** To speechify pompously.
- **Speechify:** To deliver a speech in a tedious way.
- **Roorback:** An invented rumor intended to smear an opponent.
- **Bafflegab:** Intentionally confusing jargon.
- **Gobbledygook:** Nonsensical explanation, bafflegab.
- **Snollygoster:** A politician who puts politics ahead of principle.
- **Boondoggle:** A wasteful or crooked government-funded project.
- **Mugwump:** A political maverick.

The term "soft-pedaling" refers to the piano pedal used to mute the tone.

UNCLE JOHN'S STALL OF FAME

Here are some creative ways that people have gotten involved with bathrooms, toilets, toilet paper, etc.

Honoree: Lam Sai Wing of Hong Kong

Notable Achievement: Building a pot of gold

True Story: When Lam Sai Wing was growing up in communist China, he dreamed of someday being rich. He eventually moved to Hong Kong and opened a jewelry store called 3-D Gold and by 2001 had the money to build the toilet of his dreams . . . out of gold. And he had enough money left over to build an entire bathroom of gold—wash basins, toilet brushes, toilet paper holders, towel holders, mirror frames, doors, even bathroom tiles. He topped it all off with a ceiling encrusted with precious gems. Total cost: $4.9 million, which Lam offsets by charging admission to the bathroom. Peeking into the restroom costs $4; to use the facilities, you have to spend at least $138 in the store.

Honoree: Greg Kotis, an inspired playwright

Notable Achievement: Writing a musical about urinals . . . and actually making it onto Broadway

True Story: Trying to live in Paris on $4 a day, Kotis slept on park benches and often had to choose between eating and using the city's pay urinals. One rainy afternoon while making such a choice (he chose food), a thought occurred to him: What if a single evil corporation—the Urine Good Company—controlled all of the pay urinals in a city?

"I just stood there maybe fifteen minutes. In the rain. Thinking it out," he says. Inspired, he wrote a play called *Urinetown, The Musical.* After a sold-out off-Broadway run, it opened on the Great White Way in September 2001. Highlight: A song called "It's a Privilege to Pee."

Honoree: Carl Rennie Davis, a pub owner in Stourbridge, England

Notable Achievement: Converting his men's room urinals into an electronic arcade game . . . of sorts

True Story: Davis installed paddle wheels in the drainpipes of his men's room urinals; then he hooked each one up to a row of vertical lights. How many lights flash depends on how long—and how "strong"—a person uses the urinal. Customers can compete to see who can light the most lights, and because extra rows of lights are mounted over the bar, ladies in the pub can follow the action.

Honoree: The Kimberly-Clark company

Notable Achievement: Building a better toilet paper roll

True Story: How can you improve on a classic? Kimberly-Clark took out the cardboard tube and made it a solid block of toilet paper. Now it's "coreless"! Here's the good news: The new roll has twice as much paper, so you change it half as often. Now, the bad news: It requires a special kind of dispenser and you can't have one—so far, they're strictly for commercial use in offices and restaurants. Maybe someday . . .

Honoree: Bob Ernst, a playwright and high school drama teacher in San Francisco

Notable Achievement: Writing and producing the only play ever staged in a bathroom

True Story: Ernst, 56, wrote a one-act play called *The John*, about a man named Alvin who meets Death in a theater men's room during an intermission of *King Lear*. Ernst staged the play in a men's room in the basement of the Maritime Hall in San Francisco, which he booked for $100 a day. Ernst, who plays both Alvin and Death, performed in front of 20 spectators who sat on folding chairs wedged into the space between the second and fourth stalls.

Why write a play that takes place in a bathroom? "Death can happen anywhere, anytime," Ernst says. "Elvis died in a john, you know. One minute you're here, the next you're gone. That's the way it is."

There are more than 300 patents on anti-snoring devices.

INCREDIBLE ANIMAL FACTS

Sit. Fetch. Roll over. Even more interesting than watching animals perform tricks we teach them is watching what they do naturally.

The world's longest earthworms—found only in a small corner of Australia—can grow to as long as 12 feet and as thick as a soda can.

Ancient Romans trained elephants to perform on a tightrope.

Squids have the largest eyes in nature—up to 16 inches across.

Australia's mallee bird can tell temperature with its tongue, accurate to within two degrees.

Not only does the three-toed sloth sleep 20 hours a day, it also spends most of its life upside down.

Most kangaroo rats never drink water.

The chamois—a goatlike mountain antelope—can balance on a point of rock the size of a quarter.

Robins become drunk after eating holly berries and often fall off power lines.

Octopus eyes resemble human eyes—the U.S. Air Force once taught an octopus to "read" by distinguishing letterlike shapes.

A woodpecker's beak moves at a speed of 100 mph.

By using air currents to keep it aloft, an albatross may fly up to 87,000 miles on a single feeding trip without ever touching the ground. That's more than three times around the Earth.

Polar bears are so perfectly insulated from the cold that they spend most of their time trying to cool down.

Whales can communicate with each other from more than 3,000 miles away (but the message takes over an hour to get there).

Domesticated elephants have learned to stuff mud into the cowbells around their necks before sneaking out at night to steal bananas.

A mouse has more bones than a human.

In 1977 New York hunters killed 83,204 deer . . . and seven fellow hunters.

THEY TOOK THE PLUNGE

In 1886 a man named Carl Graham rode a barrel through the rapids below Niagara Falls, starting a craze of riding the rapids in barrels. Soon, people started looking for a bigger challenge—riding the falls.

OVER A BARREL

There are three individual falls at Niagara. At American Falls, 300 tons of water drop 180 feet per second and boulders as big as houses litter the base. No one has ever survived a trip over it. Luna Falls, only 90 feet wide, is too small to ride. At Horseshoe Falls, 2,700 tons of water pass over every second. Rocks cannot withstand the constant onslaught of water, boulders are pulverized. But there is a deep plunge pool at the bottom, making it the only fall that can be ridden.

DAREDEVILS

Here are the people who have dared to go over Niagara Falls in a barrel:

• **Annie Edson Taylor** (1901). The first person ever to go over Niagara in a barrel, this widowed, unemployed schoolteacher was 63 years old when she did it. She used an oak wine barrel padded with cushions. After the plunge, she spent 17 minutes bobbing around before assistants pulled her ashore. Emerging dazed but unhurt, she said, "No one ought ever do that again." She was incoherent for several days afterward.

• **Bobby Leach** (1911). This circus stuntman went over the falls in a steel barrel and survived. Fifteen years later, while on tour with his famous barrel in New Zealand, Leach slipped on an orange peel and fell. He broke his leg, which later had to be amputated, leading to gangrene, which killed him.

• **Charles Stephens** (1920). A 58-year-old barber, he had a fair reputation as a high-dive and parachute artist, but thought a trip over Niagara Falls would make him really famous. He attached a 100-pound anvil to the bottom of his barrel for ballast and then got in and strapped his feet to the anvil. He surrounded himself with pillows and inserted his arms into two straps bolted inside the barrel. The force of the plunge caused the bottom to drop out of

Apples ripen after being picked. Oranges don't.

the barrel. The anvil, together with Mr. Stephens, sank to the bottom. The only part of the barrel recovered was a stave with an arm strap attached to it; Stephens' right arm was still threaded through the strap. A tattoo on the arm read, "Forget me not, Annie." Annie was his wife and mother of his 11 children.

• **Jean Lussier** (1928). Lussier made the trip not in a barrel but in a six-foot rubber ball lined with rubber tubes. After bobbing about at the bottom of the falls for an hour, he was pulled to shore and emerged unharmed in front of an audience of more than 100,000. Afterward, he sold small souvenir pieces of the inner tubes for 50 cents each. When he ran out of authentic pieces, he peddled rubber purchased from a nearby tire store.

• **George Strathakis** (1930). This 46-year-old Greek chef went over to generate publicity for his book, *The Mysterious Veil of Humanity Through the Ages*. His airtight barrel was trapped behind the falls for over 14 hours before rescuers could retrieve it; by then, it was out of air. Only his pet turtle, Sonny Boy, taken along for good luck, survived.

• **William "Red" Hill, Jr.** (1951). Hill, 38, should have known better: his father was a boatman who retrieved the bodies of suicide victims from the waters below the falls. Hill didn't use a barrel, he used "The Thing"—made of 13 inner tubes, a fish net, and canvas straps. Thousands of people watched as "The Thing" became trapped under the falling water. Finally a few inner tubes emerged from the mist. His mangled body turned up the next day.

• **Nathan Boya** (1961). He made the trip in a steel sphere covered by six layers of rubber, which he called the "Plunge-o-Sphere." He emerged unhurt to find the police waiting for him. He was fined $100.

• **Karel Soucek** (1984). The first Canadian to survive the plunge. His barrel had liquid foam insulation, two eye holes, and a snorkel. The fall took 3.2 seconds but left Soucek trapped in dangerous waters for 45 minutes before being pulled free. Fortunately, he suffered only minor injuries. Six months later, he recreated the spectacle at the Houston Astrodome in front of 45,000 spectators. His barrel was hoisted to the top of the dome by a crane and released into a water tank, 10 feet in diameter and

A sheep trained to turn the lights on and off will leave them on 82 percent of the time.

10 feet deep. But the barrel missed—it hit the edge of the water tank and killed him.

• **Steven Trotter** (1985). This Rhode Island bartender went over the falls in two plastic pickle barrels wrapped in inner tubes. At the age of 22, he became the youngest person ever to make the trip. He was fined $5,000 for the stunt, but he more than made up for that with his talk show fees.

• **Dave Munday** (1985). Munday has dared the falls four times to date. In 1985 a police officer saw him and immediately radioed Hydro-Control to cut the water flow, which stopped the barrel. Later that year he made the trip successfully in an aluminum barrel. In 1990 his barrel got stuck at the very brink of the falls, but in 1993 he succeeded again, this time in a converted diving bell, and at age 56, became the first person to go over the falls twice.

• **Peter DeBernardi and Geoffrey Petkovich** (1989). Canadian residents of Niagara Falls, they were the first people to go over the falls as a team, face to face in the same ten-foot steel barrel. Both men survived, suffering only minor injuries. Petkovich, who had been drinking, emerged wearing only a necktie and cowboy boots. They were arrested by the Niagara Parks Police.

• **Jessie Sharp** (1990). Twenty-eight-year-old Sharp rode the falls in a kayak. His plan was to gather so much momentum that he would avoid the thundering water and land in the pools at the bottom, then ride the rapids downstream to Lewiston, New York— where he had dinner reservations. He didn't wear a life jacket or a helmet—he wanted his face to show clearly on the videotape his friends were shooting. Minutes after he entered the water above the falls, police ordered the hydroelectric dam to shut the water flow, intending to stop him. It didn't stop him, but it slowed him down. He dropped over the falls like a sack of bricks. His kayak was recovered, but his body was never found.

• **Robert Overacker** (1995). The 39-year-old Overacker was attracted to thrill sports. He wanted a career as a stuntman and thought performing the ultimate stunt would provide him with good publicity. He went over the falls on a jet ski, wearing a self-inflating life vest, a crash helmet, and a wet suit. A rocket-propelled parachute was supposed to be deployed at the brink of the falls—but it failed to inflate. His body was recovered by the tour boat *Maid of the Mist*.

Fate of the only parking meter in Owyhee County, Idaho: A motorist shot it in 1979.

THEY WENT
THATAWAY

*We're not just fascinated by the way famous people
lived—we're fascinated by the way they die, too.
Here are a few stories from our BRI files.*

MARY TODD LINCOLN
Claim to Fame: Widow of President Abraham Lincoln
How She Died: In bed with "Mr. Lincoln."
Postmortem: Mrs. Lincoln's life was filled with tragedy: Her son
Eddie died from tuberculosis in 1850 when he was only 3; her son
Willie died of typhoid fever in 1862 when he was 11; her husband
was assassinated in 1865; and her 18-year-old son Tad died in
1871. Only one of her children, Robert Lincoln, survived into
adulthood.

Mary Lincoln never recovered from the shock of her husband's
death, and her son Tad's death sent her completely over the edge.
She suffered from hallucinations and by 1875 was so disturbed that
she attempted suicide. Robert had her committed to an asylum
that very night.

Four months later, she was released and sent to live with her
sister in Illinois, and in June 1876, a jury ruled that she had regained her sanity. In 1879 Mrs. Lincoln's health began to deteriorate. By now reclusive and nearly blind, she spent most of the last
18 months of her life locked in her bedroom, where she slept on
one side of the bed because she was convinced that her husband
was sleeping on the other side. She died on July 16, 1882, at the
age of 63, after suffering a stroke.

JOHN DENVER
Claim to Fame: A singer and songwriter, Denver shot to fame in
the 1970s with hits like "Rocky Mountain High" and "Take Me
Home, Country Road."
How He Died: He crashed his own airplane.
Postmortem: Denver was a lifelong aviation buff and an experienced

Broccoli was first introduced to the United States in the 1920s.

pilot. He learned to fly from his father, an ex-Air Force pilot who made his living training pilots to fly Lear Jets.

Denver had just bought an aerobatic plane known as a Long-EZ shortly before the crash and was still getting used to flying it. According to the report released by the National Transportation Safety Board, he needed an extra seatback cushion for his feet to reach the foot pedals, but when he used the cushion he had trouble reaching the fuel tank selector handle located behind his left shoulder. The NTSB speculates that he took off without enough fuel. When one of his tanks ran dry and the engine lost power, Denver accidentally stepped on the right rudder pedal while reaching over his left shoulder with his right arm to switch to the other fuel tank, and crashed the plane into the sea.

Final Irony: Denver's first big success came in 1967, when he wrote the Peter, Paul, and Mary hit "Leaving on a Jet Plane."

L. RON HUBBARD

Claim to Fame: Science-fiction writer and founder of the Church of Scientology

How He Died: No one knows for sure.

Postmortem: Hubbard founded his church in 1952. The larger it grew and the more money it collected from followers, the more controversial it became. A British court condemned Scientology as "immoral, socially obnoxious, corrupt, sinister and dangerous;" a Los Angeles court denounced it as "schizophrenic and paranoid."

Hubbard had a lot of enemies in law-enforcement agencies in the United States . . . the IRS suspected him of skimming millions in church funds. For a time, he avoided prosecutors by sailing around the Mediterranean, and from 1976 to 1979, he lived in hiding in small desert towns in Southern California. Then, in 1980, he vanished. He didn't resurface until January 25, 1986, when someone called a funeral home in San Luis Obispo, California, and instructed them to pick up a body from a ranch about 20 miles north of town. The corpse was identified as Lafayette Ronald Hubbard.

The FBI's fingerprint files confirmed that the man really was Hubbard. The official cause of death: a cerebral hemorrhage. But a "certificate of religious belief" filed on behalf of Hubbard prevented the coroner from conducting an autopsy, so we'll never really know.

How did grocers get their name? They sold goods by the gross.

THE HISTORY OF FOOTBALL, PART I

*If you're a fan of Monday Night Football, you may not realize
that football was invented by college students long before
the pros came along. Here's Part I. Hut, hut, hike!*

CLASS WARFARE

In 1827 the sophomores of Harvard University challenged the freshmen class to a game of "ball," to be played on the first Monday of the new academic year. The freshmen accepted.

That first game was a pretty informal affair; they just kicked around an inflated pig's bladder—a *pigskin*. There were few rules and there was no limit to how many people could play on each team, so the entire freshman class played the *entire* sophomore class, minus anyone who chickened out. The young gentlemen— many of whom were very drunk—must have had a good time, because the freshman-sophomore ball game became an annual Harvard tradition . . . a very violent Harvard tradition.

"The game consisted of kicking, pushing, slugging, and getting angry," Allison Danzig writes in *The History of American Football*. "Anyone who felt like joining in and getting his shins barked, his eyes blacked or his teeth knocked out, was free to do so." The sophomores had an advantage, because as returning students they could recognize their teammates on the field; the incoming freshmen could not.

Some years the game erupted into a full-blown riot, and even when it didn't; it was still pretty rough; game day became known as "Bloody Monday." The 1860 Bloody Monday game was so bloody, in fact, that the university banned football altogether.

PREHISTORIC FOOTBALL

Games involving teams of people kicking and throwing a ball toward opposing goals have probably been around for as long as there have been things to kick; no one knows for sure when the first football-type game was played or who played in it. Different football games are believed to have appeared independently of one

---

Thirteen percent of adults say "the last day of summer" is the "occasion they dread the most."

another in cultures all over the world. In China, for example, people were kicking around balls stuffed with human hair as far back as 300 B.C.

ENGLISH FOOTBALL

The ancient Greeks played a game called *Harpaston* on a rectangular field marked off with goal lines. When the Romans conquered Greece in 146 B.C. they picked up the game, renamed it *Harpastum*, and spread it all over the Roman Empire, including England and Ireland. (Tradition has it that the first English game, or *melee*, was played "with the head of an enemy Dane.")

By the 12th century, many neighboring towns or parishes in the British Isles played an annual football game against one another on Shrove Tuesday, the British equivalent of Mardi Gras, as a sort of last, violent hurrah before the start of Lent on Ash Wednesday.

An inflated pig's bladder or some other kind of ball was brought out to whatever served as the traditional starting point of the game: the town square, marketplace, or a field between the two towns. A local dignitary threw the ball into the crowd of hundreds or in some cases thousands of participating townspeople, who immediately surged toward it. As the quickest, strongest participants muscled their way toward the center of the action, the people at the periphery grabbed on for dear life, pushing, pulling, punching, and kicking each other as they tried to somehow steer the brawling mass of humanity toward the goal.

FREE-FOR-ALL

There were no rules or referees and no restrictions on how the ball could be kicked, carried, or thrown. Some matches restricted participation to young men only; others allowed women and children as well. Most games lasted for hours on end, with the action ending only when it became too dark to play (unless people decided to play in the dark).

"Broken shins, broken heads, torn coats, and lost hats are among the minor accidents of this fearful contest," one chronicler wrote of the annual Shrove Tuesday game between the St. Peter and All Saints parishes in the town of Derby, England, in 1795. "And it frequently happens that persons fall, fainting and bleeding beneath the feet of the surrounding mob . . . Still the

When Europeans landed in Australia, there were 300,000 aborigines. Now there are 41,000.

crowd is encouraged by respectable persons . . . urging on the players with shouts, and even handing refreshment to those who are exhausted."

US AGAINST THEM

Shrove Tuesday matches and other annual games proved to be an effective means for neighboring towns to settle scores that had arisen since the year before. It was the element of revenge, perhaps more than any other, that allowed football to survive, Stephen Fox writes in *Big Leagues*:

> Football came down the centuries less as recreation than as an expression of durable animosities between longstanding rivals. The essential point was to smite the enemy, not to play the game. Football by itself was too rough and risky to attract many players without the extra, emboldening goad supplied by smoldering feuds and hatreds.

Playing football proved such a compelling distraction that it even got in the way of other more traditional forms of violence: In 1389 King Richard II tried to ban the game, claiming that it threatened the kingdom's defenses by interfering with archery practice. He failed, as did every other monarch who tried to ban football.

CINDERELLA STORY

By the early 1800s, traditional Shrove Tuesday football games had faded into history, replaced by similar grudge-match games between rival English secondary schools. The game they played was similar to modern-day "English football," or soccer, a kicking game that did not allow touching or running with the ball. The game remained virtually unchanged until 1823, when someone broke the rules at the now-famous Rugby school. William Web Ellis happened to get the ball just as the clock began to strike five. The rules stipulated that all games ended on the final stroke of five, but Ellis was too far away from the goal to have a shot at scoring. With only seconds left, he picked up the ball and ran across the goal line, just as the clock struck five.

Carrying the ball was against the rules, but it was also fun. And as the Rugby students quickly realized, so was tackling the ball carrier. "Rugby rules" football soon began to emerge as a separate sport. Rugby even developed its own egg-shaped ball, which was easier to carry under the arm than the traditional round ball.

The average pencil will draw a line 35 miles long.

FOOTBALL IN AMERICA

Rugby enthusiasts brought the new game with them to the far reaches of the British empire, but in the United States it was still virtually unknown. By the early 1800s, many eastern universities were starting to invent their homegrown versions of football, with each college making up its own set of rules. As with Harvard, many of these games were blood-sport rituals that allowed students to bond with their own classmates against men of other classes. Princeton played a game called "ballown" as early as 1820, and Yale began playing a rowdy form of soccer in 1851.

Because each university's game was different, the schools did not play each other until 1869, when Rutgers and nearby Princeton University both adopted the soccer rules of the London Football Association and played what historians consider to be the country's first intercollegiate football game. (Rutgers won, 6–4.)

Columbia and Yale started playing Rutgers and Princeton in 1870; and in 1871, Harvard lifted their ban on football, but they played their own version, known as "the Boston Game." Unlike the soccer played at other universities, the Boston Game was more than just a kicking game. A player could pick up the ball whenever he wanted and pass it to his teammates; he was even allowed to run with it.

CANADIAN IMPORT

In 1874 the rugby team at Canada's McGill University challenged Harvard to a series of three games of football. On May 14, the two schools played the Boston Game. Harvard won, 3–0. The next day, they played rugby, which meant that tackling was allowed, and carrying the ball across the goal line and touching the ground with it—making a "touchdown"—was scored just like a kicked goal.

Switching from the Boston Game to rugby wasn't easy for the Harvard team, since no one on the team had ever even seen rugby played before. The game ended in a 0–0 tie, but the Harvard team enjoyed rugby so much that when they made a trip to Montreal later that year to play the third game, they played rugby again. This time they beat McGill 3–0, and were so taken with the new game that they abandoned the Boston Game and switched to rugby.

Cowboy star Tom Mix had tires made with his initials imprinted on them . . .

GETTING THE BALL ROLLING

In 1875 Yale decided to try rugby and challenged Harvard to a game. The game retained much of its rugby character, with a few concessions to Yale's rules thrown in for good measure: Touchdowns, for example, had no value, but gave the scoring team a chance to kick a goal.

A record crowd of 2,000 spectators showed up to watch the game that day, and Yale lost, 0–4. That didn't matter—the crowds were huge and the Yale players had fun. They switched to rugby in 1876.

Two Princeton students watching in the stands that afternoon enjoyed the Harvard-Yale game so much that they convinced the Princeton student body to change over to rugby and to invite representatives from Harvard, Yale, and Columbia to form an Intercollegiate Football Association to draw up a uniform set of rules.

THE THIRD MAN

Another person watching from the stands at that first Harvard-Yale game was a 16-year-old named Walter Camp, who would enter Yale the following year. Camp was thrilled by what he'd seen on the playing field, and as he left the game that day he made two promises to himself: 1) the next time, Yale would win, and 2) he would be on the team.

Camp got everything he wanted—he made the team and Yale beat Harvard, 1–0. And he got a lot more than that: He went on to play halfback for Yale (1877–1882), then coached the team (1888–1892), winning 67 games and losing only two. He also served on every collegiate football rules committee from 1878 until his death in 1925, and was so instrumental in guiding and shaping the new game that was beginning to evolve out of rugby that sports historians consider him the father of American football.

Ready to move the ball downfield? Turn to page 115
for Part II of "The History of Football."

. . . so that when he drove down dirt roads he would leave a trail of "TM"s.

AND THE WIENER IS…

How do you feel about wieners? They look silly and have a funny name . . . but they're loved by millions. This collection of wiener facts and quotes is from BRI stalwart Jess Brallier.

• "Some people don't salivate when they walk by a hot dog stand and smell that great symbol of American cuisine, bursting with grease and salt. But they are a very, very small group."
—**The New York Times**

• Takeru "The Tsunami" Kobayashi is the world's wiener-eating champion. His best: 53 ¾ wieners at the Nathan's dog-eating contest.

• The favorite meal of acclaimed actress Marlene Dietrich was hot dogs and champagne.

• Wieners are an economical buy. With virtually no weight loss during preparation, a pound of wieners yields a pound of edible food.

• Lucky dog: In May 2000, Larry Ross stopped for a hot dog at Mr. K's Party Shoppe in Utica, Michigan. He had a $100 bill, and bought lotto tickets with the change. One ticket was a $181.5 million winner.

• In 1970, at Camp David, the presidential retreat, wieners were served to Great Britain's Prince Charles and Princess Anne.

• NASA included hot dog as a regular menu item on its Apollo moon flights, Skylab missions, and the space shuttle.

• More hot dogs—2 million a year—are sold at Chicago's O'Hare International Airport than at any other single location in the world.

• The U.S. Department of Agriculture "officially recognizes" the following as legitimate names for the hot dog: 1) wiener, 2) frankfurter, 3) frank, 4) furter, 5) hot dog.

• Randomly slash a hot dog as it heats, and it'll curl into funny shapes.

• "Grilling wieners—or even sauteing them in a pan—makes them look nicer."
—**Julia Child**

The game Simon Says was originally called Do This, Do That.

ERROL FLYNN'S LAST STAND

*In the Second Bathroom Reader, we had a look at the accusation
that Errol Flynn was a Nazi spy during World War II (not true).
Here's the story of how he tried to revive his fading career by
starring in a screen version of* William Tell *in 1953.*

LUCKY BREAK

In 1935 the British film actor Robert Donat fell ill and had
to drop out of the starring role in the Warner Bros. swashbuckler *Captain Blood*, prompting Jack Warner to offer the part to
another actor, George Brent. Brent tried out for the role but was
rejected: he looked too silly in the period costumes for audiences to
take him seriously. So Warner offered the job to a nobody—26-year-
old Errol Flynn, a struggling actor who had had only tiny roles in a
few Hollywood films.

"I didn't know if he could act," Warner remembered in 1973,
"but he was handsomer than hell and radiated charm. So I hired
him."

RISE AND FALL

Overnight, *Captain Blood* turned Flynn into the biggest action hero
in Hollywood, and he built a reputation with films like *Charge of the
Light Brigade* (1936), *The Adventures of Robin Hood* (1938), and *The
Sea Hawk* (1940).

If anything, Flynn's private life was even more "adventurous"
than his on-screen life. He was a hard-drinking, brawling woman-
izer with a fondness for underage girls, something that caught up
with him in 1942 when he was brought up on statutory rape charges
involving two teenagers. He was acquitted, but the humiliation of
the experience reportedly broke his spirit.

Flynn was further demoralized when a bad heart kept him out of
World War II. Years of heavy drinking began to catch up with him,
eroding his good looks and sabotaging his box-office appeal. What
little clout he had left in Hollywood was destroyed by his erratic
behavior on the set and his inability to control his drinking.

Star of *Son of Captain Blood*, the sequel to *Captain Blood?* Flynn's son, Sean Flynn.

WILLIAM TELL

By the early 1950s, Flynn's career was on the ropes and he was nearly out of money. He was desperate to make a comeback and, in his hour of need, turned to the genre that had made him a star nearly 20 years before: the swashbuckler.

This time Flynn hoped that starring in a film version of *William Tell*, the legendary Swiss archer, would bring him back from the dead. But alcoholism and a recent bout of hepatitis scared serious investors away, so Flynn was forced to raise funds in Europe, where he finally cobbled together $150,000 from the Italian government and $50,000 from one Count Fossataro, a ormer police chief of Venice. It wasn't nearly enough money, so Flynn put $500,000, virtually all that remained of his fortune, on the line to get things moving.

Most of the money went toward constructing an entire Alpine village next to Mont Blanc in Italy; with the funds that were left, he was only able to film for two weeks, producing about 30 minutes' worth of footage.

ONE LAST CHANCE

Desperate, Flynn packed up his 30 minutes of film and brought it to the Venice Film Festival, where he hoped screenings of it would attract new backers. But once again, his health got in the way. "Suffering from dysentery and diarrhea," Harry Waldman writes in *Scenes Unseen*, Flynn "was more preoccupied with finding a bathroom at short notice than making polite conversation."

Flynn's frequent pit stops doomed his attempts to find financing, so one evening he pulled the only stunt he could think of that might get him some money—he staged a fall in his hotel and faked paralysis, in the hopes of winning a large insurance settlement from the hotel. The ruse backfired—all it did was illustrate just how troubled the star of William Tell was, ruining what little chance was left of getting a backer.

The film was dead, Flynn had lost his savings, and his career never did recover. He spent his final years playing the only roles that still came naturally to him—drunks—and died at the age of 50 in 1959. His 30 minutes of *William Tell* footage has been lost; about all that survives is the Alpine village itself, which today is a popular tourist attraction.

Who appeared on the first cover of *People* magazine? Mia Farrow.

AMERICA'S MONEY LAUNDRESS

When the folks behind Mrs. Butterworth's syrup came up with the name, they probably had no idea they were giving their product the same name as a colonial American counterfeiter . . . but they were.

DESIGNING WOMAN

Mary Peck Butterworth was the daughter of an innkeeper and the wife of a carpenter in colonial Massachusetts. In the early 1700s, she was raising seven children and her family desperately needed more money. Some women would have taken up sewing—Mary Butterworth became a counterfeiter. With a little bit of work and some experimentation, she invented a method of counterfeiting that not only produced passable bills but also left no incriminating evidence of the crime.

Here's how she did it: First she placed a piece of damp, starched muslin on top of the bill she wanted to copy. Then she ran a hot iron over the cloth, which caused the material to pick up a light impression of the printing from the bill. Then she ironed the muslin hard enough to transfer the pattern to a blank piece of paper in order to produce the counterfeit bill. Finally, she used a quill pen to outline the writing on the bill and touch it up. The incriminating evidence—the used piece of muslin— was then burned.

COLONIAL COUNTERFEIT RING

Butterworth set up a veritable cottage industry. Three of her brothers and a sister-in-law helped manufacture the money. The bills were then fenced for half their face value. Over a period of seven years, the Butterworth gang made and sold over £1,000 worth of bogus bills—roughly equivalent to $130,000 today—without sophisticated technology and without being detected.

In 1715 the £5 note had to be recalled because there was a flood of phony bills in circulation. At the same time, authorities eyed with suspicion the large house Butterworth and her husband had just built, but they couldn't prove anything.

An acre of potatoes can produce enough ethyl alcohol to fill 25 cars.

EXPOSED

Then in 1723, one of Butterworth's carpenters traveled to Newport, Rhode Island, to witness the mass hanging of 26 pirates. There he met three young girls. Treating them to dinner and drinks, he paid for the party with one of the many counterfeit bills he had in his wallet, but was caught by the innkeeper. After he was arrested, he quickly revealed the details of the counterfeit operation.

Mary Butterworth was imprisoned, but with no counterfeiting plates in evidence, she was promptly released. No one knows whether she gave up counterfeiting after that. Regardless, she died in 1775 at the age of 89, a respected member of the community . . . as far as anyone knew.

* * *

NUDES IN THE NEWS

- Vincent Bethell, 28, was thrown out of a British courtroom in August 2000 after he appeared in the nude to answer charges of disorderly behavior. Bethel, a nude activist, had been arrested while walking naked through the streets of London and vows to remain naked until England's antinudity laws are repealed.

- Female members of Nigeria's ruling People's Democratic Party threatened to march naked through Lagos if the party's "lack of respect" for female members continues. "We are prepared to protest by walking the streets naked and camping in our nudity in front of Commodore Bode George's house for seven days," said protest organizer Alhaja Ali-Balogun. Displays of nudity by older women, seen as "mothers of the nation" in Nigeria, are considered taboo.

- Antilogging activist Dona Nieto, who calls herself La Tigresa, has hit upon a novel way of getting lumberjacks to listen to her campaign to preserve ancient redwoods: she removes her top and recites "Goddess-based, nude Buddhist guerrilla poetry" while the loggers ogle her chest. "They stop their chainsaws and they stop their trucks and they pay attention," she says. "I've changed some of these guys' lives."

Q: What do the inventors of Coke, Pepsi, and Dr. Pepper have in common?

JUST PLANE WEIRD

*Planning a plane trip in the near future? Don't read
this! Fold over the corner of the page and save
it for another day. We warned you.*

SMOKING FLIGHT

On November 19, 2000, a drunken passenger on an
American Airlines flight from Tokyo to Seattle locked
himself into a restroom about an hour into the flight and lit up a
cigarette. Not a good idea—American Airline flights are non-
smoking. When the man refused repeated requests to extinguish
his cigarettes and come out of the restroom, the plane returned to
Tokyo, where he was removed from the flight and reprimanded
by airport police. He later made a written apology to American
Airlines and promised "never to do it again." Too late: According
to news reports, American Airlines sued him "for losses caused by
his bad behavior."

NUT CASE

In April 2001, Cathay Pacific Airlines fired pilot Scott Munro.
Reason for dismissal: He threw nuts at the company's chief executive after running into him at a bar. "He was dismissed for throwing things at me," CEO David Turnbull told the *South China
Morning Post*. "We have to operate a disciplined company, and you
do not throw things at the chief executive."

THE LATE MR. KOTIADIS

On November 21, 2000, a Greek businessman named Nikita
Kotiadis was arrested at Athens airport after phoning in a bomb
threat on his own flight. Reason: Kotiadis was running late, and he
wanted to delay the flight from taking off until he could get to the
airport. He might have gotten away with it if he'd placed the call
himself. But he had his secretary call, and she identified him by
name before putting him on the line. Kotiadis made his threat and
then raced for the airport, where he was arrested on the spot. He
was later sentenced to seven months in prison for "obstructing
transportation."

A: They were all Civil War veterans.

THE NAKED TRUTH

On March 11, 2001, police boarded an Olympic Airways flight to Paris and arrested 23-year-old Jeremy Benjamin Mauri after he stripped naked during the safety demonstration. As they removed him from the plane, Mauri offered this bizarre explanation: "I did it for a joke; I'm impotent."

YOUR TAX DOLLARS AT WORK

In June 2001 the British company Roke Manor Research announced that it had found a way to detect and track America's "invisible" stealth bombers. Their secret weapon: cell phones—when a stealth bomber flies over an area with cellular phone coverage, the aircraft disrupts the cellular signals in such a way that it's possible to calculate its location to within 30 feet using a laptop computer and a Global Positioning Satellite navigation system.

"We just use the normal phone calls that are flying about in the ether," says Roke Manor's spokesperson Peter Lloyd. "The front of the stealth plane cannot be detected by conventional radar, but its bottom surface reflects very well. It's remarkable that a stealth system that cost $158 billion to develop is beaten by mobile phone technology."

BAG LADY

An 83-year-old grandmother on an American Airlines flight from Miami, Florida, to Bogota, Colombia, was taken into custody after she made a bomb threat while the plane was taxiing for takeoff. An official with American said that Beatriz Escobar De Rodriguez, a native of Colombia, made the threat after she tried to board the plane with a carry-on bag that was too big to fit in the overhead compartment or under her seat. When told it would have to be checked and placed in the cargo bay of the plane, she replied, "Did you see the bomb in my suitcase?" What she meant is unknown, but it didn't matter—she said the "B-word." The plane returned to the gate; grandma was arrested and thrown in jail. "Her penalty depends on the judge," a court spokesman told reporters. "She might end up in jail."

DO YOU SPEAK CANADIAN?

Here's an article that was sent to us by Canadian professor Howard Richler. Of course we know that a country the size of Canada has many different regional dialects . . . but it still made us laugh.

SPEAKING CANADIAN

So you think there's no such thing as Canadian English, eh? Then tell me what this means:

> The beerslinger posted a sign warning that hosers with Molson muscles, rubbies, and sh*t-disturbers would not be welcome. No sirree. Folks were drinking bloody Caesars and brown cows at the booze can. Heck, even the Gravol was free.

Translation for the non-Canadian reader: A "beerslinger" is an informal term for a bartender; a "hoser" means a lout; a "rubby" refers to a derelict alcoholic known to mix rubbing alcohol with what he is imbibing; "Molson muscles" is a term for a beer-belly; "brown cow" and "bloody Caesar" are names for two cocktails in Canada; a "booze can" is a term for an illegal bar, usually in someone's home; a "sh*t-disturber" refers to one who likes to create trouble; and "Gravol" is the Canadian proprietary name of an anti-nausea medication.

Here are some more Canadianisms:

All-dressed: Food served with all the optional garnishes

Cuffy: Cigarette butt

Browned off: Fed up or disheartened

Two-four: A case of beer

First Peoples: The politically correct term for Canadian Indians

Bazoo: Old rusted car

Fuddle duddle: A euphemism for "go to hell"

Keener: Eager beaver

Steamie: A steamed hot dog

Gitch: Underwear

Howdy, neighbor: 36 percent of the Great Lakes lie within Canadian territory.

The Can: Canada

Schmuck: Verb meaning "to flatten," as in, "He got schmucked on the road"

Bite moose: Go away

Garburator: A garbage disposal unit

Anglophone: An English-language speaker

Francophone: A French-language speaker

Allophone: Immigrant who speaks neither English nor French

Wobbly pop: Alcohol

Keep yer stick on the ice: Pay attention

Skookum: Big and powerful (a west coast term derived from Chinook jargon)

And let's not forget unique French-Canadian English phraseology, such as "Throw me down the stairs my shoes," or "Throw the horse over the fence some hay."

So, you all you hosers from Beantown, the Big Easy, and La La Land, before you visit your neighbors to the north in T.O. (Toronto, Ontario) or up island in B.C. (British Columbia), remember that Canadians have their own way of speaking English. And although the Canadian national persona is extremely polite, don't forget that ice hockey is the national pastime and "drop the gloves," a hockey term for "prepare to fight," is also part of Canadian English.

* * *

A POLITICIAN IS BORN

In 1946 the following ad appeared in several Southern California newspapers: "Wanted: Congressman candidate with no previous political experience to defeat a man who has represented the district in the House for 10 years. Any young man, resident of district, preferably a veteran, fair education, may apply for the job." The ad had been placed by the Republican party. A man who answered the ad was awarded the job and did in fact defeat incumbent Jerry Voorhis after a dirty campaign. The man who kicked off his political career by replying to a want ad? Richard M. Nixon

---

Though deaf and blind, Helen Keller learned English, French, and German.

FAMILIAR PHRASES

Here are the origins of some common phrases.

W IN HANDS DOWN
Meaning: To win by an enormous margin.
Origin: If a racehorse jockey is so far ahead of the competition that there is no danger he will be passed again, he can drop the reins—and his hands—and let the horse finish the race without spurring it on.

BAKER'S DOZEN

Meaning: Thirteen—one more than a dozen.
Origin: In the Middle Ages, bakers who sold loaves of bread that were lighter than the legal weight were subjected to harsh penalties. To prevent being accused of cheating on the weight, bakers would often give away an extra loaf with every dozen.

CLEAN AS A WHISTLE

Meaning: Exceptionally clean or smooth.
Origin: This phrase appeared at the beginning of the 19th century, describing the whistling noise made as a sword tears through the air to decapitate a victim cleanly, in a single stroke.

LOADED FOR BEAR

Meaning: Prepared for any contingency.
Origin: American pioneers traveling alone through the woods, needed to be prepared for anything if they wanted to return intact. They carried guns powerful enough to bring down any dangerous predator they happened to meet, especially the fiercest and most territorial creature in the land—the bear.

BET YOUR BOTTOM DOLLAR

Meaning: It's a sure thing; to bet everything you have.
Origin: Just as they do today, 19th-century poker players would keep their betting chips—or "dollars"—in high stacks at the table, taking from the top when betting. When a hand was so good that a

A single, isolated heart cell will "beat" for as long as it has a fresh supply of blood.

player wanted to wager the entire stack, they would pick up or push the stack by the bottom chip—literally betting with their bottom dollar.

TO FIGHT FIRE WITH FIRE

Meaning: To respond in like manner; a desperate measure.

Origin: In order to extinguish huge prairie and forest fires in the early West, desperate American settlers would sometimes set fire to a strip of land in the path of the advancing fire and then extinguish it, leaving a barren strip with nothing for the approaching fire to feed on. Although effective, this tactic was—and still is—extremely dangerous, as the backfire itself can get out of control.

TO GET ONE'S GOAT

Meaning: To aggravate.

Origin: Hyperactive racehorses were often given goats as stablemates because their presence tended to have a calming effect on the horses. After the horse became attached to the goat, it got very upset when its companion disappeared—making it run poorly on the track. In the 19th century, when a devious gambler wanted a horse to lose, he would get the horse's goat and take it away the night before the race, thus agitating the horse.

IN THE NICK OF TIME

Meaning: Without a second to spare.

Origin: Even into the 18th century, some businessmen still kept track of transactions and time by carving notches—or nicks—on a "tally stick." Someone arriving just before the next nick was carved would arrive in time to save the next day's interest—in the nick of time.

MAKE MONEY HAND OVER FIST

Meaning: Rapid success in a business venture.

Origin: Sailors through the ages have used the same hand-over-hand motion when climbing up ropes, hauling in nets, and hoisting sails. The best seamen were those who could do this action the fastest. In the 19th century, Americans adapted the expression "hand over fist"—describing one hand clenching a rope and the other deftly moving above it—to suggest quickness and success.

In case you've forgotten: E Pluribus Unum means "from many, one."

BAD MEDICINE

Most of us take modern medical science for granted. MRIs, pain relievers, and the polio vaccine may not seem like a big deal today, but if you look back a couple hundred years, you may change your mind.

MALPRACTICE

These days you can easily find dozens of effective remedies at the local pharmacy to treat anything from a sore toe to scalp itch. So it's hard to imagine that less than 200 years ago, a person complaining to a trusted physician about a simple ailment was likely to undergo barbaric treatment that included draining of the blood, blistering of the skin, and induced vomiting.

In the 1800s, doctors were scarce and ill-trained. There were no regulations concerning the education of physicians. With just a little booklearning or information passed down by a family member, almost anyone could set up shop and call himself a doctor. There were no antibiotics, no X-rays, no vaccines, and none of the diagnostic tools we now take for granted.

Surgery was often performed by barbers. Not only did they give haircuts and shaves, but they also extracted teeth, lanced boils, and bled patients. In fact, the colors of the familiar barber's pole are derived from the practice of bloodletting: red for blood, and white for bandages. The pole itself was sometimes grasped by the patient in order to make his veins stand out and make the bloodletting easier. In the end, the patient was as likely to die from the treatment as from the illness.

KING OF PAIN

People of the 19th century accepted pain as an inevitable part of life. The aches and pains we associate with a long day of work or a touch of the flu couldn't be quelled by popping an aspirin—that wonder drug wasn't introduced until 1899. The common rationale was that pain was a punishment from God, and to endure it was good for the soul.

There were no anesthetics either. Until the 1840s all surgeries were performed without it. For this reason, not to mention the real

---

Heads up: Raindrops fall as fast as 22 mph.

possibility of death from blood loss, surgeons had to be quick. Records show that during the Battle of Bordello, Dominique Jean Larrey (1766–1842), a surgeon in Napoléon's army, performed 200 amputations in the first 24 hours. Even at that speed, the mortality rate was almost 100 percent due to shock or infection. Septicemia, or blood poisoning, was an ever-present danger. Surgeons traveled from dissection room to operating room, never once changing their coats or washing their hands.

HUMOROUS—BUT NOT FUNNY

Most physicians of the 1800s still subscribed to the ancient Greek belief that the body was made up of four "humors" corresponding to the four elements of the Earth: yellow bile (air), black bile (water), phlegm (Earth), and blood (fire). The Greeks believed that a lack or excess of these humors caused all illnesses and had to be treated accordingly. If a doctor suspected a buildup of bad blood, the patient would be "cured" by the cutting and draining of the offensive liquid. There are even records of primitive transfusions using sheep's or cow's blood.

Dr. Benjamin Rush (1745–1813), a signer of the Declaration of Independence, humanitarian, and renowned physician, was a noted believer in "humor" therapy. To maintain balance among the humors, Rush prescribed a horrifying course of bloodletting, blistering, and swinging of the body, a treatment in which the patient would be strapped into a chair, suspended from the ceiling by a rope, and swung violently back and forth to induce vomiting. Once patients vomited, they were brought down and the treatment was considered a success.

QUICK, CALL ME A QUACK

In the 1820s and 1830s, people had little faith in "scientific" medicine, due no doubt to treatments that were painful and usually produced no results other than infection or death. A new movement of treating illnesses with old folk remedies grew out of the public's fear and distrust of doctors. The medical profession called it *quackery*. The word is thought to originate either from the phrase "quicksilver doctor," which refers to the use of highly poisonous mercury as a cure, or from *kwaksalver*, an early Dutch term meaning "someone who prattles about the efficacy of his remedies."

Either way, quacks promised quick results and easy answers

without evidence to support their claims. They sold cure-all elixirs—such as Lydia Pinkham's Vegetable Compound, which was 80 percent vegetable extracts and 20 percent alcohol—and patent medicines laced with cocaine, opium, and caffeine. Morphine-based mixtures were even sold in the Sears catalog. Patients often felt better after taking a swig (or several swigs), but these patent medicines didn't cure anything.

SCIENCE IS GOLDEN

What changed? In 1865 Dr. Joseph Lister noted that almost half of patients with amputations were dying. The main cause: postoperative sepsis infections, or sepsis for short. He blamed it on unsanitary conditions, comparing the smell of an operating room to a city sewer. Inspired by Louis Pasteur's theory that decay was caused by living organisms in the air, which on entering matter made it ferment, Lister made the connection with sepsis. He had also heard that carbolic acid was being used to treat sewage, so he began using it to clean wounds and sterilize instruments.

In 1846 Scottish surgeon Dr. Robert Liston (1794–1847) introduced the use of ether as an anesthetic, making it possible for doctors to operate on patients with less pain.

Other advances included the invention of the clinical thermometer, stethoscope, and hypodermic needle; the development of anthrax, rabies, and smallpox vaccines in the 19th century; and the discovery of penicillin in the early 20th century.

When technology started catching up with advances in medicine, X-rays, the incandescent light, and even the invention of the telephone changed things dramatically for both patient and surgeon. But was it the end of quackery? Not by a long shot.

To read about Modern Quackery, go to page 235.

To read about Modern Quackery, go to page 235.

* * *

SWEET DREAMS

According to Betty Bethards in *The Dream Book: Symbols for Self-Understanding*, "toilet dreams" have to do with how well the dreamer is "flushing out negativity and wastes," including letting go of unneeded thoughts and experiences and releasing the past so as to live fully in the present.

Number-one health complaint Americans report to their doctors: insomnia.

POLI-TALKS

*Politicians aren't getting much respect these days—but
then, it sounds like they don't deserve much, either.*

"The more we remove penalties for being a bum, the more bumism is going to blossom."

**Sen. Jesse Helms
(R-NC), on welfare**

"We didn't send you to Washington to make intelligent decisions. We sent you to represent us."

**—Kent York,
a Texas pastor, to
Rep. Bill Sarpalius (D-TX)**

"President Clinton had a bill, e-i-e-i-o. And in that bill was lots of pork, e-i-e-i-o."

**—Sen. Alfonse D'Amato
(R-NY)**

"I have orders to be awakened at any time in the case of a national emergency, even if I'm in a cabinet meeting."

—Ronald Reagan

"The present system may be flawed, but that's not to say that we in Congress can't make it worse."

**—Rep. E. Clay Shaw, Jr.
(R-FL)**

"Is the country still here?"

**—Calvin Coolidge,
waking from a nap**

"We've killed health care; now we've got to make sure our fingerprints aren't on it."

**—Sen. Bob Packwood
(R-OR), in 1994, on the
GOP blocking Clinton's
health-care reforms**

"Ambiguously definitive—or is it definitively ambiguous?"

**—Sen. Bill Bradley, on
being unclear about his
presidential ambitions**

"It's no exaggeration to say that the undecideds could go one way or another."

—George H. W. Bush

"We didn't get the pay raise—why work?"

**—Bob Dole, in 1989,
on the slow pace of
Senate activity**

"Welcome to President Bush, Mrs. Bush, and my fellow astronauts."

—Dan Quayle

When George Washington was president, there were about 350 federal employees.

THE RIDDLER

What's white and black and read all over? This
page of riddles. Here are some BRI favorites.

1. What does a diamond become when it is placed in water?

2. What did the big rose say to the little rose?

3. What is it that doesn't ask questions but must be answered?

4. What does a chicken do when it stands on one foot?

5. What kind of bird has wings but can't fly?

6. What two words have the most letters in them?

7. What has neither flesh nor bone but has four fingers and a thumb?

8. How many of each animal did Moses bring on the ark?

9. What is it that grows larger the more you take away from it?

10. Poke out its eye and it has nothing left but a nose. What is it?

11. What runs all day and never walks / Often murmurs, never talks / Has a bed and never sleeps / Has a mouth and never eats?

12. Which side of a pitcher is the handle on?

13. What is the difference between here and there?

14. If two is company, and three's a crowd, how much is four and five?

15. What fruit do you find on a dime?

16. How can you divide 10 potatoes equally between three people?

17. What is no larger when it weighs 20 pounds than when it weighs 1 pound?

18. No sooner spoken than broken. What is it?

19. What falls but never breaks? What breaks but never falls?

Answers on page 742.

One-millionth trademark issued by the U.S. Patent Office: Sweet'N Low.

THE WORLD'S FIRST PHOTOGRAPH

In the first part of our story (see page 26), we told you about the camera obscura, the drawing tool that eventually evolved into the modern camera. In this installment, we introduce you to some of the people who played a role in inventing film.

SPIRITS IN THE MATERIAL WORLD

In 1674 an alchemist named Christoph Adolph Balduin performed a chemistry experiment that he hoped would help him isolate the mysterious natural force he called the *Weltgeist*, or "universal spirit." He dissolved some chalk (calcium carbonate) in nitric acid to create a sludgy substance that would easily absorb moisture from the atmosphere. Balduin believed that if he could distill the moisture from the sludge, he would capture the universal spirit in pure form.

Needless to say, Balduin didn't know much about chemistry (not many 17th-century alchemists did), because when he distilled the sludge, all he got was water. But he noticed that when he heated the dried-out crud that was left over, it glowed in the dark. He named this mysterious substance phosphorus, Greek for "bringer of light" (today it's called calcium nitrate).

What did this have to do with photography? Nothing . . . until a German anatomy professor named Johann Heinrich Schulze tried to repeat Balduin's experiment in 1727. By chance he used nitric acid that contained traces of silver. He left the chalk-acid mixture out in the sun; by the time he came back to it, it had turned a deep purple.

MESSAGE IN A BOTTLE

Schulze wasn't the first person to observe that substances containing silver salts turn dark when exposed to the sun. But it had always been assumed that it was the heat that caused the reaction. Schulze suspected that light was to blame and came up with an experiment to test his theory: He cut a stencil of some words on a piece of paper. He put the stencil on the side of a glass

Even a blind chameleon will change its color to match its surroundings.

bottle and covered the rest of the glass with dark material. He filled the bottle with the chalk dissolved in nitric acid and left it out in the sun, to see if the sunlight would "write" the stenciled words onto the material.

"It was not long," he wrote later, "before the sun's rays, where they hit the glass through the cut-out parts of the paper, wrote each word on the chalk precipitate so exactly and distinctly that many who were curious about the experiment took occasion to attribute the thing to some sort of trick." In a nod to Balduin, Schulze called the material *scotophorus*, or "bringer of darkness."

Schulze didn't understand why the substance turned dark, but today we do: When light strikes photosensitive silver crystals, some of the atoms of silver separate out from the compound. Exactly how many atoms separate depends on how much light strikes the material. With enough light, however, the silver will become visible to the naked eye, and the material becomes dark. This is the chemical principle upon which all film photography would be based.

Schulze couldn't figure out how to control the reaction—the silver salts darkened every time they were exposed to light, obliterating whatever writing or image had been created. As far as he could tell, the material had no use, but it was still interesting, and as word of his discovery spread, scientists all over Europe repeated the experiment.

PAPERWORK

One man who learned of Schulze's experiment was Thomas Wedgwood, son of the legendary English potter Josiah Wedgwood. Wedgwood thought he could use the process to make duplicates of artwork for his pottery.

He started out by soaking pieces of paper in a solution of silver nitrate to make them photosensitive (sensitive to light). He then laid his sketches on top of these materials and put them out in the sun. The sunlight would shine through the sketch where the paper was blank, but would be blocked where there was ink, creating a reverse, or "negative," image of the original sketch. The experiment worked. Wedgwood became the first person in history to transfer an image onto photosensitive paper.

Wedgwood might have become the father of photography, but his health was so poor that he had to abandon his research before

Average caloric requirement for breathing, eating, and sleeping: 1000–1500 per day.

he could reach his next goal: recording the image created by a camera obscura. And like Schulze, he died without figuring out how to arrest the photosensitive reaction so that his images would be made permanent. Even when viewed by candlelight, it was just a matter of time before they disappeared into darkness forever.

FIXING THE PROBLEM

The next major contributor to the chemistry of photography was a 19th-century French physicist named Joseph-Nicéphore Niepce.

Niepce was looking for a way to copy artwork automatically, to avoid having to pay artists to do it. He repeated the experiments of Schulze and Wedgwood and searched for chemicals that would give him positive images, but finally, after years of failed experiments, gave up on chemicals that change color and started looking for chemicals that harden when exposed to light. That's when his luck began to change.

Having worked as a printer, Niepce was familiar with "bitumen of Judea," an asphalt compound dating back to the Egyptians and commonly used by lithographers. He knew that when bitumen of Judea was exposed to sunlight, it hardened to the point that solvents would no longer dissolve it. So he smeared a metal printing plate with the stuff, placed an ink drawing on top of the plate, and left them both out in the sun. Just as he expected, the sunlight passed through the blank paper, striking the bitumen of Judea underneath and causing it to harden.

But where the sunlight was blocked by the ink, the bitumen of Judea remained soft and could be washed away with solvents. The result was a perfect copy of the original drawing. Niepce named the process heliography, after helios, the Greek word for "sun," and graphos, "writing."

THE NEXT LEVEL

Taking his discovery to the next step, one sunny morning in 1827, Niepce smeared some bitumen of Judea onto a printing plate and put it inside a camera obscura. Then he pointed the camera obscura out of an upstairs window of his country home and left it there for most of the day. In the process, he took what historians consider to be the world's first true photograph.

For part III of our history of photography, turn to page 134.

For part III of our history of photography, turn to page 134.

Distance that a silver-spotted skipper caterpillar can propel its own feces: 5 feet.

THE HOUSE CALL OF A LIFETIME

*Every collector has a Holy Grail that they hope to find at a yard sale,
or flea market someday. Baseball card collectors dream of finding
an original Honus Wagner; book collectors hope to spot a copy
of Edgar Allen Poe's* The Tamerlane *gathering dust on a
bookstore shelf. Here's the story of an amateur antique
collector who found what he was looking for.*

THE PERFECT STORM

One winter in the early 1980s, a two-day snowstorm knocked out telephone service to much of the village of East Hampton, New York. One of the people sent out into the snow to restore service was cable repairman Morgan MacWhinnie.

MacWhinnie was just finishing repairing an underground cable when an old man wearing slippers and a bathrobe came out of a run-down clapboard house and asked him to check the phones inside. MacWhinnie wanted to move on to his next repair call, but he decided it would be quicker to humor the old man than it would be to argue with him. So he went into the house.

DIAMONDS IN THE ROUGH

The old man turned out to be a pack rat: he had old aluminum TV dinner trays stacked to the ceiling in the kitchen, and mountains of trash in other parts of the dark, dusty house. MacWhinnie checked the extension in the kitchen; it had a dial tone. Then the old man insisted that he check the extension in the bedroom, too. MacWhinnie wanted to leave, but the old man was insistent, so he let the man show him the way to the upstairs room.

As MacWhinnie made his way through the cluttered dining room, he was surprised to see what appeared to be an antique tea table and a matching bonnet-top highboy chest of drawers poking out of the dust and debris. Then, after he checked the extension in the bedroom (it was fine) and prepared to leave, he saw a matching drop-leaf dining table next to the front door.

Two basketballs can fit side by side through a basketball hoop.

NEWPORT STYLE

As it turns out, MacWhinnie's hobby was collecting antiques. He knew a lot about 18th-century American furniture, and he was almost certain the pieces were valuable. In fact, he suspected they were made in Newport, Rhode Island, in the 1780s, the period considered the golden age of the Newport style. If he was right, the furniture was worth a lot of money, but he had no way of knowing for sure.

The old man told MacWhinnie that the furniture belonged to his landlady, a woman named Caroline Tillinghast. MacWhinnie called her and told her he thought the pieces were valuable and asked if she'd consider selling them. She said no—the house was a rental property and she needed the furniture for the tenants. MacWhinnie let the matter drop, but he never forgot what he saw that day.

SECOND TRY

Ten years later, MacWhinnie happened to tell his story to an antiques dealer named Leigh Keno. (Does the name sound familiar? He and his twin brother Leslie appear regularly on the PBS TV series *Antiques Roadshow*.) When he heard MacWhinnie's story, Keno thought the pieces must be reproductions but agreed that they were worth a look just in case, so they called Tillinghast to see if she would let them come over and examine the furniture. Yes, she told them, and now was a good time, because the old man had recently passed away and she was having the house cleaned for new tenants.

THE REAL DEAL

MacWhinnie was right—the pieces were genuine. They turned out to be the work of John Goddard, considered the most talented cabinetmaker of the period. Finally, nearly a decade after MacWhinnie had asked her the first time, Tillinghast agreed to put the antiques up for sale. She believed they were worth "in excess of $25,000"—and she was right. A few weeks later, Keno brokered the sale to a collector for $1 million. As for MacWhinnie, he and Keno split the hefty commission 50–50.

THE SECRET HITLER FILE

There's nothing funny about Hitler, but he is endlessly fascinating. Since Congress passed the Nazi War Crimes Disclosure Act in 1998, almost 3 million classified files have been opened to the public—including a 1942 secret profile of Adolf Hitler compiled by the OSS. Here are some excerpts.

PERSONAL APPEARANCE

- "Hitler never allows anyone to see him while he is naked or bathing. He refuses to use colognes or scents of any sort on his body."

- "No matter how warm he feels, Hitler will never take off his coat in public."

- "In 1923, Nazi press secretary Dr. Sedgwick tried to convince Hitler to get rid of his trademark mustache or grow it normally. Hitler answered: 'Do not worry about my mustache. If it is not the fashion now, it will be later because I wear it!'"

SOCIAL BEHAVIOR

- "While dining with others, Hitler will allow the conversation to linger on general topics, but after a couple of hours he will inevitably begin one of his many monologues. These speeches are flawless from start to finish because he rehearses them any time he gets a moment."

- "His favorite topics include: 'When I was a soldier,' 'When I was in Vienna,' 'When I was in prison,' and 'When I was the leader in the early days of the party.'"

- "If Hitler begins speaking about Wagner and the opera, no one dares interrupt him. He will often sermonize on this topic until his audience falls asleep."

PERSONAL HABITS

- "Hitler has no interest in sports or games of any kind and never exercised, except for an occasional walk."

- "He paces frequently inside rooms, always to the same tune that he whistles to himself and always diagonally across the room, from corner to corner."

- "He always rides in an open car for parades regardless of the weather, and expects the same of his entire staff, telling them: 'We are not bourgeois, but soldiers.'"

- "Hitler's handwriting is impeccable. When famous psychologist Carl Jung saw Hitler's handwriting in 1937, he remarked: 'Behind this handwriting I recognize the typical characteristics of a man with essentially feminine instincts.'"

ENTERTAINMENT

- "Hitler loves the circus. He takes real pleasure in the idea that underpaid performers are risking their lives to please him."

- "He went to the circus on several occasions in 1933 and sent extremely expensive chocolates and flowers to the female performers. Hitler even remembered their names and would worry about them and their families in the event of an accident."

- "He isn't interested in wild animal acts, unless there is a woman in danger."

- "Nearly every night Hitler will see a movie in his private theatre, mainly foreign films that are banned to the German public. He loves comedies and will often laugh merrily at Jewish comedians. Hitler even liked a few Jewish singers, but after hearing them he would remark that it was too bad he or she wasn't an Aryan."

- "Hitler's staff secretly made films for him of the torture and execution of political prisoners, which he very much enjoyed viewing. His executive assistants also secured pornographic pictures and movies for him."

- "He loves newsreels—especially when he is in them."

- "He adores gypsy music, Wagner's operas, and especially American college football marches and alma maters."

- "To excite the masses, he also uses American College football-style music during his speeches." His rallying cry—'Sieg Heil!'—was even modeled after the cheering techniques used by American football cheerleaders."

Frank Sinatra's father once boxed under the name Marty O'Brien.

FAMOUS LAST WORDS

If you had to pick some last words, what would they be?

"Turn up the lights. I don't want to go home in the dark."
   —O. Henry

"I've got a terrible headache."
   —Franklin D. Roosevelt

"That was the best ice cream soda I ever tasted."
   —Lou Costello

"Tell my mother that I died for my country. I thought I did it for the best. Useless! Useless!"
   —John Wilkes Booth

"I want that fifty bucks you owe me and I want it now!"
   —Carl "Alfalfa" Switzer, *shot in a bar by a drunk*

"I'm a broken machine, but I'm ready."
   —Woodrow Wilson

"¿Quien es? [Who is it?]"
   —Billy the Kid, *before being shot by Pat Garrett*

"Mozart!"
   —Gustav Mahler

"Bury me among my people. I do not wish to rise among pale faces."
   —Red Jacket, *Chief of the Seneca*

"Turn your back to me, please Henry. I am so sick now. The police are getting many complaints. Look out I want that G-note. Look out for Jimmy Valentine, for he's a friend of mine. Come on, come on, Jim. OK, OK, I am all through. I can't do another thing. Look out for mamma. Look out for her. Police, mamma, Helen, please take me out. I will settle the incident. Come on, open the soak duckets; the chimney sweeps. Talk to the sword. Shut up, you got a big mouth! Please help me to get up. Henry! Max! Come over here. French Canadian bean soup. I want to pay. Let them leave me alone."
   —Dutch Schultz, *New York gangster*

"Don't worry, be happy."
   —Meher Baba, *Indian guru*

Asian elephants are closer in relation to the extinct mammoth than to African elephants.

BEHIND THE HITS

Ever wonder what inspired some of your favorite songs?
Here are a few inside stories about popular tunes.

The **Artist:** Screamin' Jay Hawkins
The Song: "I Put a Spell on You" (1956)
The Story: Hawkins's signature tune was originally
intended as a ballad, but it came out as the haunted howling of a
jilted lover. Listeners may have guessed (correctly) that the singer
had been drinking when he laid down the vocals, and according to
Hawkins, "Every member of the band was drunk." Even the recording engineer and the A&R man, Arnold Maxin, were plastered. It
was Maxin who effectively changed the song from a torch song to
a frenzied rant by supplying the band with several cases of Italian
Swiss Colony Muscatel. "We partied and we partied," Jay recalled,
"and somewhere along the road I blanked out." When he regained
consciousness, he had a hit record on his hands but no recollection
of how he had made it.

The Artist: The Tornados
The Song: "Telstar" (1962)
The Story: This landmark recording featured the very first use of
a synthesizer and was one of the bestselling instrumentals of all
time. The song was recorded in a makeshift studio in producer Joe
Meek's apartment: the mixing board was in the living room; the
musicians performed in the bathroom, bedroom, and kitchen.
Meek came up with the tune but couldn't read or write music,
so he hummed the melody on demo tapes and then played it back
to the band. The fact that they were able to discern any tune at all
from the tone-deaf Meek's fractured, off-key humming is a testament to their musical talent. Bad luck: The song became a huge
#1 hit, but a French film composer sued Meek for plagiarism. Meek
lost the suit, which cost him millions of dollars in lost royalties.

The Artist: Serge Gainsbourg
The Song: *"Je T'Aime . . . Moi Non Plus* (I Love You . . . Nor
Do I)" (1969)

Longest word used by Shakespeare: honoroficabilitudinitatibus.

The Story: There were several "heavy breathing" songs during the sixties, but none more notorious than this one. Originally written as a love song to sex kitten Brigitte Bardot, Serge rerecorded it in 1969 with his new lover, actress Jane Birkin. It features Birkin panting and moaning, *"Je t'aime, oui je t'aime!"* ("I love you, yes I love you!"), and Serge reciting unromantic lyrics like, "Between your kidneys, I come and go." Moral authorities were outraged; the Pope even excommunicated the record executive who'd released it in Italy. But despite being banned everywhere, the single was a huge international hit. In the United States, the vocals were completely erased and it was issued as an instrumental.

The Artist: The Ramones
The Song: "Blitzkrieg Bop" (1976)
The Story: Sometimes you don't need to be on the record charts to have a hit. This early punk-rock anthem is played during almost every pro football, baseball, and basketball game. Sports fans shout out its chorus of "Hey ho, let's go!" as a rallying cry. But most stadium spectators probably don't realize that the band originally wrote the song as a celebration of gang rumbles, but with lyrics like "Shoot 'em in the back now," it fits right into today's professional sports scene.

The Artist: Patsy Cline
The Song: "I Fall to Pieces" (1961)
The Story: Few singers conveyed emotion the way Cline did, and this anguished ode to the pain of an ended love affair sounded like she'd torn her own heart out during the recording session. Truth was, she hated the tune and didn't want anything to do with it, but her record label was desperate for a hit and tricked her into believing she would be dropped if she didn't record it. It became her first #1 single and stayed on the charts for an amazing 39 weeks. Oddly enough, Cline found out it was a hit after she'd literally fallen to pieces herself. Songwriter Hank Cochran recalls, "Patsy had been in a bad car wreck. It almost killed her. She was in the hospital with her head wrapped with bandages. I told her, 'You got yourself a pop hit, girl.' I think she thought I was just fooling around. When she finally got good enough to look at the numbers, she just laid back and said, 'Damn!'"

There's a replica of Bedrock, the town where the Flintstones lived, in Vail, Arizona.

STRANGE PET LAWSUITS

*These days, it seems that people will sue each other over
practically anything . . . including their pets. Here are
a few real-life examples of unusual legal battles.*

THE PLAINTIFF: Marie Dana

THE DEFENDANT: Samantha, a 15-year-old cocker spaniel

THE LAWSUIT: When Dana's companion, Sidney Altman, died in 1996, he bequeathed his $5 million Beverly Hills mansion and $350,000 in cash to the dog, but left only $50,000 to Dana. The will did offer her $60,000 a year to mind the aging Samantha, but stipulated that upon the dog's death everything was to go to charity. Dana sued the estate for $2.7 million.

THE VERDICT: Unknown. The judge urged the parties to settle out of court.

THE PLAINTIFF: Blackie the Talking Cat

THE DEFENDANT: City Council of Augusta, Georgia

THE LAWSUIT: Carl Miles, Blackie's owner, exhibited the cat on an Augusta street corner and collected "contributions." The city of Augusta said the enterprise required a business license and a fee, which Miles categorically refused to pay. He sued, arguing that such a fee impinged on the cat's right to free speech.

THE VERDICT: The judge actually heard the cat say, "I love you," but ruled that it was not a free speech issue. Because Blackie charged money for his speech, the city was entitled to their fee.

THE PLAINTIFF: Harold Marsh, Esq.

THE DEFENDANT: Mezzaluna Café

THE LAWSUIT: Marsh sued the Los Angeles restaurant on behalf of his miniature poodle after they were asked to leave the outdoor dining section. The suit charged the restaurant with violating the dog's constitutional rights and blamed "idiot tourists and other persons similarly insane" for complaining to the health department about dogs in the restaurant.

THE VERDICT: Unknown.

The bark of the giant sequoia can be up to two feet thick.

IF YOU . . .

Life is a series of possibilities.

IF YOU . . .
are lost near a stream, your chances of finding civilization are much greater if you travel downstream.

IF YOU . . .
are suddenly buried by a snow-storm and don't know which way is up or down, spit! The spit will always head down. Now you know in which direction to start digging.

IF YOU . . .
laid all the hot dogs Americans eat between Memorial Day and Labor Day end to end, you'd circle the globe 15 times.

IF YOU . . .
parachute from a helicopter at random, 7 out of 10 times you'll hit saltwater (because 70% of the Earth is covered with saltwater).

IF YOU . . .
want to keep leaves out of your rain gutter, secure a Slinky in one end, stretch it out, and attach it to the other end. You may need two Slinkies if it's a long gutter.

IF YOU . . .
kiss under mistletoe at Christmas, that's fine. Just don't kiss the mistletoe itself—the berries are poisonous.

IF YOU . . .
and your friends meet up with a grizzly bear, stay calm and link arms with each other. This makes the bear think he's dealing with one really big creature. Confronted with a larger creature, the bear is likely to retreat.

IF YOU . . .
can spit a watermelon seed 70 feet, you're in the world-record range.

IF YOU . . .
have too many mosquitoes in your yard, you need some bats. One bat will eat up to 1,000 bugs per night.

IF YOU . . .
put a raisin in a glass of champagne, it will sink to the bottom, then float to the top, then sink to the bottom, then float to the top, then sink to the bottom. You get the idea.

The thickest tree on Earth: El Tule, a cypress in Mexico. It has a girth of 138 feet.

YOU'VE GOT MAIL!

Like anyone with an e-mail address, we at the BRI get a lot of unsolicited e-mail that seems to be too good—or bad—to be true. We've looked into the claims made by some of them, and here's what we've found. (Do any of these look familiar? We wouldn't be surprised if you've received a few of them yourself.)

YOU'VE GOT MAIL

From:	abraxas@cloudten.org
To:	djeff@home.att
Subject:	Fwd: Breasts linked to men's health

This is not a joke: Ogling women's breasts is good for a man's health and can add years to his life, experts have discovered. According to the New England Journal of Medicine, "Just 10 minutes of staring at the charms of a well-endowed female is roughly equivalent to a 30-minute aerobics work-out," declared gerontologist Dr. Karen Weatherby.

THE ORIGIN: The e-mail appeared in March 2000, not long after the *Weekly World News* tabloid ran an article making a similar claim.

THE TRUTH: It is a joke—the *New England Journal of Medicine* never published such a study, and if "Dr. Karen Weatherby" exists at all, she's never had anything published in a medical journal.

YOU'VE GOT MAIL

From:	Concerned neighbors
To:	My friends
Subject:	Missing 5-year-old

Five-year-old Kelsey Brooke Jones has been missing from her home in southern Minnesota since 4:00 p.m. on October 11, 1999. Please help find her by forwarding this e-mail—and the picture of Kelsey that's attached—to everyone you know.

THE ORIGIN: This e-mail, which originated in southern Minnesota some time after 4:00 p.m. on October 11, 1999, is believed to have been forwarded to millions of people since then.

Count 'em yourself: Every day an adult body produces 300 billion new cells.

THE TRUTH: Kelsey really did "disappear" on October 11—she went a few doors down to a neighbor's apartment to play while her mother was taking a nap, and was still playing there when her mother woke up. Mom called the police before checking with the neighbors; officers found Kelsey a few minutes later when they started knocking on doors.

Because Kelsey was never really missing, no missing child report was ever filed. No matter—by then someone had already sent out the first e-mail, and it has been circulating ever since. Apparently, the picture attached to the e-mail isn't even Kelsey, which means that millions of e-mail recipients all over the country may be keeping an eye out for a girl who never disappeared, using a picture that isn't even her.

YOU'VE GOT MAIL

From:	AllenO@CDC.gov
To:	brmail@mind.net
Subject:	Fwd: Spiked pay phones

Hello, my name is Tina Strongman and I work at a police station, as a phone operator for 911 . . . It seems that a new form of gang initiation is to go find as many pay phones as possible and put a mixture of LSD and strychnine onto the buttons. This mixture is deadly to the human touch, and apparently, this has killed some people . . . Please be careful if you are using a pay phone anywhere. You may want to wipe it off, or just not use one at all.

THE ORIGIN: The e-mail began circulating in April 1999, following months of rumors that HIV-infected drug users were hiding contaminated needles in pay phone coin-return slots. The pay phone rumors were so pervasive that the Centers for Disease Control issued an official press release debunking them.

THE TRUTH: The LSD–payphone e-mail is an April Fools' joke that draws its inspiration from a number of classic urban legends, including children's wash-off tattoos that are spiked with LSD; gangs that initiate new members by murdering the occupants of vehicles that flash their bright headlights; and AIDS-infected needles hidden in gas pump handles, movie theater seat cushions, and other seemingly innocuous places.

Once you file something, there's a 98 percent chance you'll never look at it again.

TREKKIES

Star Trek is so integrated into our culture that the word "Trekkie" is now in the dictionary. And there's no more important aspect of Trek culture than Star Trek conventions. We spoke with Trek expert Richard Arnold, of Creation Entertainment, the biggest Trek convention organizers, to get the story of how they started.

STAR WRECK

The vast *Star Trek* empire thrives today, yet back in 1966 the original TV series never did better than 52nd place in the ratings and barely clawed its way through its third season before it was cancelled. After the show's final episode in 1969, the cast and production crew disbanded, never expecting to work together again.

Two years later, Paramount syndicated the series and allowed stations to broadcast it cheaply in order to recoup part of their investment. Stations typically ran it every weekday at dinnertime, and before they knew it devoted watchers were tuning in religiously. Casual viewers also watched, giving the show a much broader audience than it had had in primetime.

Fans wanted more, but Paramount wasn't about to risk another flop by making new episodes. So people had to settle for the next best thing: hearing *Star Trek* creator Gene Roddenberry speak about it. Soon, Roddenberry was swimming in invitations for speaking engagements at colleges and science-fiction conventions.

THE WRATH OF CON

Sci-fi conventions had been around since the 1930s, but they focused on books, not movies or television. In fact, the purist organizers of the big sci-fi conventions condemned made-for-TV science fiction as a perversion of the genre. But the droves of sci-fi buffs who packed these conventions had adored Roddenberry's work ever since he previewed the *Star Trek's* pilot episode "The Cage" at the sci-fi convention WorldCon in 1966 to an explosion of cheers.

The more *Star Trek* people wanted, the more resistant organizers became. Finally, their patience ran out. In 1971 at Sci-fi Con, the

---

Scientists say the higher your I.Q., the more you dream.

committee in charge sent a clear message to Star Trek fans: "If you want Star Trek, put on your own conventions; television is not welcome here."

TO BOLDLY GO WHERE NO SHOW HAS GONE BEFORE

There had never been a convention for only one show before, so the committee thought they were putting a stop to the *Star Trek* madness. But it was a massive blunder: without Roddenberry on the bill, audiences dwindled. Still, Roddenberry was reluctant to put together a convention, so *Star Trek* actors Al Schuster and Joan Winston together with a group of devoted fans decided to do it. The world's first Trek Con was set to take place at New York City's Stadtler Hilton Hotel in January 1972. Roddenberry was to be the keynote speaker, and a few actors who had had bit parts were scheduled to make appearances.

Schuster and Winston guessed that maybe 400 fans would show up; a capacity crowd of 800 was a pipe dream. But when convention day arrived, so did 4,000 rabid *Star Trek* fans, who crowded in and around the packed hotel, among them legendary sci-fi author Isaac Asimov (a huge fan). Even NASA sent representatives.

COSTUME DRAMA

Today, a Trekkie can buy almost anything with a *Star Trek* logo on it in the "dealers' room," but in the early days only a few wares were available: T-shirts (two different designs), homemade models, and bumper stickers with phrases like "My other car is a starship" and the infamous "Beam me up, Scotty!"

Some Trekkies showed up to the first convention in full homemade Vulcan or Klingon garb. The person with the best outfit was one of the organizers, Al Schuster, who enlisted the show's head makeup artist to transform him into a Klingon. Once convention organizers realized that fans had no shame about dressing up as their favorite characters, they decided to encourage them by organizing fashion shows and awarding prizes for best costume—human or alien.

Not everyone liked wearing a costume, though. Leonard Nimoy, who played Spock, the show's most popular character, was reluctant to appear at conventions because he didn't want to be typecast. He even wrote a book entitled *I Am Not Spock*. At his first convention in 1973, his presence caused such chaos that he had to be rushed out by an army of security guards. He later came to embrace his popularity, however, and 20 years later wrote another book: *I AM Spock.*

"GET A LIFE!"

The other actors were in great demand as well, and none more than Captain James T. Kirk—William Shatner—but Shatner didn't agree to appear at a convention until 1976. When the time came to go onstage, Shatner was a nervous wreck, says Trek Con organizer Richard Arnold: "I was sort of babysitting him before he went on—for a man who doesn't smoke or drink, he had a cigarette and a drink in each hand." He recovered, then blew the audience away with his over-the-top energy.

But Shatner later turned from fan favorite to hated villain with three little words. When he hosted *Saturday Night Live* in 1986, writers wanted to lampoon Trek conventions in a skit, which ended with an exasperated plea from Shatner: "Get a life!" Shatner was apprehensive about doing the skit, but the people at SNL assured him it was all in good fun.

Right before he went on, Shatner remarked: "I hope *Star Trek* fans have a sense of humor, because if not I'm going to be in big trouble." They didn't. According to Arnold, "Some fans are still upset about it to this day because the skit was dead-on. It's true: there are fans who live in their parents' basements and never go out. These people live for the show."

LIVE LONG AND PROSPER

Since the first convention, Trek Cons have grown in frequency and popularity. In fact, it was the popularity of the conventions that convinced Paramount to resurrect *Star Trek* as a movie in 1979. By the mid-70s, Trek conventions were regularly drawing 20,000 people. Chicago's 1975 Trek Con drew a whopping 30,000 Trekkies! Today, every major city has an annual convention; many have several. On an average weekend, there are 10 to 20 Trek conventions taking place in the North America and Europe. Admission prices range from just a few dollars to over $1,000 for front-row seating.

Astronomical attendance and high ticket prices translate to big bucks for the actors. They used to speak for $500 or less—

sometimes even for free. Now big guns like Shatner, Nimoy, and *The Next Generation's* Patrick Stewart (Captain Picard) and Brent Spiner (Data) pocket as much as $50,000 per appearance. Autographs used to be free; today fans can count on forking over $5 to $30. Shatner and Nimoy charge $50 to $100 for a signature. Many former Star Trek actors make a very nice living by appearing at 30-plus conventions per year at $10,000 a pop.

And who is today's biggest draw for Trek conventions? Not Captain Kirk, not Mr. Spock, not even Jean-Luc Picard. It's Seven of Nine—the gorgeous young woman with a painted-on costume played by Jeri Ryan on *Voyager*—ensuring that Trekkies will continue to flock to *Star Trek* conventions for many years to come.

* * *

SHIPWRECKS AND ANIMALS:
THE UNTOLD STORIES

A Duck Raises Sheep. In 1964 a freighter carrying 6,000 sheep capsized and sank in Kuwait's harbor. With so many dead animals underwater, Kuwaitis worried that the rotting carcasses would pollute the water. A way had to be found to lift the ship and remove the sheep before the harbor was contaminated. Danish engineer Karl Kroyer remembered a comic book in which Donald Duck and his nephews raised a sunken ship by stuffing it full of ping pong balls. The idea was worth a try, so Kroyer had 27 million polystyrene balls injected into the hull. It worked—thanks in part to Donald Duck.

Moby's Legacy. Two Maori women were the only survivors of a canoe accident off New Zealand. As a dead whale floated by with the harpoon still stuck in it, they used the line from the harpoon to haul themselves aboard the carcass and then floated 80 miles to safety.

Horse Sense. In 1852 the British steamship H.M.S. *Birkenhead* sank three miles off the African coast. Captain Wright was one of the last to abandon ship, and when he finally made it to shore, he was greeted by another of the survivors . . . his horse.

The Japanese express mourning after the death of a loved one by wearing white.

EAT YOUR WORDS

Ever wonder where the names of certain foods or eating utensils come from? At the BRI, it's our job to wonder. Here are some origins for you to chew on:

PLATE. Comes from the Old French *plat*, meaning "flat."

CUP. From the Sanskrit word *kupa*, meaning "water well."

MUSHROOM. An English mispronounciation of *moisseron*, the Old French word for "fungus."

CABBAGE. From the French word for "head," *caboche*.

HORS D'OEUVRE. In French, *hors* means "outside" and *oeuvre* means "work;" literally "apart from the main work."

SALAD. From the Latin *salsus*, meaning "salted."

COLESLAW. Comes from the Dutch terms *kool*, meaning "cabbage," and *sla*, meaning "salad."

SPAGHETTI. From *spago*, the Italian word for "cord" or "string."

CANTALOUPE. From the place it was first grown— Cantalupo, Italy.

GELATIN. Comes from the Latin *gelo*, meaning "to freeze or congeal." So does *jelly*.

DESSERT. *Desservir* is the French word for "to clear (the table)," and that's what you do before dessert is served.

BOWL. Comes from the Anglo-Saxon word *bolla*, meaning "round."

SPOON. From the Anglo-Saxon *spon*, meaning "chip"— a curved chip of wood dipped into a bowl.

* * *

Put a pot of chili on the stove to simmer.
Let it simmer. Meanwhile, broil a good steak.
Eat the steak. Let the chili simmer. Ignore it.

—Recipe for chili from Allan Shivers, former governor of Texas

THE METRIC CLOCK

Uncle John stumbled on a strange-looking timepiece in an antique store. When the dealer told him it was a "metric clock," he just had to find out the story behind it. Here it is.

TIME FOR A CHANGE

Most of the world uses the metric system. But you probably don't know that it was invented by the French and came about as a result of the French Revolution.

After the bloody triumph over the French monarchy in 1792, the French Revolutionary government, known as "the Terror," was intent on cleansing citizens' lives of all influence of the aristocracy and the Church. They were going to create a new society based on reason and rationality.

For many years, French scientists had been trying to replace the traditional arbitrary system of weights and measures with a decimal system. This climate of reform and reason was perfect for implementing their ideas.

REASON PREVAILS

In 1793 the Committee of Public Instruction approved a bold proposal: that the basic unit of distance, the foot, be replaced with the "meter"—a unit equal to one ten-millionth of the length of the arc from the equator to the North Pole. Distance henceforth was measured in multiples of 10: centimeters, millimeters, and kilometers. The quart was replaced with the liter, and the ounce with the gram. And it opened the door for another innovation: metric time.

Under the guidance of mathematician Charles Gilbert Romme, the Committee set about the task of creating a metric clock and calendar that would reflect their belief in science over religion. After a year of tinkering by France's most distinguished poets, scientists, and mathematicians, the French Republican Calendar was officially adopted on October 5, 1793.

The new calendar still had 12 months in a year, but every month had three 10-day weeks, called decades. That accounted for only 360 days. The remaining 5 days of the year were celebrated as feast days for the common man: Virtue Day, Genius Day, Labor

. . . Buffalo, New York, governor of New York State, and president of the United States.

Day, Reason Day, Rewards Day, and, in leap years, Revolution Day.

The metric time system was even more confusing than the calendar. Each day was divided into 10 decimal hours, each hour split into 100 minutes, and each minute into 100 seconds. A decimal second was shorter than a traditional second, but a decimal minute was longer than a traditional minute.

THE NAME GAME

The new names for the months and the days were invented by poet Philippe Fabre d'Eglantine. He named the months according to the natural events occurring at that time of year and then rhymed them by season. They were *Vendemiaire* (vintage), *Brumaire* (mist), *Frimaire* (frost), *Nivose* (snow), *Pluviose* (rain), *Ventose* (wind), *Germinal* (sprouting), *Floreal* (blossoming), *Prairial* (meadow), *Moissidor* (harvest), *Thermidor* (heat), and *Fructidor* (fruit). The British press lampooned these as Wheezy, Sneezy, Freezy, Slippy, Drippy, Nippy, Showery, Flowery, Bowery, Wheaty, Heaty, Sweety.

In contrast, d'Eglantine gave the days of the week bland names: *Primidi, Duodi, Tridi, Quartidi, Quintidi, Sextidi, Septidi, Octidi, Nondidi, and Decadi.* Translation: "First Day," "Second Day," "Third Day," etc. But every day of the year was named individually, too. D'Eglantine named them for plants, animals, and tools—for example, Olive Day, Goat Day, or Plow Day—but no days were named for saints, popes, or kings.

CONFUSION REIGNS

Despite its nationalistic imagery and scientific convenience, the new calendar was rejected by the common people it was designed to benefit . . . it was just too confusing.

First strike: The calendar was designed to count from September 22, 1792, the date of the foundation of the French Republic and the abolition of the monarchy. By the time the new calendar was adopted, however, the Republic was already well into the second year, prompting immediate confusion.

Second strike: French workers detested the new calendar because it allotted only 1 rest day in a 10-day week instead of 1 per 7 days. And, to the Terror's chagrin, most people still kept track of Sundays for church.

The peanut is one of the most concentrated sources of nourishment.

Third strike: The rest of Europe was still using the Gregorian calendar, which made business increasingly difficult to conduct between French merchants and those in other countries. On top of that, the new metric clocks had faces that included markings for both traditional and metric time, which was confusing even for people who wanted to use decimal hours and minutes.

TICK . . . TICK . . . TICK . . .

As passion for the Revolution faded, aspects of the calendar were slowly abolished. By 1795 the metric clock and the year-end feast days—celebrated only once—were swept away. Napoléon Bonaparte pushed the French senate to reinstate the old calendar as soon as he was crowned emperor. At the beginning of 1806, after only reaching year 13, the French Republican calendar completely disappeared from use.

* * *

WHAT'S IN YOUR DRAIN?

Here are a few items Roto-Rooter claims they've found in clogged pipes:

Home and Garden: Broom handles, doorknobs, garden hoses, bungee cords, and a hummingbird feeder.

Health and Beauty Aids: Glass eyes, gold teeth, dentures, contact lenses, toothbrushes, hearing aids, and toupees.

Clothing and Linens: Women's lingerie, long johns, towels, robes, a complete bedspread, and, of course, a multitude of missing socks.

Electronics: TV remotes, pagers, an alarm clock, a Timex that took a licking and kept on ticking, and a Rolex that took a licking and died.

Sporting Goods and Toys: An eight ball, golf balls (30 in one drain), a shrimp net, a teargas projectile, and a Teenage Mutant Ninja Turtle doll.

Pets: Birds, bats, beavers, cats, ducks, fish, frogs, possums, skunks, a piranha, a $2^{1}/_{2}$-pound trout, and lots of snakes—including a six-foot rattlesnake.

Valuables: $400 in coins, $58 in change in a Laundromat pipe, canceled checks, a $4,000 diamond, and $50,000.

Groceries: A Cornish game hen and a six-pack of Budweiser.

Marlene Dietrich played the musical saw.

CELEBRITY GOSSIP

Here's our cheesy tabloid section—a
bunch of gossip about famous people.

LUCIANO PAVAROTTI

When Pavarotti performs for the public, he only does so under very strict conditions. His contract states that during sound check, "there must be no distinct smells anywhere near the artist." In his dressing room, he demands that all sofas be mounted on six-inch risers and that "soft toilet paper" be provided. As for his hotel accommodations, he insists that "the master bedroom must always be kept in total darkness." He refuses to go onstage for a performance before he finds a bent nail somewhere on the stage and pulls it out.

MARLON BRANDO

While filming the 2001 movie *The Score*, Brando refused to be on the set at the same time as director Frank Oz. Brando referred to Oz as "Miss Piggy" (Oz provided the voice of Muppet Miss Piggy many years ago) and teased him with lines like "Don't you wish I was a puppet, so you could control me?" Robert De Niro was forced to direct Brando instead, with Oz giving him instructions via headset.

WALT DISNEY

Before Walt Disney's 35th birthday, his brother Roy encouraged employees to throw the boss a surprise party. Two of the animators thought it would be hilarious to make a short movie of Mickey and Minnie Mouse "consummating their relationship." When Disney saw the animation at the party, he feigned laughter and playfully asked who made it. As soon as the two animators came forward, he fired them on the spot and left.

SERENA WILLIAMS

According to London's *Metro* newspaper, tennis star Serena Williams claims to have a six-hour-a-day online shopping addiction. Even while competing in the French Open, she was "stuck" online buying things she didn't need. The source of her compulsion: fame has forced her to avoid shopping in public.

During World War II, the traditionally metal Oscar statue was made of plaster.

(NOT) COMING TO A THEATER NEAR YOU

You'd be surprised by how many films in Hollywood are started . . . without ever being finished. Here's a look at a few that will probably never make it onto the big screen.

STAR TREK VI: STARFLEET ACADEMY (1990)
Starring: An entirely new cast of young actors playing James T. Kirk, Mr. Spock, and the other original *Star Trek* characters

Making the Movie: *Starfleet Academy* was intended as an "Episode 1" prequel to the original *Star Trek* TV series: the story of how Kirk, Spock, and McCoy met at Starfleet Academy. The film was the brainchild of Harve Bennett, producer of Paramount's *Star Trek* feature films.

Kiss of Doom: Bennett was also the archrival of Gene Roddenberry, creator of the original TV series. Roddenberry had his own ideas for a *Star Trek* prequel; when he learned of Bennett's plans for *Starfleet Academy*, he set out to destroy the film by spreading rumors that Bennett wanted to model it after the *Police Academy* series.

Actor George Takei (Sulu) did his part by appearing at Star Trek conventions, urging fans to protest if he and his costars were replaced with new actors. "This pressure from all sides . . . doomed the academy idea for the time being," Chris Gore writes in *The 50 Greatest Movies Never Made*. "*Starfleet Academy* as envisioned by Harve Bennett now resides amid the dust of the unproduced story pile over at Paramount."

NATIONAL LAMPOON'S JAWS 3, PEOPLE 0 (1983)
Starring: Jaws
Making the Movie: Disappointed with how poorly *Jaws 2* did at the box office, Universal Studios gave serious thought to handing their killer-shark franchise over to the folks at *National Lampoon* to see if they could do anything with it. Screenwriters John Hughes and

Tod Carroll came up with story for *Jaws 3, People 0*, a comedy about the making of a *Jaws* sequel.

Kiss of Doom: In the end, Universal dumped the idea and made *Jaws 3-D* instead. It bombed even worse than *Jaws 2*.

SOMETHING'S GOT TO GIVE (1962)

Starring: Marilyn Monroe and Dean Martin

Making the Movie: By 1962 Monroe's emotional and substance abuse problems had caught up with her. She was in no condition to work on a film, but she had to complete her four-picture deal with 20th Century-Fox. So she signed on to make *Something's Got to Give* under George Cukor, one of the few directors she was still willing to work with.

Sure enough, when filming started in May, Monroe proved impossible to work with: on the days when she bothered to show up at all, she was usually hours late and often unable to do her scenes.

Kiss of Doom: True to the film's title, something did give: Monroe. Her erratic behavior helped to push the film more than $1 million over budget in just a few weeks of filming. 20th Century-Fox was also in deep financial trouble with *Cleopatra*, already well on its way to becoming the most expensive film ever made. They couldn't afford another loser, so they fired Monroe, then rehired her when Dean Martin threatened to walk off the set. By then it was too late: Monroe died of a drug overdose in August 1962, before production could resume.

A DAY AT THE U.N. (1960)

Starring: The Marx Brothers

Making the Movie: Director Billy Wilder (*Sunset Boulevard, The Lost Weekend, Some Like It Hot*) got the idea while filming *The Apartment* near the United Nations building in New York. It occurred to him that the Cold War seriousness of the U.N. would make a great backdrop for a Marx Brothers film, even though the brothers had not worked together since their 1950 film *Love Happy*. He pitched the idea to Groucho Marx; he liked it and told Wilder to work out a deal with his brother (and agent) Gummo Marx.

Kiss of Doom: *A Day at the U.N.* came late in the Marx Brothers'

The average adult has four dreams a night and one nightmare a year.

careers . . . too late: Harpo had a heart attack while the script was being written, and although he got better, insurance companies refused to cover the Marx Brothers for the time that it would take to make the film. Sadly, the insurance companies were right: Chico died in 1961, ending the hope of one last Marx Brothers film.

THE ADVENTURES OF FARTMAN (1996)

Starring: Howard Stern

Making the Movie: *Fartman*, from a simple comedy sketch that Stern invented for his radio and TV shows, was supposed to serve as the film "vehicle" that would give Stern his big-screen debut. Screenwriter Jonathan Lawton (*Pretty Woman*) fleshed out the concept, developing *Fartman* into the story of a New York editor who gains astonishing "colonic powers" when bad guys stuff him full of mysterious goo.

Kiss of Doom: Ironically, *Fartman* was done in by a group of cartoon characters—the Teenage Mutant Ninja Turtles. New Line Pictures, which made the Ninja Turtle movies without obtaining the licensing rights to the characters, had missed out on millions of dollars in merchandising profits and wasn't about to make the same mistake with *Fartman*. The company insisted on controlling the licensing rights, offering Stern only a 5 percent share in the profits. "The deal fell through over Fartman coffee mugs," Stern said.

* * *

STAMP OF DISAPPROVAL

In 1994 the U.S. Postal Service announced that it was issuing a set of ten commemorative stamps to mark the 50th anniversary of the end of World War II. One of the stamps was going to show an atomic mushroom cloud with the caption, "Atomic bombs hasten war's end, August 1945," . . . but the insensitive message infuriated the Japanese, prompting the Japanese government to launch a formal protest with the Clinton Administration. On December 7, 1994—the 53rd anniversary of the attack on Pearl Harbor—the Postal Service announced that it was dumping the stamp in favor of one showing President Truman announcing the end of the war.

DUMB CROOKS

Here's proof that crime doesn't pay.

YOU'RE SO TRANSPARENT

"A 19-year-old convenience store employee in Shawnee, Kansas, put tape over the security camera, robbed the till, then called police to report a robbery. But since he used transparent tape to cover the camera, it was easy to see that he was the robber and he was quickly arrested."

—FHM *Magazine*

FAT CHANCE

MADRID—"Would-be burglar Pedro Cardona tried to break into a house by squeezing through a doggie door. It was something like putting two pounds of bologna in a one-pound bag as the portly Cardona became wedged in halfway through. Rescuers had to chop the door down with axes to get him out."

—*Bizarre News*

RUN FOR THE BORDER

"A criminal mastermind in a small Iowa town carefully planned a bank robbery and actually got away with the money. But he was arrested the next day at a motel near the state line, only 20 miles away.

"When asked why he had stopped so close to the scene of the crime, he explained that he was on parole and couldn't cross the state line without permission from his parole officer."

—*The World's Dumbest Criminals*,
by Daniel Butler

WHAT A DOPE

"A man in Brighton, England, jumped out of a taxi without paying and left behind a bag of marijuana. Amazingly, he called the taxi company to inquire about the bag and was told it had been turned over to the police, so he went to the local police station to claim the bag."

—*Chicago Sun-Times*

MONEY TO BURN

"Six men were charged with attempting Britain's biggest cash robbery. According to court testimony, the gang forced an armored car carrying $18.2 million to be driven to a wooded area, then used high-powered torches to open it. But the torches accidentally set off a 'bonfire' that burned $2.4 million into ashes and caused the men to flee."

—*Dumb Crooks*

BLOCKHEAD

"Seems this guy wanted some beer pretty badly. He decided that he'd just throw a cinder block through a liquor store window, grab some booze, and run. So he lifted the cinder block over his head and heaved it at the window. The cinder block bounced back and hit him on the head, knocking him unconscious. Seems the liquor store window was made of Plexiglas. The whole event was caught on videotape."

—*Darwin Awards*

WANT CHIPS WITH THAT?

"A Subway sandwich shop employee in Edmonton, Alberta, somehow managed to activate the burglar alarm and disarm two men who were attempting to rob him at knifepoint. Scared by the sandwich-maker's heroics, the felons fled the scene. The Subway employee pursued the would-be thieves, shouting that there was no harm done and that he'd gladly make them free sandwiches if they came back. Amazingly, they did! Police arrived minutes later and arrested the hungry thieves, who were patiently waiting in line for a Cold Cut Trio."

—*Stuff* magazine

* * *

ACTUAL JAPANESE CAR NAMES

- Subaru Gravel Express
- Suzuki Every Joy Pop Turbo
- Mazda Proceed Marvie
- Isuzu Mysterious Utility Wizard
- Isuzu 20 Giga Light Dump
- Toyota Master Ace Surf

Thirty million years ago, there were palm trees in Alaska.

IF YOU BUILD IT, THEY WILL COME

Some people call them roadside attractions. We call them tourist traps. Either way, it's an amazing phenomenon: There's nothing much to see there, nothing much to do there. Yet tourists go by the millions. Think we could get people to come to Uncle John's Bowl of Wonder?

WALL DRUG, WALL, South Dakota

Build It . . . One summer day in 1936, Dorothy and Ted Hustead had a brilliant idea: they put signs up along U.S. 16 advertising their struggling mom-and-pop drugstore. As an afterthought, they included an offer for free ice water. Wall Drug was situated 10 miles from the entrance to the South Dakota badlands, and on sweltering summer days before air conditioning, the suggestion of free ice water made rickety old Wall Drug seem like an oasis. When Ted got back from putting up the first sign, half a dozen cars were already parked in front of his store.

They'll Come: The Husteads knew they were on to something. Ted built an empire of billboards all over the United States, planting signs farther and farther away from his drugstore. There's a sign in Amsterdam's train station (only 5,397 miles to Wall Drug); there's one at the Taj Mahal (10,728 miles to Wall Drug); and there's even one in Antarctica (only 10,645 miles to Wall Drug).

Today, Wall Drug is an enormous 50,000-square-foot tourist mecca with a 520-seat restaurant and countless specialty and souvenir shops; if it's hokey, odds are that Wall Drug sells it. They also have a collection of robots, including a singing gorilla and a mechanical Cowboy Orchestra. Wall Drug spends over $300,000 on billboards, but every cent of it pays off. The store lures in 20,000 visitors a day in the summer and grosses more than $11 million each year. And they still give away free ice water—5,000 glasses a day.

SOUTH OF THE BORDER, Dillon, South Carolina

Build It . . . Driving south on I-95 near the South Carolina bor-

---

Gail Borden (inventor of condensed milk) is buried beneath a headstone shaped like a milk can.

der, one object stands out from the landscape: a 200-foot-tall tower with a giant sombrero on top. The colossal hat is Sombrero Tower, centerpiece of the huge South of the Border tourist complex.

SOB, as the locals call it, began as a beer stand operated by a man named Alan Schafer. When Schafer noticed that his building supplies were being delivered to "Schafer Project: South of the [North Carolina] Border," a lightbulb lit up over his head and he decided his stand needed a Mexican theme.

They'll Come: Today, SOB sprawls over 135 acres and imports—and sells—$1.5 million worth of Mexican merchandise a year. It has a 300-room motel and five restaurants, including the Sombrero Room and Pedro's Casateria (a fast-food joint shaped like a antebellum mansion with a chicken on the roof). There's also Pedro's Rocket City (a fireworks shop), Golf of Mexico (miniature golf), and Pedro's Pleasure Dome spa. Incredibly, eight million people stop into SOB every year for a little slice of Mexi-kitsch.

TREES OF MYSTERY, Klamath, California

Build It . . . When Carl Bruno first toured the towering redwood forests around the DeMartin ranch in 1931, he was awestruck by a handful of oddly deformed trees. Dollar signs in his eyes, Bruno snapped up the property and began luring in travelers to see trees shaped like pretzels and double helixes. He called his attraction Wonderland Park, and for the first 15 years of its existence, it did modest business—but something was missing.

They'll Come: He decided the park needed a 49-foot-tall statue of Paul Bunyan. In 1946 Bruno had the massive mythical logger installed near the highway and changed the park's name to Trees of Mystery. Business began to pick up. He added a companion piece, 35-feet-tall Babe the Blue Ox, in 1949. (When Babe was first introduced, he blew smoke out of his nostrils, which made small children run away screaming. The smoke was discontinued.)

Trees of Mystery prospered and is still open today. It recently added an aerial gondola ride, but the park is primarily a bunch of oddly shaped trees and a tunnel through a giant redwood. The gift shop, which sells cheesy souvenirs and wood carvings, has been hailed as a model for other tourist attractions. The park was even honored by *American Heritage* magazine as the best roadside attraction for 2001.

Every year 100,000 Americans are injured by their own clothing.

WIDE WORLD OF BATHROOM NEWS

Here are bits and pieces of bathroom trivia we've flushed out
of the newspapers of the world over the past couple of years.

GERMANY

Germany's Defense Ministry, which is looking for ways to reduce the country's military costs, has asked soldiers to use less toilet paper. "Lavatory paper is not always used just in the lavatory, it is often also used to wipe things up," a spokesperson explained. "We are asking people to think before they wipe."

UNITED STATES ABROAD

Haliburton, the oil services company that Dick Cheney headed before resigning to run for vice president, admitted during the 2000 presidential campaign that the company "maintains separate restrooms overseas for its American and foreign employees." The company defended its separate-but-equal restroom policy, saying it was done for "cultural reasons," and that Cheney was "unaware" of the practice during his five years as chief executive.

ENGLAND

• The Westminster City Council has decided to erect open-air urinals next to the National Gallery in Trafalgar Square. "Night-time revelers, waiting at a bus stop outside the gallery, have been relieving themselves against the new wing," the council said in a press release. "The gallery now fears that the stone of the building is being affected by uric acid. Urinals will be placed in problem areas where 'wet spots' have been identified."

• From Scotland Yard: "The Department of Professional Standards is investigating an incivility charge arising from the search of a home under the Misuse of Drugs Act. An allegation has been received from a person in the house that one of the male officers broke wind and did not apologize to the family for his action. The complainant felt it was rude and unprofessional."

Clue originally meant "ball of twine." That's why you "unravel" clues to solve a mystery.

CHINA

Archaeologists exploring the tomb of a king of the Western Han dynasty (206 B.C. to 24 A.D.) have unearthed what they believe is the world's oldest flush toilet, one that predates the earliest European water closet by as much as 1,800 years. The toilet, which boasts a stone seat, a drain for running water, and even an armrest, "is the earliest of its kind ever discovered in the world," the archaeologists told China's official Xinhua news agency, "meaning that the Chinese flushed first."

MEXICO

In June 2001, the Milenio daily newspaper revealed Mexican president Vicente Fox, who was elected on an anticorruption platform, has furnished the Los Pinos presidential palace with "specially embroidered" bath towels that cost $400 apiece. But they're just a tiny part of the more than $400,000 worth of household items that Fox has purchased during his first six months in office. President Fox admitted to the expenditures and even praised their disclosure by Milenio, citing the article as "evidence of progress in bringing transparency to government spending." (The minimum wage in Mexico, where 40 million people live in poverty, is about $132 a month.)

NIGERIA

A Nigerian housewife has reported seeing an apparition of the Virgin Mary in the window of her bathroom in the city of Lagos. "I walked into the bathroom at about five a.m. and was shocked and overwhelmed by fear with the visible appearance of the Virgin Mary," Christiana Ejambi told reporters. Since then, the Blessed Virgin has reappeared several times and has given Ejambi messages on a number of subjects, including religious faith and how to control the crowds that have gathered to witness the miracle. Per the instructions of the Virgin Mary, only three people are allowed into the restroom at a time; everyone else has to wait their turn.

* * *

"Red meat is *not* bad for you. Now blue-green meat,
that's bad for you." **—Tommy Smothers**

On any given day, half the people in the world will eat rice.

IRONIC, ISN'T IT?

There's nothing like a good dose of irony to put the problems of day-to-day life in proper perspective.

CRIMINAL IRONY

- New York State Assemblywoman Nancy Calhoun pled guilty to charges that she harassed her ex-boyfriend in 1999. According to the ex-boyfriend, the harassment included "bursting into his home in the middle of the night; tailgating him in a car; and posing as a cosmetics saleswoman in order to get the phone number of the man's new girlfriend." Calhoun was cosponsor of the state's antistalking legislation.

- In 2000 a branch fell off a tree in Nevada City, California, and struck a power line, cutting off power to the town for more than 30 minutes. The outage delayed the courtroom trial of the Pacific Gas & Electric Company, which was charged with "failing to trim vegetation around power lines."

- In October 2000, a gunman armed with a .38-caliber revolver held up a Head Start school in Stapleton, New York, and escaped with $11,000 in cash and jewelry. The man was later arrested . . . and identified as a local minister, who used the money to pay the rent on his church for the next six months.

MISCELLANEOUS IRONY

- In January 2000, a British professional soccer player named Rio Ferdinand strained a tendon in his leg and had to be put on the team's disabled list. Cause of injury: "He left his leg propped for too long on his coffee table while watching the Super Bowl on TV."

- A fire destroyed a $127,000 home in Maui, Hawaii; fire investigators identified the cause as a short in a fire-prevention system. "This is even worse than last year," the homeowner told reporters, "when someone broke in and stole my new security system."

Kodak founder George Eastman hated to have his picture taken.

WHY WE HAVE POSTAGE STAMPS

One of the lessons we've learned over and over again at the BRI is that there's a pretty interesting story behind just about everything, no matter how small it is or how ordinary it may seem to be in our lives. We learned it again when we started researching the history of postage stamps.

COLLECT ON DELIVERY

One afternoon in the mid-1830s, an Englishman named Rowland Hill happened to observe the response of a housemaid when the postman delivered a letter to her. In those days, the recipient of a letter, not the sender, paid the postage due on it—and the recipient could refuse to accept delivery if they wished.

That's just what the housemaid did, but there was something unusual about the way she did it: she studied the outside of the envelope, almost as if she were looking for some kind of hidden message. Then, she handed the letter back to the postman and refused to pay the postage due on the letter.

Hill knew what would happen next: The postman would take the letter back to the post office and throw it onto a pile of hundreds or probably thousands of similar "dead" letters that clogged every English post office in the 1830s. Sooner or later the post office would return that letter to the sender, free of charge.

In other words, every dead letter sent through the English mail in those days was sent through twice—first to the recipient (who refused it), and then back to the sender—even though no postage was ever collected from either the sender or the recipient. The enormous cost of delivering, storing, and returning so many dead letters was passed on to paying customers in the form of higher postage rates. Thanks to this and other glaring inefficiencies, in the mid-1830s, sending a letter across England could cost as much as an entire day's wage—historians estimate that those years saw the highest postal rates in the history of the English Post Office.

Translated from Greek, *philatelist* (stamp collector) means "lover of something untaxed."

READING BETWEEN THE LINES

The system was wide open to abuse. It was common for people to hide some kind of coded message on the outside of the envelope, which the recipient could read without having to pay the postage on the letter. Hill was sure that this was what the housemaid and the sender of her letter were up to. An educator by profession, he decided to conduct a comprehensive statistical analysis of the British postal system to see if he could improve upon it.

In 1837 Hill completed his study and published his findings in a pamphlet titled *Post Office Reform: Its Importance and Practicability*. In it, he pointed out the obvious problems associated with having the recipient of a letter pay the postage. He also criticized the practice of calculating postage by the mile: In those days a letter that traveled 15 miles or less required 4¢ postage, and a letter that traveled 500 miles or more cost 15¢. But charging by the mile meant that postal employees had to spend time measuring distances between towns and calculating postage due for every letter they delivered, a practice Hill thought was wasteful.

A BETTER SYSTEM

Hill calculated that when all of the inefficiencies were taken into consideration, on average it cost the Post Office about one and one-half cents to deliver a letter. He proposed lowering the postage rate to a uniform price of one cent per letter, regardless of how far it had to travel to get to its destination. And he proposed that the sender of the letter pay the postage in advance, so that the Post Office wouldn't waste time or money delivering letters that no one wanted to pay for. Payment in advance also saved postmen from the trouble of calculating postage due, as well as from the hassle of trying to get letter recipients to pay it. They could now devote their time to actually delivering the mail.

Better yet, by wringing dead letters and other inefficiencies out of the system, Hill believed that the Post Office's cost of delivering a letter would drop from one and one-half cents per letter to under a cent, which meant that the penny stamp would cover the entire cost of sending the letter. Reducing postage rates from four to fifteen cents down to a penny would also mean that ordinary people would be able to afford to send a letter for the first time.

Each year India's increase in population is equal to the population of Australia.

And with payment required in advance, people couldn't cheat the system.

SEAL OF APPROVAL

But how would the Post Office know for sure whether postage for a particular letter had been paid in advance or not? Hill proposed that the Post Office mark each letter using a special rubber stamp to indicate the postage had been paid. And to save customers the trouble of standing in line every time they needed a post office to stamp a piece of mail, he proposed that the Post Office sell pre-stamped envelopes that people could just drop in a mailbox whenever they were ready to send a letter.

For those who preferred to use their own stationery, Hill proposed that the Post Office sell "a bit of paper just large enough to bear the stamp," complete with gum on the reverse side that, when moistened, would allow the piece of paper to stick to the envelope. Hill didn't realize the significance of his idea at the time—he thought the prestamped envelopes would be a bigger hit than the prestamped "bits of paper," as he called them—but he had just invented the world's first adhesive postage stamp.

England's House of Commons was intrigued enough by Hill's proposals that it formed a committee to study them in 1837. Two years later, the government adopted his proposals, and on January 10, 1840, "universal penny postage" became the law of the land.

IT WORKS!

Just as he'd predicted, Hill's reforms revolutionized mail service in England. The number of letters delivered by the Post Office doubled from 83 million in 1839—the last year of the old system—to nearly 170 million the following year; by 1847 the Post Office was delivering more than 322 million letters a year. And although it had lowered its postal rates in some cases as much as 94 percent, by 1850 the Post Office was generating just as much revenue as it had in 1839.

The advantages of Hill's system were obvious, and other countries took note. In 1845 the United States reformed its postal rate structure to be in line with England's; Canada and France followed four years later. By 1870, more than 30 countries around the world had adopted Hill's system; for the rest of the world it was just a matter of time.

First stamp design selected by a vote of the U.S. public: the 1993 Elvis Presley 29¢ stamp.

FAMOUS FOR 15 MINUTES.COM

The stars below are living proof that dot-com fame can be as fleeting as dot-com profits.

THE STAR: Raphael Gray, 18, who lives with his parents in Clynderwen, a tiny village in south Wales.

THE HEADLINE: *Internet Robin Hood Scores the Ultimate Hack*

WHAT HAPPENED: Gray used to perform a "public service" by hacking into Web sites, downloading customer credit card information, and e-mailing it back to the companies to demonstrate how insecure the sites were. "It was just click, click, click, and I was downloading thousands of credit card numbers," he says. As a direct result of Gray's hacking, Visa and Mastercard had to spend nearly $3 million providing refunds and new credit cards to customers.

But what makes Gray truly unique is that one of the 26,000 credit card numbers he downloaded was for Microsoft founder Bill Gates. Gray used the information to order Gates some Viagra for delivery to Microsoft's world headquarters in Redmond, Washington. When police arrested Gray in March 2001, he became an Internet folk hero overnight. (The Bill Gates credit card was a fake—the e-commerce company had created a fake account in Gates's name to test their software. The Viagra was never shipped.)

THE AFTERMATH: In July 2001, Gray pled guilty to 10 counts of hacking and two counts of fraud; he was sentenced to three years of probation and ordered to seek counseling for his "low self-esteem."

THE STAR: Baby [Your Name Here], born to Jason Black and Frances Schroeder in New York in 2001.

THE HEADLINE: *Parents Offer Unique Name Game*

WHAT HAPPENED: In July 2001, Black and Schroeder put the

After his famous midnight ride, Paul Revere billed . . .

naming rights to their infant son up for auction on the eBay and
Yahoo! auction sites. Their hope was to attract a corporate
sponsor for their son: in exchange for naming their son "Nike,"
"Microsoft," or "A&W Root Beer," they hoped to raise money to
buy a new house and save for their children's college education.
The couple saw the promotion as a potential media moment for
the sponsor: Announcing the name of the child when the auction
was over would generate enough "free" publicity for the winning
bidder to more than justify the expense.

The couple posted their auction notices on July 18, 2001.
Minimum bid: $500,000.

THE AFTERMATH: Nobody bid—so they named him Zane.

THE STAR: Adam Burtle, a 20-year-old student at the
University of Washington.

THE HEADLINE: *It's Official: eBay Has No Soul*

WHAT HAPPENED: In February 2001, Burtle put his soul up for
auction on the eBay Web site. "Hardly used," his ad read. "I make
no warranties as to the condition of the soul. As of now it is near
mint condition, with only minor scratches. Due to difficulties
involved with removing my soul [he wasn't dead yet], the winning
bidder will either have to settle for a night of yummy Thai food
and cool indie flicks, or wait until my natural death."

The bidding started at a nickel; Burtle's ex-girlfriend bid it up
to $6.66, the number of "the Beast." In the final hour of bidding,
the price rose from $56 to $400, placed by a woman in Des
Moines, Iowa, but then eBay officials learned of the auction and
removed the listing before bidding closed—not because auctioning
a soul over the Internet is improper, but because eBay requires that
"you have a piece of merchandise that a seller can deliver to a
buyer," says eBay spokesman Kevin Pursglove. (eBay also forbids
the selling of drugs, alcohol, guns, and body parts.)

THE AFTERMATH: Burtle, who was suspended from placing
any more items for auction on eBay, is philosophical about the
canceled sale. "I don't think the winner is going to be able to collect on my soul anyway, to be honest," he says. "I was just happy
the bidding rose past $7.50."

THE STAR: DotComGuy, a.k.a. Mitch Maddox, a 26-year-old computer systems manager and self-described "cyberhermit"

THE HEADLINE: *Cyber-Cabin Fever Earns Man New Name, Dog and Fiancée; Not Much More Than That*

WHAT HAPPENED: Maddox legally changed his name to DotComGuy and on January 1, 2000, placed himself in a sort of self-imposed "house arrest" in an empty Dallas townhouse for a year. There, using only a laptop computer and a credit card, he was supposed to furnish the entire "Dotcompound" and meet all of his personal needs: food, clothing, entertainment, pets, etc., without ever leaving the house or his tiny backyard. Twenty Web cameras set up all over the house (except the bathroom) would record his every move 24 hours a day and broadcast the action on his Web site, www.dotcomguy.com. If he managed to tough it out the entire year, he would be rewarded with a bonus of $98,289 in cash, raised from the sale of banner advertising on his site.

The year-long publicity stunt had just one flaw: When it was conceived, the idea of buying everything you need online was a novel concept, but by the time DotComGuy moved into his townhouse it was already passé. "The novelty is gone," Internet analyst Patrick Keane told reporters about six months into DotComGuy's confinement. "If I'm an advertiser, there are a lot better places to put my message."

THE AFTERMATH: At one minute after midnight on January 1, 2001, DotComGuy emerged from his townhouse and announced he was changing his name back to Mitch Maddox. Then he hopped on a scooter and rode off into the darkness, having fulfilled his commitment to live in the house for one year. So what did he have to show for his experience? A dog he bought online (DotComDog) and a fiancée he met in an online chatroom (Crystalyn Holubeck, a Dallas TV reporter), but no $98,289. The banner ads barely raised enough money to keep the company afloat, let alone pay a bonus. According to a company spokesman, "DotComGuy 'forgave' his bonus at the end to keep the company's doors open."

The average American is exposed to 1,600 commercials and advertisements a day.

THE HISTORY OF FOOTBALL, PART II

Uncle John has always wondered why college football is so popular in the face of the NFL. Answer: tradition. College is where organized football started. (Part I of the story is on page 55.)

LAYING DOWN THE LAW

In 1876 representatives from Harvard, Yale, Columbia, and Princeton met to form the Intercollegiate Football Association and draft a uniform set of rules that all of the colleges would play by.

The game would be essentially rugby, with some modifications. The size of the field was set at at 140 yards by 70 yards (a modern football field is 100 yards long and 160 feet wide). And as in rugby, there would be 15 men on each team. The IFA also decided that one kicked goal counted as much as four touchdowns, and that whichever team scored the most touchdowns was the winner. If a game ended in a tie, a kicked goal counted for more than four touchdowns.

FIGHTING WORDS

The length of the game was set at 90 minutes, which was divided into two 45-minute halves separated by a 10-minute break (the clock was only stopped for scoring, injuries, and "arguments," so the games were usually shorter than football games are today). And instead of letting team captains resolve game disputes themselves, the new rules called for one unbiased referee and two opposing umpires, one for each team. That's what led to all the arguments.

"The two umpires discharged their duties like an opposing pair of football lawyers," gridiron historian Parke Davis wrote in the 1926 *Football Guide*. "In fact, they were frequently selected more for their argumentative abilities than for their knowledge of the game." Arguing with the referee became a common strategy: if an umpire noticed that his team needed a rest, he could pick a fight with the referee and drag it out for 5 or even 10 minutes, until his team was ready to play.

Prolate spheroid is the scientific name for any object that's shaped like a football.

Some more rules:

- Every member of the team played both offense and defense.

- The ball remained in play until it went out of bounds or someone scored a touchdown or goal.

- Forward passes were illegal—the ball carrier could throw the ball to teammates on either side of him or behind him, but not to players ahead of him.

FROM SCRUMMAGE . . .

In rugby, at the line of play, the ball went into what was known as "scrum" or "scrummage." Neither side had possession of the ball; the ball was tossed in between the rushers on both teams, who heaved and butted against each other as they tried to kick it forward toward the goal.

. . . TO SCRIMMAGE

Football guru Walter Camp thought the game would be more interesting if, instead of having the forwards on both teams fighting for the ball, "possession" of the ball would be awarded to one team at a time. The team in possession of the ball would have the exclusive right to attempt a touchdown or goal. One forward, called the "snapperback," would be the person designated to put the ball in play, "either by kicking the ball or by snapping it back with the foot," Camp's proposed rule explained. "The man who received the ball from the snapback shall be called the *quarterback*."

Camp pushed his proposal through in 1880. That same year he succeeded in shrinking the field size to 110 yards by 53 yards and reducing the number of players on a team from 15 to 11. Modern football finally began to diverge from rugby.

A WHOLE NEW BALL GAME

The concept of "possession" changed the nature of football considerably. It vastly increased the role of strategy, elevating the importance of the coach in the process. Because the team in possession *knew* that it was getting the ball, the players could arrange themselves on the field in particular ways to execute planned plays.

Take a step: You've just used 200 muscles.

But at the same time that possession of the ball increased the sophistication of the offensive strategy, it also weakened it. The defending team knew that every play would begin with the center snapping the ball to the quarterback, so the defensive forwards were now free to move in closer toward the center, ready to move in for the tackle as soon as the ball was snapped.

Football was already a fairly violent sport, but the new rules made it even more so by increasing the concentration of players at the center of the action. "Bodies now bumped together in massed, head-to-head alignments," Stephen Fox writes in *Big Leagues*. "Instead of glancing tackles in the open field, knots of players butted heads, like locomotives colliding, in more dangerous, full-bore contact."

BACK AND FORTH

There was a delicate balance between the strengths of the offense and defense in football, and the rule changes of 1880 upset that balance in ways the rule makers had not foreseen. Within a year they would enact new rules to restore the balance, establishing a pattern that would continue for years to come: 1) New rules to counteract new tactics; and 2) New tactics to counteract new rules.

GOING NOWHERE

The next round of changes was largely the result of outrage over the 1881 Princeton-Yale game. In those days, there was no limit to how long a team could retain possession of the ball and no way the opposing team could force them to give the ball up. A team retained possession until it scored a touchdown, made a field goal attempt, or lost the ball in a fumble. Players quickly realized that if they attempted neither a touchdown nor a field goal, they could retain possession of the ball for the entire half.

In their 1881 game, Princeton and Yale did just that: Princeton, awarded possession of the ball at the start of the first half, scrimmaged back and forth for the entire 45 minutes without attempting to score, and Yale did the same thing in the second half.

The Princeton and Yale players may have felt their do-nothing tactics were fair, but fans were outraged—and so were the newspaper sportswriters who helped whip the controversy into a national story. Within days of the game, football fans all over the country were writing to newspapers to air their disgust. According to football legend, one such fan, who identified himself only as "an Englishman" wrote a letter to the editor proposing a solution: Instead of letting a team have possession of the ball for an entire half, why not limit possession to four consecutive scrimmages?

USE IT OR LOSE IT

The newspaper printed the letter, and someone sent it to Walter Camp. He was intrigued, but he was opposed to the idea of taking the ball away from a team that was putting it to good use. If the team in possession of the ball wasn't abusing the system, why should they be forced to give it up before they scored?

Camp finally hit upon the idea of giving a team the right to possess the ball beyond three scrimmages, or "downs," but only if they *earned* that right by advancing the ball at least five yards. If they didn't, they'd have to give the ball to the other team. As long as a team continued to gain at least five yards every three downs, they were allowed to retain possession of the ball.

Camp proposed this idea when the Intercollegiate Football Association met in 1882. It passed, as did Camp's proposal that football fields be marked with chalk lines spaced five yards apart, so that it would be easy to tell if a team had gained the yardage in three downs or not. American football moved another giant step away from rugby.

TOUGH GUYS

The introduction of the downs system helped to make the game more interesting, and it changed it in another way that perhaps Camp had not intended: Now that teams had to move forward or lose the ball, agility came to be less valued than sheer mass and brawn, as teams sought to find ways to blast through the opposing team's forward line. Or as Parke Davis puts it, "The passing of the light, agile man of the seventies and the coming of the powerful young giant date from this period."

Second down. Turn to page 184 for part III of The History of Football.

The Liberty Bell was made in England.

NUDES & PRUDES

It's hard to shock anyone with nudity today. But stupidity is always a shock. These characters demonstrate that whether you're dressed or naked, you can still be dumber than sin.

NUDE . . . In April 2000, a state trooper stopped a car in the Houston suburb of Sugarland and discovered that all four passengers—three women and a three-year-old girl— were naked. God, the women claimed, had told them to burn their clothes and drive to Wal-Mart to get some new clothes. "It's always something," the state trooper says. "No two days are the same in this job."

PRUDE . . . Police in Brazil arrested a minor league soccer player named William Pereira Farias after he stripped off his uniform and threw it into the crowd to celebrate the scoring of a goal. "He broke the laws of respectful behavior," police officer Alfredo Faria told reporters. "He offended the townspeople and will likely be suspended from the team."

NUDE . . . Norway's Radio Tango has become the first radio station to offer live nude weather reports. The reports, billed as "more weather, less clothes," air on the station's morning show; listeners can view the naked weather forecasters on the Internet. "This is a world exclusive," says morning host Michael Reines Oredam. "It has never been done before. It brings a certain atmosphere to the studio which we hope our listeners are able to pick up on."

PRUDE . . . Police in Seremban, a town south of Kuala Lumpur, Malaysia, have raided several cellular phone stores and seized "obscene" plastic cellular phone covers that feature naked images of well-known celebrities. "The phones are modified to light up the private parts of actors or actresses when a user receives or makes a call," says police superintendant Abdul Razak Ghani.

NUDE . . . Portland businessman Mark Dean hopes to expand his topless nightclub business by running it as a topless doughnut shop during breakfast hours, with his strippers doubling as wait-

---

A newborn's brain will triple in weight during the first year of life.

resses. What are the odds that his new venture will succeed? Not as good as you might think—a topless doughnut shop in Fort Lauderdale, Florida, went under after less than a year; a topless car wash operated by the same businessman lasted only a few months.

PRUDE . . . The executor of the estate of the late basketball legend Wilt Chamberlain reports that he is having trouble selling the Big Dipper's Bel Air estate, even after reducing the price from $10 million to $4.3 million and tearing out the "playroom," which featured a waterbed floor covered with black rabbit fur and a wraparound pink velvet couch. (The retractable mirrored roof over the master bed has been preserved; so has the traffic light in the bedroom that signals either a green light to "Love," or a red light for "Don't Love.") Executor Sy Goldberg admits that Chamberlain's boasting that he slept with more than 20,000 women in his lifetime may be part of the problem, but he says that holding that against the house is "ridiculous."

NUDE . . . A Dutch telemarketing company has found a novel way around the tight labor market in the Netherlands: they've created a special division of the company that allows employees to work in the nude. "We had about 75 applicants in the first four hours," a spokesman for the company—which did not release its name "for fear of offending existing clients"—told reporters. "With a normal call center, you'd be lucky to get one or two applicants an hour."

PRUDE . . . Officials at Los Angeles International Airport have covered images of "bounding nude men" with brown paper pending a decision on whether to remove them permanently. The naked men, who are supposed to represent the earliest human attempts at flight, are sandblasted into the granite floor of a newly renovated terminal at the airport. American Airlines paid Los Angeles artist Susan Narduli $850,000 to create the work, which was approved by both the airline and the city's cultural affairs commission. Narduli says the figures' private parts are "completely obscured." No matter: "If the city decides it wants the artwork changed," says an American Airline spokesperson, "we'll change it."

Reykjavik, Iceland, one of the coldest cities on Earth, is heated almost entirely by hot springs.

FOR YOUR READING PLEASURE

Recently, we stumbled on Bizarre Books, a collection of weird-but-true book titles compiled by Russell Ash and Brian Lake. Hard to believe, but these titles were chosen and published in all seriousness. How would you like to spend your time reading . . .

Warfare in the Enemy's Rear, by O. Heilbrunn (1963)

Selected Themes and Icons from Spanish Literature: Of Beards, Shoes, Cucumbers, and Leprosy, by John R. Burt (1982)

What to Say When You Talk to Yourself, by Shad Helmstetter (1982)

What Do Bunnies Do All Day?, by Judy Mastrangelo (1988)

The Romance of Proctology, by Charles Elton Blanchard (1938)

How to Become a Schizophrenic, by John Modrow (1992)

Teach Yourself Alcoholism, by Meier Glatt (1975)

Nasology; or, Hints Towards a Classification of Noses, by Eden Warwick (1848)

Not Worth Reading, by Sir George Compton Archibald Arthur (1914)

Snoring as a Fine Art, and Twelve Other Essays, by Albert Jay Nock (1958)

How I Know That the Dead Are Alive, Fanny Ruthven Paget (1917)

Hepatopancreatoduodenectomy, by F. Hanyu (1996)

Jaws and Teeth of Ancient Hawaiians, by H. G. Chappel (1927)

Who's Who in Barbed Wire, by Anon. (1970)

Your Answer to Invasion—Ju-Jitsu, by James Hipkiss (1941)

Rhythmical Essays on the Beard Question, by W. Carter (1868)

How to Abandon Ship, by Phillip Richards and John J. Banigan (1942)

Adoxography is defined as "good writing about a trivial subject."

WHO FINANCED THE REVOLUTION?

Uncle John was reading an article about the Declaration of Independence and saw a brief mention of "Robert Morris, financier of the American Revolution." Having never heard of Morris, he did some research and discovered some fascinating forgotten history.

UP AGAINST THE WALL

In the late 1770s, a bunch of North American colonists got together, called themselves the Continental Congress, and decided to rid their colonies of British rule. They planned to form an army and a navy to defeat the world's most powerful nation. All they needed was the money to feed, clothe, and arm their men—about $20,000 a day. Oops.

The problems of financing the American Revolution were many. First, half of the colonists—and most of the ones with money—did not support the revolution. Next, the Continental Congress gave itself the right to tax its citizens but no power to collect the tax. And they couldn't borrow money, because no one would lend it to them—they weren't even a real country yet.

Yet behind any successful revolutionary stands a smart financier. In this case, it was Robert Morris.

SELF-MADE MAN

In 1747 Morris, a motherless 13-year-old British boy, arrived in Maryland to join his father. Three years later, Morris was orphaned when his father was killed in a gun accident. Young Morris was packed off to Philadelphia to work with Charles Willing, a shipper and merchant. Morris worked with such dedication and brilliance that at age 20 he was made full partner in the firm.

As a merchant, Morris objected to British policies of taxation more than most colonists. When news of the massacre of the colonial militia at Lexington reached him, it solidified his position against England. In 1776 Morris served in the Continental Congress as a representative from Pennsylvania. He became a signer of the Declaration of Independence and was charged with

---

Julia Ward Howe wrote "Battle Hymn of the Republic" and sold the rights for $5.

heading Congress's finance committee. Soon, with money borrowed, begged for, and taken from his own wallet, Morris was funding the American Revolution.

FORGOTTEN HISTORY

Coming up with $20,000 a day for more than five years to support the Revolution should have guaranteed Morris the heroic popularity that John Adams, Ben Franklin, and George Washington have today. But it didn't. For example:

- **History tells us . . .** how George Washington's army crossed the Delaware on Christmas night, 1776, and defeated the British. But what happened next is not so well known. The term of service for most of Washington's soldiers expired a week later, at the end of the year. And, as Morris wrote to John Hancock, "You might as well attempt to stop the winds from blowing . . . as stop them from going when their time is up." Washington was desperate. He was in a position to gain control of New Jersey, but not if his army disbanded. Worse yet, within a week, the British would regroup, defeat the depleted American army, and recapture Trenton.

Washington needed $50,000 to buy information on British troop movements and to pay each of his soldiers a $10 bonus to stay for another six weeks. He turned to Morris, who, in turn, asked a Quaker merchant to lend him the money. "But what is thy security for this large sum," asked the Quaker. "My word and my honor," replied Morris.

"Thou shalt have it," the man said. Washington got his needed funds, the soldiers stayed, and New Jersey was soon free of the British.

- **History tells us . . .** how Washington's army suffered through the winter of 1777 in Valley Forge. But it needn't have been so horrible. Against Morris's advice, Congress had issued worthless paper money and demanded, by law, that it be used. Discouraged manufacturers and sellers chose instead to cease operations, which is why 12,000 soldiers at Valley Forge were without enough shoes, blankets, and food.

- **History tells us . . .** how Washington's army arrived at the Yorktown, Virginia, peninsula on October 19, 1781, just in

Andrew Jackson was involved in over 100 duels.

time to capture the British army and effectively end the war. But the scenario might have easily played out differently.

Weeks earlier, Washington was without the money to move his army from New Jersey to Virginia. Morris quickly raised $1.4 million for flour, corn, salted meat, rum, tobacco, and hay; boats to carry the men across the many waterways; and a cash inducement for the starving soldiers to march the hundreds of miles to Yorktown. "I advanced not only my credit," Morris wrote, "but every shilling of my own money, and all which I could obtain from my friends, to support the important expedition against Yorktown."

RESIGNATION

His proposed monetary policies repeatedly rejected, a frustrated Morris resigned his position in January 1783. Eventually, in 1789, his friend Alexander Hamilton, the nation's first secretary of the treasury, was successful in securing a feasible plan to repay the huge war debt. (Almost $79 million was owed, mostly to foreign nations.)

By 1795 Morris was again fully engaged in private enterprise. Convinced that immigration would drive the nation's development westward, Morris acquired six million acres of land to resell for a sure financial killing. But the pace of European immigration and settlement slowed, and the taxes and mortgages on the unsold land overwhelmed him. Suddenly, he was broke.

HUMILIATION

In 1798 Morris was arrested and thrown in debtors prison. After more than three years of imprisonment, 68-year-old Morris was released. He died five years later in poverty and obscurity. The patriot upon whom the heroes of popular history depended, the financier who kept the Continental army in the field out of his own wallet and with his private credit, the speculator who once owned more land than any man in America, was quietly buried in a Philadelphia churchyard.

* * *

"It is fair to judge people by the rights they will sacrifice most for."

—**Clarence Day**

AN "UPLIFTING" STORY

Our long-promised history of the bra may seam padded,
but it is contoured especially for bathroom readers.
This is the real story. Thanks for your support.

MOTHER OF INVENTION

Who invented the bra? Through the 1800s, a number of people patented items of intimate apparel for women, but most were just extensions of the corset. In 1893 Marie Tucek was granted a patent on a crude "breast supporter," which had a pocket for each breast, straps that went over the shoulders, and a hook-and-eye fastener in the back.

But the modern bra was really born 20 years later. The fashion of the early 1910s was to flatten the breasts for a slim, boyish figure; the fashion also favored plunging necklines. In 1913 a Manhattan debutante named Mary Phelps Jacobs became frustrated when her chest-flattening corset kept peaking out above her plunging neckline. "The eyelit embroidery of my corset-cover kept peeping through the roses around my bosom," she wrote in her autobiography, *The Passionate Years*. The sheerness of her Paris evening gown was ruined by the lumpy, bulky corset.

WHAT'S A DEBUTANTE TO DO?

In frustration, she and her maid designed an undergarment made of two handkerchiefs and some ribbons that were pulled taut. "The result was delicious. I could move more freely, a nearly naked feeling, and in the glass I saw that I was flat and proper."

Showing off her invention in the dressing rooms of society balls, she had her friends begging for brassieres of their own. Jacobs actually sewed and gave away many bras as gifts. But when strangers started accosting her, requesting the brassieres and offering money, Jacobs went to see a patent attorney (she had her maid model the garment discreetly over the top of her uniform).

A patent was granted, and Jacobs opened a small manufacturing facility. She called her invention the "backless brassiere." It was the first ladies undergarment to dispense with corset-stiffening whalebone, using elastic instead. Jacobs sold a number of her

One out of every 270 pregnancies results in identical twins.

brassieres under the name "Caresse Crosby," but for all her ability as a designer, she had no marketing instincts. Sales were flat, and she soon shelved the business.

A few years later, she bumped into an old boyfriend who happened to mention the fact that he was working for the Warner Brothers Corset Company. Jacobs told him about her invention and, at his urging, showed it to his employers. They liked it so much they offered to buy the patent for $1,500. Jacobs took the money—she thought it was a good deal. So did Warner Brothers Corset Company—they went on to make some $15 million from Jacobs' invention.

MAIDENFORM

Ida and William Rosenthal, two Russian immigrants, came to America penniless and set up a dressmaking business in New York with a partner, Enid Bissett. They were constantly dissatisfied with the way dresses fit around the female bosom, so in frustration—and perhaps in rebellion to the popular flat-chested look of the flapper—they invented the first form-fitting bra with separate "cups." And since all women are not built equally, Ida invented cup "sizes."

The Rosenthals gave up the dress shop in 1922 and started the Maidenform Brassiere Company with a capital investment of $4,500. Four years later, they had 40 machines turning out mass-produced bras. Forty years later, they had 19 factories producing 25 million bras annually. Some of their innovations:

- The "uplift bra," patented in 1927.

- The "training bra" (no definitive word on what they were in training for).

- The "Chansonette bra," introduced in 1949. It had a cone-shaped cup stitched in a whirlpool pattern. The bra, which never changed shape, even when it was removed, was quickly dubbed the "Bullet Bra." Over the next 30 years, more than 90 million were sold worldwide.

When William died in 1958, Ida carried on and continued to oversee the company until her death in 1973 at the age of 87. The Maidenform corporation, which started with 10 employees, now has over 9,000.

Animal acts are banned from the Miss America Pageant.

PLAYTEX

Another major contributor to the development of the bra was
Abram Nathaniel Spanel, an inventor with over 2,000 patents
(including one for a garment bag designed so that a vacuum
cleaner could be hooked up to it to suck out moths). In 1932
Spanel founded the International Latex Corporation in Rochester,
New York, to make latex items such as bathing caps, slippers, gir-
dles, and bras, sold under the name Playtex.

Playtex was very aggressive with its advertising. In 1940—an
era when underwear ads in print publications were primarily dis-
creet line drawings—Playtex placed a full-page ad in *Life* magazine
with photos of models wearing Playtex lingerie alongside a mail-in
coupon. Women responded: 200,000 sales were made from the ad.
And in 1954 Playtex became the first company to advertise a bra
and girdle on TV. Those garments—the Living Bra and Living
Girdle—remained part of the line for 40 years.

In 1965 Playtex introduced the Cross Your Heart Bra. Today it
remains one of the best-known brands in the United States and is
the second best-selling brand of Playtex bra, with the 18-Hour Bra
filling out the top spot.

HOWARD HUGHES

The tycoon and film producer also had his hand in creating a bra.
In 1941 he was making a movie called *The Outlaw*, starring his
19-year-old "protégé," Jane Russell. Filming was going badly
because the bras Russell wore either squashed her breasts or failed
to provide enough support to prevent her from bouncing all over
the screen.

According to legend, Hughes designed an aerodynamic half-cup
bra, so well reinforced that it turned Russell's bosom into a veritable shelf. Censors had a fit. 20th Century-Fox postponed the
release date due to the controversy. Millions of dollars stood to be
lost, so rather than back down, Hughes went all out. He had his
people phone ministers, women's clubs, and other community
groups to tell them exactly how scandalous this film was. That
prompted wild protests. Crowds of people insisted the film be
banned. The publicity machine launched into full gear, and when
the film was finally released, it was a guaranteed hit.

On opening night, Hughes hired skywriters to decorate the

One newspaper headline described the furor over the Wonderbra as a "Tempest in a D Cup."

Hollywood skies with a pair of large circles with dots in their centers. Jane Russell, an unknown before the film, became a star overnight. Years later she revealed in her autobiography that she had found Hughes's bra so uncomfortable that she had only worn it once, in the privacy of her dressing room. The one she wore in the movie was her own bra. No one—not even Hughes—was the wiser.

THE VERY SECRET BRA

An inflatable bra introduced in 1952 had expandable air pockets that would help every woman achieve "the perfect contour." The bra could be discreetly inflated with a hidden hand pump. Early urban myth: these inflatable bras sometimes exploded when ladies wore them on poorly pressurized airplanes.

THE JOGBRA

Hinda Miller and Lisa Lindahl were friends who enjoyed jogging but didn't like the lack of support their normal bras offered. Lingerie stores had nothing better to offer them, so they decided to make their own. In 1977 they stitched together two jock straps and tested it out—it worked. Their original prototype is now displayed in the Smithsonian.

In 1978 the two inventors sold $3,840 worth of their bras to sporting apparel stores. In 1997 Jogbra sales topped $65 million.

THE WONDERBRA

Originally created in 1964 by a Canadian lingerie company named Canadelle, the Wonderbra was designed to lift and support the bustline while also creating a deep plunge and push-together effect, without compressing the breasts. Even naturally flat-chested women could achieve a full-figured look. The bra was popular in Europe but wasn't even sold in the United States because of international licensing agreements.

In 1991 fashion models started wearing Wonderbras they had purchased in London. Sara Lee Corporation (yes, the cheesecake company), who by then had purchased Playtex, bought the license to the Wonderbra and began marketing it aggressively. They spent $10 million advertising the new product, and it paid off. First-year sales peaked at nearly $120 million. By 1994 the Wonderbra was selling at the rate of one every 15 seconds for a retail price of $26.

Sharpshooter Annie Oakley once had 5,000 pennies tossed into . . .

UNCLE JOHN'S BOOBY PRIZES

- **Highest-Tech Bra:** A British inventor has come up with a bra that contains a heart rate monitor, a Global Positioning System, and a cell phone. If the wearer is attacked and her heart rate jumps dramatically, the phone will call the police and give her location as determined by the GPS. The electronic components in this "Techno Bra" are removable for laundry day.

- **Most Expensive Bra:** For $15 million you can buy a Victoria's Secret bra inset with over 1,300 gemstones, including rubies and diamonds (with matching panties).

- **Most Cultured Bra:** Triumph International, a Japanese lingerie firm, created a bra to honor Mozart on the 200th anniversary of his death. It plays 20 seconds of his music every time it's fastened and has lights that flash on and off in time to the beat. But perhaps in keeping with Mozart-era hygiene, the bra isn't washable.

- **Smelliest Bra:** In 1998, French company Neyret announced that it was marketing a bra that would release scents when stretched or caressed. Aromas included apple, grapefruit, and watermelon.

- **Biggest Celebrity Bra Collection:** If you're in Los Angeles, visit the Frederick's of Hollywood Bra Museum. It has such items as the bra Tony Curtis wore in *Some Like It Hot*; the bra Milton Berle wore on his TV show; and Phyllis Diller's training bra, marked "This side up."

- **Biggest Bra:** The Franksville Specialty Company of Conover, Wisconsin, manufactures bras for cows in order to prevent them from tripping over their udders. The bras come in four sizes and are available in only one color: barnyard brown. Design extra: They keep the udder warm.

- **Cleverest Dual-Purpose Bra:** When public opinion turned against her, former Philippine first lady Imelda Marcos reportedly wore a bullet-proof bra.

* * *

"When women's lib started, I was the first to burn my bra and it took three days to put out the fire."

—**Dolly Parton**

. . . the air one at a time in rapid succession. She hit 4,777 of them.

CIRCUS SUPERSTITIONS

*From its earliest days, the circus has been surrounded
by traditions and superstitions. Here are some of the
most widely known and often-practiced beliefs.*

Circus bands play John Philip Sousa's "Stars and Stripes Forever" in emergency situations only. The march is played as a warning signal to circus workers that something is wrong.

Never count the audience.

Accidents always happen in threes.

Always enter the ring with your right foot first.

Never whistle in the dressing room.

Boots, shoes, and slippers should never be seen in a trunk tray or on a dressing table.

Cannon-back (rounded top) tunnels are bad luck.

Never look back during the circus parade.

In pictures, elephants must always have their trunks up.

Never sleep inside the Big Top. (This belief comes from the days when the circus ring was made of dirt and people were afraid it might collapse on them.)

Never eat peanuts in the dressing room.

Never move a wardrobe trunk once it has been put into place; moving it means that the performer who owns the trunk will be leaving the show.

Never sit on the circus ring facing out.

Peacock feathers are bad luck.

Hair from the tail of an elephant is good luck.

* * *

SOME CIRCUS SLANG

Nut: The daily cost of operating a show. Legend has it that local authorities would remove a nut from the wagon wheel of the circus office and keep it to ensure that the circus didn't leave town before its local taxes were paid.

Rats can't vomit, which is why they are so susceptible to poison.

THE CURSE OF MACBETH

*Actors won't even call it by its name—they refer to it as
"the Scottish play." Why? Because they say it's cursed.
You may not be superstitious, but after reading this,
you'll never think of this play the same way.*

OUT, OUT DAMN SPOT

In a scene from Shakespeare's *Macbeth*, three witches
stand around a bubbling cauldron, brewing up a stew
which includes ingredients such as eye of newt and toe of frog,
wool of bat, and tongue of dog—"double, double, toil and trouble,
fire burn and cauldron bubble"—we all know the scene. But there's
a story behind that scene, and a curse on the play.

In 1606 King James I commissioned Shakespeare to write a play
in honor of the visit of his brother-in-law, King Christian of
Denmark. The play Shakespeare wrote was *Macbeth*.

POOR KING

James was no stranger to tragedy. He was taken from his mother
shortly after birth and never knew her. His father was murdered
soon after that. His mother was forced from the throne of
Scotland, imprisoned for 19 years in England, and beheaded by her
cousin, Queen Elizabeth I. James began his rule of Scotland at age
19, married Anne of Denmark, had nine children, and survived a
number of assassination attempts. When Queen Elizabeth died, he
ascended her throne.

Moving to England from Scotland was like turning on a light in
a dark room for James. He was particularly taken with Shakespeare's
plays. He gave Shakespeare and his company royal protection in a
time when actors were considered scoundrels. Shakespeare now
had the security, popularity, respect, and money that he needed.
He produced six new plays in the next five years.

HERE COMES TROUBLE

King James was fascinated by witchcraft and obsessed by death and

---

In the 1700s, trappers could get a dollar for a buckskin. Hence the term buck.

demons. He wrote a book about demonology and was considered the foremost authority on the subject. With this in mind, Shakespeare sat down to write a play that looked seriously at the king's favorite subject, and he did his homework. The plot was a thinly disguised accounting of the death of James's father; the witchcraft scene was crafted with care and filled with authentic details.

CURSES!

Some say the play's witchcraft spells and incantations were too faithfully reproduced, that they created a curse and that the curse is renewed every time the words are uttered. Others claim that local witches were so incensed at having their secrets revealed that they placed a perpetual curse upon the play. Whatever the case, for 400 years, *Macbeth* has been uncannily surrounded by death and disaster. So malevolent is the spell that it is said that bad luck will befall any actor who merely quotes from the play.

The curse manifested itself immediately. The young actor scheduled to play Lady Macbeth for King James came down with a fever right before the performance. Some accounts say he died. King James, who had a phobia about knives and gore, was horrified by the death scenes, which were realistically portrayed with guts and blood secured from a butcher. He immediately banned preformances of *Macbeth* for five years.

After the ban ended, the play was performed at Shakespeare's Globe Theatre. A few days later, the theater burned to the ground and with it all of the company's scenery, props, costumes, and manuscripts.

DISASTER STRIKES

Skeptical? Here is just a sampling of the disasters that have surrounded *Macbeth* in the 20th century:

- In the early 1900s, the Moscow Arts Company was doing a dress rehearsal when actor Constantin Stanislavski forgot his lines in the middle of the murder scene. He whispered for a prompt but the prompter was silent. He yelled for a prompt, but the prompter remained silent. Investigating, he found the prompter slumped over the script, dead. The show never opened.

- During a 1937 production at the Old Vic Theatre in England, the theater's founder, Lilian Baylis, suddenly died of a heart attack just before the play opened. Laurence Olivier, who was starring in the lead role, missed death by seconds when a sandbag accidentally fell from the rafters.

- In 1948, during a production at Stratford, Connecticut, Diana Wynyard as Lady Macbeth loudly announced she thought the curse was ridiculous. She also decided it was silly to play her sleepwalking scene with her eyes open, and tried it with her eyes closed. She walked off the edge of the stage during the next performance and fell 15 feet down.

- A version of the play directed by John Gielgud in 1942 was plagued by death. First, Beatrice Fielden-Kaye, in the role of one of the witches, died of a heart attack. Next, Marcus Barron, in the role of Duncan, died of angina pectoris. Another of the witches, Annie Esmond, died on stage one night while she was vigorously dancing around the cauldron. Finally, set designer John Minton committed suicide in his studio, surrounded by his designs for the *Macbeth* sets and costumes. The repainted sets were later sent on tour with matinee idol Owen Nares, who died on the tour.

- A Russian version of the play scheduled to be filmed in Georgia was canceled when nine members of the crew died of food poisoning on location.

- During a 1971 production at the Mercer O'Casey Theatre, no less than seven burglaries and one fire marred the three-month run.

A CURE

To avoid the curse, veteran actors give this advice: Walk out of the dressing room, turn around three times, spit or swear, knock on the door three times, and then humbly ask for readmittance. If that doesn't work, try quoting this line from one of Shakespeare's "lucky" plays, *The Merchant of Venice:* "Fair thoughts and happy hours attend you."

Final note: Abraham Lincoln was quoting passages from *Macbeth* to his friends the evening before he was assassinated.

* * *

Random fact: The Cairo Opera House was destroyed by fire in 1970. The Cairo fire station was located in the same building.

A typical American child sees 80,000 TV commercials by the age of 16.

"MIRRORS WITH A MEMORY"

*Here's the story of how photography pioneer Joseph Niepce's
partner, a theater owner named Louis Daguerre, turned
his name into a household word and began a worldwide
obsession with photography. (For the previous part
of the story, turn to page 76.)*

YOU HAVE TO START SOMEWHERE

The world's first photograph, the one that Joseph Niepce took in 1827, survives to this day. There's a picture of it in just about every book on the history of photography, but it's almost impossible to make out anything that's in it. If there wasn't a caption next to it identifying the objects in the scene (a courtyard, a pigeon loft, and the roofs of some buildings), you would never be able to guess what they are.

Clearly, Niepce's heliographic process was flawed. For one thing, the light-sensitive medium he used, bitumen of Judea, was very slow to react, which meant that long exposure times were required to take pictures. Very long exposure times: That first picture required an exposure of more than eight hours, during which time the sun moved most of the way across the sky. So did the shadows, obscuring much of the picture's detail.

And the sloppy way Niepce smeared bitumen of Judea on his metal plates made the resulting image even blotchier and harder to make out than it would have been otherwise.

ENTER DAGUERRE

Niepce couldn't solve these problems himself, so he joined forces with a Parisian theater owner named Louis Daguerre, who was also experimenting with photography. Daguerre's motivation: he thought that photography, if it were perfected, could be used to create better scenery for the theater.

In 1829 the two men signed an agreement to work together for 10 years, but unfortunately Niepce died from a stroke four years into the partnership. Daguerre tried to continue the work with

---

Director John Ford hired an American Indian rainmaker to get the right . . .

Niepce's son Isidore, but Isidore was convinced that if he contributed anything, Daguerre would take credit for it, so he refused to do any research on his own.

SERENDIPITY

Daguerre soldiered on by himself, and in 1835 made an amazing—and accidental—discovery. One sunny morning, the story goes, Daguerre polished a silvered copper plate and placed it in a box containing iodine. The iodine combined with the silver in the plate to form photosensitive silver iodide, which was a significant improvement over Niepce's bitumen of Judea. Then he loaded the plate into a camera.

That morning he set everything up and started his exposure, which he expected to take several hours. But a half hour later the sun disappeared behind some clouds, ruining everything. Daguerre took the plate out of the camera and tossed it into his chemical cabinet so it would be out of the way.

The following morning, when he took the plate out of the cabinet to polish it for reuse, he saw that it contained a very sharp, detailed image of the picture he had tried to take the day before.

WORTH A THOUSAND WORDS

How did the picture get there? Thirty minutes of exposure was nowhere near enough time to create an image. Daguerre guessed that the short exposure had been enough to create a hidden or "latent" image on the plate, and that one of the chemicals in the cabinet must have "developed" it to the point that it was visible to the naked eye. He tested his theory by taking another 30-minute exposure and leaving it in the chemical cabinet overnight, as well.

Sure enough, the following morning there was an image on the plate. By process of elimination, Daguerre discovered that vapors from mercury, stored in the cabinet, had developed his exposures.

Daguerre made another important discovery: Like Wedgwood and Schulze, he wanted to arrest the photosensitive reaction to stop photographic images from being obliterated from further exposure to light. He solved the problem by soaking his developed *daguerreotypes*, as he called them, in a saltwater bath to create the first permanent photographic images. (Well, almost permanent: the saltwater didn't arrest the photosensitive reaction completely, but

. . . weather for the filming of *She Wore a Yellow Ribbon* in 1949. It worked.

it did slow it down enough that daguerreotypes could be viewed in daylight and could even be preserved for many years.)

CREDIT WHERE CREDIT IS DUE

The discovery of "mercurializing," as it came to be called, was Daguerre's and Daguerre's alone—and understandably, he wanted full credit for it. In 1837 he drew up a new contract with Isidore Niepce in which he took credit for the new process but gave Joseph Niepce credit for the old process. Isidore Niepce objected to the terms but had little choice in the matter—he had not participated in Daguerre's research, did not know how the new process worked, and could not claim credit for it. So he signed.

They made plans to sell both steps of the photographic process to private investors, but when the French Academy of Sciences caught wind of the idea, it persuaded the French government to purchase the rights and give them away free to the entire world, except their traditional rival, England. Daguerre's process was now free of charge for anyone in the world—except the Brits, who had to pay him a royalty.

NOTHING LIKE IT IN THE WORLD

On January 7, 1839, Daguerre went before the Academy of Sciences to show his daguerreotypes and give a description of his process. The assembled scientists were amazed. Images that detailed did not exist anywhere on Earth and were virtually inconceivable to the 19th-century mind. They were so finely detailed that people called them "mirrors with a memory."

The American inventor Samuel Morse was in Paris when the Academy of Sciences published the news of Daguerre's process; Daguerre invited him to view the pictures. Morse described what he saw in a letter home to his brother:

> The exquisite minuteness of the delineation cannot be conceived. No painting or engraving ever approached it. For example: in a view up the street, a distant sign would be perceived, and the eye could just discern that there were lines of letters upon it, but so minute as not to be read with the naked eye. By the assistance of a powerful lens, which magnified fifty times . . . every letter was clearly and distinctly legible, and so also were the minutist breaks and lines of the walls of the buildings; and the pavements of the streets.

Jaybirds hide their food underground. They can find it even under a foot of snow.

The effect of the lens upon the picture was in a great degree like that of the telescope in nature . . . [It is] one of the most beautiful discoveries of the age.

DAGUERREOTYPE-MANIA

On July 7, 1839, six of Daguerre's daguerreotypes were put on public display in Paris; then on August 19, the full details of the photographic process were released to the world. The world's first photography fad started within days, as Parisians descended on the city's lens makers by the thousands to order the equipment that would allow them to make their own daguerreotype images. Eyewitness Marc Antoine Gaudin described the scene:

> Opticians' shops were crowded with amateurs panting for daguerreotype apparatus, and [soon] everywhere cameras were trained on buildings. Everyone wanted to record the view from his window, and he was lucky who at first trial got a silhouette of rooftops against the sky. He went into ecstasies over chimneys, counted over and over roof tiles and chimney bricks, was astonished to see the very mortar between the bricks—in a word, the technique was so new that even the poorest plate gave him indescribable joy.

A PERMANENT RECORD

Perhaps the most impressive but underappreciated early contributor to photography was Sir John F. W. Herschel, an Englishman. When Herschel learned of Daguerre's discovery, he set out to see if he could duplicate the results without knowing anything about the process, which was still a closely guarded secret.

In several weeks Herschel accomplished what had taken Daguerre several years to do; he even improved on the process by remembering an 1819 experiment in which he had observed that hyposulfate of soda dissolved silver salts. He tried the experiment again, hoping he could use the chemical to "fix" his images permanently, something Daguerre had been unable to do. It worked— and hyposulfate of soda, now known as sodium thiosulfate, is used to fix photographic images to this day.

Advance to the next frame of our story on page 210.

Galileo called Saturn "the planet with ears."

CURE FOR WHAT AILS YE

The medical profession pooh-poohs folk remedies, but who knows? Just because the cure involves fish skins or live frogs, that doesn't make it wrong, does it? Read on for some of Uncle John's favorite folk remedies.

To cure a cold, tie fish skin to your feet.

To cure mosquito bites, rub them with vinegar, oil, butter, onion, garlic, or lemon peel and then blow on them.

To get rid of freckles, rub a live frog over your face.

To cure earaches, plug the ears with a shelled snail or a slice of warm bacon. Another cure: Pour some pig's milk, warm oil, or sap from a male ash tree on them.

Drinking red pepper tea or putting dry pepper in your stockings will cure the chills.

In order to get rid of warts, put a piece of silver and some stones in a little sack and leave it on a road—the person who picks up the sack will take on the warts.

Another way to be rid of warts: steal a piece of steak and bury it where three roads cross.

You can cure throat illnesses by rubbing the soles of your feet with an unguent made of garlic cooked in lard, but some prefer spitting in a frog's mouth.

A general medicinal drink: kerosene with sugar.

Passing a child under the belly of a horse three times can cure the child's cough.

Insomniacs should rub their temples with cat fat or eat chicken feet with cooked milkweed. Or they can smoke a mixture of black tobacco, toad powder, and honey.

Pierced ears are said to cure eye trouble.

For an upset stomach, dip a comb in holy water, then leave it in a pot of wine. The comb must stay on the person's belly for 24 hours. This person must then drink a mouthful of the wine and throw away the rest.

Lemon Pledge has more lemons than Country Time Lemonade.

WHAT'S IN TOOTHPASTE?

Ever wonder what the different ingredients in your toothpaste do? Here's the basic formula for most toothpastes and how they're supposed to work.

Water. Toothpaste is 30 percent to 45 percent water. Which means you're paying about $2 a pound for that water.

Chalk. The same variety that schoolteachers use. What is chalk? It's the crushed remains of ancient ocean creatures. The exoskeletons retained their sharpness during the eons when they were buried, and they are one of the few things tough, yet gentle enough, to clean the hardest substance in the body, tooth enamel.

Titanium dioxide. This stuff goes into white wall paint to make it bright. On your teeth, it paints over any yellowing for at least a few hours, until it dissolves and is swallowed.

Glycerine glycol. To keep the mixture from drying out, glycerin glycol is whipped in. You know it as an ingredient in antifreeze.

Seaweed. A concoction made from the seaweed known scientifically as *Chrondrus crispus* is added. This oozes and stretches in all directions and holds the paste together.

Paraffin. This petroleum derivative keeps the mixture smooth.

Detergent. What good would toothpaste be without the foam and suds? The answer is: It would be perfectly fine, but the public demands foam and suds.

Peppermint oil, menthol, and saccharin. These counteract the horrible taste of detergent.

Formaldehyde. The same variety that's used in anatomy labs. It kills the bacteria that creep into the tube from your brush and the bathroom counter.

Does this recipe for toothpaste turn you off? Take heart. Studies have shown that brushing with plain water can be almost as effective.

Twenty-nine percent of men say the unstable economy "is making them watch more cartoons."

THE LEGEND OF KING ARTHUR

What do you think—was King Arthur a real person, or is he purely the stuff of legend? Either way, he makes for a good story.

TABLE TALK

In England, the most popular tales of chivalry are the Welsh legends of King Arthur and his knights of the Round Table. No one knows for sure if there was a real person who served as the inspiration for Arthur . . . or if so, which historical figure it was. The earliest known mention of Arthur is a reference to a mighty warrior in "Gododdin," a Welsh poem written about 600 A.D. Another 200 years would pass before Arthur received another mention, this time in *History of the Britons*, which credits him with winning 12 battles against Saxon invaders.

It's likely that tales of Arthur were also spread by word of mouth, because when Geoffrey of Monmouth wrote down the tales of Arthur in his *History of the Kings of Britain* in 1135, he recorded Arthur's birth in the late 5th century, childhood, military conquests, marriage to Guinevere, relationship with his mentor Merlin, and his death in 542 when he was mortally wounded in battle by his treacherous nephew Mordred. Geoffrey is also the first person to identify Arthur as a king, not just a warrior.

COOKING THE BOOKS

So where did Geoffrey of Monmouth get his information? He claimed to have gotten it from a "certain very ancient book written in the British language," but did not identify it by name. Historians now believe there was no such book. They theorize that Geoffrey simply recorded the popular tales of his day, and when needed, made up his own details to fill in any gaps, drawing from legends surrounding leaders like Alexander the Great and Charlemagne. That didn't stop readers from taking *History of the Kings of Britain* seriously—it served as the standard text on British history for more than 600 years.

Geoffrey of Monmouth wasn't the first to invent tales about

Muscle cells live as long as you do. Skin cells live less than 24 hours.

King Arthur, and he certainly wasn't the last. In 1155 another writer, Wace of Jersey, introduced the concept of the Round Table; five years later, the French poet Chrétien de Troyes wrote five Arthurian romances that are credited with introducing the Holy Grail and Sir Lancelot's love affair with Queen Guinevere. A 13th-century French poet, Robert de Boron, contributed the famous story of the orphaned Arthur winning his crown by removing a magic sword from a stone.

TIME WARP

One thing historians agree on is that even if a "King Arthur" really did live in England in the early 6th century, he and his knights did not live in castles, wear suits of armor, or fight in tournaments—because none of those things existed in the 6th century. So why is Arthur so closely associated with them? Because Geoffrey of Monmouth and other contributors to the Arthurian legend had no sense of how different life had been 600 years earlier. They, not Arthur, lived in an age of castles and knights in shining armor, and they filled their stories with the trappings of their own era. In the process, they created a world for King Arthur that he, if he did really exist, would never have recognized.

YOU CAN LEAD A KNIGHT TO WATER . . .

What about the generations of knights that grew up listening to the chivalrous tales of King Arthur and his knights of the Round Table—how well did they live up to the noble example set by their hero? Did they give to the sick and the poor? Did they protect orphans and the elderly? Did they respect women and treat captured knights with the same respect they'd bestow upon guests?

Not quite—medieval knights preached chivalry, but practicing it was another story, as Will Durant writes in *The Story of Civilization*:

> Theoretically the knight was required to be a hero, a gentleman, and a saint. All this, however, was chivalric theory. The hero who one day fought bravely in tournament might on another be a faithless murderer. He might [preach] of protecting the weak, and strike unarmed peasants down with a sword; he treated with scorn the manual worker and with frequent coarseness and occasional brutality the wife whom he had sworn to cherish and protect. He could hear Mass in the morning, rob a church in the afternoon, and drink himself into obscenity at night.

AMAZING LUCK

*Sometimes we're blessed with it, sometimes we're cursed
with it—dumb luck. Here are some examples of people
who have lucked out . . . for better or worse.*

HEAVY SLEEPER

Keith Quick, 28, a homeless man in Omaha, Nebraska, climbed into a dumpster and went to sleep. Bad move—he happened to do it on garbage pickup day and was still sleeping when the garbage truck emptied the dumpster into its compactor and crushed it. Quick cried out for help, but it wasn't until the trash had been compacted two or three more times that the garbage men finally heard him. The trash was compressed so tightly that it took firefighters more than an hour to dig him out. Incredibly, he suffered no serious injuries.

SEEING IS BELIEVING

In 1990, 14-year-old Lisa Reid went permanently blind as the result of a brain tumor. Then one night about 10 years later, she smacked her head on a coffee table as she was bending down to kiss her guide dog goodnight. When she woke up the next morning, 80 percent of the vision in her left eye had been restored. She celebrated the miracle "by telephoning her mother and reading aloud the health warning on a packet of cigarettes."

NOW THAT'S A HAPPY MEAL

In August 2001, Patrick Collier, 35, walked into a McDonald's restaurant in Holly Hill, Florida, and ordered a meal. As he was sitting down to eat it he was approached by some McDonald's corporate executives. Only weeks earlier he'd been homeless and sleeping in a cardboard box, and he was still down on his luck . . . and looked it. When the executives approached him, he said, "I thought I had done something wrong."

Not quite—the executives handed him a certificate worth $1 million. A month earlier the FBI had arrested employees of the marketing company that ran the McDonald's *Monopoly* contest for stealing more than $13 million worth of game prizes. McDonald's, concerned that the scandal would harm consumer confidence in its

Three safest modes of transportation: ship, train, and commercial airplane (in that order).

sweepstakes, chose five restaurants at random and instructed each one to award a $1 million prize to someone eating in the restaurant. At random. Apparently, Collier was the first person chosen. "I'm getting a Harley," he said, "and a couple of houses."

BODY ARMOR

In June 2001, Dana Coldwell, 31, of Frankenmuth, Michigan, was mowing her lawn when the mower blade struck a $1^1/_2$-inch-long nail and sent it hurtling toward her chest. The nail struck her on the right breast, but didn't pierce her heart—an injury that would probably have been fatal. Why? It was deflected by the "liquid-curved" Maidenform bust-enhancing bra she was wearing. "I almost didn't wear the bra, but a higher power told me to put it on," she says. "I don't know if I will be mowing the lawn after this, but if I do, I'll be wearing the bra."

THE PERFECT STORM

In June 2001, tropical storm Allison struck the township of Upper Moreland, Pennsylvania. The storm ruptured a gas main at the Village Green apartment complex, causing an explosion that destroyed much of the building and killed six people. One elderly resident lost everything she owned, but at least she had insurance. When claims adjuster Paul Markloff arrived a few days after, she asked him to search what was left of the apartment to find her purse. The woman was distraught and confused, but she believed the purse might contain as much as $8,000 in cash.

Markloff sifted through the rubble and found the purse. It contained only $35, so he looked around to see if there was any other money in the apartment . . . and found 181 envelopes filled with $50 and $100 bills stuffed into three drawers of a dressing table. "I was amazed," Markloff says. "The dressing table was the only piece of furniture that hadn't been touched by fire." It took four bank tellers more than three hours to count the money, which came out to more than $420,000.

* * *

"Tragedy is when I cut my finger. Comedy is when you fall into an open sewer and die."

—Mel Brooks

Q: How long is a million seconds? A: 11.5 days.

SALT WARS

*Today we think of salt as cheap and plentiful. But
before modern mining methods, salt was rare
and valuable—even worth fighting for.*

INDIA VS. BRITAIN

Straining under 300 years of British rule, India badly wanted
independence. The movement for self-rule began at the dawn
of the 20th century; Mahatma Gandhi led the fight.

Salt was plentiful in India, and because of the tropical climate,
where work in the hot sun depletes the body of its reserves, it was
an indispensable commodity. But British Colonial law dictated that
the sale or production of salt by anyone other than members of the
British government was a criminal offense. And British salt was
heavily taxed, forcing Indians of all castes to pay high prices for
something they could have easily gotten for free at the seashore.
Gandhi decided to use this as the focal point of his campaign for
freedom.

MARCH TO THE SEA

In 1930 Gandhi wrote to the British viceroy announcing his intention to break the Salt Laws in a campaign of civil disobedience. On
March 12, Gandhi and 78 supporters began a march, walking from
the town of Sabarmati to the coastal village of Dandi 240 miles
away. Their 23-day journey took them through the center of every
town along the way. In each town, speeches were made and people
joined the march . . . until the procession was two miles long.

On April 6, the marchers reached the Arabian Sea, where
Gandhi picked up a lump of mud and salt and boiled it to refine it,
using the ages-old method of obtaining salt. He consumed the salt
and then encouraged his thousands of followers to do the same, all
of which was illegal according to British law. By the end of the
month, the British had imprisoned over 60,000 people for making
salt illegally. Gandhi himself was imprisoned for nine months. The
salt march was one of Gandhi's most visible and successful campaigns for independence and was closely followed by the media and
the Indian people. The salt tax was eventually repealed, but it was
too late for British Colonialists. The image of Gandhi marching to

The world has been at peace only eight percent of the time over the last 3,500 years.

the sea had become a potent political symbol, adding momentum to the independence movement. In 1947 the British gave up and India finally achieved Gandhi's goal—once again becoming an independent nation.

THE REVOLT OF THE SALINEROS

For over 300 years, the Mexican salineros, or "saltmen," had been mining and selling salt from deposits near what is now El Paso, Texas. They didn't understand the concept of private ownership of what they considered public land—anyone who was strong enough to unearth the salt and and sell it was welcome to it.

That all changed in the 1870s when a young Texas district judge named Charles Howard used legal tactics to claim the land surrounding the mines as his own. Now Howard was saying he owned the property and no one was allowed to gather salt but him. At first, the salineros ignored him and continued mining as they had always done. Howard made his point clear by shooting one man who opposed him and arresting two others for merely talking about going to get salt.

Outrage spread like wildfire and a plan was made to fight back. When word came to Howard that a train of 16 wagons was being sent to get salt, he realized this meant a showdown and sent for the Texas Rangers. Howard and the Rangers were organizing when their building was surrounded by salineros and a siege began. The battle had dragged on for five days when the salineros sent word: "If Howard gives himself up willingly and gives up all claim to the salt lakes, no harm will come to him." He surrendered, but a mob shouted for his death. Howard and a few of his followers were put in front of a vigilante firing squad and summarily executed. The rest of the Rangers were released, and they fled. They are noted today for being the only Rangers who have ever surrendered.

Federal troops soon arrived, seeking revenge for Howard's murder. Anyone suspected of participating in the siege was shot on sight. Pandemonium broke out, and people began to loot and riot. A larger contingent of Texas Rangers then came on the scene and put an end to the fighting.

AT THE END OF THE DAY

A full investigation of the affair led to no definite conclusions.

The 17-year locust lives 16 years, 9 months underground.

No one was ever arrested or prosecuted. When a new agent was appointed to head up the Texas Rangers, the salineros politely applied for permission to haul salt for a reasonable fee. It was granted.

THE FRENCH REVOLUTION

In 1259, Charles of Anjou, king of Sicily, imposed the first Salt Tax on the people of France. Its original purpose was to finance a war against Naples. Every citizen over the age of eight was required to buy a certain amount of salt at a price determined by the king—but the tax wasn't equitable. People who lived close to salt-production centers paid very little, while those who lived farther away were forced to pay taxes up to 20 times the actual value of the salt, equal to a month's wages for the average family. Some provinces had special treaties that exempted them from the tax altogether, but it was illegal to buy salt in a province you didn't live in. People traveling from one place to another were searched for smuggled salt, and the penalty for possessing it was often death.

REVOLT

The Salt Tax, harsh and unfair, plagued the people of France for centuries. But the tax was hardest on butchers, who needed 30 pounds of salt to preserve a single pig. In 1413 butchers formed a union and organized a black market system to avoid the tax. Deadly skirmishes between butchers and tax collectors were common.

Ultimately, the Salt Tax was one of the factors that led to the French Revolution. During the Revolution, 32 Salt Tax collectors were executed by the peasants. The tax was repealed in 1791, but Napoléon reinstated it in 1806 in order to finance his invasion of Italy. It wasn't finally abolished until shortly after World War II ended.

* * *

HELL OF A PAGEANT

On April 29, 2001, 17-year-old Carla Renee White beat out 10 other women in a Berkeley County, South Carolina, beauty contest to win the title Miss Hell Hole. Now in its 30th year, the contest is named after a local community's "defining body of water."

It takes 6,000 gallons of paint, 60 people, and 4 months to paint the Eiffel Tower.

THE PROVERBIAL TRUTH

You know that "a bird in the hand is worth two in the bush," but there are countless other proverbs that you may have never heard. Here are some of BRI's favorites from around the world.

"A full stomach likes to preach about fasting."
Russia

"The addition is correct but where is the money?"
Japan

"The archer that shoots badly has a lie ready."
Spain

"The beetle is a beauty in the eyes of its mother."
Egypt

"A beggar who begs from another beggar will never get rich."
Jamaica

"A good bell is heard far, a bad one still farther."
Finland

"Evil knows where evil sleeps."
Nigeria

"If you want a bird and a cage, buy the cage first."
America

"If you want your dinner, don't offend the cook."
China

"Where the body wants to rest, there the legs must carry it."
Poland

"The sweetest grapes hang highest."
Germany

"Patience is an ointment for every sore."
Wales

"What is play to the cat is death to the mouse."
Denmark

"No medicine cures stupidity."
Japan

"Run after two rabbits—you won't catch either one."
Armenia

"He who is free of faults will never die."
Zaire

"Their mosquito won't bite me."
Ivory Coast

"The mud that you throw will fall on your own head."
Iran

"Don't sell the bearskin before the bear is dead."
Holland

"Better to die upright than to live on your knees."
Yiddish

"There is no phrase without a double meaning."
Kenya

Queen Anne of England (1665–1714) had 17 children; they all died before she did.

AESOP'S FABLES

Sometimes, the best way to illustrate a point is by telling a story.

THE BUNDLE OF STICKS

An old man once called his sons to him. "I shall soon die," he said, "but before I leave you, I want to show you something of great importance. But first go and gather some thin sticks for me."

His sons did as they were bid.

Then the father gave each of them a stick and said, "Please break this for me." Each of them broke a stick with great ease.

Then the father took all the remaining sticks and placed them together. "Now," he said to one of his sons, "break all these sticks at one time." The son tried and tried but could not do so. Nor could any of the other boys break the bundle of sticks.

"I am sure," said their father, "that you know what I mean to tell you by this. Each one of you, alone, is weak; but if you stay together, you will be strong."

In unity there is strength.

THE BOY WHO CRIED WOLF

There was once a shepherd boy who used to mind his sheep far out of town on a lonely hillside. The days wore heavy on his hands and one day the lad thought of a way to drum up some excitement. He ran down the hill shouting, "A wolf! A wolf!"

At this, the neighboring farmers, thinking that a wolf was devouring the boy's flock, dropped their work and ran to his aid. However, when they got to the hillside, the boy laughed and said, "I was just playing a joke." The men were quite annoyed and went back to their work.

Some few days later, the boy tried the same thing again. Again the farmers dropped their tools and ran to his assistance. When they saw that the boy had fooled them a second time, they were very angry. The next day, however, a wolf did appear.

"Wolf! Wolf!" cried the boy. But this time the farmers did not believe him. They refused to help him, and many of the boy's sheep were eaten.

A liar is not believed even when he tells the truth.

A giraffe can clean its ears with its tongue.

RUMORS
OF MY DEATH...

*Plenty has been written about how people who nearly die,
get a glimpse of the "other side," and then somehow make it
back to the land of the living. Here are some examples of
another kind of "rebirth": people who were thought
to be dead, but were actually quite alive.*

DECEASED: Ajay "Happy" Chopra, 34, of New Delhi, India

NEWS OF HIS DEATH: Several weeks after Happy disappeared from his home in 1995, his brother Ashok spotted someone he thought was his brother at a local bazaar. He walked up to the man and—no kidding—asked him, "Are you Happy?" The man nodded "yes." So Ashok took him home and bathed and fed him. He wasn't troubled by the man's apparent inability to speak, because Happy had a history of drug abuse.

That evening "Happy" died. The funeral and cremation took place the following morning.

RESURRECTION: The next evening, the real Happy Chopra returned from a religious pilgrimage, unaware that his "remains" had been cremated just that morning. The Chopra family has no idea who the dead man was, and due to the cremation no one will ever know. "The resemblance was uncanny," Ashok says. "Not only myself, but the whole neighborhood thought Happy had come back." Bonus: Happy Chopra is now seen as a sort of demigod in his neighborhood. "People touch his feet, seek his blessings, and give him offerings of money," Ashok says.

DECEASED: Abdel-Sattar Abdel-Salam Badawi, an Egyptian man suffering from fibrosis of the liver

NEWS OF HIS DEATH: In July 1997, Badawi fell into a deep coma. Thinking he was dead, doctors put his body into a coffin and sent him to the morgue.

Longest underwater kiss on record: 2 minutes, 18 seconds.

RESURRECTION: About twelve hours later Badawi came out of his coma. "I opened my eyes, but I couldn't see anything," he later told a reporter. "I moved my hands and pushed open the coffin lid, to find myself among the dead. I shouted for someone to rescue me. When no one heard me, I started to chant verses from the Koran."

Badawi remained locked in the morgue for more than twelve hours before a nurse unlocked the door. But upon seeing a "corpse" standing up and reciting from the Koran, the nurse dropped dead from a heart attack. "I left the body in the refrigerator," Badawi says, "and got out of that place."

UPDATE: The doctor who declared Badawi dead was reprimanded; Badawi says he will never go to the hospital again.

DECEASED: Jose Estrada, 48, of Baytown, Texas

NEWS OF HIS DEATH: In February 1996, Estrada went for a run on a jogging trail near his house. He didn't know it, but just a few minutes earlier paramedics had taken away the body of a man who had collapsed and died while jogging on the same trail. The dead man wasn't carrying any identification—all he had was a set of General Motors car keys. So a sheriff's deputy went back to the scene to see if the keys fit any of the cars. Somehow, the keys fit in Estrada's GM truck.

The deputy traced the license plate to the Estrada residence, broke the news to Estrada's wife, Herlinda, and took her to the hospital to identify the body. "There was a tube in the man's mouth, and tape over his mouth and eyes, so I couldn't really see his face," Herlinda says. "I thought, 'This must be Jose.' You're in such a state of shock, you're not thinking straight."

RESURRECTION: While all of this was going on, Estrada finished his jog and stopped at the grocery store before heading home. As he was putting away the groceries, his wife's boss called to offer condolences. Informed of his own death, Estrada raced to the hospital to tell his wife it was a mistake, arriving just after she signed the death certificate. "After I stopped hugging him, I started crying," Herlinda says. "And I told him, 'If you ever die on me again, I'll kill you myself.'"

THE OTHER TEXANS

George W. Bush isn't the only Texas politician who's added some unusual phrases to the English language.

"It just makes good sense to put all your eggs in one basket."
— **Rep. Joe Salem, on an amendment requiring all revenues to go into the state treasury**

"I want to thank each and every one of you for having extinguished yourselves this session."
— **Speaker Gib Lewis**

"Lemme give ya' a hypothetic."
— **Rep. Renal Rosson**

"Well, there never was a Bible in the room."
— **Gov. Bill Clements, on repeatedly lying about the SMU football scandal**

"I am filled with humidity."
— **Speaker Gib Lewis**

"It's the sediment of the House that we adjourn."
— **Speaker Wayne Clayton**

"This is unparalyzed in the state's history."
— **Speaker Gib Lewis**

"Oh good. Now he'll be bi-ignorant."
— **Ag. Commissioner Jim Hightower, when told that Gov. Bill Clements was studying Spanish**

"Let's do this in one foul sweep."
— **Speaker Wayne Clayton**

"There's a lot of uncertainty that's not clear in my mind."
— **Speaker Gib Lewis**

"No thanks, once was enough."
— **Gov. Bill Clements, when asked if he had been born again**

"If it's dangerous to talk to yourself, it's probably even dicier to listen."
— **Ag. Commissioner Jim Hightower**

Alaska alone has as much coastline as the rest of the United States.

THE DUSTBIN
OF HISTORY

Think your heroes will go down in history for something they've done? Don't count on it. These folks were VIPs in their time . . . but they're forgotten now. They've been swept into the Dustbin of History.

FORGOTTEN FIGURE: Vaughn Meader, a comedian and impersonator in the early 1960s

CLAIM TO FAME: In 1961 Meader mimicked President John F. Kennedy while kidding around with friends. His impersonation was so good that they encouraged him to incorporate it into his act. So Meader put a five-minute "press conference" at the end of his routine, taking questions from the audience and responding in Kennedy's Boston accent. The JFK shtick got him a mention in *Life* magazine, which helped him land a contract to record *The First Family*, an entire album of his Kennedy parodies.

The First Family sold more than 10 million copies, making it at the time the most successful record in history. Meader became a superstar overnight. When he appeared in Las Vegas, he pulled in $22,000 a week—not bad for a guy who'd been making $7.50 a night just a few months earlier.

Then on November 22, 1963, a year after *The First Family* made him the biggest name in comedy, Meader climbed into a taxicab in Milwaukee. The driver asked him if he'd heard about Kennedy's trip to Dallas. "No, how's it go?" Meader replied, thinking the driver was setting up a joke. No joke—in an instant Meader went from being one of the most popular acts in show business to being a pariah. No one could bear to watch him perform, even after he stopped doing JFK, the memories were just too painful.

INTO THE DUSTBIN: Meader's career never recovered; by 1965 he was broke. "That was it," Meader told a reporter in 1997. "One year, November to November. Then boom. It was all over."

FORGOTTEN FIGURE: Lucy Stone, mid-19th-century feminist, suffragist, and abolitionist

---

Most wild birds live only 10 percent of their potential lifespan.

CLAIM TO FAME: When Stone married abolitionist Henry Blackwell in 1855, she became the first woman in U.S. history to keep her own surname. Not a big deal these days, but in 1855, it was shocking. In those days, marriage laws in many states effectively awarded "custody of the wife's person" to the husband, as well as giving him sole control over the wife's property and their children. Stone and Blackwell intended the gesture as a protest against these laws, declaring that "marriage should be an equal partnership, and so recognized by law," not an institution in which "the legal existence of the wife is suspended."

Stone consulted several lawyers before taking the step; they all assured her there was no law specifically requiring her to take her husband's name. But the move was highly controversial, and in 1879, it cost Stone the thing she had fought for years to obtain: her right to vote. That year the state of Massachusetts allowed women to vote in school board elections for the first time, but the registrar refused to register her as anything other than "Mrs. Blackwell." Rather than surrender on principle, Stone chose not to vote.

INTO THE DUSTBIN: Stone died in 1893, 27 years before passage of the 19th Amendment guaranteed women's suffrage.

FORGOTTEN FIGURES: The Dionne quintuplets

CLAIM TO FAME: Born on May 28th, 1934, Yvonne, Annette, Emilie, Cecile, and Marie Dionne became world-famous as the first documented quintuplets. Their miraculous birth and survival, coming in the depths of the Great Depression, captivated the public and provided a welcome distraction from the economic troubles of the day.

What's not as well known is that the "quints" were also five of the most cruelly exploited children of the 20th century. Born to an impoverished French Canadian farm couple who already had six children, the girls were taken from their parents within weeks of birth and made wards of the government under the care of Dr. Alan Dafoe, the doctor who had delivered them. He raised them in "Quintland," a specially constructed "hospital" that was little more than a zoo with five tiny human residents.

Over the next nine years, more than four million tourists—

How did hammocks get their name? They were first made from the fibers of the *hamack* tree.

up to 6,000 a day—visited Quintland to view the children from behind two-way mirrors, pumping $500 million into the Ontario economy and turning Dafoe into one of the most famous doctors in the world. The only people who were discouraged from visiting were parents Oliva and Elzire Dionne; they weren't even allowed to photograph their own children because the rights to their image had been sold off and used to advertise products like Puretest Cod Liver Oil, Lysol, and Palmolive.

INTO THE DUSTBIN: In 1954 one of the quints, Emilie, died during an epileptic seizure. Four surviving quints weren't nearly as interesting as a complete set of five, so their fame began to fade. In 1997 the surviving women wrote an open letter to the parents of the newborn McCaughey septuplets pleading with them not to make the same mistakes.

"Multiple births should not be confused with entertainment, nor should they be an opportunity to sell products," the letter read. "Our lives have been ruined by the exploitation we suffered."

* * *

ANIMALS FAMOUS FOR 15 MINUTES

THE STAR: A blind cod living in a fjord in Norway

THE HEADLINE: *For Blind Fish, A Light At End Of Tunnel*

WHAT HAPPENED: In March 2000, Norwegian fisherman Harald Hauso caught a cod in one of the nets he uses to catch crabs and starfish. When Hauso saw that the cod was blind, he let it go out of pity.

A week later the cod was back. He let it go again, but it came back again and again . . . and again: Hauso estimates that the cod came back and deliberately got himself caught in the net on 35 different occasions. "He's found an easy place to find food," Hauso told reporters. "And he knows I let him go every time." As word of the cod's story spread, he became a local celebrity.

THE AFTERMATH: In January 2001, a marine park in Aalesund, Norway, learned of the cod's plight and gave it a home in their aquarium. Bad news, though: After two months of luxurious aquarium living, the cod suddenly and inexplicably rolled over and died.

Anne Boleyn, second wife of Henry VIII, had six fingers on her left hand.

"THE BLAST BLASTED BLUBBER BEYOND ALL BELIEVABLE BOUNDS"

We at the BRI are always on the lookout for great urban legends. For years the tale of the Exploding Whale has floated around the Internet. But it's not an urban legend—it's 100% true. Here's the story.

A WHALE OF A PROBLEM

How do you get rid of a 45-foot-long stinking dead whale? That was the bizarre question George Thornton had to answer on the morning of November 12, 1970. A few days earlier, an eight-ton rotting sperm whale carcass had washed ashore on a Florence, Oregon, beach, and the responsibility fell on Thornton—assistant highway engineer for the Oregon State Highway Division—to remove it. His options were limited. He couldn't bury the rapidly decomposing corpse on site because the tides would soon uncover it, creating a health hazard for beachgoers. And because of the whale's overpowering stench, his workers refused to cut it up and transport it elsewhere. He also couldn't burn it. So what could he do? Thornton came up with an unbelievable solution: blow the whale up with dynamite.

WHALE WATCHING

Thornton's expectation was that the whale's body would be nearly disintegrated by the explosion, and he assumed that if any small chunks of whale landed on the beach, scavengers like seagulls and crabs would consume them. Indeed, many seagulls had been hovering around the corpse all week.

Thornton had the dynamite placed on the leeward side of the whale, so that the blast would hopefully propel the whale pieces toward the water. Thorton said, "Well, I'm confident that it'll work. The only thing is we're not sure how much explosives it'll take to disintegrate the thing." He settled on 20 cases—half a ton of dynamite.

As workers piled case upon case of explosives underneath the

A typical 100-ton blue whale eats its own weight in microscopic krill every month.

whale, spectators swarmed around it to have their pictures taken—
upwind, of course—in front of the immense carcass, right near a
massive gash where someone had hacked away the beast's lower
jaw. Even after officials herded the crowds a full quarter of a mile
away for safety, about 75 stubborn spectators stuck around, most of
them equipped with binoculars and telephoto lenses. After almost
two hours of installing explosives, Thornton and his crew were
finally ready to blow up a whale. He gave the signal to push in
the plunger.

THAR SHE BLOWS!

The amazing events that followed are best described through the
eye of a local TV news camera that captured the episode on tape.
The whale suddenly erupts into a 100-foot-tall plume of sand and
blubber. "Oohs" and "aahs" are heard from the bystanders as whale
fragments scatter in the air. Then, a woman's voice breaks out of
the crowd's chattering: "Here come pieces of . . . WHALE!"
Splattering noises of whale chunks hitting the ground grew louder,
as onlookers scream and scurry out of the way. In the words of Paul
Linnman, a Portland TV reporter on the scene, "The humor of the
entire situation suddenly gave way to a run for survival as huge
chunks of whale blubber fell everywhere."

For several minutes after the blast, it rained blubber particles.
Fortunately, no one was hurt by the falling chunks, but everyone—
and everything—on the scene was coated with foul-smelling,
vaporized whale. The primary victim of the blubber was an
Oldsmobile owned by Springfield businessman Walter Umenhofer,
parked well over a quarter of a mile away from the explosion. The
car's roof was completely caved in by a large slab of blubber. As he
watched a highway worker remove the three-by-five foot hunk
with a shovel, a stunned Umenhofer remarked, "My insurance
company's never going to believe this."

THE AFTERMATH

Down at the blast site, the only thing the dynamite had gotten rid
of were the seagulls. They were either scared away by the blast or
repulsed by the awful stench, which didn't matter because most of
the pieces of blubber lying around were far too large for them to
eat. The beach was littered with huge chunks of ripe whale,
including the whale's entire tail and a giant slab of mangled whale

A full bladder is about the size of a softball.

meat that never left the blast site. And the smell was actually worse than before.

Thornton had hoped his work was done, but it was just beginning—he and his workers spent the rest of the day burying their mistake. His blunder drew the attention of news stations all over the country, but amazingly, he was promoted just six months later.

Twenty-five years later, the tale of the exploding whale is documented all over the Internet. And the Oregon Highway Division still gets calls about it today—many callers hoping to get their hands on the video. The whale is still dead, but the story took on a life of its own.

* * *

ASK THE EXPERTS

The Heart Was Taken
Q: Why do people cross their fingers for good luck?
A: "The practice may have evolved from the sign of the cross, which was believed to ward off evil." (From The Book of Answers, by Barbara Berliner)

Yee-Haw!
Q: In movie Westerns, people fire guns straight up into the air as warning shots or just to make noise during a celebration. But those bullets have to come down somewhere. How dangerous will they be if they hit somebody?
A: "Physics tells us that when it hits the ground the bullet will have the same velocity it had when it left the muzzle of the pistol, 700 to 800 mph. But that ignores air resistance. Realistically, the bullet's landing speed can be around 100 to 150 mph. That's more than enough speed to do serious or lethal damage to a cranial landing site.

And by the way, the jerk who fires the bullet isn't very likely to be hit by it. In one experiment, out of 500 machine-gun bullets fired straight upward, only 4 landed within 10 feet (3 meters) of the gun. Wind has a great effect, since bullets can reach altitudes of 4,000 to 8,000 feet (1,200 to 2,400 meters) before falling back down." (From *What Einstein Told His Barber,* by Robert. L. Wolke)

Whales dream.

DUMB JOCKS

*They give an awful lot of interviews, but sports stars
aren't always the most articulate people. Maybe
they should keep their mouths shut . . . nah.*

"The doctors X-rayed my head
and found nothing."
　　　　　　—Dizzy Dean

"Some people think football
is a matter of life and death. I
can assure you it is much more
important than that."
　　　　　　—Bill Shankly

"I want all the kids to do what
I do, to look up to me. I want
all the kids to copulate me."
　　　　　　**—Andre Dawson,
Chicago Cubs outfielder**

"Nobody in football should be
called a genius. A genius is a
guy like Norman Einstein."
　　　　　　—Joe Theismann

"I'm not allowed to comment
on lousy officiating."
　　　　　　**—Jim Finks,
New Orleans Saints
G.M., when asked what
he thought of the refs**

"You guys pair up in groups of
three, then line up in a circle."
　　　　　　**—Bill Peterson,
Florida State football coach**

"Better make it six; I can't eat
eight."
　　　　　　**—Pitcher Dan Osinski,
when asked if he wanted his
pizza cut into six or eight slices**

"We're going to turn this team
around three hundred sixty
degrees."
　　　　　　—Jason Kidd

"Left hand, right hand, it does-
n't matter. I'm amphibious."
　　　　　　**—Charles Shackleford,
NCSU basketball player**

"I'm not an athlete. I'm a
professional baseball player."
　　　　　　—John Kruk

"Are you any relation to your
brother Marv?"
　　　　　　**—Leon Wood,
to announcer Steve Albert**

"He's a guy who gets up at six
o'clock in the morning regardless of what time it is."
　　　　　　**—Lou Duva,
boxing trainer, on the
regimen of heavyweight
Andrew Golota**

More people die playing golf than any other sport. Leading causes: heart attacks and strokes.

UNUSUAL INVENTIONS

*Here's living proof that the urge to invent something—anything—
is more powerful than the urge to make sure that the invention
will be something that people will actually want to use.*

The Invention: Personal Sound Muffler
What It Does: Have you ever wanted to scream in the middle of a crowded room? With this device, you can . . . without disturbing others. About the size of a dust mask, the muffler's interior is made of sound-absorbing foam, with a saddle-shaped opening that seals tightly to the user's face. Extra bonus: A microphone mounted at the bottom of the muffler activates a light, giving the user immediate visual feedback as to the intensity of sound produced.

The Invention: Bulletproof Dress Shirt
What It Does: Just what every well-dressed gangster needs. Wear this with a tie or over a turtleneck, and no one will ever know you're actually wearing a bulletproof garment. Main features: removable bulletproof pads made of "an ultrahigh-molecular-weight extended chain polyethylene fabric for superior bullet-stopping power."

The Invention: Self-Dusting Insecticide Boot Attachment
What It Does: Like a flea collar for people, only you wear it around your boot, not around your neck. It's supposed to prevent ticks and other crawling insects from creeping up your leg.

The Invention: Tool for Imprinting on Hot Dogs
What It Does: No home should be without one. This amazing invention is actually a branding iron for imprinting messages on hot dogs ("Happy Birthday to Frank").

The Invention: Flushable Vehicle Spittoon
What It Does: Designed for use in a car or truck, this device is for anyone who likes to drive and spit at the same time. Mount the cylindrical receptacle anywhere on the dashboard with a conven-

---

Mickey quickie: Mouse sex lasts only five seconds.

ient Velcro tab. Your "fluids" flow into the funnel-shaped bottom of the spittoon, out a drainage tube, and onto the ground under the car. Then flip a switch and windshield washer fluid is automatically pumped to a spray nozzle that rinses the interior of the spittoon receptacle. You're ready to start spitting again.

The Invention: Life Expectancy Timepiece

What It Does: It looks like a watch and you wear it like a watch, but this timepiece actually displays the approximate time remaining in your life. The wearer determines his or her own life expectancy by referring to a combination of actuarial and health factor tables. How much time do you have left? Just check your watch.

The Invention: Toilet Seat Clock

What It Does: These days people like to know the time every minute of the day, even when they're in the bathroom. But where do you put a clock in the bathroom? This waterproof digital clock is mounted in the front of a U-shaped toilet seat. And the seat cover has a rectangular cutout, so the clock can be seen even when the lid is down. The clock can be reversed, so you can read it either sitting on the seat, or standing facing the toilet.

The Invention: Electrofishing Pole

What It Does: For the modern fisherman, this device is an electrified stainless-steel loop with an insulated fiberglass handle. The user wears a battery-backpack, which is connected to the loop and has another wire in the water, completing the electrical circuit. When a fish swims within the electric field created by the electrodes, ZAP! The fish quickly loses consciousness and can be easily plucked from the water. We recommend using rubber gloves.

The Invention: Electrified Tablecloth

What It Does: Plagued by picnic pests? This tablecloth has a pair of built-in electrical strips, powered by a 9-volt DC battery. An insect trying to cross the strips will get an electrical shock strong enough to discourage further travel across the table, making the world safe for potato salad. Good news: The strips are not strong enough to shock a person who accidentally touches them.

Thomas Jefferson invented a coding device called the . . .

THREE NEAR MISSES

Here at the BRI, we never fail to be amazed at the role that
chance plays in life. Take these three instances, for example.

JFK'S EAGLES

In 1985 Norman Braman, owner of the Philadelphia Eagles, was visiting the U.S. Senate when Senator Edward Kennedy told him the story of how John F. Kennedy considered buying the Eagles in October 1962. Not yet two years into his first term, JFK was already thinking about what he would do after leaving office. When he learned the Eagles were for sale, he and brother Bobby instructed Ted to go to Philadelphia to meet with the team's management and discuss a possible sale. But Ted never went, and someone else bought the Eagles. "What happened?" Braman asked. "The Cuban Missile Crisis," Ted told him.

POISONING GENERAL WASHINGTON

Phoebe Fraunces, the daughter of a New York tavernkeeper, reportedly saved the life of General George Washington after pretending to sympathize with English spies. When Thomas Hickey, a member of Washington's guard, told her to serve the general a plate of poisoned peas, she did so, and then whispered a warning to Washington. He (or she, depending on the account) immediately flipped the peas out the window, where some chickens ate them and died. Hickey was later executed for treason.

THE HUGHES H-1

In 1934 millionaire aviator Howard Hughes built an experimental plane called the H-1. In January 1937, it set a transcontinental speed record by flying at 332 mph from California to New Jersey, making it the fastest plane on Earth. Hughes proposed to the U.S. Army that they base a fighter plane on the design, but they weren't interested. Japan was. Mitsubishi engineer Jiro Horikoshi designed a fighter plane that incorporated many of the H-1's features: the "Zero" was the premier fighter plane of World War II. The United States and its allies didn't develop a plane that could match it until 1943.

CELEBRITY LAWSUITS

*These days, it seems that people will sue each other over
practically anything. Here are a few real-life examples
of unusual legal battles involving celebrities.*

T HE PLAINTIFF: Rosie O'Donnell
THE DEFENDANT: KRSK-FM, a Portland, Oregon,
radio station

THE LAWSUIT: KRSK gave itself the name "Rosie 105," a reference to Portland's nickname, "the Rose City." But O'Donnell's
lawyers sued, claiming that O'Donnell owned the name and that
the radio station was trying to cash in on her celebrity. Local newspapers blasted O'Donnell.

THE VERDICT: Not guilty.

THE PLAINTIFF: The Flying Elvi, an amateur skydiving club

THE DEFENDANT: The Flying Elvises, a rival skydiving club

THE LAWSUIT: The Flying Elvi sued the Flying Elvises for
trademark infringement: Elvi manager Richard Feeney claimed he
was marketing the concept before the Elvises were even formed.
But according to the Flying Elvises, both skydiving groups got the
idea from the 1992 film *Honeymoon in Vegas*. Furthermore, claimed
the Elvises, they have licensing rights from the Elvis Presley estate.
The Elvi responded that no such rights exist—Elvis never performed as a skydiver.

THE VERDICT: The Elvi prevailed and are now the only troup
of skydivers in wigs, sideburns, and matching jumpsuits.

THE PLAINTIFF: *The New York Times*

THE DEFENDANT: Jake Shubert, Broadway impresario

THE LAWSUIT: In 1915, Shubert decided to ban critics who
wrote negative reviews of his productions. The Shubert organization spent a lot on newspaper advertising and felt that it entitled
them to preferential treatment. At the very least, they didn't want

---

A 15-year-old burglar was charged with armed robbery after pointing his . . .

their advertising dollars to be used to pay critics to pan their plays. It all came to a head when the new *New York Times* critic, Alexander Woollcott, was denied admission to a play, even though he'd already paid for a ticket. The Times sued.

THE VERDICT: A temporary injunction allowed Woollcott to see and review the play (he liked it). The court later ruled in favor of Shubert, who continued to bar the Times critic (it actually helped make Woollcott famous). Ultimately, the New York Legislature passed a bill making it illegal for a theater to refuse admission to any sober ticketholder. The Shuberts contested the law all the way to the Supreme Court (but lost).

THE PLAINTIFF: SPAM Luncheon Meat

THE DEFENDANT: Jim Henson Productions

THE LAWSUIT: Hormel Foods Corporation, makers of SPAM, sued Henson's company over one of the characters in the movie *Muppet Treasure Island*. The character in question is the high priest of a tribe of wild boars that worship Miss Piggy. His name: Spa'am.

Hormel's suit contended that their trademark was damaged because the film "intentionally portrayed the Spa'am character to be evil in porcine form."

THE VERDICT: Not guilty. The court found that although Spa'am was "untidy," he was not evil and that, actually, the character probably enhanced the value of the SPAM trademark.

THE PLAINTIFF: Billie Jean Matay

THE DEFENDANT: Mickey Mouse

THE LAWSUIT: In 1995, Matay brought her grandchildren to Disneyland. The family was returning to their car when they were robbed at gunpoint in the parking lot. The robber got away clean with $165. While Matay reported the crime to D-land security, her grandchildren waited "backstage," where they saw several Disney characters taking off their costumes. Matay, who had actually been a Mouseketeer in 1957, sued, claiming her three grandchildren were traumatized by being exposed to "the reality that the Disney characters were, in fact, make-believe."

THE VERDICT: Case dismissed.

UNKLE JOHN'S GREATEST BLOOOPERS

One of the BRI's favorite subjects is goofs—especially by celebrities, politicians, and criminals. Napoléon had his Waterloo, Nixon had his Watergate, and guess what . . . we make mistakes, too. So here's a first—we thought we'd swallow our pride and show you a few of our own bloopers. This article is dedicated to all of you that have taken the time to write in and keep us honest.

A lot of readers pointed this one out to us: On page 88 of *The Best of Uncle John's Bathroom Reader*, in "Famous Last Words," we wrote that Ludwig van Beethoven's final utterance was, "Friends applaud, the comedy is over." But if you skip ahead to page 260, in "Final Thoughts," you'll notice that his last words were "I shall hear in heaven!" Well . . . he had a lot to say. So which one is correct? We've since discovered that no one really knows. Have proof? Send it along.

- We read that Abraham Lincoln was born in Illinois, so that's what we wrote in *Uncle John's Great Big Bathroom Reader*. But we goofed. A multitude of readers kindly pointed out that Abe was not born in Illinois—he was born in a log cabin near Hodgenville, Kentucky. (OK, but he moved to Illinois when he was very young.)

- If you own the first edition of *Uncle John's Absolutely Absorbing Bathroom Reader*, you might have noticed that there was no running foot on page 398. Actually there was . . . but it was invisible. We later replaced it with one that people could see.

- BRI member Ed J. pointed out this one: "The one-liner at the bottom of page 77 of *Great Big* is in error. It states that the odds of the average golfer making a hole-in-one are 33,676 to 1. This would make a hole-in-one very commonplace. It should read, 'The odds against the average golfer making a hole-in-one are 33,676 to 1.'"

You're right, Ed. But we think people still got the idea.

- In *Uncle John's Giant 10th Anniversary Bathroom Reader,* we state that the fuel economy of an early automobile called the Davis was 65 mph. We meant mpg. Oops.

- And for all of you who wrote in letting us know that the General Sherman tree (*Great Big Bathroom Reader,* page 391) is not the oldest living thing on Earth, we know. Well, now we do. The oldest tree is actually a bristlecone pine. Believe it or not, we got the original info from the National Park Service.

- We hoped you enjoyed our article on page 215 in the first edition of *Giant 10th Anniversary Bathroom Reader* entitled "Manimals Famous for 15 Minutes." What's a manimal? We don't know either.

- Here's a classic: We once reported that Gandhi was buried in California. Boy, did we hear it on that one. For the record, his ashes were spread in many places all over the world, including California.

- Maybe you're one of the lucky few who have the first printing of *Uncle John's All-Purpose Extra Strength Bathroom Reader.* To find out if you do, check out the copyright page at the beginning and see if yours says *Uncle John's All-Pupose Extra Strength Bathroom Reader* at the top. Just in case you're wondering, we did that on pupose.

- In our *All-Purpose Extra Strength* press release to over 5,000 BRI members, we proudly stated that the book would be available in every state in the U.S. and every providence in Canada. Thank you to everyone who informed us that Canada has provinces, not providences. We knew that.

- This one may be our all-time favorite. In *Absolutely Absorbing,* one running foot says that "Ants don't sleep." Skip ahead a few pages and you'll learn that "Ants yawn when they wake up." Well, do they sleep or not? It turns out that they only rest, but they do stretch before they resume their work.

- And finally, this is for all of you that looked up the word "gullible" and found out that it is indeed in the dictionary: it was a joke, only a joke. Apparently you fell for it.

Polo players are not allowed to play left-handed—it's too dangerous.

BRI BRAINTEASERS

We're back with another "regular" installment
of brainteasers. Answers are on page 743.

1. If you went to bed at 8 o'clock at night and wound your alarm clock to go off at 9:00 the next morning, how much sleep would you get?

2. Why can't a man living in North Carolina be buried in South Carolina?

3. If you had only one match and you entered a room in which there was a kerosene lamp, an oil heater, and a wood-burning stove, which would you light first?

4. Two men were playing checkers. Each played five games and each won the same number of games. No draws.
   How can this be?

5. You have two coins in your hands equaling 55 cents. One of them is not a nickel.
   What are the coins?

6. It is a scientific fact that a person eats over an inch of dirt at every meal.
   How is this possible?

7. Jeff bought a word processor small enough to fit in his pocket. It can add, multiply, subtract, divide, and write in all languages. It has a delete device that will correct any error, and no electricity is required to operate it. Amazingly, it costs only 12 cents. How can it be so cheap?

8. A farmer has 17 sheep. All but 9 die. How many sheep are left?

9. A man married 48 women. None of them died, he was never divorced, and he was one of the most admired men in town.
   How come?

10. If a doctor gave you 3 pills and told you to take one every half hour, how long would they last you?

11. If a farmer has 5 haystacks in one field and 4 in the other field, how many haystacks would he have if he combined them all in the center field?

The cost of a Trident submarine could cover the cost of operating the U.N. for four years.

THE AMAZING DR. BAKER

*Of all the incredible women we've ever read about, Dr. Sara
Josephine Baker is one of the most incredible. Her accomplishments
are astounding, especially when you consider the time in
which she lived. Next time you think one person can't
make a difference, remember Dr. Baker.*

RICHES TO RAGS

Sara Josephine Baker was born to a life of privilege in
Poughkeepsie, New York, in 1873. In those days there were
no water treatment plants or indoor plumbing—people pulled their
drinking water right out of the Hudson River. Unfortunately, the
Baker family lived downstream from a hospital that discharged its
waste into the same river. The hospital treated people suffering
from typhoid fever—and the typhoid germs went straight into the
water. Baker's father and younger brother both contracted the disease and died when she was 16 years old.

Although the family was left with no income and small savings,
Baker announced that she wanted to go to college to become a
doctor, so that she could combat diseases like typhoid. But not
many women became doctors in those days. Nevertheless, the
young woman insisted, and her mother finally agreed.

In 1900, after graduating from the Women's Medical College
of the New York Infirmary and completing her internship, Baker
hung out her shingle in New York City. The next year, she took
the civil service exam and scored very high—high enough to qualify for the job of medical inspector for the Department of Health.

A MISSION

Perhaps because she was a woman, she was given the worst assignment of all: reducing the death rate in Hell's Kitchen—one of the
worst slums in New York. But among rat-infested buildings
crammed with poverty-stricken immigrants, Dr. Baker found her
calling. She went from tenement to tenement, searching for people
with infectious diseases.

When astronauts returned from the moon, they had to go through customs.

She said, "I climbed stair after stair, knocked on door after door, met drunk after drunk, filthy mother after filthy mother and dying baby after dying baby." Every week, more than 4,500 people in this district died from cholera, dysentery, smallpox, typhoid, and other illnesses, fully a third of them newborn babies. Dr. Baker rolled up her sleeves and went to work.

CHILDREN'S CRUSADE

Focusing on the infant mortality rate, Baker led a team of nurses who went door to door teaching mothers the value of nutrition, cleanliness, and ventilation. She set up milk stations where free pasteurized milk was given away; she standardized inspections of schoolchildren for contagious diseases; she insisted each school needed its own doctor and nurse; she set up a system for licensing midwives; she invented a simple baby formula that mothers could mix up at home; and she devised a widespread club for young girls to teach them how to properly babysit their younger siblings. In short, she set up a comprehensive health-care program for the prevention of disease in children. Her goal: Prevent disease rather than treating it after it occurred.

Baker found that babies wrapped in cumbersome clothing were dying of the oppressive heat or from accidental suffocation. So she designed baby clothing that was light, roomy, comfortable, and opened down the front. This clothing became so popular so quickly that McCall's Pattern Company bought the design, paying Baker a penny royalty for each one sold. The Metropolitan Life Insurance Company ordered 200,000 copies of the pattern and distributed them to policy holders.

She also found that babies routinely received silver nitrate eyedrops to prevent blindness from gonorrhea. But bottles of the solution often became contaminated, or they evaporated so that the concentration of silver nitrate was at a dangerous level, thus causing the blindness it was intended to prevent. Baker invented a foolproof sanitary solution: beeswax capsules, each containing enough solution for one eye. The capsules could not become contaminated and the drops inside could not evaporate. The method was soon being used around the world, and the rate of blindness in babies plummeted.

In ancient Rome, any house hit by lightning was considered consecrated.

CHEATING DEATH

After finding that orphanages had a high rate of infant deaths, Baker became one of the first people to theorize that babies who received no cuddling and cooing simply died of loneliness. After a plan was followed to place orphaned infants with foster mothers, the death rate dropped.

Because of Baker's efforts, the city created the Division of Child Hygiene in 1908 and appointed her the chief. Within 15 years, New York City had the lowest infant mortality rate of any city in the United States or Europe. An astounding statistic: It's estimated that from 1908, when she went to work for the new division, to 1923, when she left, she saved some 82,000 lives.

EXPERT ADVICE

Dr. Baker was without doubt the leading expert of the time on children's health. In 1916 the dean of the New York University Medical School asked her to lecture his students on the subject. She agreed, on one condition—that he allow her to enroll in the school and attend classes. He refused; women weren't allowed at his college. So she told him to find someone else. But there wasn't anyone who knew as much as Baker did. He finally gave in, and because he allowed her to attend the college, he had to open the campus to other women as well. In 1917 she became the first woman to receive a doctorate in public health from the school.

World War I strained the U.S. economy, and the poor got poorer. Baker pointed out to a reporter of *The New York Times* that American soldiers were dying at the rate of 4%, while babies in the United States were dying at the rate of 12%, making it safer to be a soldier in the trenches of France than to be born in the USA. Because of the publicity this generated, she was able to start a citywide school lunch program for older children, which became a model for the world.

WORLD-CLASS

Suddenly, Dr. Baker was in high demand. An international charity asked her to take care of war refugees in France. London offered her the job of health director for their public school system. But she turned the offers down and was appointed Assistant Surgeon General of the United States, the first woman ever to receive a federal government position.

There is a species of butterfly in Brazil that has the color and fragrance of chocolate.

What else did this amazing woman accomplish? Following her retirement in 1923:

- She represented the United States on the Health Committee of the League of Nations, as the first woman to be a professional representative to the League.

- She helped apprehend Typhoid Mary—twice.

- She oversaw creation of the Federal Children's Bureau and Public Health Services, which evolved into the Department of Health and Human Services.

- She helped establish child hygiene departments in every state in the union.

- She served as a member of over 25 medical societies.

- She was a consultant to the New York State Department of Health.

- She served as president of the American Medical Women's Association.

- She wrote over 250 articles and five books, including her autobiography in 1939.

Dr. Baker's enduring legacy: by the time she died in 1945, over half of the babies born each year in New York City were cared for at the health stations she established.

* * *

AS GENTLE AS A LAMB?

• "An Egyptian sheep destined for sacrificial slaughter in a religious ceremony forestalled his owner's plans by pushing him to his death from atop a three-story building, police said . . . Waheeb Hamoudah, 56, was feeding the sheep he tethered on the rooftop, when it butted him."

• "A Bedouin shepherd was shot in the chest and killed . . . when one of his flock jostled his loaded shotgun as he slept, police said."

—Wire service reports

The 1900 Olympic Games included croquet, fishing, billiards, and checkers.

Q & A:
ASK THE EXPERTS

*More random questions, with answers
from the nation's top trivia experts.*

THE BRIGHT STUFF

Q: *How can Day-Glo colors be so brilliant? They look as if
they're actually generating their own light.*

A: "They are. There's a chemical in Day-Glo colors that takes
invisible ultraviolet radiation out of the daylight and converts it
into visible light of the same color as the object. The object is not
only reflecting light, it is actively *emitting* light, which makes it
look up to four times brighter.

What's going on is fluorescence, a natural process by which certain kinds of molecules absorb radiation of one energy and
emit it as radiation of a lower energy. The molecules in the Day-Glo pigment are absorbing ultraviolet radiation that human eyes
can't see, and reemitting it as light that human eyes can see."
(From *What Einstein Told His Barber*, by Robert L. Wolke)

WATCHIN' THE WHEELS

Q: *Why do spokes on a wagon wheel appear to move backward on
television or movie screens?*

A: "It is an optical illusion. When you watch a movie, you are
not watching a continuous flow of action, but rather a series of still
shots run at 24 frames per second. The human eye cannot detect
the gaps between each frame because they occur so rapidly. You see
a smooth-running movie.

"If the spokes were spinning at the same rate as the frames of
the movie, the wheels would appear to be stationary. But when the
spokes are spinning slower than the speed of the film, they don't
make it all the way back to their original position, and as consecutive frames are rolled, the spokes appear to move backward. This
illusion is also evident on television, which flashes the picture at
30 times per second." (From *The Book of Totally Useless Information*,
by Don Voorhees)

Sixty percent of athiests and agnostics say they own at least one Bible.

UNDERWEAR
IN THE NEWS

All the undernews that's fit to print.

AROUND THE WORLD
Cambodia: Police have broken up a notorious gang of criminals that has been terrorizing the Cambodian countryside for more than a year. "They call themselves the Underwear Gang," says Lek Vannak, chief of the country's interior ministry of police. "At night they only wear underwear and carry weapons to rob and assault people in remote villages . . . People are living in a lot of fear." So far 25 members of the Underwear Gang have been caught; seven more are still at large.

Colombia: Maria Fernanda Lopez, winner of the Miss Antioquia Province beauty pageant, was stripped of her title after posing for a magazine advertisement in underpants. Lopez admitted to posing for the ad, but insisted the garment she wore, skintight black shorts similar to the ones cheerleaders wear under their skirts, wasn't a pair of underpants—it was a "multifunctional outerwear garment" that can be worn either as underwear or as outerwear.

England: The British chain store Tesco has begun sewing labels into its underpants—instructing men on how to examine themselves for testicular cancer. "Men's insight into their own anatomy is very poor," says Ian Banks of the Men's Health Forum in England. "Having labels in their underpants gives them the information they need."

England: A British company called Brava PLC has introduced a "breast-enlarging bra" that it says can increase size by as much as one cup size. The bra uses vacuum pressure to achieve its results: hard plastic domes ringed with silicon are held in place with a sports bra; a battery-powered suction pump evacuates the air in the domes, creating a low-pressure environment that supposedly stimulates the breasts to grow. The drawbacks: The bras cost $2,000 to $2,500 apiece, and the suction cups have to be worn 10 hours a day for 10 consecutive weeks to achieve any results. "It's like buy-

---

Each mile of a four-lane freeway takes up more than 17 acres of land.

ing a gym membership or an expensive piece of home exercise equipment," says Dr. James Baker, a skeptic. "How many of us have done that and only used it a few times?"

Sweden: An inventor named Per Wallin has invented underwear with "soothing heated inserts" that he says will ease the pain and discomfort of menstruation. The inserts contain chemicals that generate their own heat for up to an hour.

RIGHT HERE AT HOME

Orlando, Florida: Costumed workers at Walt Disney World have won the right to wear their own underwear while on duty and in costume in the company's theme parks.

Why go to court over underwear? Some Disney costumes hug the body so tightly that regular underwear bunches up and can be seen through the costume. To prevent unsightly VPLs (visible panty lines), the company supplies athletic supporters, tights, or cycling shorts that are to be worn in place of undies.

But there's a catch: Employees are not issued their own garments—everyone has to share. Disney is supposed to launder them in hot water and detergent when employees turn them in at the end of a shift *before* they're put back in circulation. That apparently wasn't happening and workers had finally had enough: "Things have been passed around," says stilt walker Gary Steverson. "I don't want to share my tights, and I don't want to share my underwear."

Pueblo, Colorado: Inventor Buck Weimer has come out with underpants containing a powerful charcoal filter that removes the unpleasant smell of intestinal gas. Weimer invented the garment for his wife, who suffers from a gastrointestinal disorder called Crohn's disease. The undies, which the Weimers sell under the brand name Under-Ease, are made from airtight fabric and contain an "exit hole" fitted with a removable filter made of charcoal and Australian sheep's wool. Price: $24.95 a pair. They last for up to six months, but the filters need to be changed every two to three months, "depending on the amount and strength of gas being released."

Does Under-Ease take care of the unpleasant *sounds* associated with intestinal gas? "No," says Weimer, "This is not a muffler."

Florida officials receive 8,000 complaints each year about alligators.

VIDEO TREASURES

We've shared many of our favorite offbeat films in past Bathroom Readers. This year, we asked our readers to tell us what their favorite movies are. Use this list the next time you're at the video store staring at rows of titles, wondering which film to choose.

BEFORE THE RAIN (1994) *Foreign/Drama*
Review: "Macedonian filmmaker Milcho Manchevski tells a three-part story about the tragic, far-reaching effects of ancient blood feuds and modern-day civil strife in the remnants of Yugoslavia. Riveting and compellingly told." (*Video Movie Guide*)

HAROLD AND MAUDE (1971) *Comedy*
Review: "Oddball black comedy that has become a cult favorite. Harold is a strange young man, rich, spoiled and fascinated with the concept of death. And, that is what draws him to Maude. Maude is old, but she is also eccentric and fun-loving. The two meet at a funeral and fall in love. This is not at all a typical comedy, but the open-minded viewer will be greatly rewarded with insights into human nature." (*Mark Satern's Illustrated Guide to Video's Best*)

LIES MY FATHER TOLD ME (1975) *Drama*
Review: "Simple drama about growing up in the 1920s in a Jewish ghetto. The story revolves around a young boy's relationship with his immigrant grandfather. Quiet and moving." (*VideoHound's Golden Movie Retriever*)

THE LOVED ONE (1965) *Satire*
Review: "Correctly advertised as the picture with something to offend everyone. Britisher Robert Morse attends to his uncle's burial in California, encountering bizarre aspects of the funeral business. Often howlingly funny, and equally gross. Once seen, Mrs. Joyboy can never be forgotten." (*Leonard Maltin's Movie and Video Guide*)

WAKING NED DEVINE (1998) *Comedy*
Review: "Old Ned Devine has the winning ticket for the Irish National Lottery—unfortunately, the shock has killed him. The

Per capita, Alaskans eat twice as much ice cream as the rest of the nation.

residents of Tulaigh Morh conspire to fool a bored lottery official into thinking that Michael O'Sullivan is Devine, so that they can share the wealth . . . Warm and full of blarney, but never becomes too sappy, or contrived." (*VideoHound's Golden Movie Retriever*)

TRULY, MADLY, DEEPLY (1991) *Romantic Fantasy*

Review: "A woman grieving for the death of her husband is visited by his ghost. Unusual story of coming to terms with loss, combining wit, insight, and excellent acting. Intelligent, charming, ironic, and exceptionally well-played." (*Halliwell's Film and Video Guide*)

ROBINSON CRUSOE ON MARS (1964) *Science Fiction*

Review: "Surprising reworking of the classic Defoe story, with Paul Mantee as a stranded astronaut, at first accompanied by only a monkey. "Friday" turns out to be a similarly trapped alien. Beautifully shot in Death Valley; its intimate nature helps it play better on TV than most space films." (*Leonard Maltin's Movie and Video Guide*)

KING OF HEARTS (1966) *Foreign*

Review: "Phillippe de Broca's wartime fantasy provides delightful insights into human behavior. A World War I Scottish infantryman searching for an enemy bunker enters a small town that, after being deserted by its citizens, has been taken over by inmates of an insane asylum. In French with English subtitles." (*Video Movie Guide*)

GATES OF HEAVEN (1978) *Documentary*

Review: "(This film) is surrounded by layer upon layer of comedy, pathos, irony, and human nature. I have seen this film perhaps 30 times, and am still not anywhere near the bottom of it: All I know is, it's about a lot more than pet cemeteries." (*Chicago Sun-Times*)

SHALL WE DANCE? (1996) *Foreign/Drama*

Review: "This film proves that Japanese filmmakers can fashion charming, feel-good movies every bit as effective as their Hollywood counterparts. The film uses ballroom dancing to explore one man's struggle for freedom from the suffocating repression of Japanese society. This is a film for anyone who prefers to leave the theater smiling. Winner of 13 Japanese Academy Awards." (*ReelViews*)

Johnny Carson, Michael Douglas, and Clint Eastwood were all once gas station attendants.

ANIMALS FAMOUS FOR 15 MINUTES

When Andy Warhol said "everyone will be famous for fifteen minutes," he didn't have animals in mind. Yet even they are unable to escape the relentless publicity machine.

THE STAR: A 300 pound hog (name withheld)
THE HEADLINE: *When Pigs Fly, First Class Asks "Why?"*
WHAT HAPPENED: On October 17, 2000, two women and their hog boarded a US Airways flight from Philadelphia to Seattle. They presented a note from a doctor verifying that the animal "was a 'theraputic companion pet,' like a guide dog for the blind," so the airline cleared it to fly.

The hog snoozed through most of the six-hour flight, but got spooked when the plane landed. It charged up and down the aisle, squealing loudly, at one point even trying to smash into the cockpit. Then it hid in the galley until its owners lured it out with food and pushed it off the plane . . . at which point it fouled the jetway.

THE AFTERMATH: US Airways immediately revised its companion animal policy specifically to exclude hogs. "We can confirm that the pig traveled," a spokesperson told reporters, "and we can confirm that it will never happen again. Let me stress that. It will never happen again."

THE STARS: Drag racing hamsters of London
THE HEADLINE: *When The Chips Are Down, Bet On Hamsters*
WHAT HAPPENED: In February 2001, the highly contagious foot-and-mouth disease struck English livestock, resulting in a ban on horse races.

What was an obsessed gambler to do? The Internet betting site Blue Square, Ltd. created something new for desperate bettors—hamster drag racing. "You put an exercise wheel in the middle of a 10-inch-long dragster," a company spokesperson told reporters. "As they run in the wheel, it moves the whole thing forward."

Each race featured six hamsters in tiny plastic hot rods running along a six-foot wooden track; video cameras broadcasted the

Gorillas can't swim.

action live over the company's website. More than 2,000 people around the world logged on to watch and bet on each race.

THE AFTERMATH: The epidemic slowed, the horse races resumed, and the hamsters were put out to tiny little pastures.

THE STARS: As many as 500 Barbary apes smuggled into France from North Africa

THE HEADLINE: *Dearth Of Dogs Leads To Mobs Of Monkeys*

WHAT HAPPENED: In the late 1990s, French authorities began cracking down on youth gangs that used vicious dogs—Rottweilers, Dobermans, and Pit Bulls—to intimidate rival gangs. The crackdown was working . . . until gangs began switching to monkeys. "The apes are becoming the new weapon of choice. They're ultra-fashionable," says Didier Lecourbe, a police officer in Aubervilliers, a suburb of Paris.

THE AFTERMATH: The apes turn out to be even tougher than the attack dogs. "Removed from their natural habitat," natural historian Marie-Claude Bomsel told the *London Guardian*, "they can become highly aggressive. They bite, and their favored method of attack is to hurl themselves at people's heads."

THE STAR: A dinosaur the size of a German Shepherd

THE HEADLINE: *Dinosaur Found In Rock Named In Honor Of One Of Rock's Dinosaurs*

WHAT HAPPENED: In early 2001, paleontologists digging on Madagascar discovered a new species of dinosaur that lived 65 to 75 million years ago. "It had bizarre teeth," paleontologist Scott Sampson told reporters. "They're long and conical with hooked tips. They protrude straight forward, so it might be easier to catch fish or used to spear insects."

While digging for dinosaurs, Sampson and his colleagues listened to the music of Dire Straits, so they named the species *masiakasaurus knopfleri* in honor of Dire Straits singer/guitarist Mark Knopfler. "If it weren't for his music, we might not have found the animal in the first place," Sampson explained.

THE AFTERMATH: "I'm really delighted," Knopfler told reporters when he learned of the honor. "The fact that it is a dinosaur is certainly apt, but I'm happy to report that I'm not in the least bit vicious."

First person to receive a Social Security check: Ida May Fuller (she lived to 100).

WORD ORIGINS

Ever wonder where words come from?
Here are some more interesting stories.

BOULEVARD
Meaning: A broad avenue, often with one or more strips of plantings (grass, trees, flower beds) on both sides and/or down the center

Origin: "The name originally came from the Middle Low German *Bolwerk*, the top of the wide rampart—often 20 or more feet wide—that served as the defensive wall of medieval towns. As more sophisticated weaponry rendered such structures obsolete, they sometimes were razed to ground level and used as a wide street on the town's perimeter. Vienna has such a broad boulevard, called the Ring, circling the old town on the site of its original city walls." (From *Fighting Words*, by Christine Ammer)

QUEEN
Meaning: The wife or widow of a king

Origin: "*Queen* goes back ultimately to prehistoric Indo-European gwen-, 'woman' (from which English gets *gynecology*), Persian *zan*, 'woman,' Swedish *kvinna*, 'woman,' and the now obsolete English *quean*, 'woman.' In its very earliest use in Old English, *queen* (or *cwen*, as it then was) was used for a 'wife,' but not just any wife: it denoted the wife of a man of particular distinction, and usually a king. It was not long before it became institutionalized as 'king's wife,' and hence 'woman ruling in her own right.'" (*From Dictionary of Word Origins*, by John Ayto)

PARASITE
Meaning: An organism that lives in or on another organism at the other's expense

Origin: "In ancient Greek it meant a professional dinner guest. It came from the Greek *para* ('beside') and *sitos* ('grain, food'). Put together, *parasitos* first meant 'fellow guest' and acquired, even then, its present-day meaning." (From *Dictionary of Word* and *Phrase Origins, Vol. III*, by William and Mary Morris)

Buzz Aldrin's mother's maiden name: Moon.

TADPOLE

Meaning: The larva of an amphibian

Origin: "*Tad* was an early spelling for 'toad,' and *pol* meant 'head' in 17th-century speech. Therefore, *tadpole* means 'toad head,' an appropriate name for the early stage of a frog when it is little more than a big head with a small tail." (From *The Facts on File Encyclopedia of Word and Phrase Origins*, by Robert Hendrickson)

NAMBY-PAMBY

Meaning: Weak, wishy-washy

Origin: "Derived from the name of Ambrose Philips, a little-known poet whose verse incurred the ridicule of two other 18th-century poets, Alexander Pope and Henry Carey. In poking fun at Philips, Carey used the nickname *Namby Pamby*: Amby came from Ambrose; Pamby repeated the sound and form, but added the initial of Philips's surname. After being popularized by Pope in *The Dunciad*, namby-pamby went on to be used for people or things that are insipid, sentimental, or weak." (From *Word Mysteries & Histories*, by the Editors of The American Heritage Dictionaries)

BLESS

Meaning: To consecrate or invoke divine favor

Origin: "A gracious word with a grisly history. Its forefather was Old English *bledsian*, a word that meant 'to consecrate with blood,' this, of course, from the blood sacrifices of the day. In later English, this word turned into blessen, and the term finally came to mean 'consecrated.' So today when we give you the greeting, 'God bless you,' we are actually saying, 'God bathe you in blood.'" (From *Word Origins*, by Wilfred Funk)

KALEIDOSCOPE

Meaning: A tubular optical toy; a constantly changing set of colors

Origin: "In 1817 Dr. David Breuster invented a toy which he called a *kaleidoscope*. He selected three Greek words that when combined had a literal meaning of 'observer of beautiful forms.' The words were *kalos* ('beautiful'), *eidos* ('form'), and *skopos* ('watcher'). The term has come into prominent use in its figurative sense; namely, a changing scene—that which subtly shifts color, shape, or mood." (From *The Story Behind the Word*, by Morton S. Freeman)

Margaret Hamilton, who played the Wicked Witch of the West, was once a kindergarten teacher.

OOPS!

More tales of outrageous blunders to let us know that other people are screwing up even worse than we are.

A MOVING EXPERIENCE

MISHAWAKA, Ind.—"An Indiana couple should seriously consider hiring professional movers next time. Marsha and Niles Huntsinger threw their futon mattress out the window and it fell between two buildings. Niles lowered Marsha down on a rope to try to get the futon, but she became wedged in the 16-inch gap between the walls. Huntsinger had to be rescued by a fire crew after she spent half an hour jammed 20 feet off the ground. The rescuers also managed to save the futon."

—*Bizarre News*

ANGRY, ANGRY HIPPO

"During a *60 Minutes* interview, Mike Wallace meant to ask former Russian president Boris Yeltsin, 'Is Yeltsin thin-skinned about the press?' But the question was mistranslated as: 'Is Yeltsin a thick-skinned hippopotamus?' Yeltsin responded by saying that Wallace should 'express himself in a more civilized fashion.'"

—*San Francisco Chronicle*

STANDING ROOM ONLY

"A visitor at a Minneapolis art gallery sat in and broke a chair, which he did not realize was part of an exhibit dating to the Ming Dynasty. Value of the chair: $100,000."

—*"The Edge," The Oregonian*

SNIP-SNIP

"A minor league baseball team in Charleston, South Carolina, recently came up with a novel promotion for Father's Day. The River Dogs offered fans the chance to win a free vasectomy. They immediately withdrew the offer, however, when fans protested. Among those who complained was the Roman Catholic Diocese of Charleston, led by season ticket holder Bishop David Thompson.

'People didn't like the idea,' General Manager Mark Schuster

Michael Jackson owns the rights to "On Wisconsin," Wisconsin's state song.

said, noting the team never meant to offend anyone. 'We are sensitive to our fans' wants.'"

—*Wacky News*

SOFA, SO GOOD

"After a long night of drinking, Casey Adams ate some leftover
lasagna, took off his clothes and made himself at home on the sofa.
The problem? It was the wrong sofa—the wrong house, too.

At about 6:00 the next morning, Frances Brown, the Edge-
water homeowner, discovered Mr. Adams, 26, lounging on the sofa
in his gray boxer shorts, fast asleep. A shocked Mrs. Brown quickly called the police.

Police found no signs of forced entry on the home; residents
said a door may have been left unlocked. They charged him with
fourth-degree burglary and had his Jeep towed from the driveway.

Mr. Adams didn't know how or when he arrived there, but he
gave police a statement saying he was extremely intoxicated and
nothing like this had ever happened to him before.

'He kept saying he was sorry,' Mrs. Brown said."

—*The Capital*

NOUVEAU SCROOGE

"A Louisville, Kentucky, man who won $65 million in the state
lottery recently filed suit against a woman seeking reimbursement
after he met her in a bar and, 'while in an intoxicated state,' accidentally gave her $500,000."

—*Bloomington-Normal Daily Pantograph*

BETTER LATE THAN NEVER

EDINBURGH—"Postmen in the Scottish city of Aberdeen did
their very best to deliver a letter from Australia—112 years late.

'The card was posted on the fourth of January in 1889 and it
arrived in Aberdeen a few days ago. We have absolutely no idea
where it's been,' said Aberdeen postmaster Pete Smith.

'Whoever has this postcard should get in touch with us because we might start a new category,' a spokesman for the *Guinness
Book of Records* said. 'We've got a record for a parcel but that's only
about two or three years.'"

—*CNN Fringe*

Q: What's the only capital letter in the alphabet with exactly one end point? A: P

CREME *de la* CRUD

From the BRI files, a few samples of the worst of the worst.

WORST FOOD PRODUCT INVENTED BY MILTON HERSHEY
Beet Sherbet

Like many Americans, Milton Hershey went on a vitamin kick in the early 1940s, and he started experimenting with vegetable juices. "It's much easier to drink raw vegetables than to eat raw vegetables," he explained. Surely vegetable juice sherbets were even better.

Hershey tested onion, carrot, and celery sherbets before concluding that beet sherbet tasted the best and adding it to the menu at the Hershey Hotel. Those brave few who ordered the stuff couldn't stomach it—it tasted *terrible*, which had completely escaped the man who gave us the Hershey bar. How'd that happen? Former CEO Samuel Hinkle blamed the cigars that Hershey, then in his mid-80s, had smoked for more than 60 years. "After smoking six, eight, ten cigars a day, Mr. Hershey had absolutely burned out his taste buds," Hinkle recalled. "He couldn't taste or smell a thing."

WORST PULP FICTION NOVEL
Killer in Drag, by Ed Wood, Jr.

Yes, *that* Ed Wood, Jr. When he wasn't making movies like *Plan 9 From Outer Space*, *Glen or Glenda*, and *Bride of the Monster*, Wood was hard at work cranking out books that were every bit as bad as his films. *Killer in Drag* is the story of a transvestite assassin who "goes straight (criminally speaking) and tries to get a shady sugar daddy to pay for his sex-change operation."

WORST HOLE OF GOLF
Mrs. J. F. Meehan, Shawnee Ladies Invitational

When she got to the 16th hole (126 yards, par 3), Meehan teed up, swung . . . and hit her ball into the water. The ball was floating on the surface of the water, but rather than use another ball, Meehan got her husband to find a boat and row her out to the ball. She leaned over the front of the boat and took her swing . . . and

---

For her 40th birthday, Sophia Loren's husband gave her a 14-karat gold toilet seat.

another . . . and another. It took her more than 40 strokes just to hit the ball onto land; then she had to play through a thickly wooded area to get back to the green. Final score for the hole: 161 strokes.

WORST CHOICE OF PROPS IN A LONDON PLAY

Real champagne, in a scene of the first (and last) performance of "Ecarte" at the Old Globe Theatre

Playwright Lord Newry was a stickler for authenticity, so when his play called for a picnic, he used a real picnic basket filled with roast chicken, pies, truffles . . . and several bottles of champagne, which the actors drank to the last drop. Leading lady Nita Nicotina was soon too drunk to remember her lines; her leading man kept track of his by shouting them out at the top of his lungs. That tired him out, so he lay down in the middle of the stage and fell fast asleep as the other actors worked around him, tripping over props and leaning against scenery that was not designed to support their weight.

By now the audience had lost its composure; when Nicotina walked out onstage at the beginning of the next scene wearing one red and one green boot, the audience lost itself in howling waves of laughter. That made her mad—"What are you laughing at, you beastly fools?" she screamed. "When you have done making idiots of yourselves, I will go on with this—*hiccup*—beastly play." She never got the chance—the audience laughed and booed the entire cast off the stage. (Except for the leading man, who was still asleep.)

WORST FROZEN BREAKFAST FOOD PRODUCT

IncrEdibles Breakaway Foods

Remember those "push-up" ice cream and frozen yogurt pops? IncrEdibles, introduced in 1999, were scrambled egg push-up breakfast pops designed for eaters on the go. They came in three flavors: cheese, sausage and cheese, and bacon and cheese. The concept may seem disgusting, but what really killed IncrEdibles was the fact that when you heated them up in the microwave, the eggs became so soft, it was almost impossible to eat them without the whole superheated mess spilling onto your lap. Ouch!

In a 1936 ping pong tournament, the players volleyed for over 2 hours on the opening serve.

THE HISTORY OF FOOTBALL, PART III

In this part of our football saga, we contemplate the mysteries of safeties, offensive interference, and tackling below the waist.

MAKING HIS POINT(S)

In the early days of football, games often ended in a tie, and the referee decided the winner. Yale coach Walter Camp thought that instituting a point system, something more sophisticated than just counting touchdowns and field goals, would solve the problem by making tied games less likely. He pushed his proposal through the Rules Committee in 1883.

Beginning that year, a touchdown counted for two points, a goal kicked following a touchdown was worth four points, and a field goal was worth five points. Then there was the "safety." Whenever the ball came within 25 yards of the offensive team's own goal line, it was common practice for them to touch the ball down behind their own goal line "for safety," because this meant that the ball would be brought back out to the 25-yard line for a free kick. Henceforth, if a team was forced to resort to a safety, one point was awarded to the other team.

The new point system lasted only a year—by 1884 it was obvious that touchdowns were harder to score than field goals, so their value was raised to four points. The goal after touchdown was lowered to two points, the safety was raised to two points, and the field goal remained unchanged at five points.

GETTING IN THE WAY

Technically, "interference," or protecting the ball carrier from incoming tacklers, was illegal, just as it was in rugby. But because the introduction of the system of downs was thought to have weakened the offense, enforcement of the rules against interference began to decline.

As early as 1879, Princeton protected the ball carrier by running two players alongside him, one on either side. These shielders didn't actually block the incoming tacklers—that was still against

Passive-aggressive? In 1879, while on his honeymoon . . .

the rules—but they were an intimidating presence. Rather than complain, other teams adopted the tactic themselves.

They also began testing the limits of what else they could get away with—and quickly discovered they could get away with a lot. "A few years later," Stephen Fox writes in *Big Leagues*, "the shielders had moved out ahead of the runner, using their arms and hands to shed tacklers. The old offside rule was no longer enforced. Barely a decade old, football had lost this final vestige of rugby."

LOW BLOW

The gradual acceptance of offensive interference served to strengthen the offense, so in 1888 Walter Camp pushed through two new rules that helped strengthen the defense in response: The first banned blocking "with extended arms," a tacit acknowledgment that other forms of blocking had become legal; the second legalized tackling below the waist, as far down as the knees. The new rules shifted the balance so firmly over to the defense that the offense had to completely rethink its game.

The low tackle proved to be much harder to defend against than tackles above the waist, so forwards had little choice but to move in closer around the center, until they were standing shoulder to shoulder, as they do today. The backfield (halfbacks and fullbacks) moved further up to provide additional protection. Now, instead of being spread out all over the field, players were clumped together in the middle. It was also about this time that centers started using their hands instead of their feet to snap the ball back to the quarterback.

THE V-TRICK

With so many players crowded together, it was probably just a matter of time before someone hit upon the offensive tactic of everybody locking arms and slamming into the defense in one single, devastating mass.

One of the earliest examples of such a "mass play," as it came to be known, was the V-trick, which Princeton invented on the spur of the moment in 1884, during the second half of a game against the University of Pennsylvania. (Lehigh University claims to have invented a similar version at about the same time.)

Princeton wasn't having any luck advancing the ball with its usual strategy of having a halfback carry the ball down the field behind seven other players. Then it occurred to quarterback Richard Hodge that the seven interferers might be more effective if they locked arms together and formed a V, with the point of the V pointing downfield and the ball carrier running safely inside the formation. It worked: Princeton scored a touchdown, and went on to win the game, 31–0.

SECOND TRY

It wasn't until 1888 that Princeton used the V-trick again. This time they sprang it on Yale at the start of the second half. But it was not nearly as effective has it had been four years before, because one of the Yale guards instantly figured out a way to counter it. Author Parke Davis described the scene in his 1911 book *Football: The American Intercollegiate Game*:

> The Princeton players formed themselves into a mass of the shape of the letter V . . . The ball went into play and away went the wedge of men, legs churning in unison like the wheels of a locomotive.
>
> But on the Yale team was a young giant by the name of Walter "Pudge" Heffelfinger. He rushed at the mighty human engine, leaped high in the air, completely clearing its forward ramparts, and came down on top of the men inside the wedge, whom he flattened to the ground, among them the ball-carrier.

HUMAN CANNONBALL

Yale won the game, 10–0, and went on to win every game of its 1888 season, racking up 694 points to 0 for its opponents. Nevertheless, the V-trick was so effective that other teams quickly adopted it and began inventing other mass plays. Likewise, they adopted the defensive tactics of Pudge Heffelfinger, perfecting the art of cannonballing knees-first into chest of the lead man in the wedge. The best players were able to vault the wedge entirely to slam full force into the ball carrier.

Tactics like these led to an increase in the number of serious injuries and even deaths in the game, which led to a general increase in brutality and foul play. "We were past masters at tackling around the neck," Georgia Tech's John Heisman recalled of the period. "There was a rule against it, but that rule was broken often . . . Fact is, you didn't stand much of a chance making the line in those days unless you were a good wrestler and fair boxer."

How many leaf-cutter ants does it take to lift a 10-pound picnic basket? 60,133.

THE FLYING WEDGE

In 1890 a Boston lawyer and chess expert named Lorin F. Deland happened to see a Harvard football game. He'd never played football, but had became a fan of the sport, in large part because the strategy seemed to have a lot of parallels with battlefield tactics. His interest in the sport prompted him to read books on Napoléon Bonaparte.

One of the little emperor's favorite tricks was massing the full strength of his troops at the enemy's weakest points; Deland thought this would also work well in football. He pitched his idea for what became known as the "flying wedge" to Harvard in 1892. The flying wedge applied the principles of speed and momentum to the Princeton V-trick; Deland proposed using it during kickoffs, which would allow the wedge to get a 20-yard running head start before slamming full-speed into the opposing team.

Harvard agreed to try it against Yale in the fall and spent much of the summer secretly practicing the move. On game day they introduced it at the start of the second half, when Harvard had the kickoff. The beefiest players gathered on the right side of the field 20 yards away from the ball; the smaller players gathered 15 yards further back on the left side. When the signal was given, both groups converged in front of the ball at full speed and locked arms to form the wedge as the kicker, Bernie Trafford, tapped the ball with his foot (still legal in those days), then picked it up and passed it to teammate Charlie Brewer running alongside him.

FOOT FAULT

Running from inside the safety of the flying wedge as it plowed into Yale's defensive line, Brewer managed to advance as much as 30 yards and might even have gone all the way for a touchdown, had he not tripped over a teammate on Yale's 25-yard line. Harvard never did score a touchdown—Yale won, 6–0, but the effectiveness of the flying wedge was obvious to everyone. By 1893 almost every college football team in the country had adopted "mass momentum" plays. The golden age of football violence had arrived.

Halftime: After the BRI marching band performs, turn to page 264 for Part IV of "The History of Football."

Dallas was named after George Mifflin Dallas, U.S. vice president from 1845 to 1849.

VOLCANIC ACTION

Look out the window: everything may look calm and serene—but what's going on below the surface? The answer is . . . a lot. Here's some basic earth science.

K ABLOOM!
Why do volcanoes explode? Simply stated, because the center of the Earth is hot, while the crust is (relatively speaking) cold. This causes different pressures, which need to be equalized.

The Earth is covered by a crust of solid rock, 20 miles thick over the average continent, twice that thick under mountain ranges, and only five miles thick under the oceans. It's about 4,000 miles to the center of the Earth, and the deeper you go, the hotter it gets—90°F for every mile. The high temperature is generated by a concentration of radioactive materials, which give off heat as they deteriorate.

Gold miners in South Africa work at 11,736 feet below the Earth's surface—just a little more than two miles deep—where the rocks are hot enough to burn a naked hand. The average temperature of a typical rock on the surface is 55°F, but deep in the gold mines it is 125°. Forty miles under the surface, the heat is so great that rocks melt, forming magma. At the core, temperatures may reach 13,000°F. (Compare that to the melting point of pure iron, a mere 2,795°.)

AT THE BIRTH OF THE EARTH

In the planet's infancy, the outer part may have been a solid shell. But as it cooled, the shell cracked like an egg into nine main pieces and about a dozen smaller ones, called tectonic plates. They fit together like a jigsaw puzzle and float on top of a layer of molten magma. The plates move at the average rate of one inch per year, which is about as fast as fingernails grow. (The hour hand of a clock moves 10,000 times faster.)

Each of the tectonic plates rubs against three or more other plates. The points where the plates meet are where magma is most likely to find an escape route. Eighty percent of the world's volca-

If you work nights, you're nearly twice as likely to have an accident than if you work days.

noes and 90 percent of its earthquakes occur along the edges of these plates. That's also where we find the Earth's tallest mountains and deepest trenches.

WORLD IN MOTION

Magma is not stagnant; it moves. The same way that differences in hot and cold air cause wind, and differences in hot and cold water cause currents, differences in hot rocks in the center of the Earth and cold rocks at the surface of the Earth cause magma to move.

In addition, when rocks melt, their various materials naturally sort by weight, with heavy elements, such as iron and nickel sinking, and lighter elements rising. This also produces motion in magma. Furthermore, the gases produced when rocks melt rise to the surface, pushing magma upward. The magma forces its way through any fissure it can find. When a weak spot in the surface of the Earth is found, a pipeline forms and everything spews out. But when a pipeline becomes clogged—for example, by a plug of hardened lava from a previous explosion—nothing can escape. In that case, the pressure of the gases and magma continues to increase until it's strong enough to blow out the plug. Obviously, the tighter the plug and the greater the pressure, the more devastating the explosion.

HOT STUFF

When magma comes to the surface, it's called lava. The average temperature of lava is about 1,800°F, although it can be much hotter. When lava is churned violently, mixed to a froth with air and gases, and then thrown into the atmosphere, it comes down as pumice. When magma cools beneath the surface, it forms dense rocks such as granite and basalt. Fully 80 percent of the Earth is volcanic in origin.

There are about 600 active volcanoes in the world and an average of 20 explosions per year around the planet. North America has about 20 volcanoes, all on the west coast. Japan has over 70. (Australia has none at all, because it sits in the middle of a tectonic plate.) Over the last 10,000 years, about 1,500 different volcanoes have exploded. Over the last 1,000 years, approximately 300,000 people have died due to volcanic eruptions.

A person who collects keyrings is called a copoclephilist.

BRINGER OF LIFE

The amount of destruction that volcanoes have caused, however, is infinitesimal compared to the bounty they've given us. Basically, without volcanos there'd be no life on Earth.

When our planet was very young, it was very hot. As the outer crust cooled, volcanoes spewed out enough gas over the first billion years to create a swirling, dynamic atmosphere. The cycle kept going . . . and going . . . and going. Weather systems formed and eons of rain eventually created the oceans.

What happened next is not known for certain—here are two theories:

- Lightning may have caused certain simple chemicals, like ammonia, to form into more complicated chemicals which, in turn, may have hooked together in chains, forming molecules such as RNA and DNA, the building blocks of life.

- Fats in the primitive seas may have formed large globules enclosing "life-directing" chemicals, and these structures eventually may have formed primitive living cells.

In either case, most scientists agree that volcanoes were the spoon that stirred the primordial soup long enough to allow the chemistry of life to succeed. And they're still stirring it today. For evidence, look at any volcanic region on Earth and you'll find some of the greenest and most fertile land anywhere.

WHAT'S OUT THERE

Knowing what volcanoes have done for Earth, astronomers have looked for them on other planets. Mars has the largest known volcano in the solar system, Olympus Mons, three times higher than Mount Everest and as wide as Arizona. Samples taken from the Martian surface show trace amounts of water and biogenic elements that suggest life once existed there.

Farther away, scientists are eyeing Jupiter's moon Europa, which also shows evidence of volcanism and water. Who knows—before the 21st century is complete, we may find some new friends in the neighborhood.

Back on Earth, nothing can be done to stop volcanoes from exploding. Scientists can usually predict explosions using seismology, gas monitoring, and satellite technology. Meanwhile, mankind

Ninety percent of the world's food crops come from only 12 species of plants.

constantly works to reduce the impact of volcanoes on the population. Sometimes, it works. Sometimes, it doesn't.

BOILING RAIN

The Kelut volcano on the Indonesian island of Java tended to collect water in its crater, creating a huge lake. So, whenever the volcano erupted, an avalanche of boiling water and mud would sweep down the mountain, destroying everything in its path. In 1919 104 villages were buried and more than 5,000 people killed. Engineers decided to drain the lake. They began digging a series of tunnels through the side of the volcano, each one 30 feet lower than the last. By 1926, the lake was reduced from 85 million cubic yards of water to 4 million. When the volcano erupted again in 1951, the much smaller lake simply evaporated.

Unfortunately, the explosion also ruined the drainage system and deepened the crater. Once again, massive amounts of water collected. In 1963 an explosion killed thousands. A new drainage system was begun. Since then, the lake has been maintained at a safe level. When Kelut erupted in 1990, only 32 people were killed.

SAVING HELGAFELL

In 1973 the Helgafell volcano off the coast of Iceland began erupting. The 5,300 residents of Heimaey Island were evacuated, but 300 people remained to try to save the town. A wall of lava 120 feet high and 1,000 feet wide threatened to seal off the town's only harbor, which would effectively destroy the local economy. In desperation, the remaining citizens used their fire engines to pump water on the advancing flow. Small tongues of lava solidified under the steady barrage of water, and a small dam built up, slowing the flow. Then they used a sand dredger to pump sea water onto the flow. More high-pressure pumps were sent from the United States, and workers discovered that by piping water to points behind the flow's front, a series of small dams could be created to form internal barriers. Nineteen miles of pipe and 43 pumps were used to move water for nearly four months straight. Finally the volcano settled down. The harbor—and the town—had been saved.

For more about volcanoes, check out the stories of Mount Peleé on page 45, Mount St. Helens on page 237, and The Lost Cities on page 303.

A cubic foot of gold weighs more than half a ton.

TOILET TECH

Better living through bathroom technology.

WHY PIT-STOP . . . WHEN YOU CAN PIT-GO?
Inventor: Aston Waugh of East Orange, New Jersey
Product: An automobile urinal that flushes. The urinal
consists of three parts: a hanging water tank, a miniature padded
toilet bowl that the driver sits on while driving, and a waste storage tank that stows neatly beneath the driver's seat.
How It Works: After use, the driver flushes the device by opening
a valve; water from the hanging tank flows through a tube into the
toilet bowl, and from there into the storage tank underneath the
seat. "For privacy," the inventor advises, "the user may wrap a large
towel around him or herself from the waist to the knees before
undoing the clothing to facilitate urination." (Not recommended
for use while operating a cell phone.)

PET-O-POTTI

Inventor: Floraine Cohen of New York City
Product: A toilet conversion kit that allows dogs and cats to
use the facilities just like any other member of the family.
How It Works: A ramp leads up to a trapdoor that's installed over
the toilet bowl. An electronic sensor detects when the animal has
come and gone, so to speak; then, after the animal has left, it
opens the trapdoor, allowing the waste to fall into the bowl.
"Encircling the trap door is a perforated tube into which water is
fed, for purposes of flushing the waste material into the toilet."

PORT-O-PET-O-POTTI

Inventor: Angela Raphael of New York City
Product: A strap-on animal waste collector for dogs owned by
people too squeamish to use a pooper-scooper.
How It Works: It looks kind of like a pet harness, only backward
with two add-ons. One waste receptacle attaches beneath the dog's
tail, and one attaches beneath the dog to capture urine. Extra
bonus: both receptacles are disposable.

Ross Perot lost $450 million on the stock market in a single day—April 22, 1970

GIVES YOU STRONG MOUTH AND REFRESHING WIND

In Japan, English words are "cool"—it doesn't even matter whether they make sense, which is why they're so funny. Here are some actual English phrases found on Japanese products.

On Fresh Brand Straws: Let's try homeparty fashionably and have a joyful chat with nice fellow. Fujinami's straw will produce you young party happily and exceedingly.

Warning on a toy box: A dangerous toy. This toy is being made for the extreme priority the good looks. The little part which suffocates when the sharp part which gets hurt is swallowed is contained generously.

On Koeda brand chocolate-covered pretzels: The sentimental taste is cozy for the heroines in the town.

On a fondue set: When all family members are seated around the table, dishes are all the more tasteful. If dishes are nice, the square ceiling becomes round.

Advertisement for a restaurant: No one really goes to Aqua Bar for the drinks, but we make sure our drinks won't kill you.

On a paper coffee cup: The Art of Hot. Side by side, I'll be yours forever. Because please don't weep.

Sign for Café Miami: We established a fine coffee. What everybody can say TASTY! It's fresh, so-mild. With some special coffee's bitter and sourtaste. "LET'S HAVE SUCH A COFFEE! NOW!" is our selling copy. Please love Café Miami.

On a coat label: Have a good time! Refreshed and foppish sense and comfortable and fresh styles will catch you who belong to city-groups. All the way.

Good thing they're hauling gas: Giant oil tankers get about 31 feet per gallon.

On a package of prawn-flavored crackers: Once you have opened the packing it will be entirely impossible for you to suppress the desire to overcome such exciting challenge of your tongue. However, don't be disappointed with your repeated failure, you may continue with your habit.

In a Honda repair manual: No touching earth wire, fatal eventuarity may incur.

On a toothbrush box: Gives you strong mouth and refreshing wind!

On a package of bath salts: Humanity are fighting against tired. Charley support you.

On a washing machine: Push button. Foam coming plenty. Big Noise. Finish.

On the front of a datebook: Have a smell of panda droppings. This one is very fragrant.

On children's play microphone: Mom ma! Pap Pap! I and Lady Employees to play with it together!

On a photo developing envelope: Takes the thirst out of everyday time. A pure whiff of oxygen, painting over a monochrome world in primary colors. We all know that. It's why everyone loves fruit.

* * *

THE WRITING IS ON THE WALL

In Pompeii, the walls of every building were used as billboards on which anyone was allowed to write whatever they wanted. When the buried city was excavated, archaeologists found notices of upcoming plays at the theater, the schedule of games at the stadium, the price of goods in the market, and the comments of passersby. One message declared, "Everybody writes on walls but me."

The elections in Pompeii were coming up when the city was destroyed, so thousands of political ads were found, including this one: "Vote for Vatia, who is recommended by sneak thieves, the whole company of late drinkers, and everyone who is fast asleep."

THEY ALWAYS GET THEIR MAN

For people who grew up on John Wayne movies, where the cavalry always fought the Indians, this may be hard to believe, but Canada's cavalry, the Royal Canadian Mounted Police, was actually started to protect the Native Americans. Here's the story.

THE WESTERN FRONTIER

Canada only became an independent nation in 1867. After the American Civil War, the British colonies that now form Canada viewed the United States as a potential threat: America was a powerful nation, equipped with the tools of war and possibly willing to use them to annex Canada. Already, several fur-trading forts had been established in Western Canada and some were even flying flags that resembled the American flag. These traders posed a real threat to Canadian sovereignty, because the prairie border was not firmly established or enforced at that time. For their own protection, the colonies banded together as a single Dominion of the British Crown.

The newly formed Canadian government knew it needed a national police force to maintain friendly relations with Native American tribes and to maintain the borders at the Western territories. But there were other pressing matters, so the organization of such a police force was repeatedly postponed.

CYPRESS HILLS MASSACRE

In May 1873, a group of hunters from Fort Benton, Montana, crossed the Canadian border in search of animal pelts. One night while they slept, a band of thieves invaded their camp and stole their horses. When the hunters awoke, they were furious. They followed the tracks to the Cypress Hills in Saskatchewan and confronted a local tribe, the Assiniboine. The tribe didn't have the horses, but the hunters wanted revenge and cared little who paid for it. They raped the Assiniboine women and massacred most of the tribe.

When news of the Cypress Hills Massacre reached the east, government officials were appalled. Organizing a police force to

. . . nine colleges, ten lakes, 33 counties, and 121 towns around the world.

patrol the western territories immediately became the Dominion's top priority.

UPHOLD THE RIGHT

The government sought an educated group of men with "good moral character." By September, the recruits, called the North West Mounted Police, or "Mounties" for short, totaled 300 men. Mounted on horseback and wearing scarlet coats that mimicked the uniforms of British soldiers, the new force was stationed throughout western Canada. Their primary job: to stop Americans from slaughtering game and selling whiskey to native tribes.

By protecting the First Peoples (as the native tribes are now known) from U.S. poachers and expansionists, the Mounties quickly became friends with the Canadian Indians. In fact, by the early 1890s, there was almost no need for a mounted police force. Then gold was discovered in the Yukon.

By 1899 thousands of Canadian and U.S. citizens had invaded the Yukon in search of gold. The Mounties dispatched 250 officers to the Yukon to keep the peace and again protect Canadian sovereignty. American prospectors returning home told stories of the courageous officers on horseback who managed the potentially explosive situation with an iron fist. The romantic image appealed to newspapers, which, in turn, inspired Hollywood. Then came "Sergeant Preston of the Yukon" on radio, in comic books, and on television. The Mounties had become a Canadian icon.

MAY THE FORCE BE WITH YOU

- The Royal Canadian Mounted Police aren't mounted anymore, and they haven't been since 1966, when routine equestrian training was abandoned.

- Mounties are still issued the traditional scarlet jacket, blue jodhpur pants with gold stripes, and brown Mountie hat. But they only wear them on ceremonial occasions; most of the time they just wear standard police uniforms.

- "We always get our man" is not the RCMP motto and never has been. The phrase was invented in 1877 by an American reporter. Their real motto: "Maintain the Right."

- For that matter, Mounties don't even call themselves "Mounties." They prefer to think of themselves as "the Force."

Pigeons have three sets of eyelids.

DOG DOO! GOOD GOD!

Palindromes are phrases or sentences that are spelled the same way backward and forward. Who comes up with these things? Don't they have jobs . . . or families . . . or any other way to spend their time? Well, whether they're weird or not, we're hooked. Here are some of Uncle John's favorites.

Ana, nab a banana.

Campus motto: Bottoms up, Mac!

Dog doo! Good God!

No, Mel Gibson is a casino's big lemon.

Pasadena, Ned—ASAP!

Straw? No, too stupid a fad. I put soot on warts.

Too far, Edna, we wander afoot

He lived as a devil, eh?

Pull up, Eva, we're here! Wave! Pull up!

I saw desserts; I'd no lemons, alas no melon. Distressed was I.

Marge lets Norah see Sharon's telegram.

Ned, go gag Ogden.

No evil Shahs live on.

No lemons, no melon.

Now, sir, a war is won!

A dog! A panic in a pagoda!

Star? Come, Donna Melba, I'm an amiable man— no Democrats!

Step on hose-pipes? Oh no, pets.

Too bad, I hid a boot.

Was it a rat I saw?

We'll let Dad tell Lew.

Kay, a red nude, peeped under a yak.

Yawn. Madonna fan? No damn way.

Red rum, sir, is murder.

Don't nod.

Some men interpret nine memos.

Dammit, I'm mad!

Ed, I saw Harpo Marx ram Oprah W. aside.

Evil I did dwell, lewd did I live.

Gert, I saw Ron avoid a radio-van—or was it Reg?

Lew, Otto has a hot towel!

Lonely Tylenol.

O, stone, be not so.

Re-paper.

So, G. Rivera's tots are Virgos.

Too hot to hoot.

Was it Eliot's toilet I saw?

In 1939, Gerald Ford appeared in *Look* magazine, modeling ski clothing.

FAMILY FEUD

Here's an example of what happens when families are more interested in money and power than they are in each other.

CULKIN VS. CULKIN

The Contestants: Child actor Macaulay Culkin, his father and onetime manager, Kit Culkin, and his mother, Patricia Brentrup.

The Feud: Culkin, Brentrup, and their seven children were living in a one-room tenement when Macaulay was cast in the 1990 film *Home Alone*. Nine-year-old Macaulay suddenly found himself the biggest Hollywood child star since Shirley Temple.

"Big Mac" made only $100,000 on *Home Alone*, but made $27 million on *Home Alone 2* and went on to command huge salaries in the other roles his father chose for him. But nearly all the films that followed (*The Pagemaster*, *Getting Even with Dad*, and *Richie Rich*) were flops, and Kit Culken, "universally reviled as the stage father from hell," had burned his bridges with just about every director in Hollywood. Not that it really mattered: by 1995 the 14-year-old Macaulay was so burned out—having made 14 films in less than 10 years—that he told his parents he was through with movies. "I'd been wanting to stop since I was about eleven," he says.

As if his career problems weren't enough, Macaulay's parents split up and began a long and ugly battle for custody of the children, which included control of Macaulay's estimated $50 million in assets. Brentrup accused Kit Culkin of punching her when she was pregnant and threatening to toss her off a balcony; he accused her of being an adulterous drunk who neglected her children. Brentrup eventually won custody of the kids, and in 1997 a judge awarded oversight of Macaulay's assets to his accountant.

And the Winner Is: Macaulay, sort of. He still has plenty of cash in the bank, and after a four-year break from acting, landed the lead in a play in London's West End. As of October 2000, he and his father had not seen or spoken to each other for nearly four years. "Hopefully someday he'll realize some of the things he's done," Culkin says. "But I understand my parents put me in the financial position where I am today, and I'm grateful for that."

Male monkeys go bald just like men.

MYTH-CONCEPTIONS

*"Common knowledge" is frequently wrong. Here are
some examples of things that many people believe . . .
but that according to our sources, just aren't true.*

Myth: "Give me a home where the buffalo roam, and the
deer and the antelope play . . . "
Fact: There are no antelope in North America. The animal the song probably refers to is the pronghorn, which resembles
an antelope. Real antelope live only in Asia and Africa.

Myth: The forbidden fruit eaten by Eve was an apple.
Fact: The Bible makes reference to the "fruit of the tree" (Genesis
3:3), but names no particular fruit. Horticulturists say that apple
trees have never grown in the area where the Garden of Eden supposedly existed. She probably ate a pomegranate.

Myth: Blood is red.
Fact: This is only true part of the time. Blood is red in arteries
because it is loaded with oxygen. After the oxygen is used up,
blood travels through veins back to the heart and is usually a pur-
plish-blue. When the blood in a vein hits the air because of a cut,
it instantly oxidizes and turns red again.

Myth: Hunger is triggered by an empty stomach.
Fact: Hunger is set off when nutrients are absent in the bloodstream. In response to this, the brain begins rhythmic contractions
of the stomach and intestines, which causes stomach grumbling
and the feeling of hunger.

Myth: A limb "falls asleep" because its blood supply gets cut off.
Fact: This feeling of numbness—called *neurapraxia*—happens
when a major nerve is pinched against a hard object or bone. This
causes the harmless temporary sensation of numbness, but the
blood continues to flow normally.

Myth: Pandas are bears.
Fact: The red panda is an extremely large cousin of the raccoon.

Seventy-five percent of migrating robins will return to within five miles of their homes.

MAKING HIS MARK

*Sometimes being in the right place at the right time makes
all the difference. Here's a great story submitted by
our official BRI coincidencologist, Janet Spencer.
(See if you can guess the surprise ending.)*

A YOUNG WRITER'S BIG BREAK

In 1866, the clipper ship *Hornet* was sailing from California to New York with a cargo of kerosene and candles. A thousand miles from land and 108 days into the voyage, a careless sailor accidentally set the cargo on fire. The 33 men abandoned the ship in three life boats, each with a 10-day supply of rations. They drifted apart, and two of the lifeboats were never seen again. The third one, piloted by the captain floated 4,000 miles in 43 days until it landed safely in Hawaii.

A correspondent for a California newspaper was in Hawaii at the time, and went to the hospital to interview the men. He worked on the story all night and sent the article out on a California-bound ship the next day. His account was the first detailed report to reach the mainland—and it was a scoop. He was paid an astounding $300 bonus for it. On his return trip to California, he found that two of his fellow shipmates were survivors of the *Hornet*. He interviewed them and compiled an even more detailed article. The prestigious magazine *Harper's Monthly* purchased it.

OR WAS IT?

The writer expected to achieve instant fame and worldwide name recognition with the article's publication. Unfortunately, *Harper's* goofed—they misprinted his name. The correspondent was Samuel Clemens using his pen name, Mark Twain. But *Harper's* listed the author as "Mac Swain." Twain's dreams of fame were dashed. "I was not celebrated," Twain later lamented, "I was a Literary Person, but that was all—a buried one; buried alive."

Not quite. Within months of the *Harper's* debacle, Clemens' short story "*The Celebrated Jumping Frog of Calaveras County*" became a national hit. This time, the publisher got his name right—and Mark Twain became a star.

NAME A FAMOUS JOHN

*Where do game shows go when they die? It's called the Game
Show Network, and it's where you can catch reruns of the
Family Feud. (No cable? Don't fret—there's a new
version of the* Feud *in syndication.)*

LET'S START THE *FAMILY FEUD*!
In 1976, game show guru Mark Goodson (*The Price Is Right,
Concentration, Password, I've Got a Secret*) had an inspiration.
One segment of another of his hits, *Match Game*, featured
an Audience Match round, in which a panelist—usually Richard
Dawson—and a contestant tried to match responses to an audience
survey. The segment was so popular that Goodson decided to spin
it off as a regular show, starring Dawson as host.

Richard Dawson was a British comedian who got his first big
break in 1965 playing Newkirk on the classic TV sitcom *Hogan's
Heroes*. When the show was cancelled in 1971, he landed a gig on
Rowan & Martin's Laugh-In, and when that show died he went on
to *Match Game 73*. Then came the *Feud*.

MATCH THIS

Family Feud premiered on ABC on July 12, 1976 and quickly surpassed *Match Game* as the top-rated daytime game show, even winning an Emmy Award. And Dawson's easygoing manner, sharp wit,
and style were central to the show's success. He kissed every female
contestant, joked with the families and with the camera, and did it
with such style that audiences couldn't help but like him. The
show became so popular that Goodson created a primetime version, featuring popular celebrities feuding for charity. And that
show was so popular that he expanded it from one night a week in
1977 to two nights a week in 1979 to five nights a week in 1980.
At its peak, the *Feud* with Dawson appeared 15 times per week.

But fame went to Dawson's head. Behind the scenes he was not
so easygoing. He fought constantly with the *Family Feud* and *Match
Game* staffs. On *Match Game*, he stopped making jokes and even
refused to smile on camera. Frustrated producers were happy to let
him out of his contract when he left in 1978.

Bank robber John Dillinger used Ford cars exclusively for his getaway vehicles.

But Dawson stayed with the *Feud*, and the *Feud* stayed on top, maintaining its #1 status for years. Then, in 1983, it was eclipsed by a new show, *Wheel of Fortune*, and that was the beginning of the end. The nighttime *Family Feud* was cancelled in 1984; the daytime *Feud* was cancelled a year later. Dawson's career pretty much ended, too. His reputation for being difficult preceded him, and work was hard to find. But his rep did help him land one part: that of the evil game show host Damon Killian in the 1987 Arnold Schwarzenegger's film *The Running Man*.

NEW LEASE ON LIFE

In 1988 Mark Goodson talked CBS into reviving the *Feud*. It was the same old show, with a new host—Ray Combs, a furniture salesman turned stand-up comic. Then Goodson freshened it up by renaming it *Family Feud Challenge*, lengthening it to one hour, and adding some new features. Combs was no Dawson, but the show continued to do reasonably well until 1992, when Goodson died and ratings started to slip.

Goodson had once remarked that while he was alive, Dawson would never work with his company again, but his son, Jonathan, was desperately looking for a way to save the *Feud*. In 1994 he fired Ray Combs and asked Dawson, now 62, to return as host. It didn't help—bringing back the veteran wasn't enough to save the show, and it was cancelled a year later.

I WANT MY *FAMILY FEUD*!

Family Feud was off the air for four years. In 1997 the British conglomerate Pearson Television acquired the U.S. syndication company All American Communications, which owned the Goodson library of game show formats. Now the Brits owned the show, and they decided to bring it back once again. They needed a warm and friendly host who could work well with families. After looking at lots of options, they chose another stand-up comic, Louie Anderson. According to Tony Cohen, Pearson president, "Louie appeals to that kind of Middle American audience which we think is the *Family Feud* heartland."

In September 1999, Anderson took the helm. The revamped set, new theme music, and dollar amounts aside, the *Feud* today is played pretty much the same as it always has been. The show with Anderson gets consistently high ratings.

Top speed of astronauts traveling to the moon: 24,679 mph.

One Final Note: What happened to Ray Combs? In 1993 his 18-year marriage collapsed. Two years later, he was involved in a serious car crash, which left him partially paralyzed. He had earned $800,000 per year for his six-year stint as host of *Family Feud*, but the money was gone. In 1995 he finally landed another game show— a *Double Dare* wannabe called *Ray Combs' Family Challenge*—but it lasted only six months. In 1996, out of work, alone, and destitute, the 40-year-old Combs committed suicide.

FEUD FACTS

- The original *Feud* theme song was actually a *Price Is Right* new-car song, redone with banjos.

- In 1981 a 27-year-old *Feud* contestant, Gretchen Johnson, received more than a kiss from Dawson: the couple had a child and married 10 years later.

- Given serious consideration for *Family Feud* host: Dolly Parton.

- Louie Anderson was the victim of extortion after he allegedly propositioned a man named Richard Gordon at a California casino in 1993. Anderson reportedly agreed to pay the man $100,000 in hush money, fearing for his career. But Gordon upped the ante to $250,000, so Anderson went to the police. Gordon was convicted of extortion and sentenced to 21 months in a federal penitentiary.

* * *

SIGHT FOR SOAR EYES

Mr. See and Mr. Soar were old friends. See owned a saw and Soar owned a seesaw. Now, See's saw sawed Soar's seesaw before Soar saw See, which made Soar sore. Had Soar seen See's saw before See saw Soar's seesaw, then See's saw would not have sawed Soar's seesaw. But See saw Soar and Soar's seesaw before Soar saw See's saw, so See's saw sawed Soar's seesaw. It was a shame to let See see Soar so sore just because See's saw sawed Soar's seesaw.

Odds a child will be born albino: 1 in 9,000.

SURVEY SAYS . . .

Remember the Fast Money round on Family Feud? *Answers come easily when you're sitting on your sofa . . . but imagine the pressure you'd feel on national television. You might even say something stupid.*

Q: Name a fruit that is yellow.
A: Orange.

Q: Name something that floats in the bath.
A: Water.

Q: Name a famous cowboy.
A: Buck Rogers.

Q: A number you have to memorize.
A: Seven.

Q: Name a part of the body beginning with "N."
A: Knee.

Q: Something you do before going to bed.
A: Sleep.

Q: Name a bird with a long neck.
A: Naomi Campbell.

Q: Name something with a hole in it.
A: Window.

Q: Name a sign of the zodiac.
A: April.

Q: Name something you might accidentally leave on all night.
A: Your shoes.

Q: Name a holiday when the stores are always busy.
A: Monday.

Q: Name something some people do clothed that others do without clothes.
A: Ride a motorcycle

Q: Name something you do in the bathroom.
A: Decorate.

Q: Name the first thing you take off after work.
A: Underwear.

Q: Something that flies that doesn't have an engine.
A: A bicycle with wings.

Q: Name an occupation where you need a torch.
A: A burglar.

Q: Name an animal you might see in the zoo.
A: A dog.

Q: A job around the house that has to be done every fall.
A: Spring cleaning.

Q: Something you might be allergic to.
A: Skiing.

Q: Name a famous bridge.
A: The bridge over troubled waters.

Q: Name something a cat does.
A: Goes to the toilet.

Q: Name a song with moon in the title.
A: Blue suede moon.

Q: Name an item of clothing worn by the three Musketeers.
A: A horse.

Q: Name a famous group of singers.
A: The Simpsons.

Two countries are smaller than New York's Central Park: Monaco and Vatican City.

THE SAGE OF ATHENS

*Thoughts and observations from the ancient
Greek philosopher, Socrates.*

"The only good is knowledge and the only evil ignorance."

"Let him that would move the world first move himself."

"What you cannot enforce, do not command."

"Remember that there is nothing stable in human affairs; therefore avoid undue elation in prosperity, or undue depression in adversity."

"He who is not contented with what he has, would not be contented with what he would like to have."

"The unexamined life is not worth living."

"I know I am intelligent, because I know that I know nothing."

"Wisdom begins in wonder."

"Beauty is a short-lived tyranny."

"To do is to be."

"The way to gain a good reputation is to endeavor to be what you desire to appear."

"Fame is the perfume of heroic deeds."

"From the deepest desires often come the deadliest hate."

"If all our misfortunes were laid in one common heap, whence everyone must take an equal portion, most people would be content to take their own and depart."

"Nothing is preferred before justice."

"Better do a little well, than a great deal badly."

"As to marriage or celibacy, let a man take the course he will. He will be sure to repent."

"Life contains but two tragedies. One is not to get your heart's desire; the other is to get it."

Aristotle stuttered.

UNCLE JOHN'S
BOTTOM 10 RECORDS

*If cream rises to the top, what sinks to the bottom? These do:
records so bad, they're good. Here's an official BRI countdown—
and we do mean down. They don't sink any lower . . .*

10. EILERT PILARM: *Greatest Hits*. Anyone who's expecting
this Swedish Elvis impersonator to resemble the King will be very
disappointed. Wearing white leather and rhinestones, he comes
across like somebody's Uncle Olaf after a drunken weekend in
Vegas. His singing sounds as if he hit puberty around age 60. Our
favorite: "Yailhouse Rock."

9. MAE WEST: *Way Out West*. Is that an electric guitar in your
pocket, or are you just glad to see me? On this 1969 album, the
then-70-year-old former sex symbol tries to prove she's still relevant by talking her way through rock classics like "Day Tripper"
and "Twist and Shout."

8. PADDY ROBERTS: *Songs for Gay Dogs*. Roberts sings about
the sex life of fish in "Virgin Sturgeon" and serves up a steaming
pile of potty humor with "Don't Use the WC," a song about dirty
bathrooms. It's not just in bad taste—it's bad. By the way, this LP
has nothing to do with Spot's alternative lifestyle. So what does
the title mean? Well, most of the songs are drinking songs—maybe
he was under the influence when he picked it.

7. SAMMY PETRILLO: *My Son, the Phone Caller*. Petrillo was
an awful Jerry Lewis impersonator who starred in a few el cheapo
flicks, including the memorable *Bela Lugosi Meets a Brooklyn
Gorilla*. This album features him doing moronic phone pranks like
calling hospitals and saying that he's got a pregnant pet gorilla in
labor, then asking how to deliver the baby.

**6. THE NATIONAL GALLERY: *Performing Musical
Interpretations of the Paintings of Paul Klee*.** Four beatniks from
Cleveland introduce us to the German Expressionist painter by

performing "rock-art" song versions of his paintings. Complete with acid-drenched lyrics like "Boy with toys, alone in the attic / Choking his hobby horse, thinking of his mother."

5. HELEN GURLEY BROWN: *Lessons in Love.* The editor of *Cosmopolitan* magazine gives advice to swinging singles on the finer points of adultery. It may have been edgy back in 1963, but today it sounds like Martha Stewart reading *Affairs for Dummies.* Side 1 (for men) covers topics like "How to get a girl to the brink and . . . keep her there when you're not going to marry her."

4. LITTLE MARCY: *Little Marcy Visits Smokey the Bear.* A creepy singing ventriloquist's dummy visits Smokey and his animal pals in the woods. Part of an evangelical Christian children's act, Little Marcy had an eerie grin and a high-pitched singing voice that were probably responsible for frightening thousands of kids into becoming atheists.

3. MR. METHANE: *Mr. Methane.com.* The masked Mr. Methane is a "fartiste" in the style of Frenchman Le Petomaine. He breaks new wind by pooting his way through classics like "The Blue Danube," Beethoven's *Ninth Symphony*, and "Greensleeves," proving conclusively that he doesn't have to be silent to be deadly.

2. LUCIA PAMELA: *Into Outer Space with Lucia Pamela.* A former Miss St. Louis, Pamela claims she and her band flew to the moon in her own rocket ship to record this concept album about her trip to "Moontown." Sounding like an off-key Ethel Merman, she clucks like a chicken when she forgets the words.

1. MUHAMMAD ALI: *The Adventures of Ali and His Gang vs. Mr. Tooth Decay.* Recorded in 1976. Ali assembled an all-star bicentennial cast, including Frank Sinatra, Richie Havens, and Howard Cosell, for this "Fight of the Century" against Mr. Tooth Decay and his evil sidekick, Sugar Cuba. Old Blue Eyes sounds like he's working on his fifth martini as a shopkeeper who offers Ali's gang of hyperactive kids free ice cream. The Champ sends Frankie packing back to Vegas to "tell Sammy, and all them cats like old Dino" about the horrors of periodontal disease.

LUCKY FINDS

*Ever found something really valuable? It's one of the best
feelings in the world. Here's another installment of
a regular* Bathroom Reader *feature.*

A SHAKY PROSPECT

The Find: A dirty, moldy, wobbly old card table

Where It Was Found: At a lawn sale, for $25

The Story: In the late 1960s, a woman named Claire (no last
name—she prefers to remain anonymous) moved to a new house
and needed a small table for one of the rooms. She found one at a
yard sale but it was dirty and it wobbled; a friend advised against
buying it, telling her that "it would never hold a lamp." She
bought it anyway—after bargaining the price down from $30 to
$25, because that was all the money she had in her purse. When
she cleaned the table up, she noticed a label on the underside of it
that read "John Seymour & Son Cabinet Makers Creek Square
Boston." Claire did some research on it, but didn't learn a lot.

Nearly 30 years passed. Then in September 1997, Claire took
her table to a taping of the PBS series *Antiques Roadshow*. There
she learned that Seymour furniture is among the rarest and most
sought-after in the United States; until Claire's table showed up,
only five other pieces in original condition with the Seymour label
were known to exist. Claire thought the table might be worth
$20,000; the *Antiques Roadshow* appraiser put it at $300,000. Not
even close—the table sold at auction at Sotheby's for $490,000.
A pretty good price for a table that can't hold a lamp.

I YAM WHAT I YAM

The Find: A diamond

Where It Was Found: In Sierra Leone . . . under a yam

The Story: In 1997 three hungry boys were scrounging for food
near the village of Hinnah Malen in the African country of Sierra
Leone. The boys, orphaned since 1995 when their parents had
been killed in a rebel attack, had gone two days without food.
They spent three unsuccessful hours searching for yams that
morning and were on their way home when their luck changed.

Oldest unchanged flag in history: Denmark's has remained the same since the 1200s.

They found a yam under a palm tree and dug it up. Right under the yam they found a flawless 100-carat diamond. Estimated value: $500,000. "It was easy to see," according to the oldest boy, 14-year-old Morie Jah. "It was shining and sparkling."

NOT BAA-AA-AD

The Find: A lost Hindu shrine

Where It Was Found: In a cave in the Himalayas, in India

The Story: In September 2001, a shepherd named Ghulam Qadir lost some of his sheep and set out to look for them. He crawled into a small cave, thinking they might be there . . . but instead of his sheep, he found a 12-inch idol of the Hindu god Shiva. The cave turned out to be a 1,500-year-old shrine, one that had been forgotten and undisturbed for centuries. Government officials were so excited by the discovery that they promised to pay Qadir 10 percent of the cash offerings left at the shrine from 2002 to 2007, followed by a large final payment when the five years are up. (He never did find his sheep.)

UNLUCKY FIND

The Find: A swastika and a pile of pornographic magazines

Where They Were Found: In a brand-new Jaguar automobile—the magazines were stuffed into an interior cavity; the swastika was painted underneath a seat panel.

The Story: The discovery was made accidentally when the car was being taken apart for bomb-proofing, because this car happened to be purchased by Queen Elizabeth. The magazines and the swastika were put there during assembly by an autoworker who had no idea of the car's final destination. "It is one of those old traditions where people used to write things behind the seat panel of cars and they were never discovered unless there was an accident," another factory worker told the British newspaper *The Guardian*, "only this time it wasn't funny."

Update: The worker responsible for the "factory extras" lost his job over the incident . . . but that probably won't stop the practice of hiding things in new cars. "The chaps go to an awful lot of trouble to do the car," says the Jaguar employee. "They're there all day. What else have they got to do?"

Roughly one-third of all species of snakes are venomous.

HERE'S LOOKING AT YOU

It's easy to forget that just 160 years ago, most people lived and died without leaving a single visual record of themselves for posterity. Here's how photography began to change that.

NO-MAN'S-LAND

In 1837 Louis Daguerre discovered how to create a lasting detailed photographic image. Within months of the groundbreaking publication of his photographic process in 1839, people started taking cameras to Greece, to the Middle East, to Africa, to Central and South America, and to every other corner of the world to photograph the wonders they saw there.

But if you look at these early photographs, you'll notice that no matter what the scene, there's always one thing missing from the picture: *people*. These first photographs appear barren and empty, completely devoid of human or even animal life. It's as if each had been taken in a ghost town.

STILL SHOTS

It turns out that there were plenty of people in these scenes when the pictures were taken; they just can't be seen because they were *moving*. The early photosensitive chemicals took so long to form an image—30 minutes on a sunny day, an hour or more when it was cloudy—that pedestrians and street traffic passed in and out of the picture without registering.

The American inventor Samuel Morse noted this when he was invited to look at some of Daguerre's first photographs in 1839. One daguerreotype was a view of a busy Paris street, taken in the middle of the day when there must have been hundreds of people out. Only one person—quite possibly the first ever to be captured on film—was visible in the picture, and this only because he had been standing relatively still. Morse wrote to his brother:

> Moving objects leave no impression. The boulevard, though constantly crossed by a flood of pedestrians and carriages, appeared completely deserted, apart from a person who was having his boots polished. His feet, must of course, have remained immobile for a certain time, one of them being placed on the boot-black's box, the other on the ground.

A hippo's stomach is 10 feet long and can hold 400 pounds of food.

FACE TIME

Yet people living in the late 1830s and early 1840s wanted pictures of themselves and their loved ones more than any other photographic subject. Mortality rates were much higher then, and the pain of a death in the family was made worse by the fact that families frequently had no images of the deceased to remember them by. Only the wealthy were able to commission portraits of themselves. Now photography, with its promise of "automatic" portraits, seemed to offer the possibility of making portraiture available to everyone.

Understanding this need, photographers started looking for ways to take photographic portraits. They located their studios in rooftop glass houses to maximize available sunlight; they crammed those studios with mirrors to bring in even more light. They even filtered the sunlight through blue glass or bottles of blue liquid to take advantage of the fact that early photographic plates were especially sensitive to blue light. (Remember, the lightbulb wasn't invented until 1879.)

SAY "CHEEEEEESE"

Even with all of these measures, exposure times remained long—20 minutes or more—leaving the aspiring portraitist little choice but to resort to desperate measures. Since there was no easy way to stare at a fixed point in space for such a long time, many photographers instructed their subjects to pose with their eyes closed . . . and that was just the beginning: "Paint the face of the patient dead white," one daguerreotypist advised in 1839. "Powder his hair, and fix the back of his head between two planks attached to the back of an armchair and wound up with screws."

Posing for a portrait in such a studio was almost unbearable, something akin to having your picture taken inside a hot car with the windows rolled up and your head in a vise. The heat trapped by all that glass sent the temperature soaring, and the light from the mirrors was blinding. Looking "natural" under these conditions—sweating profusely, eyes squinting or closed, hair powdered, face painted white, head held immobile by boards while sitting perfectly still for 20 minutes or more—was just about impossible. Even when the pictures did come out, they were usually disappointing.

The United States has almost 4 million miles of roads and streets.

NEW AND IMPROVED

Fortunately, the first major improvements in daguerreotype photography came quickly. In 1840 Hungarian mathematician Jozsef Max Petzval invented a lens that let 22 times more light into the camera, reducing exposure times from 40 minutes to $2^1/_2$ minutes. That same year, English scientist John Frederick Goddard discovered that exposing daguerreotype plates to bromine vapors increased their photosensitivity, further shortening exposures to under a minute.

So what does Daguerre's process have to do with the modern photograph? Almost nothing. Daguerre became world famous, but his process was flawed—it only resulted in a single unique image. Daguerreotypes couldn't be reproduced, and ultimately the process fell into disuse.

The father of modern photography was English physicist William Henry Fox Talbot. In a sense, what Talbot did was invent the negative—a reverse image on photosensitive paper that could be used to make any number of positive prints, or "calotypes" as they came to be called. Talbot invented his process in 1835, but never published his findings or patented his original process. So when Daguerre came along two years later, he got all the credit for inventing photography. It turns out that Daguerre wasn't just smart; he was also very lucky.

OPEN FOR BUSINESS

In 1840, a photographer named Alexander Wolcot opened America's first portrait studio in New York City; the following year a coal merchant named Richard Beard opened one in London. The "nobility and beauty of England" were soon flocking to his studio to have their pictures taken; by 1842 he was making as much as £35,000 a year (in today's currency, £1,820,400, or $2,653,415) .

Other studios soon sprang up in the major cities of Europe and the United States. By the late 1840s, nearly every city in the United States had a "daguerrean artist," and smaller towns were served by itinerant photographers traveling by wagon. Photography was starting to realize its promise.

Focus on page 277 for the next part of the story.

Julius Caesar wore a laurel wreath crown to hide the fact that he was balding.

THE ORIGIN OF SOAP OPERAS, PART I

Soaps—you either love 'em or hate 'em. Either way,
you might be interested to learn where they come from.

SOAP DUD

In the early 1930s, Richard Deupree, the president of Procter & Gamble, had to make one of the most important and most difficult decisions in the history of the company: Should they continue to advertise their products, even though the country was suffering through the Great Depression?

Times were tough. Financially strapped customers were defecting to cheaper brands, forcing P&G to introduce less profitable "price brands." But for all the good that did, P&G's sales still dropped 28 percent in 1933, and the price of their stock fell more than 70 percent.

What was the point of advertising when customers (not to mention the company) were going through such hard times? Maybe it made more sense to conserve cash and wait for things to improve. A lot of the company's shareholders argued that Procter & Gamble should do just that, but Deupree had other ideas.

GOTTA HAVE IT

Deupree noticed that despite the Depression, some companies were actually prospering. The Fuller Brush Company, famous for selling its line of household brushes door-to-door, was thriving; so were many other companies that sold basic household necessities. And as crazy as it sounded, people were still buying radios even though they were a luxury. What on Earth were people doing buying luxury items in the middle of a depression?

Deupree concluded that no matter how much people had to cut back on their household expenses, some items—like soap—were so essential that families would not go without them. And if they really wanted something—like a radio—they were willing to scrimp and save their pennies for as long as it took to get one.

If people were going to spend money on things they needed or

Elephant tusks continue to grow as long as the animal lives.

wanted, Deupree figured that Procter & Gamble had no choice but to advertise . . . or lose business to competitors that did.

ON THE AIR

And since the number of households with radios was increasing, Deupree believed P&G should continue experimenting with the new medium.

Radio broadcasting was barely a decade old—KDKA, the country's first commercial radio station, had been broadcasting only since November 1920. During the day, audiences were smaller because husbands were at work and children were at school. Those few daytime shows that did exist, such as Live Stock Reports, Our Daily Food, and Mouth Hygiene, didn't attract very large audiences. Most broadcasters focused on providing evening programming, when everyone could listen.

Procter & Gamble was one of the first companies to realize that housewives working at home during the day represented a huge and potentially lucrative listening audience for the products it sold.

Remember, this was the era when most household chores had to be done by hand—few homes had washing machines or automatic dishwashers, and nearly all cooking was done from scratch. After a housewife finished preparing breakfast for her family and doing the dishes, she might spend hours washing clothes by hand with bar soap and a washboard; when she finished, she spent what was left of the afternoon cleaning the house or doing other chores. Then she prepared dinner; after that, she did the dishes. Each day was filled with hours and hours of backbreaking, tedious work, and there was little to ease the boredom. Until radio.

LEARNING CURVE

Deupree and other executives understood that if they created programming that women could listen to while they were doing their chores—many of which required the use of soap—they could advertise and sell a lot of Proctor & Gamble products in the process. But what kind of shows would work the best? It would take nearly a decade of experimentation for P&G to figure that out.

As far back as 1923, the company had created a recipe show called *Crisco Cooking Talks*, in which every recipe, naturally, called for Crisco shortening. The show was successful, and P&G

What's special about Mount Irazú in Costa Rica?

followed up with shows teaching people how to use Camay soap and Chipso laundry soap, as well as a second show (one apparently wasn't enough) on how to use Crisco.

Today these shows would probably be considered "infomercials"—their purpose was not to entertain the listener, but rather to teach them new ways to use the product being advertised. It worked, but Deupree and other executives knew the shows didn't come close to realizing radio advertising's full potential.

In 1930 Procter & Gamble created a show that featured a singer named George the Lava Soap Man. George didn't teach listeners about Lava soap; all he did was sing. It didn't matter—sales of Lava went up anyway, and the experience taught P&G execs that entertaining listeners made more sense than instructing them.

TUNE IN TOMORROW

But George the Lava Soap Man was missing something—a hook. If a listener missed George's show one day, what difference did it make? They could always tune in the next day without feeling like they'd missed anything, because one day's singing was as good as any other.

There had to be a way to create a format that would compel listeners to tune in every single day, maximizing the number of P&G ads they heard and keeping them from straying to shows sponsored by the competition.

One technique that had proven effective in Proctor & Gamble's newspaper advertising was the comic strip serial. Ivory soap's ad campaigns featured *The Jollyco Family*. Each week, the strip featured a member of the Jollyco family or a neighbor using Ivory soap. There was even a snooty villainess named Mrs. Percival Billington Folderol who used scented soaps instead of good old-fashioned Ivory. The story line continued from one week to the next, so people had to read the strip every week to keep up with what was going on.

The campaign was effective: Readers responded to the ads as if they were just another comic strip. They also bought soap—lots of it. After *The Jollyco Family* strip premiered in a New York newspaper, sales of Ivory soap jumped 25 percent in only six months.

If a continuing newspaper serial could sell soap, what about a radio serial? By 1932 Proctor & Gamble was ready to find out.

It's the only point in the Americas where one can see both the Atlantic and Pacific oceans.

AND NOW A FEW WORDS FROM OUR SPONSOR

In 1932 the company introduced a 15-minute radio serial called *The Puddle Family* on WLW in Cincinnati to advertise Oxydol laundry detergent. But that flopped. The following year, they tried again with a show called *Ma Perkins*, the continuing saga of a widowed lumber mill owner who mothers her employees and helps them solve their problems. Once again Oxydol was the sponsor.

In every 15-minute show, Ma Perkins or the other characters managed to plug Oxydol 20 to 25 times, nearly twice a minute. "We knew the repetition would be very irritating and we'd get complaints," one P&G executive said, "but the business was bad enough that we decided to try it."

Sure enough, P&G received 5,000 letters of complaint that first week alone. Within a few weeks, however, reports of another kind began arriving at company headquarters: all over the country, P&G salespeople were reporting that sales of Oxydol were picking up. Way up—in *Ma Perkins's* first year on the air, sales of Oxydol more than doubled, and they kept on climbing.

MOTHER OF HER COUNTRY

In a very short time, *Ma Perkins* grew into a national phenomenon. To many listeners, she was more than just a radio character: she was a member of the family, a close confidant, a best friend. An astonishing number of people actually believed she was real, Alecia Swasy writes in *Soap Opera*:

> Ma Perkins became America's beloved "mother of the air." Fans wrote asking her advice on their personal lives. Some sent her pot holders. One older woman suggested in a letter that the two could be companions in their "fading days." She asked Ma for directions to "Rushville Center," so she could begin packing her bags.

Proctor & Gamble had finally found a radio formula that really hooked the listening audience. The "washboard weeper," or "soap opera," as it would soon become known, had arrived.

ON A ROLL

Ma Perkins sold so much Oxydol that Procter & Gamble decided to create shows for their other products. Camay soap sponsored one called *Forever Young*; Chipso soap flakes was advertised on *Home*

A dragonfly can use its feet for perching but not for walking.

Sweet Home; and P&G White Naphtha laundry detergent sponsored *The Guiding Light*.

By producing its own shows and advertising on them as well, Procter & Gamble cut out so many middlemen that it saved as much as 75 percent of its advertising costs. So they kept creating more shows, and so did competitors like Colgate and American Home Products. By the early 1940s, there were 33 different soap operas on the radio, creating a solid block that started each morning at 10:00 a.m. and ran straight through till 6:00 p.m. Listening to the soaps during chores became a pop-culture institution—more than 40 million people were tuning in every day.

HAPPY ENDING

Richard Deupree's advertising gamble had paid off. Thanks to soap operas, Proctor & Gamble not only survived the Great Depression, it thrived: between 1933 and 1939, sales of Ivory soap nearly doubled, and sales of Crisco nearly tripled. These and other brands like Camay and White Naphtha became household words. And on the strength of their sales, Proctor & Gamble was well on its way to becoming the largest soap manufacturer in the country.

Will Proctor & Gamble stay on top? Will Ma Perkins ever be on television? Will Uncle John ever leave the bathroom? Tune in to page 352 for Part II of our saga.

* * *

SOAPY SALES

In 1951 the Swedish Film Industry was on strike, and Ingmar Bergman—already an established director—needed work. So he signed on to direct nine commercials for a new Swedish deodorant soap called Bris (Breeze). The words were the ad company's: "Bris kills bacteria!" How to get that message across was entirely up to Bergman. So how did the director of such somber classics as *Smiles of a Summer Night* and *Wild Strawberries* do it? He used his cinematic talents to create little movies in which actors dressed as microbes were defeated by Bris Man, Sweden's first antibacterial superhero.

World's largest zipper: the one that zips the turf together in the Houston Astrodome.

STRANGE LAWSUITS

These days, it seems that people will sue each other over practically anything. Here are a few real-life examples of unusual legal battles.

THE PLAINTIFF: Janette Weiss

THE DEFENDANT: Kmart Corporation.

THE LAWSUIT: Weiss was shopping for a blender. But the blenders were stacked on a high shelf, just out of her reach. Ignoring the laws of gravity, Weiss jumped up and grabbed the bottom box. Predictably, when she yanked it out, the three blenders on top came crashing down on her head. Claiming to be suffering from "bilateral carpal-tunnel syndrome," Weiss sued Kmart for "negligently stacking the boxes so high on the upper shelf."

THE VERDICT: Not guilty. After Weiss admitted on the stand that she knew the boxes would fall, it took the jury half an hour to find in favor of Kmart.

THE PLAINTIFF: Dr. Ira Gore

THE DEFENDANT: BMW America

THE LAWSUIT: In 1990, Gore purchased a $40,000 BMW. After he got it home, he discovered that the dealer had touched up a scratch in the paint on a door and never bothered to tell him he was buying damaged goods. Outraged, Gore sued.

THE VERDICT: The jury awarded Gore $4,000 compensation, even though the actual repair cost only $600. And then they slapped BMW with an unbelievable $2 million in punitive damages.

THE PLAINTIFF: Jeffrey Stambovsky

THE DEFENDANT: Helen V. Ackley

THE LAWSUIT: Stambovsky purchased Ackley's house in Nyack, New York, for $650,000. When he later discovered that the house was "haunted," he sued Ackley for failing to disclose the presence of poltergeists.

THE VERDICT: Guilty. Unfortunately for her, Ackley had bragged to friends for years that the place was spooked. She was even interviewed by *Reader's Digest* for an article on haunted houses. The judge found that Ackley should have told Stambovsky everything about the house, noting that the existence of ghosts meant that she had actually broken the law by not leaving the house vacant.

THE PLAINTIFF: Chad Gabriel DeKoven
THE DEFENDANT: Michigan Prison System
THE LAWSUIT: DeKoven, a convicted armed robber who goes by the name "Messiah-God," sued the prison system, demanding damages that included thousands of trees, tons of precious metals, peace in the Middle East, and "return of all U.S. military personnel to the United States within 90 days."
THE VERDICT: Case dismissed. While noting that all claims must be taken seriously, the judge ultimately dismissed the suit as frivolous. DeKoven, the judge said, "has no Constitutional right to be treated as the 'Messiah-God' or any other holy, extra-worldly or supernatural being."

THE PLAINTIFF: Louis Berrios
THE DEFENDANT: Our Lady of Mercy Hospital
THE LAWSUIT: Berrios, a 32-year-old quadriplegic, entered the hospital complaining of stomach pains. Doctors took X-rays to determine the cause of his pain and then called the police when the film revealed what they thought were bags of heroin in Berrios's stomach. The police interrogated Berrios and kept him handcuffed to a gurney for 24 hours, only to discover that the "bags of heroin" were actually bladder stones. Berrios, "shamed, embarrassed and extremely humiliated," sued the hospital for $14 million.
THE VERDICT: Unknown.

THE PLAINTIFF: Judith Richardson Haimes
THE DEFENDANT: Temple University Hospital
THE LAWSUIT: Haimes claimed to have had psychic abilities . . . until a CAT scan at the Philadelphia hospital "destroyed her powers." The hospital's negligence left her unable to ply her trade as a clairvoyant, she said.
THE VERDICT: Amazingly, the jury awarded Haimes $986,465. The judge disagreed and threw out the verdict.

HOW SOAP WORKS

There's so much going on in the bathroom. Take that bar of soap next to the sink, for example. For a dollar you can buy three bars. But in every bar is a thousand years of science and history. Think about it—it's amazing.

O PPOSITES DON'T ALWAYS ATTRACT
Oil and water don't mix; they repel each other like opposite ends of a magnet. When you wash your skin with water alone, the oil or "sebum" in your skin repels the water and keeps it from cleaning the skin effectively. That's where soap comes in.

Primitively speaking, soap is oil plus alkali. For centuries, that meant fat plus lye. American colonists and pioneers saved fat scraps from cooking. They also saved the ashes from their fireplaces, which they placed in a barrel with a spigot at the bottom. Water poured over the ashes and left to soak would form lye, which was then drained off from the bottom. The cooking fat would be rendered in a vat over a fire, then the lye would be added. After much stirring and cooking, a chemical reaction would take place and soap was the result. Too much lye, and the soap would be harsh on the skin. Too much fat, and the soap would be greasy. The newly formed soap would then be poured into boxes to harden and cure for several months.

But how does a combination of fat and ash take away dirt? Let's get out the microscope.

CHEMISTRY MADE SIMPLE

Water is a molecule composed of hydrogen and oxygen. The hydrogen end of the molecule has a positive charge, and the oxygen end has a negative charge. Oil has neither a positive nor a negative charge—it carries a uniform electrical distribution. That's why water and oil repel each other. Soap is actually a compound called sodium stearate and has the properties of both oil and water: partly polar, partly nonpolar. That's how it brings oil and water together.

A molecule of soap is shaped like a snake, with the head

Israel is one-fourth the size of Maine.

being the water-loving sodium compound, and the tail being the water-hating stearates. Add soap to water, and the tail end tries to get away from the water. Now add something oily to the water. The stearate tail of the soap molecules will rush to cling to the oil molecules. The oil molecule bonds with the tail and floats away, led by the water-loving sodium head.

THE HISTORY OF SOAP

So how did humans discover soap? The legend is that some time around 1000 B.C., Romans performed many animal sacrifices to the gods on Mount Sapo. The fat from the animals mixed with the ashes of the sacrificial fires. Over time, this mixture of fat and alkali flowed down to the Tiber River and accumulated in the clay soils. Women washing clothing there found that the clay seemed to help get things cleaner. Whether or not this story is true, experts say Mount Sapo is the origin of our word "soap."

The manufacture of soap actually predates this legend by a number of centuries. A recipe for soapmaking was discovered on Sumerian clay tablets dating back to 2500 B.C. And during excavations of ancient Babylon, archaeologists uncovered clay cylinders containing a soaplike substance that were around 5,000 years old. The Phoenicians were making soap around 600 B.C., and Roman historian Pliny the Elder recorded a soap recipe of goat tallow and wood ashes in the first century. A soap factory complete with finished bars was found in the ruins of Pompeii.

OUT OF REACH

In Spain and Italy, soapmaking did not become an established business until about the 7th century. France followed in the 13th century and England a century after that. Southern Europeans made soap using olive oil. Northern Europeans used the fat from animals, including fish oils.

In most places, soap was a luxury item because it was so difficult to manufacture correctly. And it was often so heavily taxed that it was beyond the budgets of most people. Furthermore, bathing was out of fashion for many centuries, being considered sinful, even unhealthy. But when Louis Pasteur proved that cleanliness cuts down on disease in the mid-1800s, bathing and the use of soap for personal hygiene began to become an accepted practice.

Q: Where won't you find the letter 'Q'? A: In any of the 50 U.S. state names.

COUNTRY HITS

*You've probably hummed some of these songs to yourself at
one time or another. Here are the stories behind them.*

Mammas, **Don't Let Your Babies Grow Up to Be
Cowboys (1978).** After nearly 20 years of writing songs
without producing a hit, 35-year-old songwriter Ed Bruce
was ready to give up. He set out to write a song called "Mammas,
Don't Let Your Babies Grow Up to Be Guitar Players," as a warning to others . . . but his wife suggested that a song about cowboys
might sell more records. (She was right.)

Folsom Prison Blues (1956). Johnny Cash didn't get the idea
for this song while doing time. He got it while watching a documentary titled *Inside the Walls of Folsom Prison.* It struck him that
most people live in a prison of one kind or another, and that they
would relate to a song about prison as much as they would to a
song about drinking, trains, or broken hearts.

If You've Got the Money, I've Got the Time (1950). In 1950 a
friend of Lefty Frizzell drove all the way from Oklahoma to West
Texas to hear him sing in a nightclub. He'd come so far that when
Frizzell was finished singing, the friend asked him to play a little
longer. "Well," Frizzell joked, "if you've got the money, I got the
time!" Frizzell knew right then he had the makings of a hit song.

Tumbling Tumbleweeds (1934). In the mid-1930s, a Los Angeles
songwriter named Bob Nolan wrote "Tumbling Leaves," a song
inspired by the blowing autumn leaves he'd seen in Arizona. His
group, Sons of the Pioneers, performed the song on the radio, and it
became a hit—of sorts: listeners requested "Tumbling Tumbleweeds,"
not "Tumbling Leaves." Nolan got so tired of correcting people that
he rewrote the song. (It was Gene Autry's first big hit.)

Your Cheatin' Heart (1953). Hank Williams came up with the
idea while he and his fiancée Billie Jean Eshlimar were driving to
Louisiana to visit her family. After rambling on about how his ex-
wife Audrey had mistreated him, Williams concluded with, "her
cheatin' heart will pay!" He thought for a moment and then said,
"that would make a good song!"

Porcupines are good swimmers . . . their quills are full of air.

HIGH VOLTAIRE

Some enlightening thoughts from, Voltaire, France's premier philosopher and satirist from the Age of Enlightenment.

"Judge a man by his questions rather than by his answers."

"One day everything will be well, that is our hope. Everything's fine today, that is our illusion."

"I have never made but one prayer to God, a very short one: 'O Lord, make my enemies ridiculous.' And God granted it."

"Prejudice is the reason of fools."

"If you have two religions in your land, the two will cut each other's throats; but if you have thirty religions, they will dwell in peace."

"The biggest reward for a thing well done is to have done it."

"Common sense is not so common."

"History is little else than a picture of human crimes and misfortunes."

"The art of medicine consists of amusing the patient while nature cures the disease."

"The progress of the rivers to the ocean is not so rapid as that of man to error."

"Our wretched species is so made that those who walk on the well-trodden path always throw stones at those who are showing a new road."

"When it's a question of money, everybody is of the same religion."

"One owes respect to the living, to the dead one owes only truth."

"If God did not exist, it would be necessary to invent him."

"One great use of words is to hide our thoughts."

"A witty saying proves nothing."

"It's dangerous to be right when the government is wrong."

MYSTERIOUS RAPPINGS

Have you ever participated in a séance or tried to contact the "spirits" using a Ouija board? You probably don't realize it, but the modern conception of communicating with the dead dates back only to the late 1840s. Here's the story of the hoax that started spirit-mania.

BUMP IN THE NIGHT

In 1848 a devout Methodist farmer named John Fox and his family began to hear strange noises in their Hydesville, New York, farmhouse. The noises continued for weeks on end, until finally on one particularly noisy evening, Mrs. Fox ordered the two children, 13-year-old Margaret and 12-year-old Kate, to stay perfectly quiet in bed while Mr. Fox searched the house from top to bottom. His search shed no light on the mystery, but afterward, Margaret sat up in bed and snapped her fingers, exclaiming, "here Mr. Split-foot, do as I do!"

"The reply was immediate," Earl Fornell writes in *The Unhappy Medium: Spiritualism and the Life of Margaret Fox.* "The invisible rapper responded by imitating the number of the girl's staccato responses."

Mrs. Fox began to make sense of what she was hearing. "Count ten," she told the spirit. It responded with 10 raps. So she asked several questions; each time the spirit answered correctly. Next, Mrs. Fox asked the spirit if it would rap if a neighbor were present; the spirit said yes. So Mr. Fox ran and got a neighbor, the first of more than 500 neighbors and townspeople who visited the home over the next few weeks to watch Margaret and Kate interact with the spirit. As long as either Margaret or Kate was present, the spirit was willing to communicate.

MURDER MYSTERY

Using an alphabetic code that Margaret and Kate devised, "Mr. Split-foot" explained that in his Earthly life he'd been a peddler, murdered by the person who lived in the farmhouse. The spirit

The higher a plane flies, the less fuel it uses.

identified the killer as "C. R." Some citizens tracked down a man named Charles Rosana, who'd lived in the house years earlier, but with no body and no evidence other than the testimony of a ghost, he was never charged.

At that point, Mrs. Fox decided to send Margaret and Kate to live with their older sister, Leah Fish, in Rochester. As soon as the girls left Hydesville, the strange noises and spirit visitations stopped.

KID STUFF

When they arrived in Rochester, Margaret and Kate let their older sister, Leah, in on a secret: the whole thing—the rappings, the spirits, "Mr. Split-foot," the "murder," and everything else—was a hoax. "We wanted to terrify our dear mother," Margaret told the *New York Herald* in 1888.

The girls started out by tying a string to an apple and bouncing it repeatedly on the floor, but soon discovered that they could make loud popping noises by cracking the joints in their big toes. They also figured out how to project the sounds around the room, in much the same way that ventriloquists throw their voices, which helped to make the rapping sounds convincing.

THE SOUND OF MONEY

By then the prank had gone on too long; Mrs. Fox was so upset by the idea of her two young girls talking to dead people that Margaret started feeling guilty and decided to put an end to it. She and Kate staged one last "farewell" rap session, then had the "spirits" announce that their Earthly work was done and that they would no longer try to make any contact with the living.

The only problem was that their sister Leah made her living running a music studio, and when Margaret and Kate had come to live with her, their notoriety scared away all of her pupils. So Leah convinced them to help her by forming a spiritualist society and staging a series of public demonstrations of spirit rapping in Corinthian Hall, the town's largest auditorium. Price of admission: $1 per person.

The audiences of these shows were fooled by the mysterious rappings, and within weeks, a number of "spirit circles" formed in Rochester and began hiring the Fox sisters to perform séances in

---

The language of Taki, spoken in parts of Guinea, consists of only 340 words.

private homes. When people began to tire of listening to Mr. Split-foot, the sisters discovered they could communicate with the spirits of such luminaries as Benjamin Franklin, Thomas Paine, and William Shakespeare.

It was from this modest beginning—two young girls figuring out how to make mysterious noises by popping their big toes, and an intimidating third sister figuring out how to exploit it—that "Split-foot" spiritualism went on to become what may have been the fastest-growing spiritual movement in the history of the United States.

IN THE RIGHT PLACE, AT THE RIGHT TIME
The Fox sisters didn't know it, but they were perfectly poised to fill the spiritual void created by advances in 19th-century science and the Industrial Revolution. According to Earl Fornell,

> The appearance of these emissaries from another world was particularly welcome, for the rise of science in the early decades of the 19th century had, to some extent, brought into question the validity of older religious dogmas. Such reform movements as Utopian socialism, temperance, abolitionism, and feminism arose from a demand for a better life on earth, since science seemed to promise no afterlife . . . Still another endeavor was a frenzied search for positive and immediate proof of the immortality that science seemed then to set aside.

TRUE BELIEVERS
The possibility of talking to the departed took the public imagination by storm. Here are a few examples of how deeply "spiritualism" pervaded the culture:

- A judge in upstate New York developed a reputation for consulting the spirits before handing down rulings.

- Some enthusiasts became so convinced that life was better "on the other side" that they commited suicide rather than waste a lifetime waiting for paradise.

- In 1853 some New Yorkers formed a group called the Free Spirit Love Society, which forbade extramarital affairs in all instances . . . except those in which the adulterer "entered into a new relation under the guidance of spiritual affinities or attractions." At its peak, the society boasted more than 600 members.

On July 4, 1776, King George III of England noted in his diary . . .

- In 1856 a Bordentown, New Jersey, man died just days before he was supposed to marry his fiancé. Rather than cancel the wedding, the man's family and his bride-to-be turned it into a wedding-funeral, hiring a medium to marry the bride to her fiancé's corpse before it was laid to rest.

SHE KEEPS GOING . . . AND GOING . . . AND GOING . . .

The public's desire to believe was so great that the Fox sisters were able to keep their hoax going for more than 40 years. The spiritualism craze faded somewhat in the late 1850s but came roaring back following the outbreak of the Civil War, as thousands of bereaved families tried desperately to get in contact with loved ones killed in battle.

Even First Lady Mary Todd Lincoln brought spiritualists to the White House so that she could speak to her dead sons Tad and Willie. In 1872, seven years after President Abraham Lincoln was assassinated, Mrs. Lincoln visited the Fox sisters several times and each time came away convinced that, through Margaret, she'd made contact with "the real presence of the spirit of her husband."

UNHAPPY MEDIUMS

One of the curses of founding this fraudulent movement was that Margaret and Kate had to spend most of their time in the presence of true believers. Both women grew to hate their lives; both became alcoholics. And though Leah Fish had grown rich off years of public performances, Margaret and Kate had not.

By the late 1870s, Margaret was still giving public performances, but she was suffering from depression and working only a few hours each week—just long enough to make the money she needed to "drown my remorse in wine," as she put it. Somehow, she managed to keep going for another 10 years.

Then in September 1888, a reporter for the *New York Herald* asked Fox to comment on the case of another spiritualist, who'd recently been exposed as a fraud. Margaret told the reporter that spiritualism was bogus and promised to one day give "an interesting exposure of the fraud."

BAD RAP

Rather than wait, the *Herald* sent a reporter the next day. As promised, Fox delivered—and over the next few hours laid out her bizarre life story in lurid detail. There was no truth to spiritualism, she told the reporter, and she said she more than anyone else should know it.

"I have explored the unknown as far as a human can," she told the reporter. "I have gone to the dead so that I might get from them some little token . . . I have tried to obtain some sign. Not a thing! No, the dead shall not return."

And in case anyone didn't believe her—in fact, many spiritualists blamed booze for the "false confession"—Fox gave a public confession and demonstration of her methods at New York's Academy of Music. *The New York Herald* described the scene:

> Everybody in the hall knew they were looking at the woman principally responsible for spiritualism. She stood upon a pine table, with nothing on her feet but stockings. As she remained motionless, loud distinct rappings were heard, now behind the scenes, now in the gallery. She had a devil's gift in a rapping ventriloquism, from which spiritualism had sprung to life, and here was the same toe rapping it out of existence.

DIDN'T SEE THIS COMING

The cash Margaret Fox made selling her story didn't last long. Neither did the money she made on tours exposing the fraud of spiritualism. When the public's interest in her exposé dried up, she became so desperate for money that she recanted her confession and went back out on the séance circuit. She toured the country for the next five years, until finally in 1893, like her sister Kate, she died drunk, broke, and alone.

The funeral arrangements were handled by a friend of Margaret's, Titus Merritt, "the mortician," Fornell writes, "at whose establishment she had often spent long nights, sitting among the corpses watching for some signs of spirit life."

The signs never came.

* * *

"The guy who invented the first wheel was an idiot, the guy who invented the other three, he was a genius."

—**Sid Caesar**

Most likely items involved in accidents at home: bicycles, stairs, and doors (in that order).

VERY SUPERSTITIOUS

*Just to be safe, Uncle John works on his
superstition pages while wearing his lucky underwear.
Here are some more classic folk superstitions.*

To tell who will be elected U.S. president, take two roosters, the evening before election, and name each for the respective candidates of the leading parties; place them together under a tub. Leave them overnight. The following morning uncover them and notice which crows first; the one crowing will indicate the election of the candidate for which he was named. It's as good a way as any.

When you get dressed in the morning be sure to put on your right sock and right shoe before you put on your left sock and left shoe, and you will have a good day.

If a red-headed woman comes to your house on Monday, there will be confusion all week.

Never sleep with the moon in your face. It will draw your mouth over and make it crooked.

Cutting a baby's nails before he is a year old makes a thief of him. Bite them off.

When sitting in on a card game, get up and twist your chair three times on its forelegs—in the direction of the sun.

If your left palm itches, money will come to you. But don't under any circumstances scratch the itch. That will break the enchantment.

If you dream of fresh pork and fish it is a sign of impending death.

If by mistake you put on a sweater or some other clothing backward or inside out, it brings good luck. But you must wear it that way all day or your good luck will turn bad. The only exception to this rule is your underwear. You can turn it right side out after lunch.

If birds weave some of your hair into their nests, you will go crazy.

Never take a broom along when you move. Throw out your old broom and buy a new one for your new home.

Hippos can run faster than humans.

THE POLITICALLY CORRECT QUIZ

*Here are eight real-life examples of "politically correct" behavior.
How sensitive are you? Try to guess which answer is the
"correct" one. Answers are on page 744.*

1. In 2001 Carol Ann Demaret launched a boycott of a film that
offended her. Which film and why?

   a) *A.I.: Artificial Intelligence.* "Abusing children, even robot
   children, is wrong."

   b) *Planet of the Apes.* "Ape actors should play the ape parts."

   c) *Bubble Boy.* "It mocks people without immunities."

2. The Brazilian city of Cascavel has banned municipal workers
from engaging in what practice?

   a) Praying. "Religion has no place in the workplace. Do it on
   your own time."

   b) Spreading gossip. "Public employees have moral rights."

   c) Drinking French roast coffee during breaks. "French roast
   encourages the perception that Brazilian roast is inferior."

3. A high priest of the British White Witches is protesting the
Warner Bros. film *Harry Potter and the Sorcerer's Stone* for what
reason?

   a) It shows witches in school. "Witches are born, not taught."

   b) It shows witches riding brooms with the brush end in the
   back—real witches ride brooms brush-end forward.

   c) It shows several black witches.

4. An organization in Florida launched a petition campaign to
amend the state constitution to protect which of the following?

   a) Pregnant pigs, to protect them from "chronic stress."

   b) Brahma bulls, to protect them from "anti-Hindu terrorism."

   c) Human souls, to protect them from "abuse by atheists."

Most ice cream is eaten in the evening, between 9:00 and 11:00 p.m.

5. College professor Jon Willand, who has taught American history for more than 30 years, was reprimanded for doing what?

a) Displaying an old recruiting poster that depicts General George Custer and seeks soldiers to fight "militant Sioux."

b) Stating that the civil rights movement was "all about ego."

c) Arranging the seating chart so that all the "hot babes" sat in front.

6. Protestors outside the U.S. Embassy in Bombay, India, criticized the Bush administration's White House website (*www.whitehouse.gov*) for which of the following reasons:

a) Describing a rash as an "Indian burn" in a press release describing George Bush's first presidential medical exam.

b) Showing a picture of the entire Bush family—parents, daughters, two dogs . . . and a cat named India.

c) Stating that Bush "feels the same way about Indian food that his father feels about broccoli."

7. A Canadian activist organization seeks to change Canada's national anthem in what way?

a) Replace "Canadians" with "North Americans." (Endorses ethnic diversity . . . and better for tourism.)

b) Remove the reference to the "milk of our sacred land." (Offends vegans and the lactose intolerant.)

c) Remove the phrase "all thy sons." (Sexist.)

POLITICALLY CORRECT BONUS ROUND

8. According to scientific research conducted by the Australian Wine Research Institute, which of the following is "the best way to preserve the quality of white wine?"

a) Use screwcaps instead of corks; they work better, plus they're easier to open and cheaper, too.

b) Drink it straight out of the bottle, wrapped in a small paper bag. The bag protects the wine against the sun.

c) Mixing a little beer into the unfermented wine, before the bottle is corked and aged at the winery. Foster's Lager works best.

A typical supermarket displays more than 25,000 items.

DUBIOUS ACHIEVERS

*People do some pretty strange things. Here are
a few of the oddest records we've ever seen.*

LONGEST DISTANCE TRAVELED BY MARSH-MALLOW FROM A NOSE INTO ANOTHER PERSON'S MOUTH

Record Holder: Scott Jeckel

The Story: Blessed from birth with the amazing ability to launch items from his nose with great precision, Jeckel once fired a marshmallow a distance of 16 feet, 31/2 inches into the waiting mouth of partner Ray Persin—who ate it.

MOST ACCOMPLISHED SEWER FISHERMAN

Record Holder: Larry Harper

The Story: Oshkosh, Wisconsin, native Larry Harper has been fishing his town's sewers in his spare time for seven years and has caught 74 fish, 13 rats, 5 old shoes, and 1 tennis racket to date. Harper has even reeled in a small alligator, using a tuna sandwich as bait.

LARGEST MASS WEDDING HELD IN PRISON

Record Holders: Inmates of Carandiru Prison, Sao Paulo, Brazil

The Story: On June 14, 2000, a record 120 prisoners and their lucky fiancées tied the knot simultaneously in a massive ceremony in romantic Carandiru Prison. Why did they do it? Carandiru was built for 3,000 inmates, but houses 7,500. Weekly riots and jail-breaks led authorities to organize the wedding, with the hope that prisoners with family ties would be less violent.

LONGEST DISTANCE TRAVELED BY FOOT WHILE CARRYING A BRICK

Record Holder: Manjit Singh

The Story: A regulation-size brick—weighing exactly nine pounds—has never traveled farther "in an ungloved hand in an

---

Only one out of every three people has 20/20 vision.

uncradled downward pincer grip" than when Manjit Singh lugged one 82.2 miles on foot from November 6 to 7, 1998.

GREATEST NUMBER OF CITATIONS FOR INDECENT EXPOSURE

Record Holder: Helga Svenstrup

The Story: Notorious in her hometown of Copenhagen, Denmark, 67-year-old Svenstrup has been arrested 45 times for indecent exposure. At one of her hearings, she even flashed the presiding judge. Her greatest stunt: at a sold-out soccer match, she ran on to the field dressed as a cheerleader and performed cartwheels without underwear before 50,000 cheering spectators.

FASTEST PEOPLE WEARING A HORSE COSTUME

Record Holders: Geoff Seale and Stuart Coleman

The Story: At a school playground in 1999, dozens of pairs of Elmbridge, England, citizens raced neck and neck in two-man horse costumes for the title of World's Fastest Horse Impersonators. The fleet-footed victors were Geoff Seale and Stuart Coleman, who "galloped" 328 feet in a record-breaking 16.7 seconds.

MOST WORMS CHARMED FROM THE GROUND

Record Holder: Tom Shufflebotham

The Story: At the first World Worm Charming Championship in Cheshire, England, in 1980, entrants tried to entice as many worms out of the ground as possible on a 32.3-square-foot lot. Using his amazing powers of worm appeal, Shufflebotham charmed 511 worms from the ground in just 30 minutes. How does he do it? He coaxes them to the surface by "vibrating garden forks."

LONGEST TIME SPENT SITTING ON A BLOCK OF ICE

Record Holder: Gus Simmons

The Story: During the Depression, people would do almost any-thing for fun—if it was cheap. On October 17, 1933, at Chicago's White City Casino, contestants tested the warmth of their nether regions in an "ice sitting" championship. Contest winner Simmons sat on a two-foot cube of ice for 27 hours, 10 minutes before finally being disqualified for having a 102-degree fever.

Disney World is twice the size of Manhattan.

AMAZING ANAGRAMS

In previous BRs, we've included a page of anagrams . . . words or phrases that are rearranged to form new words and phrases. We particularly like the ones that end up with more or less the same meaning.

THE ACTIVE VOLCANOS
becomes . . . **CONES EVICT HOT LAVA**

ADOLF HITLER
becomes . . . **HATED FOR ILL**

AN ALCOHOLIC
BEVERAGE *becomes . . .*
GAL, CAN I HAVE COOL BEER?

THE ASSASSINATION OF
PRESIDENT ABRAHAM
LINCOLN *becomes . . .*
**A PAST
SENSATION
CHILLS ME, OR
A FIEND SHOT
IN A BARN**

CLOTHESPINS *becomes . . .*
SO LET'S PINCH

THE COMING
PRESIDENTIAL
CAMPAIGN
becomes . . . **DAMN!
ELECTING TIME
IS APPROACHING**

MUTTERING *becomes . . .*
EMIT GRUNT

NOVA SCOTIA AND
PRINCE EDWARD
ISLAND *becomes . . .*
**TWO
CANADIAN
PROVINCES:
LANDS I DREAD**

POSTPONED *becomes . . .*
STOPPED? NO.

RECEIVED PAYMENT
becomes . . . **EVERY
CENT PAID ME**

A ROLLING STONE
GATHERS NO MOSS
becomes . . . **STROLLER
ON GO, AMASSES
NOTHING**

SLOT MACHINES
becomes . . . **CASH LOST
IN 'EM**

A STRIPTEASER
becomes . . . **ATTIRE
SPARSE**

THE PUBLIC ART
GALLERIES *becomes . . .*
**LARGE PICTURE
HALLS, I BET**

A typical banana travels 4,000 miles before being eaten.

MODERN QUACKERY

Though the days of such gruesome 19th century medical practices as bloodletting and blistering are over, quack medicine is still going strong. Do oxygen bars battle the effects of air pollution? Do magnetic bracelets cure arthritis pain? We can't say for sure, but here are af few modern "treatments" that leave us wondering.

EAR CANDLING

Description: The user sticks a hollow, cone-shaped candle into his ear canal and lights it. As the candle burns, it supposedly creates a vacuum that sucks out earwax, debris and other "toxins." Claimed benefits include improved senses of smell and taste, clearer eyesight, purified blood, and even a "strengthened brain."

Truth: Sure enough, when you stick the candle in your ear, light it, and let it burn down, some crud forms inside the cone. What's it made of? Candle wax. If there was any crud in your ear to begin with, it's still in there.

FRESH CELL THERAPY

Description: "Fresh cell therapy, also called live cell therapy or cellular therapy, involves injections of fresh embryonic animal cells taken from the organ or tissue that corresponds to the unhealthy organ or tissue in the patient." Some reported recipients: Marlene Dietrich, Winston Churchill, Nelson Mandela, and Fidel Castro.

Truth: If you're having trouble with your rump, injecting cells from a rump roast isn't going to do you any good and may do harm. According to the American Cancer Society, the therapy "has no benefit, and has caused serious side affects such as infection, immunologic reactions to the injected proteins, and death."

PSYCHIC SURGERY

Description: This procedure takes the power of positive thinking to extremes: the "surgery" is performed by a healer, using psychic powers alone.

Truth: It's pure sleight of hand. The most skilled "psychic surgeons" go as far as to use a false fingertip filled with artificial blood so

To lose a pound of fat, you need to walk at least 35 miles (briskly).

blood so that when they draw the finger across your skin it leaves a red, "bloody" line that has the appearance of a surgical incision. Then they supposedly reach into your body and present you with what they claim are "diseased organs" or other body parts. What are they really? Usually chicken guts or cotton wads soaked in the fake blood. According to the American Cancer Society, "all demonstrations to date of psychic surgery have been done by various forms of trickery."

COLON HYDROTHERAPY

Description: Also called colonic irrigation, this one plays on the theory that if a treatment hurts, it must be doing some good: A rubber tube is passed into the rectum for a distance of up to 30 inches (ouch!). Then as much as 20 gallons of warm water, coffee, herbal tea, or some other solution is gradually pumped in and out through the tube to remove "toxins."

Truth: "No such 'toxins' have ever been identified; colonic irrigation is not only therapeutically worthless, but can cause infection, injury, and even death from fatal electrolyte imbalance."

TREPANATION

Description: Trepanation, also known as "drilling holes in your head," is believed to be the oldest surgical practice in history. Archeologists have found skulls with holes drilled in them dating as far back as 5,000 B.C. Modern advocates of the procedure claim that drilling holes "relieves pressure permanently," and in the process increases blood flow to the brain and expands consciousness. One Englishwoman named Amanda Fielding performed the "surgery" on herself in 1970; she not only lived to tell the tale but ran for Parliament in 1978 . . . and received 40 votes. "Although I trepanned myself in 1970, having unsuccessfully for several years looked for a doctor to do it for me, I have always been very against self-trepanation," Fielding says now. "It is a messy business, and best done by the medical profession."

Truth: This form of treatment is not just dangerous, it's also totally unnecessary. "This is nonsense," says Dr. Ayub Ommaya, professor of neurosurgery at George Washington University.

Doctors in the 1700s prescribed ladybugs, taken internally, to cure measles.

MOUNT ST. HELENS

*May 18, 1980 was a day that people living in
southern Washington state will never forget—the day
that Mount St. Helens blew its top. Here's the story.*

FIRST COME, FIRST SERVED

In 1774, Spanish captain Juan Josef Perez Hernandez sailed the harbors along the coast of what is now Washington State and British Columbia. Apparently he didn't see much of interest and never bothered to stop. Four years later, English captain James Cook dropped anchor in one of those harbors, now known as Nootka Sound. Cook landed to stock up on fresh water and to trade with the natives. He took a few sea otter pelts back to Europe, and soon otter pelts were being sold there for $4,000 each, worth more than their weight in gold. Thus began the Otter Rush.

The Spanish claimed that since they had been the first to sail through the sound, the Nootka area belonged to them. The English said that since they had been first to set foot on the land, they owned the territory. The English built a fort; the Spaniards seized an English ship in retaliation. War seemed certain until England sent Ambassador Alleyne Fitzherbert, Baron St. Helens, to Spain to negotiate a treaty. In 1790, the Nootka Convention was crafted to give both countries access to the area. Several years later, Captain George Vancouver was exploring the Northwest, he saw a majestic mountain in the distance and named it after St. Helens. The native name was *Loo-wit-lat-kla*, meaning "keeper of the fire." It was an appropriate name for a volcano.

On May 18, 1980, it exploded.

IMPENDING DOOM

Scientists knew an explosion was imminent in April 1980, when a bulge 320 feet high appeared on the side of the mountain, indicating that magma was pressing outward. The bulge was moving up at the sustained rate of five feet per day. Finally, the movement triggered an avalanche, which shook off the top of the bulge, exposing the white-hot interior to the air.

Wettest place on Earth: Tutunendo, Colombia. Average rainfall: 38.6 feet per year.

Under normal conditions, water can't be heated beyond the boiling point because then it turns to steam. But when it's kept under pressure (as in a pressure cooker) it can be heated beyond the boiling point and still remain liquid. When the pressure is removed, the super-hot water flashes into steam. Because steam takes up a lot more room than water, an explosion occurs. It's like carbon dioxide in soda: shake the bottle or can, and the gas wants to escape. Pop the top, and the release of pressure results in a mini-volcano of soda. That's what happened to Mount St. Helens.

AMAZING STATISTICS

The blast was heard all the way to Canada. The main eruption continued for 10 minutes, followed by 9 hours of explosive ashfall. The energy released was equal to 27,000 Hiroshima-sized bombs dropped at the rate of one per second, for 9 hours. The volcano hurled 1.3 billion cubic yards of ash and rock into the air, enough to cover a piece of land a mile wide, a mile long, and as high as three Empire State Buildings.

The volcanic ash mixed with the water of surrounding rivers and lakes to form mud the consistency of wet concrete; it flowed downstream, wrecking everything in its path. An area stretching 8 miles out from the volcano and fanning to a width of 15 miles was flattened. But the damage extended much farther than that. Eleven hundred miles of Washington roads were impassable, stranding 10,000 people. Police cars were stalled, train service halted, shipping channels clogged, and power lines knocked out.

GONE IN AN INSTANT

Two hundred square miles of wildlife habitat were destroyed. One-and-a-half million animals and birds lay dead, as well as half a million fish. A hundred miles of streams were wiped out entirely, and another 3,000 miles of streams were contaminated by ash. Twenty-six lakes were removed from the map. One hundred twenty-three riverside homes were washed away, and 75 cabins were wrecked. More than 1,000 people were left homeless. In all, $2.7 billion in damage was caused in a single day.

Fifty-seven people died; the only survivor in the blast area was a dog who had been on a camping trip with his family. One man who died instantly when the blast hit was found in the front seat

---

After spending 84 days in *Skylab*, astronauts found that they were two inches taller.

of his car with his camera still held up in front of his face. Two young lovers in a tent were blown into a mass of fallen trees hundreds of feet away. They were found with their arms still around each other. Two other people were killed in their car as they tried to outrace the ash cloud. Most of those who died in the explosion were killed by inhaling hot, toxic volcanic gases and ash. And most had violated orders to stay away from the area.

ASH FALLOUT

Nearly half the state of Washington received visible ashfall. As much as 800,000 tons of it fell on the city of Yakima alone, 85 miles east of the volcano. In fact, so much ash was flushed into the Yakima sewer system that the treatment plant was shut down for fear of permanent damage. All over the region, water reservoirs were drained by communities trying to clean city streets and water rationing had to be imposed.

In Pasco, Washington, paper envelopes full of ash (mailed from residents to friends and relatives around the country) kept breaking open during processing, ruining the machinery. Someone in Seattle suggested dropping the "W" from the state's name and calling it Ashington. The ash cloud from the blast took 17 days to go completely around the globe. One disc jockey joked, "If you were planning on visiting Washington this year, don't bother. Washington is coming to visit you!"

BACK TO NATURE

Today, bluebirds are plentiful as they nest in the abundant cavities found in the mountain's snags. Pocket gophers dig holes in the ash, tilling it. Elk, which returned to the area only a few weeks after the blast, leave droppings, which fertilize the ash. Fireweed, with roots that reach the fertile soil beneath the ash, turns entire hillsides pink with flowers. Mosses, grasses, shrubs, and trees all took root again soon after the blast. The trees now stand over 20 feet tall in some areas. Nature recovers, and the moutain is heading back to normal. Except for one thing: the majestic vista that inspired Vancouver is not quite as majestic now. Mount St. Helens is 1,200 feet lower than it was before the eruption.

MOTHER OF THE BOMB

You've heard of physicist J. Robert Oppenheimer, the "father of the A-Bomb." But have you heard of Lise Meitner? Her discovery of nuclear fission opened the door to the creation of the atom bomb, much to her regret. Here's her story.

OUT OF SCHOOL

O Lise Meitner was born in 1878 in Vienna, Austria. She was very bright, but in those days it didn't matter—education was for boys only. People thought that if the delicate female brain were subjected to too much education, the result would be mental illness and infertility. (Schooling for girls ended at age 13.) Fortunately for Meitner in the 1890s, the Viennese government began to permit women to attend high school and college, making it possible for her to pursue her passion—physics.

After graduating from the University of Vienna in 1906, Meitner went to Berlin to attend lectures by Max Planck, later winner of the Nobel Prize for his work in quantum mechanics. The existence of the atom had only recently been discovered and the study of radiation was new and exciting—and Berlin was where these sciences were being advanced most vigorously. She decided to stay.

A WOMAN'S PLACE

At the University of Berlin, Meitner had to ask permission to attend classes. Planck was reluctant to allow a woman in, but begrudgingly gave his permission, saying, "It cannot be emphasized strongly enough that Nature itself has designated for woman her vocation as mother and housewife, and that under no circumstances can natural laws be ignored without grave damage." Planck later recognized that Meitner had great talent, and she became his assistant. Eventually she was offered a position doing research . . . though she was not allowed to work in the same lab as the men and was instead given a makeshift workshop in the basement. Her parents supported her financially, but she wrote scientific articles to earn additional income, signing her name "L. Meitner." (Journals would not publish work written by a woman.)

At the university, Meitner began working with another scientist, Otto Hahn. Together they made numerous discoveries about

---

If you had a million $1 bills, you'd need a box as big as a small coffin to carry them in.

the nature of the atom and radiation. They remained scientific partners for the rest of their lives.

SECOND-CLASS CITIZEN

When the modern Kaiser-Wilhelm Institute opened a new wing devoted to radiation research, Hahn was offered a job and Meitner accompanied him . . . officially listed as his "unpaid guest." (Hahn got paid for his work; she did not.) At the institute, Meitner discovered the element *protactinium*. Though she did the majority of the work, Hahn's name appeared as the senior author on their scientific papers. Consequently, the Association of German Chemists presented him with their highest award, the Emil Fischer Medal. Meitner received only a copy of his medal.

It was only after World War I that Meitner's value began to be recognized: She became the first woman professor ever in Germany and was finally paid a living wage (though still less than Hahn). In 1926 she was appointed full professor of physics at the University of Berlin. There, she continued to study beta and gamma rays, isotopes, atomic theory, radioactivity, and quantum physics.

A NEW COUNTRY

By 1937 Meitner and Hahn had identified at least nine different radioactive elements. A scientist named Fritz Strassmann joined them, and together the three of them began working to find out what happens when the nucleus of an atom splits. But at this time, the Nazis were rising to power. Meitner was forced to fill out papers admitting that her grandparents were Jewish. It didn't matter that she was raised a Protestant—she was fired from her job.

Jews made up less than one percent of the German population, yet they accounted for 20 percent of the scientists. Researchers all over Germany began to follow Albert Einstein's lead, and fled the country. Meitner announced that she was taking a "holiday," but instead escaped to safety in Sweden. At the age of 59, after living and working in Germany for 31 years, she was forced to leave her money, possessions, research papers, friends, and career. Starting over from scratch, she went to work at the Nobel Institute of Physics in Stockholm, where she spent the next 22 years. It was there that she made the discovery that rocked the world.

Supermarket items most likely to be shoplifted: cigarettes, beauty aids, and batteries.

SPLIT DECISION

Scientists knew that radiation is released when the nucleus of an atom decays. Every nucleus has protons, which have a positive charge, and electrons, which have a negative charge. When a nucleus loses protons, radiation is emitted and the atom transforms into a new kind of atom. This new atom, or "daughter atom," splits and spirals away with enough force that the original atom recoils, like a rifle recoils after firing a bullet. (Radium releases a million times more energy during radioactive decay than when it is burned like coal.) Then scientists discovered that every atom also has a neutron, which has no electrical charge at all. Enrico Fermi discovered that when he bombarded heavy elements such as uranium with neutrons, he ended up with new elements that were even heavier than the ones he started with.

Protons and neutrons in a nucleus cling very tightly together, but they cling more tightly in some elements than in others. Iron is the most stable element and therefore the hardest to split. Uranium is the least stable and the easiest to split. When Meitner and Hahn had tried bombarding uranium with slow-speed neutrons, they ended up with barium—which is lighter than uranium, not heavier. They were confused: neither of them realized they had just split the atom.

EARTH-SHATTERING

In Sweden, Meitner discovered that when a nucleus splits, the mass of the two new atoms added together is less than that of the original atom, because some of the mass is released as energy. That energy is what causes the two pieces of the split atom to repel from each other. She calculated, using Einstein's formula of $E=MC^2$, exactly how much energy would be given off every time a single atom split and predicted that this could happen in a chain reaction, releasing an enormous amount of energy in a very short period of time. If millions of atoms could be split at once, the power would be unimaginable: splitting the nucleus of a uranium atom, for example, releases 20 million times more energy than exploding an equal amount of TNT.

When she shared this news with Hahn, he did experiments to prove her theory. Then he published a paper (leaving her name off, for fear he would get in trouble if the Nazis found he was still in contact with her). Meitner also published a report in a British journal in 1939. Suddenly the world was in a race to see who would be first to harness atomic energy in the form of a bomb.

Einstein wrote a letter to President Roosevelt warning him about what would happen if Germany got the bomb first. Roosevelt set American scientists to work on the project—called the Manhattan Project—and invited Meitner to help. She turned the job down, repulsed by the idea that her discovery might be used to kill people. She told them she hoped they failed.

BAD CREDIT

The Nazis, in the meantime, had been removing all traces of the Jews, and Meitner's name was erased from all the research she had done. Perhaps because of this, Otto Hahn managed to convince himself—and the world—that the discovery of nuclear fission (Meitner coined the term) had been his. Hahn received the Nobel Prize in 1944. (Meitner never did.) For years, Hahn was listed as the inventor, with Lise Meitner occasionally mentioned as his assistant.

When the atom bomb was dropped on Japan, Meitner was upset, not only by the devastation but also by the sudden publicity: reporters on her doorstep; cameras in her face; phone messages and telegrams waiting for her reply. She had little to say. The bomb had killed 100,000 people, and suddenly she was being portrayed in the media as the person who had come up with the blueprint for it.

RECOGNITION

Lise Meitner finally did receive her share of attention for her discoveries. She was named "Woman of the Year" by the Women's National Press Club; received the Max Planck Medal from the German Chemical Society; received honorary doctorates; published 135 scientific papers; won the Enrico Fermi Award; and was elected to the Swedish Academy of Science—only the third woman in history to achieve that honor. She was even offered a movie deal by MGM. (She turned it down, horrified that the script called for her to flee from Germany with an atom bomb hidden in her purse!) Meitner continued her research into her mid-70s and helped Sweden design its first nuclear reactor, which was the way she wanted her discovery to be used. Despite continual exposure to massive amounts of radiation, she lived to be nearly 90 years old, dying in 1968, just three months after Otto Hahn. In 1992 physicists named the newly discovered 109th element in her honor: *meitnerium*.

... U.S. unemployment rose from 1.5 million to 7 million.

FABULOUS FLOPS

Next time you see the hype for some amazing,
"can't-miss" phenomenon, hold on to a healthy sense
of skepticism by remembering these duds.

THE NATIONAL BOWLING LEAGUE

If people were willing to pay to watch professional football, baseball, and basketball teams, they'd pay to watch teams like the New York Gladiators and the Detroit Thunderbirds compete against each other, right? That was the thinking behind the 10-team National Bowling League, founded in 1961. The owner of the Dallas Broncos poured millions of dollars into his franchise, building a special 2,500-seat "Bronco Bowl" with six lanes surrounded by 18 rows of seats arranged in a semicircle; space was also set aside for a seven-piece jazz band to provide entertainment between games. But he couldn't even fill the arena on opening night, and things went downhill after that. The league folded in less than a year.

GERBER SINGLES

This was Gerber Baby Food's attempt to sell food to adults. Launched in the 1970s, the line of gourmet entrees like sweet-and-sour pork and beef burgundy had two major problems: the food came in baby food–style jars, and the name "Singles" was a turnoff to customers who were lonely to begin with.

HERSHEY'S CHOCOLATE SOAP

Milton Hershey didn't like to let anything go to waste. There were times in the chocolate business when he found himself with millions of pounds of cocoa butter that he didn't know what to do with, and he spent years trying to find a product that would put it to use. In the early 1930s, he finally settled on cocoa butter soap.

Three months later, the factory that he built behind the Cocoa Inn in Hershey, Pennsylvania, began producing 120 bars of chocolate-scented soap a minute. Finding 120 customers a minute to buy the stuff proved to be much more daunting: people were used to eating their chocolate, not bathing in it, and were put off by the

A housefly born today will be dead within two months.

strong chocolate smell of the soap. (Some even tried to eat the bars, thinking it was candy.)

More than a million bars of the stuff piled up in the basement of the Hershey Sports Arena waiting to be sold; nevertheless, Hershey kept the assembly line running at full speed. "Don't worry about my money," he told his executives, "You just sell all you can." Seven years and several million dollars later, he finally pulled the plug. Interestingly, cocoa butter—unscented—is a popular ingredient in soap today.

SOLAR-POWERED PARKING METERS

City officials in Nottingham, England, spent more than £1 million (about $2 million) installing solar-powered parking meters on city streets after reading reports that the meters saved a fortune in maintenance costs in Mediterranean countries. The only problem: Mediterranean countries get a lot of sun; England doesn't, not even in summer. As of August 2001, more than 25 percent of the parking meters were out of commission, allowing hundreds of motorists to park for free.

HITS SNACK FOOD

Here's one of the few products whose demise can be blamed solely on its packaging. When lined up end-to-end on store shelves, the packages read: "HITSHITSHITSHITSHITSHITSHITS."

NO FURTHER EXPLANATION REQUIRED

See if you can figure out why these products bombed:

- Buffalo Chip chocolate cookies
- Mouth-So-Fresh Tongue Cleaner
- Incredibagels—microwave bagels "stuffed with egg, cheese, and bacon"
- Gillette's For Oily Hair Shampoo
- Hagar the Horrible Cola
- Burns & Rickers freeze-dried vegetable chips
- Jell-O for Salads (available in celery, tomato, mixed-vegetable)
- Tunies (hot dogs made from tuna fish)

Germans eat more potatoes per capita than any other people. They average 370 pounds per year.

THE FINAL EDITION

Still waiting for your 15 minutes of fame? Don't worry—
as these folks would attest (if they could), you don't
have to be alive to get your name in the paper.

NO DEPOSIT, NO RETURN

In January 1995, a small-claims court commissioner in Mill Valley, California, ruled that the landlord of a man who died in his apartment could keep the $825 security deposit. Tenant James Pflugradt passed away from a heart attack in 1994; his son Rick cleaned out the apartment five days later and then asked for the security deposit back, but landlord Fred Padula refused to hand it over, arguing that the deposit was needed to cover rent during the time it would take to find a new tenant.

Court Commissioner Randolph Heubach sided with landlord Padula. "I am not unsympathetic, but it is really a straightforward financial situation," he said after making his decision. His reason: The deceased "failed to give the 30-day notice required before vacating his apartment." Rick Pflugradt didn't see it that way. "This sends my faith in the human race to an all-time low," he said.

FAIRWAY TO HEAVEN

In 2001 the city of Columbia, South Carolina, began building a driving range on what they thought was an open field, but it wasn't long after construction got underway that they discovered the plot was actually the unmarked graveyard of a 19th-century insane asylum. At last count, there were at least 1,985 graves of mental patients at the site, some dating as far back as 1848. Rather than abandon its plans, city officials simply redesigned the driving range "to ensure that no golf balls land on graves."

HE URNED IT

In August 2001, a two-bedroom apartment in London was put up for sale after the previous owner, described in newspapers as an "unnamed pensioner," passed away. Asking price: $728,000, not a bad amount for apartments in the area. Added "bonus": the

---

Dustin Hoffman used to type entries for the yellow pages.

apartment comes complete with the dead man's ashes, in a stone urn on the mantlepiece. In his will, the man stipulated that he wanted the apartment to serve as his final resting place. "I have to tell people before they go to view the flat," realtor James Bailey told *The Sun* newspaper. "Luckily most just laugh."

STARTING OVER

When 70-year-old James Ross asked girlfriend Maryo Griffin to marry him in 1993, there was just one thing keeping her from saying yes: more than 12 years after the death of his first wife, Judy, Ross still kept her ashes in his home. Ross and Griffin decided to solve the problem by getting married in Las Vegas and then scattering Judy's ashes in the Grand Canyon.

Everything was going according to plan until a thief broke into Ross's car in the Las Vegas World Casino parking lot and stole the box containing Judy's ashes. At last report, the wedding was postponed, perhaps indefinitely, until the ashes are returned. "They got Judy," said Griffin. "I don't see how we can be married until we get Judy taken care of."

BODY OF EVIDENCE

When Rodney Williams, 21, appeared in Washington State's Cowlitz County District Court in April 1994 to explain why he'd missed an earlier court date on an assault charge, he brought an unusual witness to substantiate his claims—the cremated remains of his mother, which he carried in a plastic box. Williams explained that he had missed the earlier court appearance because he was caring for his mother during her final illness.

Judge Robert Altenhof, who accepted Williams's excuse, said he'd never seen anything like it in 12 years on the bench. "They bring engine parts, rugs that are urine stained, but this is the first time they've brought in human remains," he said. "You think you've heard it all, but somebody always comes up with something new."

* * *

BEARS REPEATING

"We don't know one millionth of one percent of anything."

—Thomas Alva Edison

Hottest place on Earth: Dallol, Ethiopia. Average temperature: 94°F . . . in the shade.

BATHROOM FACTS AND FIGURES

Amazingly, government agencies, public interest groups, and private industry all collect statistics on bathrooms and the people who use them. Here is some of what they've found.

PASSING TIME

- According to a study by the National Association for Continence (NAFC), the average American spends about an hour in the bathroom per day, including time spent bathing. That comes to about two weeks per year.

- How do people pass the time in the bathroom? About half of survey respondents said they thought about "serious issues." A third said they were daydreaming, making phone calls, or singing in the shower.

- Nearly two-thirds of Americans surveyed say they engage in "toilet mapping" when they're out in public—scouting out the locations of restrooms in advance of actually needing them, just in case nature makes an unexpected call. People over 50 are more likely to engage in this practice than people under 50.

HOME AND AWAY

- Do you avoid using public restrooms? According to Quilted Northern's 2001 "Bathroom Confidential" Survey, 30 percent of Americans avoid public restrooms, citing "fear of germs" as the primary reason.

- Of those who do venture in, up to 60 percent say they don't sit—they hover over the public toilet without ever touching it.

- Then, when the deed is done, 40 percent say they flush the toilet by kicking the handle with their feet, rather than touching it with their bare hands. Another 20 percent reach for paper to "protect" themselves before touching the handle.

- What about when you're at home—are you bashful? Hard to believe, but 70 percent of Americans say they always close the

---

How did the golden silk spider get its name? It's the only spider that spins a gold web.

bathroom door even if they live alone or are the only ones at home.

- Once they're behind closed doors, people are a little more at ease—50 percent of Americans talk on the phone in the bathroom and more than 90 percent read on the pot or in the tub. Meditating, balancing checkbooks, and even eating are also popular bathroom activities.

NEWS FROM ENGLAND

- England's Department of Trade and Industry conducted a survey of emergency room admissions for the year 1999. Among their findings: "trouser accidents" (when anatomy and zippers collide) resulted in more visits to the country's emergency rooms—5,945—than any other bathroom-related accident. That's up from 5,137 in 1998.

- Other winners: Accidents involving sponges resulted in 787 trips to the hospital; accidents involving toilet roll holders, 329.

MODERN PLUMBING

- According to the U.S. Census Bureau, Alaska ranks first among the 50 states in the percentage of homes without indoor plumbing. The bureau estimates that in 2000, 3.8 percent of Alaska's occupied homes lacked "complete plumbing" (hot and cold running water, a flush toilet, and a tub or shower). That's a significant improvement from just 10 years earlier, when an amazing 12.5 percent—more than 1 in 10 Alaskan homes—were without.

- The remoteness of many small Alaskan towns is a big part of the problem; so is the state's arctic climate. "At the risk of stating the obvious, water is a solid in our communities for up to nine months a year, and that makes it hard to transport," says Dan Easton, an official with the state. In many parts of the state, water pipes have to be installed above ground, with their own heating systems and plenty of insulation to keep the water from freezing and bursting the pipes.

- New Mexico has more homes without complete plumbing than Alaska—14,228—but they make up only 2.2 percent of the total number of households in the state.

In pro Ping-Pong, if players use white balls, they can't wear white shirts. Why? Can't see 'em.

HANG UP AND DRIVE!

*Every year, BRI member Debbie Thornton sends in a list of
real-life bumper stickers. Have you seen the one that says . . .*

*As long as there are tests,
there will be prayer in
public schools*

**Forget About World Peace
. . . Visualize Using
Your Turn Signal!**

Consciousness: That
annoying time between naps

I Are Illeterate And I Vote

**SO MANY CATS,
SO FEW RECIPES**

THERE'S NO SUCH THING
AS A DUMB BLONDE (*seen
placed upside down on
the bumper*)

Jesus is coming . . .
everyone look busy.

**A bartender is just a
pharmacist with a
limited inventory.**

Out of my mind . . . back
in five minutes.

VEGETARIAN: Indian Word
for "Lousy Hunter"

Warning: I have an attitude
and I know how to use it.

PLEASE DON'T MAKE
ME KILL YOU.

**Meandering to a
different drummer.**

I drive way too fast to
worry about cholesterol.

DON'T PISS ME OFF! I'M
RUNNING OUT OF PLACES
TO HIDE THE BODIES.

**You are depriving some
poor village of its idiot.**

**Everyone has a
photographic memory,
some just don't
have film.**

Why am I the only person
on Earth who knows
how to drive?

*Don't like my driving?
Then quit watching me.*

I may be slow, but
I'm ahead of you.

The average person speaks 450 words in a typical three-minute phone call.

LOONEY LAWS

Believe it or not, these laws are real.

In Tuscumbia, Alabama, it is against the law for more than eight rabbits to reside on the same block.

In Birmingham, Alabama, it is illegal to drive a car while blindfolded.

In Arizona, it is illegal to hunt or shoot a camel.

In Atlanta, it is illegal to make faces at school children while they are studying.

In Hawaii, no one may whistle in a drinking establishment.

A law in Zion, Illinois, prohibits teaching household pets to smoke cigars.

According to Kentucky law, women may not appear on the highway in bathing suits unless they carry clubs.

In Marblehead, Massachusetts, each fire company responding to an alarm must be provided a three-gallon jug of rum.

Undertakers are prohibited from giving away books of matches in Shreveport, Louisiana.

It is illegal to fish for whales in any stream, river, or lake in Ohio.

It is unlawful to tie a crocodile to a fire hydrant in Detroit.

In Minnesota, it is illegal to dry both men's and women's underwear on the same clothesline.

In Natchez, Mississippi, it is unlawful for elephants to drink beer.

It is illegal for barbers in Waterloo, Nebraska, to eat onions between 7 a.m. and 7 p.m.

In Yukon, Oklahoma, it is illegal for a patient to pull a dentist's tooth.

In Portland, Oregon, it is illegal to shake a feather duster in someone's face.

A South Carolina statute states that butchers may not serve on a jury when a man is being tried for murder.

In Knoxville, Tennessee, it is illegal to lasso a fish.

Tendons, which anchor muscle tissue to bones, have half the tensile strength of steel.

LAWYERS ON LAWYERS

Believe it or not, some lawyers are actually quite clever. Here are some quotes from the world's most famous attorneys.

"I bring out the worst in my enemies and that's how I get them to defeat themselves."
—**Roy Cohn**

"The court of last resort is no longer the Supreme Court. It's *Nightline*."
—**Alan Dershowitz**

"We lawyers shake papers at each other the way primitive tribes shake spears."
—**John Jay Osborn, Jr.**

"[The] ideal client is the very wealthy man in very great trouble."
—**John Sterling**

"An incompetent lawyer can delay a trial for months or years. A competent lawyer can delay one even longer."
—**Evelle Younger**

"I've never met a litigator who didn't think he was winning . . . right up until the moment the guillotine dropped."
—**William F. Baxter**

"I'm not an ambulance chaser. I'm usually there before the ambulance."
—**Melvin Belli**

"This is New York, and there's no law against being annoying."
—**William Kunstler**

"I get paid for seeing that my clients have every break the law allows. I have knowingly defended a number of guilty men. But the guilty never escape unscathed. My fees are sufficient punishment for anyone."
—**F. Lee Bailey**

"I don't want to know what the law is, I want to know who the judge is."
—**Roy Cohn**

"The 'adversary system' is based on the notion that if one side overstates his idea of the truth and the other side overstates his idea of the truth, then the truth will come out . . . Why can't we all just tell the truth?"
—**David Zapp**

Blue eyes have less pigment in them than brown eyes.

CLASSIC HOAXES

Here are a few more of our favorite classic hoaxes.

THE WAR IS OVER!

Background: On November 8, 1918, the United Press Association became the first news organization to report that Germany had signed an armistice agreement, bringing World War I to an end. From there the news spread quickly, as papers all over the country ran the story beneath banner headlines. "The public response was what might have been expected," Curtis D. MacDougal writes in *Hoaxes.* "Factory whistles blew, church bells rang, parades were organized, public leaders addressed jubilant crowds, and bonfires were lighted. It was a wild, nationwide demonstration."

Exposed: Unfortunately, it was also a deliberate hoax, which started when "someone, now commonly believed to have been a German secret agent," telephoned the French and American intelligence offices to report that Germany had signed the armistice. From there the story was passed to United Press president Roy Howard in Europe, who cabled the story back to his offices in the United States.

Within the hour, Howard discovered the story was false, but it was too late—cable traffic was backlogged, and a second message with instructions to disregard wasn't delivered until 24 hours later. By then, MacDougall writes, the story had became "the most colossal journalistic blunder" of World War I. The real armistice was signed a few days later, on November 11, 1918.

MESSAGES FROM GOD

Background: In 1725, Dr. Johannes Beringer, dean of the medical school at the University of Würzburg, astonished the scientific world by announcing the discovery of hundreds of tiny fossils as well as a number of clay tablets, "including one signed by Jehovah." In 1726, Dr. Beringer published a book theorizing that the tablets and the fossils had been carved from solid stone by God.

Exposed: Beringer's book took the academic world by storm . . .

until rumors began to surface that the tablets were fakes, the work of two of Beringer's enemies on the faculty of the University of Würzburg: J. Ignatz Roderick, a geography professor, and Georg von Eckhart, the university's librarian. When Roderick and von Eckhart confessed to staging the hoax, Beringer accused them of spreading false rumors to undermine the importance of his discovery. Then he examined the tablets a little more closely and found his own name inscribed on some of them.

Rather than admit he'd been had, Beringer tried to cover up the scandal by buying all outstanding copies of his book. He might have succeeded, had word of what he was doing not leaked out. Suddenly, the book became a collector's item. Beringer's professional reputation was destroyed and the man once considered "one of the preeminent scholars of the day" went to his grave a laughingstock.

Final Note: The hoax actually contributed to the advancement of science: Beringer's theory of the divine origin of fossils (which unlike the tablets, were authentic) was so thoroughly discredited, Carl Sifakis writes in *Hoaxes and Scams*, that "scholars began more and more to embrace Leonardo da Vinci's suggestion that fossils were the remains of a former age."

HARVARD'S ANTI-SMUT WEEK

Background: In 1926 a Harvard University student newspaper announced an "Anti-Smut" campaign, calling it "an organized attempt to aid the police in their diligent prosecution of filth in Harvard University." They sponsored a campus rally and hung posters reading HELP THE OFFICERS TO KEEP YOU CLEAN and DON'T BE DIRTY! all over campus.

Exposed: The newspaper sponsoring Anti-Smut Week was actually the *Harvard Lampoon,* and the campaign was their prankish response to the Boston Police Department's seizure of the Lampoon parody of the *Literary Digest,* after the *Boston Telegraph* attacked it as "obscene."

The *Telegraph* fell for the stunt, crediting their own "vigorous denunciations of the moral uncleanness in the atmosphere of Harvard, as shown by the publication of obscenity that nauseated the public," as the inspiration for Anti-Smut Week.

IRONIC DEATHS

*You can't help laughing at some of life's—and death's—
ironies . . . as long as they happen to someone else.
These stories speak for themselves.*

BOB TALLEY, *centenarian*
Final Irony: Talley passed away in London during his 100th birthday party, moments after receiving a telegram of congratulations from the Queen and telling friends, "Yes, I made it to 100."

RALPH BREGOS, *heart patient*
Final Irony: Bregos, 40, spent more than two years wondering if a suitable donor heart would ever become available. Finally in 1997, doctors told him that one had been found. Bregos became so excited at the news that he suffered a massive heart attack and died.

STANLEY GOLDMAN, *candidate for mayor of Hollywood*
Final Irony: At one campaign stop, Goldman chided his opponent for being "too old for the job." Moments later, he dropped dead from a heart attack.

ROBERT SHOVESTALL, *gun enthusiast in Glendale, California*
Final Irony: Shovestall, 37, died from an accidental gunshot wound. According to news reports, he placed a .45-caliber pistol he thought was unloaded under his chin and pulled the trigger. The incident took place "after his wife's complaints about his 70 guns prompted him to demonstrate they were safe."

ANONYMOUS MAN, *from West Plains, Missouri*
Final Irony: According to news reports, the suicidal man set himself on fire, only to change his mind moments later and jump into a pond to extinguish the flames. Cause of death: drowning.

ELIZABETH FLEISCHMAN ASCHEIM, *pioneering X-ray technician at the turn of the 20th century*
Final Irony: Ascheim often X-rayed herself to show patients that the treatment was safe. Cause of death: "severe skin cancer."

Chance that a peanut grown in the United States will end up as peanut butter: 33 percent.

URBAN LEGENDS

*Here's our latest batch of urban legends—have you heard any of these?
Remember the BRI rule of thumb: If a wild story sounds a little
too "perfect," it's probably an urban legend . . . or is it?*

THE LEGEND: Chocolate milk is made from tainted milk.
Dairies too cheap to throw away unusable milk add chocolate to hide the bad taste.

HOW IT SPREAD: This story started out as a schoolyard rumor,
spread by kids. But it took on new life in the 1990s, when the
introduction of prepared coffee drinks in bottles and cans inspired
people to extend the children's tale to adult beverages.

THE TRUTH: The milk in chocolate milk and coffee drinks is as
carefully tested and regulated by the U.S. Food and Drug
Administration as any other form of milk.

THE LEGEND: When the Missouri Ku Klux Klan won a lengthy
court battle to participate in the Adopt-a-Highway program—
which would have required the state to use taxpayer dollars to
"advertise" the KKK on those little roadside Adopt-a-Highway
signs—the state legislature responded by naming the Klan's designated stretch of road after civil rights activist Rosa Parks.

HOW IT SPREAD: By word of mouth and over the Internet.

THE TRUTH: What makes this urban legend different from
most others? It's true. In March 2000 the Missouri KKK really did
win a legal battle to adopt a mile-long stretch of I-55 south of St.
Louis, and the state legislature really did name it the Rosa Parks
Highway in response.

PROBLEM SOLVED: No one ever showed up to clean the road
either before or after the name change, so the state dropped the
KKK from the program in April 2000.

THE LEGEND: A few years before the Gulf War, Barbara
Walters did a news story on gender roles in Kuwait in which
she reported that Kuwaiti wives traditionally walk several paces
behind their husbands. She returned to Kuwait after the war and

There are 27 chemicals that can be added to bread without being listed on the label.

noticed that women were now walking several paces *ahead* of their husbands. When Walters asked a Kuwaiti woman how so much social progress had been accomplished in so little time, the woman replied, "Land mines."

HOW IT SPREAD: By word of mouth and e-mail, starting shortly after the end of the Gulf War.

THE TRUTH: This is the latest version of a classic urban legend that has been around as long as land mines themselves. The subjects of the story—Kuwaitis, Korean and Vietnamese peasants, and in the case of World War II, nomads in North Africa—change to fit the circumstances of each new war.

THE LEGEND: You can help oil-soaked Australian penguins by knitting tiny sweaters for them to wear and mailing them to an address in Tasmania, off the southern coast of Australia.

HOW IT SPREAD: By word of mouth, e-mail, and cable news broadcasts, following an oil spill near Tasmania on New Year's Day 2000.

THE TRUTH: Another example of an urban "legend" that's actually true, this one is a request for public assistance that snowballed out of control. In 2001 the Tasmanian Conservation Trust and State Library asked knitters to put their leftover yarn to good use by knitting it into penguin sweaters. It even posted a pattern on the Internet so that knitters would know how to make one in just the right shape and size. (The sweaters keep oil-soaked penguins warm and prevent them from ingesting oil until they regain enough strength to be scrubbed clean.)

The story received international news coverage, prompting concerned knitters all over the world to begin sending penguin sweaters to Tasmania. The Conservation Trust had hoped to create a stockpile of 100 in preparation for the next oil spill, but more than 800 arrived in the first few weeks alone; from there, the number just kept growing. "They're all one size," says a volunteer. "But at least the penguins have a choice of color."

* * *

"Life is tough, but it's tougher when you're stupid."

—John Wayne

Left alone, a dog will spend up to three hours a day remarking its scent posts.

THE CHOCOLATE HALL OF FAME

In previous Bathroom Readers we've told you the stories of Milton Hershey, Henri Nestlé, Frank Mars, and other notables in the chocolate world. Here are a few more.(Hint: Baker's chocolate wasn't named with bakers in mind, and German chocolate doesn't come from Germany.)

HARRY BURNET REESE

In the early 1920s, Reese worked in one of the dairies owned by Milton Hershey. Inspired by Hershey's success, he decided "if Hershey can sell a trainload of chocolate every day, I can at least make a living making candy." Reese struck out on his own and by the mid-1920s had an entire line of candies, including dinner mints, dipped chocolates, caramels, and coconut candies. In 1928, he added peanut butter cups; they were so popular that when World War II rationing put a dent in his business in 1942, he dumped the rest of his product line and focused exclusively on them. Today, Reese's Peanut Butter Cups are part of Hershey Foods.

L. S. HEATH

In 1914 an Illinois schoolteacher named L. S. Heath mortgaged his house for $3,000 to buy his sons a soda shop. A year later, he quit his teaching job to join them and expanded the business into homemade ice cream and candy. One afternoon in the mid-1920s, a salesman told them about a candy called Trail-Toffee that he'd seen in another store. The Heath brothers took the basic recipe—almonds, butter, and sugar—and spent the next several months experimenting. In 1928 they finally came up with a chocolate-covered English toffee bar—the Heath Bar.

DR. JAMES BAKER

In 1765 Dr. Baker and an Irish immigrant chocolate-maker named John Hannon formed a chocolate company in Dorchester, Massachusetts. In 1772 they started advertising their chocolate under the brand name Hannon's Best Chocolate . . . but when

---

In 1907, egret plumes were worth twice their weight in gold.

Hannon was lost at sea in 1799, Dr. Baker assumed full control of the company and renamed the product Baker's Chocolate.

SAM GERMAN

The guy that German chocolate is named after worked for the guy that Baker's chocolate is named after. No kidding. Sam German was an employee of the Baker Chocolate Company in the 1850s, when he created a mild dark chocolate bar for baking. The bar was named Baker's German's Sweet Chocolate in his honor.

About a century later in 1957, a Dallas, Texas, newspaper published a recipe for German Chocolate Cake, sparking a local baking craze. When General Foods, then-owner of the Baker's Chocolate company, noticed a spike in German's Chocolate sales, they investigated. And when they learned that German Chocolate Cake was responsible, they sent copies of the recipe and photos of the cake to food editors all over the country. Sales of German's Chocolate jumped 73 percent in the first year alone, and German Chocolate Cake became an American dessert classic.

JOHN AND RICHARD CADBURY

In 1822 John Cadbury opened a tea and coffee shop in Birmingham, England. He expanded into chocolate manufacturing, and in 1853 became purveyor of chocolate to Queen Victoria. In 1861 his son Richard Cadbury hit upon the idea of increasing sales of Valentine's Day chocolate sales by packaging Cadbury chocolates in the world's first heart-shaped candy box.

DAVID LYTLE CLARK

In 1883 Clark, an Irish immigrant, hired a cook and started a candy business in Pittsburgh. While the cook prepared the candy, Clark sold it out of the back of a wagon to local merchants. In 1886, he tasted chewing gum for the first time; a short while later, he added it to his product line. Countless other products followed; in time, Clark became known as the Pittsburgh Candy King. But his biggest claim to fame came in 1917, when he invented a nickel candy bar similar to a Butterfinger—honeycombed ground, roasted peanuts coated with milk chocolate—that America's World War I fighting men could carry with them into battle. Clark liked his new product so much he named it after himself: the Clark Bar.

World's most recognizable smell: coffee.

IRONIC, ISN'T IT?

*Some more irony to put the problems of
day-to-day life in proper perspective.*

VOCATIONAL IRONY

- In August 2000, a 44-year-old woman named Angel Destiny fled for her life dressed only in pajamas after half of her house in Cardiff, Wales, collapsed into rubble. Destiny, who makes her living as a psychic, told reporters, "I just didn't see it coming."

- A circus contortionist who goes by the name Berkine got his right foot stuck on his left shoulder . . . and did not immediately receive the medical attention he needed to get unstuck. Reason: Circus workers who heard him screaming for help "thought he was joking."

- In May 2000, a save-the-whales activist was forced to call off his sailing voyage across the Pacific Ocean, which he had hoped would call attention to his cause. Reason: "His 60-foot boat was damaged by two passing whales."

- In an unrelated incident, in July 2001, the 50-foot yacht *Peningo* was struck by a whale while sailing about 350 miles off the coast of Newfoundland. What was crew member John Fullerton doing when the incident occurred? Reading a copy of *Moby Dick*.

- According to Industrial Machinery News, an (unnamed) company with a five-year perfect safety record tried to demonstrate the importance of wearing safety goggles on-the-job by showing workers a graphic film containing footage of gory industrial accidents. Twenty-five people injured themselves while fleeing the screening room, 13 others passed out during the film, and another required seven stitches "after he cut his head falling off a chair while watching the film."

GOVERNMENTAL IRONY

- In June 2000, an 87-year-old man dropped dead while standing in line at a government office in Bogotá, Colombia. Reason for visiting the office: to "apply for a government certificate to prove he was still alive."

Toilet Rock, a natural rock formation shaped like a flush toilet, is in City of Rocks, New Mexico.

- In 1919, *The New York Times* commissioned a poll asking people who they thought were the 10 most important living Americans. Herbert Hoover won first place. Franklin Roosevelt, then assistant secretary of the Navy, saw the poll and wrote a colleague, "Herbert Hoover is certainly a winner, and I wish we could make him President of the United States."

- In January 2000, a Florida seventh-grade teacher had his 70 students write their elected representatives a letter. Purpose of the exercise: to demonstrate that "their opinions matter." As of the end of the school year, none of the students had received a reply.

HOLLYWOOD IRONY

- *Hellcats of the Navy,* a 1957 film starring Ronald Reagan and Nancy Davis (the future Mrs. Reagan), was co-written by screenwriter Bernard Gordon. Gordon used the name Raymond T. Marcus because he'd been blacklisted during the McCarthy era, during which Reagan had served as a government informant.

- A production company won a $1.8 million judgment against a former employee accused of stealing the concept for a television game show. Name of the stolen show: *Anything for Money.*

MISCELLANEOUS IRONY

- A 15-year-old Zimbabwe boy named Victim Kamubvumbi lived up to his name when he became stranded on an island in the middle of the Ruya River during a flood. Victim's last name, when translated into English: "slight drizzle that does not end."

- In 1982, Bill Curtis, an electronic technician at the Vancouver airport, became convinced that a nuclear war was imminent. So convinced, in fact, that he moved his family to the place his research told him would be the safest on Earth: the Falkland Islands, an English colony off the east coast of South America. The following April, 4,000 Argentinian troops attacked the islands and claimed them for Argentina, in the process starting a war with England that lasted more than three months.

* * *

"I've always hated that damn James Bond. I'd like to kill him."

—Sean Connery

Poison oak is not an oak, and poison ivy is not an ivy. Both are members of the cashew family.

RUMORS
OF MY DEATH...

*Here are more examples of "rebirth": people who were
thought to be dead, but were actually quite alive.*

DECEASED: Jayaprakash Narayan, Indian "patriot and
elder statesman"
NEWS OF HIS DEATH: On March 22, 1979, Prime
Minister Morarji Desai announced to the nation that Narayan had
died. Desai delivered an emotional eulogy; Parliament was
adjourned. Flags were lowered to half-mast nationwide, schools and
shops closed, and funeral music was broadcast over All-India Radio
in honor of the fallen giant.

RESURRECTION: Later that day, Jayaprakash Narayan heard
the news of his own death while convalescing in the hospital,
where he was still very much alive. Prime Minister Desai apologized for the mistake and brought the official mourning to an end,
blaming the false report on the director of the Indian Intelligence
Bureau, "one of whose staff had seen a body being carried out of
the hospital."

DECEASED: Sam Kalungi, a private in the Ugandan army

NEWS OF HIS DEATH: In the late 1990s, Private Kalungi was
one of more than 10,000 Ugandan soldiers sent to the Congo to
aid rebels trying to overthrow Congolese president Laurent Kabila.
Several months later, the Ugandan Army contacted Kalungi's family, telling them that Kalungi had died in battle. Family members
went to the morgue of the Mbuya military hospital, positively identified the body, and had it delivered to their home village of
Mbukiro for burial.

RESURRECTION: When his two-year tour was up, Kalungi
returned home to Mbukiro, where shocked and relieved relatives
took him to see the grave that bore his name. So who's buried
there? Private James Kalungi (no relation), delivered to the wrong
family and misidentified by Sam Kalungi's own parents. "The body
had spent one and a half months in the military hospital. It had an

The flowers of Africa's baobab tree open only in the moonlight. They're pollinated by bats.

ice coating on the face which made us believe it was our son," Sam's mother explained.

DECEASED: An unidentified man from Almaty, Kazakhstan

NEWS OF HIS DEATH: According to the Reuters news agency, the man was trying to steal electrical power cables in eastern Kazakhstan, when he touched a live wire and was electrocuted. Thinking he was dead, his family wrapped him in a cloth shroud and buried him in a shallow grave.

RESURRECTION: The grave must have been really shallow, because two days later the man "regained consciousness and rose naked from the ground," whereupon he hitched a ride back to his village . . . and got there just in time to attend his own funeral feast. That was no easy task—according to local news reports, the naked, electrocuted man "had trouble flagging down a vehicle to take him home."

DECEASED: Cesar Aguilera, 58, of Nicaragua

NEWS OF HIS DEATH: In May 2001, Aguilera went to tend some property he owned in the countryside. More than a week passed and he did not return. His relatives, fearing the worst, went around to local morgues looking for his body . . . and thought they had found it when they discovered a man about Aguilera's height and weight who'd been run over by a car.

RESURRECTION: Aguilera returned home from his trip just as his family was preparing to bury the deceased. You would expect they would have been happy to see him, but they didn't exactly show it. "One kid screamed at me, 'Are you from this life or the other?'" Aguilera said.

* * *

A REAL SHOW STOPPER

In a version of the opera *Carmen* performed in Verona in 1970, 38 horses were used live on stage. All went well until the conductor gave a violent upswing of his baton, startling a horse and causing a stampede. Sole fatality: one of the horses jumped into the orchestra pit and landed on top of the kettledrum.

Lincoln survived two assassination attempts before being killed by John Wilkes Booth.

THE HISTORY OF FOOTBALL, PART IV

Here's the part of our story on the history of football that "red-meat"
sports fans have been waiting for: how one of America's most violent
sports became even more violent. So violent in fact, that for
a time it looked like some colleges would ban it forever.

FOOTBALL IN THE NEWS

The "Hospital Box Score" printed by the *Boston Globe* following the Harvard-Yale game of 1894 (Yale won, 12–4):

> **YALE:** JERREMS, KNEE INJURY; MURPHY, UNCONSCIOUS FROM A KICK IN THE HEAD; BUTTERWORTH, CARRIED FROM THE FIELD.
>
> **HARVARD:** CHARLEY BREWER, BADLY BRUISED FOOT; WORTHINGTON, BROKEN COLLARBONE; HALLOWELL, BROKEN NOSE.

By the mid-1890s, due in large part to the introduction of mass plays like the V-trick and the flying wedge, serious injuries had become such a routine part of football that newspapers began publishing injury reports as part of their sports coverage. How violent was it? In the early 1890s, a player was actually allowed to slug another player three times with a closed fist before the referee could throw him out of the game.

THE NAKED TRUTH

The situation was made even worse by the fact that players wore almost no protective padding—not even football helmets, which were not mandatory until 1939. The football players of the late 1880s and early 1890s wore little more than canvas or cotton knickers, a football jersey, high-top shoes with leather spikes, and hard leather shin guards worn underneath wool socks. They topped off the look with a knitted cap with a tassle or pom-pom on top. If a player was worried about getting his ears torn from the grabbing style of tackling popular at the time, he could wear earmuffs. "Anyone who wore home-made pads was regarded as a sissy," early football great John Heisman remembered.

Football has more rules than any other American sport.

One acceptable piece of protective wear: ff a player worried about breaking his nose, he could wear a black, banana-shaped rubber nose mask. "Sometimes all 11 players wore them," Robert Leckie writes in *The Story of Football*. "They were indeed a ferocious sight with the ends of their handle-bar mustaches dangling from either side of that long, black, banana-like mask, and their long hair flying in the breeze."

GAME OVER

Thanks to the introduction of mass-momentum plays, the 1893 season was surprisingly brutal, even to hardened football fans. That year's Purdue-Chicago game was so violent that the Tippecanoe County District Attorney, who was watching from the stands, ran out onto the field in the middle of the game and threatened to indict every single player on charges of assault and battery. The departments of the Army and Navy were so disturbed by the violent direction that football was taking that they abolished the annual game between their military academies.

Public sentiment was also beginning to turn sharply against mass-momentum plays—not just because people were being hurt and killed, but also because they made the games boring to watch (unless you were there to watch people break bones). So many players crowded around the ball during the mass plays that it was difficult for spectators to see what was going on.

MAKING SOME CHANGES

In 1894 the University Athletic Club of New York invited the "Big Four" football powers—Yale, Princeton, Harvard, and Pennsylvania—to meet in New York to form new rules that would curb the violence in football.

Banning mass-momentum plays outright was out of the question—they were too popular with too many football teams—but the Big Four did agree to a few restrictions. They limited the number of players who could gather behind the line of scrimmage in preparation for a play, and they passed a rule requiring that a ball had to travel at least 10 yards at kickoffs to be considered in play, unless it was touched by a member of the receiving team.

They also made it illegal to touch a member of the opposing team unless the opponent had the ball, and reduced the length of

Seventy-five percent of all murder victims knew their killer.

the game from 90 minutes to 70, in the hopes that shorter games would mean less violence.

The new restrictions effectively banned the flying wedge and similar plays during kickoffs, but in the end, they were not very effective, because teams kept inventing new mass plays that got around the rules. Injuries continued to mount.

THE BIG TEN IS BORN

The following year, Princeton and Yale proposed banning mass-momentum plays altogether, by requiring a minimum of seven players on the line of scrimmage and by allowing only one back to be in forward motion before the snap. Harvard and Penn refused to go along, and rather than sign on to the new rules, they broke off from the Big Four and drafted their own set of rules, allowing mass-momentum plays.

When the Big Four split in 1895, the presidents of Chicago, Illinois, Michigan, Minnesota, Northwestern, Purdue, and Wisconsin universities stepped in to fill the breach by meeting and forming what grew into the "Big Ten" Western Conference. (Iowa and Indiana joined in 1899, and the 10th school, Ohio State, signed on in 1912.)

The rise of a competing football conference motivated the students of the Big Four to resolve their differences. In the summer of 1896, Harvard and Pennsylvania returned to the fold, and the Big Four moved a step closer to banning mass-momentum plays with a rule that forbade players from taking more than a single step before the ball was in play, unless they came to a complete stop before taking another step. But it wasn't enough, as Robert Leckie writes in *The Story of Football:*

> As the twentieth century began, football was still a game of mass-momentum . . . The flying wedge was not completely gone. Hurdling and the flying tackle were common. Slugging was still a familiar tactic up front, and the most acceptable method of getting the ball carrier through the line was to push, pull, or haul him through. Thus the only participant surviving the contest undamaged was apt to be the ball.

Fortunately, reading is not a contact sport, so while we go off to the infirmary to get a few bandages, you may turn to page 313 for Part V of The History of Football.

Fastest action in the animal world: The common midge beats its wings 133,000 times/min.

Q & A:
ASK THE EXPERTS

*Everyone's got a question or two they'd like answered—basic stuff,
like "Why is the sky blue?" Here are a few of those questions,
with answers from some of the nation's top trivia experts.*

SEA-SONING
Q: *Why are the oceans salty?*
A: One theory: "When rain falls on rocks it dissolves some
of the minerals in them, particularly salt. The rainwater washes into
streams and rivers, carrying away the salt with it. There is not
enough salt in most rivers to make them taste salty, but after millions of years the salt carried to the oceans has made them quite
salty. During all these years, ocean water has been evaporating, leaving the salt behind, increasing the saltiness of the oceans. There are
beds of salt throughout the world, sometimes hundreds of feet thick,
probably formed by the evaporation of ancient seas." (From *The
Question and Answer Book of Nature*, by John R. Saunders)

ESSENTIAL BATHROOM KNOWLEDGE
Q: *Why is there a crescent moon on outhouse doors?*
A: "The main reasons for carving anything into an outhouse door
are light and ventilation.

"In olden times, outhouse builders used cutouts of the moon
and sun to let people know which outhouse to use. The moon
represented women, the sun represented men. The symbols also
helped foreign travelers. It didn't matter what language they spoke
because the symbols were universal.

"But if one of the outhouses at an inn was damaged and could
no longer be used, it was automatically assumed to be the men's
outhouse. The reasoning was that men could always go behind a
tree, so the crescent moon was put on the remaining usable structure for use by women. For economy, many inns only constructed
an outhouse for women. This custom soon became so widespread
that eventually the moon became the symbol used for all outhouses." (From *What Makes Flamingos Pink?*, by Bill McLain)

Pound for pound, radium is worth more than gold.

FROZEN STIFF

Q: *Why do ice cubes crack?*

A: "They're trying to shrink! When water freezes, it gets bigger and lighter. As soon as you put an ice cube in a drink, the outside of the cube wants to turn back into water. So the cube tries to shrink—quickly. The shrinking squeezes hard on the inside of the ice cube and, all of the sudden . . . the inside part goes crack." (From *Why Does Popcorn Pop?*, by Catherine Ripley)

STALE MATE

Q: *Why don't birds sing in the winter?*

A: "One reason is that many species are gone, having migrated south for the winter. But some birds, such as starlings, mourning doves, and sparrows, are around all winter. Yet even they are silent.

"For birds, singing is associated with mating. As birds mate and begin to build their nests, one of their first tasks is to stake out a territory where other birds are not welcome. By keeping competitors away from a particular area, a nesting bird ensures that there will be enough food for both parents and the growing chicks. Singing is a very efffective way of announcing to other birds, 'This territory is occupied.'

"Since most birds set up territories and mate in the spring, this is the time you are most likely to hear birdsong." (From *101 Questions and Answers About Backyard Wildlife*, by Ann Squire)

CAUGHT A LIGHT SNEEZE

Q: *How come whenever I go out into bright light I sneeze?*

A: "You say you don't have this problem? Well, between one-sixth and one-quarter of the population do. They have what's known as photic sneeze reflex ('sneeze caused by light').

"What causes it? Nobody knows. What we do know is that the nerves for the eye and the nose run pretty close together. Some think what we've got here is a case of nerve signals getting crossed. If it bugs you . . . well, there's always brain surgery. But personally, I'd learn to live with it." (From *Know It All!*, by Ed Zotti)

If you feed a rhesus monkey a "typical American diet" it will die within two years.

WOMAN TO WOMAN

*Some thoughtful observations on womanhood from
some of the world's most interesting women.*

"From birth to age 18 a girl needs good parents. From 18 to 35 she needs good looks. From 35 to 55 she needs a good personality. From 55 on, she needs cash."
—**Sophie Tucker**

"Whatever women do they must do twice as well as men to be thought half as good. Luckily, this is not difficult."
—**Charlotte Whitton**

"The hardest task in a girl's life is to prove to a man that his intentions are serious."
—**Helen Rowland**

"My idea of a superwoman is someone who scrubs her own floors."
—**Bette Midler**

"We haven't come a long way, we've come a short way. If we hadn't come a short way, no one would be calling us 'baby.'"
—**Elizabeth Janeway**

"I refuse to think of them as chin hairs. I think of them as stray eyebrows."
—**Janette Barbery**

"I will feel equality has arrived when we can elect to office women who are as incompetent as some of the men who are already there."
—**Maureen Reagan**

"Woman's virtue is man's greatest invention."
—**Cornelia Otis Skinner**

"Who ever thought up the word 'mammogram'? Every time I hear it, I think I'm supposed to put my breast in an envelope and send it to someone."
—**Jan King**

"I'm furious about the women's liberationists. They keep getting up on soapboxes and proclaiming women are brighter than men. That's true, but it should be kept quiet or it ruins the whole racket."
—**Anita Loos**

"The especial genius of women I believe is to be electrical in movement, intuitive in function, spiritual in tendency."
—**Margaret Fuller**

Woodrow Wilson's second wife, Edith, learned to ride a bike in the White House halls.

BEHIND BAR CODES

We see them on every item we buy, but we don't know
what they mean or what they're used for. Here's
the story of the Universal Product Code.

STEP UP TO THE BAR

The story of the bar code begins in 1948, when the president of the Food Fair chain of grocery stores went to see the dean of Philadelphia's Drexel Institute of Technology. Food Fair wanted Drexel to do research into the feasibility of some kind of device that could collect product information automatically at checkout counters. The dean said no—but a graduate student named Bernard Silver overheard the conversation. Silver was intrigued and mentioned it to his friend Joseph Woodland, a teacher at Drexel. The two men decided to work together on creating a device.

After some moderately successful experiments using ultraviolet light, Woodland quit his teaching job and moved to his grandfather's apartment in Florida to devote more time to the project. One day while lounging on Miami Beach, Woodland was thinking about the problem and absentmindedly pulled his fingers through the sand, leaving lines. That gave him the brainstorm to work with Morse code and to extend the lines, so that dots would become skinny lines and dashes would become fat lines—the prototype of the first bar code.

OPTICAL ALLUSION

To read the code, Woodland used technology from another project he was working on—improving Muzak using the technology from movie sound tracks. Sound for movies was printed in a light-and-dark pattern along the edges of film, read by a light, transformed to electric waveforms, then converted to sound. Woodland and Silver adapted the technology to read their morse code lines and filed a patent application on October 20, 1949.

In 1951 Woodland got a job with IBM, where he hoped to push his invention forward. In his spare time, he and Silver built the first actual bar code scanner. The finished product was the size of a desk and used a 500-watt lightbulb and a "photomultiplier tube"

A snapping turtle can swallow only when its head is under water.

designed for movie sound systems, hooked up to an oscilloscope. When the bar code on a piece of paper was moved across the beam of light, it caused the oscilloscope signal to move. It was crude, it was huge, and it was so hot that it set the paper on fire . . . but it worked. Woodland and Silver had created an electronic device that could read a printed code. Their patent was granted in 1952.

In 1962 IBM offered to buy the patent, but Woodland and Silver thought the offer was too low. A few weeks later, Philco made a better offer and they sold it. Philco later sold it to RCA.

UNMARKED CARS

At the same time, the railroad industry was developing its own bar-code system. Tracking freight cars created an impossible tangle of paperwork; bar coding each car looked like a cheaper, easier way to do it. Unfortunately, it wasn't (and eventually they scrapped the idea)—but by the time that became obvious, the technology had progressed significantly, and it could be used to address some of the bugs in Silver and Woodland's system.

By the late 1960s, lasers and microchips made it possible to greatly reduce the size of the code reader. The bars of the code were also revised to record the numbers 0 through 9 instead of Morse code dots and dashes.

In 1969 the General Trading Company of New Jersey started using bar codes to direct shipments to their loading docks. Then the General Motors plant in Michigan began to use them to monitor production of axle units. Meanwhile, RCA was working on a bull's-eye-shaped code for grocery stores. IBM saw a huge potential market and wanted to get into it, too. Then someone at IBM remembered that the bar code's inventor, Joseph Woodland, was still working for IBM. Woodland was transferred to the project and became instrumental in developing what we know today as the UPC—the Universal Product Code.

STANDARD RESPONSE

In 1973 the Uniform Grocery Product Code set nationwide standards for bar coding. National Cash Register began building efficient scanners and introduced their first model at the 1974 convention of the Super Market Institute. Six weeks later, on June 26, 1974 at the Marsh Supermarket in Troy, Ohio, a package of Wrigley's chewing gum was the first item ever scanned. Why a

In 1790, there were 66 slaves for every 100 Europeans in the state of Virginia.

pack of gum? It just happened to be the first item out of the shopping cart of a now-nameless shopper. Today it is on display at the Smithsonian Institute.

HOW IT WORKS

The UPC is composed of 12 digits. A single digit on the left identifies which type of product the item is: meat, produce, drug, etc. The next five digits identify the manufacturer, followed by five digits that identify the actual product. Every item scanned has its own unique ID number. A single digit on the right acts as a "check digit." It adds up some of the previous numbers to come up with a magic "everything's OK" number. For example, if someone has altered the code with a marker, the numbers won't add up and the product will be rejected.

The identifying numerals are also printed along the bottom of the bar code for the sake of the cashiers, in case the scanner is down or the bar code has been partially obscured and the numbers need to be entered by hand.

The UPC contains only the manufacturer and the product, but this information is fed to a computer (the cash register), which knows the price of the item. It also acts as an inventory system, telling management how much of any given item is still on hand, how fast it's being sold, when it will need to be reordered, how many coupons have been redeemed, and community purchasing patterns.

CHECK THIS OUT

Bar codes are not just for pricing products. They are used

- For tracking inventory on aircraft carriers
- For coding blood in blood banks
- For following applications in the Patent Office
- For identifying people in places like hospitals, libraries, and cafeterias
- For sorting baggage at airports
- For monitoring radio-collared animals
- For keeping track of logs in lumberyards

A cashier entering digits by hand will average one error for every 350 characters, . . .

- For tracking the mating habits of bees (researchers put tiny bar codes on their backs)

- For tracking packages (Federal Express is probably the world's largest single user of bar code technology)

- For identifying ships in the Navy

- By runners in the New York City Marathon—they don bar codes on their vests, and a computer records the order in which they cross the finish line

- To prevent scalping and theft of badges at the Masters Golf Tournament in Georgia

- By NASA to make sure the backs of heat-resistant tiles are installed on the correct spots of the space shuttles

- By the Occupational Safety and Health Administration to track the characteristics of hazardous materials (such as whether they're explosive and how to control them), in case there's an accident

MONETARILY SPEAKING

More than a million companies worldwide use the UPC to identify their products. Equipment used to print, scan, and program bar codes amounts to a $16 billion-a-year business. It's estimated that the codes are scanned five billion times a day across the planet.

Bernard Silver, who died in 1963 at the age of 38, never got to see his invention reach such phenomenal proportions. But Joseph Woodland was awarded the National Medal of Technology by President Bush in 1992. Neither man made very much money from his invention.

* * *

HOW DO THEY KNOW WHAT IT IS?

Scientists in Spain have discovered what they believe to be dinosaur vomit. According to a paleontologist from the Natural History Museum of Los Angeles County, it is the world's oldest specimen. Age of the prehistoric puke: about 120 million years.

—*Wireless Flash News Service*

. . . but a bar code scanner will make an error only once every 3,500,000 characters.

THE BIGGEST CULT MOVIE OF ALL TIME

Imagine the boy next door trading in his Levi's for fishnet stockings, his all-American sister sporting a sexy French maid's outfit. It's a scene that's played out at movie theaters around the world every Saturday at midnight—all because starving actor/playwright Richard O'Brien needed to pay the rent.

DON'T DREAM IT, BE IT

In the early 1970s, Richard O'Brien had just been fired as a chorus boy in a musical at London's West End. With no money, a wife and child to support, and lots of time on his hands, O'Brien penned a bizarre musical about cross-dressing, sex-starved aliens. He called it *The Rocky Horror Show*. And somehow, this weird show actually got produced. It opened at London's Royal Court Theatre in 1973 and was an amazing success; it was even named the best musical of the year.

Shortly after its debut, producer Lou Adler bought the play and moved it across the Atlantic to Los Angeles' Roxy Theater, where it met with critical and audience acclaim. It also caught the eye of filmmakers at 20th Century Fox, who were sure they they could transform it into a hit movie. The film version starred newcomers Tim Curry, Susan Sarandon, Barry Bostwick, and the singer Meat Loaf. It took eight weeks to shoot and cost $1 million to make. But before the movie was released, the play opened in New York . . . and flopped.

COLD FEET

Because the play had bombed, 20th Century Fox spent little on publicity for the film, and it played in very few theaters. The movie initially had about as much success as the Broadway show—critics hated it and audiences stayed away in droves. It appeared that *The Rocky Horror Picture Show* was dead in the water.

But because of the play's early success at the Roxy, the movie did well in Los Angeles, so Adler and a few others were convinced that the film just hadn't found its audience. In 1976 a

---

A butterfly's taste organs, located on its feet, are 2,400 times as sensitive as the human tongue.

20th Century Fox employee named Tim Deegan persuaded New York's Waverly Theater, in the heart of bohemian Greenwich Village, to begin midnight showings. The tactic was tried in other select cities across the country as well. The hope was that it would catch on with cult audiences, just as offbeat films like *El Topo* and George Romero's horror classic *Night of the Living Dead* had done.

JUST A JUMP TO THE LEFT

Within months, a phenomenon began to take hold. Audiences decided to tear down the invisible wall that separated them from the on-screen action. They weren't content just watching the movie from their seats—they began to dress as their favorite characters and perform along with the film, creating a show within a show. Seeing the movie became an interactive adventure; the *Rocky* experience was now part movie, part sing-along, part fashion show, and all party. Being in the audience at *The Rocky Horror Picture Show* now involved shouting lines at the screen, covering up with newspapers during scenes with rain, squirting water pistols to simulate rain in the theater, throwing rice during the wedding sequences, and dancing in the aisles doing the "Time Warp," the film's contagious anthem.

The *Rocky* phenomenon spread across the United States, giving birth to a midnight movie industry that spanned from major metropolitan areas right through to the straightlaced suburbs of America's heartland.

More than 30 years after its initial debut in the attic of London's Royal Court Theatre, *Rocky* still plays every weekend at midnight in theaters across the United States and around the world. And in November 2000 *The Rocky Horror Show* returned to Broadway . . . this time to critical praise and commercial success. It was nominated for several Tony Awards, including Best Revival.

LAUNCHING PAD

Can you picture actor Russell Crowe in high heels and a black bustier? In the 1980s, the Academy Award–winning star of *Gladiator* toured Australia and New Zealand singing and dancing through more than 400 performances of *The Rocky Horror Show*, including several times as the cross-dressing Dr. Frank N. Furter.

There are more churches per capita in Las Vegas than in any other U.S. city.

TESTOPHOBIC?

*Do you have testophobia, the fear of taking tests? If you don't, then test
your skills at the meanings of these other fears. They're 100 percent real.*

1. coulrophobia

2. phalacrophobia

3. automatonophobia

4. liticaphobia

5. myxophobia

6. geniophobia

7. cacophobia

8. atychiphobia

9. selenophobia

10. coprastasophobia

11. phobophobia

12. Francophobia

13. didaskaleinophobia

14. caligynephobia

15. arachibutyrophobia

16. decidophobia

17. automysophobia

A. failure

B. slime

C. making decisions

D. France

E. the moon

F. ventriloquist dummies

G. beautiful women

H. lawsuits

I. clowns

J. phobias

K. being dirty

L. becoming bald

M. school

N. ugliness

O. constipation

P. chins

Q. peanut butter sticking
to the roof of your mouth

Answers:

11. J, 12. D, 13. M, 14. G, 15. Q, 16. C, 17. K.
1. I, 2. L, 3. F, 4. H, 5. B, 6. P, 7. N, 8. A, 9. E, 10. O,

The enamel on a human tooth is only 1/1,000th of an inch thick.

PHOTOMANIA

If you had lived in the 1840s, you probably wouldn't have owned even a single photograph. Here's the story of how—and why—photos became affordable. (Turn to page 210 for the previous part of the story.)

GETTING IT BACKWARD

For all of the improvements that had been made to them, daguerreotypes and calotypes still had a lot of problems. Daguerreotype images not only could not be duplicated, they were also reverse images: any writing that appeared in the picture, be it on a street sign, in a shop window, or on the stern of a ship, appeared backward, something that was terribly distracting to the viewer.

Calotype images didn't have those problems—they were printed from negatives, so 1) the images were not reversed, and 2) you could make as many prints as you wanted. But calotype negatives were made of opaque paper. The resulting image was blurrier than a daguerreotype, and the grainy surface of the photographic paper used to make prints only made things worse.

People wanted the best of both worlds: pictures as sharp and clear as a daguerreotype that could be easily duplicated like a calotype. The obvious solution was to replace the calotype's paper negatives with negatives made of smooth-surfaced glass. Figuring out how to do this was a challenge, however, because the non-porous surface of the glass was so slippery that photographic chemicals wouldn't stick to it. Scientists tried everything to get them to stick (including smearing glass with snail slime), but nothing seemed to work.

EGGING THEM ON

Then in 1847, Claude-Félix-Abel Niepce de Saint-Victor, nephew of photographic pioneer Joseph Niepce, finally found something that did the trick: egg whites, also known as albumen. It got the chemicals to stick, and the images that resulted were as crystal clear as daguerreotypes and as easy to duplicate as calotypes. But the exposure times for albumen plates were so long that the plates couldn't be used for portraits.

One out of every 10 people surveyed claim to be satisfied with their jobs.

In 1851 English sculptor and photography buff Frederick Scott Archer used a substance called collodion to glue together some broken glass photographic plates. Made from guncotton (an explosive) dissolved in ether and alcohol, collodion formed a tough, waterproof skin when it dried; doctors used it to seal burns and wounds while new skin grew in underneath.

As Archer pieced together the broken glass, it occurred to him that collodion might be as good as egg whites for getting photosensitive chemicals to stick. He used it to apply a photosensitive emulsion to some photographic plates . . . and it worked. Not only that, but the plates had exposure times that were 20 times shorter than daguerreotypes (two minutes) or calotypes (one-and-a-half minutes). With good lighting, an exposure of just a few seconds would result in a good picture.

THE WET LOOK

The only drawback to the collodion process was that the photographic plates only worked while the collodion was still wet, because once it dried into its tough waterproof skin it was impervious to the developing chemicals. Photographers had to prepare their plates before they took photographs, and develop them immediately afterward. There was no time to waste.

That meant that a photographer had to bring all necessary equipment—chemicals, darkroom, and everything else—along for every picture. This, of course, was a huge hassle, but the "wet-plate process," as it came to be known, produced such beautiful photographs that it quickly passed the daguerreotype and the albumen calotype to become the most popular form of photography. It remained so for more than 30 years.

Now there was only one thing left that kept people from having their pictures taken: the price.

ACCENTUATE THE NEGATIVE

As he worked on his wet collodion process, Archer noticed that when he held one of his negatives against a black piece of paper, it didn't look like a negative—it looked like an ordinary photograph, very similar to a daguerreotype.

Archer made note of his observation, but didn't do much with it. But other photographers did—they grabbed the idea as a way to

There are 3,000 quintillion living things on this planet. Of these, 75 percent are bacteria.

make portraits cheaper. Why go to the trouble and expense of making a positive print, when a negative backed with black paper or some other dark material—soon to become known as an "ambrotype"—worked just as well?

In 1854 Boston photographer James Cutting patented an improved method of making ambrotypes and began selling them. Other photographers followed suit, and in the price war that followed, pressure from ambrotype photographers drove the price of a single daguerreotype from $5 down to 50 cents. Ambrotypes sold for as little as a dime, and though they were lower in quality they were much easier and quicker to produce: a person could pose for an ambrotype and receive the finished portrait in less than 10 minutes. Higher-quality daguerreotypes quickly began to lose ground to the speed and affordability of the ambrotype.

THE TINTYPE

If viewing a glass negative against a black background gave it the appearance of a photograph, why not just make the negative out of something black to begin with, like a thin sheet of tinned iron painted with black varnish? You'd get the same effect for less money because you would be leaving out the glass, which was expensive.

That's what Hamilton Smith was thinking when he invented what became known as the "tintype process" in 1856. Tintypes were cheap—they sold for a fraction of the cost of an ambrotype—and because they were made of iron they could take a lot of abuse. You could carry them in your pocket, send them through the mail, and collect them in photo albums. The images were still reversed, but with simple portraits no one seemed to mind.

As it turned out, you could even carry tintypes into war: in four years' time, Union and Confederate soldiers would bring tintypes of their loved ones with them into battle; between skirmishes they would line up outside the photographer's tent to pose for pictures of themselves to send back home.

MULTIPLE PERSONALITIES

As popular as they were, tintypes never came close to matching the craze of another type of photograph, the *carte-de-visite*. Invented by French photographer Andre Disdéri in 1854, the *carte-*

In the densest jungle, only one percent of sunlight ever reaches the forest floor.

de-visite was, like the ambrotype and the tintype, an extension of the collodion process. Disdéri's idea was to use a special camera with four lenses to divide a single large photograph into many smaller photographs. Some *carte-de-visite* cameras only let the subject pose for one photograph, which was then duplicated eight or more times; others allowed several poses. Either way the effect was the same: for the price of a single photograph, the customer got as many as 24.

Disdéri intended that the tiny pictures, which were printed on paper and backed by stiff cardboard, would serve as photo versions of traditional calling cards to be given as a memento of a visit with friends.

THE ROYAL TOUCH

Then in 1860, Queen Victoria, her husband Prince Albert, and their children posed for some *cartes-de-visite*. These images were the first photographs of the royal family ever commissioned for the public. They were sold individually, in sets, and in a book called the *Royal Album*. And they were hugely popular.

Photo studios took note. They started printing photographs of other famous people—Sarah Bernhardt, Abraham Lincoln, and Gen. Ulysses S. Grant among them—to see if they would sell. They did, prompting what came to be known as "cardomania." Cartes-de-visite covered a huge variety of subjects, including animals, politicians, military leaders, famous works of art, scenes of faraway places . . . even Barnum's circus freaks. Collectors bought them all. During the Civil War, people bought pictures of Maj. Robert Anderson, the hero of the battle of Fort Sumter, at a rate of 1,000 prints a day.

HOUSE OF CARDS

Cardomania was so powerful that it may be the reason the White House still stands in Washington D.C. The Founding Fathers never intended the White House to be a permanent presidential residence; it was just supposed to serve until something bigger and better would be built.

Few Americans had ever seen the White House, until Lincoln's assassination in 1865, when photos of the fallen president—as well as of the house where he had lived—circulated in great numbers.

Researchers have been able to teach ravens to count as high as six.

These popular images established the White House as a symbol of the presidency . . . and of the United States. After that, no one would have suggested tearing it down.

PICTURES, PICTURES, EVERYWHERE

After decades of development and innovation, photographs had become part of pop culture. They sold for only pennies apiece. People wore them as jewelry in brooches, lockets, and pocket watches. They projected them onto the walls of their homes using gas-lit "photographic lanterns" and drank from china cups decorated with photographic images fired into the porcelain. They bought picture postcards of the places they visited and mailed them home to friends.

Huge albums overflowing with photographs were as common a fixture in late-19th-century households as televisions are today. So were stereographs, double pictures about the size of postcards that, when viewed through a special viewer (like a View-Master), formed a single 3-D image. Portraits were still popular, too, especially now that photographers could retouch negatives to remove wrinkles, moles, and other blemishes.

Journalists incorporated photographs into news coverage, publishers pasted them into books, cartographers used them to improve maps, and Scotland Yard fought crime by photographing criminals for the first time. Photographs were everywhere.

LEAVE IT TO THE PROFESSIONALS

These pictures all had one thing in common: they were taken by professionals or by serious amateurs. If you wanted to be a photographer in the 1860s, you had to be a chemist, too. And you had to have a fair amount of money. This began to change in 1871, when a British physician named Richard Leach Maddox decided he'd had enough of the wet-plate process and started looking for something better.

Part VI of the photography story is on page 320.

Part VI of the photography story is on page 320.

* * *

"You don't take a photograph, you make it."

—**Ansel Adams**

Frank Lloyd Wright wore elevator shoes.

NUDE LAWSUITS

As The Peoples Court's Doug Llewellyn might say,
"If you're naked and angry, don't take matters into
your own hands. Take 'em to court."

THE PLAINTIFF: Two Philadelphia Eagles cheerleaders, identified in court papers as Jane Doe #1 and Jane Doe #2

THE DEFENDANTS: Twenty-three NFL teams who played games in Philadelphia between 1986 and 2000

THE LAWSUIT: The cheerleaders claim that for 15 years, visiting teams spied on Eagles cheerleaders in their dressing room by peeking through cracks in walls and doorways and even drilling holes in walls.

"These players viewed the Eagles cheerleaders in various stages of undress, including in complete nudity, when preparing for showering," the lawsuit alleges. "It was common knowledge among virtually the entire National Football League, while at the same time a carefully guarded secret, known only to the players and team employees." The women seek $150,000 from each team for "invasion of privacy, trespass, and intentional infliction of emotional distress."

THE VERDICT: Pending.

THE PLAINTIFF: Nicole Ferry, formerly an art major at the University of South Florida

THE DEFENDANT: The University of South Florida

THE LAWSUIT: In September 1999, Ferry attended a lecture on controversial art; one of the examples shown to the class was a suggestive photograph of a nude male posterior being embraced by female hands. Attending the lecture was optional—students were warned in advance that controversial art is controversial, and were told that they were free to skip class if they wanted to. Ferry attended the lecture anyway, was offended, and later filed a lawsuit against the school, alleging "sexual harassment."

THE VERDICT: USF settled the case for $25,000, but school officials insist the settlement is not an admission of wrongdoing. "For us as an institution, not to present that type of work would be something far more worthy of a lawsuit," said a spokesperson.

Central Africa has the largest variety of animals dangerous to man. Ireland has the smallest.

WHY ASK WHY?

Sometimes the answer is irrelevant—it's the question that counts.
These cosmic queries have been sent in by BRI readers.

Do hungry crows have ravenous appetites?

If a lawyer can be disbarred and clergymen defrocked, can electricians be delighted, musicians denoted, cowboys deranged, models deposed, and tree surgeons disembarked?

When cheese gets its picture taken, what does it say?

Why is *brassiere* singular and *panties* plural?

Why are builders afraid to have a 13th floor, but book publishers aren't afraid to have a chapter 11?

If a word is misspelled in a dictionary, how would we ever know?

Why is it that writers write but grocers don't groce and hammers don't ham?

Why do "slow down" and "slow up" mean the same thing?

Why doesn't onomatopoeia sound like what it is?

Why do *fat chance* and *slim chance* mean the same thing?

If humans evolved from monkeys and apes, why do we still have monkeys and apes?

How can the weather be hot as hell one day and cold as hell another?

Why doesn't glue stick to the inside of the bottle?

Why don't you ever see the headline "Psychic Wins Lottery"?

Why is it called *lipstick* if you can still move your lips?

When you lose your temper, shouldn't that mean that you get happy?

If someone is deceased, did they just come back from the dead?

How do you get off a non-stop flight?

If blind people wear dark glasses, why don't deaf people wear earmuffs?

Lewis Carroll wrote *Alice's Adventures in Wonderland* standing up.

FAMILY FEUD

You can't always get along with everyone in your family,
but these guys just out and out declared war on each other.

HAFT VS. HAFT VS. HAFT
The Contestants: Herbert Haft, who bought his first drug-store in 1955; his wife, Gloria; their daughter Linda; and their sons Robert and Ronald.

The Feud: Over the years Herbert Haft built his single drugstore into a huge regional chain called Dart Drugs. He also built up the Trak Auto chain of auto parts stores and Consolidated Properties Inc., the family's real estate division, all of which were part of the Dart Group conglomerate.

In the 1970s, he invited his sons into the business. Robert signed on in 1977 and founded Crown Books. He became famous as the chain's spokesman, telling TV viewers, "If you paid full price, you didn't buy it at Crown Books." By 1993 the Dart Group was worth more than $500 million . . . but it wouldn't be for long.

In June 1993, *The Wall Street Journal* published an article that speculated that Robert Haft was the child most likely to take over as head of the family business when Herbert retired. The article infuriated Herbert—he saw it as his "business obituary"—and he responded by firing Robert, Linda, and even Gloria from the company. He and Ronald tried to run the Dart Group together but were soon at each others' throats. In September 1994, four outside directors seized control of the Dart Group in an attempt to save it from the feuding Hafts.

They were too late. By the time the smoke cleared, Dart Group was no more. Consolidated Properties Inc. filed for bankruptcy in 1995, and Crown Books went under in 1998. (Herbert and Gloria's marriage was another casualty—they divorced in 1994 after 45 years of marriage.)

And the Winner Is: Nobody. As of February 2000, Herbert and Robert were still duking it out, this time with dot.com drugstores. Robert founded Vitamins.com; Herbert runs HealthQuick.com. Says Herbert, "I wish Robert well."

Of the 80,000 known species of plants, only 50 are cultivated regularly.

WHY IS *CITIZEN KANE* THE MOST IMPORTANT MOVIE OF ALL TIME?

In 2000, Kane was voted the best film of all time by the American Film Institute. Good choice. Here's why.

BACKGROUND

When *Citizen Kane* premiered on May 1, 1941, the *New York Times* film critic called it "far and away the most surprising and cinematically exciting motion picture in many a moon. As a matter of fact, it comes close to being the most sensational film ever made in Hollywood."

But in early 1941 it seemed like the film would never even make it to the theaters, let alone win public acclaim. Newspaper baron William Randolph Hearst, the inspiration for the film's main character, Charles Foster Kane, waged a no-holds-barred campaign to destroy the film. He offered RKO president George Schaefer $800,000 to burn the negative and all the prints in a bonfire; Schaefer refused. When that failed, Hearst tried to prevent it from being widely released.

For the most part, he succeeded. Because of Hearst's influence the major theater chains refused to book it, forcing *Kane* to premiere in smaller, independent theaters. The film was a commercial flop, and Orson Welles—the genius who made it—never recovered from the disaster. RKO never again gave him the artistic freedom he'd had in making *Citizen Kane*, and most of his later film projects were commercial flops.

RESURRECTION

To the few who saw *Citizen Kane* in its initial run, it was a masterpiece. To the rest of America, it was quickly forgotten. As Harlan Lebo writes in *Citizen Kane: The Fiftieth Anniversary Album*,

> Through 1950, *Citizen Kane* played here and there, principally in the scattered revival theaters in larger cities that showed "oldies." But that was all. *Citizen Kane* disappeared in the United States almost entirely, and it didn't emerge again for more than five years.

Why is honey so easy to digest? Because it has already been digested by the bee.

In the United States, *Citizen Kane* finally reappeared in 1956—on television. And there it developed a following. "Its time had finally come with the general audience," Lebo writes. "Several polls of film fans placed *Citizen Kane* at the top of the picks of screen favorites."

Citizen Kane's TV showings also made it a hit with a new generation of film critics. Over the next several years, the film's stature continued to grow. In 1962 the British magazine *Sight and Sound* released a critics' poll of the best films of all time. *Citizen Kane* was #1.

WHAT'S THE BIG DEAL?

In a world where no one can agree on anything, most serious critics seem to agree that *Citizen Kane* is the best film ever made. Why?

For one thing, "talkies" had only been around for 14 years when *Kane* made its debut, and in that time filmmaking had become predictable. Virtually all movies used the same stale camera angles, the same lighting, and the same types of sets. *Citizen Kane* broke all the rules. It introduced avant-garde storytelling and cinematography methods to Hollywood. And the film was crafted with Welles' incredible attention to detail, from the music to the lighting.

INNOVATIVE FILMMAKING

- Before *Citizen Kane*, most films were organized chronologically: they began at the beginning and ended at the end. Kane famously begins at the end, when a dying Charles Foster Kane whispers "Rosebud." From there the film moves back to Kane's childhood, and tells the story of his life . . . from the perspectives of five different people. Welles explains: "They tell five different stories, each biased, so that the truth about Kane, like the truth about any man, can only be calculated, by the sum of everything that has been said about him."

- Welles also compressed much of Kane's life story into a fictional newsreel segment that was incredibly realistic for its time. Editor Robert Wise blended 127 different clips of film into the newsreel: Some were clips of actual news footage, others were staged shots of Welles and other actors. Wise "aged" the new footage by dragging the negatives across a concrete floor, giving them authentic-looking scrapes.

- In another famous sequence, Welles illustrates the breakdown of Kane's first marriage with a montage of scenes of Kane and

Liza Minnelli, daughter of Judy Garland, married Jack Haley, Jr., the . . .

his wife at the breakfast table. The first shot shows the newly-weds madly in love with each other; over the next several scenes, they age gradually, denoting the passage of time, and become increasingly distant. In the last scene, they sit at opposite ends of a long table in stony silence. The sequence is less than three minutes long, but it took six weeks to put together.

- Welles and cinematographer Gregg Toland spent weeks setting up *Citizen Kane's* scenes and planning camera angles. "This is un-conventional in Hollywood," Toland wrote in *Popular Photography* in 1941, "where most cinematographers learn of their next assignments only a few days before the scheduled shooting starts."

- Toland used "deep-focus" camera techniques, including special film, lenses, and lighting developed especially for *Citizen Kane*, that made everything on screen appear in focus at the same time, an unheard-of practice in Hollywood. "The normal human eye sees everything before it clearly and sharply," Toland wrote. "But Hollywood cameras focus on a center of interest and allow the other components of a scene to 'fuzz out' . . . The attainment of approximate human-eye focus was one of our fundamental aims . . . in some cases we were able to hold sharp focus over a depth of 200 feet."

MUSICAL SCORE

It was no accident that the musical score fit the film like a glove. Unlike other films, *Citizen Kane* and its music were created side by side. "I worked on the film, reel by reel, as it was being shot and cut," composer Bernard Herrmann wrote in 1941. "Most musical scores are written after the film is entirely finished, and the composer must adapt his music to the scenes on the screen. In many scenes in *Citizen Kane*, an entirely different method was used, many of the sequences being tailored to match the music."

MAKEUP

Since the story takes place over 50 years, the actors age greatly throughout the film; Kane, for example, ages from 25 to 78. Makeup artist Maurice Seiderman invented many techniques to age the characters in the film. Rather than just cover Welles with latex wrinkles and gray hair, he made a complete body cast and

. . . son of Jack Haley, who played the Tin Man in *The Wizard of Oz*.

used it to create custom-fitting body pads and facial appliances that show Kane aging gradually over 27 different stages of his life.

The level of detail is astonishing: Welles wore special milky, bloodshot contact lenses to make his eyes look old, and 72 different facial appliances, including hairlines, cheeks, jowls, bags under his eyes, and 16 different chins. Some pieces even had artificial pores that matched those in Welles's own skin.

CEILINGS

If you look for ceilings in most movie scenes, you won't find them. The powerful lamps needed to light a scene are usually hung above the set, where a ceiling would normally go. But scenes in Citizen Kane used a cloth canopy that simulated an actual ceiling. "The sets have ceilings," Toland wrote, "because we wanted reality, and we felt it would be easier to believe a room was a room if its ceiling could be seen in the picture. Furthermore, lighting effects in unceilinged rooms generally are not realistic because the illumination comes from unnatural angles." Since ceiling lights were not possible, most shots were lit using floor lights.

ACTING

- Most of the actors in Citizen Kane, Welles included, had never been in a movie before. They had only appeared on stage and on radio as members of Welles's Mercury Theater company. They were not a part of the Hollywood culture and did not feel bound by the conventions of 1940s filmmaking.

- Citizen Kane had almost no close-up shots of the actors, which were extremely common at the time. But the Mercury actors were used to performing with the audience at a distance. Welles was afraid their exaggerated gestures and boisterous theatrical acting style—which were calculated to be seen and heard in the most distant seats of a large theater—would look artificial at close range. So he left the close-ups out.

FINAL WORD

"Fifty years later, Citizen Kane is as fresh, as provoking, as entertaining, as funny, as sad and as brilliant as it ever was. Many agree it is the greatest film of all time. Those who differ cannot seem to agree on their candidate."

—**film critic Roger Ebert**

IT'S A WEIRD, WEIRD WORLD

More proof that truth really is stranger than fiction.

I'M NOT DEAD YET

TOPEKA, Kansas—"A 53-year-old Kansas woman reportedly shot herself in the head and then called 911 for help. Firefighters found her unconscious and assumed she was dead, without checking for a pulse. An ambulance was cancelled, and firefighters and deputies waited outside the home to protect it as a crime scene. Meanwhile, the woman regained consciousness and called 911 again. Firefighters outside the home were told of the call and rushed inside to provide medical care."

—*Bizarre News*

ADDING INSULT TO INJURY

"A 51-year-old London man, out of work 14 weeks with broken ribs after being hit by a bus, was billed $850 for damage to the bus."

—*Funny Times*

COME TOGETHER . . .

"In one of the strangest alliances ever, members of the Pagans Motorcycle Club allegedly conspired with some young Amish men to sell cocaine to Amish youth groups. According to their plan, the drugs were to be sold during hoedowns."

—*Wacky News*

N IS FOR NUTJOB

"Prominent Vermont hunter Thomas Venezia, 41, was finally brought to justice after several shooting sprees, marauding through Canadian woods. An undercover agent quoted Venezia after one illegal shooting: 'I have the K chromosome. I love to kill. I have to kill.' Once, Venezia spontaneously leaped from a truck and started firing at ducks, then later at pigeons because, he said, he had gone an hour without killing anything. At a hearing in Saskatoon, Saskatchewan, Venezia, sobbing, admitted the incidents and was

---

Devon is the only county in Great Britain that has two coasts.

permanently barred from Canada. However, he remains licensed to hunt in Vermont."

—*News of the Weird*

KINDERGARTEN COPS

"Children at a kindergarten in Nelson, New Zealand, are now required to carry a pretend weapon permit if they want to carry a pretend weapon to play pretend cops and robbers."

—*"Quick Takes," Chicago Sun-Times*

AWW, YEAH BABY

"According to Sasquatch researcher David Shealy, who also owns an RV park in Ochopee, Florida, love is in the air for a Florida Bigfoot known as the 'skunk ape.' Shealy claims as many as nine of the creatures roam the Everglades, and reports their love calls sound 'something like Barry White doing a dove call.'"

— *"The Edge," The Oregonian*

HOLE IN THE HEAD

"Poet William Adrian Milton, 59, told reporters that his recent CAT scan revealed to his complete surprise that he had a bullet in his head. Searching his memory, Milton recalled a 1976 incident in which he wandered too close to a street fight, heard a noise, and was knocked down. He said he staggered home bloody and went to bed, but failed to seek medical treatment because the bleeding soon stopped and the remaining lump was consistent with being hit by a brick. Milton said he'll leave the bullet there."

—*New York Post*

SWING YOUR TRACTOR . . .

"Eight farmers in the town of Nemaha, Iowa, have taught themselves to perform various square-dancing routines (do-si-dos, promenades, etc.) on their tractors. However, since all the farmers are men and square-dancing is a couples activity, four of the dancers operate their tractors while dressed in calico skirts."

—**Universal Press Syndicate**

The average American ate the equivalent of 23 whole chickens in 2000.

THE NAME GAME

Did you hate your name when you were growing up? Maybe that's because you didn't know what it means. See if you can match the following names with their meanings.

NAME	MEANING
1) George	a. God is gracious
2) Amy	b. Farmer
3) Michael	c. Beloved
4) Barbara	d. Lovable
5) Daniel	e. Bright fame
6) Edward	f. Bee
7) Amanda	g. Foreign
8) Henry	h. Lily
9) Joel	i. God is God
10) Susan	j. Beautiful
11) Linda	k. God is my judge
12) Melissa	l. Grace
13) Ann	m. Ruler of the home
14) Robert	n. Rich guard
15) Stephen	o. Who is like God
16) John	p. Crown

Answers:

10. h, 11. j, 12. f, 13. l, 14. e, 15. p, 16. a

1. b, 2. c, 3. o, 4. g, 5. k, 6. n, 7. d, 8. m, 9. i,

For more info about the answers, see page 745.

For more info about the answers, see page 745.

Ladybugs are named after the Virgin Mary; they used to be called "Beetles of Our Lady."

DISGUSTING FACTS

*With a title like this one, you can't help yourself . . . you have
to read this page. These facts really are disgusting, but, well,
now you have something to share as dinner conversation.*

The average human foot has about 20,000 sweat glands and can produce as much as half a cup of sweat each day.

Cockroaches can flatten themselves almost to the thinness of a piece of paper in order to slide into tiny cracks, can be frozen for weeks and then thawed with no ill effect, and can also withstand 126 g's of pressure with no problem (people get squished at 18 g's).

Most of the dust in your house is made up of dead human skin cells—every day, millions of them float off your body and settle on furniture and floors.

The average municipal water treatment plant processes enough human waste every day to fill 72 Olympic-sized swimming pools.

According to a recent survey, over 10 percent of Americans have picked someone else's nose.

Most people generally fart between 10 and 20 times a day, expelling enough gas to inflate a small balloon.

Your mouth slows production of bacteria-fighting saliva when you sleep, which allows the 10 billion bacteria in your mouth to reproduce all night; "morning breath" is actually bacterial B.O.

Tears are made up of almost the exact same ingredients as urine.

Leeches have mouths with three sets of jaws and between 60 to 100 teeth.

A tapeworm can grow to a length of 30 feet inside human intestines.

The crusty goop you find in your eyes when you wake up is the exact same mucus you find in your nose—boogers.

Spiders don't eat their prey; they paralyze the victim with venom, vomit a wad of acidic liquid onto them, and then drink the dissolved body.

The average person will produce 25,000 quarts of saliva in a lifetime—enough to fill up two swimming pools.

Three out of every four creatures living on Earth are insects.

CIRCUS SLANG

Uncle John was at the circus earlier this summer, when it occurred to him that circus performers probably have their own language. Well, it turns out they do. Here's a list of his favorite terms.

Clown Alley: The dressing area for the clowns.

Blow Off: Immediately following the end of a performance, when the crowd mills out of the tent and onto the midway.

Butcher: A concessionaire who sells food—hot dogs, sodas, ice cream, etc.—to the audience.

Dry Butcher: A butcher who sells toys and souvenirs.

Groundhog: A slow butcher.

Greyhound: A fast butcher.

Razorbacks: The workers who set up the big tents.

Roustabout: A laborer for the circus.

Deemer: A dime; 10 cents.

Mud Show: A small circus or carnival.

Cloud Swing: Aerial act performed on a loop of rope suspended from the top of the tent.

Kinker: Any circus performer.

Grease Joint: A food stand.

Grubers: Peanuts.

Spool Truck: Truck that carries the tent canvas.

Joey: Any clown, after Joseph Grimaldi's character, Joey.

Fine Ways: Twenty-five cents.

The Disaster March: "Stars and Stripes Forever" (see "Circus Superstitions," page 130).

Fancy Pants: The master of ceremonies (often incorrectly referred to as the *ringmaster*).

First of May: A rookie on the circus.

John Robinson: A shortened performance.

Pie Car: Place where circus people eat. Also *cookhouse*.

Risley: An acrobatic act in which one person juggles another on their feet.

Cherry Pie: Extra work for extra pay.

Home Sweet Home: Last show of the season.

Straw House: A sold-out performance.

Windjammer: Circus musician.

Twenty-Four-Hour Man: The scout who plans the route to the next town and determines where the circus will be set up.

Q: How many hair follicles on an average adult? A: 5 million.

THREE'S COMPANY

Critics called Three's Company *"mindless" and "smarmy."
But it was one of the longest running and highest rated shows
in TV history. We're not sure why, either, but here's the story.*

COME AND KNOCK ON OUR DOOR

You might not know it, but two popular American TV shows were actually rip-offs of British sitcoms: *All in the Family* is an Americanized version of *Till Death Do Us Part*, and *Sanford and Son* is a copy of *Steptoe & Son*.

Donald Taffner, U.S. representative for Thames Television, wanted to export other shows for American audiences so he hooked up with American TV executive Ted Bergmann. In 1975 Bergmann took a Thames hit, *Man About the House*, to the networks. ABC's programming chief, Fred Silverman, ordered a pilot.

He advised Bergmann to get an experienced television writer, and he found one in Larry Gelbart, developer of the TV show M*A*S*H. Gelbart declined at first, but an unprecedented offer of $50,000 convinced him. Gelbart devised characters in their late 20s who were intelligent and witty: David Bell, an aspiring filmmaker; Jenny, a witty brunette who worked at the DMV; and Samantha—Sam for short—a cute blonde model aspiring to be an actress. And of course there was a landlord, George Roper, and his sex-starved wife, Mildred.

FALSE START

But Gelbart's pilot didn't make the 1976 fall season lineup— Silverman wanted the show recast. He'd already picked John Ritter for the male lead. A relatively unknown Norman Fell was cast as the nosy landlord, with veteran actress Audra Lindley as Mildred. But the original female leads were fired and another pilot was ordered.

Before moving to ABC, Silverman was president of CBS Entertainment. So Silverman got NRW Company, producers of *All in the Family* and *The Jeffersons*, to develop *Three's Company*. He instructed them to make it "the same kind of breakthrough in sexiness that *All in the Family* was in bigotry."

NRW renamed the roommates and gave them ordinary jobs that people could relate to: David Bell became cooking student Jack Tripper; civil servant Jenny became florist Janet Wood, played by Joyce DeWitt; and aspiring actress Sam became naive jiggle queen Christmas Snow—Chrissy for short—played by an unknown Suzanne Somers.

A SMASH HIT

The show premiered on March 15, 1977 and ABC's ratings immediately went through the roof: *Three's Company* ranked #11 among all the network shows for the 1976–77 season. Combined with *Happy Days* and *Laverne & Shirley*, the show made ABC's Tuesday-night lineup the most-watched night on TV from 1977 to 1980.

The success of *Three's Company* astounded ABC execs. It broke ratings records, even beating CBS's M*A*S*H, a feat no other show could accomplish. But critics hated it. *The New York Times* suggested that a blank television screen was better than tuning in to the show.

THE KISSES ARE HERS, HERS, HERS!

In February 1978, the same week that *Three's Company* hit #1 in ratings, *Newsweek* magazine did a feature on the trio that would forever mar the ensemble's relationship. The article reported that the National Religious Broadcasters was lobbying against the show's "immoral programming." But it wasn't the negative publicity that bothered Ritter and DeWitt, it was the cover—featuring Suzanne Somers most prominently, with the two others behind her.

The veteran actors feared that Somers was compromising the cooperative effort to secure her own stardom. She was being aggressively marketed by her star-maker agent, Jay Bernstein—who had helped launch Farrah Fawcett's career—and began hawking hammers for Ace Hardware, posing for *Playboy* (twice), and performing in Las Vegas and Atlantic City. But when she fired Bernstein in 1980 so hubby Alan Hamel could take over, it was the beginning of the end. "After that, it all went to hell in a handbasket," said Ted Bergmann. "Hamel was about as ill-equipped to do the job as anybody could be."

The husband-and-wife team pushed for more money: they

... and Halsted Streets in Chicago. It has to be emptied six times a day.

wanted $150,000 per episode, the same amount Alan Alda was getting for M*A*S*H, and demanded part ownership of the show. Somers believed she was the secret of the show's success, but the producers said it was the pratfalling Ritter . . . and he was only getting $50,000 an episode.

CHRISTMAS PAST

So Somers went on strike—she didn't show up for work, claiming "back injuries," which infuriated her co-stars. Then she threatened to sue the producers and her on-screen roommates for conspiracy. Negotiations crumbled, and by the time Somers did return to work, the producers had had it—they wanted to get rid of her.

But ABC execs feared ratings would drop if the jiggle queen was dropped completely, so her role was cut to one minute a week. Chrissy suddenly went away to care for her sick mother. Somers was secluded to a small set, where Chrissy talked to Janet on the telephone from her mother's. Slowly and quietly, Chrissy Snow was phased out of the show.

Somers left the show in 1981, but it proved a costly mistake: She walked away from $4.5 million in residuals, and DeWitt and Ritter wouldn't even speak to her.

WE'VE BEEN WAITING FOR YOU

Somers's replacement, ex-L.A. Rams cheerleader Jenilee Harrison, played Chrissy's country cousin, Cindy Snow, and the writers tried to develop her character without using the trademark suggestive jokes. Bad move: ratings dropped. Harrison was dropped, too.

A new blonde was brought in to facilitate the dirty talk. As Terri Alden, Priscilla Barnes gave *Three's Company* the shot in the arm it needed to regain its #1 status. But the success was short-lived: the producers didn't want to repeat the experience they had had with Somers, so they didn't let the writers develop Barnes's character. Another bad move. The show couldn't sustain its ratings, and ABC cancelled it.

The one-hour series finale aired on May 15, 1984 as a hurried attempt to provide closure to the millions of viewers who had watched the show and the characters develop over the years. Janet married her boyfriend Phillip, Jack fell in love with their neighbor Vicky, and Terri moved to Hawaii to care for sick children.

Female rabbits can mate as early as 12 hours after giving birth.

WHERE ARE THEY NOW?

John Ritter went on to star in more than 20 TV projects, including the spin-off bomb, *Three's a Crowd*. He also appeared in motion pictures, most notably Billy Bob Thornton's *Sling Blade*. He passed away in 2003. Joyce DeWitt dropped out of sight after *Three's Company*, going on a 13-year spiritual odyssey around the world.

Audra Lindley and Norman Fell were lured off *Three's Company* to star in their own show, *The Ropers*. They left at the height of *Three's Company's* popularity; *The Ropers* flopped after a single season. Throughout the 1980s, Fell worked steadily in supporting roles on the big and small screens. Lindley returned to the stage and made guest television appearances on *Friends* and *Cybill*. She died of complications from leukemia in 1997. Fell died of natural causes the following year.

When Fell and Lindley left *Three's Company*, they were replaced by Don Knotts. Knotts played the leisure suit–wearing bachelor, Mr. Furley, and the audience loved him. The producers actually had to edit Knotts's lines because his laughs were so long. After *Three's Company*, Knotts made several films, including *Return to Mayberry*.

And Suzanne Somers? The networks wouldn't touch her for almost a decade after her battle with ABC. She rehabilitated herself as a bankable commodity when she became the spokesperson for the ThighMaster exerciser in 1990. The attention landed her the lead in the sitcom *Step By Step* in 1991 and a job as co-host of *Candid Camera* in 1998. But since then she's been marketing a line of exercise equipment—the FaceMaster and the ButtMaster.

* * *

A PLACE-NAME ORIGIN

"California was named by the Spanish, not from their language but from their literature. In 1510 Garcia Rodriquez de Montalvo wrote a book entitled *Sergas de Esplandian (Feats of Esplandian)*, in which he created the imaginary realm of *California*: an island ruled by Black Amazons 'at the right hand of the Indies . . . very close to that of the Terrestrial Paradise.' When the first Spaniards arrived in the southern portion of California in the 1530s, they believed it to be an island and so called it *California*." (From *Inventing English: The Imaginative Origins of Everyday Expressions*, by Dale Corey)

One out of every 14 women in America is a natural blonde (and one out of every 16 men).

THE PRICE WAS RIGHT

You've heard people talk about how much things cost back in the "good ol' days"—heck, you might even remember them yourself (Uncle John does). Talk about nostalgia . . . check out these prices.

IN 1900:

Seven-shot revolver: $1.25

Bicycle: $20

Grand piano: $175

Men's leather belt: 19¢

Alligator bag: $5

IN 1910:

All-expenses-paid trip to Bermuda for nine days: $37.50

Bottle of Coke: 5¢

Imported spaghetti: 12¢/box

Cigarettes: 10¢/pack

Wage for postal workers: 42¢/hr.

IN 1920:

Life insurance premium: $16.40/yr.

Chocolates: 89¢/lb.

Eggs: 64¢/doz.

Box of 50 cigars: $2.98

Public school teacher's salary: $970/yr.

IN 1930:

Christmas tree light set (eight bulbs): 88¢

Electric toaster: $1

Motor oil: 49¢/gal.

Washing machine: $58

IN 1940:

Coffeemaker: $2

Movie ticket: 25¢ (day); 40¢ (night)

Golf balls: $1.88/doz.

Bayer aspirin: 59¢

Minimum wage: 30¢/hr.

IN 1950:

Jackie Robinson's salary ('51): $39,750/yr.

Roll of film: 38¢

Toilet paper (20 rolls): $2.39

Corvette ('53): $3,498

Combination 19" television/FM radio/phonograph: $495

IN 1960:

Refrigerator: $200

Polaroid Camera: $100

Mercedes Benz 220S: $3,300

Breakfast (two hot cakes and two strips of bacon): 33¢

Clearasil: 98¢/tube

IN 1970:

Answering machine: $50

Sirloin steak: 97¢/lb.

Tennis racket: $25

Movie projector: $80

Orange juice: 35¢/qt.

IN 1980:

Cordless telephone: $300

Six-pack of Budweiser: $1.99

Video camera: $360

Cadillac El Dorado: $19,700

Herbert Hoover never accepted his presidential salary.

AMERICAN CANNIBAL

A previous Bathroom Reader included an "Oops!" about a government cafeteria named after Alferd Packer. After our friend Jeff Cheek read it, he sent us this amazing story.

A DUBIOUS DISTINCTION

Alferd G. Packer holds a unique spot in American jurisprudence. He is the only U.S. citizen ever charged, tried, and convicted for the crime of murder and cannibalism.

Born in rural Colorado in 1847, Packer drifted into the Utah Territory, supporting himself as a small-time con artist, claiming to be an experienced "mountain man." In the fall of 1873, he persuaded 20 greenhorns in Salt Lake City to grubstake an expedition to the headwaters of the Gunnison River in Colorado Territory. He swore that the stream was full of gold and promised to lead the party to it if they would finance the operation.

GOLD FEVER

With Packer leading, they plunged into the San Juan Mountains and promptly got lost. The party was near starvation when they stumbled into the winter quarters of the friendly Ute tribe. The Indians nursed them back to health, but the leader, Chief Ouray, advised them to turn back. Winter snows had blocked all trails. Ten of the party listened and returned to Utah. The other 10, still believing Packer's tales of gold-filled creeks, stayed with him.

Ouray gave them supplies and advised them to follow the river upstream for safety, but Packer ignored this counsel and plunged back into the mountains. The party split up again. Five turned back and made their way to the Los Pinos Indian Agency. Fired up with gold fever, the others continued on with their con man guide. Days later, exhausted, half frozen, and out of food, they found refuge in a deserted cabin. Most of them were now ready to give up and go back to Salt Lake City.

The exception was Alferd Packer. He was broke, and returning to Salt Lake City would cost him his grubstake. When the others fell asleep, Packer shot four of them in the head. The fifth woke and tried to defend himself, but Packer cracked his skull with the barrel of his rifle. Then, he robbed them . . . He also used them for food.

Most Americans say that if they had to resort to cannibalism, "they'd eat the legs first."

When his strength returned, he packed enough "human jerky" to get back to the Los Pinos Agency. Several miles from the agency, he emptied his pack to conceal his crime. He was welcomed by General Adams, commander of the agency, but shocked everyone by asking for whiskey instead of food. When he flashed a huge bankroll, they started asking questions.

WELL, YOU SEE, OFFICER . . .

Packer's explanations were vague and contradictory. First, he claimed he was attacked by natives, then he claimed that some of his party had gone mad and attacked him. On April 4, 1874, two of Chief Ouray's braves found the human remains Packer had discarded. General Adams locked him up and dispatched a lawman named Lauter to the cabin to investigate. But while Lauter was away, Packer managed to escape.

He made his way back to Utah and lived quietly for 10 years as "John Schwartze," until a member of the original party recognized him. Packer was arrested on March 12, 1884 and returned to Lake City, Colorado, for trial.

Packer claimed innocence but as the evidence against him mounted, he finally confessed. Apparently, he reveled in the attention his trial gave him and even lectured on the merits of human flesh. The best "human jerky," he said, was the meat on the chest ribs. The judge was not impressed.

"Alferd G. Packer, you no good sonofabitch, there wasn't but seven Democrats in Hinsdale County, and you done et five of 'um," he thundered. "You're gonna hang by the neck until dead!"

SAVED BY A TECHNICALITY

His lawyer appealed the decision, citing a legal loophole. The crime was committed in 1873, in the *territory* of Colorado. The trial began in 1884, in the new *state* of Colorado. The state constitution, adopted in 1876, did not address such a heinous crime, so the charge was reduced to manslaughter and Packer was sentenced to 40 years in prison. He was a model prisoner and was paroled after 16 years. Freed in 1901, he found work as a wrangler on a ranch near Denver.

On April 21, 1907, Alferd G. Packer, horse wrangler and cannibal, died quietly in his sleep.

What was John Tyler doing when he was informed that Pres. William Henry Harrison . . .

OOPS!

*It's comforting to know that other people are screwing
up even worse than we are. So go ahead and
feel superior for a few minutes.*

LIGHT MY FIRE

JERUSALEM—"It was, to say the least, a very unfortunate mistake. German chancellor Gerhard Schroeder accidentally extinguished Israel's eternal memorial flame for the six million Jews killed in the Nazi Holocaust.

"At a somber ceremony in Jerusalem's Yad Vashem Holocaust Memorial, Schroeder turned a handle that was supposed to make the flame rise. It went out instead. Israeli prime minister Ehud Barak stepped forward to try to help, but was unsuccessful. Finally, a technician used a gas lighter to bring the flame to life again, but by then the damage had been done."

—**Reuters**

REAL-LIFE LESSON

"A Grand Rapids, Minnesota, SWAT team, scheduled a drill at a local high school with actors and actresses playing the part of terrorists. But they mistakenly stormed another school next door. One of the teachers terrorized in the 'raid' said she was sure she was about to be killed as she was led from the building at gunpoint by the officers, who never identified themselves."

—**Bonehead of the Day**

SANTA CROOK

PHILADELPHIA—"Construction workers recently did a 'chimney sweep' of a vacant building and found the remains of a serial burglar who had tried to rob the place several years ago. According to Detective Romonita King, workers were knocking down the chimney Saturday when they smelled a foul odor. On closer inspection, they noticed a pair of sneakers, jeans, a Phillies cap, and what appeared to be human remains. The medical examiner's office tentatively listed the cause of death as accidental compression asphyxia. It was reported that the remains could be at least five years old and it was not known how long the business—ironically, a theft-prevention business—was closed."

—*Bizarre News*

THREE STRIKES, YOU'RE OUT

"Lorenzo Trippi, a lifeguard in Ravenna, Italy, lost his job when three people drowned after he hit them with life preservers. Police said his aim was too accurate."

—*Strange World #2*

HOE NO!

"Leonard Fountain, 68, got so fed up with having his gardening tools stolen from his shed that he rigged a homemade shotgun booby trap by the door. A year later, he was in a hurry to get some pruning done and opened the door, forgetting about the modification. He received severe flesh wounds to his right knee and thigh from the ensuing blast, and was charged with illegal possession of firearms."

—*Stuff* magazine

THE YOUNG AND THE WRESTLESS

TACOMA, Wash.—"A seven-year-old boy practicing wrestling moves he had seen on TV bounced off his bed and tumbled out a second-story window. The boy sustained minor cuts and bruises after smashing through the bedroom window and tumbling two stories onto a cushion of grass. 'He was jumping from the dresser and doing a back-flip to the bed and went straight out the window,' said his mother.

"The boy was treated for minor internal injuries and hospitalized in satisfactory condition Friday. 'It hurts to wrestle,' he said. 'I'm not doing any more wrestling moves.'"

—*CNN Fringe*

* * *

"I watched the Indy 500 and I was thinking—if they left earlier they wouldn't have to go so fast."

—**Steven Wright**

The only fish that swims upright: the seahorse.

THE LOST CITIES

Everyone fantasizes about accidentally uncovering a treasure.
Pompeii and Herculaneum were such treasures. They existed for
a thousand years until, in one brief moment, they disappeared.
Here's the story of how they were lost . . . and found.

VESUVIUS BLOWS

Two thousand years ago, the prosperous cities of Pompeii and Herculaneum thrived near Rome, 10 miles from the foot of the volcano Mount Vesuvius. Vesuvius hadn't exploded for over 1,000 years; no one even knew it was a volcano. Then on August 24 in the year 79 A.D., it erupted, completely burying both cities under mountains of ash. Pompeii and Herculaneum were lost.

Mount Vesuvius continued to erupt sporadically over the centuries that followed, each time adding to the volcanic debris that covered the former town sites; each layer leaving the two cities more hidden than before. Four hundred years later, the Roman Empire collapsed, and legends about the two lost cities went with it. For 15 centuries, they lay forgotten and undisturbed, their stories untold. Then clues about their existence began to turn up. For example, around 1594, a Roman architect named Domenico Fontana was digging a canal to supply water to a rich man's home when workmen uncovered pieces of ruined buildings and a few ancient coins. But nothing much came of the discovery.

RUMORS OF TREASURE

In 1707 part of Italy came under Austrian rule, and Prince d'Elboeuf came to command the cavalry. He heard rumors of treasures being brought up from underground, so he promptly purchased a large parcel of land in the immediate vicinity. Over the next 30 years, he had shafts and tunnels dug and uncovered vases, statues, and even a number of polished marble slabs (once the floor of the theater in Herculaneum) all of which he used to decorate his villa.

Word of the prince's finds spread and other treasure hunters came looking. When the first skeleton—complete with bronze and silver coins—was unearthed in 1748, treasure fever hit hard. For

---

A museum dedicated to nuts in Old Lyme, Connecticut, also has the world's largest nutcracker.

the next several years, artifacts were continually looted from the area. But it wasn't until 1763, when workers unearthed an inscription reading *"res publica Pompeianorum"*—meaning "the commonwealth of Pompeians"—that the ancient city was identified.

SAVED AT LAST

The looting of Pompeii and Herculaneum continued for 100 years until a new ruler, King Victor Emmanuel II, became interested in preserving the sites. In 1860 he put archaeologist Giuseppe Fiorelli in charge of excavations. From that time until the present, the treasures of Pompeii have been treated with the care and respect they deserve, and, in turn, they have taught much about daily life in ancient times.

Ironically, the explosion of Vesuvius occurred the day after the annual celebration of Volcanalia, festival of the Roman god of volcanic fire. When Vesuvius began quaking, spouting ash, and spewing rivers of lava on August 23, 79 A.D., most of Pompeii's 20,000 inhabitants fled the area. For the next 12 hours, ash and pumice rained down on the town, accumulating at the rate of six inches per hour. About 2,000 people remained in the city. Perhaps they refused to abandon their treasures. Or possibly they were slaves ordered to stay behind. Early in the morning of August 24, Vesuvius really blew its top. By then, it was too late.

GHOSTS

Crouching, crawling, and clinging to loved ones, the people were buried by ash, which perfectly preserved their positions at the moment of death. When rain came, the layer of ash turned to concrete, entombing the bodies in an undisturbed environment. The bodies themselves then slowly decayed. When archaeologist Fiorelli found the hollow cavities where the bodies had once been, he realized that by pumping wet plaster into what were essentially molds and letting it harden, he could make perfect casts of the dead.

A beggar with a new pair of shoes died at the city gate. Perhaps he had recently swiped the shoes from a corpse. The owners of a house were hiding their valuables in their well when they fell in and died. A dog was still chained up to a fence. A woman held an infant in her arms while two young girls clung to the hem of her dress. A man was trying to pull a goat by its halter outside the city wall. Thirty-four people were hiding in a wine vault with food that they never got a chance to eat.

A man, seeking refuge in a tree, died holding a branch. A young girl clutched a statue of a goddess. A man, lying next to a woman seven months pregnant, reached out to cover her face with his robe in the moment before death. A group of priests were about to sit down to a meal of eggs and fish. One of the priests had a hatchet and chopped his way from room to room as lava rushed after him. He was trapped in the last room, which had walls too thick to chop through. The remains of a woman were found next to a wine vat. Inside the vat were over 100 silver dishes and 1,000 pieces of gold. One of the silver cups bore this inscription: *Enjoy life while you have it, for tomorrow is uncertain.*

CIVILIZATION INTACT

Here was an entire thriving city caught exactly at the peak of its prosperity and perfectly preserved—eggs unbroken, bread baking in an oven, coins left on a countertop. Pots on cookstoves still contained meat bones. Shops displayed onions, beans, olives, nuts, and figs. A heap of discarded fish scales was uncovered near a fish shop. A meal of bread, salad, cakes, and fruit was set on a table. Ropes and nets used by unknown fishermen were preserved, as was the straw padding recently removed from a shipment of glasswares.

Papyrus scrolls, charred but still readable, revealed dissertations on music and other subjects. There were taverns, snack shops, gambling halls, a stadium that could hold 20,000 spectators, theaters, public baths, streets with sewer systems and raised sidewalks, homes with plumbing, and thousands of works of art. Everyday objects such as perfume bottles and glass jars, sewing needles and brooms, muffin pans and cooking pots were found in the homes. Also uncovered: glass vases, tile mosaics, painted murals, marble statues, golden jewelry, bronze lanterns, jeweled amulets, religious icons, and exquisite furniture.

POMPEII TODAY

The excavation of Pompeii continues today; it's estimated that only about a third of the town has been uncovered. Yet Vesuvius continues to rumble, most recently erupting in 1944.

Will it bury Pompeii again?

The seed cones of the cycad tree can weigh up to 90 pounds.

MYTH-SPOKEN

Some of the best-known quotes in history weren't said by the people they're attributed to . . . and some weren't said at all!

Line: "If you can't stand the heat, get out of the kitchen."
Supposedly Said By: Harry Truman
Actually: Although Truman decided to take credit for this saying in his autobiography, he didn't coin the phrase. He was actually quoting his good friend and chief military aide, Major General Harry Vaughan.

Line: "Say it ain't so, Joe."
Supposedly Said By: A little boy to "Shoeless" Joe Jackson
Actually: Baseball legend has it that when White Sox left fielder "Shoeless" Joe appeared to testify before the Grand Jury about his part in fixing the 1919 World Series, a heartbroken little boy gazed up at his hero and pleaded: "Say it ain't so, Joe." It never happened. The line was made up by a journalist.

Line: "What's good for General Motors is good for the country."
Supposedly Said By: Charles Wilson, former GM president and U.S. secretary of defense
Actually: Wilson was misunderstood and misquoted. He really said: "For years I thought what was good for our country was good for General Motors—and vice versa." Wilson was trying to say that GM wanted to look out for the American people and not just make a profit, but over time it has been corrupted to mean the reverse.

Line: "I disapprove of what you say, but I will defend to the death your right to say it."
Supposedly Said By: Voltaire, French philosopher and author
Actually: This saying first appeared over 100 years after Voltaire died. Using the pen name S. G. Tallentyre in her 1906 book *The Friends of Voltaire*, writer E. Beatrice Hall created this aphorism to paraphrase a section in one of Voltaire's essays.

With enough training, an elephant can throw a baseball faster than a human can.

MAKING SMALL TALK

Here are the origins of some common abbreviations.

£ or lb.

Meaning: Pound

Origin: The abbreviation originates with the Latin phrase *libra pondo*, which means "a unit of measurement by weight." The Romans shortened the phrase to *pondo*, which ultimately became *pound* in English, but the abbreviation of the first word—*lb.*, for *libra*—endured. The symbol for British currency is a stylized L, or £, which comes from the same source. The value of the British pound was originally equal to one pound of silver.

V.I.P.

Meaning: Very important person

Origin: This frequently used contraction was created during World War II by a British officer in charge of organizing flights for important military leaders. In order to conceal the names from enemy spies, each of these were referred to as a "V.I.P." in the flight plan.

Mrs.

Meaning: A married woman

Origin: Originally, *Mrs.* was a shortened version of *mistress*, a word that used to mean "wife" but has since acquired a very different meaning. Strictly speaking, because the word it once abbreviated has changed its meaning, *Mrs.* is no longer an abbreviation—unlike *Mr.*, its male counterpart, which can be spelled out as *Mister*.

K

Meaning: A strikeout in baseball

Origin: In the 1860s when a batter struck out, it was proper to say that he "struck." It was during this era that a newspaperman named Henry Chadwick created symbols for use with his new invention—the box score. He gave each play a letter: S for sacrifice, E for error, and so on. Since S was already taken, he used the last letter of "struck" instead of the first to abbreviate it: K.

The Australians used to name hurricanes after unpopular politicians.

Rx

Meaning: A drug prescription

Origin: Actually, there is no *x* in *Rx*. In Medieval Latin, the first word in medicinal prescriptions directing one to take a specific quantity of a concoction was *recipe*, meaning "take" or "receive." This was later symbolized as an R with a slash across its leg. The spelling *Rx* is an attempt to represent this symbol in English letters.

B.O.

Meaning: Body odor

Origin: In 1933 the Lifebuoy Health Soap Company ran a series of radio advertisements containing their new slogan: "Lifebuoy stops B--- O---." A heavy two-note foghorn warning was synchronized with the "B.O.," giving the phrase a negative spin it has retained ever since.

D-Day

Meaning: June 6, 1944, the day Allied forces invaded France during World War II

Origin: The *D* in D-day does not stand for "designated" or "defeat," as many believe, but simply for "day." *D-day* actually means "day day." The redundancy comes from the common practice in army correspondence of referring to a top secret time as *H-hour* or *D-day*.

XXX

Meaning: Marking on bottles in cartoons to indicate that they contain alcohol

Origin: According to one theory, during the 19th century, breweries in Britain marked their bottles X, XX, or XXX as a sign of alcohol content. The number of Xs corresponded to the potency of the drink.

* * *

"What a life. When I was a kid, I asked my dad if I could go ice skating. He told me to wait until it gets warmer."

—Rodney Dangerfield

Cyclosporine, which prevents organ transplant rejections, comes from a fungus grown in dirt.

UNCLE JOHN'S PAGE OF LISTS

Uncle John has a list of ten reasons why
the Bathroom Reader *should have lists in it.*
(The list is confidential.)

7 "Official" Attributes of the Pillsbury Doughboy:
1. His skin must look like dough: "off-white, smooth, but not glossy"
2. Slightly luminous, but no sheen
3. No knees, elbows, wrists, fingers, ears, or ankles
4. Rear views do not include "buns"
5. Walks with a "swagger"
6. Stomach is propotional to the rest of his body.
7. He is not portly.

4 Strange Tourist Attractions
1. The Hall of Mosses (WA)
2. Phillip Morris Cigarette Tours (VA)
3. The Soup Tureen Museum (NJ)
4. The Testicle Festival (MT)

7 Nicknames Given to President Grover Cleveland
1. Big Beefhead
2. The Buffalo Hangman
3. The Dumb Prophet
4. The Stuffed Prophet
5. The Pretender
6. His Accidency
7. Uncle Jumbo

Origins of 4 Native American tribal names:
1. *Apache*: the Zuni word for "enemy."
2. *Cherokee*: the Creek word for "people of different speech."
3. *Hopi*: from *hopituh*, or "peaceful ones"
4. *Sioux*: Chippewa name for a kind of snake.

State With the Most Pollution:
Texas

5 Most-Read U.S. Newspapers
1. *Wall St. Journal*
2. *USA Today*
3. *L.A. Times*
4. *New York Times*
5. *Washington Post*

26 Things Elvis Demanded Be Kept at Graceland at all Times
Fresh ground beef, Hamburger buns, Case of Pepsi, Case of orange soda, Brownies, Milk, half & half, 6 cans of biscuits, Chocolate ice cream, Hot dogs, Sauerkraut, Potatoes, Onions, Bacon, Fresh fruit, Peanut butter, Banana pudding, Meat loaf, 3 packs each of Spearmint, Juicy Fruit, Doublemint gum, Cigarettes, Dristan, Super Anahist, Contac, Sucrets

---

Only female ducks quack; the males coo, hoot, honk, and grunt, but they don't quack.

TOILET TECH

Better living through bathroom technology.

YOU'RE CLEARED TO LAND

Inventor: Brooke Pattee of Lake Forest, California

Product: Toilet "landing lights"—a lighting system that illuminates the inside of your toilet bowl so you can see it in the dark.

How It Works: A transparent tube containing wiring and several lights is positioned beneath the upper rim of the toilet bowl. When you lift or lower the lid, the lights come on, bathing the inside of the bowl in light so that you can take care of business without blinding yourself in the middle of the night by turning on the bathroom light. An automatic timer turns the lights off after several minutes.

AS GOOD AS GOLD

Inventor: Japanese electronics giant Matsushita

Product: An electric toilet seat that uses gold dust to filter out unpleasant smells.

How It Works: When a person sits on the toilet seat, an electric fan begins blowing the air in the toilet bowl into a "deodorization device" containing the gold dust and zeolite; they act as a catalyst to oxidize and deodorize ammonia and other compounds. Another filter containing manganese removes compounds containing sulfur. Toilet seat air filters are popular in Japan, where "lavatories at home are often so small and airless that smells hang around for some time."

DIAPER ALARM

Inventor: Karel Dvorak of Toronto, Ontario

Product: A disposable diaper with a moisture sensor that sets off a flashing LED light when wetness is detected.

How It Works: A clothespin-like moisture sensor is clipped to the baby's diaper in such a way that it makes contact with the baby's skin. The sensor compares the electrical conductivity of

---

Half of all coffee drinkers drink it black.

the skin to that of a special layer of material inside the diaper. When the diaper becomes wet, the voltage changes and the LED light begins to flash, notifying mom that it's time for a new diaper.

THE TOILET THAT SHOPS

Inventor: Twyford, a toilet manufacturer in Cheshire, England

Product: The Versatile Interactive Pan (VIP), a toilet that analyzes your urine and stool samples for dietary deficiencies, compiles a shopping list of needed nutritional items, then e-mails your local supermarket to order the foods.

How It Works: "If, for example, a person is short on roughage one day," says Twyford spokesperson Terry Wooliscroft, "an order of beans or lentils will be sent from the VIP to the supermarket and delivered the same day." The toilet can also e-mail a doctor if it detects health problems. Added bonuses: The seat is voice activated and the toilet flushes automatically.

BLAST PAD

Inventor: UltraTech Products of Houston, Texas

Product: The Flatulence Filter Seat Cushion—a foam seat cushion that doubles as a rear-end odor eater.

How It Works: The foam cushion contains a hidden "super-activated" carbon filter that absorbs unfortunate odors as soon as they are created. The filter is hidden inside the cushion's gray tweed fabric, so no one has to know it's there—for all anyone knows, it's just another seat cushion. The company also makes a smaller filter pad that you can wear inside your underpants, "for protection when you are not at your seat."

By Any Other Name: "Originally the seat cushion was named the TooT TrappeR. At the time, it seemed like the perfect name. In time, doctors became interested in the cushion, but felt that some would think it was a joke. For this reason, we changed the name to the Flatulence Filter Seat Cushion. This resulted in a more clinical-sounding name."

George H. W. Bush was the youngest Navy pilot of World War II.

POLI-TALKS

More proof that politicians don't deserve much respect these days.

"We are ready for any unforeseen event that may or may not occur."

—Al Gore

"Statistics show that teen pregnancy drops off significantly after age 25."

—Sen. Mary Anne Tebedo (R-CO)

"I can't believe that we are going to let a majority of people decide what's best for this state."

—Rep. John Travis (D-LA)

"What is the state of North Carolina going to do about its bludgeoning prison population?"

—Sen. Maggie Tinsman (R-IA)

"We don't want to open a box of Pandoras."

—Gov. Bruce King (D-NM)

"What right does Congress have to go around making laws just because they deem it necessary?"

—Marion Barry

"She's a wonderful, wonderful person, and we're looking to a happy and wonderful night . . . uh, life."

—Sen. Ted Kennedy, about his then-fiancee

"It's like an Alcatraz around my neck."

—Thomas Menino, Boston mayor on the shortage of city parking

"Our cabinet is always unanimous—except when we disagree."

—British Columbia premier William Vander Zalm

"I don't know anyone here that's been killed by a handgun."

—Rep. Avery Alexander (R-LA)

"What's a man got to do to get in the top fifty?"

—President Bill Clinton, on a survey ranking the Lewinsky scandal as the 53rd most significant story of the century

John Quincy Adams and Dwight D. Eisenhower were the only bald presidents (so far).

THE HISTORY OF FOOTBALL, PART V

Here's a sports trivia question for you: Which U.S. president threatened to ban college football on the grounds that it was becoming too violent? Answer: Theodore Roosevelt. Here's the story of how football nearly pummeled itself into extinction.

BIG TIME

By the late 1880s, American football was beginning to spread from the original handful of eastern colleges to schools in other parts of the country. Notre Dame started its football program in 1887, and the University of Southern California followed a year later; Stanford and the University of California both launched programs in 1893. By 1897 teams were popping up all over the country.

Yale University remained the dominant force in American football—it lost only three games in the first 10 years of intercollegiate play. And because coach Walter Camp dominated Yale's program and had been so influential in shaping the modern game, his authority at the center of American football was unchallenged.

A VICTIM OF ITS OWN SUCCESS

But football was too much fun to remain the exclusive preserve of pampered "college boys." As the sport caught on in universities across the nation, athletic clubs in the surrounding communities began to form their own football leagues. So did church parishes, community groups, businesses, and small towns itching to earn big reputations. Regular play between such teams soon led to the same kinds of traditional rivalries and fierce grudge matches that by now were an entrenched part of the college game.

As the violence of these "semi-pro" leagues escalated beyond even that of college football, the sport returned ever closer to the anarchy of its medieval roots. In some areas of the country, Stephen Fox writes in *Big Leagues*, semi-pro football became little more than "a formalized excuse for beating up men from other communities."

Honeybees are not native to North America. They were introduced by explorers and colonists.

BAD NEWS

Twenty-one people died playing football during the 1904 season; another 23 would die the following year. Only a handful of those killed had been playing on college teams—the majority had been playing on semi-pro teams. But the college teams were still the organizing force behind football, and in the middle of the 1905 season, President Theodore Roosevelt, himself a football fan, summoned representatives from three of the major football powers—Harvard, Yale, and Princeton—to the White House and ordered them to clean up the sport. "Brutality and foul play," he told them, "should receive the same summary punishment given to a man who cheats at cards."

Roosevelt was no shrinking violet when it came to physical contests: The president broke his right arm while "stick fighting" and would eventually lose the sight in his left eye from a boxing injury. And he resumed stick fighting and boxing as soon as these injuries "healed." So if *he* was concerned about violence in football, there really was a problem.

NOTHING NEW

Harvard, Yale, and Princeton reps left the White House meeting promising to do better, but football didn't really change. And football's image was so tattered that some colleges were ready to ban the game with or without presidential support: Columbia abolished its football program in 1905 and did not reinstate it until 1915. Stanford and the University of California replaced their programs with rugby the same year. "The game of football," U.C.'s president Benjamin Wheeler declared, "must be made over or go."

For years, one of the biggest obstacles to cleaning up football had been Walter Camp himself. As chairman of the Intercollegiate Football Rules Committee, he had been able to fend off any fundamental changes to the game. Elliott Gorn writes in *A Brief History of American Sports*:

> Calls for "reform" of the game occasionally met with public approval, but they had little impact on the conduct of the game itself. Walter Camp saw no contradiction between honor and brutality. He defended—nearly always successfully—the game he loved against all efforts at significant reform; he remains one of the central figures whose efforts increased the game's violence.

Keep dreaming: The average person has more than 1,400 dreams a year.

YALEGATE

Camp's iron grip on football loosened considerably beginning in 1905, following the publication of a number of articles in the *New York Evening Post*, and in *McClure's* and *Outlook* magazines detailing scandalous financial abuses in the Yale football program.

As amateur athletes, Yale players weren't supposed to receive compensation of any kind for playing football, a system that Camp enthusiastically endorsed . . . in public. "We do not make exceptions to the rules," he said, "hence our men are not eligible if they have received money or compensation for ball playing."

But what went on behind the scenes was another story entirely. As treasurer of the Yale Financial Union, Camp controlled the funds of all of Yale's major sports programs—not just football—and unknown to anyone, he had stashed more than $96,000 in a secret fund that he used to coddle his star players, putting them up in expensive dorms, paying their way through school (there were no football scholarships at the time), and even sending them on paid vacations, all of which he hid in the budget as "miscellaneous expenses."

And though as head of the Yale football program he served ostensibly as a part-time volunteer, Camp secretly paid himself a $5,000 annual salary, while full-time Yale professors earned only $3,500 a year. He buried this expenditure under the heading "Maintenance of the field."

Yale's shady financial practices were no different from any other college at the time. Recruiting the country's best players and fielding championship teams year after year took a lot of money, and it had to come from somewhere. But the revelations about Yale came just as the pressure to clean up football violence was intensifying, and Camp, with his reputation as a "rock-ribbed standard bearer of Victorian honor in the midst of corruption" now seriously in question, was no longer able to block the reforms that others were determined to push through.

CHANGING OF THE GUARD

When Camp tried to resist Roosevelt's demand to clean up football, Chancellor Henry MacCracken of New York University decided he'd had enough. He organized a conference of 13 colleges not represented on Camp's tightly controlled rules committee to

A full-moon is nine times brighter than a half-moon.

discuss whether college football should be abolished altogether or whether one last attempt at cleaning it up should be made.

The original group of 13 schools that met on December 9, 1905 expanded to 62 schools by the time they met a second time, on December 28. At this meeting the schools voted to form an organization called the Intercollegiate Athletic Association, which in 1910 changed its name to the National Collegiate Athletic Association (NCAA). The group also voted to create its own rules committee, headed by Captain Palmer Pierce of West Point, to push through the reforms that Camp had resisted for so long.

CAN'T WE ALL JUST GET ALONG?

Rather than compete against the old Intercollegiate Football Association, when the Intercollegiate Athletic Association met for the third time in January 1906, they agreed to merge, electing a reformer named E. K. Hall to serve as chair of the new joint rules committee. Camp was out as chairman—for good.

"Ever the good sportsman, Walter Camp stayed involved at the highest levels of football," Stephen Fox writes in *Big Leagues*. "But his reign had ended."

"Lavatory! Lavatory! Sis, boom, bah! Uncle John! Uncle John! Rah, rah, rah!" Now turn to page 735 for the final installment of The History of Football.

* * *

GET IN FORMATION

It was in about the 1880s that the current names of football positions were beginning to come into use.

- Because the "snapperback" stood at the center of the line of scrimmage, he became known simply as the "center."

- The forwards standing at either end of the line of scrimmage became known as "end men" and later as "ends."

- The back who played deepest became the "fullback," and the two backs who stood between the quarterback came to be known as "halfbacks."

In 1888 Yale football coach Walter Camp fell ill. His wife coached for the entire season.

THE FOOD QUIZ

*You shop for food, you cook it, you eat it . . . But
how much do you really know about it? Take
our food quiz and find out.* Bon appétit!

1. Which is heavier: light cream or heavy cream?
   a) Light cream
   b) Heavy cream
   c) Neither—all milk products, including cheese, are the same
      weight by volume. The only exception is Swiss cheese,
      which is lighter because it's filled with holes.

2. When a meal is served on an airline, how is it likely to differ
   from the same meal served on land?
   a) It is likely to contain added sucrose, which has natural
      mellowing agents that reduce stress during long flights.
   b) Entrees are likely to contain gelatin, which helps the food
      retain its natural shape in the pressurized cabin.
   c) It probably contains more seasonings, but less salt. People
      taste food differently when flying, so extra seasoning is
      added. But they also dehydrate easily, so less salt is used.

3. In addition to adding their own flavor, how else do onions
   alter the taste of food?
   a) They release a caffeinelike stimulant. The diner experi-
      ences a mild euphoria that enhances their enjoyment of
      the meal and perceives the food as being tastier than it
      actually is.
   b) They release oils that coat the tongue, dulling the taste of
      everything except the onion.
   c) They irritate tastebuds, making them more sensitive to
      taste.

4. How can you judge the quality of ice cream before you buy it?
   a) Weigh it.
   b) Twirl the container in midair. Well-balanced ice cream is
      of higher quality than ice cream that wobbles when
      thrown.
   c) Squeeze it—ice cream, like fruit, isn't "ripe" until it's soft.

Cat milk is 10 percent protein. Cow's milk is only three percent protein.

5. Botanically speaking, what is the difference between a fruit and a vegetable?
   a) Color. Green or yellow means it's a vegetable. Red, blue, or purple means it's a fruit.
   b) Seeds. If it has seeds, it's a fruit. If it doesn't, it's a vegetable.
   c) Sugar content. A good rule of thumb is if it's sweet enough to be eaten for dessert, it's a fruit.

6. Apple seeds contain which of the following?
   a) Cyanide
   b) Lactose
   c) LSD

7. When, if ever, is it safe to refreeze food?
   a) It's never completely safe. Thawing and refreezing can "wake up" certain bacteria.
   b) It's always safe, but texture and flavor may deteriorate.
   c) Only when the food is refrozen within 90 minutes of thawing.

8. Most of the vitamins in a potato are located where?
   a) In the skin
   b) Near the skin
   c) In the starch

9. Where does Mocha-Java coffee originally come from?
   a) The Yemen port of Mocha. (*Java* means "coffee" in Yemeni.)
   b) The Indonesian island of Java, where cacao beans are also grown.
   c) The Yemen port of Mocha *and* the Indonesian port of Java.

10. In addition to adding flavor, how does a marinade change meat?
    a) The cooked meat will be juicier.
    b) The cooked meat will be drier.
    c) The cooked meat will be better preserved. On average, it will remain fresh in the refrigerator three times as long as unmarinated cooked meat.

Answers on page 746.

Mesquite bushes growing in Death Valley can have roots reaching 100 feet down for water.

NUDES & PRUDES

Even more proof that whether you're dressed
or naked, you can still be dumber than sin.

NUDE . . . The Florida Board of Medicine has indefinitely suspended the medical license of physician William Charles Leach after he examined at least three patients in the nude or nearly nude. "He took off his lab coat and his shirt and pants," one patient writes. "He then stood naked in front of me and asked me to comment on his appearance." The suspension has forced Dr. Leach to put on hold his plans for establishing the first nude medical clinic in the state of Florida.

PRUDE . . . Finnish cellular phone maker Nokia and the Dutch phone company KPN Telecom are protesting a decision by Tring, an Amsterdam cell phone retailer, to give away a sex toy with each cell phone purchase. "We've asked that it be stopped," says a KPN spokeswoman. "It's not our style at all."

NUDE . . . Arne and Oeystein Tokvam, two elderly brothers living in Oslo, Norway, got the show of a lifetime when a blonde-haired woman they didn't know talked her way into their home and began stripping off her clothing. The woman, who was in her 30s, was soon joined by an older woman who also stripped naked and began dancing around the brothers' home. "The older one was the wildest of the two," Arne, 73, told a local newspaper. "We saw everything."

After about 15 minutes, the mystery women put their clothes on and left; that was when Oeystein, 80, discovered that the brothers' safe was missing, and along with it $6,600 in cash and two government checks for $1,700. "Never mind," says Arne. "It's been a long time since we had that much fun."

PRUDE . . . Senegalese police detained two journalists for questioning after they published a photomontage that showed the head of Prime Minister Mame Madior Boye, Senegal's first female prime minister, pasted onto the body of a nude model. "We did not aim to hurt the prime minister," a spokesperson for *Tract* newspaper said following the arrests. "It was just meant as a joke."

It takes four hours to weave a hula skirt from 60 ti plants. The skirt will only last about five days.

PHOTOGRAPHY BEGINS TO GEL

Photography was a 19th-century technological wonder, and the early years of its development were incredibly productive. It turned another corner in 1878, with the introduction of the dry plate.

STILL WET AFTER ALL THESE YEARS

In the fifteen years since the invention of the daguerreotype in 1837, photography had made amazing progress. The collodion process and its descendants—ambrotypes, tintypes, and cartes-de-visite—were huge improvements, but they were still "wet-plate" processes.

Photographers had to apply fresh collodion to their glass photographic plates right before they took a picture, and then develop the plates immediately afterward, before the chemicals dried. That meant lugging all their chemicals and equipment, including a portable darkroom, wherever they went to take a picture. Every photo shoot was an expensive camping trip . . . which made photography off-limits to everyone except professionals and a handful of dedicated amateurs.

Someone either had to find a substitute for collodion or find a way to stop it from drying out so quickly, perhaps by mixing in substances that were slower to dry. They tried everything they could think of—honey, glycerine, raspberry syrup, beer—but nothing worked.

THE SMELL OF SUCCESS

The person who finally stumbled onto the answer, English physician Richard Leach Maddox, wasn't even trying to solve the problem. Maddox didn't mind the inconvenience of the wet-plate process, he just hated the way it smelled. His photography studio was set up in a glasshouse, and when it heated up, the smell of the ether in the collodion was overpowering. He became determined to find a process that did not require ether.

In 1871 Maddox found one that showed a lot of promise: a silver-gelatin emulsion. He believed this was the key to a

---

T. D. Rockwell had his name and address tattooed on his body in . . .

non-smelling "dry-plate process," but the demands of his medical practice prevented him from spending the time needed to refine it. So, in a letter to the *British Journal of Photography*, Maddox invited others to pick up where he had left off.

Seven years later another Englishman, Charles Harper Bennett, refined the process and proved Maddox right. He discovered that he could "ripen" the gelatin emulsion by heating it to 90°F and holding it at that temperature for several days. Then, after washing the plate to remove excess chemical salts, Bennett discovered that he could create a "dry plate" that was 60 times more sensitive to light than one made with the collodion or any other photographic process.

IN THE BLINK OF AN EYE

For decades, photographers had yearned to capture all that the human eye could see. Now, in a single stroke, Bennett had invented plates that worked faster than the human eye, allowing people to see things that it had never been possible to see before: horses in mid-gallop, birds flapping their wings in flight, children jumping rope, water droplets falling in mid-air. Before gelatin plates, all of these images had appeared as blurs—now they were crystal clear.

The invention of gelatin plates prompted new camera designs: bulky wooden tripod-mounted cameras were replaced by smaller units that photographers could easily hold in their hands. The new cameras were also more sophisticated. In the past people took pictures by removing the lens cap and replacing it a few seconds later, but gelatin plates were too sensitive for that. Precise exposure speeds, accurate to within a fraction of a second, were necessary. So camera makers added shutter systems that allowed for short and accurate exposure times. By 1900 it was possible to take exposures as short as 1/5000 of a second.

SCIENTIFIC METHOD

Just as important as the speed of the new gelatin plates was the fact that they remained photosensitive for months on end, which meant that they could be prepared well in advance of being used. Photographers no longer had to prepare plates themselves; they could buy them from the hundreds of small companies that sprang up to sell ready-made plates. They still had to develop the plates themselves, but at least now they could do it at their leisure.

Gelatin plates also helped bring standardization to the photography industry. In the past, each photographic plate was prepared from scratch moments before being put into use, so photosensitivity varied from plate to plate and from photographer to photographer. Not anymore: Now plates could be made under more controlled conditions, making their performance more predictable and reliable.

This mass production made it possible for two British scientists, Vero Charles Driffield and Ferdinand Hurter, to begin some of the first serious scientific studies of the chemistry and physics of photography. Through their research they calculated the optimum exposure time for photographic plates depending on lighting, temperature, and other factors, and they perfected the developing process to the point that people could develop exposures in absolute darkness, just by timing how long the exposures soaked in developing chemicals. As Driffield and Hurder unlocked photography's secrets, they helped to make it more accessible to ordinary people.

ONE MORE THING

The introduction of smaller, more sophisticated cameras and standardized, ready-made supplies simplified photography, but there were still a few hurdles that kept most people away.

For one thing, people still needed a darkroom or at least a *dark room*, because the gelatin plates had to be loaded into a camera in absolute darkness. The plates were so sensitive that exposing them to even a small amount of light caused them to fog over. And they were still made of glass, which was expensive, fragile, and heavy. Glass plates and plate holders added several pounds to the weight of a camera, which meant that no matter how small the cameras got, photography was still a costly and unwieldy affair.

But the most daunting problem of all was that most people still had to develop exposures themselves. If you wanted to *take* a picture, you had to *make* the picture. And if you weren't willing to do that, you were out of luck.

Then in 1880, George Eastman, a bookkeeper at the Rochester Savings Bank in Rochester, New York, decided to go into the gelatin-plate business.

To capture the rest of the story, turn to page 363.

The Earth spins 1,000 mph faster at the equator than at the poles.

MYTH-AMERICA

Some of the stories we recognize today as American myths were taught as history for many years. The truth might surprise you.

MYTH: Witches were burned at the stake during the Salem witch trials of 1692.

TRUTH: No witches were ever burned in Salem. One hundred and fifty men and women were arrested under suspicion of witchcraft. In all, 19 people and two dogs were put to death as "witches and warlocks," all of them hanged except for one person, who was pressed to death by stones. Ten others were convicted, but not put to death. A few months later, the governor of Massachusetts dissolved the witch court. The judges didn't mind; they were running out of people to accuse.

MYTH: While writing *Walden*, Henry David Thoreau lived in isolation in the woods of Massachusetts.

TRUTH: Thoreau's two-year retreat to Walden Pond was like a little boy pretending that his backyard tree house is in the middle of the jungle. In truth, Thoreau built his famous cabin a scant two miles from his family's home and spent very little time in isolation. "It was not a lonely spot," wrote Walter Harding in *The Days of Henry Thoreau*. "Hardly a day went by that Thoreau did not visit the village or was visited at the pond." Thoreau was even known to return home on the weekends to raid the family cookie jar.

MYTH: The westward expansion of the 1800s offered American pioneers millions of acres of fertile farmland.

TRUTH: The American frontier was not an organized democracy in which every "sodbuster" could own a piece of land with the promise of prosperity. The money of big corporations dominated the West. Although the federal government did in fact permit pioneers to stake large claims in the Great Plains, the arid climate and dry infertile soil rendered this land almost impossible for individuals to raise crops or maintain livestock on. To escape starvation, most pioneers were forced to sell their land to the corporations. In return, the corporations often offered the pioneers

---

President Grant appointed 13 of his relatives to federal posts.

jobs as low-paid miners and farmhands. By the 1890s, almost 90 percent of the farmland west of the Mississippi River was owned by corporations.

MYTH: The American bald eagle, symbol of the United States, is a noble creature.

TRUTH: The American bald eagle, whom Benjamin Franklin referred to as "a bird of bad moral character," is an aggressive species that, according to news reports, has recently begun to terrorize people. Since they were removed from the endangered species list in the late 1990s, the birds have been using their large talons and sharp beaks to attack fishermen and picnickers. Eagles have also been known to snatch puppies from suburban backyards.

MYTH: To escape Union capture, Confederate president Jefferson Davis fled Richmond disguised in his wife's dress.

TRUTH: Rather than admit defeat by surrendering to the Union army, Davis fled to Texas with the hope of reorganizing his troops. However, on May 10, 1865, he was apprehended in Georgia. Clad in a gray suit as he hastily greeted the Union troops, he accidentally grabbed his wife's cloak to protect him from the cold. Secretary of War Edwin M. Stanton presented the false story of Davis disguising himself in a dress to the *New York Herald*, which published it on May 16, 1865.

MYTH: "Jesse James was a man who killed many a man. / He robbed the Glendale train. / He stole from the rich and he gave to the poor. / He'd a hand and a heart and a brain."

TRUTH: Jesse Woodson James, who was born in Missouri in 1847, did indeed rob from the rich. Most of the money that he stole, however, he kept for himself. A child of slave-owning aristocrats, Jesse James made a name for himself as one of the Confederate marauders known as Quantrell's Raiders during the Civil War. His move to robbing banks after the war was inspired by a deep hatred of the Northern industry that was becoming widespread in the pastoral South. It is true that he killed many a man—most of them innocent bystanders.

Comedian Stan Laurel was married eight times, but had only four wives.

MIRROR, MIRROR ON THE WALL

*Not that we're vain or anything, but we at the BRI find mirrors
endlessly fascinating. Here are some important facts about
the second-most important object in the bathroom.*

POOLS OF LIGHT

How do mirrors work? Generally speaking, by reflecting light. Most objects don't give off any light of their own. They can only be seen because light from other sources—the sun, a candle, a lightbulb—hits them and bounces off. Not all of the light bounces, though. Some is absorbed by the object and some is transmitted through the object. The part that does bounce back is the reflection. Flat shiny surfaces like water, metal, and mirrors reflect light well because very little of the light is absorbed or transmitted—most of it is reflected.

When light hits a mirror, it bounces off in the opposite direction, but at the same angle it came from. It appears as if the image is coming from behind the mirror, but it's not. What we see is a virtual image.

THE FIRST MIRRORS

For centuries, mankind's only mirrors were pools of water or polished metal. The first glass mirrors were made by Venetian craftsmen in the 1300s. Their method: They covered the back of a piece of glass with an amalgam of tin and mercury, rubbed flat and smooth. A piece of wool cloth would then be laid on top of the mercury and pressed with iron weights for more than a week. Then the excess mercury would be drained off. This method remained a carefully guarded secret, and for centuries Venice had a monopoly on mirrors.

In 1665 the chief minister to Louis XIV of France went to Italy and—at the risk of death—bribed 18 Venetian mirrorsmiths to move to France. Soon after their defection, the French passed a law making it illegal to import Venetian mirrors.

Three years later, a Frenchman named Louis Lucas beat the Venetians at their own game—he invented plate glass. Venetians

---

The pouch on a pelican's beak can hold up to two gallons of water.

only knew how to make blown glass, so each mirror started out as a bottle or cylinder that was slit open and flattened while hot. The size of mirrors was, therefore, very limited.

But Lucas discovered how to pour molten glass onto an iron table where it could be flattened with an iron roller. Now mirrors could be made that were much larger. Soon France became famous for its mirrors. A very pleased Louis XIV purchased 700 mirrors and lined an entire hallway at the Palace of Versailles with them in a stunning display.

UPON FURTHER REFLECTION

In 1835, German chemist Justus von Liebig discovered a way to make a better mirror. He invented a process for using silver as a backing instead of tin and mercury. He flushed the glass with silver salts and then covered it with a solution of silver nitrate. After being heated and left undisturbed for an hour, a chemical reaction caused the metallic silver to separate and adhere to the glass. Then it was coated with shellac and painted with a black backing. And that's how mirrors were made for the next 150 years.

In mirrormaking today, silver or aluminum is vaporized then sprayed onto glass. For finer mirrors—such as those used in telescopes—aluminum, chromium, or gold are heated in a vacuum tank. When they reach the critical temperature, they "flash" into vapor, filling the tank with metallic gas. A film is then deposited on whatever material is inside the tank.

MIRROR FACTS AND TRIVIA

- In the 1600s, the Dutch used to cover their mirrors with curtains when not in use, lest the reflectiveness be used up!

- In ancient China, reflective pieces of polished brass were placed over doorknobs so that evil spirits would scare themselves away.

- Ben Franklin mounted mirrors outside his second-story window so he could secretly see who was knocking at his door.

- The vanity license plate "3M TA3" was banned after someone looked at it in the mirror.

- A middle school in Oregon was faced with a unique problem: A number of girls were beginning to use lipstick and would

Close but no cigar. The thinnest man-made thread is a gold filament . . .

apply it in the bathroom. That was fine, but for some reason, they would also press their lips to the mirrors, leaving dozens of little lip prints. Finally the principal called all the girls to the bathroom. She explained that the lip prints were a major problem for the custodian and asked the custodian to demonstrate how difficult it was to clean one of the mirrors. He proceeded to take out a long-handled brush, dip it into the nearest toilet, and scrub the mirror. After that, there were no lip prints on the mirrors.

- The world's largest mirrors (to date) sit inside the twin Keck Telescopes—the world's largest telescopes—at the W. M. Keck Observatory in Hawaii. Each mirror is made of 36 hexagonal segments which work together as a single piece. Diameter: ten meters (32 feet) across.

- People once thought that the reflection of the body in a shiny surface or mirror was an expression of the spiritual self and if anything happened to disturb that reflection, injury would follow. This was the origin of the superstition that breaking a mirror would bring seven years of bad luck.

- Trade secret: Building managers install mirrors in lobbies because people complain less about waiting for slow elevators when they're occupied looking at themselves.

- In 1994 Russian astronauts orbiting in the Mir spacecraft tried using mirrors to reflect sunlight into northern areas of their country in an attempt to lengthen the short growing season. It didn't work.

- Ever wonder if the mirror in the dressing room is a real mirror or a two-way mirror? Here's as simple test: Place the tip of your fingernail against the reflective surface. If there's a gap between your fingernail and the image, it's a *genuine* mirror. But, if your fingernail *directly touches* the image, watch out—it very well could be a two-way mirror. Remember, though, that mirror technology is always changing, so no test is 100 percent foolproof.

* * *

Word Origin: Clock comes from the Latin *clocca* meaning "bell," since clock tower bells were rung on the hour. The same root gives us *cloak* which is shaped like a bell.

. . . four microns (millionths of a meter) thick. Spiders webs are as thin as one micron.

YOU'RE MY INSPIRATION

It's always fun to find out what—or who—inspired
cultural (and pop cultural) milestones like these.

YELLOW JOURNALISM. In 1895 publisher William Randolph Hearst broke into the New York newspaper world by buying the *New York Journal* and copying feature-by-feature Joseph Pulitzer's New York *World*, then the nation's most popular paper. Hearst even hired away *World* cartoonist R. F. Outcault, who drew "The Yellow Kid" comic strip for the color comics section. Pulitzer retaliated by hiring another cartoonist to create a second "yellow" kid; the dueling strips attracted so much attention that the sensationalist style of journalism practiced by both papers became known as "yellow journalism."

MITSUBISHI LOGO. Today Mitsubishi is best known for its cars, but in the 1930s and 1940s it was better known for its infamous Zero, the warplane that was used to launch the attack on Pearl Harbor. Although the company no longer produces airplanes, it still uses the same logo—*mitsu bishi*, or "three diamonds," arranged in the shape of an airplane propeller.

STATUE OF ST. MICHAEL. Located at Norway's Trondheim Cathedral, it is considered one of the greatest Gothic structures in all of Northern Europe. Sculptor Kristofer Leirdal created the statue for the 12th-century cathedral when it was being restored in 1969. He says he based the figure—that of a winged angel with a spear poised to slay a dragon—on singer Bob Dylan. "I saw him as a representative of American opposition to the Vietnam War," he recounted. "I thought it was appropriate to have a great poet on top of the tower."

SUBARU LOGO. In 1953 six Japanese companies merged to form one automobile company. They modeled their six-star logo after the Pleiades constellation, which also has six stars. In Japan the star cluster is known as *Subaru*.

Homing pigeons can't find their way home if a magnet is tied to their necks.

IT'S A WEIRD, WEIRD WORLD

Proof that truth really is stranger than fiction.

I'LL GET YOU, MY PRETTY

"High school student Brandi Blackbear has filed a federal lawsuit against the Broken Arrow, Oklahoma, school district. The suit claims Blackbear was unfairly suspended because the assistant principal believed her Wiccan 'curse' actually caused a teacher to become ill. 'I, for one,' said the Oklahoma director of the American Civil Liberties Union, 'would like to see the evidence that a 15-year-old girl made a grown man sick by casting a magic spell.'"

—**Bizarre News**

LIFE IN THE FAST LANE

WALTHAM ABBEY, Essex—"A senior citizen was involved in a low-speed chase after he decided to go for a cruise in his electric wheelchair along the M25, Britain's busiest motorway. According to Police Inspector Keith Fitzjohn, the man, whose name was not disclosed, was intercepted and taken home after being 'lectured on the folly of driving an electric wheelchair on the M25.'"

—**Funny Times**

MONK-ING AROUND

BANGKOK—"Two Buddhist monks are suspected of ignoring their vows by drinking in a bar 62 miles north of Bangkok. According to police, bar employees said the monks—disguised in wigs and hats—had been there several times, drinking and singing karaoke. Buddhist monks are supposed to shave their heads and live simple lives devoid of materialism, forswearing wordly pleasures such as alcohol, sex and, apparently, karaoke."

—**Associated Press**

A CASE OF COWLICK

PEREIRA, Colombia—"A Colombian hairdresser says he has found a way to lick baldness—literally. His offbeat scalp treatment

Only six percent of land on Earth is suitable for growing crops.

involves a special tonic and massage—with a cow's tongue. 'I feel more manly, more attractive to women,' says customer Henry Gomez. 'My friends even say "What are you doing? You have more hair. You look younger."'"

—CNN *Fringe*

TRICK AND TREAT

"Home-invading robbers tied up a Westminster, California, family on Halloween night, 2000, and loaded up their valuables, diligently pausing several times to pass out candy to trick-or-treaters."

—*News of the Weird*

THE CRYING GAME

BANGKOK—"Kesaraporn Duangsawan captured the hearts of the judges and walked away with 6,000 baht (about $135) as first runner-up in a Thai beauty contest. When pageant organizers discovered the beauty queen was a man, the disgraced 22-year-old admitted his fraud and handed back the prize money, but asked to keep the Miss Media runner-up sash 'as a memento.'"

—*Reuters*

TOOTH IS STRANGER THAN FICTION

"Singing hymns and praying for peace and luck, thousands of Buddhists greeted a holy tooth, believed to have belonged to Buddha, when it arrived in Taiwan. Monks in saffron robes escorted the tooth, encased in a miniature golden pagoda, off a flight from India. Dozens of women prostrated themselves. Others knelt, clasping their hands in front to express their reverence. Buddhists say the tooth brings blessings and keeps them from disaster."

—*Wacky News*

A FAREWELL TO ARMS

"Police in Manchester, England, stunned Louis Makin, 27, when they went to his home and asked if they could throw away his arm. Makin had the arm amputated two years ago after being attacked by thugs. It had then been frozen to be used as evidence, and police needed permission to destroy it. 'I didn't know they still had it,' said Makin."

—*"The Edge," The Oregonian*

GOING POSTAL

Sending a letter through the mail seems so simple—put a stamp on it and drop it in a mailbox—that it's difficult to imagine that it took centuries for postal service to evolve into the form we recognize today. Here's a look at how it happened.

THE ROMAN EMPIRE

When the Roman republic was founded in 509 B.C., it was little more than a city-state. But after centuries of conquest, it grew into an empire that included large parts of North Africa, most of Western Europe, and the entire Mediterranean.

Maintaining control over such a large area required that the central government in Rome be in regular contact with its representatives in every corner of the empire. This required a good system of roads and, just as importantly, a reliable and speedy postal system. Rome had both.

The emperor Augustus (27 B.C.–14 A.D.) is credited with establishing the imperial postal service, the *cursus publicus*, which consisted of relays, or *posts*, of runners stationed at intervals of 5 to 12 miles apart along the empire's military roads. Later, boats were employed to carry mail from port to port across the Mediterranean Sea, and the runners were replaced by horse-drawn carriages. At the system's peak, a message could travel as far as 170 miles in 24 hours, a speed unsurpassed in Europe until the 19th century.

THERE'S A CATCH

There was, however, one major difference between the Roman postal system and our modern one: the *cursus publicus* was for official government communications only. If private citizens wanted to send a message to another part of the empire, they had to hire a courier to deliver it in person.

The collapse of the Roman Empire in 476 A.D. marked the end of centralized authority in Europe and split the continent into numerous kingdoms who waged war not only against each other, but also against their own subjects as they strived to establish authority. Parts of the *cursus publicus* lasted for more than 400 years after the Roman Empire collapsed, but in the centuries that

---

. . . mail to more than 500 different addresses along their route each day.

followed, travel and trade across Europe declined, and so did literacy, which became the almost exclusive preserve of clerks and the clergy. By the time the last vestiges of the Roman system disappeared in Western Europe in the 9th century, it didn't even matter—there wasn't much demand for a public postal system since few people could read or write.

A NEW ERA

But things began to change in the 11th century. With the founding of numerous universities, monasteries, and cathedrals across Europe, correspondence began to increase somewhat, prompting many institutions to set up their own private corps of foot-messengers. Few of these services carried private mail, though, because the level of literacy was still low.

It wasn't until after Johannes Gutenberg invented the movable-type printing press in about 1450 that literacy rates began rising to the point where letter carrying could become a profitable business. Local messenger services began popping up in towns and cities all over Europe. Some of these expanded into regional and nationwide services—the largest was founded in 1290 by an Italian named Amadeo Tasso.

Tasso introduced courier service to one Italian city after another. After he died, his descendants continued to add new routes . . . *lots* of new routes. His family married into another prominent courier family, the Della Torres, and as the years passed, their combined business continued to expand. By the late 1500s, the family business, now known by the Germanicized name Thurn and Taxis, employed more than 20,000 couriers and delivered mail quickly, reliably, and very profitably, all over Europe.

By now a number of the royal houses of Europe, not comfortable with the idea of entrusting government communications to private courier services, began setting up their own national postal systems. In 1477 King Louis XI of France established the French Royal Service with 230 mounted couriers; England's Henry VIII followed in 1516.

COMMON CARRIER

Neither of these systems attempted to provide service to the entire country, and neither accepted private mail . . . at first. But by 1600

You need four tons of grapes to make a ton of raisins.

it had dawned on the French government that charging private citizens to carry their mail would help offset the cost of operating the system, so it began accepting private mail for the first time. In 1627 a schedule of regular fees and timetables was put in place. Eight years later, the English set up a similar postal service for the general public, completely independent from the one used by the government.

As these and other government-run mail services expanded, they began to restrict the activities of privately owned enterprises like Thurn and Taxis, forbidding them to compete in areas served by the national post. Thurn and Taxis managed to hang on until 1867, when, after 577 years in business, it sold its last remaining postal lines to the Prussian government. The era of large-scale, privately owned postal systems was over; by 1875, virtually every postal service in the world was a government monopoly.

THE NEW WORLD

Initially, there were no post offices in the New World. When a ship pulled into port, it dropped bags of mail at a nearby tavern or coffeehouse, where the European colonists would go to pick it up. Most such places also had a bag for outgoing mail—for a penny you could drop a letter in the bag, which an outgoing ship would deliver to a similar tavern or coffeehouse on the other side of the Atlantic.

It took a while for regular mail service to get established in the colonies. This was due in large part to the fact that individual colonies didn't trust one another, and the need for communication between residents in neighboring colonies was minimal. It was much more common for colonists to send letters home to Europe.

Then, in 1737, a struggling 31-year-old printer named Benjamin Franklin became the postmaster of Philadelphia. Franklin distinguished himself in the position, and in 1753 was appointed one of two joint postmasters general for the colonies. In the two decades that followed, Franklin did much to improve and expand the colonial postal service. He reorganized the system, personally inspecting post offices, conducting surveys, and laying out newer, shorter routes. During these years, postal riders traveling between New York and Philadelphia began carrying mail at night as well as during the day, cutting the delivery time in half.

A field bee flies 50,000 miles to collect enough nectar to produce a pound of honey.

By the time the British fired him for pro-Revolutionary sympathies in 1774, Franklin had established regular, scheduled mail service from Maine to Florida and into Canada, and had also significantly improved mail service to England. (Although Franklin is better known as the first U.S. Postmaster General, he served for little more than a year before leaving the job to become ambassador to France.)

PROGRESS

One of the hardest things about running the postal service in the new republic was keeping up with the rapid growth of the country. If anything, the U.S. Post Office grew faster than the country it served. As late as 1789, there were only 75 post offices in the entire country. Over the next 40 years, the number grew to more than 8,000, and by 1901 there were 76,945.

As the U.S. Post Office grew, the industrial revolution was vastly increasing the speed at which mail could be transported across the country. Mail that had once been transported on foot and by horseback along narrow dirt trails came to be delivered first by stagecoach, then by canal boat and steamboat, and then beginning in the 1830s, by railroad.

HURRY UP AND WAIT

Transporting mail quickly and broadening the range of services offered was one thing; figuring out how to sort mail more quickly proved to be a much greater challenge. At the turn of the 20th century, the U.S. mail was still sorted almost entirely by hand, just as it had been nearly 200 years before. Tentative steps toward automating the sorting process were made in the late 1920s, but the Great Depression and World War II put off real modernization for another 15 to 20 years.

The first automated mail-sorting equipment was finally put in place in the 1950s, and in 1963 the Postal Service introduced the ZIP Code (ZIP for "Zoning Improvement Plan") to further speed mail processing. But these improvements barely kept pace with the steadily increasing volume of mail, especially business mail, which by 1963 made up 80 percent of the total. In 1966 the Chicago Post Office ground to a halt under tons of mail it could not process quickly enough.

Cost of mailing a letter more than 400 miles in 1816: 25¢.

A large part of the problem was that the U.S. Post Office had grown into a huge, inefficient, money-losing government agency subject to the whims and politics of Congress. In the late 1960s, a federal commission recommended reconstituting the U.S. Post Office as a nonprofit corporation wholly owned by the government but managed by an independent board of directors, and in August 1970, President Nixon signed the Postal Reorganization Act into law. On July 1, 1971, the old U.S. Post Office became the U.S. Postal Service.

BRAVE NEW WORLD

This reorganization effectively removed Congressional pressure to maintain low stamp prices—and along with it, taxpayer subsidies. The price of stamps began to climb, both to cover the full cost of delivering the mail and also to finance continuing modernization and automation. In 1971 a first-class stamp cost 8¢; the price rose to 13¢ in 1975, to 20¢ in 1981, 29¢ in 1991, 34¢ in 2001, and 39¢ in 2007.

Besides the increase in the price of stamps, another way the U.S. Postal Service attempted to cover its costs without taxpayer support was to change stamp subjects to make them more appealing to collectors.

"That's how Tweety Bird and Sylvester have come to displace George Washington and Abe Lincoln," says Michael Laurence, publisher of a stamp-collecting newspaper in Ohio. "It didn't take the Post Office long to realize that revenue from stamps retained and not used was money in the bank."

Perhaps the best example of this was the 1993 Elvis stamp. An estimated 38.5 million of the 500 million Elvis stamps sold were never used to send a letter, the highest unused percentage of any stamp ever issued by the U.S. Postal Service.

WE'RE NUMBER ONE

Today, the U.S. Postal Service delivers mail to more than 134 million addresses around the country, and provides service to a larger geographical area than any other postal service in the world. It delivers more than 200 billion pieces of mail every year, which makes up more than 46 percent of the world's card and letter mail volume. Who's number two? Japan, which handles less than seven percent.

Stamp collecting is the most popular hobby in the world.

BEHIND THE HITS

Ever wonder what inspired some of your favorite songs?
Here are a few more inside stories about popular tunes.

The Artist: Beck
The Song: "Loser"
The Story: One day, Beck was fooling around at producer Karl Stephenson's house. Beck started playing slide guitar, and Stephenson began recording. As Stephenson added a Public Enemy–style beat and a sample from Dr. John's "I Walk on Gilded Splinters," Beck attempted to freestyle rap—something he had never done before. Frustrated at his inability to rap, Beck began criticizing his own performance: "*Soy un perdedor*" ("I'm a loser" in Spanish). Beck wanted to scrap it, but Stephenson thought it was catchy. Stephenson was right—"Loser" made Beck a star.

The Artist: David Bowie
The Song: "Fame"
The Story: In 1975, as Bowie and his band were playing around in the studio with a riff that guitarist Carlos Alomar had come up with, former Beatle John Lennon dropped in. When they played the riff for Lennon, he immediately picked up a guitar, walked to the corner of the room and started playing along and muttering to himself, "Aim . . . aim!" When he said, "Fame!" the song started to come together. Bowie ran off to write some lyrics while the band worked out the music. Bowie gave writing credit to Lennon, saying: "It wouldn't have happened if John hadn't been there."

The Artist: The Byrds
The Song: "The Ballad of Easy Rider"
The Story: In an effort to convince Bob Dylan to write the theme song for *Easy Rider*, Peter Fonda gave him a private screening of the movie. Dylan didn't like the movie and wouldn't write the song. But he scribbled the words "The river flows, it flows to the sea, wherever the river flows, that's where I want to be" on a napkin and told Fonda: "Give this to McGuinn," referring to Roger McGuinn of the Byrds. Fonda gave McGuinn the napkin, and McGuinn immediately finished the song. But when Dylan learned

---

The 1983 movie Cujo used 5 St. Bernards, a mechanical head, and an actor in a dog costume.

that he had gotten songwriting credit, he called McGuinn and chewed him out, saying he didn't want to be associated with it in any way. Dylan cowrote the song, but McGuinn got all the credit.

The Artist: Aerosmith
The Song: "Walk This Way"
The Story: Guitarist Joe Perry and bassist Tom Hamilton were exhausted from rehearsing the new riff they had written, so they took a break to see a movie—*Young Frankenstein*. Says Hamilton, "There's that part in the movie where Igor says 'Walk this way,' and the other guy walks the same way with the hump and everything. We thought it was the funniest thing we'd ever seen." After the movie, they told singer Steven Tyler that the name of the song had to be "Walk This Way." Tyler rushed out and scribbled the lyrics to the song on the walls of the studio's stairway, and the band recorded the song right then.

The Artist: The Crystals
The Song: "He's a Rebel"
The Story: Phil Spector wanted to record "He's a Rebel," but the publisher told him it was taken—another producer, Snuff Garrett was preparing to record it with singer Vikki Carr. Spector ran out in a panic and dragged vocalist Darlene Love and a bunch of musicians into the studio to cut the song. That evening, Garrett was preparing to record the song when his studio guitarist walked in. He glanced at the music and exclaimed, "Hey, man, I just played this!" Garrett asked "Where?" "In Studio C," the guitarist replied. By the time Garrett got to the studio to see what was going on, Spector had already put the finishing touches on his version—the version that became the hit.

The Artist: The Rolling Stones
The Song: "Jumpin' Jack Flash"
The Story: One rainy winter morning, Mick Jagger and Keith Richards were in Richards's living room when Jagger suddenly jumped up, frightened by a stomping noise. Richards explained, "Oh, that's just Jack, the gardener. That's jumpin' Jack." The two laughed and Richards began fooling around on the guitar, singing, "Jumpin' Jack." Inspired by the lightning, Jagger added "Flash!"

About 45 percent of all prescription drugs contain ingredients originating in the rainforest.

THEY WENT THATAWAY

*A few more stories about the final days
of the famous, from our files.*

BENEDICT ARNOLD

Claim to Fame: Revolutionary War general and turncoat whose name became synonymous with treason

How He Died: In exile, suffering from asthma, dropsy, and gout.

Postmortem: Described as "the very genius of war" by his men, General Arnold helped turn the tide of the war in favor of the Americans at the second battle of Saratoga in 1777.

But Arnold became bitter at having been passed up for a promotion and for other perceived slights, and in 1779 switched his allegiance to the British. He conspired to surrender West Point to them in exchange for £20,000, but failed when his British accomplice, Major John André, was captured.

André was hanged as a spy, but Arnold managed to escape, and he later led a raid against American soldiers in his own home state of Connecticut before fleeing to England. There, "inactive, ostracized, and ailing," he lived with his wife and children until his death in June 1801 at the age of 60.

According to one account of Arnold's last days, shortly before he died he asked to be dressed in his Revolutionary uniform. "Let me die in my old uniform," he wheezed through his asthma, "God forgive me for ever putting on any other."

TYRONE POWER

Claim to Fame: Swashbuckling Hollywood actor best known for his action-adventure films

How He Died: From a heart attack caused by a sword fight.

Postmortem: In 1958 he was filming *Solomon and Sheba* on location in Madrid, Spain. One scene called for Power (playing Solomon) and actor George Sanders (playing Solomon's brother) to fight a duel on a staircase using 15-pound swords. Because

---

In 1986, 183 Adams were christened in the state of Oregon, but not a single Eve.

Sanders was a pathetic swordfighter, Power's scenes had to be filmed twice—close-ups with Sanders, and wide shots with a double who knew how to use a sword. It doubled his workload. After eight takes of one shot, Power was so exhausted that he walked off the set, refusing to film a ninth take. "I've had it," he told the director.

He began trembling uncontrollably and had to be helped back to his trailer. His makeup man made him some tea, but Power was unable to lift his arms to drink it. When no one could find the studio's doctor, Power was bundled into a car and driven to a nearby U.S. airbase for treatment. But he never made it—he had a heart attack in the car and was dead before he ever reached the hospital. *Solomon and Sheba*, refilmed with Yul Brynner playing Solomon, was released in 1959.

LUDWIG VAN BEETHOVEN

Claim to Fame: German composer

How He Died: Possibly by lead poisoning

Postmortem: Beethoven's last years were filled with excruciating pain: He suffered from abdominal pains, bad digestion, headaches, diarrhea, rheumatism, fever, irritability, and depression. He never knew the cause of his myriad maladies, despite having consulted with numerous doctors. On March 26, 1827, he died as he had lived for so many years: in agony. He was 57.

Snipping a lock of hair from the recently deceased was a popular custom in the 19th century. Fortunately for us, Beethoven had a lot of fans—and a lot of hair. Admirers snipped him nearly bald, and several confirmed samples of his hair survive to this day. A few strands were recently subjected to an X-ray fluorescence spectroscopy, which revealed lead concentrations of more than 100 times the level considered normal. It was enough lead to account for nearly all of Beethoven's symptoms, including his deafness. During his lifetime no one knew that lead was toxic—it was used in paint and in pottery, and was even added to wine to remove any bitterness. Beethoven could have poisoned himself with lead in any number of ways.

"If he had a favorite pewter mug that he drank from all his life, that alone could clearly be the culprit," says Russell Martin, author of *Beethoven's Hair*.

The speckles on a bird's egg are as individual as a fingerprint.

FAMOUS FOR
15 MINUTES

*Here's more proof that Andy Warhol was right when he said that
"in the future, everyone will be famous for 15 minutes."*

THE STAR: Danny Almonte, 12-year-old pitcher for the
Rolando Paulino All-Stars Little League team in the Bronx

THE HEADLINE: *Little League Champ Pitches Perfect
Game; Too Bad He's Not as Little as His Parents Say He Is*

WHAT HAPPENED: Almonte became an instant celebrity after
he pitched a no-hitter in the opening game of the Little League
World Series, the first since 1957. His major league heroes Randy
Johnson and Ken Griffey, Jr. called to congratulate him, and New
York mayor Rudolph Giuliani gave the entire team the key to
the city.

But there was trouble brewing: For months, Almonte had been
dogged by rumors that he was actually 14, not 12, which would have
made him ineligible to play in Little League. Two rival teams even
hired private investigators to look into the rumors, but it wasn't
until *Sports Illustrated* obtained a birth certificate that showed Danny
was born on April 7, 1987, not April 7, 1989 as his parents claimed,
that things started to unravel. Dominican government officials confirmed the authenticity of the certificate, just as investigators in the
U.S. discovered that 14-year-old Danny not only wasn't enrolled in
school as his father claimed—a violation of the law—but that he
and his father were in the country illegally, on expired tourist visas.

THE AFTERMATH: Danny's father was banned for life from any
association with Little League; so was team founder Rolando
Paulino. The All-Stars were stripped of their third-place title in
the Little League World Series, and all of their records—including
Almonte's no-hitter—were expunged from the Little League record
book. About the only thing the team didn't lose was its key to the
city of New York—Mayor Giuliani said he wouldn't ask for it back,
explaining that "it would only add to the hurt and the pain that
the innocent children of this team are experiencing."

The World's Largest Office Chair is in Anniston, Alabama. It's 33 feet tall.

THE STAR: Ilanit Levy, the Israeli contestant in the 2001 Miss Universe pageant

THE HEADLINE: *Beauty Queen Takes Flak for Wearing Flak Jacket*

WHAT HAPPENED: Citing a desire to "reflect the current tension in the Middle East," Miss Israel made news all over the world by incorporating body armor into the formal wear she wore during the pageant: She modeled a diamond-encrusted blue flak jacket over a camouflage evening gown. "It's very Israeli," she explained to reporters. "We have to show ourselves the way we really are."

THE AFTERMATH: The armored look won Levy plenty of headlines, but it didn't win her the Miss Universe crown. She made it all the way to the finals before being eliminated in the swimsuit contest and losing to Miss Puerto Rico.

THE STAR: Samuel Feldman, a 37-year-old Pennsylvania advertising executive

THE HEADLINE: *Adman Avoids Squeezing the Charmin—but Squeezes Just About Everything Else*

WHAT HAPPENED: In 1997 local media outlets in suburban Bucks County, Pennsylvania, began reporting a rash of "assaults" on baked goods in supermarkets and bakeries. Somebody was squeezing, crumbling, and poking thousands of dollars worth of baked merchandise, damaging it to the point that it was no longer sellable. The reign of bakery terror went on for two years before Samuel Feldman was identified as the culprit, thanks to security cameras that caught him in the act on seven different occasions. Dubbed the "Cookie Crumbler" by local reporters, Feldman went on trial in November 2000, charged with destroying $800 worth of cookies and more than $7,000 worth of bread, including 175 bags of bagels, 227 bags of dinner rolls, and 3,087 loaves of bread.

Feldman's wife, Sharon, came to his defense at the trial. "Freshness is important," she told the jury, hoping to convince them that her husband only wanted what was best for his family and was a little too picky in how he went about it. She almost succeeded: Jurors actually tried to acquit Feldman on the bread charge, but the judge overruled them, finding him guilty and telling Feldman that his conduct was "not just odd, it was criminal."

THE AFTERMATH: Feldman was sentenced to 180 days of probation, was ordered to pay $1,000 in restitution, and was advised to seek psychological counseling.

THE STARS: Princess Meriam Al Khalifa of Bahrain and Lance Corporal Jason Johnson of the U.S. Marines

THE HEADLINE: *Love-Struck Couple Ignites Royal Headache for U.S. State Department, Bahrain Royal Family*

WHAT HAPPENED: In January 1999, Johnson met his future wife by chance in a shopping mall while stationed in Bahrain. The two soon fell in love, but Princess Meriam's family forbade her to date Johnson and even put her under police surveillance when they suspected she was seeing him anyway. She was, and when her family found out, they ordered her to end the relationship.

Rather than obey, the couple eloped—on November 2, 1999, Johnson snuck Princess Meriam out of Bahrain using a fake military ID and brought her to the United States, where they were later married in a Las Vegas wedding chapel.

There were just two problems: the princess had entered the country using the same fake ID she had used to sneak out of Bahrain; and her father is the second cousin of the ruling Emir of Bahrain. That made her case an international incident. As her relatives in Bahrain used diplomatic channels to demand her return, American politicians began lining up on Princess Meriam's side, calling on the U.S. Immigration and Naturalization service to allow her to remain in the United States. Their story made headlines all over the world, and a Hollywood studio began production of a TV movie based on it even before knowing how it would end.

THE AFTERMATH: If the INS moved to deport Princess Meriam, she was prepared to request asylum on the grounds that if she returned home she faced persecution for marrying a non-Muslim. Neither Bahrain nor the United States wanted a public trial, and in the end her family dropped their demand that she be returned to Bahrain. The INS issued her a green card, which allows her to remain in the U.S. permanently. As for Lance Corporal Johnson, he was reduced in rank to private for helping his fiancée leave Bahrain without permission, and given an early honorable discharge. The couple now lives in Las Vegas.

Q: What was the first tropical storm named after a male? A: Bud.

YOU'RE MY INSPIRATION

It's fascinating to find out the inspirations
behind cultural milestones like these.

POPEYE. A real Popeye? Apparently so. E. C. Segar's character was based on a beady-eyed, pipesmoking, wiry old barroom brawler named Frank "Rocky" Feigle—a legend in Segar's hometown of Chester, Illinois, around 1915. Like Popeye, Feigle was reputed never to have lost a fight. But he was no sailor; he earned his drinking money by sweeping out the local saloon.

Note: There was a real Olive Oyl, too: Dora Paskel, a shopkeeper in Chester. She was tall and skinny, wore her hair in a bun, and even wore tall, button-up shoes.

ROCKY. In March 1975, Chuck Wepner fought Muhammad Ali for the heavyweight boxing title. Wepner, a second-rate fighter from Bayonne, New Jersey, was considered a joke. Ali didn't even bother training full-time for the match. But to everyone's surprise, Wepner lasted 15 rounds with the champ and even knocked him down. Sly Stallone saw the fight on TV and was inspired to write his Oscar-winning screenplay about Rocky Balboa.

THE SHINING. Inspired by John Lennon . . . or at least the term was. Stephen King came up with the idea of the "shining" as a description of psychic power after hearing Lennon's tune, "Instant Karma." King recalls: "The refrain went, 'We all shine on.' I really liked that, and used it. The [book's] name was originally *The Shine*, but somebody said, 'You can't use that because it's a pejorative word for Black' . . . So it became *The Shining*."

STAGE NAMES
- Nicholas Coppola "always loved the comic book character, Luke Cage, Power Man." So he changed his name to Nicholas Cage.
- Roy Scherer got his stage name by combining two geographical spots: the Rock of Gibraltar and the Hudson River: Rock Hudson.

No matter what anyone tells you, elephants are not afraid of mice.

DUMB CROOKS

More proof that crime doesn't pay.

GONE TO POT

INDIANA—"An Indiana farmer was the victim of a cruel prank when he received a phone call from the 'authorities,' busting him for growing marijuana in his backyard. During the conversation, the man was told that if he brought the plant, roots and all to the station, charges would not be pressed. Believing the call to be real, he cut down the eight-foot plant and carried it into the lobby of the sheriff's office. He was then placed into custody for suspected felony cultivation by surprised officers."

—*Bizarre News*

BLESSINGS FROM ABOVE

"A Tampa, Florida, burglar who decided to rob a 24-hour convenience store didn't know the store was open 24 hours. He cut a hole in the roof, then fell through and onto the coffee pot just as a police officer was buying some coffee."

—*"The Edge," The Oregonian*

LET'S MAKE A DEAL

"Kidnappers who abducted Gildo dos Santos near his factory in a suburb of São Paulo, Brazil, demanded $690,000 in ransom, but Santos escaped. The next day, Santos got a phone call asking for $11,500 to defray the cost of the abduction. After negotiating a discount of 50 percent, Santos called police, who were waiting when Luiz Carlos Valerio showed up to collect payment."

—*Dumb Crooks*

"HE WAS REALLY HANDSOME . . . "

"A Kwik-Fill gas station attendant in Syracuse, New York, stole $300 from the till, then tried to cover it up by calling police and reporting that the station had been robbed. His plan was foiled, however, when police asked him to describe the robber and he gave them a perfect description of himself."

—*Syracuse Post-Standard*

Most dangerous animal in Ireland: the bumblebee.

BAD TIMING

"Sherman Lee Parks of Arkansas escaped from jail on the day he was scheduled to be released. He was re-arrested and is now back in jail."

—FHM *Magazine*

EGO TRIP

"Andrew T. Burhop of Des Moines, Iowa, was arrested after robbing a bank in Muscatine. Police didn't have much trouble finding the culprit, since Burhop's getaway car had a vanity license plate, which read 'Burhop.'"

—*Des Moines Register*

PAINT IT BLACK

"Constable Duncan Dixon, from Naskup, British Columbia, was called to a mischief in progress. A young male was witnessed spray-painting the roof of a gazebo.

"'When I arrived, the witnesses pointed him out,' says Dixon, but the alleged perpetrator denied it.

"'I looked at his hands, which were covered in gold spray paint. I noted he had the cap to a spray paint can in his pocket.'

"'He continued to insist that he wasn't responsible. I also noticed his friends' shoes were painted with, of course, gold paint. This wasn't the biggest nail in the coffin of the young man: he had painted his name on the gazebo roof—first and last names.'"

—*The Valley Voice*

ACCIDENTAL IDIOT

"James Brian Kuenn, 40, on trial in Largo, Florida, for murder, said the victim's death was accidental and that he was so embarrassed at the accident that he 'made it look like murder to throw police off.' Must have worked. He was convicted."

—*Universal Press Syndicate*

NO FORE-THOUGHT

"Robbery suspect Denis Jesper, 20, was arrested at a Miami country club, where he had been hiding from police in a ficus tree next to the golf course. He revealed himself by calling out to a golfer who hit into the rough, 'Hey, hey, your ball is over there.'"

—*Wacky News*

Half of the members of the Rodeo Cowboys Association have never worked on a ranch.

WEIRD CANADA

*Canada: land of beautiful mountains, clear lakes, bustling
cities . . . and some really weird news reports. Here are some
of the oddest entries from BRI member Therese Morin.*

HOW MUCH FOR NOT ROBBING SOMEONE?

Over the 2000 holiday season, officials in Edmonton, Alberta, tried to encourage motorists to obey the rules of the road by having police officers in unmarked cars find and reward the safest drivers in town. Traffic officers tailed drivers for as long as half an hour to determine if they were truly law-abiding, then pulled the puzzled motorists over and offered them a free steak dinner for two at "Tom Goodchild's Moose Factory."

TOKEN OF OUR APPRECIATION

Over a period of 13 years, Edmonton transit worker Salim Kara patiently built a fortune of $2.3 million (Canadian) by stealing coins from fare machines using a rod with a magnetized tip. No one suspected the 44-year-old delinquent until he purchased an $800,000 house on a yearly salary of $38,000. He was sentenced to four years in prison in 1996.

OUTHOUSE NEWS

* In Tiverton, a tiny island community in Nova Scotia, "Outhouse" is the most common last name.
* In Quesnel, British Columbia, it's still a legal requirement to have an outdoor out house, at least 20 feet (6 metres) from your house, but not more than 100 feet (30 metres). It has to be "fly tight" too.

BETTER BY THE BAGFUL

Back in the 1980s, the citizens of Desmond, Ontario, needed to raise money to renovate their school. A raffle? A rummage sale? No, "Manurefest." They filled 600 bags with manure and sold them for $3 each. Some were sheep manure (sold as "Ewedunnit"), some were cow manure, and some were a guinea fowl-hen blend. "Some of it," says spokesman Henk Reininck, "was vintage—eight years old. And it don't smell at all." Manurefest has become an annual event. Next to the manure, they now sell baked goods.

In 1971 it rained in Chile's Atacama Desert for the first time since the 16th century.

FLYING CAKES

Every January, residents of the small community of Manitou Springs, Saskatchewan, get together to see who can fling their Christmas fruitcake the farthest. In the Great Fruitcake Toss, there are no rules; contestants can use catapults, slingshots, and even specially designed guns, but most prefer the "Olympic-style" discus throwing method.

WATCH WHERE YOU'RE GOING

It should be obvious to everyone, but in Ontario it's illegal for motorized vehicles to have a television on the dashboard or the front seat.

RUB-A-DUB-DUB

The Yukon isn't just the capital of the Klondike Gold Rush, it's also the capital of Bathtub Racing. They've been doing it since 1992. Every August, "tubbers" race 5 by 3-ft regulation size bathtubs 480 miles from Whitehorse down the Yukon River to Dawson City. There's another bathtub race in Nanaimo, British Columbia. The Loyal Nanaimo Bathtub Society has been holding a 36-mile race every July since 1967.

HOLE-Y COW!

Canada has more doughnut shops per capita than any other country on earth—one for every 9,000 of its 30 million residents.

LOONEY LAWS

- It is legal for women to go topless in public in Ontario.
- In Oak Bay, British Columbia, garbage crews don't have to pick up your trash if it "oozes."
- It's against the law to have a toilet room smaller than 1 square meter (10 square feet) in Halifax, Nova Scotia.

STICKS AND STONES

In 1991, a GM assembly line foreman in Ontario reprimanded a worker for having bad body odor. The worker complained to the Workers Compensation Tribunal about loss of appetite, lack of sleep, and sexual dysfunctions brought on by the foreman's insensitive remarks. The Tribunal awarded him $3,000 for "job stress."

What do turtles and honeybees have in common? They're both deaf.

CLASSIC HOAXES

Here's another classic hoax for you to enjoy.

THE SIR FRANCIS DRAKE ASSOCIATION

Background: In 1913 thousands of people with the last name Drake received a letter from the "Sir Francis Drake Association," an organization founded for the purpose of settling the estate of the legendary British buccaneer who had died 300 years earlier. The letter claimed that the estate was still tied up in probate court and that, since Drake's death in 1596, the value had grown to an estimated $22 billion. Any Drake descendant who wanted a share of the estate was welcome—all they had to do was contribute toward the $2,500-a-week "legal expenses" needed to pursue the case. When the estate was settled, each contributor would be entitled to a proportional share. There was no time to waste—the fight was underway and any Drake descendant who hesitated risked being cut out entirely.

Exposed: The Sir Francis Drake Association was the work of Iowa farmer-turned-conman Oscar Merrill Hartzell. But he didn't invent the hoax—the first of hundreds of similar swindles took place within months of Drake's death in 1596. Hartzell got the idea for his version after his mother was conned out of several thousand dollars in another Drake estate scam. When he tracked down the crooks who had swindled her and realized how much money they were making, Hartzell decided that rather than call the police, he would keep quiet . . . and launch his own scam. Using the money he'd recovered for his mother, Hartzell promptly sent out letters to more than 20,000 Drakes. Thousands took the bait. Hartzell eventually expanded the scam to target people who weren't even named Drake.

Final Note: By the time the feds caught up with him 20 years later, Hartzell had swindled an estimated 70,000 people out of more than $2 million. Rather than admit they'd been duped, many of the victims donated an additional $350,000 toward his legal defense. Hartzell was convicted of mail fraud and sentenced to 10 years in federal prison; a few years later, he was transferred to a mental institution, where he died in 1943.

Deion Sanders is the only man to play in the World Series and the Super Bowl.

SWAN SONGS

*Why are we so intrigued by death? Because it's a part
of life . . . And besides, we've all got to go sometime.
So why not enjoy a chuckle while we're here?*

DEATH AND TAXES

In late 1997, homeowner Eugene Bearringer stopped paying taxes on his home in Toledo, Ohio. Repeated attempts to contact Bearringer and his out-of-state relatives were futile, so in November 2000, county officials foreclosed on the property and sold it at auction—sight unseen—to William Houttekier of Temperance, Michigan. The following week, Houttekier went to Toledo to tour his new home . . . and found Bearringer's skeletal remains on the living room floor, where they had laid undiscovered and undisturbed for more than two years—about the same length of time that he'd gone without paying his property taxes. Bearringer, an asthmatic, had apparently died from natural causes.

County Auditor Larry Kaczala explained that the foreclosure and auction went according to standard procedure—without anyone from the county ever stepping foot on the premises. "The government would have no right to go onto that property," he explained, "because we don't own it. We just sell it for the back taxes."

"I always wondered what happened to that dude," a neighbor told reporters. "It got awful quiet over there."

LAST STOP

In September 2001, the city of Calcutta, India, announced that it would begin playing calming classical music in each of the city's 17 subway stations "to discourage passengers from trying to commit suicide." Since 1984 fifty-nine passengers have tried to kill themselves by jumping onto the tracks in front of trains; 26 of the attempts succeeded. The campaign also includes posters with slogans like "I don't like to die in this beautiful world."

"Hopefully, people contemplating suicide will listen to our music and see our posters and get diverted from killing themselves at the stations," says subway system spokesman S. C. Banerjee.

Polar bears are left-handed.

CELEBRITY GOSSIP

*Here's the BRI's cheesy tabloid section—a
bunch of gossip about famous people.*

MARTHA STEWART
Twenty-three-year-old landscaper Matthew Munnich filed
a lawsuit against Martha Stewart, claiming that the
design magnate had attacked him with her car. Reportedly, as
Munnich and his crew worked on property next door to Stewart's
New York estate, she pulled up in a dark Suburban and asked if
they had put up a fence. When Munnich replied, "No," Stewart
grew angry and began yelling things like "F***ing liar!" and "You
and your f***ing illegal aliens are no good!" Looking directly at
Munnich, Stewart then backed her Suburban into him, briefly
pinning him against an electronic security box before tearing off.
Stewart denies everything.

BURT REYNOLDS
Burt Reynolds spends more on his toupees than most people make
in a year. In late 1996, he filed for bankruptcy. Among his $4.5
million in liabilities was a $12,200 bill from Edward Katz Hair
Design—his custom hairpiece designer.

JANE FONDA
In 1970 the actress, activist, and fitness guru was arrested for kick-
ing a police officer when he found her with a large amount of pills.
All charges were dropped when it was discovered that the pills
Fonda was carrying were vitamins.

WILLIAM SHATNER
William Shatner once starred in a movie called *Incubus*, filmed
entirely in the failed "universal language," Esperanto.

JERRY SEINFELD
When Seinfeld went onstage for his first-ever stand-up perform-
ance, he was paralyzed by stage fright and forgot his entire routine.
He ran off the stage in a panic, mumbling a few lines to the crowd,
"The beach. Driving. Shopping. Parents."

Your liver—the largest organ inside your body—processes about a quart of blood a minute.

SEEING DOUBLE

The bare bear asked the dear deer, "What do you call two words that sound alike but are spelled differently?" Of course, a deer can't speak bear, but if it could it would have said, "A homophone." The phrases below describe some of our favorite homophones. Can you figure out what they're trying to say?

1. Bad-smelling chicken

2. Candy-coated hotel room

3. Moby Dick's cry

4. Revenue on little nails

5. Bullwinkle's chocolate delight

6. Rabbit fur

7. Funny bone

8. No Shakespeare allowed

9. A bumpy way to go

10. Counting your smells, sights, tastes, sounds, and feelings

11. The scared guy hid low

12. They talked about gross stuff

13. Almost speechless Mr. Ed.

14. Promised lyric poem

15. Letterhead and envelopes going nowhere

16. Spirit of a fish

17. Worried wigwams

ANSWERS

1. Foul fowl; 2. Sweet suite; 3. Whale wail; 4. Tacks tax; 5. Moose mousse; 6. Hare hair; 7. Humorous humerus; 8. Barred bard; 9. Coarse course; 10. Senses census; 11. Coward cowered; 12. Discussed disgust; 13. Hoarse horse; 14. Owed ode; 15. Stationary stationery; 16. Sole soul; 17. Tense tents

Floods cause more destruction in the United States than any other natural disaster.

THE ORIGIN OF SOAP OPERAS, PART II

Part II of our story on the creation of a truly American form of storytelling . . . and soap peddling. (See page 213 for Part I.)

TV OR NOT TV?

In 1949 Procter & Gamble formed an entire corporate division to "produce, or acquire, and produce, radio, television and motion picture shows, programs, and other forms of entertainment." And by the early 1950s, they were producing more content than any of the major Hollywood studios. TV airwaves were filled with Procter & Gamble–produced shows, including *Truth or Consequences*, *This Is Your Life*, Westerns, sitcoms, adventure shows, variety shows, and children's shows.

But not a single TV soap opera.

TV shows cost so much more to make than radio shows that Procter & Gamble preferred to focus on programs that would be broadcast in the evening, when viewing audiences were largest. Furthermore they wondered whether women would stop doing their housework long enough to sit down and watch a televised soap. And even if they did, some executives worried, was it right for the company to encourage them to do so? "It was almost a decadent implication that we were taking housewives away from their work and families," said P&G executive Ed Trach.

MAKING THE SWITCH

Finally, Procter & Gamble filmed an experimental pilot for a TV version of *Ma Perkins*. They quickly realized that making the transition from radio to TV would be even more difficult than they had imagined. After 15 years of listening to *Ma Perkins* on the radio, listeners had formed their own ideas of what she should look like. The TV version couldn't help but seem inauthentic and disappointing; sure enough, it flopped.

So they decided to create a TV soap from scratch. This, too, proved to be a challenge—*The First Hundred Years*, P&G's first original TV soap, lasted only nine months.

In 1986, in the very last scene of *Search for Tomorrow*, after . . .

P&G's next effort, *Search for Tomorrow*, debuted in September 1951. By the end of its first year on the air it had five million regular viewers. (And once it found an audience, it kept it: the show finally went off the air in December 1986, it was the longest running daily show in the history of American network television.)

THE TELEVISION ERA BEGINS

Once *Search for Tomorrow* convinced P&G that TV soaps could work, they created a TV version of its radio soap "The Guiding Light," which ran on both radio and TV until 1956. It was another huge hit, so they added still more soaps to the daytime lineup. By the mid-1950s, they had more than a dozen TV soaps on the air.

Then Irna Phillips, creator of *"The Guiding Light"* (and the person credited with introducing organ music and the amnesia storyline to soaps) suggested that P&G switch from the traditional 15-minute length to a 30-minute format. She figured that one 30-minute soap would be cheaper to produce than two 15-minute soaps, each with their own sets and staff.

P&G balked. Would viewers sit still for one half-hour soap when they could change channels and get two of the 15-minute soaps they were used to? Company execs resisted the idea for more than two years before they finally caved in and allowed Phillips to create *As the World Turns* and commissioned another soap called *The Edge of Night* from another producer, both to be 30 minutes long.

The two shows premiered on the same day in 1956 and by 1957 were the two highest rated soaps on television. That was all it took—every single soap opera on the air switched to the half-hour format. And as soap fans—and advertisers—made the switch to TV, the era of radio soaps came to an end. The last of the radio soaps went off the air on November 25, 1960.

FROM FANTASY . . .

Story lines had changed a great deal over 25 years. Depression-era listeners had preferred escapist themes that allowed them to forget their troubles. *Our Gal Sunday*, for example, was about an orphan girl from a Colorado mining town who marries "England's richest, most handsome lord, Lord Henry Brinthrope," and *Mary Noble:*

Backstage Wife was about a common Iowa girl who marries a movie star. Other soaps showcased the lives of men and women with interesting careers: ministers, doctors and nurses, and glamorous movie actresses.

... TO FEELING THEIR PAIN

For whatever reason, housewives of the 1950s were much more interested in commiserating with characters than they were in escaping with them or watching them in their careers. Fantasy-themed soap operas steadily lost viewers to soaps featuring people battling terrible illnesses, coming to terms with miserable child-hoods, and going on trial for murders they did and did not commit. *The Secret Storm*, one of the most popular early TV soaps, focused almost entirely on the suffering of the Ames family after Mrs. Ames died in a car accident in the first episode.

LOVE IN THE AFTERNOON

But the most obvious change over the years was the Great Unmentionable—s-e-x. The earliest radio soaps had featured romance, but no sex. In her 27 years on the radio, Helen Trent, the fictional heroine of the show *The Romance of Helen Trent* never consummated a single romance. From 1933 until she went off the air in 1960, her intimate life consisted of an occasional quick kiss and, once in a while, a sigh or two.

The subject of adultery, when it first appeared in radio soaps in the 1940s, was limited to married women suspecting that their husbands were cheating (invariably, they weren't). Even divorce remained a taboo subject until the late 1940s; soap opera writers could only end marriages by killing off one of the characters.

By the early 1950s, most soaps had a lone, unmarried "bad girl" character who had affairs. But these encounters were never depicted onscreen, only hinted at with kisses, knowing glances, and the occasional dance with the offending male character. Once an affair was established in this way, it could be discussed, but never shown, and the "bad girl" was always punished for her transgressions in the end.

MARRIAGE PROBLEMS

Another barrier fell in 1956, when a story line on *As the World Turns* called for an unhappily married character to divorce his wife and marry his mistress. Procter & Gamble forced the show's producers to kill the story line before it got too far, but there was no turning back.

The next love triangle came in 1957, when a male character on *Search for Tomorrow* fell in love with his wife's sister. The tale was made deliberately short in case viewers complained, but they didn't—and the theme of morally weak husbands lured into sin by immoral temptresses became a daytime staple. By the late 1960s, such love triangles often resulted in illegitimate children; the paternity secrets and child custody disputes that followed could keep a story line going for years.

SOAP GLUT

By March 1970, there were 20 soaps on the air—10 full hours every afternoon; and with the soap audience spread so thin over so many shows, ratings began to sag. In the cutthroat battle for viewers, two new themes began to emerge as audience pleasers.

The first was "young love"—romance and affairs between central characters who were younger than 35, the average age of soap opera viewers. The second was "relevancy"—soaps that dealt realistically with controversial issues of the day, such as drug abuse, abortion, interracial relationships, and the Vietnam War. (*One Life to Live* spent five months on a story line involving Pap tests, and another eight months on one involving venereal disease.)

GENERATION GAP

Unlike its competitors, Procter & Gamble stuck to its official policy of avoiding controversial subjects. Big mistake: Racier soaps like *General Hospital* and *All My Children* won the lion's share of high school and college-age women (and not a few men) who discovered soaps in the 1970s; meanwhile, P&G's traditional audience—housewives—was shrinking as increasing numbers of women entered the workforce.

Eventually, Procter & Gamble spiced up its soaps, but only succeeded in alienating traditional viewers without attracting new ones. By the 1980s, many of its longest running soaps were in trouble: *The Edge of Night* was cancelled in 1984, and *Search for Tomorrow* went off the air two years later.

The highest temperature ever reached in Britain was 98.2°F on August 9, 1911, in Surrey.

SOAPS ON THE ROPES?

By the 1980s, much of the action and excitement in the soap opera world had moved from daytime television to primetime. The trend started in 1978 when *Dallas* premiered on CBS. The first successful primetime serial since *Peyton Place* (1964–1969), *Dallas* inspired a host of imitators, including *Dynasty*, *Knots Landing*, *Falcon Crest*, *The Colbys*, and *Flamingo Road*.

Between 1995 and 1999, the daytime soap opera audience shrank by more than a third, this time because of a real-life soap opera—the O. J. Simpson murder trial.

The case, which unfolded live on TV for more than a year, had as many heroes and villains, twists and turns as any soap opera could dream of having, and yet it was real. Millions of soap opera fans abandoned their shows to follow the Simpson trial and the numerous legal shows and talk shows that followed in its wake. How could a fictional drama hope to compete?

Just as importantly, networks and cable channels discovered that true-crime shows and tabloid talk shows could be produced for a fraction of the cost of a soap opera and could thus earn huge profits even when they didn't attract as many viewers.

YOU BE THE JUDGE

Today, "lapsed" soap opera fans—people who used to watch soaps but no longer do—outnumber fans who still watch the shows. Networks and soap opera producers are working hard to get them back: ABC launched a 24-hour all-soap cable channel so that people who can't watch soaps during the day can tune in and watch them in the evenings or over the weekend. *All My Children* and other soaps let viewers decide the outcome of story lines by voting on possible outcomes over the Internet. *Days of Our Lives* let viewers vote to determine the paternity of a character's baby. And *Passions* even let fans decide whether a character should live or die. (Viewers chose death.)

Will any of these measures work? Will soap operas pull out of their current slump and be restored to their former glory? Or will they continue a slow slide into oblivion? The answer is as unpredictable as the soaps themselves. All you can do is "tune in tomorrow . . . "

A giraffe can run faster than a horse and can go longer without water than a camel.

OFF YOUR ROCKER

*We'll bet that you didn't know your favorite
singers could talk too. Here are some of the
profound things they have to say.*

"I get a lot of influences from
electric shavers."

—**Iggy Pop**

"We can fly, you know. We
just don't know how to
think the right thoughts
and levitate ourselves off the
ground."

—**Michael Jackson**

"A performer to me is like
a racehorse, except that I
don't eat hay."

—**Neil Young**

"If women didn't like
criminals, there would be no
crime."

—**Ice-T**

"My attitude, in purely
intellectual terms, was
'screw you.'"

—**Neil Diamond**

"I totally appreciate being
able to buy, say, this thou-
sand-dollar cashmere blanket
. . . because if I couldn't, I
would hate to have to go back
to regular blankets."

—**Stevie Nicks**

"Folk singing is just a bunch
of fat people."

—**Bob Dylan**

"The ocean scares me."

—**Brian Wilson**

"A lot of Michael's success
has been timing and luck. It
could just have easily have
been me."

—**Jermaine Jackson**

"I think the highest and
lowest points are the important ones. All the points in
between, are, well, in
between."

—**Jim Morrison**

"You can write a book on
each of my thoughts."

—**Vanilla Ice**

"I'd like to get a beer-holder
on my guitar like they have
on boats."

—**James Hetfield**

"Hair is the first thing. And
teeth is the second. Hair and
teeth. A man got those two
things he's got it all."

—**James Brown**

The most popular fruit in the United States: apples (followed by oranges and bananas).

UNCLE JOHN'S STALL OF FAME

*You'd be amazed at the number of articles BRI members
send in about the creative ways people get involved with
bathrooms, toilets, toilet paper, etc. So we've created
Uncle John's "Stall of Fame" to honor them.*

Honoree: Thomas Suica of Monaca, Pennsylvania
Notable Achievement: Beating the system with toilets
True Story: In November 2000, the Sky Bank announced
it was building a branch on a vacant lot next to Suica's home.
Suica, a plumber, didn't like the idea of a bank moving in next
door—so he fought back by installing 10 "decorative" toilets on
the roof of his garage. About every month or so after that, he
rearranged them to create scenes commemorating the changing
seasons. (His Christmas display: Santa's sleigh being pulled by 10
toilet reindeer.)

When the borough of Monaca fined Suica $135 and cited him
for creating "unsanitary and unsafe conditions" on his roof, Suica
fought back in court . . . and won: Judge Thomas Mannix threw
out the citation, finding that the borough "had not proved the
toilets, which Suica bought new, were unsanitary."
Update: Sky Bank eventually abandoned its plans to build a
bank next to Suica's house. So is he taking his toilets down? Not
a chance—Suica "says he will continue his protest, because he does
not trust the bank."

Honoree: Joseph Taviani of Bath, Pennsylvania
Notable Achievement: Decorating his rental properties in a
fashion worthy of a town named Bath
True Story: In July 2001, Taviani planted toilets on the lawns in
front of three rental properties he owns in Bath. Two were stolen
immediately; one, at last report, is still there. Why toilets? "When
you think of Bath, you think of a bathroom," Taviani explains.
"Tubs were too big."

The first president to act in movies: Teddy Roosevelt starred as himself in a 1908 comedy.

Honoree: Alberoni, a "low-born, clever opportunist" who worked for the bishop of Parma, Italy, in the late 1700s

Notable Achievement: Promoting himself using bathroom diplomacy

True Story: One of the French king's most obnoxious underlings was the Duc de Vendôme; he was notorious for conducting business while seated on the pot and "offering visitors a view of his backside as he got up to wipe himself." Most people had to put up with this rude treatment, but the bishop of Parma refused and sent Alberoni as his potty-proxy.

Where others saw only a French moon, Alberoni saw opportunity. "Upon seeing this spectacle," Barbara Kelatsas writes in *Inside the Pastilles of the Marquis de Sade*, "Alberoni exclaimed, 'O! culo de angelo!' and rushed to embrace the ducal posterior. This worshipful attitude, and his ability to make good cheese soups, enabled him to attach himself to the Duc de Vendôme and make his fortune."

Honoree: Irene Smith, a member of the St. Louis Board of Aldermen in Missouri

Notable Achievement: Taking care of business . . . while taking care of business

True Story: In July 2001, Smith and three other lawmakers were staging a filibuster over a redistricting plan that they felt would hurt their constituents. Smith had to go to the bathroom, but the president of the board told her that if she left the room for any reason, she would lose the floor and her filibuster would end. Rather than abandon her cause, Smith held out for 40 minutes; then, when she couldn't put off nature's call any longer, "her aides surrounded her with a sheet, tablecloth, and quilt while she appeared to use a trash can to relieve herself," according to one account. "What I did behind that tablecloth was my business," she explained afterward.

No word on whether Smith won her redistricting fight, but she certainly won the day—the Board of Aldermen adjourned without voting on the controversial plan . . . but not without condemning Smith. "The people in Missouri must think we're a bunch of morons," Mayor Francis Slay told reporters.

Seventy-two percent of Americans don't know the people who live next door.

IT'S A WEIRD, WEIRD WORLD

More proof that truth really is stranger than fiction.

WHY DIDN'T WE THINK OF THAT?

"A Denver woman has filed for divorce after finding out her husband of seven years had been faking being deaf and mute. In recently-filed court papers, Bill Drimland admitted to the ruse to escape what he called 'incessant nagging' from his wife."

—*Bizarre News*

OH, DEER

"A Pennsylvania couple woke up to find a strange intruder in their home. A deer had run into the house and into the bathroom, somehow managing to turn on the water and knock over a bottle of bubble bath. He then submerged himself in the frothy water. The Becks called state the Game Warden, who arrived with tranquilizers. 'The guy said: "There's nothing wrong. He's just in there taking a bubble bath,"' said Beck. The animal was subdued, removed from the house and released back into the wild."

—*Ananova.com*

YOU ANIMAL!

"Many Nigerians hold to the belief that people can be turned into animals and vice versa. Over the last two years, Nigerian newspapers have covered many such incidents, including the turning of two children into dogs, the turning of a vulture into a man, and the turning of a schoolboy into a yam."

—*Discovery News*

ROBBIN' HOOD

"In Australia, a man named Rob Banks, who was convicted of robbing banks, has been given a new trial because the judge said the jury may have been swayed by his name. This time he will be tried under an alias."

—*"The Edge," The Oregonian*

It would take 27,000 spiderwebs to produce a single pound of spider silk.

BRIDGE OVER DUBLIN WATER

"Irish hospital worker Willie Nugent decided he would raise money for charity by swimming across a river in downtown Dublin. There was only one problem: Nugent can't swim. So instead he crawled across a bridge, in movements 'resembling a breast stroke.'"

—*Universal Press Syndicate*

MINTY FRESH

"A farmer in India has been charged with manslaughter after allegedly killing a police officer with his rancid breath. While attempting to arrest Raji Bhattachara of Bhopal, the officer smelled the curry on the farmer's breath and died from an asthma attack."

—*Maxim magazine*

THAT'LL LEARN YA

"After being charged £20 for a £10 overdraft, 30-year-old Michael Howard of Leeds legally changed his name to "Yorkshire Bank are Fascist Bastards." The bank has now asked him to close his account. Mr. Bastards has asked them to repay his 69-pence balance by check made out in his new name."

—*Manchester Guardian*

VEGETABLY INCORRECT

"Kathy Szarko, the artist who created the 6-foot-tall Mr. Potato Head as a symbol for Rhode Island's tourism campaign, was upset after it was removed . . . for being racist because it was brown. 'He's a potato,' she said. 'That's why he's brown.'"

—*Universal Press Syndicate*

PISTOL PACKIN' PADRES

"Last week it became legal for Kentucky ministers to pack heat inside a house of worship, as long as they have a concealed weapons permit. Not all religious officials agree with the change. 'A friend of mine said it, and I'm going to repeat it,' said the Rev. Nancy Jo Kemper, 'Jesus would puke.'"

—*Wacky News*

The CIA once called an assassination team the "Health Alteration Committee.

IF YOU . . .

Life, as a series of possibilities.

IF YOU . . .
are brushing your hair, it's best to stop after about the 25th stroke. That's the right number for the best distribution of your hair's natural oils. Much more brushing than that can cause damage.

IF YOU . . .
have hair growing out of your armpit, you've got hirci. That's the fancy word for armpit hair.

IF YOU . . .
are stuck in the grip of a crocodile's jaw, jam your thumbs in its eyeballs. (Good luck.)

IF YOU . . .
get a "mustache" from drinking grape or cherry juice, you can quickly wipe it off with a bit of toothpaste dabbed on a washcloth.

IF YOU . . .
are an average American, your butt is 15 inches long.

IF YOU . . .
sneeze your most powerful sneeze, it'll come flying out of your face at a little more than 100 mph.

IF YOU . . .
have to choose between total lack of sleep or food for the next 10 days, go with lack of food. You'll die from total lack of sleep sooner (in about 10 days) than from starvation (a few weeks).

IF YOU . . .
are the electrician in charge of the lighting on a movie or TV set, you're a "gaffer." If you're an assistant to the gaffer, you're known as the "best boy."

IF YOU . . .
weigh 120 pounds on Earth, you'd weigh about 20 pounds on the moon.

IF YOU . . .
listen to a cricket chirp, you can figure out the temperature. Count the number of chirps per 15 seconds and add 40. That'll give you the temperature (Fahrenheit).

IF YOU . . .
are trying to find a tiny object on the floor, put a bare light at floor level. The light will cause the object to cast a shadow, making it easier to spot.

A freshly hatched crocodile is three times longer than the egg from which it emerged.

"YOU PRESS THE BUTTON, WE DO THE REST"

In this installment of our history of photography, we tell you about the man who is to photography what Colonel Sanders is to fried chicken: George Eastman, founder of Eastman Kodak.

CAMERAMAN

On November 13, 1877, a 23-year-old bank clerk named George Eastman walked into a camera store in Rochester, New York, and paid $49.58 for a camera and some equipment. Eastman bought only the essentials, but in those days "the essentials" included a tripod, glass plates, a plate holder, containers of photographic chemicals, and more than a dozen other items, including a tent to serve as a darkroom.

Eastman took his camera with him on a trip to Mackinac Island in Lake Huron, where he photographed some of the local sights. But as fascinated as he was by photography, he loathed the amount of equipment that was required. "It seemed," he said, "that one ought to be able to carry less than a pack-horse load."

MADE IN ENGLAND

Eastman began to experiment to see if he could simplify the process. He bought a subscription to the *British Journal of Photography*, and by chance, his first issue was the one reporting Charles Harper Bennett's perfection of the gelatin dry-plate process. The article prompted him to abandon the collodion "wet process" and start making his own gelatin plates.

"The English article started me in the right direction," he wrote. "At first I wanted to make photography simpler merely for my own convenience, but soon I thought of the possibilities of commercial production."

Like most other commercial plate makers, Eastman started out making them one at a time. He heated chemicals in an old teakettle, poured them over glass plates, then smoothed out the emulsion with a rod. It was a cumbersome, time-consuming process, and that made precoated plates expensive. Eventually, Eastman invented a

The notebooks used by Marie and Pierre Curie are still too radioactive to be handled safely.

machine to coat gelatin plates automatically, then, in April 1880, started manufacturing them to sell to local photographers and photo supply stores.

ON A ROLL

The Eastman Dry-Plate Company grew rapidly on the strength of gelatin plate sales, but that didn't stop Eastman from introducing a product in 1884 that he believed would make glass plates obsolete: it was a roll of photosensitive paper, or "film," that could be used instead of glass plates. Eastman sold this film in a box that could be attached to existing cameras, in place of the box that held the glass plates.

Using glass plates, photographers could take at most a few shots before having to reload the camera, which usually required a darkroom; with Eastman's roll film there was enough paper for 50. Added bonus: roll film wasn't heavy. "It weighs two and three-quarters pounds," Eastman explained. "A corresponding amount of glass plates and holders would weigh fifty pounds."

A TOUGH SELL

Eastman's new film seemed such an obvious improvement over glass plates that he believed it would take the photographic world by storm. He was wrong. Professional photographers had too much money invested in glass-plate technology. Besides, glass plates made negatives as large as 20 by 24 inches, which captured an incredible amount of detail and produced beautiful photographs. Eastman's film couldn't duplicate the quality.

At first, Eastman tried to adjust his product line to accommodate the needs of professional photographers, but he soon realized that this was exactly the opposite of what he should be doing. And that was when he changed photography forever.

"When we started out with our scheme of film photography," he recalled in 1913, "we expected that everybody who used glass plates would take up films, but we found that in order to make a large business we would have to reach the general public."

JUST PLAIN FOLKS

Eastman was one of the first people to understand that the number of people who wanted to take pictures was potentially much larger than the number of those who were interested in developing their own film. He realized that if he was the first person to patent a complete and simple camera "system" that anyone could use, he would have that market all to himself.

In 1888, Eastman patented what he described as a "little roll holder breast camera," so called because the user held it against their chest to take a picture. But what would he call it? He wanted the name of his camera to begin and end with the letter K—he thought it a "strong and incisive" letter—and to be easy to pronounce in any language. He made up a word: Kodak.

CLICK

Just as Eastman intended, his camera was easy to use. The photographer simply pulled a string to set the shutter, pointed the camera at the subject, pushed a button to take the picture, then turned a key to advance the film. The user didn't even have to focus: the lens was designed so that anything more than six feet away was always in focus. Price: $25—a lot of money in those days, but half what Eastman had paid for his first camera equipment 11 years earlier.

But the most important selling point of this new system was that Eastman offered to develop and print all of the pictures taken with Kodak cameras—something no camera maker had ever offered before. He sold the Kodaks loaded with enough film for 100 pictures, and when these were used up the owner could, for $10, mail the entire camera back to Rochester. The company would remove the film, process and print the pictures, and return them to the owner along with the camera, freshly loaded with enough film for 100 more pictures.

"You press the button," the company's slogan went, "We do the rest."

PICTURE PERFECT

The Kodak camera went on sale in June 1888. It was followed by an improved model, the Kodak No. 2, in 1889. By September of that year, Eastman had sold more than 5,000 cameras in the United States and was developing an average of 7,000 photographs a day.

Eastman quickly came to understand that the real money in the photography business wasn't in selling cameras—each customer needed only one—it was in selling and processing film. This gave him an incentive to lower the cost of his cameras, so that more

. . . of Decency because it contained the words "mistress" and "virgin."

people could afford to buy the film. In 1895 he introduced a Pocket Kodak camera, which at five dollars was Kodak's first truly affordable camera. Then in 1900 he introduced the Brownie, which sold for a dollar. Eastman sold more than 100,000 Brownies in the first year.

KODAK MOMENTS

Most photographers had approached photography as an art form, but Eastman worried that if his customers did the same thing, they might get bored with their new hobby and find something else to do. He believed that if he could convince the public to use their cameras to document birthdays, summer vacations, and other special moments of their lives—once a family purchased a camera they would never go without one again.

Accordingly, Kodak's advertisements featured parents photographing their children, and children photographing each other. The Kodak Girl, one of the most popular advertising icons of the early 20th century, was shown taking her camera everywhere: to the mountains and the beach, on yachts, and on bicycle rides in the country.

"Don't let another weekend slip by without a Kodak," the magazine ads cooed. "Take a Kodak with you." And millions of people did.

PATENTS PENDING

Eastman believed that the best way to stay ahead of the competition was to constantly improve his products and to protect his improvements with patents, which would guarantee sole ownership of those markets. In 1886 he became one of the first American businessmen to hire a full-time research scientist, Henry Reichenbach.

One of Reichenbach's first triumphs was a roll film that used a solution of guncotton or *nitrocellulose*—the same substance that served as the basis for the collodion process—as a base, instead of paper. The first rolls went on sale in August 1889; when it did, film as we know it was born, and the word *snapshot* entered the language.

BROUGHT TO YOU BY THE LETTER K

True to form, Eastman patented the chemistry and every step of the manufacturing process so that Kodak would have the roll film market all to itself; then, when the profits started rolling in, he used the money for more research and more patents—so that the company would continue to dominate the industry it had played such a huge part in creating.

In 1891 Kodak marketed its first "daylight-loading" camera, which allowed the user to reload film into a camera without a darkroom. In 1896, just a year after the discovery of X-rays, Eastman began manufacturing plates and paper for X-ray photographs; that same year, Kodak began selling the first motion picture film. Film for "talkies"—motion pictures with sound—followed in 1929.

These advancements continued long after Eastman's death in 1932. In 1936 Kodak brought Kodachrome Film to market, the world's first amateur color slide film; they introduced color print film in 1942. Instamatic cameras, which used easy-to-load film cartridges instead of rolls, came out in 1963; the company sold more than 50 million Instamatics in the next seven years alone. Super-8 home movie cameras hit the market in 1965, and Kodak dominated that market too.

KING OF THE HILL

Decades of continuous innovation have turned Kodak into a household word, synonymous with photography itself. When astronaut John Glenn became the first American to orbit Earth in 1962, a Kodak camera in the space capsule recorded the event. When Neil Armstrong walked on the moon seven years later, he had a Kodak with him.

Eastman accomplished what he had set out to accomplish—he brought photography to the masses. Now, with the advent of digital technology, film photography may soon disappear, like the disposable cameras Kodak makes today. But that doesn't take away from the miracle of what the pioneers of photography achieved—capturing actual images from the air and preserving them for all time, an amazing feat that once seemed impossible.

* * *

Random Fact: King James IV banned golf from Scotland in 1491 for the simple reason that it "looketh like a silly game."

Find a worm in your apple? Don't worry—it means the apple has no pesticides.

FAMILY FEUDS

Is blood thicker than water? Not when there's money
and power involved. Here are two feuds from
the BRI files that prove the point.

MURRY WILSON VS. THE BEACH BOYS

The Contestants: Murry Wilson, father of three of the Beach Boys—Dennis, Brian, and Carl Wilson—and the uncle of Mike Love. He was also the band's first manager . . . and according to his three sons, he was also an abusive tyrant.

The Feud: Murry managed the band for the first three years of its existence, from 1962 until 1964. By then the Wilsons and the Loves had had enough of his explosive temper, and they fired him while working on the tracks for "I Get Around."

At first Murry refused to accept that his sons were even capable of firing him. Then, convinced that he was the one responsible for their success, he retaliated by forming a new group, the Sun Rays, and set out to "teach those ungrateful little bastards a lesson."

And the Winner Is: The Beach Boys—although for a short time it seemed that the Sun Rays might actually make it big. Their third single, "I Live for the Sun," actually made it onto the pop charts, but that was the best they ever did. "After several more singles," Dennis Wilson writes, "they faded into the background."

From Beyond the Grave: Before he died in 1973, Murry Wilson reconciled with his son, Brian . . . they even wrote a song together in 1969, called "Break Away." But behind Brian's back, Murry had sold Brian's publishing company, Sea of Tunes, which he controlled. Murry got $700,000; Brian got nothing. Brian sued, and won $10 million, but never got the publishing rights back. The final winner: Murry Wilson.

CHARLES AND J. FRANK DURYEA

The Contestants: Charles and his brother J. Frank, two bicycle makers living in Springfield, Massachusetts, in the 1880s.

The Feud: The Duryea brothers are generally credited with building the first working automobile in the United States. After read-

---

The Wok began as a Bronze Age Mongolian helmet that doubled as a cooking pan.

ing a description of German automaker Karl Benz's car in an 1889 issue of *Scientific American*, they set out to make a car of their own; on September 1, 1893, they drove their car 600 feet down the streets of Springfield.

One question still haunts the Duryea family today: which of the brothers deserves the most credit for inventing the car? Not long after they started building it—and before they had one that actually worked—Charles went back to his bicycle business in Peoria, Illinois, and did not return for more than a year. By the time he got back, J. Frank had solved all of the technical problems by himself, without any help from Charles.

Unfortunately, for all his talent as a mechanic, J. Frank neglected to make sure he received credit for his contributions. He let Charles file the patent for their engine . . . and Charles listed himself as the only inventor. For the rest of his life he took full credit for the Duryea automobile, dismissing J. Frank as "simply a mechanic" he'd hired to execute his designs. The resulting feud shortened the life of their auto company. The brothers managed to make only 13 cars before they closed up shop and went their separate ways.

And the Winner Is: Nobody, not even after all these years. Charles and Frank's descendants are still fighting over which brother is the true inventor of the first American car.

* * *

THE AMAZING FASTING GIRL

Background: In the 1870s, a Welsh teenager named Sarah Jacobs became famous for her ability to fast for months on end. Her parents put her on exhibit, claiming she'd gone more than two years without eating a single piece of food.

Exposed: Concerned that the exhibit was a fraud, Welsh officials decided to test the Jacob family's claims by putting young Sarah in the care of a professional nurse, who would verify whether the girl ate anything or not. When she died from starvation nine days later, her parents were arrested and went to prison for fraud.

A groaner: What do you call Santa's helpers? Subordinate clauses.

E PLURIBUS UNUM

*This phrase appears on every U.S. coin . . . but what does
it mean? Don't think too hard—the answer's right here.*

THE NATIONAL SEAL

Shortly after the signing of the Declaration of Independence
in 1776, the Continental Congress created a committee of
three—John Adams, Thomas Jefferson, and Benjamin Franklin—to
design an official seal for the United States.

Adams wanted a picture of Hercules standing between two alle-
gorical figures representing Virtue and Sloth; Jefferson wanted a
depiction of "The Children of Israel in the Wilderness"; and
Franklin suggested a representation of Moses parting the Red Sea.
They couldn't agree, so they hired Swiss-born artist Pierre Eugene
du Simitiere to come up with a compromise design. Du Simitiere
combined the three themes, then added his own flourishes to the
goulash. They hated it.

Seal of Approval. Frustrated, they hired a Philadelphia lawyer
named William Barton to come up with something better. Barton
proposed his mishmash of symbols, including an eagle and crest on
one side of the seal and an unfinished pyramid on the other. But
that wasn't right, either. Finally, Secretary of Congress Charles
Thomson stripped away everything except the eagle and the pyramid, and added his own symbols, including a shield over the eagle's
chest, an olive branch in one of the eagle's claws (symbolizing
peace), and a bundle of arrows (symbolizing war) in the other. That's
the seal that was finally adopted; you can see it on the $1 bill.

Salad Days. As it turns out, two elements of du Simitiere's
original design did make it into the final seal: the all-seeing eye of
Providence, which was placed atop the unfinished pyramid, and
the motto *E Pluribus Unum:* "From Many, One," which is printed
on a banner the eagle holds in its mouth. Where did du Simitiere
get the motto? Believe it or not, historians speculate that he borrowed it from the masthead of *Gentleman's Magazine,* a popular
publication in the late 1700s. The editors of the magazine, in turn,
took it from *color est e pluribus unus,* a line in Virgil's poem
"Moretum" that "refers to the making of a salad."

The average American consumes 22 gallons of beer a year.

COURT TRANSQUIPS

We're back with one of our regular features. Do court transcripts make good bathroom reading? Check out these real-life quotes. They're things people actually said in court, recorded word for word.

Lawyer: "Okay, we've talked at length about how the accident happened, is there anything we haven't covered that you can think of, anything in your mind that you're thinking about how the accident happened that I haven't asked you and you're thinking 'He hasn't asked me that' and 'I'm not going to tell him because he hasn't asked me,' is there anything?"

Witness: "Have you lost your mind?"

Q: "Mr. Slatery, you went on a rather elaborate honeymoon, didn't you?"
A: "I went to Europe, sir."
Q: "And you took your new wife?"

Q: "Doctor, as a result of your examination of the plaintiff, is the young lady pregnant?"
A: "The young lady is pregnant, but not as a result of my examination."

Q: "Why do you handle the family finances?"
A: "Because my mom and sister ain't that bright."

Q: "Is there a difference between a reconditioned and rebuilt piece of equipment in your mind, if you have one?"

Q: "How far apart were the vehicles at the time of the collision?"

Q: "Are you being selective about what you remember and what you don't remember as to the details of your previous record?"
A: "I don't remember."

Q: "Now, doctor, isn't it true that when a person dies in his sleep, he doesn't know about it until the next morning?"

Q: "She had three children, right?"
A: "Yes."
Q: "How many were boys?"
A: "None."
Q: "Were there any girls?"

Defendant: "You know, I hate coming out here at seven in the morning and sitting downstairs with a bunch of criminals."
Judge: "I have to do the same thing every day."
Defendant: "Yeah, but you don't have to sit down in a holding tank with 'em."
Judge: "Every day I come in and I meet the dregs of society, and then I have to meet their clients."

Q: "The youngest son, the twenty-year-old, how old is he?"

The movie *Grease* was released in Venezuela under the name *Vaselina*.

ORIGINS

Once again, the BRI asks—and answers—the
question: Where did all this stuff come from?

GRANOLA

In the 1860s, a "fanatical vegetarian hydrotherapist"
named Dr. James Caleb Jackson created a breakfast food
consisting of twice-baked whole-wheat graham dough, crumbled
into pebble-sized clusters. He named his creation Granula . . . and
attracted the attention of Dr. John Harvey Kellogg. Years away
from inventing Corn Flakes, Kellogg was looking for something to
serve for breakfast at his Battle Creek, Michigan, sanatorium
besides crackers and dry toast. Dr. Kellogg made his own crumbly
cereal using a baked mixture of wheat flour, cornmeal, and oatmeal . . . and like Dr. Jackson, he called his new food Granula.
Jackson sued. Kellogg lost—and changed the spelling of his cereal
to *Granola*.

BUTTON-DOWN SHIRTS

In the 1920s it became fashionable for wealthy vacationers on the
French Riviera to wear "polo shirts"—lightweight knit shirts with
collars adapted by polo players from a shirt worn by Basque fishermen. The polo players added button-down collar points so that
collars wouldn't fly up in their faces during a hard gallop . . . and at
the turn of the century a New York haberdasher named John
Brooks saw the shirts in England. He sent some home to his family
business—Brooks Brothers—which incorporated the collar into a
line of dress shirts.

NEWSPAPERS

The first medium used to spread news and information is believed
to be the *Acta Diurna* ("Daily Events"), founded by Julius Caesar
in 59 B.C. Posted in prominent areas and gathering places all
over Rome, the daily paper contained news items as well as birth,
death, and marriage announcements, updates on criminal trials
and executions . . . and even news of sporting and theatrical
events.

No surprise—Brightest city, when seen from space: Las Vegas, Nevada.

PARACHUTES

The trouble with inventing parachutes is that if you test them yourself, you only have one chance to get it right. Andre-Jacques Garnerin became the first person to invent a *successful* parachute in 1797, when he took a hot-air balloon up to 3,000 feet and then floated back to earth in a basket tethered to a parachute similar to a large umbrella.

TRAFFIC LIGHTS

The world's first blinking green-and-red traffic light is believed to be the one erected on the corner of George and Bridge streets in London, near the Houses of Parliament. The manually operated signal featured a red gaslight for "stop" and a green light for "caution." The sign was operated by a constable standing watch for members of Parliament who wanted to cross the busy street.

The first American traffic light was installed at Euclid Avenue and 105th Street in Cleveland, Ohio, on August 4, 1904. It had red and green lights, and a warning buzzer to let motorists know when the light was about to change. Why red and green lights? They're believed to be descended from the practice of hanging red lights on trains that weren't moving.

CHOPSTICKS

"According to one theory of their origin, food was cooked in large pots, which held the heat long after everything was ready to be eaten. Hungry people burned their fingers reaching into the pot, so they sought alternatives, and grasping the morsels with a pair of sticks protected the fingers. Another version credits Confucius with advising against the use of knives at the table, since they would remind the diners of the kitchen and the slaughterhouse, places the 'honorable and upright man keeps well away from.'"

—*The Evolution of Useful Things,* by Henry Petroski

* * *

"It may be the cock that crows, but it's the hen that lays the egg."

—Margaret Thatcher

OOPS!

Everyone is amused by tales of outrageous blunders—probably because it's comforting to know that someone's screwing up even worse than we are. So go ahead and feel superior for a few minutes.

A FINE BOUQUET?

"Wine merchant William Sokolin had paid $300,000 for a 1787 bottle of Châteaux Margaux once owned by Thomas Jefferson. He presented it before a group of 300 wine collectors at Manhattan's Four Seasons restaurant in 1989, hoping that one of them might offer $519,000 for it. Before bidders could get out their checkbooks, he dropped the bottle and broke it."

—Oops!, by Smith and Decter

WHAT A CLOWN

"On its July 30 'Family Fun' page, the *Kansas City Star* ran a blurb on National Clown Week. Accompanying the text, naturally enough, was a photo of a clown. But the editor selecting the file photo neglected to look at the flip side, which would have revealed that the clown in question was John Wayne Gacy, a Chicago serial killer (and onetime clown) executed five years ago for killing 33 boys and young men. The *Star* apologized the next day in an editor's note."

—Brill's Content

1-900-JACK-ASS

"Harold Reinke in Troy, New York, called a European 900 sex line that charged $9.95 per minute. There was only one problem— Reinke was drunk and fell asleep. He woke up hours later still connected. The bill? $7,164."

—Bizarre News

COULD WE DROP THE DROP?

"The Joseph A. Bank Clothiers, Inc., of Atlanta, Georgia, requested that the word 'Inc.' be dropped from its listing in the 1982 telephone directory yellow pages. As a result, the store was listed as 'Drop Inc.'"

—Atlanta Constitution

There are over 1,000 nicknames for marijuana.

SINCERELY YOURS . . .

"The Clinton Legal Expense Trust, set up to defray President Clinton's legal expenses, sent fund-raising letters to names on a Democratic mailing list. Apparently no one screened them—one went to Bernard Lewinsky, Monica's father. His written response: 'You must be morons to send me this letter!' "

—*Time* magazine

NOT JUST ANY MAN

"At a White House reception for the nation's mayors, President Ronald Reagan went up to a black man, shook his hand and said, 'How are you, Mr. Mayor? I'm glad to see you. How are things in your city?' The man Reagan didn't recognize was Samuel Pierce, the Secretary of Housing and Urban Development, who regularly attended Cabinet meetings at which Reagan was present."

—*Oops!*, by Smith and Decter

WEEKNIGHT AT BERNIE'S?

"Last October, Ian Clifton of Sheffield, England, slumped over in a pub after consuming 11 pints of lager and untold amounts of bathtub punch. Pub regulars [who assumed he had passed out] shaved off his hair and took pictures of him posed with an inflatable doll. Actually, Clifton had died of acute alcoholic poisoning. By the time [his mates realized their mistake] and called paramedics, Clifton had been dead for about an hour."

—*Bizarre News*

SUB-CONTRACT

"To make a few extra bucks, Canada sold two old navy destroyers, the *Kootenay* and the *Restigouche*, to Richard Crawford of Florida. However, they inadvertently transformed him into a military power because they forgot to remove a 10-foot-tall, eight-barreled anti-submarine launcher from one of the ships. Embarrassed Defense Department officials announced that Crawford wouldn't be allowed to leave Canadian waters until he turned in his guns."

—*In These Times*

There are 34 bathrooms in the White House.

THE CLASSIFIEDS

Have you ever been in a place where all you can find to read in the bathroom is an old newspaper? Try flipping to the classifieds and look for unintentionally goofy ads and notices like these. (Then send them to us!)

FOR SALE

Mixing bowl set designed to please a cook with round bottom for efficient beating.

Snow blower for sale . . . only used on snowy days.

Great Dames for sale.

Four-poster bed, 101 years old. Perfect for antique lover.

Free puppies . . . part German Shepherd, part dog.

'83 Toyota hunchback— $2,000.

Free puppies: Half cocker spaniel, half sneaky neighbor's dog.

Free Yorkshire Terrier: Eight years old. Unpleasant little dog.

Full-sized mattress, 20 yr. warranty. Like new. Slight urine smell.

Nordic Track: $300. Hardly used. Call Chubbie.

WANTED

Mother's helper—peasant working conditions.

Attractive Girl Needed. Exciting interesting work. Lucrative. Nudity required.

Wanted: Unmarried girls to pick fresh fruit and produce at night.

Girl wanted to assist magician in cutting-off-head illusion. Blue Cross and salary.

MISCELLANEOUS

Notice: To person or persons who took the large pumpkin on Highway 87 near Southridge Storage. Please return the pumpkin and be checked. Pumpkin may be radioactive. All other plants in vicinity are dead.

Open house: Body shapers, toning salon. Free coffee and donuts.

Publicize your business absolutely free! Send $6.

Found: Dirty white dog . . . looks like a rat . . . been out awhile . . . better be reward.

Lost: Small apricot poodle. Reward. Neutered. Like one of the family.

Get a Little John: The traveling urinal holds 2 1/2 bottles of beer.

Nearly 60 percent of adults say they would like to walk without shoes in New York City.

WORD ORIGINS

Ever wonder where words come from?
Here are some interesting stories.

BOOTLEGGER

Meaning: Someone who distributes alcohol illegally

Origin: "In the 19th century, bootleggers actually carried illicit merchandise in the legs of high boots when making deliveries. The term was well-known and since their most common commodity was liquor, it gradually became applied exclusively to distributors of illegal booze." (From *Dictionary of Word and Phrase Origins*, by William and Mary Morris)

SHREWD

Meaning: Clever, cunning

Origin: "Probably derives from the mouselike shrew, which will fight for the smallest morsel . . . and finish the meal by eating its defeated foe. Original meaning: 'wicked, dangerous, ugly.' By the 16th century, it had its current meaning." (From *Take My Words*, by Howard Richler)

PLAYING HOOKY

Meaning: Skipping school

Origin: "First appeared in the late 1840s. It probably comes from the Dutch *hoekje*, a name for the game of hide and seek. The derivation is obviously one of skipping school to play games." (From *Etymologically Speaking*, by Steven Morgan Friedman)

CADDIE

Meaning: A person hired to carry a golfer's clubs

Origin: "From the French word *cadet*, for 'younger son.' In noble families the second son inherited neither title nor fortune and consequently often joined the army. The word *cadet* retained this military meaning, but acquired the connotation of someone who hung around waiting to be called on to do errands. This kind of cadet was abbreviated to caddie." (From *Fighting Words*, by Christine Ammer)

Termites are not related to ants. They are a member of the cockroach family.

CLASSIC (B)AD CAMPAIGNS

Every year, we feature stories of ad campaigns or promotions that backfired. There seems to be an endless supply—which leads us to believe either that Murphy's Law is alive and well (see page 393) or there are an awful lot of clueless marketing people. What do you think?

SKY HIGH

Brilliant Marketing Idea: In 1999 the Healthy Choice diet food line offered 1,000 frequent flier miles to anyone who sent in 10 proof-of-purchase seals from *any* of their products.

Oops: The company made the classic blunder of awarding a prize worth more than the item being sold. David Philips of Davis, California, figured that out. When he saw the proof-of-purchase seals on Healthy Choice's 25¢ pudding cups, "I quickly realized that for 25¢, I was getting 100 free miles," he says. So Philips bought $3,140 worth of the diet pudding cups (which he donated to food banks), and earned 1.25 million frequent flier miles, good for $25,000 worth of airline flights. The promotion was discontinued.

I'M NOT A DRINKER, BUT I PLAY ONE ON TV

Brilliant Marketing Idea: Hire superstar musician Eric Clapton to be a part of Anheuser-Busch's "The Night Belongs to Michelob" advertising campaign.

Oops: Clapton was an alcoholic. Shortly after the ad was filmed, the guitarist checked himself into a drug rehab clinic . . . and was actually in treatment in Minnesota when the ad premiered on TV. The first time he saw it, he says, "I was in a room full of alcoholics, myself being one of them, and everybody went, 'Is that *you?*'" Anheuser-Busch quickly pulled the ad.

HEIL HEATER

Brilliant Marketing Idea: In 1999 the Taiwanese trading company K.E. and Kingstone ran a promotion for German heaters, using the lighthearted slogan, "Declare War on the Cold Front!"

In 1923 French sports reporter Pierre Labric rode his bicycle down the 347 stairs . . .

Oops: The war they had in mind was World War II. According to news reports, "The company's posters had a smiling caricature of Adolf Hitler in a khaki uniform and black jackboots, his right arm raised high in a salute." Faced with a storm of protest, the company's shell-shocked marketing manager explained that he hadn't intended to show support for Hitler—only to show that the heaters were made in Germany. "We thought it was just a comic picture," he said.

OFF WITH HIS . . .

Brilliant Marketing Idea: Court TV scheduled a series of specials on Super Bowl Sunday, hoping to attract women uninterested in the game.

Oops: Every single one of the specials turned out to be a story about a woman who attacked her husband—starting with the trial of Lorena Bobbitt, accused of cutting off her husband's genitals. To make things worse, the network advertised the shows with a commercial depicting a disgruntled wife reaching for a knife to get revenge on a football-obsessed husband. The weekend before the Super Bowl, they issued a public apology.

CRASH COURSE

Brilliant Marketing Idea: Show a celebrity endorsing South Korea's Kia automobile.

Oops: The celebrity was Princess Diana, who was dead . . . and the company's TV ad re-created the car crash that killed her. London media reported that the commercial showed a "Diana lookalike in a Kia being chased through the streets by paparazzi . . . then emerging from the wreck unhurt and giving the camera a knowing wink." Kia withdrew the ad.

* * *

IT'S A WEIRD, WEIRD WORLD
"Alaskan authorities have been hunting a gunman who has held up 21 people and forced them to whistle 'Hail, Hail, the Gang's All Here.' He has never hurt anyone or stolen any property."

—The Oregonian

. . . of the Eiffel Tower. It took him 3 minutes and 17 seconds. His bike was wrecked.

"SPECIAL" EVENTS FOR TOURISTS

We're always on the lookout for bizarre tourist attractions, and these events—which attract tens of thousands of people every year—definitely qualify.

THE BUG BOWL

Location: Purdue University, West Lafayette, Indiana

Background: In 1990, a Purdue professor named Tom Turpin organized a cockroach race on campus to attract students to the field of entomology (the study of insects). Like roach problems, the Bug Bowl grew; today the Bug Bowl draws more than 12,000 people a year. But now there's a new attraction—tourists come not only to look at bugs, but to eat them.

Don't Miss: The exotic menu. Items include: mealworm chow mein; caterpillar crunch (a trail mix made with waxworms); chocolate chirpy chip cookies, which contain crickets; and basic bug quiche, made with sauteed bee larvae "or crickets, depending on your mood." There's also a cricket-spitting contest.

THE WORLD'S LARGEST RATTLESNAKE ROUNDUP

Location: Sweetwater, Texas

Background: Started in 1958, it takes place on the second full weekend of March. Inspired by area farmers and ranchers trying to get rid of the rattlers "that were plaguing them and their livestock." About 30,000 people show up each year to hunt and eat rattlesnakes. As of 1996, an astounding 231,636 pounds of western diamondback rattlesnakes had been collected.

Don't Miss: The Rattlesnake Review Parade, the Miss Snake Charmer Queen Contest, rattlesnake dances, a snake-handling demonstration, instructions on snake-milking techniques, and, of course, guided snake hunts. After the snakes are gutted and eaten, "the severed heads are adorned with blue wigs and Dallas Cowboys helmets."

During the 16th century, drinking coffee was punishable by death in Turkey.

THE REDNECK GAMES

Location: East Dublin, Georgia

Background: The only rule for tourists: if you don't like rednecks, stay home. "Some folks would prefer we didn't have this celebration of being a redneck," says East Dublin mayor George Goruto, "but they don't have to come down here. I mean, man, I wouldn't go to an opera!"

Don't Miss: The Mudpit Belly Flop, the Hubcap Hurl, Bobbing for Pigs' Feet, and the Armpit Serenade—a talent competition in which "pimply faced prepubescents stick one hand up their T-shirts, flap the other arm, and perform flatulent renditions of classics like 'Old MacDonald' and 'Green Acres.' " First prize: "a crumpled can of Bud."

THE MOSQUITO COOKOFF

Location: Crowley's Ridge State Park, Arkansas

Background: If the Bug Bowl whets your appetite, here's the next event to put on your itinerary. It's part of the annual World Championship Mosquito Cooking Contest. Participants try to top one another with recipes containing mosquitoes. (Cooking the bugs for at least 30 minutes makes the mosquitos safe to eat.) "I'd also suggest using dry mosquitoes," says park superintendent Larry Clifford, "so you don't get the gummy quality to it."

Don't Miss: The mosquito meat pie, mosquito supreme pizza, and mosquito paté.

AND DON'T FORGET . . .

- **The Annual Casket Race**, Goodwater, Alabama. "Pallbearers manhandle a coffin over an obstacle course, including a pile of sawdust and a mud-pit. The 'corpse' within must carry a cup of water through the course, not spilling one drop."

- **The National Hollerin' Contest**, Spivey's Corner, North Carolina. "Traces its origin to the tradition of local farmers yodeling hello to each other in the morning."

- **The International Worm Fiddling Contest**, Caryville, Florida. The challenge: "Drive a stake into the ground to entice worms to come up" and check out what's happening.

Whenever actress Joan Crawford remarried, she replaced all the toilet seats in her house.

IT'S SERENDIPITY

The word "serendipity" means "making happy and unexpected discoveries by accident." The more we study the details of history— scientific, pop, political . . . or any kind at all—the more we realize just how many things that impact our lives are basically accidents.

THE FIRST SYNTHETIC FIBER

In 1854 a devastating silkworm epidemic struck the silk industry in France, wiping it out, and in 1865 the renowned French scientist Louis Pasteur was asked to study the disease. One of his assistants, a young chemist named Hilaire de Chardonnet, became convinced that France needed some kind of artificial substitute for silk. Unfortunately, he had no idea how to find one.

In 1878 Chardonnet was working in a darkroom with some photographic plates when he knocked over a bottle of a photographic chemical called collodion (cellulose nitrate). He didn't bother to clean it up right away, and by the time he got around to it, much of the spill had evaporated. What was left? A sticky mess that produced "long, thin strands of fiber" as he wiped it up. The strands reminded him so much of silk fibers that he spent the next six years experimenting with the substance. Finally he invented what he called "artificial silk." In 1924 the name was changed to Rayon. It was the first commercially viable synthetic fiber, and paved the way for the entire synthetics industry.

THE FIRST ARTIFICIAL SWEETENER

In 1879 Constantin Fahlberg, a chemist at Johns Hopkins University, put in a long day at the lab. Then he washed up and went home for dinner. As he sat at the dinner table, Fahlberg noticed that the bread was surprisingly sweet. Then he realized that it wasn't the bread at all—it was something on his hands . . . and even his arms. He went back to the lab and tasted every beaker and basin he'd worked with that day (chemists weren't as cautious about poisoning themselves then). He finally found the source of the sweetness—a chemical called ortho-sulfobenzoic acid imide, which is 200 to 700 times as sweet as granulated sugar. Fahlberg patented the substance—the world's first artificial sweetener—in 1885 under the name saccharin, from *saccharvm*, the Latin word for sugar.

A FEW POP ICONS

A Classic Movie: When Frank Capra's *It's a Wonderful Life* was released in 1946, it was dismissed by critics as sappy and sentimental; by the 1950s it was largely forgotten. In the mid-1970s the movie's copyright lapsed and nobody remembered—or bothered—to renew it. That made the film "public domain"—i.e., legally, TV stations could broadcast it for free. That's why so many stations started showing it every holiday season . . . which is what turned it into the "Christmastime classic" it is today.

A Popular Radio Show: In 1977 the Program Director at Boston's public radio station WBUR invited five Boston-area mechanics to sit on a panel for a call-in talk show about cars. Two of the mechanics he asked were brothers Tom and Ray Magliozzi, owners of the Good News Garage in Cambridge, Massachusetts. Ray was busy, but Tom accepted the offer . . . and turned out to be the only person who showed up. He answered callers' questions so well that he was asked to return the next week. The week after that, he brought Ray along—and they've been doing "Car Talk" together (as Click and Clack the Tappet Brothers) ever since.

A Movie Star: In 1983, Martha Coolidge, director of a film called *Valley Girl*, was angry with the casting director, who kept auditioning "pretty boys" for the lead role. So Coolidge went to the reject pile, pulled the first photo off the top, held it up, and said. "Bring me someone like this." The picture was of Nicholas Cage, and he got the part. It was his first lead role.

EVEN WORLD WAR I

"Private Henry Tandey had the man in his rifle sights at point-blank range. It was September 28, 1918, on the French battlefield of Marcoing . . . and Tandey's courage in battle that day would earn the young soldier [a medal]. Yet when Private Tandey realized the German corporal he was aiming for was already wounded, he couldn't bring himself to pull the trigger. Only years later did he realize that the object of his mercy was none other than Adolf Hitler." (*Bizarre*)

The human brain can hold five times as much information as is in the *Encyclopedia Brittanica*.

WISE WOMEN

Some thoughtful observations from members of the stronger sex.

"If the world were a logical place, men would ride side saddle."
—**Rita Mae Brown**

"Creative minds have always been known to survive any kind of bad training."
—**Anna Freud**

"Blessed is the man who, having nothing to say, abstains from giving worthy evidence of the fact."
—**George Eliot**

"If you just set out to be liked, you would be prepared to compromise on anything at any time, and you would achieve nothing."
—**Margaret Thatcher**

"If you don't risk anything, you risk even more."
—**Erica Jong**

"How wonderful it is that nobody need wait a single moment before starting to improve the world."
—**Anne Frank**

"It is not true that life is one damn thing after another. It's one damn thing over and over."
—**Edna St. Vincent Millay**

"The heresy of one age becomes the orthodoxy of the next."
—**Helen Keller**

"Regret is an appalling waste of energy; you can't build on it; it is only good for wallowing in."
—**Katherine Mansfield**

"In the face of an obstacle which is impossible to overcome, stubbornness is stupid."
—**Simone de Beauvoir**

"Spend the afternoon. You can't take it with you."
—**Annie Dillard**

"You can be up to your boobies in white satin, with gardenias in your hair and no sugarcane for miles, but you can still be working on a plantation."
—**Billie Holiday**

"You take your life in your own hands, and what happens? A terrible thing: no one to blame."
—**Erica Jong**

"Just remember, we're all in this alone."
—**Lily Tomlin**

In 1916 Cumberland College's quarterback was knocked unconscious in the first play . . .

FLUBBED HEADLINES

*These are 100 percent honest-to-goodness headlines. Can
you figure out what they were trying to say?*

*Lebanon Will Try
Bombing Suspects*

**Officials Warn Clams,
Oysters Can Carry Virus**

Man Shoots Neighbor
with Machete

**STRIPPER RESENTS
EXPOSURE**

*Multiple-Personality Rapist
Sentenced to Two Life Terms*

Iran Claims Success in Its
Attack on Iran

RETIRED PRIEST TO
MARRY SPRINGSTEEN

**Defendant's Speech Ends
in Long Sentence**

*Old School Pillars Are
Replaced by Alumni*

**19 Feet Broken in
Pole Vault**

Kicking Baby Considered
to Be Healthy

*Henshaw Offers Rare
Opportunity to Goose Hunters*

TERMINAL SMOG
NOT LETHAL

Police Kill Man with TV
Tuner

**Milk Drinkers Are
Turning to Powder**

*Bible Church's Focus
Is the Bible*

TWO CONVICTS EVADE
NOOSE, JURY HUNG

Stiff Opposition Expected to
Casketless Funeral Plan

**Council to Examine
Impotant Problems**

LITERARCY WEEK
OBSERVED

*Prosecutor Releases Probe
into Undersheriff*

Queen Mary Having Bottom
Scraped

LARGE CHURCH
PLANS COLLAPSE

**Potential Witness to
Murder Drunk**

NJ JUDGE TO RULE
ON NUDE BEACH

Official: Only Rain Will
Cure Drought

. . . against Georgia Tech. They went on to lose, 222–0, the worst defeat in football history.

REEL LIFE

They say art imitates life, but sometimes the facts get screwed up. And in Hollywood, truth inevitably takes a back seat to drama. Here are a few examples.

THE BRIDGE ON THE RIVER KWAI (1957, Alec Guinness, William Holden, Sessue Hayakawa)

The movie plot: British POWs in World War II Burma are forced to build a railway bridge for their cruel Japanese captors. Using superior British know-how, they succeed. The British commander, Col. Nicholson, takes such pride in the construction that at first he defends it against saboteurs, but then comes to his senses and blows it up himself.

The real story: The POWs actually built two bridges. And they used Japanese know-how, not British. The Japanese weren't all cruel. In fact, the real British commander, Lt. Col. Toosey, testified on behalf of Japanese commander Major Saito at his war crimes trial, saving him from a death sentence. The bridges were destroyed two years later, by the RAF, not saboteurs.

THE ENGLISH PATIENT (1996, Ralph Fiennes, Kristin Scott Thomas, Juliette Binoche)

The movie plot: French-Canadian nurse cares for dashing Count Laszlo Almasy (Ralph Fiennes), a burn victim, in a Tuscan villa at the end of World War II. Using flashbacks, the film recounts Almasy's illicit love affair with a friend's wife (Kristin Scott Thomas), his devotion to her and her tragic death. As he lays dying, his last thoughts are of her.

The real story: The real Count Almasy was a puny man with bad teeth. He was gay and in love with a German Army officer. He wasn't burned and did not die at the end of World War II. Actually, after the war, he worked as a Soviet spy.

THE STING (1973, Robert Redford, Paul Newman, Robert Shaw)

The movie plot: Two con artists, Gondorf (Newman) and Hooker (Redford) set up an elaborate betting parlor scam on an Irish racketeer to avenge the murder of a fellow grifter. The sting works and the lovable conmen get away with it.

The real story: There really was a Gondorf (but no Hooker). He and his brother really did work this scam. But they did it for money, not for justice. The real "sting" was pulled in 1914 on an Englishman who was cheated out of $10,000. He went to the real police and Gondorf went to a real prison.

SATURDAY NIGHT FEVER (1977, John Travolta, Karen Lynn Gorney)

The movie plot: Bored with his day-to-day life, Tony Manero, a Brooklyn teenager (played by John Travolta) becomes the local disco king.

The real story: The movie was based on an article in *New York* magazine by writer Nik Cohn, who supposedly met and interviewed the real Tony Manero. But it turned out to be a lie—there was no real Tony Manero. In 1997 Cohn admitted he had made the character up.

RAIDERS OF THE LOST ARK (1981, Harrison Ford, Karen Allen, John Rhys-Davies)

The movie plot: Swashbuckling, whip-wielding archeologist Indiana Jones battles the Nazis to locate the mythical Ark of the Covenant, which contains the original Ten Commandments. Good triumphs over evil, and Indie returns to his job as college professor awaiting his next adventure.

The real story: Jones's character is based on the 18th-century inventor-turned-archaeologist (and circus performer), Giovanni Belzoni, who discovered several lost tombs in Egypt's Valley of the Kings. He battled French Egyptologists, not Nazis. And he didn't live happily ever after—he died from dysentery at the age of 55 while searching for the lost city of Timbuktu.

* * *

Weird World: "120 men named Henry attacked each other during a "My Name Is Henry" convention in Australia. The melee was set off when one Henry accused another of not being a Henry at all but an Angus, provoking an instant fistfight." —*Bizarre* **magazine**

Some species of ants have five noses.

WHAT'S THE NUMBER FOR 911?

*Here are some of our favorite transcripts of 911
calls. Believe it or not, they're all true.*

Dispatcher: "Nine-one-one. What's your emergency?"

Caller: "I heard what sounded like gunshots coming from the brown house on the corner here."

Dispatcher: "Do you have an address."

Caller: "No, I'm wearing a blouse and slacks. Why?"

Dispatcher: "Nine-one-one. What's your emergency?"

Caller: "Someone broke into my house and took a bite out of my ham-and-cheese sandwich."

Dispatcher: "Excuse me?"

Caller: "I made a ham-and-cheese sandwich and left it on the kitchen table, and when I came back from the bathroom, someone had taken a bite out of it."

Dispatcher: "Was anything else taken?"

Caller: "No. But this has happened to me before, and I'm sick and tired of it."

Dispatcher: "Nine-one-one."

Caller: "Hi, is this the police?"

Dispatcher: "This is 911. Do you need police assistance?"

Caller: "Well, I don't know who to call. Can you tell me how to cook a turkey? I've never cooked one before."

Dispatcher: "Nine-one-one. Fire or emergency?"

Caller: "Fire, I guess."

Dispatcher: "How can I help you, sir?"

Caller: "I was wondering... does the Fire Department put snow chains on their trucks?"

Dispatcher: "Yes, sir. Do you have an emergency?"

Caller: "Well, I've spent the last four hours trying to put these darn chains on my tires and...well...do you think the Fire Department could come over and help me?"

Dispatcher: "Help you what?"

Caller: "Help me get these damn chains on my car!"

If you're an average adult, you'll eat 2,000 pounds of food this year.

WERE YOU RAISED IN A BARN?

Tell the truth—how are your manners? Maybe you need some help from these old etiquette books. You may not believe it, but we really didn't make them up.

"Although asparagus may be taken in the fingers, don't take a long drooping stalk, hold it up in the air, and catch the end of it in your mouth like a fish."
—***Etiquette*** (1922)

"Do not move back and forth on your chair. Whoever does that gives the impression of constantly farting or trying to fart."
—***On Civility in Children*** (1530)

"If a dish is distasteful to you, decline it, but make no remarks about it. It is sickening and disgusting to explain at a table how one article makes you sick, or why some other dish has become distasteful to you. I have seen a well-dressed tempting dish go from a table untouched, because one of the company told a most disgusting anecdote about finding vermin served in a similar dish."
—***Martine's Handbook of Etiquette*** (1866)

"It is not the correct thing to put the spoon or fork so far into the mouth that the bystanders are doubtful of its return to the light."
—***The Correct Thing in Good Society*** (1902)

"No decent person laughs at a funeral."
—***The Bazar Book of Decorum*** (1870)

"When you have blown your nose, you should not open your handkerchief and inspect it, as though pearls or rubies had dropped out of your skull. Such behavior is nauseating and is more likely to lose us the affection of those who love us than to win us the favor of others."
—***The Book of Manners*** (1958)

"Never put your cold, clammy hands on a person, saying, 'Did you ever know anyone to have such cold hands as mine?'"
—***Manners for Millions*** (1932)

"It is unmannerly to fall asleep, as many people do, whilst the company is engaged in conversation. Their conduct shows that they have little respect for their friends and care nothing either for them or their talk. Besides, they are generally obliged to doze in an uncomfortable position, and this nearly always causes them to make unpleasant noises and gestures in their sleep. Often enough they begin to sweat and dribble at the mouth."
—*The Book of Manners* (1958)

"Peevish temper, cross and frowning faces, and uncomely looks have sometimes been cured in France by sending the child into an octagonal boudoir lined with looking glasses, where, whichever way it turned, it would see the reflection of its own unpleasant features, and be constrained, out of self-respect, to assume a more amiable disposition."
—*Good Behavior* (1876)

"If you ask the waiter for anything, you will be careful to speak to him gently in the tone of request, and not of command. To speak to a waiter in a driving manner will create, among well-bred people, the suspicion that you were sometime a servant yourself, and are putting on airs at the thought of your promotion."
—*The Perfect Gentleman* (1860)

"It is bad manners, when you see something to nauseate you by the roadside, as sometimes happens, to turn to your companions and point it out to them. Still less should you offer any evil smelling object for others to sniff, as some people do, insisting upon holding it up to their noses and asking them to smell how horrible it is."
—*The Book of Manners* (1958)

"When not practicable for individuals to occupy separate beds, the persons should be of about the same age, and in good health. Numerous cases have occurred where healthy, robust children have 'dwindled away' and died within a few months, from sleeping with old people.
—*The People's Common Sense Medical Adviser* (1876)

"Applause is out of order at any religious service."
—*Your Best Foot Forward* (1955)

Most adults believe we will make "first contact" with alien life by the year 2100.

A 'TOON IS BORN

*TV cartoons used to be tame and bland. But now, with cable,
there's a whole new breed of 'toons. Here are the stories
of how a couple of new cable classics were created.*

R UGRATS
Background: Arlene Klasky and her husband, Gabor
Csupo, owned the studio that animated *The Simpsons* in the
late 1980s. One afternoon in 1989, Klasky was at home trying to
plan for a meeting the following day with Nickelodeon. The kids'
cable channel was looking for new Sunday morning programming,
but Klasky and Csupo didn't have any viable ideas.

Inspiration: As Klasky sat watching her three-year-old and 15-
month-old playing with each other, the idea suddenly came to her:
create a cartoon that explored childhood from a toddler's point of
view. She called Csupo and their creative director, Paul Germain,
and the trio fleshed out the *Rugrats* concept that night.

"People kept telling me, 'Everybody's done babies already,'"
recalls the exec who bought the show, "but this was perfect." The
first six-minute *Rugrats* test cartoon featured a big-headed, pigeon-
toed baby (inspired by Klasky's son Jarett) "staring up at a toilet as
though it were the monolith from *2001: A Space Odyssey.*"

On the Air: *Rugrats* premiered in August 1991. It ran for four
years on Sunday mornings, then Nickelodeon stopped buying new
episodes. Ironically, that's when the show became a hit.
Nickelodeon began airing reruns twice a day on weekdays, and kids
finally discovered it. Today, according to surveys, the *Rugrats* characters are more recognizable to small children than even Mickey
Mouse and Bugs Bunny.

SOUTH PARK

Background: In 1994, a Fox executive named Brian Graden saw a
film called *Cannibal: The Musical*, created by Trey Parker and Matt
Stone, two Colorado State University film students. Graden was
impressed and tried to develop a few show ideas for Fox with the
pair. But nobody at the network was interested in either *Cannibal*

Columbus traveled at an average speed of 2.8 mph on his first voyage across the sea.

or *Conifer*, a show based on kids Parker had grown up with in Conifer, Colorado.

Inspiration: In the meantime, Graden hired Parker and Stone to make him an animated video Christmas card—partly out of admiration for their talents . . . but also to help them pay their rent. He gave them $2,000. Rather than burn the money on sophisticated animation, the pair spent $750 animating construction paper cutouts and pocketed the difference. Result: A five-minute cartoon called "The Spirit of Christmas," in which Jesus and Santa Claus curse each other out and battle to see who has the biggest claim on the holiday.

"I was supposed to send it to 500 people on my executive kiss-a—list," Graden says. "Then I saw it and thought, OK, this is the funniest thing I've ever seen, but I can't send it to studio heads. So I sent it to about 40 friends, most of them not even in the business." Graden's friends passed it on to their friends, and so on, and from there the video was distributed to tens of thousands of people over the Internet, generating such a buzz in Hollywood that people who'd earlier turned down Parker and Stone's work took a second look.

On the Air: Comedy Central eventually bought *Conifer* . . . but by then the name of the show had changed. "*Conifer* just wasn't a great name for a show," Parker explains, "so we named it after the town of South Park," a real town about an hour away from Conifer. Why South Park? "Because," says Parker, "that was where all the weird stuff was happening."

It aired for the first time on August 13, 1997. Thirteen episodes later, *South Park* had become the highest-rated series in Comedy Central's history; it has gone on to become the top-rated series on cable, seen by five million people every week.

* * *

WEIRD CLAIM TO FAME

"In 1973, Amar Bharti of India raised his right arm—and has kept it there ever since. This 26-year-and-counting endeavor supposedly shows respect for the Hindu god Shiva." (*Stuff*)

THE REAL STORY OF MURPHY'S LAW

The amazing thing about Murphy's Law is that it's true. In other words, whatever can go wrong, actually will go wrong. Scientific experiments have proven it. For example, if we weren't careful, this paragraph might get printed backward. Boy, wouldn't that be embarrassing. Well . . . it could happen. Here's why.

HISTORY

The sentiment expressed in Murphy's Law, "Anything that can go wrong, will go wrong," has probably been around as long as there have been things to go wrong. In 1786, for example, Scottish poet Robert Burns wrote, "The best laid schemes o' mice an men gang aft agley [are prone to go awry]."

But the official Murphy's Law is much more recent. In fact, it's barely 50 years old.

HOT SEAT

In 1949, the U.S. Air Force conducted a series of tests on the effect of rapid deceleration on pilots, so they could get a better understanding of how much force people's bodies can tolerate in a plane crash. The tests, part of what was known as Project MX981, consisted of strapping volunteers into a rocket-propelled sled, accelerating the sled, and then slamming on the brakes—bringing the sled to a very abrupt stop. The volunteers wore a special harness fitted with 16 sensors that measured the acceleration, or G-forces, on different parts of their body.

The harness was the invention of an Air Force captain named Edward A. Murphy . . . but the 16 individual sensors were installed by someone else.

BRAKE DOWN

On the day of the fateful test, a volunteer named John Paul Stapp was strapped into the sled and the rockets were fired. The test went off as expected—the sled accelerated to a high speed and

. . . which he lost, than he got in the 1884 presidential election . . . which he won.

then abruptly braked to a stop, subjecting his body to such enormous forces that, according to one account, when he stumbled off the sled, his eyes were bloodshot and his nose was bleeding. Stapp's body is believed to have endured forces equivalent to 40 Gs, or 40 times the force of gravity. But no one will ever know for sure, because all 16 of the sensors failed, each one giving a zero reading for the test.

When Murphy examined the harness to see what had gone wrong, he discovered that the technician who had installed the sensors had wired every single one of them backward. Because of a simple human error, Stapp's life had been put at risk in vain.

There are varying accounts of what Murphy said next—he may have cursed out the technician responsible for the mistake, saying "If there is any way to do it wrong, he'll find it." Whatever he said originally, at a press conference a few days later Stapp quoted him as having said, "If there are two or more ways to do something and one of those results in a catastrophe, then someone will do it that way."

Within months, this expression became known throughout the aerospace industry as "Murphy's Law."

FIRST VICTIM

This first version of Murphy's Law might never have become known beyond the participants of Project MX981 had it not been a very sound design and engineering principle. The sensors in Murphy's harness failed not just because they had been installed backward, but also because they were *capable* of being installed backward. Had they been designed so they could not be installed in the incorrect way—they would never have failed in the first place.

A few days later, Murphy himself redesigned the sensors so that they could only be installed one way, and the problem never came up again. (Murphy's Law is why two-pronged electrical plugs are now designed with one prong slightly larger than the other—so they can only be plugged in the proper way.)

Murphy's Law became a popular principle throughout the aerospace industry, and from there it spread to the rest of the world. But as it spread it also evolved into the popular, more pessimistic form, "If anything can go wrong, it will go wrong."

Over 2,500 lefties die each year "using products meant for right-handed people."

THE SCIENCE OF MURPHY'S LAW

Since 1949, any number of permutations of Murphy's Law have arisen, dealing with subjects as diverse as missing socks and buttered bread falling to the floor. As the BRI's own research has shown us, some of these laws are grounded in very solid science:

- **Murphy's Law of Buttered Bread**: "A dropped piece of bread will always land butter-side down."
  Scientific analysis: The behavior of a piece of bread dropped from table height is fairly predictable: As it falls to the ground it is more likely than not to rotate on its axis; and the distance to the ground is not sufficient for the bread to rotate the full 360 degrees needed for it to land faceup. So more often than not, it will land facedown.

- **Murphy's Law of Lines**: "The line next to you will move more quickly than the one you're in." (Also with a line of traffic.)
  Scientific analysis: On average, all the lanes of traffic, or lines at a K-Mart, move at roughly the same rate. That means that if there's a checkout line on either side of you, there's a two in three chance that one of them will move faster than the one you're in.

- **Murphy's Law of Socks**: "If you lose a sock, it's always from a complete pair."
  Scientific analysis: Start with a drawer containing 10 complete pairs of socks, for a total of 20 socks. Now lose one sock, creating one incomplete pair. The drawer now contains 19 socks, 18 of which belong to a complete pair.
  Now lose a second sock. If all of the remaining socks have the same odds of being lost, there's only 1 chance out of 18 that this lost sock is the mate of the first one that was lost. That means there's a 94.4% chance that it's from one of the complete pairs.

- **Murphy's Law of Maps**: "The place you're looking for on the map will be located at the most inconvenient place on the map, such as an edge, a corner, or near a fold."
  Scientific analysis: If you measure out an inch or so from each edge of the map and from each fold, and then calculate the total area of these portions of the map, they'll account for more than half the total area of the map. So if you pick a point at random, there's a better than 50 percent chance that it will be in an inconvenient-to-read part of the map.

ZAPPA'S LAW & OTHER FACTS OF LIFE

You know Murphy's Law: "Anything that can go wrong, will go wrong." Here are some other immutable laws of the universe to consider.

Zappa's Law: There are two things on earth that are universal: hydrogen and stupidity.

The Murphy Philosophy: Smile. Tomorrow will be worse.

Baruch's Observation: If all you have is a hammer, everything looks like a nail.

Lowe's Law: Success always occurs in private, and failure in full public view.

Todd's Law: All things being equal, you lose.

Thompson's Theorem: When the going gets weird, the weird turn pro.

Vac's Conundrum: When you dial a wrong number, you never get a busy signal.

The Golden Rule of Arts and Sciences: Whoever has the gold makes the rules.

The Unspeakable Law: As soon as you mention something . . .

- if it's good, it goes away.

- if it's bad, it happens.

Green's Law of Debate: Anything is possible if you don't know what you're talking about.

Hecht's Law: There is no time like the present to procrastinate.

Sdeyries's Dilemma: If you hit two keys on the typewriter, the one you don't want hits the paper.

The Queue Principle: The longer you wait in line, the greater the likelihood that you are standing in the wrong line.

Johnson's Law: If you miss one issue of any magazine, it will be the issue that contained the article, story, or installment you were most anxious to read.

Issawi's Law of Progress: A shortcut is the longest distance between two points.

Ginsberg's Theorem:

1. You can't win.

2. You can't break even.

3. You can't even quit the game.

When Martin Van Buren was vice president . . .

Perkins's Postulate: The bigger they are, the harder they hit.

Johnson and Laird's Law: A toothache tends to start on Saturday night.

The Salary Axiom: The pay raise is just large enough to increase your taxes and just small enough to have no effect on your take-home pay.

Hutchin's Law: You can't out-talk a man who knows what he's talking about.

Wellington's Law of Command: The cream rises to the top. So does the scum.

Todd's Two Political Principles:

1. No matter what they're telling you, they're not telling you the whole truth.

2. No matter what they're talking about, they're talking about money.

Kirby's Comment on Committees: A committee is the only life form with 12 stomachs and no brain.

Harrison's Postulate: For every action, there is an equal and opposite criticism.

Murphy's Paradox: Doing it the hard way is always easier.

* * *

WORD ORIGINS

BUTTERFLY
Meaning: An insect
Origin: "The most generally accepted theory of how this insect got its name is a once-held notion that if you leave butter or milk uncovered in a kitchen, butterflies will land on it . . . and eat it. Another possibility is that the word is a reference to the color of the insects' excrement." (From *Dictionary of Word Origins*, by John Ayto)

GENUINE
Meaning: Real, not fake
Origin: "Originally meant 'placed on the knees.' In ancient Rome, a father legally claimed his new child by sitting in front of his family and placing his child on his knee." (From *Etymologically Speaking*, by Steven Morgan Friedman)

THE MINIATURE GOLF CRAZE

*Most of us have played this "sport" at least once, but today we can't
imagine how popular it was in the late 1920s. Here's the story of
one of the most popular American fads of all time.*

LILLIPUTIAN LINKS

It all started in 1927 at a hotel perched on Tennessee's
Lookout Mountain, the picturesque site of a major Civil War
battle. The owner, Garnet Carter, wanted to find a way to promote
his resort and golf course. He decided to build a new golf course
that anyone could play—a cheap version of the tiny courses that
used to appear in front of English Inns. The hazards on the course—
tree roots, sand traps, and water hazards—were arranged so that
even the most pathetic golfer could handle them. His plan worked
so well that the mini-links soon eclipsed the resort's other attractions, and he had to charge a "greens fee" to keep the massive
crowds down.

BOOM

Carter was an astute businessman—he immediately recognized
the potential profits in miniature golf. So he founded the
Fairyland Manufacturing Company and began constructing "Tom
Thumb" courses all over Tennessee and, eventually, the entire
South.

In the fall of 1929, the pygmy links invaded California and
New York, and then the rest of the nation. For only $2,000,
Carter's company would lay down a course that would be opera-
tional in less than a week, and they proved so popular (and profitable) that many courses would earn back their initial investment
in only a few days. The game was the first of many recreational
fads of the Great Depression, successful mainly because it was so
inexpensive to play.

Within a year, you could find mini golf courses everywhere—
from highway filling stations to vacant city lots. And by the mid-
1930s, 20 million Americans were regular players. On any given

night, there were close to four million people flooding over 40,000 courses nationwide. People joked that the only industry still hiring during the Depression was miniature golf, which in 1930 employed 200,000 workers and generated profits of over $225 million in a single year.

Not only that, the fad helped bolster the flagging Depression-era cotton and steel industries. How? Crushed cotton seed hulls were used as a surfacing material for the greens and steel pipes were used for trick shots and hazards.

IT'S A SIN

Even a pastime as harmless as miniature golf was not without controversy. The courses were banned within 50 feet of churches, hospitals, and public schools, and the nongolfing element of the population complained nightly that the late-night revelry of reckless young golfers—who would spike their sodas with bootleg liquor— disturbed their sleep. The game also sparked a debate between physicians and pastors. Doctors liked it—miniature golf took young folks out of stuffy movie theaters at night and put them in the fresh outdoor air for some healthy activity. But church officials claimed that playing on the Sabbath—the most popular day for recreation—was a sin. Ironically, a few churches around the country saw a chance to help pay off their debts and went over to the dark side, encouraging one and all to come and play (but never on the Sabbath).

BUST

In the end, too many entrepreneurs saw a cheap, profitable Tom Thumb course as their road out of financial hardship. The fatal combination of market saturation and dwindling interest in the game brought about its swift end. In 1931 *Miniature Golf Management*, a one-year-old publication, noted that every California course was in the red financially.

But its shrewd inventor survived the fall. In 1929, he had the foresight to sell out to a Pennsylvania pipe manufacturer and settle for royalties from future miniature courses. At the end of the tiny sport's three-year heyday, he emerged unscathed. A half-century later, the game retains a small following in more than one sense of the word—it has been bequeathed to children.

. . . (only 6) that the prize has been called "the kiss of death for college players."

Q & A:
ASK THE EXPERTS

Everyone's got a question or two they'd like answered—basic stuff like "Why is the sky blue?" Here are a few of those questions, with answers from books by some of the nation's top trivia experts.

WRONG TURN

Q: Why do so many earthworms come out on the sidewalk when it rains?

A: "Most people assume that earthworms come to the surface during heavy rains to avoid drowning in their tunnels. In fact, worms can live totally submerged in water, so drowning isn't the problem. But the rainwater that filters down through the ground contains very little oxygen, so the real reason earthworms come to the surface is to breathe.

"Once above ground, earthworms are very sensitive to light, and even a brief exposure to the sun's rays can paralyze them. Unable to crawl back into their burrows, they eventually dry out and die on the sidewalk." (From *101 Questions & Answers About Backyard Wildlife*, by Ann Squire)

FUZZY LOGIC

Q: Why are tennis balls fuzzy?

A: "The fuzz is to slow the balls down. Tennis balls are made to exacting standards so players have a decent chance of hitting them. The fuzz makes the ball softer and less bouncy and increases wind resistance. In addition, the fuzz adds to a player's racket control because the strings hold onto the surface of the ball longer." (From *Just Curious, Jeeves*, by Jack Mingo and Erin Barrett)

ASLEEP AT THE WHEEL

Q: You are driving in bumper-to-bumper traffic on the highway. Then, suddenly, inexplicably, traffic clears. What caused the jam? What caused the traffic to clear?

A: "It's the shock-wave effect. Highway drivers operate best at

World's most popular "laptop": the Etch-a-Sketch.

speeds of 35 mph and higher. When highway traffic volume nears its capacity, some stragglers begin driving under 35 mph and a traffic jam is born.

"Slower speeds, theoretically, should increase control and maneuverability, but drivers grow fearful as their pace declines. The shock-wave effect occurs because drivers look for the reason they had to slow down in the first place: they overreact to any stimuli, particularly the brake lights of cars ahead of them. A few drivers at 25 mph can set off a shock-wave effect for miles behind them and create bumper-to-bumper traffic without any ostensible reason.

"Why do these traffic jams suddenly disappear? Usually, it's because there is enough breathing room ahead to prompt even slow-poke victims of the shock-wave effect to risk peeling away at 35 mph or more." (From *Imponderables*, by David Feldman)

CAPTAIN'S LOG, SUPPLEMENTAL

Q: *Star Trek* episodes often refer to the "star date." What exactly is a star date?

A: "Who knows? Star dates were among hundreds of unexplained space terms invented by *Star Trek* scriptwriters.

"The dates in the original show (1966–1969) were of the form 0000.0 and were assigned pretty much at random, the producers merely keeping a list to avoid duplication. Eventually it was agreed that the units were roughly equivalent to Earth days and decimals were tenths thereof. For *Star Trek: The Next Generation*, one production staffer was actually 'keeper of the star dates' . . . but everybody is still pretty vague on what the numbers mean." (From *Return of the Straight Dope*, by Cecil Adams)

SWEET SCIENCE

Q: Why can I melt sugar, but not salt?

A: "Who says you can't melt salt? Any solid will melt if the temperature is high enough. Lava is molten rock, isn't it? If you want to melt salt, all you have to do is turn your oven up to 1474°F. Sugar, being made from a living thing, is an 'organic' compound and melts at a much lower temperature—365°F. Salt, being a mineral, is inorganic. Inorganic compounds require more energy (in this case, heat) to break apart." (From *What Einstein Didn't Know*, by Robert L. Wolke)

MADE IN SWITZERLAND

*If you've ever owned a Swiss army knife, chances are
you've asked yourself these two questions: Is there a Swiss army?
And if so, do they really use these knives? The short answer
is yes . . . and yes. Here's the long answer.*

BACKGROUND. In 1891 Karl Elsner, owner of a company
that made surgical instruments, got a rude shock—he found
out that the pocket knives used by the Swiss army were
made in Germany. Outraged, he founded the Association of Swiss
Master Cutlers. Their purpose: Swiss knives for Swiss soldiers.
Elsner designed a wood-handled knife that also contained a screw-
driver, a punch, and a can opener. He called it "the Soldier's Knife"
and sold it to the Swiss army.

But Elsner wasn't done yet—he also wanted to develop a better
knife for officers. It took five years, but he finally found a way to
put blades on both sides of the handle, using the same spring to
hold them in place—something no one had done before. This
made it possible to put roughly twice as many features on the knife.
Elsner replaced the wood handle with red fiber (which lasted
longer), then added a second blade and a corkscrew.

CHANGES. Elsner had the market all to himself until 1908.
Then a preacher named Theordore Wenger, from the French-
speaking region of the country, started selling a similar product.
The Swiss government, sensitive to regional favoritism, started
buying half their pocketknives from him . . . and they still do.
Today, the two companies are rivals. Elsner's company, Victorinox
(after his mother, Victoria) calls its knife the "original" Swiss army
knife. The Wenger Company calls its knife the "genuine" Swiss
army knife. Each is allowed to put the Swiss white cross on its
knife—but no other company is.

Swiss army knives became popular in the United States after
World War II; returning GIs brought them home by the thousands.
Today, the United States is the world's largest market for them.
And ironically, Victorinox, founded to prevent the Swiss army
from buying German pocketknives, is now the official supplier of
pocketknives to the German army.

Join the crowd: 75 percent of all Americans live in cities.

HOW TO AVOID GETTING HIRED

Your résumé is a carefully crafted chronicle of what you've achieved . . . and how indispensable you'll be to prospective employers. That's what it's supposed to be, anyway. This list of real-life résumé bloopers appeared in Fortune *magazine.*

"I demand a salary commiserate with my extensive experience."

"I have lurnt Word Perfect 6.0, computor and spreadsheat progroms."

"Received a plague for Salesperson of the Year."

"Reason for leaving last job: maturity leave."

"Wholly responsible for two failed financial institutions."

"Failed bar exam with relatively high grades."

"Let's meet, so you can 'ooh' and 'aah' over my experience."

"You will want me to be Head Honcho in no time."

"Marital status: single. Unmarried. Unengaged. Uninvolved. No commitments."

"Reason for leaving last job: They insisted that all employees get to work by 8:45 every morning. Could not work under those conditions."

"Note: Please don't misconstrue my 14 jobs as 'job-hopping.' I have never quit a job."

"I am loyal to my employer at all costs . . . Please feel free to respond to my résumé on my office voice mail."

"I procrastinate, especially when the task is unpleasant."

"As indicted, I have over five years of analyzing investments."

"Personal interests: donating blood. Fourteen gallons so far."

"Instrumental in ruining entire operation for a Midwest chain store."

"The company made me a scapegoat, just like my three previous employers."

"Finished eighth in my class of ten."

"References: None. I've left a path of destruction behind me."

"It's best for employers that I not work with people."

Horned toads like to be petted.

STRANGE LAWSUITS

These days, it seems that people will sue each other over practically anything. Here are a few real-life examples of unusual legal battles.

THE PLAINTIFF: Rene Joly, 34

THE DEFENDANT: Canadian Defense Minister Art Eggleton, Citibank, and several drugstore chains

THE LAWSUIT: In 1999 Joly filed suit claiming that the defendants were trying to murder him because he is a Martian.

THE VERDICT: Case dismissed. The judge ruled that since Joly said he isn't human, he "has no status before the courts."

THE PLAINTIFF: Gerald Overstreet

THE DEFENDANT: Gibson's Discount Store

THE LAWSUIT: In 1979, Overstreet, of Del Rio, Texas, was shopping at Gibson's. He reached for a jar of jelly . . . and a rattlesnake bit him. He sued for negligence.

THE VERDICT: Overstreet lost. According to a report by Donald Sobol, the court ruled that "a store's duty to protect its customers from wild animals does not begin until the store knows the animal is there."

THE PLAINTIFF: Joel R. Bander, a lawyer and Deadhead

THE DEFENDANT: Malek H. Shraibati, a lawyer who rented office space from Bander

THE LAWSUIT: Grateful Dead leader Jerry Garcia died on August 9, 1995. Bander's suit claimed that shortly after he heard the news of Garcia's passing, he spotted a cardboard tombstone on Shraibati's shelf. It read: "R.I.P./Jerry Garcia (a few too many parties perhaps?)" Bander was already upset . . . and that was the last straw. He sued, contending that Shraibati "should have known how such a joke would impact him." He claimed to have suffered "humiliation, mental anguish, and emotional and physical distress" after seeing the sign.

THE VERDICT: Unknown.

Survey says: In 71 percent of "baby boomer" households, both spouses work.

THE PLAINTIFF: Mrs. Margaret Taylor

THE DEFENDANT: Randle & Sons Funeral Home, St. Louis, Missouri

THE LAWSUIT: The casket for William Taylor's 1997 funeral was closed until after the pastor finished his eulogy. Then it was opened . . . and people yelled "That's not Willie, you got the wrong man!" Mrs. Taylor called the police to keep the funeral home "from literally burying their mistake," and the body was taken to the morgue. It was identified as Frederick Ware—whose own funeral had passed without anyone noticing he wasn't really there. Taylor's body was finally located, but Mrs. Taylor was enraged. She sued for $2.2 million for emotional distress and "fear of not knowing the whereabouts of her husband's body for more than one week."

THE VERDICT: Unknown.

THE PLAINTIFF: Cleanthi Peters

THE DEFENDANT: Universal Studios

THE LAWSUIT: In 1998 Peters visited the Halloween Haunted House at Universal Studios in Orlando, Florida. She expected to be scared—but a costumed guy chasing her with a chainsaw was too scary. She sued for $15,000 for unspecified physical injuries, "extreme fear, emotional distress, and mental anguish."

THE VERDICT: Unknown.

THE PLAINTIFF: Joan Hemmer

THE DEFENDANT: Ronald Winters, owner of a chimpanzee named Mr. Jiggs

THE LAWSUIT: Hemmer was eating at a restaurant in Freehold, New Jersey, when she looked up and saw Mr. Jiggs walk in—dressed in a Boy Scout uniform. She freaked out and bumped into a wall, injuring her shoulder. So she sued. Winters told the jury that Mr. Jiggs was no danger to anyone: he was thoroughly domesticated, lived in a house, could even feed himself . . . and besides, he was actually on his way to a Boy Scout party in the restaurant.

THE VERDICT: The jury sided with Mr. Jiggs.

Alberta, Canada, is said to be completely free of rats.

HISTORY OF
THE IQ TEST, PART I

Do you think IQ tests really measure intelligence?
Don't answer now—wait until you read this dark,
strange history. Then see what you think.

ORIGIN

In 1904, the minister of public instruction in Paris became concerned that mentally retarded children in the French capital were not receiving an adequate education. He also feared that teachers were dumping disruptive children into retarded classes—not because they were retarded, but because they were distracting other children.

The minister appointed a commission to study the problem. It hired Alfred Binet, head of the Sorbonne's psychology laboratory. Binet's mission was to come up with some kind of intelligence test that could be used to identify which children had learning problems severe enough to justify placing them in special schools.

PULL MY FINGER

Binet was not the first person to take on the job of creating a test to measure people's intelligence. In 1884, Sir Francis Galton, a cousin of Charles Darwin and father of the eugenics movement—which advocated the use of "selective breeding" techniques to improve the human race (see "Tarzan, Part I," page 510)—opened the Anthropometric Laboratory at the South Kensington Museum in London. There, for a small fee, he would administer his own version of an intelligence test.

Like most scientists of his day, Galton reasoned that since all knowledge of the surrounding world is transmitted to the brain through sight, sound, and the other senses, the people with the most acute senses would also have the most developed minds. So he devised a number of "Galtonian tasks" that measured the senses. One measured the listener's ability to hear high-pitched sounds; another measured sensitivity to subtle differences in color of pieces of dyed wool. There was also a test that measured how accurately a

---

Q. What was Little Red Riding Hood's first name? A. Blanchette.

person could approximate the weights of different objects. In the six years that Galton's laboratory was open, he tested 9,337 people. While that isn't a large sample by modern IQ test standards, historians consider Galton's research to be the first large-scale attempt to measure human intelligence.

THE OLD COLLEGE TRY

One of Galton's students was an American named James Cattell. When Cattell returned to the United States, he brought Galton's test with him and used it to test the intelligence of students entering the University of Pennsylvania and Columbia University. Then he tracked the students' grades to see if the test results related in any way to academic performance. He wanted to find out whether the Galtonian tasks really did measure intelligence.

But it turned out there was no correlation—for that matter, the individual Galtonian tasks weren't even good at predicting a person's ability to perform other Galtonian tasks. This led Cattel to the conclusion that Galton's sensory tests were of no use in measuring intelligence . . . and they soon fell out of favor.

A NEW APPROACH

Binet's attempts to measure intelligence a few years later were no more successful than Galton's. "I began with the idea, impressed upon me by the studies of so many scientists, that intellectual superiority is tied to superiority of cerebral volume," Binet wrote. So the first thing he tried was measuring children's skulls. The smartest kids must have the largest heads because they contain the biggest brains . . . or so the logic went.

The logic was wrong. Binet found virtually no difference in skull size between good and poor students. So he began looking for some other way to measure intelligence. He tried studying the shapes of children's ears, reading their palms, and even testing their ability to perform Galtonian tasks. Nothing worked. Finally, he decided to test more sophisticated skills such as judgment, comprehension, reasoning, memory, academic aptitude, and how quickly kids could absorb new information and concepts.

HOW OLD ARE YOU?

Binet and a colleague, Theodore Simon, studied the abilities of "normal" schoolchildren and institutionalized retarded children.

Twice as many people live in Shanghai, China as in New York City.

They compiled a long list of intellectual tasks, or "stunts," for the children to perform, starting with very simple ones and increasing them in complexity. After three more years of testing children, they were able to group the stunts by age level. Normal three-year-olds, for example, should be able to point to their eyes, nose, and mouth; and normal four-year-olds should be able to repeat three digits in the same order as the person giving the test had recited them.

Once Binet and Simon had the questions sorted according to age, they were able to measure what they called the "mental age" of the children they tested. The examiner began by asking questions that corresponded to the child's chronological age or slightly younger, and then progressed to more complicated questions to see how high the child could go before they could no longer answer questions correctly. If an eight-year-old could answer questions at the 10-year-old level, they were said to have a "mental age" of 10. Likewise, if a 13-year-old was only able to answer at the 11-year-old level, they had a mental age of 11.

HELPING HAND

The Binet-Simon tests didn't attempt to distinguish between children whose low scores were caused by external factors (such as poor education) and those whose scores were caused by learning disabilities. All the tests did was measure how much children "knew," so those who didn't know very much—for whatever reason—could receive the special attention they needed and reach their full intellectual potential.

Binet vehemently objected to the notion that a person's intelligence is predetermined. In his writings, he lashed out at "some recent philosophers," as he called them, "who appear to have given their moral support to the deplorable verdict that the intelligence of an individual is a fixed quantity . . . . We must protest and react against this brutal pessimism."

"With this orientation," Leon J. Kamin writes in *The Politics of IQ*, "it is perhaps as well that Binet died in 1911, before witnessing the uses to which his test was speedily put in the United States."

For Part II of "The History of the I.Q. Test," see page 520.

Marilyn Monroe's dog was named Maf. It was a gift from Frank Sinatra.

UNCLE JOHN'S STALL OF FAME

You'd be amazed at the number of newspaper articles BRI members send in about the creative ways people get involved with bathrooms, toilets, toilet paper, etc. So we've created Uncle John's "Stall of Fame."

Honoree: David Garza of Henrietta, Texas

Notable Achievement: Owns "The Toilet of Mystery"

True Story: Between 1991 and 1993, Garza fished more than 75 Papermate ballpoint pens out of his toilet—sometimes as many as five pens a day—and still has no idea how they got there. It has made him into a local celebrity. "Everywhere I go people say to me, 'Hey, have you got a pen?'"

Honoree: Ann Landers

Notable Achievement: Demonstrated how passionate people are about even the most trivial bathroom issues

True Story: In the mid-1980s, Landers innocently printed a letter in her advice column that raised the issue of whether toilet paper should come off the top or the bottom of the roll. A flood of letters ensued. In fact, Landers revealed in 1986 that "in 31 years, this question has been the most controversial" of all the issues ever raised in the column. Her own conclusion: the paper should come over the top. Why? "Fine quality toilet paper has designs that are right side up," she explained.

Honorees: Paul and Virginia Alee of Boulder, Colorado

Notable Achievement: Solved—once and for all—the "top or bottom" toilet paper issue (see above)

True Story: The couple couldn't agree. So, "When we built our house," they told the *Rocky Mountain News*, "we had the builder put two dispensers in each bathroom, with one unrolling in one direction, and the other rolling in the other direction. The builder told us he got more contracts as a result of showing our home to the public than any other 'show home' they'd ever put on display."

The average cost of a house on Jupiter Island, Florida: $3.9 million.

Honoree: A Halifax bar called Number 15

Notable Achievement: The only pub in England built in a public restroom

True Story: Halifax is considered the pub capital of Britain. According to news reports, Halifax has more pubs per household than anywhere in the country. "The local paper, the *Evening Courier*, even boasts its own Pub Correspondent." The demand for pubs is so strong that when an underground public lavatory became available, someone bought it and converted it into a pub called W.C.'s. When it was recently sold, the name was changed to Number 15. (This makes us wonder: Why not Number 2?)

Honoree: Edmond Rostand (1868–1918)

Notable Achievement: Author of the most famous play ever written in a bathroom

True Story: Rostand didn't like to be rude to his friends, but didn't like to be interrupted when he was working, either. Rather than risk having to turn away any friends who might drop by to visit, "he took refuge in his bathtub and wrote there all day." His biggest bathroom success: *Cyrano de Bergerac*.

Honoree: Yang Zhu, a young mother in China

Notable Achievement: Gave birth in a train bathroom . . . and lost the baby down the toilet (she got it back).

True Story: Yang Zhu was nine months pregnant and headed home by train on May 4, 1999, when she began to suffer stomach pains. Her husband took her to the washroom where, "to her great surprise," she gave birth to her first child into the toilet "as soon as she squatted down . . . The panic-stricken and screaming Yang ripped off the umbilical cord with her hands, and the baby immediately slipped down through the toilet and fell onto the rails." Three security guards spotted the baby, covered in blood and lying in the middle of the tracks, but before they could reach him, another train sped by right over him. Miraculously, he only had slight bruises and a small cut on his head that needed three stitches.

President Clinton was allergic to Socks the cat.

EXECUTIVE DECISIONS

They may be in positions of responsibility . . . they may be captains of industry . . . they may be among the world's most successful business people. But that doesn't mean they can't make really dumb decisions, just like the rest of us. Here are some classics.

SHOULD WE SIGN THEM UP?

Mike Smith and Dick Rowe, executives in charge of evaluating new talent for the London office of Decca Records

Background: On December 13, 1961, Mike Smith traveled to Liverpool to watch a local rock 'n' roll band perform. He decided they had talent, and invited them to an audition on New Year's Day 1962. The group made the trip to London and spent two hours playing 15 different songs at the Decca studios. Then they went home and waited for an answer.

They waited for weeks.

Decision: Finally, Rowe told the band's manager that the label wasn't interested because they sounded too much like a popular group called the Shadows. In one of the most famous of all rejection lines, he said: "Not to mince words, Mr. Epstein, but we don't like your boys' sound. Groups are out; four-piece groups with guitars particularly are finished."

Impact: The group was the Beatles, of course. They eventually signed with EMI Records, started a trend back to guitar bands, and ultimately became the most popular band of all time. Ironically, "Within two years, EMI's production facilities became so stretched that Decca helped them out in a reciprocal arrangement, to cope with the unprecedented demand for Beatles records."

SHOULD WE LET THAT DIRECTOR USE OUR CANDY IN HIS FILM?

John Mars and Forrest Mars Jr., owners of Mars Inc., makers of M&Ms

Background: In 1981, Universal Studios called Mars and asked for permission to use M&M's in a new film they were making.

There are more creatures in your mouth than there are humans on earth.

This was (and is) a fairly common practice. Product placement deals provide filmmakers with some extra cash or promotion opportunities. In this case, the director was looking for a cross-promotion. He'd use the M&M's, and Mars could help promote the movie.

Decision: The Mars brothers said no.

Impact: The film was *E.T. The Extra-Terrestrial,* directed by Steven Spielberg. The M&M's were needed for a crucial scene: Elliot, the little boy who befriends the alien, uses candies to lure E.T. into his house. Instead, Universal Studios went to Hershey's and cut a deal to use a new product called Reese's Pieces. Initial sales of Reese's Pieces had been light. But when *E.T.* became a top-grossing film—generating tremendous publicity for "E.T.'s favorite candy"—sales exploded. They tripled within two weeks and continued climbing for months afterward. "It was the biggest marketing coup in history," says Jack Dowd, the Hershey's executive who approved the movie tie-in. "We got immediate recognition for our product. We would normally have had to pay 15 or 20 million bucks for it."

HOW DO WE COME UP WITH SOME QUICK CASH?
Executives of 20th Century Fox's TV division (pre-Murdoch)

Background: No one at Fox expected much from M*A*S*H when it debuted on TV in 1972. Execs simply wanted to make a cheap series by using the M*A*S*H movie set again—so it was a surprise when it became Fox's only hit show. Three years later, the company was hard up for cash. When the M*A*S*H ratings started to slip after two of its stars left, Fox execs panicked.

Decision: They decided to raise cash by selling the syndication rights to the first seven seasons of M*A*S*H on a futures basis: local TV stations could pay in 1975 for shows they couldn't broadcast until October 1979—four years away. Fox made no guarantees that the show would still be popular; the $13,000 per episode was nonrefundable. But enough local stations took the deal so that Fox made $25 million. They celebrated . . .

Impact: . . . but prematurely. When M"A*S*H finally aired in syndication in 1979, it was still popular (in fact, it ranked #3 that year). It became one of the most successful syndicated shows ever, second only to *I Love Lucy.* Each of the original 168 episodes grossed over $1 million for local TV stations; Fox got nothing.

THEY WENT THATAWAY

Malcolm Forbes wrote a fascinating book about the deaths of famous people. Here are some of the weirdest stories he found, along with some from the BRI's own files.

STEPHEN FOSTER

Claim to Fame: 19th-century American songwriter; composer of "Oh! Susanna," "Camptown Races," and "Swanee River"

How He Died: Broke.

Postmortem: Foster was a reckless spender who apparently never realized the value of his songs. In 1848, for example, he sold the rights to the classic "Oh! Susanna" for $100.

In 1857, Foster was so desperate for cash that he sold the rights to all the songs he'd written for $1,900. Three years later, Foster left his wife and moved to a run-down rooming house in New York City. Sinking into alcoholism, tubercular and broke, he cranked out 105 songs over the next three years—most of them mediocre.

On the morning of January 13, 1864, Foster awoke with a fever and fell onto his porcelain washbasin while washing himself. The basin shattered, and one of the sharp pieces gouged deeply into his neck. He died, anonymous and alone, three days later. His body was sent to a morgue for "John Doe" corpses, where it remained until friends realized what had happened and came to claim the body.

Ironically, his last song, "Beautiful Dreamer," written only a few days earlier, became one of his greatest hits.

CASEY JONES

Claim to Fame: Legendary railroad man and inspiration for the popular folk song

How He Died: In a trainwreck, just like the song says.

Postmortem: On the night of April 29, 1900, Jones pulled into Memphis aboard the *Cannonball Express*, one of the fastest trains of the Illinois Central. It should have been his last stop, but Jones was working a double shift.

. . . the one in Island Park, Idaho. It's more than 33 miles long.

The *Cannonball* was more than an hour late. Casey decided to make up for lost time by pushing the passenger train to over 100 mph on the 50-mph route to Canton, Mississippi. Fifteen minutes outside of Canton, Jones was only two minutes behind schedule. But he was tired, and as he roared down the tracks that foggy night, Jones missed a flagman's signal—a freight train was stopped on the tracks ahead. By the time he saw the red taillights on the caboose, it was too late. Jones pulled the air brakes, slammed the train into reverse, and, as the ballad says, blew the whistle just before he crashed.

The engine was destroyed and Jones was killed—an iron bolt pierced his neck—but no one else was . . . and none of the *Cannonball's* passenger cars were even damaged. Less than a week later, a railroad worker named Wallace Saunders started singing about the crash. The song spread from one worker to another, and people added new stanzas. It was published in 1909 and became a huge hit on the vaudeville circuit.

MERIWETHER LEWIS

Claim to Fame: 18th-century explorer who, together with William Clark, led the first overland expedition to the Pacific Northwest

How He Died: Was it suicide . . . or murder?

Postmortem: Lewis was better at exploring than he was at politics. President Thomas Jefferson appointed him governor of the upper Louisiana Territory in 1807, but dealing with corrupt officials, settlers, and Indian tribes took its toll on Lewis. He became increasingly troubled by the pressures of his office. In September 1809, Lewis traveled to Washington to deal with some unreimbursed expenses that had left him in debt. On the return leg of the journey, he had a nervous breakdown, and spent the next few weeks recovering at Fort Pickering. Then he set out for Nashville along the trail called the Natchez Trace. On October 10, Lewis and two servants stopped for the night at a cabin owned by Mrs. Robert Grinder. According to Mrs. Grinder, Lewis appeared to be very troubled, pacing back and forth late into the night, mumbling about his problems and occasionally screaming out loud.

That night, Mrs. Grinder heard a gunshot coming from Lewis's cabin, then a thud, then Lewis shouting, 'Oh, Lord!' and then another shot. Lewis staggered from his cabin to Mrs. Grinder's and pounded on the door, shouting to be let in.

U.S. law requires that Yankee bean soup be served in the Congressional dining room at all times.

Terrified, Mrs. Grinder refused to open the door. The following morning, she and Lewis's servants found Lewis in his bed, dying from bullet wounds in the chest and head. He died a short time later.

Did he commit suicide or was he murdered? Lewis had $200 with him when he left Fort Pickering, but only 25¢ was found on his body after he died . . . which led to speculation that Lewis was killed by Indians, by his servants (who were underpaid), by highway robbers who plagued the Natchez Trace, or even by Mrs. Grinder. What really happened? No one will ever know.

* * *

RANDOM LISTS

TEN INTERNATIONAL WORDS FOR "FART"
1. Afrikaans—*maagwind*
2. Israeli—*nuhfeechah*
3. Japanese—*he*
4. Cantonese/Chinese—*fang*
5. German—*furz*
6. Bantu—*lu-suzi*
7. Hindu—*pud*
8. Polish—*pierdzenic*
9. Italian—*peto*
10. Russian—*perdun*

6 EVERYDAY LIES FROM THE BOOK OF LIES
1. "I'll just be a minute."
2. "Let's get together for lunch. I'll give you a call."
3. "Everything's fixed."
4. "The check is in the mail."
5. "I'll return your book as soon as I finish reading it."
6. "The doctor will be with you shortly."

3 MOST PRIZED AUTOGRAPHS OF ALL TIME
1. Shakespeare (only six known to exist)
2. Christopher Columbus (eight exist)
3. Julius Caesar (none known to exist)

FIRST 7 ROCK RECORDS TO WIN GOLD DISCS
1. *"Hard Headed Woman,"* Elvis Presley (1958)
2. *Pat's Greatest Hits*, Pat Boone (1960)
3. *Elvis*, Elvis Presley (1960)
4. *Elvis' Golden Records*, Elvis Presley (1961)
5. *Encore—Golden Hits*, The Platters (1961)
6. *Blue Hawaii*, Elvis Presley (1961)
7. *Can't Help Falling in Love*, Elvis Presley (1962)

Beavers' teeth are so sharp that Native Americans used them as knife blades.

NOT WHAT THEY SEEM TO BE

We take an awful lot of things for granted, based on image. But things (and people) aren't always what we think they are. Here are some examples.

BEATRIX POTTER

Image: A sentimental, animal-loving author who named her Peter Rabbit children's stories after her own pet rabbit, Peter.

Actually: Well, she did love animals, but she wasn't sentimental about them. Potter also wrote—in her diaries—about killing, boiling, and dissecting rabbits so she could study their organs.

FREDERIC REMINGTON

Image: Perhaps more than the work of any other artist, Frederic Remington's vivid, action-packed sculptures, paintings, and illustrations of the Old West have defined the look and feel of American cowboys and Indians and the world in which they lived.

Actually: Remington's works "were in fact largely studio creations based on a lively imagination," Bill Bryson writes in *Made in America*.

> He never saw any real cowboys in action. For one thing, he was too fat to get on a horse, much less ride it into the midst of Indian battles. Even more crucially, by the time he made his first trip to the West, the age of the cowboy was all but over.

PAUL CÉZANNE

Image: A Post-Impressionist painter known for his "attachment to nature," which manifested itself in his landscapes and still lifes. His paintings of fruit in a bowl are among the most famous still lifes ever produced.

Actually: Many of Cézanne's still lifes were much more *still* than life: it took him so long to paint a bowl of fruit that the fruit often rotted before he could finish. So he used wax fruit.

Time magazine's man of the year for 1988: "Endangered Earth."

BELA LUGOSI

Image: Lugosi's groundbreaking role as the bloodthirsty Count Dracula in the early 1930s helped establish him as Hollywood's leading horror star.

Actually: Lugosi wasn't quite as bloodthirsty as he looked. According to one biographer, "He became sick and fainted at the sight of his own blood."

ROBERT E. LEE & ULYSSES S. GRANT

Image: Grant, who commanded the Union Army, was against slavery; Lee, who commanded the Confederate Army, was for it.

Actually: According to David Wallechinsky in *Significa*, both were slave owners—"and the Southern general, Lee, freed his slaves before the Northern general, Grant, freed his." When Grant married his wife, Julia, she had four slaves, and although he freed his own slave in 1849, Julia's slaves "were not freed until the end of the Civil War. Mrs. Grant was an apologist for slavery all her life, and her husband stood up to her."

On the other hand, Robert E. Lee once wrote: "Slavery as an institution is a moral and political evil." In the late 1840s, Lee reportedly freed his four slaves. And he released his wife's slaves, whom he had inherited from his father-in-law in 1863—two years before those owned by Julia Grant gained their freedom.

NEWSREEL FOOTAGE

Image: In the early black-and-white newsreel days of broadcast journalism, covering traffic accidents was as common a practice as it is today; yet somehow, the footage somehow seemed even gorier.

Actually: "Newsreel camera crews would sometimes pour several gallons of water on the roadway before filming. In black-and-white film, the water looked like blood." (*If No News, Send Rumors*, by Stephen Bates)

FOSTER'S LAGER

Image: Sold under the slogan "Australian for beer," Foster's Lager has become one of the most easily identifiable Australian imports.

Actually: The Foster's Lager sold in the U.S. is imported, but not from Australia—it's brewed in Canada.

The planet Mercury is 800°F at its equator, but has ice at its North and South Poles.

RANDOM ORIGINS

Once again, the BRI asks—and answers—the
question: where did all this stuff come from?

THE TELEPHONE BOOTH

Alexander Graham Bell invented the telephone, but it was his assistant, Thomas Watson ("Come here, Mr. Watson"), who invented the phone booth. The reason: his landlady complained that he made too much noise shouting into the phone during his calls. Watson remedied the situation by throwing blankets over some furniture and climbing underneath whenever he needed to make a call; by 1883 he'd upgraded to an enclosed wooden booth with a domed top, screened windows, a writing desk, and even a ventilator.

THE SLOT MACHINE

Other types of gambling machines date back as far as the 1890s, but the first one to really catch on was a vending machine for chewing gum introduced by the Mills Novelty Company in 1910. Their machine dispensed three flavors of gum—cherry, orange, and plum—depending on which fruits appeared on three randomly spinning wheels. If three bars reading "1910 Fruit Gum" appeared in a row, the machine gave extra gum; if a lemon appeared, it gave no gum at all (which is why "lemon" came to mean something unsatisfactory or defective). You can't get gum in a slot machine anymore—the 1910 Fruit Gum machine was so popular that the company converted them to cash payouts—but the same fruit symbols are still used in slot machines today.

THE CINEMA MULTIPLEX

Invented by accident by theater owner Stan Durwood in 1963, when he tried to open a large theater in a Kansas City, Missouri, shopping mall. The mall's developer told Durwood that the support columns in the building could not be removed to build a single large theater . . . so Durwood built two smaller theaters instead. He showed the same movie on both screens—until it dawned on him that he'd sell more tickets if he showed two different films. It was a huge success; the national attention he got spurred a "multiplex boom" in other cities.

If the sun were an inch in diameter, the nearest star would be 445 miles away.

ANIMAL SUPERSTITIONS

Superstitions are intriguing, even if you don't believe in them. Here are some pretty bizarre ones that people actually did believe.

"A swarm of bees settling on a roof is an omen that the house will burn down."

"It's bad luck for a miner to say the word 'cat' while down in the mine."

"More than seven spots on a ladybug is an omen of famine."

"Killing a bat shortens your life."

"It's bad luck to see three butterflies on one leaf at the same time."

"A swan feather sewn onto a husband's pillow will make him faithful to his wife."

"Carrying a badger's tooth brings good luck, especially at gambling."

"Cows lifting their tails is a sure sign that rain is coming."

"A white horse is a harbinger of bad luck—worse luck if a redheaded girl is riding it."

"It's unlucky to burn a haddock."

"A bull's heart stuck with thorns and put in the fireplace wards off witches."

"To make a sleeping woman talk, put a frog's tongue on her heart."

"Seeing an owl during the daytime is bad luck."

"If you make a wish when you see the first robin of spring, it will come true—but only if you complete the wish before the robin flies away."

"Pictures of an elephant bring good luck, but only if they face a door."

"Rats leaving one house and running into another mean good luck for the new house and bad luck for the old."

"If a frog hops into your house, it will bring good luck."

"Stuffing a cat's tail up your nose will cure a nosebleed."

"Don't let a pig cross your path—it's unlucky."

A Karaoke singing of "We Are the World" burns 20.7 calories.

THE BIRTH OF THE SUBMARINE, PART I

Trivia question: In what American war was the submarine first used in battle? Answer: The American Revolution. (No, we're not kidding.) Here's Part I of the BRI's story of the submarine.

DIVE BOMBER

In 1774, a Yale University student named David Bushnell invented an underwater bomb to use against England's Royal Navy. Bushnell's plan: Sneak up beside the enemy ship, drill the hull, and attach the bomb. After activating a time-delayed detonator, you had 30 minutes before the bomb went off. But the bomb weighed over 150 pounds—too heavy for a swimmer to tow . . . and in wartime any approaching boat carrying a big bomb was sure to be fired on and sunk. Bushnell realized that a new kind of boat was needed to deliver his bomb: a "submarine," a ship that could travel unseen under the water. He set out to build one.

THE FIRST SUBMARINES

Bushnell was not the first to look for a way to travel beneath the waves. In the early 1500s, Leonardo da Vinci drew plans for a submersible boat made of goat skins stretched over a wooden frame. In 1620, Dutch inventor Cornelius Drebbel actually built one. Drebbel's boat was leather stretched over a wooden frame, and was powered by oars poked through waterproof flaps on both sides. Between 1620 and 1624, Drebbel made several trips up the Thames River, as much as 15 feet below the surface.

But Bushnell was the first to build a sub designed to be used in battle. Bushnell's 1776 vessel was 7 1/2 feet long, 8 feet tall, and 4 feet wide, not much bigger than a barrel—barely large enough to hold one man and 30 minutes' worth of air. Made of iron, brass, and wood, it looked like "two gigantic tortoise shells joined together and stood on end," as Robert Burgess writes in *Ships Beneath the Sea*.

HANDS ON

The *American Turtle*, as it came to be known, weighed more than a

Left to its own devices, a ton of iron can turn into three tons of rust.

ton but had no motor (it was 1776, after all)—so the pilot had to move it with foot pedals and manual controls.

Opening a valve let water into a ballast tank and caused the submarine to sink; a foot-powered pump pushed the water out and enabled the *Turtle* to surface. Foot pedals connected to a propeller moved the vessel forward and backward; a hand crank connected to a second propeller moved it up and down. As if there weren't already enough to do, the pilot also had to use a hand rudder to steer and another hand crank to drill a hole in the enemy ship. A candle used too much precious air, so phosphorescent fungus was smeared on the instruments to make them glow in the dark. George Washington was impressed enough by the effort to fund it. "Bushnell is a man of great mechanical powers," he wrote to Thomas Jefferson, "fertile in invention and a master of execution."

BOMBS AWAY!

In 1775, England and the American colonies went to war. And in September 1776, the *American Turtle* was sent into action against the 350 ships and 10,000 sailors of the Royal Navy massing along the Eastern seaboard. The *Turtle*'s first target: the HMS *Eagle*, anchored near Governor's Island. The *Eagle* was the 64-gun flagship of British admiral Earl Howe, who was in charge of the blockade of New York.

In the early morning hours, longboats towed the *Turtle* within a few hundred yards of the *Eagle*. The *Turtle* then submerged and traveled the rest of the way under its own power. The pilot, Ezra Lee, managed to make it underneath the *Eagle*, but when he tried to drill the hull, he missed and struck an impenetrable iron crossbar. Dawn was approaching and he was running out of air, so rather than risk another attempt, he decided to make a getaway. Too late—Lee was spotted by some British sailors, who gave chase in rowboats. Since he still had a bomb, Lee released it in the middle of New York Harbor, where it detonated and scared his pursuers away.

THAT SINKING FEELING

The attack had failed miserably, and so did the two that followed. British ships were not sunk, the blockade was not lifted, and the *Turtle* itself was captured by the British and destroyed.

When pronounced correctly, Chinese surnames never have more than one syllable.

Bushell's later attempts to sink British warships with floating mines also failed; he never managed to sink a single British ship.

Perhaps because he was embarrassed by his failure, Bushnell disappeared from view around 1783. According to Alex Roland in *Underwater Warfare in the Age of Sail*, he relocated to Georgia, where he lived under the assumed name of Dr. David Bush. There, Bushnell "lived out his life as a teacher and a physician, and died in 1826, anonymous to all but a few close friends."

Want to immerse yourself in more of the story?
Turn to page 525 for part II.

* * *

PRIMATE HALL OF FAME: BONZO

Background: In the 1951 film *Bedtime for Bonzo*, Bonzo the chimp (real name: Tamba) became the only animal star ever to share top billing with a future president of the United States. The film was one of Ronald Reagan's few box office successes.

The Plot: Reagan plays a psychology professor whose father was a crook. To prove that environment, not heredity, is to blame, he borrows a chimp from the zoology department and raises it like a son. It backfires. When the chimp pilfers some jewelry, Reagan is accused of training it to steal. Reagan winds up in jail until Bonzo's blonde nurse (Diana Lynn) convinces the chimp to come clean. Bonzo returns the loot, Ronnie marries the nurse, and they all live happily ever after.

Tricks and Training: Reagan recalls: "The normal procedure called for the director, Fred de Cordova, to tell the trainer what he wanted from the chimp. But after a time Freddie was so captivated by Bonzo's acting that he'd forget and start to direct Bonzo as he did the human cast members. He'd say, 'No, Bonzo, in this scene you should . . . ' Then he'd hit his head and cry, 'What the hell am I doing?' "

- Reagan made light of the experience, but it wasn't always safe. Once, on the set, Bonzo suddenly grabbed Reagan's necktie and almost strangled him with it.

"WE WANT MORE OF YOUR MONEY" DAY

You want to take a day off, but can't think of an excuse? No problem—there are hundreds of "holidays" to celebrate that you've probably never heard of. This article might even inspire you to create your own.

IT'S A HOLIDAY!

Banks did not shut their doors and the mail still arrived on May 18. For the record, though, it was "Don't Do Dishes Day." This "holiday" was not, as one might guess, dreamed up by two-career couples rebelling against domesticity; it was the creation of the makers of Dixie paper plates and Reynolds Wrap, two products that, as it happens, would sell very nicely if Americans turned their backs on the kitchen sink.

How to celebrate? Well, the sponsors envisioned a moment of silence in kitchens around the country as overworked Americans ignored their dishwashers and dined on paper and foil.

The goal, according to the Fort James Corporation, maker of Dixie products, and the Reynolds Metals Company, was to cut down on the time consumers spend scrubbing melted cheese and sticky pie filling off plates and pans, which the companies went to the trouble of estimating at 7,000 minutes a year.

"That is three full workweeks tackling dirty dishes," said Bill Schultz, a general manager at Fort James. "For most of us, that's more time than we spend on vacation each year. Our whole reason for being is to make washing dishes obsolete."

CHECK YOUR CALENDAR

That is a visionary goal, indeed, but even if it is never reached, the company will not complain. "Naturally, we want to sell product," Schultz acknowledged. So, Fort James teamed up with Reynolds Metals to promote the day with sweepstakes, national television advertising, and supermarket displays.

And the calendar is getting crowded. A growing number of companies that make and market everything from pain relievers to

---

Since 1850, world population has increased 600 percent.

refrigerators are creating "national days," ostensibly for consumers to reflect on weighty issues and trends. Others go for a week or even a full month, like "Toilet Tank Repair Month" in October, sponsored by Fluidmaster Inc., which makes toilet valves.

The beauty of this is that anyone can do it. If you have something to sell, just proclaim a special day—and hope someone listens. Authentic proclamations must come from the president or state or local elected officials, who generally deny requests to support events that are too obviously commercial. But that doesn't stop states from declaring events like "National Mule Appreciation Day" (observed in Tennessee) or companies and their trade groups from promoting official-*sounding* holidays.

HERE'S RELIEF!

And if the thought of adding more days to remember to your calendar is enough to give you a headache, don't fret. Now there is a "Migraine Recognition Day," designated by Bristol-Myers Squibb, the pharmaceutical company.

The day, which is observed on May 5, was scheduled just four months after the company received regulatory approval to market a new migraine formula of Excedrin, and Bristol-Myers Squibb says the event was created to educate the public about the differences between migraines and, say, stress or sinus headaches.

Some marketing experts scoff at this approach. "You've got to be kidding; I don't need a day of the year to tell me I have a headache," said Clive Chajet of Chajet Consultancy, which advises corporations on brand-building strategies. "I would definitely discourage my clients from spending their money that way." The risk, as Chajet sees it, is that consumers may be turned off by such obvious selling strategies.

OUR DAY WILL COME

Tell that to Burger King, which early in 1998 was unapologetic in its use of a manufactured special day to drum up business. Looking for an edge in its long-running burger battle with McDonald's, the company introduced what it touted as a tastier french fry and proclaimed January 2 as national "Free Fryday." Then they gave away an estimated 15 million orders of fries as part of a $70 million advertising and marketing campaign.

"Kryptonite" made its first appearance on the Superman radio show . . . not in the comic book.

Even marketers of goods that people give little thought to have found an angle to wrap a day around. The Whirlpool Corporation sponsors "National Clean Out Your Refrigerator Day" each November.

Whirlpool times its annual event to fall the week before Thanksgiving, when most people need extra space in their refrigerators anyway. On clean-out day, refrigerator technicians and nutritionists operate a toll-free information line to answer questions about defrosting and food mold. Whirlpool also has customer service representatives standing by to explain to callers the virtues of its latest appliances and to offer a list of stores that carry them.

"Nobody is trying to sell them anything," Carolyn Verweyst, manager of marketing communications for the company, said without a hint of irony.

Last year, Whirlpool recorded about 1,000 calls to its special line and hundreds of hits on its Web site. "We hope if and when they need a refrigerator, the first name that comes to mind will be the Whirlpool folks," she added.

THEY'RE ALL SPECIAL DAYS

Chajet says people have a hard enough time remembering their own anniversaries, let alone trying to keep track of who sponsored what corporate commemoration.

Even so, he predicted, "I can't help thinking that next we'll have a 'Viagra Day.'"

Trying to stand out from the clutter of advertising, marketers have created a calendar crowded with sponsors. Here are some examples:

Free Fryday
Jan. 2
Sponsor: Burger King

Prune The Fat Month
January
Sponsor: California Prune
Board

Egg Salad Week
April 13–19
Sponsor: American Egg Board

**Clean Out Your
Refrigerator Day**
Nov. 18
Sponsor: Whirlpool

One fourth of the land on Earth is classified as desert.

HAPPY DONUT DAY!

*Like to party? Well, here are some more special days,
weeks, and even months that you can celebrate!*

JANUARY: Bread Machine Baking Month (*Sponsor: Continental Mills*)

Jan. 1: Get a Life Day

Jan. 27: Thomas Crapper Day (*BRI Offices Closed*)

FEBRUARY: Return Shopping Carts to the Supermarket Month (*Sponsor: Illinois Food Retailers*)

Feb. 11: Be Electrific Day

Feb. 29: Gravity Observance Day (*Very Heavy*)

MARCH: National Sauce Month

Mar. 1: National Pig Day (*Oink!*)

Mar. 5: National Pancake Week (*Sponsor: Bisquick Baking Mix*)

Mar. 9: Panic Day

APRIL: Holy Humor Month

Apr. 14: Polkabration Weekend (*South Fallsburg, New York*)

Apr. 28: National Hairball Awareness Day

Apr. 30: Hairstylist Appreciation Day

MAY: National Salsa Month (*Sponsor: Pace Foods*)
. . . *and* National Egg Month (*Sponsor: The Egg Council*)

May 17: National Be a Millionaire Day

May 26: Morning Radio Wise Guy Day

JUNE: National Frozen Yogurt Month (*Sponsor: TCBY*)
. . . *and* National Accordion Awareness Month

June 2: Yell "Fudge" at the Cobras in North America Day

June 2–3: Donut Day (*Sponsor: The Salvation Army*)

June 8: World Pork Expo (*Sponsor: National Pork Producers Council*)

JULY: National Hot Dog Month

July 1–4: Spam Town USA Festival (Austin, Minnesota)

July 2–8: Be Nice to New Jersey Week

July 10–16: Nude Recreation Week

July 15: Cow Appreciation Day

July 18: National Baby Food Festival (Fremont, Michigan)

AUGUST: National Hypnosis Awareness Month

Aug. 5: National Mustard Day (*Sponsor: Mt. Horeb Mustard Museum*)

Shirley Temple made $300,000 in 1938 but her allowance was only $4.25 a week.

Aug. 8: Sneak Some Zucchini onto Your Neighbors' Porch Night

Aug. 10–16: Elvis Week

SEPTEMBER: National Chicken Month (*Sponsor: The National Chicken Council*)

Sept. 6: Do It! Day (Fight Procrastination Day)

Sept. 10: Old Timers Day (Lisco, Nebraska)

Sept. 11: No News Is Good News Day

OCTOBER: National Toilet Tank Repair Month (*Sponsor: Fluidmaster, Inc.*)

Oct. 4: Ten-Four Day

Oct. 13: Skeptics' Day (Don't believe it)

Oct. 15: National Grouch Day

NOVEMBER: National Bone Marrow Awareness Month

Nov. 5: National Split Pea Soup Week (*Sponsor: Dry Pea and Lentil Council*)

Nov. 6: Shallow Persons Awareness Week

DECEMBER: Bingo's Birthday Month (the game, not the dog)

Dec. 5: Bathtub Party Day

Dec. 15: Underdog Day

Dec. 26: National Whiner's Day

* * *

BRI "FAVORITE ROLE MODELS"

Role Model: Patricia Downey, Nebraska's Mother of the Year

Setting an Example: In April 2000 "she surrendered her title after one of her sons accused her of nominating herself for the honor, and forging his signature on a letter of support. According to press reports, 'only five of Downey's seven sons actually supported her nomination.'"

Role Model: Koo-Koo the Klown

Setting an Example: In 1993 the Legal Aid Society of Santa Clara County filed charges against the man who portrayed Koo-Koo for nearly 30 years, entertaining children at parties, for routinely violating state law at an apartment complex he owned. Which law? According to the society, Koo-Koo "refused to rent to tenants with children."

The "Pretend Cafe" in Tel Aviv served empty plates. (They've since closed down.)

A TOY IS BORN

Here are the origins of some toys you may have played with.

THE ERECTOR SET

Inventor: A. C. Gilbert, an Olympic pole-vaulter who owned the Mysto Company, which sold magic tricks and magicians' equipment

Origin: The market for magic tricks was pretty narrow, and Gilbert was hoping to break into the toy business. But he couldn't think of a product. Then one day in 1911, while riding a commuter train to New York City, Gilbert saw some new power lines being strung from steel girders. It suddenly occurred to him that kids might enjoy building things out of miniaturized girders. So he went home, cut out prototype girders from cardboard, and gave them to a machinist to make out of steel. "When I saw the samples," Gilbert wrote in his autobiography, "I knew I had something."

Selling It: Gilbert brought the prototypes to the big toy fairs of the year, in Chicago and New York . . . and walked out with enough orders to keep his factory busy for a year. So Gilbert took a chance and the following year, he made the Erector Set the first major toy ever to be advertised nationally. It sold so well that the Gilbert Toy Company became one of America's largest toy manufacturers almost overnight.

THE BABY ALIVE DOLL

Inventor: The Kenner Products Company

Origin: Baby dolls that wet themselves were nothing new in the early 1970s, and they were popular sellers. So in 1972 Kenner decided to take the concept to the next level with a doll called Baby Alive. When someone held a spoon or a bottle up to the doll's mouth, she took in the food . . . and after "a suitable interval," she pooped it back out again. The baby's "food" consisted of cherry, banana, and lime "food packets" that were actually colored gel. "And to answer the obvious question," writes Sydney Stem in *Toyland*, "yes, what went in red, yellow, or green came out red, yellow or green."

Selling It: At the time, Kenner was owned by food giant General

---

It's against French law to reveal the true identity of a member of the French Foreign Legion.

Mills—which meant that Kenner president Bernie Loomis had to get approval from the chairman of General Mills before he could put the doll into production. He nearly blew it, Stem writes:

> Unfortunately, he forgot to put a disposable diaper on the doll before feeding it, and it extruded poo-poo gel all over his boss's arm. "Who in the world would ever want such a messy thing?" asked the disgruntled chairman. As it turned out, there were fast hordes of children eager to own a defecating dolly. Baby Alive was the number-one-selling doll in 1973, and Kenner went on to sell three million of them.

RISK

Inventor: Albert Lamorisse, a French filmmaker

Origin: In 1957, a year after winning an Academy Award for his (now-classic) film *The Red Balloon*, Lamorisse created the game he called La Conquête du Monde (Conquest of the World).

Sales Tales: La Conquête du Monde was a big hit in France, prompting U.S. game maker Parker Brothers to snap up the rights to the American version. They immediately ran into a problem: many of the executives at Parker Brothers were veterans of World War II and the Korean War, and they were uncomfortable with the game's title. So Parker Brothers ordered their R&D department to come up with a less warlike name. No luck—nobody could think of a name until a salesperson happened to hand the Parker Brothers president a piece of paper with the letters R-I-S-K written on it. A divine inspiration? No. According to company lore, the four letters were merely the first letters of the names of each of the president's four grandchildren. Historical footnote: Risk was banned in Germany for years . . . until the object of the German version was changed from "conquering the world" to "liberating the world."

* * *

KOOSH BALLS

Koosh balls were invented when Scott Stillinger, an engineer, was looking for a safe ball for playing catch with his small children. Foam balls bounced out of their hands, and bean bags were too heavy. So he made a ball from more than 2,000 rubber strings, joined together at the center.

Nobody knows who invented eyeglasses.

WORD ORIGINS

Here are some more interesting word origins.

THIRD DEGREE

Meaning: Intense, often brutal questioning, especially by police

Origin: "Dating to the 1890s in America, it has no connection with criminal law. The third degree is the highest degree in Freemasonry. Any Mason must undergo very difficult tests of proficiency before he qualifies for the third degree and it is probably from these 'tests' that the exhaustive questioning of criminals came to be called the third degree." (From QPB *Encyclopedia of Word and Phrase Origins*, by Robert Hendrickson)

HANGNAIL

Meaning: A small piece of a fingernail that's partially detached from the rest of the skin

Origin: "Had nothing to do with a hanging nail—the original word was angnail. The ang referred to the pain it caused—as in anguish." (From *Take My Words*, by Howard Richler)

GYPSY

Meaning: A nomad, or a member of a nomadic tribe

Origin: "In the early 16th century members of a wandering race who called themselves Romany appeared in Britain. They were actually of Hindu origin, but the British believed that they came from Egypt, and called them *Egipcyans*. This soon became shortened to *Gipcyan*, and by the year 1600, to *Gipsy* or *Gypsey*." (From *Webster's Word Histories*)

SIEGE

Meaning: A prolonged battle or period of oppression

Origin: "Comes from the Latin *sedere*, to sit. It refers to a basic tactic of ancient warfare—that is, an army surrounds a fort or castle and remains there ('sits') until enemy resistance breaks down because the defenders are cut off from aid and supplies." (From *Fighting Words*, by Christine Ammer)

Pound for pound, oysters have 20 times as much cholesterol as eggs.

BEDLAM

Meaning: Madness, uproar, or confusion

Origin: "*Bedlam* is a Middle English form of *Bethlehem* (the city where Jesus is said to have been born). Its current meaning comes from the Hospital of Saint Mary of Bethlehem in London, which was incorporated as a lunatic asylum in 1547." (From *Wilton's Etymology*, by Dave Wilton)

ADDICT

Meaning: A person with an uncontrollable (usually bad) habit

Origin: "Slaves given to Roman soldiers as a reward for performance in battle were known as *addicts*. Eventually, the term came to refer to a person who was a slave to anything." (From *Etymologically Speaking*, by Steven Morgan Friedman)

FIZZLE

Meaning: To make a hissing sound; to fail or end weakly

Origin: "Derives from the word *fisten*, 'to fart.' Its original definition, according to the *Oxford English Dictionary*, is 'the action of breaking wind quickly.'" (From *Take My Words*, by Howard Richler)

LEWD

Meaning: Vulgar or lascivious

Origin: "Comes from the Anglo-Saxon *loewede*, which meant 'unlearned,' and referred to the mass of the people as opposed to the clergy, just as we now talk of laymen in this sense. From 'unlearned' it came to mean 'base, coarse and vulgar.'" (From *To Coin a Phrase*, by Edwin Radford and Alan Smith)

HALIBUT

Meaning: A bottom-dwelling fish

Origin: "A Middle English term for any flatfish, including flounder and fluke, was *butte*. Fish was often eaten on holy days, so butte was compounded with haly, a form of 'holy,' thus giving Middle English *halybutte*, which became our modern halibut." (From *Webster's Word Histories*)

One speck of dust contains a quardrillion atoms.

COURT TRANSQUIPS

Here's more real-life courtroom dialogue.

Q: "How did you get here today?"
A: "I had a friend bring me."
Q: "The friend's name?"
A: "We call him Fifi."
Q: "To his face?"

Q: "When you said that, there was some hesitation. Have you heard of others that you haven't heard about yet?"

Q: "What did you do to prevent the accident?"
A: "I just closed my eyes and screamed as loud as I could."

Judge: "What's the problem?"
Bailiff: "Oh, a cockroach was on the exhibit table, Your Honor."
Plaintiff's Counsel: "Motion to quash."
Judge: "Granted."

Mr. Jacobs: "Don't wave at me, or I will wave at you."
Mr. North: "You did wave."
Mr. Jacobs: "You can wave and I'll wave. Why don't we take five minutes to wave at each other."
Mr. Black: "Why don't we stipulate that all waves will be waived."

Defendant: "But, Judge, I can't do 61,500 years!"
Judge: "Well, just do as much of it as you can. And have a nice day."

Q: "Do you remember the context in which your husband brought the issue up?"
A: "Not really. I try not to listen when he talks."

Q: "Do you speak Spanish, Officer?"
A: "Yes, I do."
Q: "Are you fluent in Spanish?"
A: "Yes, I do."

Q: "Doctor, before you performed the autopsy, did you check for a pulse?"
A: "No."
Q: "Did you check for blood pressure?"
A: "No."
Q: "Did you check for breathing?"
A: "No."
Q: "So, then it is possible that the patient was alive when you began the autopsy?"
A: "No."
Q: "How can you be so sure, Doctor?"
A: "Because his brain was sitting on my desk in a jar."
Q: "But could the patient have still been alive nevertheless?"
A: "It is possible that he could have been alive and practicing law somewhere."

Q: "How many times have you committed suicide?"

Before he became an actor, Sean Connery had a job polishing coffins.

MISTAKEN IDENTITY

The next time someone says, "Y'know, you remind me a lot of (insert name here)." Don't simply laugh it off—get paranoid! According to the BRI's extensive files, a case of mistaken identity can lead to . . .

HARRASSMENT

Background: Slobodan "Dan" Milosovic (spelled with an "o"), has lived in London, England, since 1980. Unfortunately for him, he has the same name—more or less—as Serbian ex-president Slobodan Milosevic (spelled with an "e").

What Happened: During the Kosovo war, reporters assumed there was some connection between the two, and camped out on Milosovic's doorstep. They not only harangued him with questions, they even began quizzing his neighbors. Eventually, Milosovic had to file a complaint with England's Press Complaints Commission to protest all of the attention. "Milosovic was fed up with being hounded by the media," said the media.

LAWSUITS

Background: Kevin Moore, a 45-year-old Florida resident, was contacted some years ago by a woman named Anne Victoria Moore, who assumed she had finally located her ex-husband, also named Kevin Moore. He assured her she had made a mistake.

What Happened: Ms. Moore refused to believe him. At last report, Ms. Moore had spent more than eight months filing legal actions against Kevin Moore. First, she placed a claim on his house . . . then on his bank account . . . and then charged him with failure to pay child support. She persists, although numerous government agencies have informed her that this Kevin Moore is "11 years older than, six inches shorter than, and facially dissimilar to, her ex-husband."

UNEMPLOYMENT

Background: In 1990 Bronti Wayne Kelly of Temecula, California, had his wallet stolen. The guy who stole it was then caught for shoplifting, and "pretended to be Kelly when he was arrested."

Nissan has invented an artificial butt to test car seats.

What Happened: Kelly wound up with a criminal record. And according to news reports, after losing his wallet in the theft, he also "lost his apartment, car and most of his belongings between 1991 and 1995 because no one would hire him . . . Every time potential employers did a background check, they found the shoplifting arrest . . . The same man apparently also pretended to be Kelly when he was arrested for arson, burglary, theft, and disturbing the peace." Today Kelly carries a special document that distinguishes him from the impostor, but—amazingly—"he cannot have the criminal record carrying his name erased unless the fake Kelly is found."

IMPRISONMENT

Background: In 1993, a "woman with long blond hair" broke into the house of a Mississippi man named Darron Terry. He caught her in the act . . . but she escaped. Following the burglary, Terry looked through some photographs and identified Melissa Gammill, "a carefree single woman working at a mall food court" as the culprit. Three months later, Gammill was arrested.

What Happened: Gammill could not provide an alibi, because she couldn't remember where she'd been on the night of the burglary. She was charged with the crime, convicted, and sentenced to ten years in prison. Luckily for Gammill, her lawyer, Debra Allen, believed that her client was innocent and developed a hunch that a lookalike had actually committed the crime. She pursued her theory until she stumbled across a mug shot of Pauline Meshea Bailey, who looks so much like Gammill that their photographs are practically interchangeable. In April 1995, Terry admitted he'd mistakenly identified the wrong person, and Gammill was set free after serving 10 months in prison.

ASSASSINATION

Background: During World War II, England's prime minister, Winston Churchill, was targeted by Nazi agents for assassination. They were constantly on the alert, waiting for an opportunity to strike. In 1943, their moment came. At an airport in Lisbon, Portugal (a neutral country), they saw Churchill, famous as "a portly, cigar-smoking Britisher," board a commercial flight to England.

What Happened: According to Churchill in his 1950 memoir, *The Hinge of Fate*:

> The daily commercial aircraft was about to start from the Lisbon airfield when a thickset man smoking a cigar walked up and was thought to be a passenger on it. The German agents therefore signaled that I was on board. Although these neutral passenger planes had plied unmolested for many months between Portugal and England and had carried only civilian traffic, a German war plane was instantly ordered out, and the defenseless aircraft was ruthlessly shot down. Fourteen civilian passengers perished, among them the well-known British film actor, Leslie Howard.

The "portly, cigar smoking Britisher" was in reality one Alfred Chenhalls. "The brutality of the Germans was only matched by the stupidity of their agents," Churchill wrote. "It is difficult to understand how anyone could imagine that with all the resources of Great Britain at my disposal, I should have booked passage on a neutral plane from Lisbon and flown home in broad daylight."

THE DESTRUCTION OF AN ENTIRE CIVILIZATION

Background: When Hernán Cortés landed in Mexico with his 600 soldiers in 1519, the Aztecs were in control of most of present-day Mexico. They had been since around the year 1200.

Religion was a major part of Aztec life . . . and according to legend, the god Quetzalcoatl, who had light skin, light eyes, and a beard (just like Cortés) was supposed to return to earth. So when Cortés and his men started to march toward the Aztec capital city of Tenochtitlán (now Mexico City), word passed that Quetzalcoatl had come back.

What Happened: In the capital city, the Aztec king, Montezuma, received the visitors "in fulfillment of the ancient prophecy." The Spaniards were greeted with food, gold, and women. Montezuma is quoted as saying to Cortés, "Our lord, you are weary. The journey has tired you, but now you have arrived on the earth. You have come to your city . . . You have come here to sit on your throne, to sit under its canopy." Cortés, in reply, assured Montezuma he had come in peace. Actually, he had come to conquer, and quickly took Montezuma hostage. The Spaniards then proceeded to wipe out the Aztec civilization.

A squirrel can fall as much as 600 feet to the ground without injuring itself.

DUMB JOCKS

They give an awful lot of interviews, but sports stars aren't always the most articulate people. Maybe they should keep their mouths shut. Nah.

"Some of the great Oedipuses in the world have been built by Donald Trump."
—**Don King**

"Sure I've got one. It's a perfect 20–20."
—**Dallas Cowboy Duane Thomas, on his IQ**

"Even Napoleon had his Watergate."
—**Baseball manager Danny Ozark**

"I'm a four-wheel-drive-pickup type of guy, and so is my wife."
—**Outfielder Mike Greenwell,** *describing his personality*

"That was the nail that broke the coffin's back."
—**Basketball coach Jack Kraft,** *after his star player fouled out*

"He'll take your head off at the blink of a hat."
—**Joe Theismann,** *on an NFL draft pick*

"I look up in the stands and I see them miss balls, too."
—**Outfielder Devon White,** *after fans booed him for dropping a fly ball*

"Next up is Fernando Gonzalez, who isn't playing tonight."
—**Broadcaster Jerry Coleman**

"My grandmother told me it was good for colds."
—**Outfielder Kevin Mitchell,** *on why he eats Vick's VapoRub*

"You mean the great home-run hitter?"
—**N.J. Net Yinka Dare,** *asked about Beirut*

"I'm in favor of it, as long as it's multiple choice."
—**L.A. Laker Kurt Rambis,** *on drug tests*

"Maybe I'm not getting enough saltwater to my brain."
—**Frankie Hejduk, U.S. soccer team member and surfer,** *on his hamstring injuries*

"If a guy is a good fastball hitter, does that mean I should throw him a bad fastball?"
—**Pitcher Larry Anderson**

"David Cone is in a class by himself with three or four other players."
—**George Steinbrenner,** *on his ace pitcher*

Benjamin Franklin invented Daylight Savings Time.

BEHIND THE HITS

Here are a few "inside" stories about popular songs.

The Artist: The Champs
The Song: "Tequila"
The Story: An accidental hit. In 1958, a group of studio musicians recorded an instrumental called "Train to Nowhere" for Gene Autry's Challenge label. For the flip side, Danny Flores, the saxophone player, suggested a song he'd written in Tijuana. While arranging the song, someone jokingly told Flores to shout "Tequila!" in a low voice during the breaks. None of the musicians took it seriously . . . or even stuck around the studio long enough to hear a playback. On a whim, they named the group after Gene Autry's horse, Champion.

"Train to Nowhere" went nowhere . . . until DJs discovered the flip side. "Tequila" shot to number one, and the Champs won the first Grammy ever awarded for Best R&B performance.

The Artist: R.E.M.
The Song: "Losing My Religion"
The Story: When R.E.M. recorded their album *Out of Time*, in 1991, this was the song that stood out as an obvious single. The only problem was Warner Bros. executives didn't want to release a record with religious symbolism. But according to lead singer Michael Stipe, the song actually has nothing to do with religion. "The phrase 'losing my religion' is Southern slang," he explained. "It means 'fed up' or 'at the end of your rope.'" R.E.M. insisted that it be released, and Warner Bros. finally gave in. Good decision: it was a Top 5 single that won a Grammy for Best Song in 1992.

The Artist: Todd Rundgren
The Song: "I Saw the Light"
The Story: Many of the biggest hits of all time were created spontaneously, in a few minutes—including this Top 20 hit. But just because a song is popular doesn't mean that the writer likes it. "I wrote this song in fifteen minutes from start to finish," Rundgren said, "and it was one of the reasons that caused me to change my

---

Record for most haircuts given in an hour: 18, by Englishman Trevor Howard.

style of writing. For me, the greatest disappointment in the world is not being able to listen to my own music and enjoy it. 'I Saw the Light' is just a string of cliches. It's absolutely nothing that I ever thought, or thought about, before I sat down to write the song."

The Artist: Los Del Rio
The Song: "Macarena (Bayside Boys Mix)"
The Story: Spanish duo Los Del Rio wrote this song about a girl named Macarena, a common name in their native Seville. Their original version was already a big hit in Spanish-speaking countries when Miami radio stations started getting requests for it. A local DJ and two friends made this American version because it was the only way the program director would play the song on the air. They wrote English lyrics, restructured the melody (they used the Los Del Rio chorus and music tracks) and rerecorded it with a new singer— all in two days. It became a huge local hit, then a huge national hit, and was on the charts for an amazing sixty weeks. The DJ and his crew never even met Los Del Rio.

The Artist: Bob Dylan
The Song: "Lay Lady Lay"
The Story: There's nothing profound in this song—and that's the story. Dylan has always been known for his meaningful lyrics. But when he gave up smoking in the late 1960s, he was taken with the new sound of his voice, and suddenly seemed to care more about the music than the words. "Lay Lady Lay" typified the change. Dylan came up with the chord progression first. Then he added the melody, singing "la-la-la-la," which he conveniently turned into "lay lady lay." The song was originally commissioned as the theme for the film *Midnight Cowboy*. But Dylan didn't finish it in time . . . so the producers used Harry Nillson's *Everybody's Talkin'* instead.

The Artist: The Beatles
The Song: "Yesterday"
The Story: This song just popped into Paul McCartney's head when he woke up one morning. He ran to the piano immediately and plunked out the tune so he wouldn't forget it. His sleepy-eyed lyrics: "Scrambled eggs . . . / Ooooh baby how I love your legs." It was only after people close to the band convinced them that the song had real potential that Paul rewrote the lyrics.

The last TV cigarette ad appeared on *The Tonight Show* on December 31, 1970.

THE BIRTH OF THE COMPACT DISC

When CDs were introduced, we thought it was a conspiracy to make us replace our record collection with CDs. Well, maybe it was, but we have to admit that CD quality is pretty good. Here's the story of how they were invented.

AS SEEN ON TV

In 1974, the Philips Electronics company of the Netherlands started a revolution. They invented a laser video disc—the first product to make use of the "general induction laser" that had been developed at MIT in the early 1960s.

But LaserVision, as it was called, was a brand-new technology and it had a problem: poor error detection and correction—which resulted in inconsistent sound and picture quality. Philips built a prototype to show to several Japanese manufacturers, but the LaserVison player performed so poorly that only one of the Japanese companies—Sony—was willing to work with Philips to fix their new product.

At the time, Sony was a leader in both magnetic tape and digital recording technology. They had already built the world's first digital sound recorder—which used magnetic tape, weighed several hundred pounds, and was as large as a refrigerator . . . but it worked. And it gave Sony a head start in figuring out how to correct the problems that Philips was now experiencing with LaserVision.

DISC JOCKEYS

Sony put its digital magnetic tape system on the back burner and began developing a system that would record audio directly to a laser disc. It wouldn't be easy—on top of all the technical problems that had to be worked out, there was also strong opposition within the company to spending money on risky new technology.

Norio Ohga, the company's earliest and most enthusiastic proponent of digital sound recording, faced resistance from company founder Masaru Ibuka and all but three of Sony's audio engineers.

Dolphins sleep with one eye open.

Creatures of the analog age, they had little faith in the basic concept of digital technology—converting sound into numbers and then converting the numbers back into sound—and doubted it would ever improve on conventional analog recording. But Ohga, a former musician and aspiring symphony conductor, likened digital recording to "removing a winter coat from the sound," and insisted that the project be given the highest priority no matter what the cost.

STEP BY STEP

By the spring of 1976, most of the audio compact disc's bugs had been worked out, and the compact disc development team proudly presented Ohga with an astonishing technical marvel: a compact disc the same size as an LP record; but instead of having the same recording capacity as its vinyl counterpart, the CD could hold 13 hours and 20 minutes of sound.

So why aren't today's compact discs as big as an LP and capable of holding 13 hours of music? Because they'd cost too much to produce—something Ohga realized after taking one look at the prototype.

THE SIZE OF THINGS

Ohga sent his engineers back to the drawing board to come up with something that made more financial sense—a smaller CD that approximated the *capacity* of a vinyl record instead of its physical size. But exactly what size? The decision was still a few years off.

Back in the Netherlands, Philips Electronics was at work on its own version of a compact disc that was 11.5 centimeters (about $4^1/_2$ inches) across and capable of holding exactly 60 minutes of sound. Sixty minutes was a nice round number, and the discs were small enough to fit easily into players the size of automobile tape decks. But drawing from his background in classical music, Sony's Ohga pointed out a problem with the 11.5-centimeter standard that others had missed, as John Nathan writes in *Sony: The Private Life*:

> Ohga was adamantly opposed on grounds that a 60-minute limit was "unmusical": at that length, he pointed out, a single disc could not accommodate all of Beethoven's Ninth Symphony and would require interrupting many of the major operas before the end of the

What's a singulthus? A hiccup.

First Act. On the other hand, 75 minutes would accommodate most important pieces of music, at least to a place where it made musical sense to cut them . . . The disc would have to be 12 centimeters to accommodate 75 minutes. In the end, Philips agreed to Sony's specifications.

FINAL TOUCHES

In March 1980, Sony and Philips tested their competing error-correction systems on discs that had been deliberately scratched, marked with chalk, and smeared with fingerprints. Sony's system worked better and was adopted by both companies.

Three months later, they submitted their prototype to the Digital Audio Disc Conference, which had been formed in 1977 to select a single worldwide standard for recording digital audio sound.

Two other companies submitted competing technologies: Telefunken, which recorded digital information mechanically, and JVC, which recorded digital sound electrostatically, the same way that a standard cassette recorder puts analog sound onto tape.

The conference adopted both the Sony/Philips "Compact Disc Digital Audio System" and the JVC system, leaving Telefunken out in the cold. But the compact disc system quickly surpassed JVC's system because, unlike the JVC system, the compact disc's laser read the information on the CD without actually touching it—which meant that discs would last almost forever.

JUST SAY NO

While both companies continued work on perfecting their players, Sony's Norio Ohga and a Philips executive named Hans Timmer began preparing the recording industry for the introduction of CD technology. In May 1981, they brought Sony's prototype CD player to the International Music Industry Conference in Athens, Greece.

While they expected to dazzle the record company executives with CD technology, Ohga and Timmer also realized that they would encounter some opposition. But they were astonished by just how much opposition they did run into. The record companies had millions upon millions of dollars invested in LP record technology—all of which could become worthless if CDs ever took off. And because every compact disc manufactured was, in essence, a

Longest national coastline in the world: Canada's, at 151, 400 miles long.

perfect "master" recording, counterfeiters could use them to make perfect bootleg recordings, something that had not been possible with LPs.

"Ohga must have been shaken, but he didn't show it," Timmer recalls. "He was calm and kept explaining that CDs would never scratch and that the sound was superior. But they shouted him down." Toward the end of Ohga's presentation, the executives stood up and began chanting, "The truth is in the groove! The truth is in the groove!"

"We barely escaped physical violence," Timmer says.

KEEP ON TRUCKIN'

Ohga was determined to continue developing CD technology, even if the entire industry was against him. Not that he had any choice: Sony's fortunes were now inextricably linked to the success of compact discs. Sony had taken a financial bath on its Betamax video recorders, which had been driven out of the marketplace by the VHS format, and the company sorely needed a hit product. Now they had invested tens of millions of dollars in CD technology. Compact discs *had* to succeed.

CD-DAY

On October 1, 1982, the world's first CD player—the Sony CDP 101—went on sale in Japan . . . and with it, the world's first CD albums, courtesy of CBS/Sony records.

The CDP 101 sold for $1,000 and compact discs sold for $16 to $18, twice the price of LPs. At those prices, the CDP 101 was a hit with audiophiles, but out of reach for most consumers. The *New York Times* wrote in March 1983:

> Some question whether the audio-disc will succeed. Even if prices come down—and industry experts expect they will—some analysts doubt whether consumers will be willing to sacrifice substantial investments in turntables and stacks of traditional recordings . . . The compact disc and player . . . is being likened in the music industry to the advent of stereophonic sound or the long-playing recording. Still, the CD's effect on record makers, manufacturers of audio equipment, and—most importantly—the music-loving consumer will probably be more gradual than the two previous revolutions, according to analysts.

The typical violin contains more than 70 separate pieces of wood.

SUCCESS AT LAST

The analysts were wrong. In November 1984, Sony introduced a new CD player, the D-50, that was half the size of the CDP-101 and cost only $230. "The market came roaring back to life," John Nathan writes. By 1986, CD players were selling at a rate of more than a million per year and consumers had purchased more than 45 million compact discs. And that was just the beginning. Sales doubled to 100 million CDs by 1988 and quadrupled to 400 million CDs in 1992, compared to 2.3 million LPs sold that year, making them the fastest-growing consumer electronic product ever introduced.

* * *

REALLY BAD, AWFUL, TERRIBLE JOKES

Yes, we know these jokes are bad and you'll groan when you read them . . . and then you'll tell them to someone else.

A man walks into a psychiatrist's office with banana up his nose and says, "What's the matter with me, Doc?"
The psychiatrist says, "You're not eating properly."

Q: What do you call a cow with no legs?
A: Ground beef.

Q: Why couldn't the sesame seed leave the gambling casino?
A: Because he was on a roll.

Upon seeing a flock of geese flying south for the winter, the bird watcher exclaimed, "Migratious!"

Q: How many surrealists does it take to screw in a lightbulb?
A: To get to the other side.

Q: Did you hear about the dyslexic devil worshipper?
A: He sold his soul to Santa.

Q: What do you get if you don't pay your exorcist promptly?
A: Repossessed.

If you're swimming in the creek and an eel bites your cheek, that's a moray.

The Chinese commonly drink donkey's milk.

LUCKY FINDS

*Ever found something really valuable? It's one of the best
feelings in the world. Here's another installment of
a regular Bathroom Reader feature.*

UP IN SMOKE
The Find: A bunch of cigars
Where It Was Found: In the wine cellar of Temple
House, a 97-room manor built in Ireland in 1864
The Story: For more than 30 years, lord of the manor Sandy
Perceval had been going into the cellar to scrounge up old cigars,
which had been there for as long as anyone in the family could
remember.

Perceval never gave the smokes much thought until 1995,
when a friend, impressed by their quality, asked if he could take a
few to be appraised. It turned out that the cigars had been rolled in
1864, making them the oldest smokable cigars in the world. They
were imported from the Orient by Perceval's great-great-grandfa-
ther. As Sondra Bazrod writes in *The Hunt for Amazing Treasures*,
"Thanks to the mist from a nearby lake, the Irish damp, and the
temperature of the wine cellar, the cigars survived in perfect condition in their own natural humidor," until Perceval and his friends
started smoking them again 100 years later. Originally there were
thousands of cigars, but by 1995 the collection had dwindled to a
few strays plus one unopened box of 500. Estimated value of that
one box: $1,000,000.

OFF THE WALL

The Find: "Large, poster-like cards" with movie stars on them
Where They Were Found: In the walls of a Victorian house in
Three Oaks, Michigan
The Story: About a week after Bill Moorehouse and Joseph
Foxhood bought the vintage house, a huge storm hit and rain
seeped in through the leaky roof, ruining the plaster walls.

As workers tore down the plaster, they discovered old movie
posters—thousands of them stuffed into walls in every room. It
turned out that the house had belonged to the manager of the

town's movie theater during the Great Depression. For years he'd brought several "window cards" home each day . . . and used them as insulation, because they were just the right size to fit between the studs in the walls. Some of the window cards featured *The Girl From 10th Avenue*, starring Bette Davis (the only one known to exist); *I'm No Angel*, starring Mae West; and *Song of Songs*, starring Marlene Dietrich. "These cards were intombed in the walls for sixty years," says Dwight Cleveland, a Chicago movie poster dealer, "and their condition was so good it was like they were in a time capsule."

Estimated value of the entire collection: hundreds of thousands of dollars. "It was like winning the lottery," Moorehouse said.

CANNED GOODS

The Find: A fire extinguisher canister

Where It Was Found: In a house in Ontario, Canada

The Story: Shortly after her husband died, Jean Weitzer sold her home of 30 years to Wilbert Herman, a local businessman. A few weeks later, the 89-year-old Mrs. Weitzner overheard some gossip at the hairdresser: cash had been found in her house.

Weitzner approached Herman to see if the rumor was true, and he admitted that $12,000 "plus a little bit more" was found in a fire extinguisher under the section of the house that had been her husband's office. Herman suggested that he, the contractor who found it, and Mrs. Weitzner split the loot three ways—$4,000 apiece. But when he showed up at her house with a document which said that the $4,000 represented "full payment" for any money found "in or around the house," Mrs. Weitzner refused to sign. Instead, she filed suit to recover the entire amount, which Herman later admitted was not $12,000, but actually $130,000, mostly in $50 and $100 bills. Apparently, Mr. Weitzner had been stashing away in small amounts for more than 40 years and never told his wife about it.

The judge ruled that the money belonged to Mrs. Weitzner, citing case law more than 300 years old that found that "finders keepers" only applies when the original owner's identity cannot be determined. Bonus: after interviewing the Weitzners' bookkeeper, the judge concluded that Harry Weitzner had already paid his full income taxes on the income—Mrs. Weitzner inherited the entire stash tax free.

Among other things, to see if they throw up.

THE HATFIELDS VS. THE McCOYS

The facts about one of the most famous feuds in U.S. history.

The Contestants: Neighboring clans living on opposite sides of a stream that marked the border between West Virginia and Kentucky. The Hatfields, headed by Anderson "Devil Anse" Hatfield, lived on the West Virginia side. The McCoys, whose patriarch was Randolph "Ole Ran'l" McCoy, lived on the Kentucky side.

How the Feud Started: There was already animosity between the two clans by 1878. For one thing, during the Civil War, the Hatfields sided with the Confederacy and the McCoys sided with the Union. But in 1878 Ole Ran'l sued Floyd Hatfield for stealing a hog—a serious offense in a farm-based economy—and McCoy lost. In 1880 relations worsened when McCoy's daughter Rose Anne became pregnant by Devil Anse's son Johnse and went across the river to live—unmarried—with the Hatfields.

Then, on August 7, 1882, Randolph's son Tolbert stabbed Devil Anse's brother Ellison multiple times in a brawl that started during an election day picnic; when Ellison died a few days later, the Hatfields retaliated by tying three of the McCoy brothers to some bushes and executing them.

The feud continued for six more years. It ended after a night-time raid on the McCoys on January 1, 1888. That night, a group of Hatfields surrounded Ole Ran'l McCoy's house (he was away) and ordered the occupants to come out and surrender. When no one did, they set the house on fire. Ole Ran'l's daughter Allifair finally ran out and was gunned down; so was her brother Calvin. The house burned to the ground.

And the Winner Is: No one. This last attack was so brutal that officials in both Kentucky and West Virginia finally felt compelled to intervene. One Hatfield who participated in the raid was convicted and hanged for the crime. Several others were sentenced to long prison terms. With most violent offenders behind bars and the rest of the clan members weary of years of killing, the feud petered out.

When the airbag in your car goes off, it expands at a rate of 150 miles per hour.

WHERE'D THEY GET THAT NAME?

Ever wonder where the names of cities, towns, and other places come from? Think you know? Let's see how good you are—take this quiz and find out.

1. **BOSTON, MASSACHUSETTS.** This state capital was founded by Puritans in 1630. It's named after:
   a. One of its original Puritan settlers
   b. A stone
   c. The tea company that owned much of the city until the 1800s

2. **LITTLE ROCK, ARKANSAS.** Founded in 1722, this state capital is named after:
   a. A little rock
   b. The French town of the same name (La Petite Roche)
   c. The Frenchman Pierre de Rocqueville

3. **IDAHO.** This state's name means:
   a. Good place to grow potatoes
   b. Look, the sun is coming down the mountain
   c. Place of refuge

4. **HONG KONG, CHINA.** This city's name means:
   a. Fragrant harbor
   b. Land of dreams
   c. River of water

5. **KALAMAZOO, MICHIGAN.** This city, settled in 1829, is named after:
   a. A Native American god
   b. A word meaning "he who smokes" or "boiling water"
   c. A dried, salted fish

A female flea can drink 15 times her weight in blood a day.

6. BATON ROUGE, LOUISIANA. This state capital was founded in 1882. It's named after:

   a. A local redheaded beauty

   b. A boundary marker

   c. A Creole word for "lipstick"

7. CONEY ISLAND, NEW YORK. The name is derived from:

   a. Bugs Bunny's ancestor

   b. The evergreen forest once located there

   c. The huge snow cones sold at the famous amusement park

8. ALCATRAZ. This island's name is derived from:

   a. A kind of bird

   b. A Native American word for "rocky island"

   c. The huge trash heaps—mainly empty alcohol bottles— deposited there by settlers; Native Americans thought they were "traz heaps"

9. TOPEKA, KANSAS. The name of this city means:

   a. Home of the singing bushes

   b. Fermenting swamp

   c. Good place to grow potatoes

10. BOCA RATON, FLORIDA. This city's name comes from:

   a. A game of chance

   b. A rock formation

   c. A nasty comment about the Native tribes living there

11. WALLA WALLA, WASHINGTON. The name of this port city comes from:

   a. A Native American fishing god

   b. A bird

   c. A swift, little river

Answers on page 748.

ACCORDING TO THE LATEST RESEARCH...

It seems as though practically every day there's a report on some scientific study with dramatic new info on what we should eat, or how we should act, or who we really are underneath. Some are pretty interesting. Did you know, for example, that science says . . .

YOU'D BETTER WATCH WHAT YOU SAY ABOUT PEOPLE

Researchers: Psychologists from Ohio State University, Purdue University, and Indiana University

Who They Studied: College students

What They Learned: When a person attributes positive or negative traits to someone else, the listener will frequently attribute those same qualities to the speaker, a process known as "spontaneous trait transference."

"In other words," the researchers conclude, "politicians who allege corruption by their opponents may themselves be perceived as dishonest, critics who praise artists may themselves be perceived as talented, and gossips who describe others' infidelities may themselves be viewed as immoral . . . The gist of our research is that when you gossip, you become associated with the characteristics you describe, ultimately leading these characteristics to be transferred to you."

YOUR MEMORY GETS WORSE WITH LESS SLEEP

Researcher: Dr. Robert Stickgold, an assistant professor of psychiatry at Harvard Medical School

Who He Studied: Harvard undergraduates

What He Learned: Memory retention is linked to how much sleep you get. Stickgold tested this by conducting an experiment where Harvard undergraduates were trained to spot visual targets on a computer screen, and then press a button as soon as they were certain they had seen one. Conclusion: students who were tested 3–12 hours later on the same day showed "absolutely no improvment" in

What part of the cinnamon tree is used to make cinnamon? The bark.

speed or accuracy; neither did students who were tested the following day after getting six hours of sleep or less. "Only those who slept more than six hours," the study found, "seemed to improve in speed and accuracy."

YOUR MOOD INFLUENCES YOUR APPETITE
Researchers: Bernard Lyman and Janet Waters, two psychologists at Simon Fraser University in British Columbia

Who They Studied: Unknown

What They Learned: A person's mood influences the kinds of food they like to eat. "When people are lonely, they like liquid foods like soup or milk. When they 'want to be amused,' they like to eat spicy, salty, and crunchy foods. When they're worried, they prefer 'unheated sweets,' like candy bars and cookies. When they're angry, they like 'unheated solids' (whatever that means); and when they're happy, they like soft foods such as ice cream and yogurt."

SHOULD PEOPLE PRAY FOR YOU?
Researcher: William Harris of the Mid America Heart Institute in Kansas City, Missouri

Who He Studied: Heart patients

What He Learned: It seems as though having people pray for you when you're sick can help you get better. In the study, heart patients who had strangers praying for them had fewer complications than those who didn't. "It's potentially a natural explanation we don't understand yet," Harris says, "or, it's potentially a super- or other-than-natural mechanism."

THERE IS A KEY TO HAPPINESS
Researchers: David Blanchflower of Dartmouth College in Massachusetts and Andrew Oswald of the University of Warwick in Great Britain

Who They Studied: 100,000 people of different ages and backgrounds

What They Learned: Blanchflower and Oswald concluded that happiness tends to be the lowest around age 40, and goes up after that. Furthermore, "a lasting marriage brings about the same amount of happiness as an extra $100,000 in yearly income."

It took daVinci about five years to paint the Mona Lisa. (He took a lot of breaks.)

"TRUST IN GOD, BUT TIE YOUR CAMEL"

You know that "a watched pot never boils," but there are countless other proverbs that you may have never heard. Here are some of BRI's favorites from around the world.

"Remember to dig the well long before you get thirsty."
Chinese

"If you cannot catch a fish, do not blame the sea."
Greek

"It is not for the blind to give an opinion on colors."
Italian

"Trust in God, but tie your camel."
Persian

"Measure forty times, cut once."
Turkish

"He that blows into the fire must expect sparks in his eyes."
German

"Six feet of earth makes us all of one size."
Italian

"Fault denied is twice committed."
French

"Never send a chicken to bring home a fox."
Irish

"To lose a friend, make him a loan."
Greek

"Do not hit the fly that lands on the tiger's head."
Chinese

"A lovesick person looks in vain for a doctor."
West African

"Pearls are of no value in the desert."
Hindustan

"When one has no needle, thread is of little use."
Japanese

"When the elephant sinks in a pit, even the frog gives him a backward kick."
Indian

"The sky is the same color wherever you go."
Persian

"When the fox preaches, look to your geese."
German

"He that cannot dance claims the floor is uneven."
Hindustan

"When the ship has sunk, everyone knows how she could have been saved."
Italian

"Even the powerful ox has no defense against flies."
Chinese

"A good archer is known not by his arrows but by his aim."
English

"The road of by and by leads to the house of never."
Spanish

"The longer the explanation the bigger the lie."
Chinese

If you have a backbone, there's about a 50 percent chance you're a fish.

THE BARBADOS TOMBS

The island of Barbados is known for its tropical climate, its sandy beaches—and its restless dead. Here are two legendary, unexplained mysteries surrounding people who have been buried on the island.

THE CHASE FAMILY CRYPT
Background

Col. Thomas Chase and his family were wealthy English settlers living on Barbados in the early 1800s. They owned a large burial crypt in the graveyard of Christ Church. In 1807, Thomasina Goddard, a relative of the Chases, died and was interred in the crypt. A year later, Mary Chase, Thomas Chase's infant daughter, died mysteriously. (It was widely believed that Thomas Chase beat her to death; he was known as a violent man who beat his children—a number of whom showed signs of mental illness.) She, too, was placed in the crypt. But unlike Thomasina, who was placed in a wooden coffin, Mary's body was placed in a heavy lead coffin. After her casket was interred, the vault was sealed shut with a massive marble slab.

A Mysterious Happening

A few months afterward, Dorcas Chase, Thomas Chase's teenage daughter, starved herself to death. Like her infant sister, Dorcas was placed in a heavy lead casket and brought to the crypt. But when the family unsealed and opened the vault, they saw that something peculiar had happened: Mary Chase's tiny coffin had moved to the opposite side of the crypt—and it was standing on one end. Thomasina Goddard's casket had not been moved.

The family was shocked, but assumed the crypt had been broken into by grave robbers. They returned Mary's casket to its proper place, laid Dorcas's coffin next to it, and sealed the crypt even tighter than before—this time pouring a layer of molten lead over the marble capstone.

A Moving Experience

Thomas Chase committed suicide a month later. As with Mary and Dorcas, his body was placed in a heavy lead casket. This time when the crypt was opened, all the coffins were still in place. The

---

Queen Victoria's first act as queen: moving out of her mother's room.

crypt was again tightly sealed; it would not be opened again by the family for another eight years.

In 1816 another child related to the Chase family died. This time when the vault was unsealed, the hinges on the doors were so rusty, they would not open; it took two strong men to finally pry them open wide enough to get the coffin inside. But when the family peered into the dark vault, they saw that the caskets had again been strewn about the crypt . . . except for Thomasina Goddard's, which was left untouched a second time.

The mourners were dumbfounded: the adult-sized lead coffins weighed more than 500 pounds each, and the child-sized ones weren't much lighter. It took four strong men to return each of the caskets to their proper places, and it seemed inconceivable that any natural forces could have tossed them around the tomb.

Keep on Moving

Less than a month after this latest interment, a woman visiting another grave heard groans and "loud cracking" noises coming from the Chase family crypt. Her horse became so agitated by the noises that it began foaming at the mouth and had to be treated by a veterinarian. And a week after that, something spooked several horses tied up outside Christ Church; they broke free, ran down the hill, and jumped into the sea, where they drowned.

By now the goings-on in the vault were public knowledge and the source of wild speculation; when the next member of the Chase family died, more than 1,000 people came to the funeral—some from as far away as Cuba and Haiti. They weren't disappointed: when the crypt was unsealed, all of the coffins were out of place, each one standing on end against the walls of the crypt—except for Thomasina Goddard's.

You Move Me, Governor

After this funeral, the governor of the island decided to investigate. He attended the next funeral, and once again the coffins had been strewn about. This time, he tested the crypt's walls for secret passages (there were none), had the floor of the crypt covered with sand to detect footprints and other marks, had a new lock installed in the crypt's door, and had the crypt sealed with a layer of cement to be sure the door would not be opened. To top it off, he and other officials stamped the wet cement with their

One reason why Fidel Castro grew a beard: The U.S. embargo cut off his razorblade supply.

signet rings, making sure that it couldn't be tampered with without being detected.

On April 8, 1820, the vault was reopened to inter another member of the Chase family. The cement was still in place, but when the family removed it, something heavy leaning against the door of the crypt prevented it from being opened. Several strong men tried to force the door open . . . and when they finally succeeded, something crashed down inside the crypt. They opened the door all the way . . . and saw that it had been held shut because one of the coffins had been leaning against it. This time all the coffins had been disturbed—including Thomasina Goddard's.

The governor and several others examined the crypt closely to try and find an explanation. There was none; there were no footprints in the sand and none of the jewelry on any of the bodies had been stolen. Completely mystified, the governor ordered that the bodies be removed from the crypt and interred in another crypt on the island. They were never disturbed again; they rest in peace to this day.

THE McGREGOR CRYPT
Background
The Chase crypt wasn't the only one on Barbados to have strange things happen to it. In August 1943, a group of Freemasons unsealed a crypt containing the body of Alexander Irvine, the founder of Freemasonry on Barbados. (Irvine's remains were interred in the 1830s in the same crypt as Sir Even McGregor, the owner of the crypt, who was laid to rest in 1841.)

Strange Happenings
The McGregor crypt was even more tightly sealed than the Chase crypt: the inner door was locked tight and cemented with bricks and mortar, which itself was covered with a huge stone slab. When they unsealed the crypt, the inner door of the tomb would not open. Peeking in through a hole, they saw that a heavy lead coffin was standing on its head, leaning against the inner door. The masons carefully moved it and opened the door—only to discover that Irvine's coffin was missing; McGregor's was the one up against the door. The mystery was never solved; the island's burial records confirmed that both men had been interred in the crypt nearly 100 years before, but no evidence was ever found to explain the missing coffin.

The Arctic tern flies as far as 10,500 miles when it migrates.

TV'S MOST TASTELESS SITCOM?

Tasteless television is pretty common these days—from Baywatch
to Who Wants to Marry a Millionaire? *Many critics think* Hogan's
Heroes—*a 1960s sitcom based in a Nazi POW camp—belongs
in the same group. In fact, its outrageous premise might
qualify it as the most tasteless sitcom ever aired.*

CON JOB

C In the early 1960s, two men named Bernard Fein and
Albert Ruddy teamed up to write a pilot for a TV sitcom.
Neither had any experience writing pilots—Fein was an actor
who'd costarred in the *Sergeant Bilko* TV series, and Ruddy was an
architect—but that turned out to be an asset. If the pair had known
how difficult it was to sell a TV pilot in Hollywood, they probably
would not have bothered. "If someone were to ask me today what
their chances of selling a television pilot are, I would say you might
as well go to Vegas," Ruddy says. "It's a million-to-one shot."

The pair came up with a sitcom about inmates in an American
prison who outwit the buffoonish warden and guards and are
secretly running the prison. Instead of stamping license plates and
exercising in the yard, the cons manufacture cigarette lighters and
engage in other moneymaking schemes to bankroll escape
attempts.

The script was genuinely funny, but when Fein and Ruddy
began shopping it around, they realized the prison concept had an
innate problem: American audiences were not inclined to sympathize with hardened criminals and probably wouldn't enjoy watching them escape each week. And potential advertisers knew it. "No
one wanted to sponsor 'a night in the slam,'" Ruddy says.

TURNABOUT

The pilot might have died right then and there—and with it, Fein
and Ruddy's writing careers—if the two men hadn't heard about a
show called *Campo 44* that was going into production at NBC.
"We read in the paper that NBC was doing a World War II sitcom
set in an Italian prisoner-of-war camp, and we thought—perfect,"

According to food researchers, thyme helps prevent tooth decay.

Ruddy says. "We rewrote our script and set it in a German POW camp in about two days."

The revised script featured the exploits of Colonel Robert Hogan, recruited to lead an espionage/sabotage group behind enemy lines. Hogan and his men allow themselves to be captured by the Germans so they can set up a base of operations at the Stalag 13 POW camp—which is run by comically inept Nazis. From there, they sabotage the Germans while helping Allied prisoners escape.

HARD SELL

Fein and Ruddy pitched *Hogan's Heroes* to NBC, but the network turned it down—not because they thought the pilot was terrible, but because they thought it was so good that the series couldn't possibly live up to it. "If the pilot is this good," one NBC executive asked Ruddy after his sales pitch, "how could they sustain it week after week?"

CBS also rejected the series, but for an entirely different reason. After sitting through the sales pitch, CBS founder William Paley told Fein and Ruddy: "I find the idea of doing a comedy set in a Nazi prisoner-of-war camp reprehensible." But Ruddy kept pitching the show. "I literally acted out a half-hour of the show—the barking dogs, the machine-gun sound effects . . . It was hilarious!" At the end of it, Paley bought the show.

Hogan's Heroes premiered on September 17, 1965, and quickly became the most popular new show of the year. In fact, for several seasons it ranked in TV's top 20 programs . . . but it never escaped the controversy its premise engendered: Was it immoral to portray history's most evil killers as bumbling—even lovable—buffoons week after week, just to make a buck? One critic wrote: "Granted, this show is often funny and well-acted. But there's simply no excuse for turning the grim reality of Nazi atrocities into fodder for yet another brainless joke." Another wrote simply: "What's next? A family sitcom set in Auschwitz?"

CAST ASIDE

Ironically, the biggest apologists for the show were its Jewish cast members—including all four of the actors who played the regular Nazi characters—Colonel Klink, Sergeant Schultz, General Burkhalter, and Major Hochstetter. Not only were they Jewish, but three were actually refugees from Nazi Germany:

- Werner Klemperer (Colonel Klink) was the son of conductor Otto Klemperer, a Jew who left Germany in 1933 when Hitler came to power.
- John Banner (Sergeant Schultz), an Austrian Jew, was touring with actors in Zurich, Switzerland, in 1938, when Hitler invaded Austria. Unable to return home, he emigrated to the United States.
- Leon Askin (General Burkhalter) was an actor in Germany when Hitler became chancellor. He was dismissed from the theater and was later arrested and beaten by the Gestapo. He fled to Paris, and emigrated to the United States in 1938.

A STRANGE CHOICE

If that's not weird enough, it turns out that Robert Clary, who played a character named LeBeau, had actually been imprisoned for three years in a Nazi concentration camp. His comment: "A lot of people have asked me how I could work on *Hogan's Heroes*. I tell them that '*Hogan's Heroes* was very different' . . . We were not really dealing with Nazism." Howard Caine, who played Major Hochstetter, was also Jewish. His defense: "I've had, over these years, many fellow Jews say to me, 'How could you play a comic Gestapo like that?' Because I played him as a madman . . . My willingness to do it was to remain true to the concept that they wanted of the vicious killer, potential Nazi."

However, not everyone who worked on the show was comfortable with the concept. Actor Paul Lambert got out after only four episodes. "I always felt a little queasy about doing this show about 'funny Nazis,'" he says. "If it wasn't for the money, I wouldn't have done *Hogan's* at all." And Leonid Kinskey, who played a Russian POW in the pilot, turned down a regular part in the series. "The moment we had a dress rehearsal and I saw German SS uniforms, something very ugly rose in me," he said. "I visualized millions upon millions of innocent people murdered by Nazis. One can hardly in good taste joke about it. So in the practical life of the TV industry, I lost thousands of dollars, but I was, and am, at peace with myself concerning my stepping out of the series."

Ironic note: When *Campo 44* finally debuted on NBC (September 9, 1967), critics denounced it as a *Hogan's Heroes* rip-off, not realizing that it was really the other way around.

Twenty million bats live in Texas's Bracken Cave. They eat 100 tons of insects every night.

FOUNDING FATHERS

You already know the names. Here's who they belong to.

RICHARD REYNOLDS

Background: The nephew of cigarette mogul R. J. Reynolds. He spent ten years working for his uncle's tobacco company, then in 1912 struck out on his own. After several setbacks, he went back to his uncle and borrowed enough money to start the U.S. Foil Company—which made foil cigarette packaging for R.J. Reynolds Co.

Famous Name: In the mid-1930s, Richard learned of a new type of foil made from aluminum. Sensing the product's potential, he built a plant to manufacture it. He began selling it as Reynold's Wrap.

TOM AND LOUIS BORDERS

Background: In 1971, they opened a college bookstore in Ann Arbor, Michigan. To manage the huge inventory, they developed one of the book industry's first computer systems. It helped them develop a reputation as the store where people could find almost any book imaginable . . . and made expansion possible.

Famous Name: By 2007, the Borders Books chain had expanded to more than 1,300 stores around the world, with annual book (and music, added in the early 1990s) sales of more than $4 billion.

WARREN AVIS

Background: In the 1930s, he was a Ford salesman. Then, during World War II, he joined the Air Force and became a combat flying officer. He found that often the hardest part of flying was figuring out how to get from the airport to his final destination.

Famous Name: In 1946, he started a car rental company at Detroit's Willow Run Airport. He talked Ford into selling him cars at a discount by convincing them that having renters test-drive new Fords would help the automaker sell its cars. By the time he sold Avis Rent-A-Car in 1954, the chain had expanded to 154 locations around the country.

Longest recorded Monopoly game: 1,680 hours, the equivalent of 70 days of uninterrupted play.

GLEN W. BELL
Background: After he got out of the Marines in 1946, Bell sold his refrigerator for $500 and used the money to start Bell's Drive-In in San Bernardino, California. San Bernardino is also the birthplace of McDonald's, and when Bell realized how well the McDonald brothers were doing, he decided it would be easier to switch to Mexican food than it would be to compete against them directly.

Famous Name: His first restaurants were called Taco Tia. But after a while he renamed them Taco Bell, after himself.

MAJOR GENERAL OLIVER OTIS HOWARD
Background: Howard commanded troops in important battles during the Civil War—including the First Battle of Bull Run and Antietam. After the war, he demonstrated such interest in the fate of the nearly four million recently freed slaves that President Andrew Johnson appointed him commissioner of the Bureau of Refugees, Freedmen, and Abandoned Lands.

Famous Name: As commissioner, Howard oversaw the establishment of numerous schools and training institutes for African Americans, including Howard University, named in his honor.

HEINRICH STEINWEG
Background: In 1815 Steinweg, who couldn't play a single musical instrument, got a job at an organ builder's shop in the German duchy of Braunschweig. In 1850 he and his wife and children emigrated to the United States, and in 1853 he opened his own piano manufacturing business that he named after himself . . . sort of.

Famous Name: Rather than stick with the original German spelling, Steinweg "Americanized" his name, calling his company Henry Steinway and Sons.

DR. KLAUS MAERTENS
Background: In the 1940s he made orthopedic support shoes for older women. He expanded his line to include shoes for people suffering from skiing injuries, and simple, functional work boots that could stand up to almost anything.

Famous Name: In 1959, Maertens licensed his designs to a small British shoe company, R. Griggs, which began selling English versions of the shoes under the anglicized trade name Dr. Marten's.

If you're an average U.S. male, you'll spend 2,965 hours shaving in your lifetime.

FAMOUS FOR 15 MINUTES

Here it is—our feature based on Andy Warhol's prophetic remark that "in the future, everyone will be famous for 15 minutes." Here's how a few folks have used up their allotted quarter-hour.

THE STAR: Tony Wilson, 29, a British light heavyweight boxer in the late 1980s

THE HEADLINE: *Boxer Wins Bout . . . With Help From Mom*

WHAT HAPPENED: In September 1989, Wilson fought a bout with Steve McCarthy. Wilson was losing: in the middle of the third round, McCarthy landed a punch that sent Wilson to the canvas for an eight count and then pinned him against the ropes as soon as he got up.

That was all Wilson's 62-year-old mother could take. Somehow she managed to jump over rows of spectators, get past security guards, and climb into the ring. She removed her high-heeled shoe and began clubbing McCarthy on the head with it, opening a wound in his scalp. The referee stopped the fight for a few minutes, then ordered McCarthy and Wilson to resume fighting. McCarthy, bleeding profusely from his head, refused . . . and the referee disqualified him. He awarded the match to Wilson.

THE AFTERMATH: Newspapers all over the world ran the story the following day, turning Wilson from a promising fighter into a laughingstock—the first boxer in the history of the sport to win a match with help from his mother. He barred her from attending any more of his fights, but it was too late; his career was already on the ropes.

THE STAR: Daron Malmborg, a Utah motorist

THE HEADLINE: *Vanity Plate Injures Utah's Vanity*

WHAT HAPPENED: In 1999, it was disclosed that Salt Lake City officials had given cash and other gifts to members of the International Olympic Committee, trying to secure the 2002 Olympics for their city. Outraged, Malmborg ordered commemora-

---

More U.S. flags are manufactured in New Jersey than in any other state.

tive "Olympics" license plates for his car . . . and customized the tag number to read SCNDL.

Malmborg had the special plates for 11 months when he received a letter from the Department of Motor Vehicles ordering him to give them back. Malmborg's lawyer—license plate "ISUE4U"—referred him to the American Civil Liberties Union, which took the case public.

THE AFTERMATH: The Associated Press picked up on the story, and it became fodder for TV and radio talk show hosts all over the country. Ultimately, the state backed down and let Malmborg keep his plates. According to press reports, "SCNDL was Malmborg's second choice for the plate. His first—'BRIBE'—was turned down because someone else already had it."

THE STAR: "Miracle" Morris Lieberman, a furniture salesman from Queens, New York, who was addicted to being "famous for 15 seconds."

THE HEADLINE: *Salesman Sneaks His Way Into High Society*

WHAT HAPPENED: In 1928, 16-year-old Morris picked up his unusual hobby by accident. He went to a political rally for presidential candidate Al Smith, saw an empty seat in the front row next to Smith's family, and sat in it. When Smith's entourage left the rally, Lieberman followed close behind—so close, in fact, that the following morning a photograph of Smith and Lieberman together appeared on the front page of at least two newspapers.

Lieberman was hooked. He began crashing parties in his spare time and getting photographed with presidents, royalty, and movie stars.

"I could look up at Adlai Stevenson, Eleanor Roosevelt, the Duke of Windsor arriving at a tribute diner," a *New York Post* columnist wrote in 1974, "and there would be Miracle Morris chatting intimately with them as though he was reception chairman."

THE AFTERMATH: In the late 1970s, Lieberman hung up his tuxedo and retired to Florida . . . and that's when he became famous. He proudly told reporters that in his 50 years of gate-crashing, he was never once asked to leave . . . and he was never once accompanied by his wife, Fay, who refused to go anyplace she wasn't invited. "It was his thing," she explains. "He didn't smoke, drink, or fool around. He liked being around important people."

THE STAR: Rollin Stewart, a.k.a. Rainbow Man

THE HEADLINE: *Clown-Wigged Crusader Says: John 3:16!*

WHAT HAPPENED: During a 1976 trip to Mardi Gras, Stewart had a vision. It told him to take a sign that read "John 3:16" (a passage in the Bible) to nationally televised sporting events and wave it for the television cameras while wearing a rainbow-colored clown wig.

"I wanted to go into show business," he explained a few years later, "and I got this idea for a character who could be a people pleaser. My ultimate goal was to be an actor and spend an occasional day shooting a commercial, then sit back and collect the residual checks."

Stewart never made much money off of his clown-wig crusade for Christ, but by 1980, the year he gave up the sign, he'd become one of the most recognized figures in the sports world, even if nobody knew who he was.

AFTERMATH: Stewart couldn't bear to be out of the limelight. He blew an air horn on the 16th green of the 1991 Masters golf tournament, set off some stink bombs in Robert Schuller's Crystal Cathedral during a service, and then did it again during the title fight between Evander Holyfield and George Foreman. His final "stunt" (so far) was in 1992, when, brandishing a .45-caliber assault rifle, he barricaded himself in a hotel room near the Los Angeles International Airport and threatened to shoot down arriving jumbo jets "if he wasn't given three hours of network television prime time to offer his views of world politics, the weather situation, and the Second Coming of Jesus." The seige ended when a SWAT team broke down the door and took him into custody. Today Stewart is serving three concurrent life sentences in the California prison system.

* * *

"If you can't beat them, arrange to have them beaten."

—George Carlin

New Zealand sheep outnumber New Zealanders 13 to 1.

WEIRD GAME SHOWS

According to experts, the most important aspect of a game show is . . . the game. So what were the designers of these ridiculous shows thinking?

TV Champions (Japan). A different bizarre contest each week. One week contestants chug "rancid, evil-smelling soy bean gruel;" another week they "allow themselves to be locked in cages and sworn at."

The Game of the Goose (Spain). Contestants move around a game board; each space represents a different challenge. One challenge: release a semi-nude model from an exploding bed. Another: try to escape from a box that's slowly filling with sand.

Dream House (U.S.). Young married couples move from room to room, competing to win furniture. Grand prize: An entire mobile home, "put anywhere in the USA."

Finders Keepers (U.S.). "Each day, the show is filmed on location at a different contestant's house. The film crew hides a prize in the contestant's living room, sets up cameras, and then lets viewers watch the contestant tear the room apart looking for it."

Italian Stripping Housewives (Italy). "A strange game show takeoff on strip poker. Wives strip while their husbands gamble."
100 Grand (U.S.). Hollywood's response to the quiz show scandals of the 1950s: Contestants spend part of the show in an isolation booth writing their own questions. Amazingly, the first time the show aired, one contestant missed every single question. "*100 Grand* aired twice before sinking into oblivion."

Endurance (Japan). "Contestants are literally tortured . . . One of the stunts, for example, involves dragging contestants across gravel until they are injured." In another, they crawl through a cage of scorpions. When a contestant fails, the studio audience shouts, "Go Home!"

Gonzo Games (U.S.). A gentler version of *Endurance*. "Overanxious contestants vie to see, for instance, who can attach the most clothespins to their face." In another test of strength, "contestants stand on a barbecue grill until the pain forces them off."

Until the 20th century, the people of Fiji used whale teeth as currency.

RAMBO, STARRING AL PACINO

Some roles are so closely associated with a specific actor that it's hard to imagine he or she wasn't the first choice. But it happens all the time. Can you imagine, for example . . .

G ENE HACKMAN AS HANNIBAL LECTER (*The Silence of the Lambs*—1991) Hackman wanted to direct the film and write the screenplay, so Orion Pictures bought the rights to the novel. Then Hackman dropped out. Director Jonathan Demme signed Anthony Hopkins for the part without telling Orion head Mike Medavoy, who was furious that "an Englishman" would play Lecter. Medavoy agreed on one condition: that Jodie Foster be cast as FBI agent Clarice Starling instead of Meg Ryan. Demme agreed; Foster won her second straight Oscar.

GOLDIE HAWN AND MERYL STREEP AS THELMA AND LOUISE (*Thelma and Louise*—1991) Streep wanted to test her comedic talents; Hawn's film *Private Benjamin* had made $100 million at the box office. They seemed perfect for the film, and wanted to work together. But their schedules were full. "We weren't available right then," Hawn says, "and the director, Ridley Scott, wouldn't wait." Michelle Pfeiffer and Jodie Foster turned down the film; so did Cher. So Scott gave the parts to Geena Davis—who had only two films to her credit—and Susan Sarandon.

ELVIS PRESLEY AS THE MIDNIGHT COWBOY (*Midnight Cowboy*—1969) Desperate to be taken seriously as an actor, the King went shopping around for "a more serious movie role." The part of the male prostitute in *Midnight Cowboy* was one of the parts he considered, but he ultimately turned the film down and did one called *A Change of Habit* instead. Reason: "Since it was about a doctor (Elvis) and a nun (Mary Tyler Moore) in the ghetto, that qualified as being more 'serious.'" *A Change of Habit* was Elvis's biggest box office dud; *Midnight Cowboy* won the Oscar for Best Picture and turned Jon Voight into a star.

The population of Washington, D.C. is greater than the population of Wyoming.

AL PACINO AS RAMBO (*First Blood*—1982) Pacino wasn't the first major star interested in the part of John Rambo. (Eastwood, De Niro, and Paul Newman turned it down.) He wanted Rambo to be "a little more of a madman" and had the script rewritten. But the new draft made the character too dark and nutty, so Pacino passed on the role. So did John Travolta, Michael Douglas, and Nick Nolte. Then Carolco Pictures bought the script and offered it to Sly Stallone, who rewrote the insane Vietnam vet into a misunderstood American hero, "kind of like a *Rocky* movie." *First Blood* was Stallone's first non-*Rocky* film that didn't bomb. It saved his career. The sequel, *Rambo*, established it for good.

DORIS DAY AS MRS. ROBINSON (*The Graduate*—1967) Day's Hollywood image was as "the perennial virgin." "There was something about taking that All-American housewife image and turning it all around," says producer Larry Turman. "I sent the script to her, but we never heard a thing." Day later explained that she read the script but just couldn't see herself playing the role. So it was offered to Anne Bancroft, who could.

BURT REYNOLDS AS RANDALL P. McMURPHY (*One Flew Over the Cuckoo's Nest*—1975) When Marlon Brando turned down the part, director Milos Forman had breakfast with Burt Reynolds and told him he was one of two actors being considered for the part. Reynolds was thrilled. "If the other guy isn't Jack Nicholson," he replied, "I've got the part." When Forman stopped eating dead in his tracks, Reynolds knew he wasn't going to get the part. Nicholson got the role and won the Oscar for best actor.

BURT REYNOLDS AS GARRETT BREEDLOVE (*Terms of Endearment*—1983) About ten years after Reynolds was turned down for *Cuckoo's Nest*, director James L. Brooks sent him the script for *Terms of Endearment*. The lead had been created especially for him, but Reynolds rejected it. "I'd promised . . . that I'd star in *Stroker Ace*," Burt explained later. So Brooks offered the part to Jack Nicholson, who jumped at it. "How many scripts make you cry?" he said. "I read hundreds of screenplays every year and this one made me think, 'Yeah, I know just how this guy feels.' It was terrific." *Stroker Ace* was one of the forgettable films of the year; *Terms of Endearment* won Nicholson his second Oscar.

HOW TO READ TEA LEAVES

It used to be a common thing—go into a tea room or coffee shop and as you reached the end of your cup, a dark, mysterious stranger would offer to read your future for a few coins. After a ritual of stirring and dumping the cup's dregs, the reader would point out pictures in the leaves and tell you what they meant. It's a lost art. But now, thanks to the BRI, you can be the first on your block to practice it.

THE HISTORY OF TEA LEAF READING

Tasseography—the art of telling the future by reading tea leaves and coffee grounds—has been around for so long there's no way to trace its history accurately. Legend, though, says it originated in China. The ancient Chinese foretold the future by reading the marks on the inside of bells. Apparently someone noticed that a teacup is shaped like an inverted bell—and that tea leaves left in a cup resemble the marks on a bell's interior. Since teacups were easier to handle than bells, reading tea leaves became more popular.

HOW DOES IT WORK?

Well, you have to use loose tea—not tea bags. And it's an art, not a science—like interpreting ink blots in a psychologist's office. This becomes obvious when you realize that it's awfully hard to differentiate between, for example, a tea leaf dog ("faithful friends") and a wolf ("jealous friends"), or between a toad ("unknown enemy") and a frog ("arrogance").

Throw in a reader who is also a good and intuitive judge of people, and you may have an effective "fortune-teller."

GETTING READY

- Use a cup with a wide opening, the kind that comes with a saucer—not a mug. The inside of the cup should be light colored and patternless so you can see the leaves clearly.

- Use loose tea, preferably with big leaves. If you can't find it in the store, cut open a tea bag or two and dump the contents into a cup. If you're making coffee, dump the loose ground

Q. What do Bob Hope and Billy Joel have in common? A. They were both once boxers.

coffee (instant coffee won't work) right into the cup. Add hot water and wait for a few minutes before adding cream or sugar.

- The room should be peaceful, if possible. Clear your mind and relax, concentrating on your future and asking whatever power is involved for an accurate reading.

NOW SEE THIS

1. Don't drink to the last drop. Save the leaves or grounds with a little liquid in the bottom (one or two teaspoons is plenty).

2. Take the cup in your left hand and spin it three times clockwise.

3. Immediately after swirling it, turn the cup over on a saucer or plate. After all the liquid drains out, set it upright, with the handle pointing toward you. Note: The handle is like a YOU ARE HERE arrow on a map—it represents you and your home. So a symbol found near the handle indicates something that will strike close to home. Leaf configurations stuck near the rim represent your present; the walls, your immediate future; and the bottom, the distant future.

4. Look carefully into the cup, tipping it and noting the leaves or grounds stuck to the walls and the bottom from all angles. At first they may look like random clumps and glops, but see if their shapes remind you of anything. This will take some imagination (like looking for pictures in clouds). Also notice their size and relative positioning, because two images next to each other can influence each other.

INTERPRETING THE LEAVES

- The bigger and clearer an image is, the more significant it is. A small or blurry image has substantially less significance. If all the images are blurry, it indicates a delay before the events come to pass. If the cup itself is blurry too, it signifies that you'll soon be receiving bad news from your optometrist.

- You may see just a few symbols, or dozens in one cup. The idea is to note all of them in a big picture and see how they interact with each other. As in life, each component influences and is influenced by the others.

Dogs are mentioned 14 times in the Bible. Cats aren't mentioned even once.

- For example: Bad omens may be weakened or canceled out by nearby good omens and vice versa. A snake ("bad luck") that appears near the letter M may indicate that you should be on guard against an enemy whose name begins with M. A number 6 next to a travel symbol may mean you'll be gone for that many days, weeks . . . or even years.

- Start with the images near the rim ("the present"), then work your way into the bottom of the cup ("the future").

SYMBOL KEY

Below, we list some of the images you might see, along with their traditional meanings. In most guides there are literally hundreds to choose from. So when you see something in your cup, just ask yourself what it means to you and determine whether it's a good or bad omen. Have fun, and remember . . . they're only tea leaves!

Acorn: Good health, good luck

Airplane: Unexpected journey; shattered wings—danger

Alligator: Strength and power

Angel: Good news, lucky love

Apple: Long life, gain in business (maybe incompatibility with other PCs)

Arch: Trip abroad (or maybe just to McDonald's)

Arrow: A letter; if bent, bad news

Ax: Trouble

Basket: New family member

Bat: Fruitless endeavor (unless it's a fruit bat)

Bell: Good news, or a wedding

Birds: Good news

Boat: Friendly visitor

Bridge: Pleasant trip; if blurry, unfortunate ending

Bull: Enemies are out to get you

Bush: Success, fulfillment, presidential aspirations

Butterfly: Frivolous pleasure, squandered savings

Candle: Love, goodwill, education

Castle: Marrying into money

Cat: Treachery, insincere friends

Chain: Early marriage; if broken, an unhappy one

Coffin: Death of a person or one of your dreams

Comet: Unexpected visitor (or maybe clean sinks)

Cross: Trouble

Crown: Success

Dog: Faithful friend

Dot: Money

Egg: Some say good fortune; others, that you'll lose your savings

---

Los Angeles has more judges than France.

Elephant: Good luck, health, happiness

Envelope: Good news; if blurred, bad news.

Eye: Watch out, especially around money

Fan: Good luck with opposite sex

Feather: Frivolity, lack of responsibility

Fence (or other barrier): Obstacles

Fish: Good news from far away

Flag: Danger

Flowers: Loyal friends, happy marriage, success

Frog: Beware excessive pride, arrogance

Fruit: Success in new venture

Goat: You're surrounded by enemies

Grasshopper: A friend will leave, maybe not return (or you'll be cast in a remake of *Kung Fu*)

Gun: Trouble

Hand: Friendliness

Hat: Small success

Heart: A letter or lover is coming

Hen: New addition to family

Hourglass: Danger nearby

Key: Problems solved

Kite: Trip that will lead to valuable friendship

Knife: Danger

Ladder: Success, travel

Lizard: Treacherous friends

Monkey: Success

Moon: Fame and riches

Mouse: Thief nearby

Mushroom: Quarrel with lover

Owl: Failure, sickness, poverty, maybe death (but have a nice day anyway)

People: Generally good omen

Pig: Good luck, new member of family

Pitchfork: Deceitful opposite sex

Question mark: Beware all major decisions

Ring: Marriage

Screw: Just as implied, you'll be victim of injustice

Ship: Good news on its way

Snake: Enemy or threat

Spider: Unexpected inheritance

Square: Peace, or no marriage (actually, the two may go together)

Star: Achievement and success

Sun: Joy and power

Toad: Unknown enemy

Tree: Success, fulfillment

Tree branch: Better health

Umbrella: New opportunities

Volcano: Major upheaval

Wheel: Unexpected gift or inheritance

Windmill: Someone you helped will help you

Wolf: Jealous friends

Worms: Secret enemies

Wreath: Loss of loved one

How would you know a Cherophobe if you met one? They'd be "afraid of having fun."

OFF YOUR ROCKER

More wisdom from your favorite rock singers.

"I'm a mess and you're a mess, too. Everyone's a mess. Which means, actually, that no one's a mess."
—**Fiona Apple**

"It's really hard to maintain a one-on-one relationship if the other person is not going to allow me to be with other people."
—**Axl Rose**

"I only answer to two people—myself and God."
—**Cher**

"I'm not a snob. Ask anybody. Well, anybody who matters."
—**Simon LeBon, Duran Duran**

"There's a basic rule which runs through all kinds of music, kind of an unwritten rule. I don't know what it is."
—**Ron Wood**

"I want to go out at the top, but the secret is knowing when you're at the top. It's so difficult in this business—your career fluctuates all the time, up and down, like a pair of trousers."
—**Rod Stewart**

"I can't think of a better way to spread the message of world peace than by working with the NFL and being part of Super Bowl XXVII."
—**Michael Jackson**

"Damn, I look good with guns."
—**Ted Nugent**

"We use volume to drive evil spirits out the back of your head, and by evil spirits I mean the job, the boss, the spouse, the probation officer."
—**David Lee Roth**

"I should think that being my old lady would be all the satisfaction or career any woman needs."
—**Mick Jagger**

"God had to create disco music so that I could be born and be successful."
—**Donna Summer**

"I can do anything. One of these days I'll be so complete I won't be a human. I'll be a god."
—**John Denver**

"Just because I have my standards, they think I'm a bitch."
—**Diana Ross**

Q. How to tell you if an Amish man is married? A. He has a beard.

DUMB CROOKS

Here's proof that crime doesn't pay.

A BAD CALL

"When two service station attendants in Ionia, Michigan, refused to hand over the cash to an intoxicated robber, the man threatened to call the police. They still refused, so the robber, true to his word, called the cops and was arrested."

—"The Edge," *The Oregonian*

SHOULD'VE ELOPED

"Tennessee man Winston Swaggerty, 32, had an outstanding arrest warrant (on a theft charge), but that didn't stop him from having his wedding on the lawn of the Newport, Tennessee, courthouse. A deputy sheriff walking to work recognized the groom, handcuffed him, and led him upstairs to a cell. The bride's reaction? Said the deputy, 'She was really upset.'"

—*Associated Press*

DISAPPEARING THINK

"A pair of Indiana 19-year-olds thought they'd devised the perfect scam: signing checks with disappearing ink. They forgot to make something else disappear though: the name of Jeffrey J. Pyrcioch permanently printed at the top of the bogus checks. Pyrcioch and Heather M. Green were arrested on suspicion of fraud and theft."

—*Atlanta Journal*

ANGER MANAGEMENT

"Johnny Miller, 32, allegedly walked into a First Utah Bank, pulled a gun out of an envelope and robbed the teller. Miller got away with $34,000—but left behind the envelope. It contained a certificate for his completion of an anger-management course run by Utah's Department of Corrections. Miller was apprehended and currently awaits trail."

—*Stuff*

Australia has a robot that shears sheep; Japan has one that makes sushi.

LEAST-COMPETENT CROOK AWARD

"Dennis Sullivan, 23, was arrested in January for the robbery of what he thought was an armored car, according to Manassas, Virginia, police. In reality, it was a laundry truck delivering towels and mops to a Bowl America. Said a police officer, '(Sullivan, holding a sawed-off shotgun), ran up to the (driver) and said, "Give it up." The (driver) said, "What?" Sullivan grabbed a bag and ran but soon realized he had a bag of mopheads.' Police spotted him running for his getaway car, and arrested him."

—*News of the Weird*

HE DIDN'T SEE THE ERROR OF HIS WAYS

"A blind man tried to rob a bank as a security guard who helped him to the teller's window stood nearby, police say.

"Bruce Edward Hall, 48, entered the bank Tuesday, accepted the guard's help, then gave a teller a note demanding money, police said. The teller mouthed 'It's a robbery' to a guard," and Hall was apprehended."

—**Associated Press**

ROAD RAGE

"A motorist was infuriated by the ticket that a Santa Monica traffic officer had just left on his windshield. So he reached into the officer's vehicle, pulled its keys from the ignition, and then sped off in his own car. Police nabbed him and the keys the next day. A police sergeant explained the easy arrest: 'We had his license plate number from the citation.'"

—*Only in L.A.*, Steve Harvey

HE'S GOT A ROOM FOR THREE TO FIVE YEARS

"A man registered for a motel room at the Meader Inn in Van Buren, Arkansas, then followed the clerk into the back room, robbed her, and fled. When police checked the registration card, they found that the thief had registered under his own name, Scott Brady, and even listed his address, which was local. The police went to Brady's home and arrested him."

—**"The Edge,"** *The Oregonian*

"I put a dollar in a change machine. Nothing changed."—George Carlin

VIDEO TREASURES

Ever found yourself at a video store staring at thousands of films you've never heard of, wondering which ones are worth watching? It happens to us all the time—so we decided to offer a few recommendations.

SWINGERS (1996) Comedy
Review: "This highly entertaining low-budget comedy features five young, Rat-Pack showbiz wanna-bes on the prowl for career breaks and beautiful 'babies.' Witty script and clever camera work make this one 'money, baby, money." (*VideoHound's Golden Movie Retriever*)

THE KILLING (1956) Mystery/Suspense
Review: "Strong noir thriller from Stanley Kubrick has Sterling Hayden leading a group of criminals in an intricately timed racetrack heist. Excellent performances and atmospheric handling mark Kubrick, even at this early stage of his career, as a filmmaker to watch." (*Video Movie Guide*)

GET CARTER (1970) Drama
Review: "British gangster film set in the 1970s. The inspiration is Hollywood [in the] 1940s. Michael Caine is a cheap hood who returns home to investigate his brother's death. One of Caine's finest performances." (*Movies on TV*)

DEJA VU (1998) Romance
Review: "An unabashed love story, a glorious fantasy that's all the more meaningful because it involves grown-ups instead of the post-adolescents who usually star in movie romances. Unafraid to be sentimental, it has a certain wisdom about life, about the way we have to take chances and make hard decisions." (*Roger Ebert & The Movies—Capsule Summaries*)

EATING RAOUL (1982) Comedy
Review: "Delicious black comedy about the Blands, a super-square couple who lure wealthy swingers to their apartment and kill them, which both reduces the number of 'perverts' and helps finance their dream restaurant. A bright, original, and hilarious satire." (*Leonard Maltin's Movie & Video Guide*)

Hummingbirds hold their nests together with spiderwebs.

Q & A:
ASK THE EXPERTS

*Here are some more random questions, with answers
from books by some of the nation's top trivia experts.*

IN A LATHER
Q: Do I really have to shampoo twice?

A: "Of course not. Soaps are really efficient; one washing
removes about 99 percent of the oil. But initially, that dirt and oil
prevent the shampoo from forming the nice firm bubbles, which
together make up lather. In fact, the only point of reapplying
shampoo is that it's psychologically pleasing." (From *Why Things
Are, Vol. II*, by Joel Achenbach)

POL POSITION
Q: How did "left" and "right" come to represent the ends of the
political spectrum?

A: "According to the Oxford English Dictionary: 'This use originated in the French National Assembly of 1789, in which the
nobles as a body took the position of honor on the President's
right, and the Third Estate sat on his left. The significance of these
positions, which was at first merely ceremonial, soon became political." (From *Return of the Straight Dope*, by Cecil Adams)

EAU DE CAR
Q: What exactly is that "new car smell"?

A: "There's nothing quite like it, and all attempts to reproduce it
artificially for colognes and air fresheners have fallen short. It is a
combination of scents from things one wouldn't normally smell
voluntarily, condensed in intensity by the size of the relatively airtight passenger compartment. The odor components that go into it
include fresh primer and paint, plastic, leather, vinyl, rubber, glues,
sealers, and carpeting. The smell fades with time, as residual solvents leech away from exposure to light, heat, and air." (From *Just
Curious, Jeeves*, by Jack Mingo and Erin Barrett)

How did the kerosene fungus get its name? It eats kerosene and lives in jet fuel tanks.

CONCRETE JUNGLE

Q: How do city street trees survive with only foot-square holes in the pavement?

A: Actually, many of them don't. The average life of a street tree surrounded by concrete and asphalt is only 7 to 15 years—compared to the 30 to 40 years of similar trees in the wild. Why? "Tree roots are very superficial, occupying only the top three feet of soil—they spread out, not down. When the soil gets so compacted that the roots can't get in, the tree dies. But if the roots can get into the soil (or sewer), the tree has a decent chance of getting the water and nutrients needed to survive. People can help street trees by watering during dry periods and protecting them from dogs, bicycle chains (which can rub the thin bark that covers the tree's growth layers), bleach water from the scrub bucket, and motor oil." (From *The New York Times Book of Science Questions & Answers*, by C. Claiborne Ray)

APPLES AND ORANGES

Q: What's the difference between horns and antlers?

A: "The horns of antelopes and the antlers of deer, although comparable in function, differ considerably in structure. Horns, usually possessed by both sexes, are permanent features that continue to grow throughout the animal's life. They are bony projections from the skull, covered with keratin, which is tougher than bone. Antlers, by contrast, are pure bone and are formed and shed every year. They are normally grown only by male deer, with the exception of reindeer and caribou, whose females have them as well." (From *Can Elephants Swim?*, by Robert M. Jones)

HE GO BOOM!

Q: How do they shoot off a "human cannonball" at the circus without blowing the poor guy to pieces?

A: "Human cannonballs aren't blasted from the cannon with gunpowder. They're propelled by a catapult. The flash, loud noise, and smoke are supplied by firecrackers and such." (From *The Straight Dope Tells All*, by Cecil Adams)

Only about three percent of mammals practice monogamy.

FAMILY FEUDS

*You can't always get along with everyone in your family . . . but
these guys just out and out declared war on each other.*

MARS vs. MARS
The Contestants: Frank Mars, founder of Mars, Inc.,
chocolate company, and his son Forrest Mars.
The Feud: The candy bars that Frank Mars invented—Snickers,
Milky Way, and Three Musketeers—made him a wealthy man.
He lived in a mansion, drove expensive cars, and owned race
horses and an airplane. He had plenty of money, but the country
was in the middle of the Depression, so he wouldn't expand the
company.

Forrest Mars was another story. He worked in his father's company and wanted to expand it. "I wanted to conquer the world," he
explained years later, and he soon began to chafe under his father's
authority. "Things got bitter. I told my dad to stick his business up
his ***. If he didn't want to give me one-third right then, I said,
I'm leaving.' He said leave, so I left."

When Frank Mars died from kidney failure 15 months later
(Forrest did not attend the funeral), his second wife, Ethel, inherited control of Mars, Inc. The will stipulated that Forrest would
not inherit any Mars, Inc. stock until Ethel died, and even then he
would get only half her shares. He was on his own.

Moving to France, Mars started a business selling shoe trees.
When this failed, he went back to the candy business. He moved
to Switzerland and took jobs in the world's great chocolate companies—Tobler and Nestle—to learn everything he could about
chocolate from the best minds in the industry. (Frank Mars never
knew anything about how to make chocolate—his candy bars were
made with Hershey's chocolate.) "I was an hourly paid guy," Mars
recounted years later. "They didn't know who I was. They never
asked. They didn't care."

In 1933, Mars moved to London, reformulated his father's Milky
Way recipe to suit English tastes, and began selling them under the
name "Mars bars." By 1939, he had built his company into the third
largest candy manufacturer in Britain. But when England passed a

special tax on resident foreigners to raise money for World War II, Mars put his senior manager in charge of the company and returned to the United States to avoid paying the tax.

By now Forrest's stepmother and her family were firmly in control of Mars, Inc. So rather than go back to the family firm, Mars founded a new company, M&M, Inc., and began manufacturing candy-coated chocolates like the ones he'd seen during a visit to Spain. Just as he'd done in England, Mars built M&M, Inc. into one of the largest candy companies in the country. But it wasn't enough—he still had one last score to settle.

And the Winner Is: Forrest Mars. When Ethel Mars died in 1945, he inherited half of her Mars, Inc. shares, making him a part-owner of the company he'd been shut out of. But he wanted it all. Mars spent the next 19 years battling executives for control. And he got it. In 1964—32 years after his father kicked him out of the company—it was his.

KRASILOVSKY VS. KRASILOUSKY VS. KRASILOSKY

The Contestants: Uncles, nephews, and cousins who worked at S. Krasilovsky & Brothers, a moving company in Brooklyn, New York.

The Feud: In 1939, nephew Mike Krasilovsky left the firm and started his own moving company, which he named Mike Krasilovsky Trucking & Millwright Company. The two companies began stealing each other's customers . . . and Mike began spelling his last name with a "u" instead of a "v" so his company would appear ahead of his uncle's in the telephone listings.

That was only the beginning: When cousin Milton started his moving company, he changed his name to Mick (because it looks like Mike), and spelled his last name Krasilosky so that it would appear ahead of both his uncle and his cousin. Mike retaliated by buying the Atlas-York Safe Corporation so that he would also appear in the "A" listings; then another cousin got into the business—the Acme Safe company—which prompted Mike to buy the Ace Trucking Company.

And the Winner Is: No one. But at the peak of the feud, Milton had 13 different listings in the phone book; Mike had 18. When another cousin, Marvin, came up with the idea for the AAA Acme Krasilovsky Safe Company, Mike finally gave up.

DON'T LEAVE
HOME WITHOUT IT

*You're at a restaurant and the waiter brings your check. You reach
in your pocket and suddenly realize your wallet is at home. Or,
you hand the waitress a credit card; she comes back and tells you,
apologetically, that it's expired (or maxed out). Sound familiar?
We figure there are two things to learn from the stories here: 1)
Don't worry, it happens to everyone; and 2) Don't panic.
If you're resourceful, you can deal with it.*

EVEN THE PRESIDENT . . .

"President Bill Clinton was visiting Park City, Utah, on Monday. He picked out several books at Dolly's Books and handed over his American Express card for the $62.66 bill—only to be informed it had expired the day before." He paid cash.

—**Medford, Oregon,** *Mail Tribune*

SORRY, NO CHECKS ACCEPTED

In April 1997, former British Prime Minister Margaret Thatcher tried to purchase $40 worth of groceries with a check. The clerk wouldn't accept it. "I can't override the system, so there was no way I could take her check," said cashier Shirley Taylor. "She was very good about it, tore the check up and paid cash. It was a bit embarrassing for her, I think."

—***Wire service reports***

THAT'S ME!

"After a young woman wrote a check at a clothes store in Marina del Rey, the clerk asked to see her driver's license. She explained apologetically that her wallet had been stolen. But, she added, she did have one form of ID. 'I was the May centerfold in *Playboy* magazine,' she said. 'I have the centerfold here in my purse if you want to see it.' She took it out. The smiles matched."

—*Only In L.A.,* **by Steve Harvey**

Fastest-growing plant on earth: Bamboo, which can grow as much as 35 inches a day.

SAVED BY THE BUCK

"In 1979 Treasury Secretary Michael Blumenthal found himself in an embarrassing situation in Beethoven's, an expensive San Francisco restaurant. Blumenthal was confronted with a sizable dinner bill, an expired Visa card, and a waiter who wanted proof of signature to back up an out-of-town check. Blumenthal solved his predicament in a way only he could: He produced a dollar bill and pointed out his own signature, W.M. Blumenthal, in the bottom right-hand corner. The signatures matched, and Blumenthal's personal check was accepted."

—*The Emperor Who Ate the Bible,* **Scott Morris**

X-RATED

"NEW YORK—Sharon Mitchell, heroine of the X-rated *Captain Lust,* was having trouble cashing a check at a New York bank because she was not carrying a driver's license or any other identification.

"She was, however, carrying a magazine in which she appeared in the nude. She handed over the magazine, hitched her sweater up to her chin, and arranged herself in the same pose. "They cashed her check."

—*London Sunday Telegraph Magazine*

* * *

BRI "FAVORITE ROLE MODELS"

Role Model: Abigail Boettcher, Pork Queen of Buena Vista County, Iowa

Setting an Example: In her farewell speech as reigning Pork Queen, the college freshman admitted to area pork producers that she "is, and always has been, a vegetarian."

Role Model: Diane Smith, of the Texas Dept. of Agriculture

Setting an Example: In 1996 Smith, the official in charge of promoting Texas's $8 billion beef industry, revealed that she'd been a vegetarian for the past 14 years.

UNCLE JOHN'S FLATULENCE HALL OF FAME

*It used to be that no one talked about farts . . . now, it's no big deal.
You can't get away from it. Which is fine by us. Here we honor
people who have made an art out of passing gas. (By the way—
if this is your favorite part of the book, we recommend a
tome called* Who Cut the Cheese? *by Jim Dawson.)*

Honorees: Simon Brassell, Karen Chin, and Robert Harman
Notable Achievement: Finding a way to discuss dinosaur
farts without making people laugh
True Story: In 1991, the three scientists published a paper proposing that millions of years' worth of dinosaur farts may have helped
make the Earth more hospitable for humans and other mammals.
How? The methane gas passed by dinosaurs during the Cretaceous
period, they suggested, "may have been a . . . contributor to global
warming."

Honoree: King Louis XIV of France
Notable Achievement: Turning a fart into a compliment
True Story: "It is said," Frank O'Neil writes in *The Mammoth Book
of Oddities*, "that Louis XIV expressed his admiration for the
Duchess of Orleans, by doing her the honor of breaking wind in
her presence."

Honoree: Randy Maresh, an employee at the Albertson's supermarket in Gresham, Oregon
Notable Achievement: Making someone so mad at his farting that
they sued him
True Story: In the mid-1990s, Tom Morgan sued co-worker
Randy Maresh for $100,000, claiming in court papers that Maresh
"would continually and repeatedly seek out the plaintiff on the
premises of Albertson's [supermarket] while plaintiff was engaged
in his employee duties. That defendant, after locating plaintiff,

The ancient Chinese would swing their arms to cure a headache.

would position himself in the proximity of plaintiff so as to direct his 'gas' toward plaintiff, humiliating plaintiff and inflicting severe mental stress upon plaintiff." (In his written response to the suit, Maresh's lawyer argued that farts are "expressive behavior," and as such, are protected by the First Amendment.) No word on the outcome.

Honoree: Dr. Michael Levitt of Minneapolis, Minnesota
Notable Achievement: Inventing a Breathalyzer-type test that can detect a propensity for excessive farting
True Story: Dr. Levitt's test checks for elevated levels of hydrogen in a patient's breath. If it's there, the patient is likely to be gassy. (Not everyone is impressed with Dr. Levitt's scientific break-through. "If Levitt is checking his patients' breath for flatulence," Jeffrey Kluger writes in *Discover* magazine, "I wouldn't even ask how he'd propose to conduct dental work.")

Honoree: Canelos Indians of Ecuador
Notable Achievement: Turning a fart into a supernatural experi-ence . . . and a free meal
True Story: "The Canelos Indians," Eric Rabkin writes in *It's a Gas*, "are particularly scared by their farts because they believe the soul escapes the body along with the smell. They have developed a ritual to counter this escape. When in a group someone breaks wind, one of the rest, the quickest, will clap him on the back three times and say, 'Uianza, uianza!' The meaning of this word is unknown but it does signify a feast by that name which the person who farted is obliged to prepare . . . Alternatively, he can discharge his obligation by rewarding the clapper's kindness with three big clay vessels of manioc beer."

Honoree: Ned Lowenbach, assistant district attorney in Tuolumne County, California
Notable Achievement: Using farts as a legal strategy
True Story: In 1988, a defense attorney appealed his client's con-viction, protesting that Lowenbach had disrupted trial proceedings by passing gas. 'He farted about one hundred times,' the attorney said. 'He even lifted his leg a few times.'"

WHY WE EAT OATMEAL

It seems like people have been eating oatmeal forever, but that isn't the case. If it wasn't for the efforts of three men—one who figured out how to make it, another who figured out how to steal it, and a third who figured out to sell it—oatmeal might never have become a popular breakfast food at all.

STRONG MEDICINE

For thousands of years, humans have created meal and flour by grinding grain between two millstones—flat stones that lay atop one another and rotate in opposite directions. In the process, the grain trapped between them is ground into flour.

But when raw oats are ground between millstones, the result is a floury meal that takes three or four hours to cook . . . and produces a lumpy, pasty gruel. Benjamin Franklin and others touted "oatmeal gruel" as a health food. But it tasted so terrible, and was so difficult to make, that it remained something sold by druggists and kept in the medicine closet, to be brought out only when necessary for "invalids and convalescents." With the exception of German, Scottish, and Irish immigrants who'd eaten it as a staple food in the old country, anyone healthy enough to eat something else usually did. Oats were something you fed to horses, not people.

MAN OF STEEL

Then in 1877 a miller in Akron, Ohio named Ferdinand Schumacher developed a process that used steel knives to convert hulled oat kernels into coarse meal. Because the knives cut the oats into flakes instead of grinding them into floury powder, the resulting porridge no longer had the consistency or taste of lumpy paste, and was much easier to prepare.

Schumacher's German American Oatmeal Factory had the improved method of milling oats all to itself . . . but not for long. Within a year, an employee named William Heston figured out how to improve the machine's cutting process. Then he went and secured a patent for the improvement—in effect using patent law to steal control of the machine. Heston quickly licensed the

---

Jellyfish are 99 percent water.

improvement back to Schumacher to prevent him from retaliating, but the damage was done—now someone else had the ability to mill oats into something that people actually wanted to eat.

Heston didn't waste any time setting himself up in business. He opened a mill 16 miles away in Ravenna, Ohio, and began producing steel cut oats to compete directly Schumacher. Heston was of Quaker descent, and understood that the Quaker reputation for simplicity, thrift and hard work would reflect well on his product. So he named his company the Quaker Mill Company and in 1877 registered as a trademark "the figure of a man in Quaker garb"— the first trademark for a breakfast cereal in the United States.

In spite of all his advantages, Heston proved to be a terrible businessman, and in 1881 the mill went bankrupt.

That November an evangelical Christian named Henry Parsons Crowell bought Heston's mill, his oatmeal patents, and his Quaker trademark. The world of breakfast foods would never be the same.

DIVINE INTERVENTION

Crowell was on a mission from God. Seven years earlier when he was at death's door with tuberculosis (which had also killed his grandfather, father, and two brothers), he'd made a pact with God: If his health were restored, he'd devote the rest of his life to raising money for Christian causes. His health was restored, and Crowell became focused on raising as much money as possible . . . then donating 65 percent of it to Christian charities. (There is little evidence to suggest that he ever gave any of his money to the Quakers, however).

By now, thanks largely to Schumacher's efforts, demand for steel cut oatmeal was enormous. In 1883 he built a huge new five-story mill, appropriately named the Jumbo Mill, to meet it. His oatmeal production increased to 360,000 pounds a day; and because demand for oatmeal was growing so fast, other millers were trying to enter the business—usually by infringing on Schumacher's and Crowell's patents. As the supply of oatmeal increased, prices fell and profits disappeared.

Crowell realized he needed a better way to sell oatmeal. He tried to form a cartel of the largest oatmeal producers—which would have limited productions and raised prices—but Schumacher refused to join. Then in 1886, Schumacher's Jumbo Mill burned to the ground. It was not insured against fire.

The average smell weighs 760 nanograms.

THINKING OUTSIDE OF THE BOX

Crowell was determined to take advantage of Schumacher's misfortune, and he was in good position to do so.

In the mid-1880s, all oatmeal was sold in bulk—the shopkeeper had a huge, 180-pound wooden barrel of oatmeal in his store, and when a customer wanted to buy some, it was scooped into a bag.

Crowell decided it made more sense to package oatmeal in individual 2-pound cardboard cartons—which had been invented only seven years earlier. The cartons were a revolution in packaging. Because they lay flat when unfolded, they could be fed into a printing press and became miniature billboards for the product inside.

Crowell made the most of this new advertising space. He used a colorful printing process that featured a picture of a Quaker on the box, plus cooking instructions and recipes for new dishes that helped increase demand. A free spoon was included in every box to encourage brand loyalty, and customers were invited to cut the Quaker off of the box and mail it in for more freebies.

YOU DIRTY RAT

Crowell also blanketed his sales territories with advertising, painting the Quaker Oats trademark on the sides of buildings and posting it on billboards, on the sides of streetcar cards and in grocery store windows—even on the back of Sunday church bulletins. "In the space of only a few years," Thomas Hine writes in *The Total Package*, "Quaker Oats became the most promoted product ever."

At the same time, Crowell launched an assault on millers who still sold their oatmeal in bulk barrels. "This grocer dumps oats into a bin," the company's magazine *The Daily Quaker* reported, "Sets his rat traps on top of oats. Catches two rats the first night."

Quaker Oats was now set on the path that would make it America's best-selling cereal by the turn of the century . . . but there was still one thing left to do. In 1888 Crowell finally succeeded in convincing seven of the country's largest millers—including Schumacher, who'd been humbled by the Jumbo Mill fire—to join together as the American Cereal Company.

Schumacher and Crowell battled for control of the company for the next eleven years, until Crowell finally shoved Schumacher out in 1899 and made himself president. Then in 1901, American Cereal changed its name . . . to the Quaker Oats Company.

Do you close your eyes when you dive? So does a frog.

CLASSIC HOAXES

*We've got a whole library full of books on hoaxes. It's amazing how
many times people have pulled off clever scams . . . and how much
fun it is to read about them. Here are a few more favorites.*

THE BOSTON BABY MEDIUM

Background: In the 1880s, a Boston "spiritualist" named
Hannah Ross became famous for her ability to bring
deceased infants back to Earth temporarily, so grieving parents
could not only talk to them, but also see and touch them. Ross's
séances were always held in dark rooms: She would go into a large
cabinet and pull a curtain closed behind her, at which point she
would summon the baby back from beyond the grave. Moments
later, the baby's head—but never the rest of its body—would poke
through the curtain. Ross would then call the parents forward to
kiss, cuddle, and caress the ghostly baby's head, which was as warm
to the touch as if it were still alive.

Exposed! In 1887, some news reporters teamed up with the Boston
police to look into the séances . . . and exposed them as a hoax.
Ross had accomplished the illusion by "painting the face of a baby
on her breast and poking it through a slit in the cabinet curtain."

THE COUNTRY CLUB ELIMINATION ACT

Background: In 1971, the *Saturday Review* published in its April 3
issue a Letter to the Editor from a reader concerned about H. R.
6142, a little-known piece of legislation "introduced by
Congressman A. F. Day and cosponsored by some 40 members of
the House," that would abolish all private parks larger than 50
acres in size and all public recreation areas larger than 150 acres
and used by fewer than 150 people a week.

The concerned reader, who identified himself as K. Jason
Sitewell, explained that he'd grown up with Congressman Day and
knew that Day suffered "a long history of golf-related family
tragedies," including a grandfather who "perished in a sand trap,"
and his father, who died from a heart attack after hitting 19 balls
in a row into a pond. The following week, the magazine printed a
letter from Congressman Day himself, which cited statistics that in

---

The first CD to sell one million copies: Dire Straits' *Brothers in Arms*.

an average year, golf caused 75,000 coronary occlusions, 9,300 golf-cart fatalities, and 60,000 ruined marriages.

News of the bill sent the golfing world into an uproar. Concerned golfers all over the country contacted their congressmen, golf clubs held emergency meetings, and a popular weekly golfing magazine reprinted Sitewell's letter.

Exposed! Then in its May 8 edition the Review's editor Norman Cousins admitted the whole thing was a hoax—Congressman A. F. Day's name was short for "April Fool's Day," and K. Jason Sitewell was an "imperfect anagram for 'It's a joke, son.'"

THE CORNELL RHINO

Background: One winter morning in the 1920s, students at Cornell University discovered a set of large footprints in the snow around the campus. Zoology professors examined the prints and declared that, beyond a doubt, they were rhinoceros tracks. But where did the animal go? A horde of students followed the tracks across campus and out across the frozen surface of Beebee Lake, the source of the university's drinking water. There the tracks stopped . . . right next to an enormous hole in the ice. It seemed obvious that the rhino had walked onto the lake, fallen through the ice, and drowned. Many students and faculty swore off drinking tap water for the foreseeable future. Those who continued drinking it swore they could taste a subtle hint of rhino.

Exposed! A few days later, university officials received an anonymous letter from a Cornell student admitting he and a friend had made the tracks . . . using a rhinoceros-foot wastebasket.

THE GREAT SOVIET FUR SWINDLE

Background: Minks and sables are among the most valuable fur-bearing animals in the world. In the early 1950s, the Soviet Union had sables; Canada had minks. The Soviets proposed a swap: in exchange for two breeding pairs of Canadian minks, they would give the Canadians two pairs of sables. Sable furs were worth more than minks, so the Canadians accepted and sent the minks to Russia.

Exposed! They were ecstatic when the four Soviet sables arrived in return . . . until they realized that the two females had been sterilized prior to shipment.

Over 6 billion copies of the Bible have been sold.

LIFE AFTER DEATH

*These folks have glimpsed the "other side" and
made it back to the land of the living.*

DECEASED: 32-year-old Ali Abdel-Rahim Mohammad, of
Alexandria, Egypt

NEWS OF HIS DEATH: In 1999 Mohammad blacked
out while swimming off the coast of Alexandria. His body was
recovered and taken to the morgue.

RESURRECTION: After about three hours in the morgue refrigerator, Mohammad was awakened by a loud banging sound—an
attendant was trying to close the refrigerator drawer in which
Mohammad had been placed. So the "corpse" reached up and
grabbed the attendant's hand. According to one news account, "his
firm grip sent the attendant and a family who had apparently come
to identify the body of a loved one stampeding out of the morgue
yelling, 'Help us!'"

DECEASED: Henry Lodge, a 63-year-old California man

NEWS OF HIS DEATH: In 1986 Lodge was fixing some fuses
when he had a heart attack. He was pronounced dead, and his
remains were transported to the Los Angeles morgue.

RESURRECTION: Just as the morgue's Dr. Philip Campbell was
preparing to make an incision in the remains, Lodge opened his
eyes and screamed, "HELP!" Lodge made a speedy recovery and
was soon released from the hospital; Dr. Campbell took a leave of
absence from work for "nervous exhaustion."

DECEASED: Xue Wangshi, an 81-year-old Chinese woman

NEWS OF HER DEATH: On December 2, 1995, Ms. Wangshi
collapsed and stopped breathing. She was pronounced dead and
sent to a nearby crematorium.

RESURRECTION: Workers put Ms. Wangshi on a conveyor belt
that fed the deceased into the furnace, but in classic cliffhanger
fashion, moments later they saw her move her right hand. So they
stopped the conveyor belt, "and Mrs. Wangshi sat up."

Elvis's underpants are estimated to be worth $1,300.

DECEASED: Musyoka Mutata, 60, who lived in the village of Kitui in Kenya

NEWS OF HIS DEATH: In 1985 Mututa contracted cholera and was thought to have died. Funeral arrangements were made, and at the appointed hour pallbearers arrived in his home to take the body away for burial.

RESURRECTION: When the pallbearers sprayed Mutata with insecticide to ward off flies, he suddenly sat up and asked for a drink of water. According to newspaper reports, this was Mutata's second near-death experience: in 1928 his parents mistook him for dead after an illness, and when "his body, wrapped in sheets and blankets, was being lowered into its grave, the three-year-old let out a scream and was saved."

Update: Four months after his 1985 near-death experience, Mutata died again, this time for real. Rather than bury him right away, however, his family waited two days to be sure that he was really, really dead.

DECEASED: The entire Naua tribe, which until the turn of the 20th century had made its home in the Amazon rain forest in Brazil

NEWS OF THEIR DEATH: No word on precisely when the tribe is thought to have gone extinct; the last known report on the tribe was a 1906 newspaper article titled, "Last Naua Woman Marries."

RESURRECTION: The Naua weren't dead—as far as anyone can tell, they were just hiding. After avoiding contact with the rest of the world for nearly a century, in August 2000, more than 250 members of the tribe emerged from deep in the rain forest to protest the Brazilian government's plan to incorporate the Naua native lands into a national wildlife park. It's too early to tell what will happen, but as the law stands now, the Naua are considered trespassers on their own land. "We thought there were no more Naua," one Brazilian government told reporters. "Our job now is finding them land. No humans are allowed in the park, just the forest and the animals."

MORE BRAINTEASERS

We're back with another installment of brain-testing puzzles.

1. During a high-stakes bridge tournament preceded by a sit-down dinner, Jay, Jennifer, Jeff, and John played together. At the end of the night, all four had more cash than when they had arrived. In other words, none of them lost, although they were playing for money. How could this be?

2. What belongs to you alone, but is mostly used by others?

3. Two French diplomats who have never seen each other meet at the French embassy in New York and decide to have a drink together in a nearby bar. Incidentally, one is the father of the other one's son. How is this possible?

4. You're at a cocktail party with your date. Strangely enough, there's something in the room that everybody can touch—and so can you, but only with your left hand. What is it?

5. What word is always spelled incorrectly?

6. I dig out tiny caves, and store gold and silver in them. I also build bridges of silver and make crowns of gold. Sooner or later everybody needs my help, yet many people are afraid to let me help them. Who am I?

7. What is greater than God, more evil than the devil, poor people have it, rich people need it, and if you eat it, you die?

8. You have to get to the hospital. At a fork in the road you meet Joe and Moe, a pair of identical twin boys. You can't tell them apart, but you know that Joe always tells the truth and Moe always lies. You can ask one of them only one question. What question will guarantee that you take the correct fork . . . and which twin do you ask?

9. The person who made it had no use for it; the person who bought it didn't want it; and the one who finally ended up with it, never even knew about it. What was it?

Answers are on page 750.

A typical porcupine has about 30,000 quills.

BRAM STOKER'S
DRACULA

*It was a dark and stormy night . . . no, it really was. And that
was the perfect setting for telling one of the scariest
stories of all time. Here's how it happened.*

CABIN FEVER

It all started in the summer of 1816. Percy Bysshe Shelley,
the famed English poet, was vacationing along the shores of
Lake Geneva in Switzerland with his 18-year-old future wife, Mary
Wollstonecraft. In adjoining villas were their friends, the poet Lord
Byron, and Lord Byron's personal physician Dr. John Polidori. "It
was a wet, ungenial summer," Mary Shelley later wrote, and the
rain "confined us for days."

The group passed some of their time reading German horror
stories. Then, inspired by the tales, Lord Byron announced to the
group, "We will each write a ghost story." And with that challenge,
two of the most enduring monsters in English literature came into
being.

DYNAMIC DUO

Mary Wollstonecraft wrote a tale about a mad scientist who assem-
bles a monster out of body parts stolen from cadavers and then
brings the monster to life. Polidori, she recounted later, "had some
terrible idea about a skull-headed lady, who was punished for peeping through a keyhole." Percy Shelley came up with a story
"founded on the experiences of his early life" . . . and Lord Byron
created a story about a vampire.

Wollstonecraft spent the rest of the summer turning her story
into a novel—*Frankenstein*. Lord Byron never did complete his
story, but Dr. Polidori was so intrigued by the vampire idea that
he scrapped the skull-headed lady and, borrowing from Byron,
later wrote *The Vampyre*, the first vampire novel of any substance
to appear in English literature. *The Vampyre* was published in
the April 1819 edition of *New Monthly Magazine* and earned
Polidori £30.

The Statue of Liberty's fingernails each weigh about 100 pounds.

REVENGE!

The Vampyre might have been just another simple retelling of the traditional vampire legends of Eastern Europe were it not for the fact that Polidori and Lord Byron had once been lovers. Cooped up in the villa in Geneva that summer, they were driving each other crazy. Polidori was jealous of Byron's increasingly close friendship with Percy Shelley, and, perhaps because of this, he decided to make the vampire character a parody of Lord Byron.

The vampires of Eastern European lore were not that different from today's conception of werewolves: they were scary, uncivilized creatures, more animal than human. But Polidori's character was different. His vampire was a nobleman, and an immoral, sinister antihero named Lord Ruthven—not unlike Lord Byron, whose numerous sexual liaisons were the scandal of Victorian society.

The name Ruthven was another dig at Byron. Polidori took the name from Ruthven Glenarvon, the main character of *Glenarvon*, a popular novel, written by Lady Caroline Lamb, another of Byron's former lovers. Lamb, too, had intended her character to be a satirical slap at Byron.

PULP FICTION

The Vampyre was modestly successful, but not a hit. Two years after it was published, Polidori, despondent over his failures both as a physician and a writer, committed suicide. Yet, for all its failings, *The Vampyre* was indirectly responsible for launching Europe's first vampire fad.

"In Paris," David Skal writes in *Hollywood Gothic*, "the theatrical possibilities of Polidori's tale were quickly grasped." The first offering—a play entitled *Le Vampire*—generated huge interest. "The production was reportedly thrilling, controversial—and an immense success," Skal writes. "The public appetite for vampire dramas prompted a veritable stampede of imitations." Within just a few years, one Parisian theater critic would complain:

> There is not a theatre in Paris without its Vampire! At the Potre-Saint-Martin we have *Le Vampire*; at the Vaudeville *Le Vampire* again; at the Varietés *Les trois Vampires ou le clair de la lune*.

The nobleman-vampire was a common theme in these French works. By the time an Irish writer and civil servant named Bram

Stoker arrived in London, England, in 1878, vampires had become a common theme in English drama and popular literature, as well.

NUMBER-ONE FAN

Stoker had been hired to manage the Lyceum Theatre, the most famous theater in London. He was also the personal assistant of Henry Irving, owner of the Lyceum and the man considered the greatest actor on the Victorian stage. And on top of that, Stoker also liked to write novels in his spare time. He had already written three: *The Snake's Pass*, *The Watter's Mou'*, and *The Shoulder of Shasta*. None of them had sold very well or won him much acclaim.

Some time around the year 1890, Stoker decided to try his hand at writing his own vampire story.

TRUE TO LIFE

Stoker decided to make the novel seem more authentic by setting the story in the present and inserting as many authentic details as possible. But where would the story take place? Who would the main character be?

Like Polidori, Stoker made his vampire a nobleman, and gave him the name Count Wampyr . . . but the name didn't sound right. Stoker renamed him Count Ordog, from the Romanian word for Satan . . . and then Count Pokol, from the Romanian word for Hell. That didn't work either.

At some point, as he was sketching the outlines of his vampire tale, Stoker stumbled upon the name of Prince Vlad "The Impaler" Dracula, a tyrannical 15th century warlord. No one knows for certain when or where Stoker learned of the existence of Dracula, but according to one theory, he made the discovery in 1890 while vacationing in the seaside town of Whitby, North Yorkshire. Stoker, who made the village the center of action for much of his vampire story, reportedly found a book on Vlad the Impaler in the Whitby Library.

Some time later while researching his novel, Stoker met Arminus Vambrey, a professor from the University of Budapest. Vambrey had traveled extensively in Eastern Europe and Central Asia, and knew many Dracula tales, which he shared with Stoker over dinner. "After Vambrey returned to Budapest," Raymond

---

In which country were the most World War II battles fought? The USSR.

McNally writes in *In Search of Dracula*, "Bram wrote to him, requesting more details about the notorious 15th-century prince and the land he lived in. Transylvania, it seemed, would be an ideal setting for a vampire story."

Working in the circular Reading Room of the British Museum Library, Stoker read up on the superstitious beliefs of Romanian peasants, and scoured every book and map he could find that described the geography and features of Transylvania (which he'd never visited). He also placed much of the story in Whitby, and even named the ship in the story the *Dmitri*, after a Russian ship that had run aground there in 1885. He may also have drawn some "inspiration," from the crimes of Jack the Ripper, who terrorized London from August to November 1888.

FINISHED!

After spending more than seven years researching and writing *Dracula*, Stoker finally finished the book in early 1897.

By the time he'd completed his novel, Stoker had worked for Henry Irving for nearly 20 years. He idolized Irving, and is said to have modeled Dracula's character after some of Irving's finest stage performances. Stoker hoped to turn his novel into a theatrical vehicle for Irving, and even arranged for a dramatic reading of *Dracula* at the Lyceum Theatre in May 1897.

The book, Stoker must have hoped, would demonstrate that he was as talented a writer as Irving was an actor. But it was not to be. "Legend has it," Stoker's grand-nephew and biographer Daniel Farson writes, "that Sir Henry Irving entered the theater during the reading and listened for a few moments with a glint of amusement. 'What do you think of it?' someone asked him as he left for his dressing room. 'Dreadful!' came the devastating reply, projected with such resonance that it filled the theater."

CURSE OF THE VAMPIRE

Stoker had hoped that even if Irving rejected *Dracula*, the novel might be a financial success. His wife Florence expected as much, predicting that *Dracula* would earn a lot of money for the family, perhaps even enough for Stoker to quit his job at the Lyceum Theatre and either retire or take up writing full time.

"The prediction turned out to be mistaken," Leonard Wolf

President John Tyler (1841–45) had 15 children by two wives.

writes in *Dracula: The Connoisseur's Guide*. "Though it had a steady small sale, in Stoker's lifetime it did not earn enough to change the Stokers' standard of living."

Stoker continued writing an average of one novel a year—none of which were very successful—and working at the Lyceum Theatre until October 1905, when Henry Irving died suddenly and the theater closed. He spent the next few years moving from one theatrical project to another until May 1909, when he suffered a stroke that made it impossible for him to continue working. By 1911 he was virtually destitute, and had to apply to the Royal Literary Fund for assistance (he received £100). He died broke on April 20, 1912, at the age of 64. A year later, Florence Stoker was forced to sell her husband's working notes for Dracula at a public auction. They sold for under £3.

For more on Dracula, turn to page 562.

* * *

IT'S NOT A WORD, IT'S A SENTENCE
Some comments about marriage.

"Marriage is a great institution, but I'm not ready for an institution."
—Mae West

"Marriage is the best magician there is. In front of your eyes it can change an exciting, cute little dish into a boring dishwasher.
—Ryan O'Neal

"Love is blind—marriage is the eye-opener."
—Pauline Thomason

"Whatever you may look like, marry a man your own age—as your beauty fades, so will his eyesight."
—Phyllis Diller

"Only two things are necessary to keep one's wife happy. One is to let her think she is having her own way, and the other, to let her have it."
—Lyndon B. Johnson

BAD JOKES

Heard any good jokes lately? Not here, you haven't.
Our jokes are awful and we love them that way.
Heard any bad ones? Send them to us.

Q: What has four legs and one arm?
A: A rottweiler.

Q: Hear about the ship that ran aground carrying a cargo of red paint and black paint?
A: The whole crew was marooned.

Q: What is the difference between ignorance, apathy, and ambivalence?
A: I don't know and I don't care one way or the other.

Q: Did you hear about the Buddhist who refused novacaine during his root canal?
A: He wanted to transcend dental meditation.

Q: What do the letters DNA stand for?
A: National Dyslexics Association.

Q: Did you hear about the two antennas that got married?
A: The wedding was terrible, but the reception was great.

Q: What's the difference between mashed potatoes and pea soup?
A: Anyone can mash potatoes.

Q: How much do pirates pay for their earrings?
A: A buccaneer.

Q: What is bright orange and sounds like a parrot?
A: A carrot.

Q: How many narcissists does it take to change a lightbulb?
A: One. He holds the bulb while the world revolves around him.

Q: If you're American when you go into the bathroom, and American when you come out, what are you when you're in the bathroom?
A: European.

Q: What do you call a midget fortune-teller who escaped from prison?
A: A small medium at large.

You can lose up to a third of your blood and still survive.

FRIENDS IN HIGH PLACES

We don't believe that the key to success is who you know.
But connections sure can help. And, as you will see from the
following accounts, it doesn't matter whether the help is behind
the scenes or in public . . . as long as it's from the right person.

SCRABBLE

Powerful Friend: Jack Strauss, chairman of Macy's department store, one of the nation's largest and most influential retailers in the 1940s and 1950s

Background: Alfred Botts and James Brunot launched Scrabble in 1949 . . . and saw it go virtually nowhere. By 1952, they'd sold a little more than 15,000 copies of the game and were barely breaking even.

A Friendly Hand: In 1952 Strauss happened to play Scrabble with some friends during a summer holiday. He loved it—but when he returned to work and found that Macy's didn't even stock the game, he was shocked. He ordered the store to buy a quantity of the game, and run a big promotion for it—which sparked a Scrabble craze in New York City. Soon the craze spread to the rest of the country, and more than 4.5 million copies of the game were sold in less than five years. Sales have remained strong: today Scrabble is the most popular word game and the #2 board game (after Monopoly) in the country.

M&M's

Powerful Friend: William Murrie, president of the Hershey Chocolate Company, the #1 chocolate manufacturer in the United States and exclusive chocolate supplier to the U.S. Armed Forces

Background: Forrest Mars was the son of the candymaker who invented the Snickers and Milky Way bars. They had a falling out (see page 476), and the elder Mars banished his son to Europe where, in the late 1930s, Forrest founded his own candy company. He had big plans to market a candy-coated chocolate he'd "invented" after

---

In her entire lifetime, a female hummingbird will lay no more than two eggs.

seeing similar candies in Spain. The thick sugary shell kept the chocolate from melting, even on hot summer days. Mars had everything he needed to start the company—money, experience, candy-making equipment—except for access to sugar and cocoa. Both were rationed during World War II, and without these ingredients, the new company would go nowhere.

A Friendly Hand: The Hershey Company had plenty of sugar and cocoa because it manufactured chocolate for the war effort, and Murrie was happy to sell some to Mars. Why? Because he wanted to help his son Bruce Murrie, who'd recently graduated from college.

Murrie had known Mars's father, so Forrest Mars used the connection to approach him with a proposal: In exchange for 20 percent of the startup capital and a steady supply of raw materials from Hershey, he'd make Bruce the executive vice president of the new company. Mars even offered to name the candy after him. "We'll call them M&M's, for Mars and Murrie," he explained. William Murrie took the deal and even threw in technical assistance from Hershey engineers.

M&M's went on to become the most popular candy worldwide . . . but Bruce Murrie was gone by then. Once Mars had the company up and running, he forced Murrie out.

"Bruce expected to manage the company, much the way his father had managed Hershey for the past 50 years," writes Cynthia Brenner in *The Lords of Chocolate*. "But as time wore on it became painfully obvious that Forrest never wanted a real business partner; he just needed Murrie's connections."

PROFILES IN COURAGE

Powerful Friend: Arthur Krock, influential *New York Times* columnist and friend of the Kennedys

Background: Freshman Senator John F. Kennedy of Massachusetts had presidential ambitions in 1952, but his reputation was more that of a wealthy playboy than a future president. "By all outward appearances," Christopher Matthews writes in *Kennedy and Nixon*, "Kennedy seemed a genial dilettante destined for a long, no-heavy-lifting career in the Senate."

While recovering from back surgery in 1954, however, Kennedy, (with help from aide Ted Sorensen) wrote a book called

Profiles in Courage, an account of eight different American political leaders who took principled but unpopular stands on controversial issues . . . and paid heavy political prices for their integrity.

A Friendly Hand: Years earlier, Krock had served on the Pulitzer Prize committee. When he read an early, unfinished draft of *Profiles in Courage*, he suggested that it might win a Pulitzer—and Kennedy rushed to finish the book. Then Krock went to work, lobbying members of the Pulitzer board, most of whom he knew personally. "I thought *Profiles* had better be taken in hand by somebody and it might as well be me," Krock recalled years later.

Profiles in Courage did win the Pulitzer in 1957, establishing JFK as one of the Democratic Party's intellectual heavyweights and an up-and-comer for the presidency.

"In January 1957, the Gallup Poll showed that . . . 41 percent of all Democrats preferred Senator Estes Kefauver as the party's next nominee and 33 percent favored Jack," Peter Collier writes in *The Kennedys*. "In March, after *Profiles in Courage* had been awarded the Pulitzer Prize, the order was reversed: 45 percent for Jack, and 33 percent for Kefauver."

THE HUNT FOR RED OCTOBER

Powerful Friend: President Ronald Reagan

Background: In 1984, a Maryland insurance broker named Tom Clancy wrote *The Hunt for Red October*, a naval thriller about a Soviet submarine captain who tries to defect to the United States. Clancy, a military buff, had never published a book before—his only "author" credits were for a three-page article on the MX missile and a single Letter to the Editor. And the *Naval Institute Press* had never published a work of fiction. But they liked Clancy's manuscript, so they bought it and printed 14,000 copies.

A Friendly Hand: President Ronald Reagan read *The Hunt for Red October* after it was recommended to him by a friend . . . and that's when a reporter just happened to ask what he was reading. Reagan praised the book as "the perfect yarn" and "non-put-downable." That did the trick. *The Hunt for Red October*, which until then had received little attention and was selling slowly, shot up the bestseller lists. Ultimately, it sold more than 5.4 million copies, setting Tom Clancy on a course to become one of the best-selling authors of the 20th century.

WINE BY THE FOOT

*We can't help you pick out a good bottle of wine . . . but here
are a few vintage facts you can use to fool your friends into
thinking you're an oenophile (pronounced "ee-nuh-file"
—that's your first fact; it means "wine connoisseur").*

STEP BY STEP

What's the first thing that comes to mind when you think of
Italian wine? Grape stomping, right? You've seen it in old
paintings, *Fantasia,* and that classic "*I Love Lucy*" episode where
Lucy turns purple after a brawl in an Italian treading vat.

But do winemakers really crush grapes with their feet? Well,
they don't anymore. And it's probably just as well, because stomping grapes is harder than you'd think.

For example, keeping your footing is difficult because the grape
mass gets really slippery. Ancient Egyptians invented a grid of
overhead bars for treaders to hold onto because they kept falling in
and drowning. Wine treaders making port in Portugal kept from
falling in by linking their arms around their neighbors' waists in a
tightly linked chain that looked like a chorus line. And drowning
isn't the only potential danger: over long days and nights of treading, the grapes would start to ferment, releasing large quantities of
carbon dioxide that sometimes asphyxiated treaders.

THAT WINE HAS LEGS

Still, despite the hazards, stomping the grape harvest sounds like
fun. Songs were sung to keep a regular pace. Sometimes a little
band played. But there was nothing romantic about it—it was hard
work—tiring and monotonous. And when the grapes were finally
completely crushed, treaders ended up stepping on pips and stalks
at the bottom of the vat—described in 1877 as "something like the
pilgrimages of old when the devout trudged wearily along, with
hard peas packed between their feet and the soles of their shoes."

VIN DE SWEAT

A visiting American winegrower described this scene from Burgundy,
in the late 1800s:

Ten men, stripped of all their clothes, step into the vessel, and begin to tread down the floating mass, working it also with their hands. This operation is repeated several times if the wine does not ferment rapidly enough. The reason . . . is that the bodily heat of the men aids the wine in its fermentation.

The American later declined his host's offer of a glass of red wine, choosing an untreaded white instead. Fortunately, foot treading is now just a historical footnote, as it were. Today, almost all grapes are pressed by machines.

Want another taste of wine? See page 650.

* * *

WINE TRIVIA: A DROP OF THIS, A DROP OF THAT

- King Louis XVI of France believed that a refusal to drink wine was a sign of fanaticism. In his last letter before he lost his head in the French Revolution, he blamed the political savagery of the revolutionaries on the fact that their leader, Robespierre, drank only water, not wine.

- Louis Pasteur first developed pasteurization in the 1850s as a way to prevent the spoiling of wine. Afterward, he realized it could also be used on other substances, such as milk.

- The first large-scale American winegrowing region was not on either coast, but in Cincinnati, Ohio. In fact, in the 1850s, it was known as the "Rhine of America." In 1870, America's largest winery was located on Middle Bass Island, just off the grape-growing town of Sandusky, Ohio.

- Many people think that California wine is a relatively recent phenomenon. However, both the Napa and Sonoma wine industries were started by Franciscan monks, who in 1824 started growing grapes and making wine at the Solano Mission in Sonoma. The winemaking they began continues to the present, interrupted only by Prohibition early in the last century.

How much would you weigh at the exact center of the Earth? Nothing.

WHY DIDN'T WE THINK OF THAT?

It's the ultimate American fantasy—invent a hot product and become a zillionaire overnight. That's why people work long, hard hours on their pet projects. Have you ever heard of any of these? They're available.

Entrepreneur: Bruce Lambert, Swedish inventor
Brilliant Idea: The See-through Refrigerator
Description: The door is a one-way mirror—so when a light is switched on inside the fridge, you can see what's inside without opening the door. You save energy . . . and pounds, Lambert figures, "The mirror encourages dieting, because people can see their reflections as they approach the door."

Entrepreneur: John D. Haley, of Boise, Idaho

Brilliant Idea: Rape-L

Description: Haley manufactures skunk scent vials that wearers can clip to their undergarments to fend off sexual assaults. When attacked, the wearer simply pinches the vial and douses themselves with the scent, which is harvested from real skunks at a skunk ranch in upstate New York. The kit also contains a second vial filled with ordinary tap water—"For practice," Haley explains. Suggested retail price: $19.95.

Entrepreneurs: John Lisanti and Cary Schuman, founders of Peace Missile, Inc.

Brilliant Idea: The Peace Missile II Putter And Driver

Description: The golf clubs are manufactured out of material recycled from American A-3 Polaris and Soviet SS-23 nuclear missiles. Lisanti says he got the idea while golfing with Schuman. "I mentioned how Cary hits the ball like a rocket," Lisanti says, "and then we thought, 'wouldn't it be great if we could melt down discarded Russian nuclear missiles and make some fabulous golf clubs out of them?'" Suggested Retail Price: $79 for the putter, $199 for the driver.

Each year insects eat a third of the Earth's entire food crop.

Entrepreneur: Lino Missio, a 26-year-old Italian physics student

Brilliant Idea: Beethoven Condoms

Description: The condom will play a bit of Beethoven if it breaks during use. According to news reports, "the condom is coated with a substance that changes electrical conductivity upon rupture, setting off a microchip that produces sound." Missio has also proposed an alternative to music: a verbal warning to the participants to stop what they're doing immediately.

Entrepreneur: The Sigma Aldrich chemical company, which manufactures products for search-and-rescue-dog training

Brilliant Idea: Pseudo Scents

Description: Scents that mimic the odor given off by cadavers, to assist in the training of search-and-rescue-dogs. The product line includes Pseudo Corpse I (deceased less than 30 days); Pseudo Corpse II (more than 30 days); Drowned Victim Scent; and Distressed Body Scent Trauma and Fear (the victim is injured but not deceased). According to one report, trainers like the pseudo scents "because they're easier to tote around than the blood, bones, or bits of corpse typically used in training. That's less muss, less fuss, and no threat of hepatitis infection." No smell, either: only canines can detect them.

Entrepreneurs: Scientists at five German zoological institutes

Brilliant Idea: Raise money for scientific research by "selling sponsors the right to name newly-discovered plant and animal life"

Description: The scientists got the idea when Manfred Parth, a researcher, tennis fan, and admirer of Boris Becker, named a new species of snail bufonaria borisbeckeri after the tennis great. (No word on whether Becker knows about his snails.) Suggested Retail Price: $5,000 "minimum."

And don't forget . . . Pedal and Play, "a slot machine mounted on an exercise bicycle," available in casinos in Atlantic City and Las Vegas, and on Carnival cruise ships.

British explorer Robert Swan's claim to fame: first person to walk to the North and South poles.

UNDERWEAR IN THE NEWS

Here's a question you've probably never considered: When is underwear newsworthy? We've got the answer because we've been studying the news to find out. The answer is, when it's . . .

ROYAL UNDERWEAR

In February 2000 Captain Nick Carrell, once a member of the queen of England's elite bodyguard unit, "admitted trying to steal Queen Elizabeth's underwear and being caught red-handed by the monarch."

The incident occurred in 1992 during a fire at Windsor Palace, when Carrell was helping remove belongings from the queen's private apartments (which were threatened by the fire). "I was planning to steal a pair of the queen's knickers," Carrell admitted to London's *Sunday People* newspaper. "I was helping to clear out her private apartment when I pulled open a chest of drawers. I was amazed to see it was filled with the queen's underwear and I put out my hand to take a pair. Suddenly, I realized she was standing right behind me, watching my every move. I don't know what she thought, but she didn't say a word. It was all very embarrassing."

LIFE-SAVING UNDERWEAR

"In 1994, fisherman Renato Arganza spent several days at sea clinging to a buoy after his boat capsized off the Philippines. Once rescued, he remarked that he had survived by eating his underpants."

DEADLY UNDERWEAR

In 1999, two women sheltering under a tree in London's Hyde Park during a thunderstorm were killed when lightning struck the tree. According to medical examiners, the two women died because the metal underwire in their bras acted as an electrical conductor. "This is only the second time in my experience of 50,000 deaths where lightning has struck the metal in a bra causing death," Westminster coroner Paul Knapman told the media. "I do not wish to overemphasize any significance." (*In These Times*)

What happened to Cleopatra's mummy? It was probably thrown out by accident.

CELEBRITY UNDERWEAR

- "At the 1998 auction of Kennedy memorabilia, Richard Wilson paid $3,450 for a pair of JFK's long johns. Mr. Wilson plans to exhibit the underwear next to a slip and a pair of panties formerly owned by Marilyn Monroe." (*Presidential Indiscretions*)

- In the early 1990s, an upset young man paid a visit to Father Fambrini, pastor at Hollywood's Blessed Sacrament Church. The man confessed that he'd raided Frederick's of Hollywood's lingerie museum and stolen some celebrity undies. Now, consumed with guilt, he wanted to return them, but didn't have the courage . . . so he asked Father Fambrini to do it. Father Fambrini agreed and returned the two stolen items: a bra belonging to actress Katey Sagal, and "the pantaloons of the late actress Ava Gardner." ("The Edge," *Oregonian*)

LIFESTYLE-ENHANCING UNDERWEAR

- In 1998, Monash University's (Australia) Institute of Reproduction and Development announced the invention of air conditioned mens' briefs, which the Institute says will prevent heat buildup in the nether regions that is believed to inhibit fertility. Why not just ask infertile males to switch from snug-fitting briefs to looser, cooler boxer shorts? "Because," says the Institute's David de Kretser, "some men don't like the freedom."

- In 1998, Florida entrepreneur Victoria Morton announced that she'd invented a bra that she claims can increase a woman's breast size by repositioning body fat, and she doesn't mean just body fat on the chest. "If a woman has extra tissue anywhere above her waist," Morton explained in a press release, "even on her back, she can use this bra to create bigger, firmer breasts." (Universal Press Syndicate)

ARTISTICALLY INSPIRED UNDERWEAR

American artist Laurie Long wasn't just offended when she learned that some vending machines in Japan dispense panties worn by schoolgirls, she was also inspired: she stocked a vending machine with her own used panties, "which have labels describing what she did while she wore them." (*Stuff* magazine)

WORD ORIGINS

Here are some more interesting word origins.

FEISTY
Meaning: Spunky, quarrelsome
Origin: "A 'fart' word. First appeared in the 13th century meaning 'a breaking of wind' or 'to break wind.'" (From *Take My Words*, by Howard Richler)

PUNDIT
Meaning: A critic/commentator on current events or politics
Origin: "Comes from the Hindu word pandit, meaning 'learned man.'" (From *Word Mysteries and Histories*, by the Editors of the *American Heritage Dictionary*)

SINCERE
Meaning: True to your word, not lying
Origin: "Came from two Latin words sine, 'without,' and cera, 'wax.' Legend has it that Roman artisans used wax for filling cracks or holes in furniture, so sine cera would mean 'without flaw': pure, clean." (From *Thereby Hangs a Tale*, by Charles Earle Funk)

NIGHTMARE
Meaning: A very bad dream
Origin: "Mare is an Old English term for a demon, known as incubus (male) or succubus (female), that descended on a sleeper, paralyzing and suffocating them . . . and sometimes having sexual relations with them. Over the centuries the meaning—'night demon'—has become generalized to any frightening dream." (From *Wilton's Etymology*, by Dave Wilton)

KHAKI
Meaning: A light shade of brown; cloth or pants of that color
Origin: "The name comes from the Urdu word for dust or dust-colored . . . which came from the Persian khak, for dust. First introduced into English in the mid-19th century by British troops serving in India." (From *Fighting Words*, by Christine Ammer)

One in twelve men is color-blind . . . but only one woman in a hundred is.

MODERN MYTHOLOGY

These mythological characters may be as famous in our culture as Hercules or Pegasus were in ancient Greece. Here's where they came from.

NIPPER (THE RCA DOG). Nipper, a fox terrier, was originally owned by the brother of English painter Francis Barroud; when the brother died, Francis inherited the dog. According to legend, when a recording of the brother's voice was played at his funeral, the dog recognized his master's voice and looked into the horn of the phonograph. "Barroud depicted this incident in a painting that showed his brother's coffin, with the dog sitting on top listening to the Victrola. The image (minus the coffin, of course) became the symbol of RCA Victor."

PAUL BUNYAN. Paul Bunyan is commonly thought to be a character from traditional folklore, but he is actually what is known as "fakelore"—"an ersatz creation developed to meet the American need for instant homegrown folk heroes." Paul Bunyan was actually created in 1920 by an advertising agent named W. B. Laughead, to serve as a fictional spokesperson for the Red River Lumber company. "As such," Richard Shenkman writes in Legends, Lies and Cherished Myths of American History, "Paul is about as authentic a folk hero as Mr. Clean or the Jolly Green Giant—that is to say, not very authentic at all."

SPUDS MACKENZIE. "Some guy in our Chicago agency drew a rough sketch of a dog called the Party Animal, for a Bud Light poster," Anheuser-Busch's marketing director told *Sports Illustrated.* "So we had to find a real dog that looked like this drawing." They picked Honey Tree Evil Eye, a female English bull terrier. The poster was only supposed to be distributed to college students, but "orders for the poster of this strange-looking dog were monumental. We still can't explain it. It's like everything else in advertising. You just hope you get it right, but you never know for sure." After Spuds made his (her) TV debut during the 1987 Super Bowl, Bud Light sales shot up 20 percent. But Spuds was retired in controversy a few years later when Anheuser-Busch was accused of using him (her) to encourage underage drinking.

In the Congo, professional corpse painters charge admission to see their work.

THE TACO BELL CHIHUAHUA The most famous fast-food character of the 1990s was invented by chance, when two advertising executives named Chuck Bennett and Clay Williams were eating lunch at the Tortilla Grill in Venice, California. "We saw a little Chihuahua run by that appeared to be on a mission," Bennett says. "We both looked at each other and said, 'That would be funny.'"

THE CALIFORNIA RAISINS In 1986 California raisin growers were facing a double whammy: declining raisin sales and a bumper raisin harvest coming—which would depress prices. So the California Raisin Board asked their ad agency, Foote, Cone & Belding, to come up with a campaign to help increase sales. The agency turned the assignment over to two young copywriters, Seth Werner and Dexter Fedor . . . who couldn't think of anything. One evening they confessed their worries to some friends. "We'll probably do something stupid like have raisins sing 'Oh, I Heard it Through the Grapevine,'" Werner told the friends. That got a laugh . . . so the next morning Werner and Fedor began thinking about really doing the commercial that way—never realizing what a huge hit the characters would become. "No one can really explain the idea," Werner says. "In fact, the more people try to put their finger on it, the stupider it sounds."

Our Little Secret: In most press reports, Claymation pioneer Will Vinton, who filmed the ads, is credited with creating the raisin characters. But the truth is—and you'll never read this anywhere but here—by the time Vinton was hired, the raisins were already designed. The artist who designed them, Michael Brunsfeld, has also created every *Bathroom Reader* cover.

Fedor and Werner didn't have any idea what the raisins should look like, and Brunsfeld, a director at Colossal Pictures, submitted a design for an animated test commercial. "Raisins were difficult to make into appealing characters," Brunsfeld recalls. "It was like putting eyes on a wrinkled blob." The solution: Drawing them in the "rubber hose" style of the '30s and giving them oversized sneakers for balance. "That made them feel loose and funky." By the time the test ad was done, everything was in place. Vinton could just copy it. Everyone else got rich from the ads—but all Brunsfeld got were the original drawings—which are mounted on his wall today.

A horse will win a sprint against a camel, but a camel will win a marathon against a horse.

WHY ASK WHY?

Sometimes the answer is irrelevant—it's the question that counts. These cosmic queries have been sent in by BRI readers.

Why isn't there mouse-flavored cat food?

Shouldn't there be a shorter word for *monosyllabic*?

Why is *dyslexic* so hard to spell?

Why are they called *stands* when they're made for sitting?

Why are there flotation devices under plane seats instead of parachutes?

If it's illegal to drink and drive, why do bars have parking lots?

Do you need a silencer if you are going to shoot a mime?

How does the guy who drives the snowplow get to work in the mornings?

If nothing sticks to Teflon, how do they make Teflon stick to the pan?

Why do they call it a *building*? Why isn't it a *built*?

Why is *verb* a noun?

Are there seeing-eye humans for blind dogs?

What does Geronimo say when he jumps out of a plane?

Do pediatricians play miniature golf on Wednesdays?

How can a house burn up while it burns down?

Why is the third hand on the watch called the *second hand*?

Is it good if a vacuum really sucks?

Why do we sing "Take me out to the ball game" when we're already there?

Why is it called *after dark* when it really is *after light*?

Why do we press harder on the buttons of a remote control when we know the batteries are dead?

Before drawing boards, what did they go back to?

Teddy Roosevelt's opinion of Winston Churchill: A "shady self-promoter."

HONK IF YOU LOVE PEACE AND QUIET

More real-life bumper stickers.
Have you seen the one that says . . .

When everything's coming your way, you're in the wrong lane and driving against traffic.

A DAY WITHOUT SUNSHINE IS LIKE NIGHT.

You never really learn to swear until you learn to drive.

If you think nobody cares, try missing a couple of payments.

Originality is the art of concealing your sources.

You have the right to remain silent.

Shin—Device for finding furniture in the dark

WHICH IS THE NON-SMOKING LIFEBOAT?

COLE'S LAW:
Thinly sliced cabbage.

Experience is something you don't get until just after you need it.

I CAN RESIST ANYTHING BUT TEMPTATION

No sense being pessimistic. It wouldn't work anyway.

I intend to live forever.
So far, so good.

You're just jealous because the voices only talk to me.

DYSLEXICS OF THE WORLD, UNTIE.

Beauty is in the eye of the beer holder.

Be nice to your kids. They'll choose your nursing home.

Clones are people two.

Does the name Pavlov ring a bell?

EVER STOP TO THINK, AND FORGET TO START AGAIN?

If you can read this, I can slam on my brakes and sue you.

A typical raindrop falls at about seven miles per hour.

THE BIRTH OF TARZAN, PART I

Tarzan was the first modern superhero—the first pop icon whose fame spread to every corner of the globe. That makes him the forefather of Superman, Batman, Star Wars, Madonna, and Michael Jordan. "Before Tarzan," writes one critic, "nobody understood just how big, how ubiquitous, how marketable a star could be." Here is the inside story of how—and why—Tarzan came to be.

OCCUPATIONAL HAZARD

In 1911, a paunchy, balding, 35-year-old named Edgar Rice Burroughs took a job selling pencil sharpeners. He wasn't very good at it; for that matter, he didn't seem to be very good at anything. As a young man he was denied admittance to West Point, and from there he'd gone on to fail at a number of professions, including cowpunching, goldmining, selling lightbulbs, running a newstand, advertising, and peddling quack medicine door-to-door.

"Two decades later," John Taliaferro writes in *Tarzan Forever*, "when Burroughs drew up an outline for his autobiography, he summarized the period between 1905 and 1911 with the simple, dreary statement: 'I am a flop.' "

KILLING TIME

A few years earlier, while selling a "remedy" for alcoholism door-to-door, Burroughs had been responsible for reading magazines to make sure the company's ads appeared as promised and were error-free. "After our advertisements were checked," he recalled later, "I sometimes took the magazines home to read"—a habit he kept up even after he switched jobs and began selling pencil sharpeners.

"There were several all-fiction publications among them," Burroughs remembered, "and although I had never written a story, I knew absolutely that I could write stories just as entertaining, and probably more so, than any I read in those magazines. If people were paid for writing such rot as I read, I could write stories just as rotten."

The standard U.S. drinking straw is 7 3/4" long.

BEDTIME STORIES

Coming up with story ideas was no problem; the troubled Burroughs had become an insomniac. To distract himself as he lay in bed each night, he had developed the habit of telling himself adventure stories featuring heroes whose lives were nothing like his own. "While drifting through the unsatisfactory real world," Gabe Essoe writes, "Burroughs would console himself with a fantasy world in which he was handsome, virile, and capable of success, the idol of whole civilizations, beyond the limits of credulity."

"Most of the stories I wrote," he later admitted, "were stories I told myself just before I went to sleep."

OUT OF THIS WORLD

Burroughs started work on his first story in July 1911, and by mid-August he'd completed a 43,000-word manuscript he called *A Princess of Mars*, about a Civil War veteran who falls into a trance in Arizona, wakes up on Mars, fights a war against the Martians, and then marries a Martian princess.

Burroughs was actually latching onto a popular topic of the early 1900s. In 1879, Italian astronomer Giovanni Schiaparelli detected what he thought were canali ("canals") on the Martian surface, and in 1906 another astronomer, Percival Lowell, wrote a book that proposed that the canals were irrigation ditches built by an advanced race of Martians. People were excited by the prospect of life on the Red Planet . . . which is probably why Burroughs decided to write about it. He couldn't afford typing paper—he had a wife and two babies to support and had just lost his job selling pencil sharpeners—so he wrote on the backs of old letterhead that he picked up at his brother's stationery company.

PAYDAY

Burroughs finished the story, and sent the manuscript to Argosy magazine, and with a few changes, "A Princess of Mars" was accepted for serial publication in Argosy's sister publication, the *All-Story*. Price: $400. "I shall never make a million dollars," Burroughs wrote in his autobiography, "but if I do, it cannot possibly give me the thrill that that four-hundred dollar check gave me."

Thomas Newell Metcalf, managing editor of the *All-Story*,

If you have keraunothnetophobia, you're afraid of satellites falling to Earth.

invited Burroughs to submit another story, "a serial of the regular romantic type, something Like, say, *Ivanhoe*." Three weeks later, Burroughs turned in a short story called "The Outlaw of Torn," a 13th-century tale about a fictitious son of England's King Henry III. But Metcalf didn't like it, so it was shelved.

GOING APE

In March 1912, Burroughs wrote back to Metcalf that he was already at work on his next tale:

> The story I am now on is of the scion of a noble English house—of the present time—who was born in tropical Africa where his parents died when he was about a year old. The infant was found and adopted by a huge she-ape, and was brought up among a band of fierce anthropods.
>
> The mental development of this ape-man in spite of every handicap, of how he learned to read English without knowledge of the spoken language, of the way in which his inherent reasoning faculties lifted him above his savage jungle friends and enemies, of his meeting with a white girl, how he came at last to civilization and to his own makes most fascinating writing and I think will prove interesting reading . . . The boy-child is called Tarzan, which is ape talk for "white skin."

Metcalf was impressed: "I think your idea for the new serial is cracker-jack and I shall be very anxious to have a look at it. You certainly have the most remarkable imagination of anybody whom I have run up against for some time."

SIGN OF THE TIMES

Again, Burroughs's story was built around popular topics of the day: Charles Darwin's theory of evolution and the mysterious continent of Africa, which had only recently begun giving up its secrets to Western explorers.

It also reflected his interest in another popular theory of the day: eugenics. In 1869, 10 years after Darwin published *On the Origin of Species*, his cousin, Francis Galton, wrote *Hereditary Genius*. In it, he argued that some human bloodlines were, by the law of natural selection, more advanced than others. According to Galton, the way a person could tell how advanced their bloodline was was to count the number of distinguished ancestors they had in their family tree: If you were descended from kings, Pilgrims, or the Founding Fathers, you were a member of a very advanced

The average American family spends more than $2,000 a year dining out.

bloodline. If you were descended from criminals or peasants, you weren't very evolved at all.

This book made Galton the father of "eugenics," the theory that "selective breeding" could be used to improve the bloodlines of the human race. By 1912, the eugenics movement was so strong that universities all over the country offered courses in it; one organization called the American Breeders Society had even begun compiling a list of "America's Most Effective Blood Lines," a Who's Who of natural selection.

Perhaps in response to his own personal failings, Burroughs liked to brag that he came from exceedingly "good stock"—he shared a common Pilgrim ancestor with American Red Cross founder Clara Barton, Morse code inventor Samuel Morse, and (future) president Calvin Coolidge. The greatest gift his mother gave him, he later wrote, was "the red blood of the Puritan and the Pioneer, bequeathed . . . uncontaminated."

It was this fascination with bloodlines and natural selection that drove the new story. Could good breeding triumph over adversity?

GOING TO PRESS

In May, Burroughs finished work on "Tarzan of the Apes" and sent it to Metcalf. "I did not think it was a good story," Burroughs recalled, "and I doubted it would sell." As he'd done so many times before, Burroughs was also beginning to doubt whether he really wanted to be a writer. "I was sort of ashamed of it as an occupation for a big, strong, healthy man," he admitted later.

Metcalf disagreed with Burroughs's appraisal of the story: "Tarzan" was good—very good, he wrote to Burroughs later that summer:

> If you will stop and realize how many thousands and thousands of stories an editor has to read, day in, day out, you will be impressed when we tell you that we read this yarn at one sitting and had the time of our young lives. It is the most exciting story we have seen in a blue moon, and about as original as they make 'em.

Neither Burroughs nor Metcalf had any idea just how good "Tarzan of the Apes" was until October, when the "Tarzan" issue hit the newsstands. Within just a few days, "Tarzan" fan letters began pouring into the *All-Story* offices praising the story . . . and begging for more.

Aaaiieeeahhh! Grab a vine and swing to page 586 for Part II.

The word tragedy comes from *tragos* and *ode*, Greek words for "goat" and "song."

MILITARY SURPLUS: THE STORY OF CARROT CAKE

Our good friend Jeff Cheek has been writing about food ever since he left the CIA (the spy agency, not the food institute—no kidding!). He wrote this column for a local newspaper; we decided it was worth sharing with all our BRI members.

THE FRUIT MAN

George C. Page was a Nebraska farm boy who arrived in Los Angeles in the mid-1920s with a dream . . . and $2.30 in his pocket. He found a job as a busboy/dishwasher and worked double shifts until he'd saved $1,000. Then he rented a vacant store and founded Mission-Pak, shipping exotic Southern California fruits as holiday gifts. It was an overnight success. Ten years later, he was a millionaire, with eight packing plants and over a thousand workers.

In 1941, after the Japanese bombed Pearl Harbor, Page volunteered for active duty. He discovered, however, that the government had classified him as an "essential industrialist" and wouldn't let him serve in the military. Instead, they arranged for him to go to the University of California at Berkeley to learn how to dehydrate vegetables. With German submarines sinking our ships, every shipload had to count. Dehydration, and rehydration after delivery, seemed like the answer.

WAR SURPLUS

When the atomic bomb brought the Pacific war to an end, Page's government contracts were canceled. He was left with thousands of five-gallon cans of dehydrated carrots . . . and no place to sell them.

Page went back to his old boss at the restaurant where he'd started out. They tried everything. Baked carrots. Stewed carrots. Fried carrots. No luck; customers sent these tasteless dishes back. Finally, they dumped a few cups of shredded dried carrots into a cake mix. It was an instant hit. Other restaurants and bakeries wanted to add carrot cake to their menus. Page sold them five-gallon cans of dehydrated carrots, along with a printed recipe for carrot cake. Within a few months he'd gotten rid of his surplus carrots, and carrot cake was being served as dessert all over America.

President John Adams was so short and fat that his nickname was "His Rotundity."

MYTH-CONCEPTIONS

Here are more examples of things that many people believe . . . but according to our sources, just aren't true.

Myth: Stepping on a rusty nail will give you tetanus.
Fact: The bacteria that causes tetanus, or "lockjaw," can enter the body through any cut, including a puncture from a nail. It has nothing to do with rust.

Myth: Crickets chirp by rubbing their legs together.
Fact: They rub their wings.

Myth: In the Old West, pioneers circled their wagons to protect against Indian raids.
Fact: When they did circle the wagons, it was to keep livestock in.

Myth: Mosquitoes bite.
Fact: They can't bite—they have no teeth. They punch a needle-like proboscis into the skin of their victim.

Myth: Lightning comes out of the sky and strikes the ground.
Fact: Scientists now believe that the lightning bolt we see is actually moving from the ground up to the sky.

Myth: Some people are double-jointed.
Fact: No one is truly double-jointed. Some people are just more flexible than others.

Myth: You can eat oysters only in months that have an "r" in their name.
Fact: Before refrigeration, oysters (and other foods) were more likely to spoil in May, June, July, and August. It is no longer the case.

Myth: The lion is the king of the jungle.
Fact: The lion doesn't live in the jungle; it lives on the plains, where it can run and chase its prey.

Some beaver dams are more than 1,000 years old.

Myth: A strong cup of coffee will help a drunk person get sober.
Fact: It's the alcohol in a person's bloodstream that makes him drunk, and no amount of coffee, no matter how strong, will change that.

Myth: A sudden fright can turn a person's hair white overnight.
Fact: The age at which your hair turns white is determined by heredity. Seeing a ghost will have no effect on your hair color.

Myth: On a clear night, you can see millions of stars.
Fact: The most stars you could *possibly* see without a telescope is about 4,000.

Myth: Dogs sweat through their panting tongues.
Fact: Panting may help them cool off, but they sweat through their feet.

Myth: The sky is blue.
Fact: The sky is black. Dust particles and droplets of moisture in the air reflect the sun's light and make it appear blue.

Myth: A penny is made of copper.
Fact: Pennies minted after 1982 are 97.5 percent zinc and 2.5 percent copper.

Myth: Constant cracking of your knuckles will make them get bigger.
Fact: Go ahead and crack them—it's harmless.

Myth: In the French tale written by Charles Perrault in 1697, Cinderella's slippers were made of glass.
Fact: They were made of fur. The goof comes from a poor translation; someone interpreted *vair*, "fox fur" as *verre*, "glass."

Myth: St. Bernards wear kegs of brandy around their necks when they go out to rescue stranded travelers.
Fact: They never have. The popular idea comes from a series of paintings by Sir Edwin Landseer in the 1800s that depicted the dogs wearing brandy casks.

The Gold Reserve Act of 1934 made it illegal for private citizens to own gold bullion.

THE GOLDEN RULE

Every once in a while we throw in something serious—you can take it, can't you? Did you know that there's a version of the Golden Rule in most (maybe all) major religions? Here are eight translations of religious texts . . . and one secular commentary.

CHRISTIANITY

"Therefore all things whatsoever ye would that men should do to you, do ye even so to them, for this is the law of the prophets."

—*Matthew 7:12*

JUDAISM

"What is harmful to you, do not to your fellow men. That is the entire Law; all the rest is commentary."

—*Talmud, Shabbat, 312*

HINDUISM

"This is the turn of duty; do naught unto others which could cause you pain if done to you."

—*Mahabharata, 5, 1517*

CONFUCIANISM

"Surely it is the maxim of loving-kindness: Do not unto others that you would not have them do unto you."

—*Analects, 15, 23*

TAOISM

"Regard your neighbor's gain as your own gain and your neighbor's loss as your own loss."

—*T'ai Shang Kan Ying P'ien*

BUDDHISM

"Hurt not others in ways you yourself would find hurtful."

—*Udana-Varga 5, 18*

ZOROASTRIANISM

"That nature alone is good which refrains from doing unto another whatsoever is not good for itself."

—*Dadistan-i-dinik, 94, 5*

ISLAM

"No one of you is a believer until he desires for his brother that which he desires for himself."

—*Sunnah*

SECULAR VIEW

"Do not do unto others as you would that they should do unto you. Their tastes may not be the same."

—*George Bernard Shaw*

The "WD" in WD-40 stands for "Water Displacer."

ACCORDING TO THE LATEST RESEARCH...

More "scientifically proven" info about you and your world.
(See page 449 for other important scientific studies.)

AMERICANS ARE REALLY GULLIBLE
Researchers: DiMassimo Brand Advertising
Who They Studied: Friends and neighbors of
200 volunteer liars

What They Learned: "Americans will believe anything, as long as
it comes from a friend or a neighbor." The ad company recruited
200 people to tell fibs to their friends, then polled the friends a
week later. Sample results: "Twenty-seven percent repeated the lie
that 'Just Do It!' was the slogan of Ex-Lax instead of Nike; 22 percent believed that milk was 'the other white meat,' rather than
pork; 23 percent thought Amazon.com was a fashion Web site for
large women; 29 percent agreed that Kenneth Starr was the president of Starbucks."

POETS REALLY ARE CRAZY
Researcher: Professor Arnold Ludwig, M.D., of the University of
Kentucky

Who He Studied: 1,000 "original thinkers" of the 20th century

What He Learned: "Crazy people tend to choose creative jobs,"
and the most consistently off-kilter are poets. To be more precise:
"Ludwig's study, 'Method and Madness in the Arts and Sciences,'
reports that nearly 9 out of 10 poets surveyed have had diagnosable
mental disorders." On the other end of the spectrum, only about
28 percent of physicists and biologists have mental disorders—the
lowest percentage tested. The crazy runners-up: fiction writers are
second, at 77 percent; theater people are at 74 percent; visual arts,
73 percent; musicians, 68 percent.

YOUR PETS KNOW WHEN YOU'RE COMING HOME
Researcher: Rupert Sheldrake, a British biologist
Who He Studied: Dogs in 1,500 different homes around the world

In 1970, an Englishman named A. P. Herbert cashed a check written on the side of a cow.

What He Learned: "Animals appear to sense when their owners are returning home and actually prepare for the event." He observed that almost half the dogs he studied actually "began preparing for their owner's return an hour before they got home . . . Besides becoming visibly agitated, the animals started going to the window to watch for their owner." He noticed cats and birds doing it, too.

ONIONS ARE GOOD FOR YOUR BONES
Researchers: Swiss scientists

Who They Studied: Female rats

What They Learned: "An onion a day keeps bone fractures away." Newsweek reported in its October 11, 1999 edition: "To study the effects of herbs and vegetables on osteoporosis, [the scientists] removed the ovaries from female rats. That made the rats' hormone fluctuations resemble those of post-menopausal women, who are at most risk for bone loss. After four weeks, the rats that were fed a gram of dried onion a day had significantly thicker and stronger bones. An onion, as well as other typical salad ingredients, reduced bone loss by 20 percent—slightly more than the popular anti-osteoporosis drug called calcitonin."

MARRIAGE CAN BE DEPRESSING
Researchers: Professor of psychology Daniel K. O'Leary and colleagues at the State University of New York at Stony Brook

Who They Studied: Women with significant marital problems who had no history of depression in their families

What They Learned: If you're depressed, you might need to do something about your marriage rather than simply take anti-depressants. "For decades, people—particularly women—have been treated with antidepressants by well-meaning practitioners," explains O'Leary. "They get on medication, and nobody does a thing about the relationship." In the study, O'Leary and his crew interviewed women who were in the throes of marital difficulty. "We were able to pretty clearly conclude that if they were depressed, the depression was caused by the marital problems," he says. "They should seek help not only for the depression, but for the relationship problem."

World's fastest flying insect: The deer botfly, capable of flying 36 miles per hour.

THE HISTORY OF
THE IQ TEST, PART II

As you read in Part I (page 406), the IQ test had its origins
in Victorian England and France. But it came into
its own when the Americans got their hands on it.
Here's another piece of the controversial story.

SO THAT'S WHAT IT MEANS

In 1916 a Stanford University psychologist named Lewis Terman modified the Binet-Simon test to create a new test. He called it the Stanford-Binet test . . . and if you've ever taken an IQ test, you may have experienced it firsthand. The original 1916 test and its descendants are still among the most widely-used intelligence tests in use today.

Drawing from a concept first suggested by German psychologist, William Stern, Terman developed a new formula for comparing a child's intelligence to that of other children the same age. He did it by dividing the test taker's "mental age," as determined by the test, by the test taker's chronological age. Then he multiplied the result by 100 to get a whole number:

$$(\text{Mental Age} \div \text{Chronological Age}) \times 100$$

Terman called this number the "intelligence quotient," or IQ for short. According to this formula, a 10-year-old child with a mental age of 12 would have an IQ of $(12/10) \times 100 = 120$. Likewise, a ten-year-old child with a mental age of eight would have an IQ of 80, and any child with the same mental and chronological age— indicating normal intelligence—would have an IQ of 100.

WISE GUY

Though Terman based his test on Alfred Binet's, he had an entirely different purpose in mind. Binet's test was designed to identify children who needed extra help in learning, so that they could be placed into special "mental orthopedics" courses that would bring them up to speed with kids whose scores were higher.

Terman had a different theory: He believed very strongly in the

---

The word "million" was invented sometime around the year 1300 A.D.

concept of "innate intelligence," the idea that a person's intelligence was as unchangeable as the color of their eyes. Thus, he concluded, there was no point providing assistance to slow learners, because it wouldn't do any good. Since intelligence was immutable, educating the unintelligent was a waste of time.

A BREED APART

Like Francis Galton before him, Terman was an enthusiastic supporter of the eugenics movement. He believed that "selective breeding" of intelligent people with one another, combined with discouraging—or even forbidding—unintelligent people from reproducing at all, would increase the general intelligence of the human race.

Terman was also convinced that the Stanford-Binet test was an important breakthrough in psychological research. Unlike Binet, who saw his test as a rough measure of a child's level of knowledge relative to his peers, Terman believed that he had invented a diagnostic tool that could accurately and precisely measure the intellectual capacity of the human brain. He was determined to put the test to work for the benefit of mankind. As he wrote when the first Stanford-Binet test was published in 1916:

> There is no investigator who denies the fearful role played by mental deficiency in the production of vice, crime, and delinquency . . . In the near future, intelligence tests will bring tens of thousands of these high-grade defectives under the surveillance and protection of society. This will ultimately result in curtailing the reproduction of feeblemindedness and in the elimination of an enormous amount of crime, pauperism, and industrial inefficiency . . .

There is no possibility at present of convincing society that they should not be allowed to reproduce, although from a eugenic point of view they constitute a grave problem, because of their unusually prolific breeding.

"Organized charities," he observed the following year in a paper titled "The Menace of Feeble-Mindedness," "often contribute to the survival of individuals who would otherwise not be able to live and reproduce."

Feeling smart enough to read more?
Turn to page 573 for Part III.

MOVIE BOMB:
LAST ACTION HERO

*Some films don't set out to be disaster films, but they still end
up that way. This one, for example, starred Hollywood's most
bankable actor. He could do no wrong . . . until he picked this.*

UNLIKELY SCENARIO

It was the kind of thing that's supposed to happen only in
the movies: In 1991, two recent graduates of Weslyan
University, Zak Penn and Adam Leff, wrote a script called
Extremely Violent, about a troubled boy who goes to adventure
movies to escape his problems and one day finds himself in the
middle of a film starring his favorite action hero. "Their friends in
the lower ranks of show business helped promote it," Thom Taylor
writes in *The Big Deal*. "The script landed Penn and Leff with the
agent of their choice . . . and suddenly it became a priority-event
movie for Columbia Pictures." Then came Ah-nold.

Fresh from the success of *Total Recall* and *Terminator 2: Judgment
Day*, Arnold Schwarzenegger was one of the world's biggest movie
stars in 1992. At Columbia's urging, he read the script—and liked
it. He agreed to do the film . . . as long as there were changes.

What Arnold wanted, Arnold got. He was considered "bulletproof" in the industry—everything he touched turned to money. So
the studio eagerly had the script redone by new writers, who gutted
it beyond recognition. Under Schwarzenegger's direction, they
turned what had been a promising script into *Last Action Hero*, the
Schwarzenegger vehicle that made it onto the screen. (The script
was so thoroughly reworked that Penn and Leff lost their screen-
writing credit and are credited only with developing the story.)

Meanwhile, acting as producer, Schwarzenegger set to work giving the film his own personal touch. Using his newfound box office
clout, Schwarzenegger assumed a greater degree of creative control
than he'd had on any other film. "Before, I always felt a little bit
like I was butting in," he told a reporter, "I always felt I was stepping over the line." Not this time— Schwarzenegger was in the driver's seat. As Nancy Griffin and Kim Masters write in *Hit & Run*:

On an average day, McDonalds feeds 43 million people.

Acting as a producer for the first time in his career, Schwarzenegger operated like a field marshal out of his 40-foot trailer on the Sony lot. Equipped with a special telephone that allowed him to punch directly into [the studio's offices], he would summon executives—who would immediately be seen streaking out of their offices and tearing across the lot to Camp Arnold.

Destroying the original script and letting Schwarzenegger call the shots seemed like a good idea at the time, even as *Hero's* cost nearly doubled from $65 million to $120 million—making it the most expensive film ever made at the time.

The first hint of trouble came on May 1, 1993, when a rough cut of the film was shown to a test audience to gauge their reactions. The audience roared with approval when told they were there to watch Arnold Schwarzenegger's latest movie, but as the film progressed, the excitement degenerated into boredom; by the end of the film the audience was "almost catatonic," according to one account. "The movie lay there like a big fried egg," one witness remembers, "and the executives (including Schwarzenegger, who was present) looked like a group of people who had just gotten on a ship and saw the name *Poseidon*."

Normally the studio would have tabulated audience survey cards to see how many people rated the film "good" or "excellent," but this time nobody bothered—the cards were quickly fed, unread, into a paper shredder before word of how bad the film was could get out.

Too late—within hours Hollywood was swirling with rumors that Schwarzenegger's magnum opus was doomed. Weeks of round-the-clock editing and the addition of newly filmed scenes didn't change a thing: When *Last Action Hero* opened on June 13, audiences stayed away from theaters and critics tore the film apart.

In its opening weekend *Last Action Hero* came in second place behind *Jurassic Park*, which had already been in theaters a week. *Hero* dropped to fourth place the second week, behind *Jurassic Park*, *Sleepless in Seattle*, and even *Dennis the Menace*, and dropped out of sight soon after that. Estimated loss: $35 million.

"It's a bad feeling to stand around a giant premiere when they spend $200,000 on a blow-up doll of Arnold," says Chris Moore, the agent who sold Penn and Leff's original script to Columbia, "and feel, 'Wow, it's just not that good.'"

Nanook of the North was the first documentary film ever made.

JOIN THE CLUB:
THE SALVATION ARMY

The Salvation Army may be the most famous charitable organization in the world. Here's how it got started.

FOUNDED BY: William Booth, a London preacher in the 1860s. Booth's experience as a pawnbroker's apprentice gave him insight into the problems of England's underclass, and he made it his mission to minister to the poor.

HISTORY: Booth became a Methodist minister in the mid-1850s, but after several years he came to feel that God wanted more from him. He also felt that he should do more to reach ordinary people. So he began preaching in the streets of the East End of London, one of the city's poorest districts.

Booth never had any intention of starting his own church—his original goal was to convert "the poor and wretched" and send them to the established churches nearby. But he soon realized that many his converts didn't feel welcome in other churches "because they could not afford a special Sunday suit . . . and many of the regular churchgoers were appalled when these shabbily dressed, evil-smelling people came to join them in worship."

So in 1865 Booth formed the East London Christian Mission (later shortened to the Christian Mission) and began focusing on meeting his converts' clothing and other material needs—as well as their spiritual needs.

How did the Christian Mission become known as the Salvation Army? In May 1878 Booth asked his son, Bramwell to read the draft of the Christian Mission's Annual Report. Bramwell took one look and immediately objected to the first statement on the first page, which read:

"The Christian Mission is a Volunteer Army."

Bramwell argued that he wasn't a volunteer, because he felt compelled by God to work with the poor. So Booth crossed out the word; in its place, he wrote the word "Salvation." And the Salvation Army had its name.

The Man-o-War jellyfish can have tentacles up to 60 feet long.

THE BIRTH OF THE SUBMARINE, PART II

Sixty-eight years before Jules Verne wrote about an imaginary submarine called the Nautilus *in his book* 20,000 Leagues Under the Sea, *a failed-artist-turned-inventor named Robert Fulton invented a real submarine called the* Nautilus. *Does the name Fulton sound familiar? It was only after his sub failed to attract any interest from the leading naval powers of the day that Fulton went on to invent the thing he is most famous for: the steamboat. Here's part two of our history of the submarine. Part I is on page 420.*

RUE BRITTANIA

Twenty years after David Bushnell built the *American Turtle*, another American inventor, Robert Fulton, took the concept a step further when he drew up plans for a submarine he called *Nautilus* (Greek for "sailor"). Fulton, a pacifist at heart, hated the way the British were able to use the Royal Navy to control international trade in the mid-1790s, so he approached France, then at war with England. Convinced that submarines could be used to break the Royal Navy's blockade of French ports, he thought that France would jump at the chance to buy them. But he was wrong—France wasn't interested in his submarines, at any price. After all, while Fulton had drawn plans for his submarine, he'd never actually built one, and the French were skeptical that such a strange boat—even if it could be built—would ever be as effective in battle as Fulton claimed.

Fulton sweetened his offer: he'd build and man the subs at his own expense and send them into battle against the British. All France had to do was pay him 4,000 francs for every large English warship he sunk, and 2,000 francs for every small one. Still no deal . . . but Fulton persisted, and finally, three years later, in 1799, France agreed to pay him 10,000 francs to build a single experimental submarine.

THE *NAUTILUS*

By June 1800, Robert Fulton had completed his submarine and was

---

More road-rage incidents occur on Friday between 4 and 6 p.m. than at any other time.

ready for a public demonstration. To the crowds that gathered on the Seine River to witness the spectacle, the *Nautilus* might have looked like something from another planet, as Robert Burgess writes in *Ships Beneath the Sea*:

> She was twenty-one-feet-three-inches long and six-foot-four-inches wide . . . With her forward-mounted observation dome, the *Nautilus* bore a remarkable resemblance to a modern-day research submersible. She was operated by a three-man crew.
>
> Power was provided by a hand crank geared to a screw propeller at the rear. The boat would submerge upon flooding her hollow iron keel . . . Pumping the water ballast from the keel brought her to the surface, where she could be sailed.

After sailing a short distance up the Seine, the two men on deck folded up her fan-shaped sail, lowered the mast onto the deck, and disappeared inside the ship. As the *Nautilus* continued to make its way upstream without any visible means of propulsion, the vessel slowly sank beneath the waves. Five minutes later, it resurfaced a little farther up the river, proceeded for a short distance, then sank again. Minutes later, the *Nautilus* surfaced even farther up river, after which the two men came back up on deck, raised the mast, unfolded the sail, and sailed away.

No one had ever seen anything like it.

BOMBS AWAY

In his next demonstration, Fulton attacked a 40-foot "target" ship. Towing a bomb containing 20 pounds of gunpowder on a long rope, Fulton sailed to within 650 feet of the target ship and then dove below the surface and continued underwater, passing underneath the target ship and continuing onward until the towed bomb made contact with the hull and exploded.

The French were finally impressed; Napoleon himself asked for a demonstration. But Fulton replied with a bombshell of a different sort. He told Napoleon that he had dismantled and destroyed the sub. Furthermore, he refused to rebuild it or even show his drawings until he and Napoleon came to a financial agreement. Otherwise, he feared France would use his idea without paying him.

Destroying the submarine was a huge gamble and Fulton lost. "Napoleon did not even give Fulton the courtesy of a reply," Robert Burgess writes in *Ships Beneath the Sea*. "As time passed,

---

In English, "four" is the only digit that has the same number of letters as its value.

Fulton heard that the French dictator was calling him a charlatan and a swindler bent on obtaining money under false pretenses."

SWITCHING SIDES

By now Fulton had shed his idealism and was determined to earn fame and fortune from his submarines, even if that meant building submarines for the hated Royal Navy. Having worn out his welcome in France, he accepted an offer from the British government to continue his work in England.

But on October 21, 1805, the Royal Navy destroyed the combined Spanish and French fleets in the Battle of Trafalgar, before Fulton had a chance to build even a single sub for Britain.

"Victory at Trafalgar," Cynthia Owen Philip writes in *Robert Fulton: A Biography*, "made Great Britain the undisputed ruler of the seas and secured the island kingdom from the threat of French invasion. It also abruptly changed the government's attitude toward Fulton. His unorthodox weapons, still unproven in battle, were now superfluous. So that there would be no chance of misunderstanding his position, the government stopped paying his monthly salary."

STEAMED UP

After more than a decade of futile effort, Fulton finally gave up on the submarine and returned to the United States to work on another interest of his—the steamboat. "With wealthy backer Robert Livingston he built the famous steamboat *Clermont*," Burgess writes, "and with the assistance of a steamboat monopoly, it brought him the fame and fortune he had long sought elsewhere." The submarine was dead . . . until it found a new champion.

See page 632 for Part III of the story.

* * *

A REEL QUOTE

"I told you 158 times I cannot stand little notes on my pillow. 'We are out of corn flakes, F.U.' It took me three hours to figure out F.U. was Felix Unger."

—Walter Matthau, *The Odd Couple*

In an emergency, Coca-Cola can replace oil in cars.

Q & A:
ASK THE EXPERTS

Here are some more random questions, with answers from books by some of the nation's top trivia experts.

VERY CAREFULLY

Q: *How do they get all that shaving cream into an aerosol can?*

A: "They don't. Shaving cream is basically soap and water, put into the can along with compressed butane gas. Without the gas, all you have is soapy liquid. When the valve is pressed, some of the gas mixes with the soap and water and expands to make foam." (From *The New York Times Book of Science Questions & Answers*, by C. Claiborne Ray)

PARTLY SILLY

Q: *What is the difference between "partly cloudy" and "partly sunny" in a weather report?*

A: "The expression 'partly sunny' was brought to you by the same folks who brought you 'comfort station' and 'sanitary engineer.' As a technical meteorological term, 'partly sunny' doesn't exist. So while you might assume that a partly sunny sky should be clearer than a partly cloudy one, the two terms signify the same condition. You have merely encountered a weathercaster who prefers to see the glass half full rather than half empty." (From *Imponderables*, by David Feldman)

QUIT WINE-ING

Q: *What are the "sulfites" I see listed on some wine labels, and why do all American wines seem to have them?*

A: "They are preservatives. In wine they're used to prevent discoloration, bacterial growth, and fermentation. They're also used to prevent discoloration in shrimp, raisins, potatoes, lettuce, and other vegetables. But that's not all they do. Sulfites are the only additives now in use that are known to kill people. Fortunately, deaths are rare and result from what amounts to an extreme

---

Three out of four college students expect to become a millionaire.

allergic reaction. If you've drunk your share of wine and you're still breathing, you're probably safe." (From *Return of the Straight Dope*, by Cecil Adams)

YOU'RE GROUNDED!

Q: *In a lightning storm, will rubber tires insulate a car from being hit by lightning?*

A: "No. Lightning is strong enough to travel through or around the rubber. According to the Boston Museum of Science, your tires would have to be solid rubber a mile thick to actually insulate you from a lightning bolt. Does that mean, then, that you should avoid your car in a thunderstorm? No, the good news is that your car is the safest place to be if you're outside during a storm—the lightning will most likely travel around the metal shell of your car and not do any damage to it or you. That is, if you have a metal car and don't park under a tree or touch the metal. The bad news is that if you have a convertible or plastic car, or if you touch the metal skin of your automobile when lightning strikes, you may be in for a profoundly shocking experience." (From *Just Curious, Jeeves*, by Jack Mingo and Erin Barrett)

BEE-HAVE

Q: *How can I tell whether I was stung by a wasp or a bee?*

A: "The easiest way to tell if a wasp or a bee caused the sting is to look at the perpetrator. Both yellow jackets (the most common) and honeybees have yellow-and-black markings, and they look very much alike, but honeybees have hairy bodies, whereas the bodies of yellow jackets are smooth.

"If the insect that stung you has flown away, you can sometimes identify the culprit by looking at the sting. Wasp stingers are smooth like needles. After piercing your skin and injecting its venom, the wasp slides its stinger out and flies away. Honeybees have barbed stingers that remain even after the bee has gone. When the bee leaves behind its stinger, it also leaves its venom sac. The muscles in the sac can continue pumping venom into the wound for up to 20 minutes." (From *101 Questions & Answers About Backyard Wildlife*, by Ann Squire)

Why did Grace Hopper coin the term "computer bug"? A moth shorted out her computer.

THE DUSTBIN
OF HISTORY

*Think today's big newsmakers will go down in history for
what they've done? Don't count on it. These folks were
well known in their time . . . but they're forgotten now.
They've been swept into the Dustbin of History.*

FORGOTTEN FIGURE: John Billington, "a foul-mouthed
miscreant" who came to America in 1620 on the *Mayflower*
CLAIM TO FAME: Billington, his wife, and their two sons
were among the 67 non-Pilgrim passengers on the ship. The
Billingtons were, Governor William Bradford later wrote, " . . . one
of the profanest families aboard the ship." They made enemies of
just about everyone during the 66-day voyage and things did not
improve on land.

In the summer of 1630, Billington shot a man, John
Newcomen, in the woods near Plymouth Colony. Apparently he
thought he'd finished him off . . . but he was wrong. When
Billington returned to the colony, he learned that Newcomen was
still alive and had identified him as the assailant. Newcomen died
a few days later and Billington was charged with murder—the first
ever in the colonies. Tried and convicted, Billington was hanged in
September 1630.

INTO THE DUSTBIN: Amazingly, writes Peter Stevens in *The
Mayflower Murderer and Other Forgotten Firsts in American History*,
"Some Americans tracing their bloodlines back to the *Mayflower*
proclaim proudly their kinship to the lout. And on the *Mayflower
Compact*, the hallowed names of Brewster, Mullins, Alden,
Bradford, and Standish abide for posterity with the scrawl of
America's first convicted murderer: big, bad, John Billington."

FORGOTTEN FIGURE: Barney Oldfield, a race car driver
CLAIM TO FAME: In 1902, an obscure Detroit automaker
named Henry Ford built a race car which he dubbed the "999."
When his partner refused to drive it, Ford hired daredevil bicycle
racer Barney Oldfield.

New York City's Broadway was once known as Bloomingdale Road.

Oldfield had never been behind the wheel of an automobile in his life, but it didn't matter—Ford entered him in a race against Alexander Winton, then considered the fastest race car driver in the world.

"When race day came," Robert Lacy writes in *Ford: The Men and the Machine,*

> Oldfield charged 999 into battle with the happy ignorance of a neophyte. He slammed his foot down on the accelerator at the start and didn't raise it until he had crossed the finish line, not slackening in the slightest. Winton, who had christened his car "The Bullet," held the pace for a lap or so, then gave up.

The victory put Ford on the map and set Oldfield on a course to become America's first superstar race car driver. He became the first man in America to drive a gasoline-powered car at an average speed of 60 mph and by 1910 had pushed the land speed record all the way to an astonishing 131.25 mph, "the fastest ever traveled by a human being."

INTO THE DUSTBIN: Oldfield retired in 1918 at the age of 40 and spent the rest of his life watching one record after another fall to younger drivers in faster cars. "There is a story," Kernan writes, "that in old age he was stopped for speeding after a wild chase featuring three motorcycle cops. He watched calmly as the toughest of them strode up. 'Who do you think you are?' the cop snarled at him. 'Barney Oldfield?'"

FORGOTTEN FIGURE: Joshua Lawrence Chamberlain, Union general during the Civil War

CLAIM TO FAME: When the Civil War broke out, 33-year-old Chamberlain left his quiet life as a college professor to volunteer for the Union Army. Entering the army as a Lt. Colonel, he rose to the rank of Brigadier General. He fought with bravery in 24 major battles, including the battle of Gettysburg; he was wounded six times and had six horses shot out from under him.

On March 29, 1865, for example, a bullet went through his horse's neck, ricocheted off his arm, and struck him in the chest just below the heart. It probably would have killed him had it not been deflected by a pocket mirror. Instead, Chamberlain was knocked unconscious. When he came to, he was disgusted to see some of his men retreating. Bleeding profusely, Chamberlain grabbed his sword and charged the enemy. His men abandoned their retreat and joined him in the charge, turning the tables and winning the battle.

INTO THE DUSTBIN: General Grant rewarded Chamberlain's bravery by designating him to receive the formal surrender of the Confederacy at Appomattox. He later served four terms as governor of Maine and in 1893 was awarded the Congressional Medal of Honor. Nevertheless, historian Charles Calhoun writes, "Chamberlain largely faded from national view for most of the 20th century. No statue of him was ever erected at Gettysburg; few historians ever studied his campaigns."

* * *

FORGETTABLE FLOPS

- **Porcupine-flavored Potato Chips.** In 1984, Welsh bar owner Phil Lewis was discussing potato chip flavors with some Romanian customers. They told him of an old gypsy delicacy—porcupine baked in clay—and suggested the possibility of porcupine-flavored potato chips. Using a closely guarded recipe, Lewis set to work in his kitchen to produce the first packages. Customers compared the taste to smokey bacon but, as the venture attracted more and more publicity, animal-lovers protested. Lewis was forced to abandon it for more traditional flavors.

- **Attack Clock.** In 1919, John Humphrey of Connecticut invented an unusual alarm clock: The apparatus consisted of a timepiece attached to an adjustable rod with a rubber ball on the end. When the alarm on the clock went off, instead of a bell ringing, the rod would be activated, causing the ball to hit the sleeper. Humphrey deemed his device to be of great benefit to deaf people or invalids who might be upset by bells . . . but who presumably didn't mind being whacked over the head with a ball.

FAMILY FEUDS

Is blood thicker than water? Not when there's money involved.
Here are two feuds from the BRI files that prove the point.

KOCH vs. KOCH

The Contestants: Charles and Bill Koch, two sons of Fred Koch, the founder of Koch Industries, an oil refining company with annual revenues of $35 billion—making it the 2nd-largest privately-held company in the U.S.

How the Feud Started: When Fred Koch died in 1967, Charles Koch became company president. Two other sons, Bill and David, joined the company in the 1970s. Bill, who owned 21 percent of the company, became increasingly bitter about the way Charles ran things—he felt he was entitled to more power. He also was upset at being "limited" to a $10,000 expense account, and at having to report to non-family executives.

Then, in 1979, Bill learned that his brother Charles had commissioned a plan on how Bill's stake in the company would be distributed at his death. Enraged, he enlisted his brother Frederick—an "artist" who'd been written out of his father's will (but still owned 14 percent of the company)—to join him in a proxy fight against Charles. But they lost the fight.

Charles retaliated by firing Bill and then consolidated his control over the company by issuing shares to loyal executives. After that, it was tit-for-tat: Bill filed his first lawsuit against the company in 1982; Charles filed a $167 million countersuit for libel, also charging that Bill was "mentally unstable." In one of the lawsuits, the Koch's 80-year-old mother was dragged into court to testify only days after she is believed to have suffered a small stroke.

In 1983, Charles took out more than $1 billion in bank loans and bought Bill's and Frederick's shares, which should have been the end of it . . . but wasn't. In 1985, Bill sued again, accusing Charles of shortchanging him on the sale of his stock. Bill lost the suit, filed another one, then lost again in 1988. Then, armed with evidence that the company was shortchanging oil producers, Bill revived his 1985 lawsuit and also turned the information over to the U.S. Senate Select Committee on Indian Affairs.

Do all dogs bark? Almost. The Basenji, an African breed, is the only kind that doesn't.

And the Winner Is: Split decision. Bill didn't get any more money for his shares . . . but he won the "shortchanging" lawsuit. A jury ruled that Koch Industries had defrauded the government in oil payments and had to pay over $200 million—25 percent of which Bill got. The company also had to pay his legal fees. Equally important, the verdict damaged the company's reputation. Bill announced that he was so pleased, he was celebrating with a backyard barbecue for his family and neighborhood kids.

JOHN KELLOGG vs. WILL KELLOGG
The Contestants: John Harvey Kellogg, a physician and bowel-obsessed health guru at the turn of the century, and his brother Will Keith Kellogg, an accountant.

The Feud: While searching for a new kind of breakfast food to help his patients get "regular," Dr. Kellogg invented the recipe for bran flakes; then he invented the recipe for corn flakes.

But he was an idealist: he saw corn flakes as purely medicinal and began selling them under the brand name "Sanitas," after his Seventh Day Adventist Sanitarium.

Will Kellogg was a businessman—he thought that Sanitas was a stupid name for a breakfast food (it reminded him of a disinfectant), and he thought the flakes would sell better if they contained a little sugar, which his brother opposed for health reasons.

While John Kellogg was on a trip to Europe, Will formed a cereal company and launched his own brand of corn flakes to compete against Sanitas. To add insult to injury, his packaging suggested that "Kellogg's Corn Flakes" were linked to his brother's famous sanitarium. John was furious when he found out. He filed suit to block the corn flakes and put his brother out of business.

And the Winner Is: Will Kellogg. John lost the suit. Not only that, when he retaliated by introducing "Kellogg's Sterilized Bran" to capitalize on his brother's thriving cereal business (just as his brother had earlier cashed in on the sanitarium's fame), Will filed suit to stop *him* from using the family name . . . and *won*. "The Battle of the Brans" had lasted more than a decade; by the time it was over, Dr. John Kellogg's sanitarium had fallen on hard times, while Will Kellogg's breakfast cereal business was booming, all thanks to an idea he'd stolen from his brother. The brothers rarely spoke to each other for the rest of their lives.

The musical *Cats* ran on Broadway for 18 years.

WOULD YOU BELIEVE?

Advice to our younger readers. It's a good idea to pick your role models carefully. Here's why.

CRUSADERS AGAINST CRIME

Role Model: Richard Pimental, a captain in the Taunton, Massachusetts Police Department, known as "Captain Good." He was the no-nonsense host of *Crime Watch*, a cable TV show in which he profiled local crimes and denounced criminals as "toilet-licking maggots."

Setting an Example: In March 1999, Captain Good was convicted of stealing a gun from the department and sentenced to two years' probation. The following year he was sentenced to six months' house arrest after pleading guilty to obstruction of justice. He'd apparently been tampering with witnesses while trying to fix the assault trial of his nephew, who was charged with punching a bouncer in a bar.

Role Models: Art McKoy and Abdul Rahim, heads of a Cleveland, Ohio, anti-crime organization

Setting an Example: In 1998, they were sentenced to prison for spending $617,597 that the city of Cleveland, Ohio, accidentally deposited in the bank account of their organization. According to news reports, the money landed in their account "when a city data operator punched in the wrong wire-transfer number while intending to pay a utility bill."

CRUSADERS AGAINST ALCOHOL ABUSE

Role Model: Susan John, chairperson of Rochester, New York's Committee on Alcohol and Drug Abuse

Setting an Example: In March 1997, she pleaded guilty for "driving while impaired"—in other words, drunk driving. Her public statement: "This will give me additional insights into the problem of drinking and driving, and I believe will allow me to do my job even more effectively." Sure.

Role Model: Bethany Tosh, 21-year-old Miss Northeast Arkansas for 2000

Fastest-growing religion in Ireland: Buddhism.

Setting an Example: She won the pageant on an anti-drunk driving platform. In March 2000, she surrendered her title after being convicted of driving under the influence of alcohol.

DEFENDERS OF PEOPLE'S RIGHTS
Role Models: Age Concern, a British organization "devoted to concerns of the elderly"

Setting An Example: In June 2000, a 69-year-old Englishman named Hector McDonald applied for a job at Age Concern. He was turned down for the job—because he was too old.

Role Models: The Texas Commission for the Blind, which was set up to provide workplace support to the visually impaired

Setting An Example: In 1999, it paid $55,000 to settle lawsuits filed by two blind employees. The commission had neglected to make "Braille and large-type employee manuals available to employees."

EXPERTS ON CONTROLLING ANGER
Role Model: A German youth worker who teaches anger control, identified only as "Herman K"

Setting An Example: In June 1999, Herr K was fined about $1,000 and given a 10-month suspended sentence. What for? He punched a policeman in the face, shouting "Here's something for your mouth!" after the officer ticketed his illegally parked car.

Role Model: Charles Mahuka, an anger management instructor
Setting an Example: In 1995, 32-year-old Miguel Gonzales was ordered to attend an anger management class after he assaulted his girlfriend. He showed up at the class drunk, which made his instructor so angry that he beat Gonzales to death.

HITS AND MISSES
Role Model: The Reverend George Crossley, a televangelist

Setting An Example: In 1997, Crossley was convicted of trying to hire a hit-man to kill his arch-rival, whose estranged wife he was having an affair with. He'd inadvertently "hired" an undercover agent of the Bureau of Alcohol, Tobacco, and Firearms to do it.

The male red colobus monkey nurses for three or four years.

TRISKAIDEKAPHOBIA

Triskaidekaphobia is "the fear of 3 plus 10," and millions of people suffer from it. According to experts, it costs America more than a billion dollars a year in absenteeism, train and plane cancellations, and reduced commerce on the 13th of every month. We decided to take a look at the affliction.

Fear of the number 13 originated in Norse mythology. Aegir summoned 12 gods to a banquet in Valhalla. Guest number thirteenth showed up uninvited: Loki, god of evil.

Another possible connection comes from Christianity. Jesus and the 12 apostles dined together at the Last Supper, Judas, Christ's betrayer, being the 13th.

Predating the Christians, the Turks hated the number 13 so much that it was almost expunged from their vocabulary.

The Romans associated the number 13 with death and misfortune. There were 12 months in a year and 12 hours in a day (according to the Roman clock), so 13 was seen as a violation of the natural cycle.

For ancient Egyptians, 13 represented the final rung of the ladder by which the soul reached eternity.

Even before that, at religious feasts in ancient Babylon, 13 people were selected to represent the gods. At the end of the ceremony, the 13th "god" was put to death.

Thirteen is the number of members in a witch's coven.

The 13th card in the Tarot deck is the skeleton—Death.

According to *The Encyclopedia of Superstitions*, if 13 people gather in a room, one will die within a year. In 1798, *Gentleman's Magazine* explained the superstition by saying, "It seems to be founded on calculations adhered to by insurance offices."

On the other hand, consider the ill-fated Apollo 13 lunar mission, which left the launch-pad at 13:13 hours on April 13 . . . and then exploded, almost killing the entire crew.

"Lenin" was only one of 151 pseudonyms that Vladimir Ilyich Ulanov used in his lifetime.

MORE EXECUTIVE DECISIONS

More dumb business decisions, made by U.S. executives.

SHOULD WE BUY THIS INVENTION?

Executive: William Orton, president of the Western Union Telegraph Company in 1876

Background: In 1876, Western Union had a monopoly on the telegraph, the world's most advanced communications technology. This made it one of America's richest and most powerful companies, "with $41 million in capital and the pocketbooks of the financial world behind it." So when Gardiner Greene Hubbard, a wealthy Bostonian, approached Orton with an offer to sell the patent for a new invention Hubbard had helped to fund, Orton treated it as a joke. Hubbard was asking for $100,000!

Decision: Orton bypassed Hubbard and drafted a response directly to the inventor. "Mr. Bell," he wrote, "after careful consideration of your invention, while it is a very interesting novelty, we have come to the conclusion that it has no commercial possibilities . . . What use could this company make of an electrical toy?"

Impact: The invention, the telephone, would have been perfect for Western Union. The company had a nationwide network of telegraph wires in place, and the inventor, 29-year-old Alexander Graham Bell, had shown that his telephones worked quite well on telegraph lines. All the company had to do was hook telephones up to its existing lines, and it would have had the world's first nationwide telephone network in a matter of months.

Instead, Bell kept the patent and in a few decades his telephone company, "renamed American Telephone and Telegraph (AT&T), had become the largest corporation in America . . . The Bell patent—offered to Orton for a measly $100,000—became the single most valuable patent in history."

Ironically, less than two years after turning Bell down, Orton realized the magnitude of his mistake and spent millions of dollars challenging Bell's patents while attempting to build his own telephone network (which he was ultimately forced to hand over

---

Sports myth: Footballs are made of cowhide, not pigskin.

to Bell). Instead of going down in history as one of the architects of the telephone age, he is instead remembered for having made one of the worst decisions in American business history.

HOW DO WE COMPETE WITH BUDWEISER?

Executive: Robert Uihlein, Jr., head of the Schlitz Brewing Company in Milwaukee, Wisconsin

Background: In the 1970s, Schlitz was America's #2 beer, behind Budweiser. It had been #1 until 1957 and has pursued Bud ever since. In the 1970s, Uihlein came up with a strategy to compete against Anheuser-Busch. He figured that if he could cut the cost of ingredients used in his beer and speed up the brewing process at the same time, he could brew more beer in the same amount of time for less money . . . and earn higher profits.

Decision: Uihlein cut the amount of time it took to brew Schlitz from 40 days to 15, and replaced much of the barley malt in the beer with corn syrup—which was cheaper. He also switched from one type of foam stabilizer to another to get around new labeling laws that would have required the original stabilizer to be disclosed on the label.

Impact: Uihlein got what he wanted: a cheaper, more profitable beer that made a lot of money . . . at first. But it tasted terrible, and tended to break down quickly as the cheap ingredients bonded together and sank to the bottom of the can—forming a substance that "looked disconcertingly like mucus." Philip Van Munching writes in *Beer Blast:*

> Suddenly Schlitz found itself shipping out a great deal of apparently snot-ridden beer. The brewery knew about it pretty quickly and made a command decision—to do nothing . . . Uihlein declined a costly recall for months, wagering that not much of the beer would be subjected to the kinds of temperatures at which most haze forms. He lost the bet, sales plummeted . . . and Schlitz began a long steady slide from the top three.

Schlitz finally caved in and recalled 10 million cans of the snot beer. But their reputation was ruined and sales never recovered. In 1981, they shut down their Milwaukee brewing plant; the following year, the company was purchased by rival Stroh's. One former mayor of Milwaukee compared the brewery's fortunes to the sinking of the *Titanic*, asking, "How could that big of a business go under so fast?"

Odds that you will be dealt four of a kind in a five-card draw: 1 in 4,165.

THE ORIGIN
OF THE FORK

Of the three eating utensils we normally use, only forks have a modern origin. Knives and spoons are prehistoric—but as recently as 1800, forks weren't commonly used in America. Some food for thought.

KNIVES, BUT NO FORKS

Centuries ago, few people had ever heard of a "place setting." When a large piece of meat was set on the table (sometimes on a platter, sometimes directly on the table), diners grabbed the whole thing with their free hand . . . then pulled out a knife and sliced off a piece with the other hand. Most eating was done with fingers: Common people ate with all five, while nobles—who understood sophisticated table manners—ate with only three (thumb, forefinger, and middle).

At that time, there were no utensils. In fact, most men owned just one multipurpose blade, which, in addition to carving food, was used for fighting, hunting, and butchering animals. But wealthy nobles had always been able to afford a different knife for each purpose, and by the Middle Ages, they had developed a setting of two knives, for very formal dining. One knife was thrust into a large piece of meat to hold it in place on a plate, while the second was used to cut off a smaller piece, which the eater speared and placed in his mouth.

FORKS

One of the drawbacks of cutting a piece of meat while holding it in place with a knife is that the meat has tendency to "rotate in place like a wheel on an axle," Henry Petroski writes in *The Evolution of Useful Things*. "Frustration with knives, especially their shortcomings in holding meat steady for cutting, eventually led to the development of the fork." The name comes from *furca*, the Latin word for a farmer's pitchfork.

The first fork commonly used in Europe was a miniature version of the big carving fork used to spear turkeys and roasts in the kitchen. It had only two "tines" or prongs, spaced far enough apart to

---

After the U.S. Civil War, the U.S. charged England $15.5 million for not annexing Canada.

hold meat meat in place while cutting it; but apparently it wasn't something you stuck in your mouth and ate with—that was still the knife's job.

A FOOLISH UTENSIL

These first table forks probably originated at the royal courts of the Middle East, where they were in use as early as the seventh century. About A.D. 1100 they appeared in the Tuscany region of Italy, but they were considered "shocking novelties," and were ridiculed and condemned by the clergy—who insisted that "only human fingers, created by God, were worthy to touch God's bounty." Forks were "effeminate pieces of finery," as one historian puts it, used by sinners and sissies but not by decent, God-fearing folk.

"An Italian historian recorded a dinner at which a Venetian noblewoman used a fork of her own design," Charles Panati writes in *The Extraordinary Origins of Everyday Things*, "and incurred the rebuke of several clerics present for her "excessive sign of refinement.' The woman died days after the meal, supposedly from the plague, but clergymen preached that her death was divine punishment, a warning to others contemplating the affectation of a fork."

FORK YOU

Thanks to these derogatory associations, more than 250 years passed before forks finally came into wide use in Italy. In the rest of Europe, they were still virtually unheard of. Catherine de Medici finally brought them to France in the 1500s when she became queen. And in 1608, an Englisman named Thomas Coryate traveled to Italy and saw people eating with forks; the sight was so peculiar that he made note of it in his book *Crudities Hastily Cobbled Up in Five Months*:

> The Italians . . . do always at their meals use a little fork when they cut their meat . . . Should [anyone] unadvisedly touch the dish of meat with his fingers from which all at the table do cut, he will give occasion of offense unto the company, as having trangressed the laws of good manners, insomuch that for his error he shall be at least browbeaten if not reprehended in words . . . The Italian cannot by any means indure to have his dish touched with fingers, seeing all men's fingers are not alike clean.

More than half of all the bones in your body are in your hands and feet.

Coryate brought some forks with him to England and presented one to Queen Elizabeth, who was so thrilled by the utensil that she had additional ones made from gold, coral, and crystal. But they remained little more than a pretentious fad of the royal court. Forks became more common during the late 17th century, but it wasn't until the 18th century that they were widely used in continental Europe as a means for conveying food "from plate to mouth." The reason: French nobles saw forks as a way to distinguish themselves from commoners. "The fork became a symbol of luxury, refinement, and status," writes Charles Panati. "Suddenly, to touch food with even three bare fingers was gauche." A new custom developed—when an invitation to dinner was received, a servant frequently was sent ahead with a fine leather case containing a knife, fork, and spoon to be used at dinner later.

MAKING A NEW POINT

But before this revolution took place, the fork had to be redesigned. The first forks were completely useless when it came to scooping peas and other loose food into the mouth—the gap between the two tines was too large. So cutlery makers began adding a third tine to their forks, and by the early 18th century, a fourth. "Four appears to have been the optimum [number]," Henry Petroski writes in *The Evolution of Useful Things*. "Four tines provide a relatively broad surface and yet do not feel too wide for the mouth. Nor does a four-tined fork have so many tines that it resembles a comb, or function like one when being pressed into a piece of meat."

COMING TO AMERICA

One of the last places the fork caught on in the Western world was colonial America. In fact, forks weren't commonly used by the average citizen until the time of the Civil War; until then, people just ate with knives or their fingers. In 1828, for example, the English writer Frances Trollope wrote of some generals, colonels, and majors aboard a Mississippi steamboat who had "the frightful manner of feeding with their knives, till the whole blade seemed to enter the mouth." And as late as 1864, one etiquette manual complained that "many persons hold forks awkwardly, as if not accustomed to them."

A penguin with a six-inch stride can run as fast as an average man.

OOPS!

*More tales of outrageous blunders to let us know that
someone's screwing up even worse than we are. So
go ahead and feel superior for a few minutes.*

NAKED AMBITION

"Thirty-one-year-old stripper Roberto Pamplona suffered a broken nose and multiple injuries after performing his act in Milan, Italy. He was supposed to be stripping for a party in one room, but showed up next door . . . where the Catholic Mothers Against Pornography were meeting. The innocent mix-up angered the 'Mothers' and Pamplona's act erupted into a riot halfway through the show."

—**"The Edge,"** *Oregonian*

THE LIGHTS ARE ON, BUT . . .

"Police in Oakland, California, spent two hours attempting to subdue a gunman who'd barricaded himself inside his home. After firing 10 tear gas canisters, officers discovered that the man was actually standing right beside them, shouting pleas to come out and give himself up."

—*Bizarre News*

ROYAL CLOTHES

"On a visit to Kuala Lumpur, [former First Lady Nancy] Reagan was invited to tea with the Queen of Malaysia at the royal palace. The First Lady's entourage was cautioned not to wear yellow or blue, the royal colors, or white, because it is a funeral color. On the appointed hour, a misinformed Mrs. Reagan showed up in a white dress with blue flowers, blue shoes, and a blue straw hat."

—**Not a Good Word,** *by Jane Goodsell*

FIRE DOWN BELOW

"More than two hearts were enflamed as a couple became engaged on the night of November 13 near Medford, New Jersey. The groom-to-be—we'll call him Clifford—bought enough hay bales to spell 'Marry Me Ruth' and paid $200 more to hire a plane. As he and the lady flew over the bales, friends were supposed to illuminate them with car headlights. But the pals didn't arrive on time, so Clifford's brother Ric did the next best thing: He set the hay on fire. Fortunately for Clifford, Ruth saw the message and said 'yes.' Unfortunately for his brother, the flames also ignited surrounding vegetation. Firemen put out the blaze, but Ric was arrested and Clifford had to put up additional money—for that other type of bail."

—Christian Science Monitor

FRIENDS IN LOW PLACES

"As he pulled his car into the Yankee Stadium VIP parking lot, a driver claimed to be a friend of Yankee owner George Steinbrenner. He didn't realize the parking-lot attendant *was* Steinbrenner. 'He looked at me, and said, "Guess I've got the wrong lot,"' said Steinbrenner, who had decided to personally investigate traffic problems at the stadium."

—Parade magazine

RUSSIAN ROULETTE

"For high-ranking bureaucrats in the old USSR, nearly any special privilege was available. The mayor of Leningrad wanted nothing but the best for his daughter's wedding in January 1980. He used his clout to get the Hermitage Museum, which stores many of the nation's art treasures, to let him use Catherine the Great's china tea set, a prized antique, for the occasion.

"As the evening wore on, and the guests grew more exuberant, one reveler got to his feet and accidentally dropped one of the priceless teacups. Assuming that he had proposed a toast, the rest of the guests took this as a signal for the traditional Russian gesture of good luck, stood up and threw their teacups into the fireplace, smashing them."

—Oops!, by Smith and Decter

MAYBE IT WORKED

"Callers to a suicide hotline got a surprise when they heard a voice promising 'the naughtiest girls around.' The toll-free number had been given to an adult phone service after the suicide prevention folks stopped paying for it. This is not the kind of message a suicidal person needs to hear,' said a spokeswoman for the Alliance for the Mentally Ill in South Carolina."

—Bizarre News

Most crowded U.S. state: New Jersey, with an average of 1,000 people per square mile.

AMAZING ANAGRAMS

We've noticed that anagrams (words or phrases that are rearranged to form new words with—more or less—the same meaning) are all over the Internet. We don't know who writes these things, but we love them.

ASTRONOMERS *becomes . . .* **MOON STARERS**

DESPERATION *becomes . . .* **A ROPE ENDS IT**

CLOTHESPINS *becomes . . .* **SO LET'S PINCH**

A DECIMAL POINT *becomes . . .* **I'M A DOT IN PLACE**

THE CHECK IS IN THE MAIL *becomes . . .* **CLAIM "HECK, I SENT IT (HEH!)"**

TIRED NERVES *becomes . . .* **DRIVE TENSER**

VALENTINE POEMS *becomes . . .* **PEN MATES IN LOVE**

LATE-NIGHT CHINESE FOOD PARTY *becomes . . .* **HEATING THE CRISPY NOODLE FAT**

A SHOPLIFTER *becomes . . .* **HAS TO PILFER**

A DOMESTICATED ANIMAL *becomes . . .* **DOCILE, AS A MAN TAMED IT**

THE EYES *becomes . . .* **THEY SEE**

PAYMENT RECEIVED *becomes . . .* **EVERY CENT PAID ME**

NEW YORK TIMES *becomes . . .* **MONKEYS WRITE**

CIRCUMSTANTIAL EVIDENCE *becomes . . .* **CAN RUIN A SELECTED VICTIM**

MALES NEVER ASK FOR DIRECTIONS *becomes . . .* **KEEN CRISIS OF MEN'S ROAD TRAVEL**

The all-time champion: TO BE OR NOT TO BE: THAT IS THE QUESTION, WHETHER 'TIS NOBLER IN THE MIND TO SUFFER THE SLINGS AND ARROWS OF OUTRAGEOUS FORTUNE *becomes . . .* **IN ONE OF THE BARD'S BEST-THOUGHT-OF TRAGEDIES, OUR INSISTENT HERO, HAMLET, QUERIES ON TWO FRONTS ABOUT HOW LIFE TURNS ROTTEN**

A newborn baby's body contains 26 billion cells; an adult has 50 trillion.

UNCLE JOHN'S
BOTTOM 10 RECORDS

Most people have a list of Top 10 songs they listen to. But Uncle John has a Bottom 10. Here's another Official BRI Countdown— and we mean down. *They don't get much worse than this.*

10. MERRY CHRISTMAS FROM THE BRADY BUNCH.
"The six [Brady] kids were herded into a studio, where a producer barked out a list of songs that each would perform. He didn't bother to ask if they could sing, or even to learn their real names." Barry Williams, who played Greg Brady, tells the story of being forced to sing the difficult "O Holy Night," despite the fact that his pubescent voice kept cracking. His comment: "I think I made the recording guy's ears bleed." He adds: "Should you ever come across this particular album in a record store, I suggest you run screaming in the opposite direction."

9. RHAPSODY OF STEEL. From U.S. Steel. "A beautiful symphonic score over which people promote steel products."

8. ADRIAN MUNSEY AND THE LOST SHEEP. "A new category of popular music: Middle of the Field (MOF)." The album features Munsey and a bunch of baaa-ing sheep recorded live in a small English studio. "There are 30 million sheep and 19 million lambs in the U.K.," he intones, "This record is about three of them." Munsey's follow-up: a disco tune called "C'est Sheep."

7. THE CANARIES. *The Songs of Canaries with Music by the Artal Orchestra.* "mixes canary songs with waltzes such as 'Jeannie with the Light Brown Hair' and 'Wine, Women and Song.'"

6. PLANT TALK. The jacket says it all: "Have you ever found yourself lying in bed at night and an idea hits you like a cold slap in the face?" Jim Bricker, owner of Reel Productions did, and this album is the result . . . "Treat yourself by listening to Molly Roth (plant shop owner) talk to your Philodendron, Schefflera, Palm

Vanilla comes from orchids.

Tree, and many others." Sample: "Do you speak English, Ivy? What's the matter, why are you so droopy? Oh I see, your person really poured water to you. You don't like wet feet, do you?" (Not recommended for people with suicidal tendencies.)

5. THE ELVIS TRIBUTES. A variety of awful tunes. For example: "Welcome Home Elvis," by Daddy Bob ("All the angels have been waiting for their rock and roll star"); "Elvis," by Jenny Nicholas ("Where are you, Elvis? . . . Where is the past that I embrace?"), "The Gate" by George Owens, in which the gate at Graceland sings about how sad it is since Elvis died.

4. SEBASTIAN SPEAKS! Your Watchdog on a Disc (Grr-r-records). Approximately 30 minutes of mean, growling dog sounds. The jacket says: "Sebastian was recorded live, at work in his own home. No stand-in dogs or sound effects were used."

3. LEARN CHARM THE WENDY WARD WAY! A two-hour, two-album, 20-day course in CHARM. OK, everybody sing along: "If she's perky and she's pretty and sparkles . . . if she's confident and knows what to say . . . she's a girl who knows about beauty . . . bet she learned it the Wendy Ward Way!"

2. WHY. Not included just because it is, as critics George Grimarc and Pat Reeder say, "one of those gooey, 'We Are the World'-type projects that naively seeks to alter 10,000 years of basic, vicious human nature with just a limp, sing-song melody, a children's chorus, and a lyric sheet that oozes sap like a Vermont maple tree." No, it's one of Uncle John's favorites because the lead voice is *Fantasy Island*'s inimitable Herve Villechaize ("De plane! De plane!"). And, yes, he sings the way he talks: "Why? Do pipple hef to fight? . . . Why don't dey know what cheeldren know?"

1. LET'S LOOK AT GREAT PAINTINGS. Feel inadequate when you visit art museums? No problem! "Understanding paintings is like learning how to swim or ice skate—it might be hard at first, but once we learn how, we can have fun for years!" Narrated by "the *rich, friendly* voice of Miss Ann Loring, who makes the paintings about which she talks *come to life*."

About 1 million people drink cola for breakfast.

CREME *de la* CRUD

From the BRI files: A few samples of the worst of the worst

HOLLYWOOD'S WORST CASTING DECISION

The Conqueror, starring John Wayne as Genghis Khan

John Wayne signed a two-picture deal with RKO Pictures in the mid-1950s and owed the studio another film. He expected it to be a Western.

Unfortunately, RKO had a big-budget epic about Genghis Khan scheduled for theaters in 1956, and no star for it. They wanted Marlon Brando and even wrote a screenplay for him—filled with the kind of "stylized, slightly archaic Elizabethan English" that Brando had mastered in the film *Julius Caesar*. But Brando wasn't available. "Faced with an expensive project with no leading man," writes Damien Bona in *Hollywood's All-time Worst Casting Blunders*, "the studio called in its chits." Wayne was Khan.

How did the Duke plan to play a 12th-century Mongol warlord? The same way he played most of his characters—as a cowboy. "The way the screenplay reads," Wayne explained at the time, "it is a cowboy picture, and that is how I am going to play Genghis Khan. I see him as a gunfighter.

Who knows? It might've worked . . . except that Wayne was no match for the Brando screenplay. He sounded ridiculous saying things like "I am bereft of spirit," and "I feel this Tartar woman is for me. My blood says take her." He didn't look the part, either. As Bona writes, the Duke's Mongol warlord costume was an embarrassment:

> Wayne sports a Fu Manchu moustache and a toupee that calls to mind Moe Howard; his eyes are taped to give him a slight Asian flavor . . . The look does not become him. Clearly uncomfortable—and reportedly sauced much of the time—Wayne . . . is so unsteady in the role that ultimately he comes across like an amateur John Wayne impersonator wearing a funny costume.

Note: *This was one of the first movies we ever wrote about—it's not only terrible, but cursed. See BR#1, page 30.*

Ex-President Gerald Ford's favorite food: Cottage cheese with A-1 Sauce.

THE WORST NURSERY RHYME BOOK
The Struwwelpeter (Slovenly Peter), by Dr. Heinrich Hoffmann (1845)

We found this in William Maloney's book, *The Worst of Everything*. Maloney writes: "If you're a latent sadist and get your jollies from scaring small children, *The Struwwelpeter* is the book for you. Tuck the little ones in, turn down the light, and open to '*the Story of Little Suck-a-Thumb*.' The kids will never suck their thumbs again, and they'll have lots of interesting stuff to tell their psychiatrists when they grow up . . . Editions of *Slovenly Peter* usually have some 35 stories in which children meet hideous ends for such naughtiness as romping, discontent, idleness, fidgeting, and crying. In '*The Cry-Baby*,' a little girl who cries a lot goes blind, then her eyeballs fall out . . . The book was first published, as you might guess, in Germany." Want more? Probably not. But Maloney has kindly reprinted a page from an old edition anyway:

THE STORY OF LITTLE SUCK-A-THUMB

One day, Mamma said: Conrad dear,
I must go out and leave you here.
but mind now, Conrad, what I say.
Don't suck your thumb while I'm away.
The great tall tailor always comes
to little boys who suck their thumbs.
And ere they dream what he's about,
He takes his great sharp scissors out
And cuts their thumbs clean off—and then,
You know, they never grow again.
Mamma had scarcely turn'd her back,
the thumb was in, Alack! Alack!
The door flew open, in he ran,
the great, long, red-legg'd scissor man.
Oh! Children, see! The tailor's come
And caught out little Suck-A-thumb.
Snip! Snap! Snip! The scissors go;
And Conrad cries out Oh! Oh! Oh!
Snip! Snap! Snip! They go so fast,
That both his thumbs are off at last.
Mamma comes home; there Conrad stands.
And looks quite sad, and shows his hands.
"Ah!" said Mamma "I knew he'd come
To naughty Little Suck-A-Thumb."

Babe Ruth's bat was nicknamed Black Betsy.

IT'S A WEIRD, WEIRD WORLD

More proof that truth really is stranger than fiction.

THAT VOODOO THAT YOU DO

"When her seventh-grade students refused to calm down, Monique Bazile, a substitute teacher in Irvington, New Jersey, threatened to burn down their houses and performed voodoo, causing some children to complain of itching."

—*Esquire*

BEAN COUNTER

"A Nairobi physician, after removing a bean from a young girl's ear, jammed it back in when her parents came up short on cash for the $6 operation."

—**"The Edge,"** **The Oregonian**

DUCK, DUCK, GOOSE

"A Tulsa, Oklahoma, physician, writing in a 1992 issue of the *Irish Journal of Psychological Medicine*, reported on a 32-year-old woman whose neighbors had a large satellite dish installed in their yard. The woman became convinced she was being wooed by Donald Duck and that the dish was put there to facilitate his communicating with her. After 'hovering' around the dish, she eventually undressed and climbed into it . . . where she later said she consummated marriage to Mr. Duck."

—*News of the Weird*

JUST CALL ME DAFFY

"A Wisconsin psychiatrist was accused of malpractice by one of his patients, Nadean Cool, who claimed he had convinced her that she had 120 separate personalities, including that of a duck, and then billed her health-care provider $300,000 for group therapy."

—*TV Guide*

People have been living in Damascus since 2000 B.C.—longer than any other city in the world.

IRONIC, ISN'T IT?

There's nothing like a good dose of irony to put the problems of day-to-day life in proper perspective.

LIFE'S LITTLE IRONIES

- In 1999 the Mississippi state capitol in Jackson put up an artificial Christmas tree instead of a real one, out of concern for the fire hazard posed by real trees. "The artificial tree promptly caught fire, forcing the evacuation of the building."

- Tired of the other hunters who crowded into his favorite squirrel hunting grounds, in 1963 Pete Pickett strapped on some fake gorilla feet and tramped all over the place, hoping the prints would scare everyone else away. "Instead, the footprints drew mobs of Big Foot hunters."

- In 1999 Roger Russell began a 2,600-mile walk across South Africa to promote crime prevention. Two days into his walk, Russell was robbed at gunpoint.

IRONIC LIFE . . .

On a Friday the 13th, a man identified only as a 30-year-old Swede began choking on a piece of steak while at a restaurant in Norrkoping, Sweden. Paramedics could not dislodge the steak, and the man was dying in the back of the ambulance as it rushed to the hospital. Then, according to a Swedish newspaper account, "a few hundred yards from the hospital, the ambulance collided with a car. It was not a serious collision and no one was hurt. But the impact dislodged the chunk of beef, and the man resumed breathing."

. . . AND IRONIC DEATHS

- English novelist Arnold Bennett died in Paris in 1931. Cause of death? "Drinking a glass of typhoid-infected water to demonstrate that Parisian water was perfectly safe to drink."

- U.S. Army Surgeon John Blair Gibbs died while conversing with a reporter during the Spanish-American War. Gibbs was standing just inside his tent when he remarked to Thomas Steep, a correspondent with *Leslie's* magazine, "Well, I don't want to die in this place . . ." Before he could finish his sentence, a bullet struck him in the head, killing him.

- "A Swedish man escaped from a blaze at a hunting cabin in central Sweden but froze to death as he fled, naked, on a snowmobile, a Swedish newspaper reported on Monday." (Reuters)

- "A 22-year-old man sliding down a ski run in California, crashed into a lift tower and died. He was sliding on a makeshift sled of yellow foam. The lift towers are meant to be cushioned by this foam, and the tower he hit was the one from which he had stolen the foam to make his sled." (*Fortean Times*)

CELEBRITY IRONY

- In 1995 singer Michael Jackson wrote to the British ambassador to the United States "to request a British knighthood." When asked what he should be knighted for, representatives of the "King of Pop" replied, "for his work with little children."

- "In the 1974 film *Chinatown*, Faye Dunaway's character famously tells Nicholson, 'She's my sister, she's my daughter . . . ' Just as the film was about to open, Nicholson learned that the woman he thought was his older sister, 16 years his senior, was, in fact, his mother." (*Newsweek*)

- In the mid-1980s, sports fan and former President Richard Nixon was named to arbitrate a salary dispute between baseball owners and umpires. "Baseball needs clean, honest, well-paid umpires," Nixon told reporters.

- In the summer of 2000, English Prime Minister Tony Blair launched a public campaign against rowdy "yob culture" in England, in which he called for tougher laws against people who are drunk and rowdy in public. About three weeks into the campaign Blair's 16-year-old son Euan (who is too young to drink in public bars in England) was picked up by police after he was found "lying drunk and vomiting in a central London square."

- In 1988 Geraldo Rivera threatened to sue a couple who appeared on his show under false pretenses. "I'm very thick-skinned," Rivera told reporters, "but this is different. It affects the credibility of my program."

How did Picasso keep warm in his early days? By burning his paintings.

YOU'RE MY INSPIRATION

More inspirations for famous fictional characters.

CROCODILE DUNDEE. In 1977, Rodney William Ansell was rescued from a remote part of the Australian outback. Against impossible odds, he'd survived on his own for two months after a giant crocodile attacked his boat and left him stranded. Watching him on TV, actor Paul Hogan and cowriters Ken Shadie and John Cornell were inspired to create Mick "Crocodile" Dundee for their 1986 film. Ansell was killed 22 years later in a shootout with police.

MURPHY BROWN. Inspired by Candace Bergen's friend, real-life newscaster Diane Sawyer.

CHARLIE'S ANGELS. The TV series was going to be called "Alley Cats" . . . until costar Kate Jackson suggested "Charlie's Angels." Producer Aaron Spelling asked where she got the idea, and Jackson pointed to a picture of three female angels—right behind him, on the wall of his office. It wasn't even Spelling's picture; he'd inherited the office (and the picture) from Frank Sinatra.

PEPE LE PEW. The Looney Tunes skunk was inspired by smooth talking French actor Charles Boyer, who played a character named Pepe Le Moko in the 1938 film *Algiers*.

POE'S "THE RAVEN." Believe it or not, the immortal poem was inspired by a real raven. The bird was a gift to Charles Dickens in 1840, when he was researching ravens for *Barnaby Rudge*. "In 1841 Edgar Allen Poe, then a literary critic in Philadelphia, savaged Dickens's use of the raven in *Rudge*, saying a raven could be put to far better literary use." That's when he started working on his poem. Meanwhile, Dickens's pet raven died in 1842 and was stuffed. It was passed among collectors until 1971, when it was donated to the Philadelphia Library, "where the raven remains today, locked in a closet, next to a sign: *The Most Famous Bird in the World*." (From *Wild Things*, by Mike Capuzzo)

First American novel to sell more than a million copies: *Uncle Tom's Cabin*.

LUCKY FINDS

*Here's another look at some folks who found really valuable
stuff . . . and got to keep it. We should all be so lucky!*

PICTURE PERFECT

The Find: An ink-and-water color drawing of a dancer
Where It Was Found: In a thrift shop in Fort Myers, Florida
The Story: Jean Comey-Smith, 64, found the picture in 1998 and
bought it for $1.99. She left it in her car for nearly a month.
"What caught my eye was the frame," Comey-Smith says. I flipped
it over and saw the name A. Rodin . . . I thought, 'I know that
name . . .' and remember thinking, 'I couldn't be that lucky. It's
got to be a copy. It's got to be a print.'" Auguste Rodin is the
French artist best known for his 1904 sculpture *"The Thinker."*

Comey-Smith *was* that lucky—Several appraisers turned down
her offer to let them study her find, so she e-mailed the *Oprah
Winfrey Show* after learning they were planning a program called
"Hidden Treasures." They invited her on the show to have the
water watercolor appraised by experts. "I was almost ready to cry
when I found out how much it's worth," Comey-Smith said. The
experts' finding: her $1.99 painting, a genuine Rodin, was worth at
least $14,000.

UNDERGROUND

The Find: Some coins
Where It Was Found: In a cornfield in Somerset, England
The Story: Since childhood, Martin Elliott had enjoyed playing
with metal detectors. He never found more than junk—belt buckles, buttons, etc.—but he never lost enthusiasm for his hobby and
was still going at it years later.

One afternoon in 1999, he paid a visit to his cousin Kevin
Elliott and taught him how to use the metal detector. Kevin started
sweeping across his father's cornfield. He was just trying the detector out and didn't expect to find anything: the field, which was
planted with corn, had been plowed over many times. But about
four minutes later the metal detector sounded an alarm, so Elliott
started digging. About a foot below the surface, he found an old

---

Most popular sport on earth: Soccer—played by 100 million people in over 50 countries.

Roman silver coin. Then he found another one . . . and then another, and another and another, eventually finding so many that he had to run and get some buckets to hold them all. In the end, he found 9,213 silver coins, worth an estimated $400,000—the largest hoard of Roman coins ever uncovered in Britain. Historians estimate that someone buried them in the field in about 230 A.D.

That was only the beginning—further excavations beneath the cornfield revealed "the presence of a major complex of Roman buildings," including an entire villa where the coins were buried, "a previously unknown and important Roman site."

STUCK IN THE MUD

The Find: A boat

Where It Was Found: Buried in the mud of the Sea of Galilee, in Israel

The Story: For years, two fishermen, brothers named Yuval and Moshe Lufan, had dreamed of finding the remains of an ancient boat in the Sea of Galilee. But such boats, if there were any, would have been buried in the mud at the bottom of the sea and impossible to find. Then, in the 1980s, a severe drought struck Israel, and the water level in the Sea of Galilee dropped considerably. Much of the sea-floor that ordinarily would have been under water was temporarily exposed. So Yuval and Moshe spent the summer of 1986 combing the shore, looking for the oval outline of a boat . . . And amazingly, they actually found one. It appeared to be very old and, what's more, it was in very good condition.

The boat turned out to be even older than anyone imagined—carbon dating showed that it was built in the time of Christ, about 2000 years ago. How'd it last that long without rotting away? Apparently the mud had acted as a preservative, keeping out corrosive elements in the air that would have caused the boat to disintegrate. It is the oldest example of its type ever found . . . and a true archaeological treasure.

* * *

REEL QUOTE

"He has every characteristic of a dog except loyalty."
—**Henry Fonda,** *The Best Man*

It takes Pluto 25 years to receive as much solar energy as the Earth receives in one minute.

WHO SMELT THE IRON?

We all make dumb comments now and then, which we hope nobody notices . . . or that if they do, they're not writing them down. The people who made these bloopers weren't so lucky. Believe it or not, these are real.

KIDS' FAKE EXCUSES FOR SCHOOL ABSENCE

"Please excuse Mary for being absent. She was sick and I had her shot."

"Please excuse Ray Friday from school. He has very loose vowels."

"Please excuse Jimmy for being. It's his father's fault."

"Please excuse Harriet for missing school yesterday. We forgot to get the Sunday paper off the porch, and when we found it on Monday, we thought it was Sunday."

DOCTORS' MEDICAL REPORTS

"Patient was tearful and crying constantly. She also appears depressed."

"Patient has left his white blood cells at another hospital."

"When she fainted, her eyes rolled around the room."

"Discharge status: Alive but without permission."

COMMENTS FROM VISITORS TO U.S. NATIONAL PARKS

"We had no trouble finding the park entrances, but where are the exits?"

"The coyotes made too much noise last night and kept me awake. Please eradicate those annoying animals."

"Too many rocks in the mountains."

"Where does Bigfoot live?"

STUDENT SCHOOLWORK

"The inhabitants of Moscow are called Mosquitoes."

"A census taker is a man who goes from house to house increasing the population."

"Most of the houses in France are made of plaster of Paris."

"Iron was discovered because someone smelt it."

"The four seasons are salt, pepper, mustard, and vinegar."

QUESTIONS FOR CANADIAN FOREST RANGERS

"Where does Alberta end and Canada begin?"

"Can you help me? My husband's driving me crazy and he won't shut up."

"Do you have a glacier at this visitor center?"

"Is this a map I'm looking at?"

"Don't all Canadians wear raccoon hats? Where can I buy one?"

He wasn't blind, but Thomas Edison preferred reading in Braille.

MOVIE BOMB:
CUTTHROAT ISLAND

*Some films don't set out to be disaster films, but they still
end up that way. Take this one, for example—it's
the most expensive flop in Hollywood history.*

CUTTHROAT CASTING

Fresh from his success directing *Cliffhanger* and *Die Hard 2*, Finnish director Renny Harlin was searching for a script that would help his future wife, actress Geena Davis, make the leap from light comedies into big-money action films. Harlin found his script in *Cutthroat Island*, an *Indiana Jones*-type epic about a pirate's daughter who searches for her murdered father's treasure. But Harlin worried that Davis didn't have enough star power to attract the large audiences needed to justify the cost of a big-budget action film. So he began looking for a male star to complement her. He picked Michael Douglas, who agreed to do the film on two conditions: 1) It had to start filming immediately, because he was only available for a short period of time; and 2) His part had to be rewritten to give his character the same amount of "screen time" as Davis.

THE FIRST SIGN OF DISASTER

Harlin agreed, hired "script doctor" Susan Shaliday, and began building sets. He decided to film it in Thailand and on the Mediterranean island of Malta—two beautiful locations, but more than 5,000 miles apart . . . adding greatly to the expense and complexity of completing the picture. The film's budget was set at $65 million, making it one of Carolco Picture's most expensive films to date.

Several rewrites later, Geena Davis' role was actually expanding at the expense of Douglas . . . so Douglas dropped out. "We spent money like crazy, and the script was being rewritten like crazy," one executive recalls. "But it was becoming Renny's film for Geena. Michael got upset when he realized what was happening. I don't fault him; it was an impossible situation."

Now that Douglas was out, Geena Davis wanted out too. "Let's be serious," one production executive says, "Everyone wanted off

---

F. Scott Fitzgerald died on February 12, 1942 . . . the same day Frank Zappa was born.

this picture when Michael Douglas left." But Davis was contractu-ally obligated to finish the film whether Douglas was in it or not. So she stayed.

Harlin, left with expensive, half-built sets in two foreign coun-tries, and no male lead, began working his way down the roster of Hollywood's "A-list" stars, trying to find someone—anyone—will-ing to take the part. Nobody would—Liam Neeson turned down the role; so did Ralph Fiennes, Keanu Reeves, and every other major star. So Harlin pulled out the "B-list" and began looking for second-tier actors to fill the part.

At this point in the film, Harlin should have been supervising the construction of the sets, the rewriting of the scripts, and other details. But he was so occupied by his mad scramble to find a male star that the work went forward without him. By the time he cast actor Matthew Modine for the part, much of the work was done.

ONE DISASTER AFTER ANOTHER

Unfortunately, it wasn't to Harlin's liking. He decided that the shooting script was "totally unshootable," and the enormously expensive sets all had to be redone. And that was only the begin-ning: one of the directors of photography broke his leg falling off a crane, some broken pipes caused raw sewage to pour into the water tank where the actors were supposed to swim, and when Harlin fired the chief camera operator following a dispute, more than two dozen crew members quit with him.

By the time *Cutthroat Island* limped into theaters its cost had mushroomed from $65 million to more than $115 million. Even worse: the critics hated it. "This film is too stupidly smutty for children," a *New York Times* film critic wrote, "and two cartoonish for sane adults." Ticket sales were disappointing even for a movie that everyone knew was bad and that no one wanted to make. Pulled from theaters after only a few weeks, *Cutthroat Island* made only $10 million at the box office, bringing the total loss to more than $105 million. Not only was it the most expensive film ever made at the time, but also the most expensive flop in Hollywood history. But the studio responsible for this bomb, Carolco Pictures, wasn't around to see it: in the hole to the tune of $47 million, Carolco filed for bankruptcy six weeks before *Cutthroat Island* reached theaters.

Who has appeared on the most covers of *People* magazine? Princess Diana—53 times.

LITTLE THINGS MEAN A LOT

"The devil's in the details," says an old proverb. And in the profits, too. The littlest thing can cost big bucks. Here are a few examples from our files.

A PAINT SCRAPER

The Story: In September 1978, a sailor accidentally dropped a 75¢ paint scraper into the torpedo launcher of the nuclear sub, U.S.S. *Swordfish*. The sub was forced to scrap its mission so repairs could be performed in drydock. Cost to U.S. taxpayers: $171,000.

A DECIMAL POINT

The Story: In 1999, Lockheed Martin signed a contract to sell military aircraft to "an international customer." (The company won't say who.) Unfortunately, whoever drew up the contract misplaced a decimal point in the formula for determining the price. The mistake wasn't discovered until after the contract was signed, and the customer insisted on sticking to the wording of the contract exactly. Cost to Lockheed Martin: $70 million.

THE WORD "PLEASE"

The Story: In 1995 Pacific Bell Telephone told its 4,500 directory assistance operators to answer calls with either: "Hi, this is ——, what city?" or "Hi, I'm ——, what city?" According to Pac Bell, these new greetings take 1.2 seconds to say, compared to 1.7 seconds when "please" is used. The phone company calculated that shaving half a second off of each call makes it possible for operators to handle 135,000 more calls per hour.

A FEW WASHERS

The Story: The $1.6 billion Hubble Space telescope was launched into orbit on April 24 1990, and immediately needed repairs. Cost of the rescue mission: $86 million. Cause of the problem: a few 25¢ washers that technicians used to fill in a gap in an optical testing device. No one noticed they were there . . . until they shook loose.

Each cell in your body has more molecules than there are stars in the entire Milky Way galaxy.

MORE STRANGE LAWSUITS

Here are more real-life examples of unusual legal battles.

THE PLAINTIFF: Lorenzo Grier
THE DEFENDANT: The United States of America
THE LAWSUIT: In 1995, Grier sued the government for fraud, breach of contract, and discrimination. The basis for his suit? "Appellant alleged that former President Ronald Reagan did not respond when Appellant invented the multiplication tables and sent them to the White House, but instead stole Appellant's invention and implemented it in the public schools." Grier asked for $900 billion in damages.
THE VERDICT: Case dismissed

THE PLAINTIFF: Edna Hobbs
THE DEFENDANT: The Joseph Company, makers of The Clapper (a device that activates appliances when someone claps)
THE LAWSUIT: Hobbs filed suit because she had to clap so hard, she injured her hands trying to get the appliances to go on. In fact, she was in so much pain, she said, "I couldn't peel potatoes," adding "I never ate so many baked potatoes in my life."
THE VERDICT: Case dismissed. The judge ruled that Hobbs "had merely failed to adjust the sensitivity controls."

THE PLAINTIFF: The parents of Daniel Dukes, "a 27-year-old drifter with a criminal record"
THE DEFENDANT: Sea World in Orlando, Florida
THE LAWSUIT: When Dukes' body was found in the park in 1999, he was wearing only underwear and was draped on the back of a killer whale. Cause of death: drowning. His parents sued for millions, claiming Dukes had been *pulled* into the water (though that wouldn't explain how his clothes were removed). Plus, they insisted the park should have posted a sign warning that a killer whale can kill. The *San Antonio Express-News* commented, "If his

parents couldn't teach Dukes the dangers of playing with a five-ton whale, Sea World cannot be expected to do much better."
THE VERDICT: Unknown

THE PLAINTIFF: Larry W. Bryant
THE DEFENDANT: Governor James Gilmore of Virginia
THE LAWSUIT: In June 2000, Bryant filed suit to get Gilmore to call a grand jury to look into alien abductions and to make sure the National Guard knew how to deal with alien attacks. Bryant was quoted as saying he was especially concerned about some "dark, silently floating triangles," which Gilmore had done nothing about.
THE VERDICT: Case dismissed

THE PLAINTIFF: The mother of a newborn girl in an unnamed Tennessee hospital
THE DEFENDANT: The hospital
THE LAWSUIT: About 12 hours before the woman went into labor, she was injected with blue dye as part of a test for a urinary tract infection. Result: when the baby was born, it was dyed blue (only temporarily). Amused hospital workers referred to the baby as "Smurfette." The not-so-amused mother sued the hospital for $4 million, saying their "callous remarks" about "Smurfette" caused "permanent emotional damage, humiliation, and ridicule."
THE VERDICT: Unknown

THE PLAINTIFF: S, a California lawyer
THE DEFENDANT: R, his next-door neighbor—also a lawyer
THE LAWSUIT: In 1991, R asked S, whose family was playing basketball, to quiet down. S refused . . . so R sprayed the family and their basketball court with a hose. S sued, claiming emotional distress. Then R countersued, saying S had reduced the value of his home. And to prove it, he introduced "scientific testimony from acoustical engineers, architects, and real-estate appraisers."
THE VERDICT: At first the court restricted S to six hours of basketball a day . . . But an appeals court ruled that R should just close his window.

Nearly everyone's right lung is a little bigger than their left lung.

VLAD THE IMPALER: THE REAL DRACULA

On page 490, we told you about Bram Stoker's book,
Dracula. Here's a short history of the man
who inspired it, Vlad the Impaler.

SEEING IS BELIEVING

In 1431, Holy Roman Emperor Sigismund invited Prince Vlad II of Wallachia (part of modern-day Romania) to join the Order of the Dragon, a religious order of knights sworn to defend Christendom from the Muslim Turks. The Prince traveled to Nuremburg to accept the honor, and returned carrying a large flag with the image of a dragon on it.

"It seems probable," Raymond McNally and Radu Florescu write in *In Search of Dracula,* "that when the simple, superstitious peasants saw Vlad bearing the standard with the dragon symbol, they interpreted it as a sign that he was now in league with the devil." Prince Vlad soon became known as Vlad Dracul—Vlad the "dragon" or, since dragons and devils were synonymous in 15th-century Romania, Vlad the Devil. Prince Vlad's son, who was also named Vlad, was nicknamed Dracula, "son of the devil."

The nicknames weren't too far from the truth: both Vlads were bloodthirsty tyrants.

YOUNG TURKS

Born sometime between 1428 and 1431, Dracula had a fairly uneventful childhood. Then in 1442—when Dracula was a teenager—Sultan Murad II of the Turks, suspecting the loyalty of Vlad Dracul, imprisoned his family. Dracul managed to talk his way out of prison, but his sons, Dracula and Radu, were forced to remain hostages as a further "guarantee." There they were educated by some of the finest tutors of the Ottoman Empire and learned to speak Turkish with near-perfect fluency. At the same time, McNally and Florescu write, Dracula "developed a reputation for trickery, cunning, insubordination, and brutality, and inspired fright in his own guards."

Most popular hard liquor in Scotland: Vodka.

IN AND OUT OF POWER

In 1447, Vlad Dracul was assassinated on the orders of the Prince of nearby Transylvania. Dracula, still a hostage of the Sultan, managed to escape the following year and was installed as the new Prince of Wallachia. He was overthrown two months later and didn't reclaim the throne until 1456.

It was during this second reign that Dracula earned his legendary reputation for cruelty. In fact, for centuries Vlad Dracula was better known as Vlad Tepes—"The Impaler"—for his method of torturing and executing thousands of his enemies and even his own countrymen—by impaling them on wooden poles.

Dracula was a certifiable psycho. He enjoyed watching people suffer and made sure an impalement took several hours—sometimes even days. There were even various forms of impalement depending upon age, rank, or sex.

Yet amazingly, in spite of his legendary cruelty, Dracula is thought of as a hero in Romanian history because he used the terror of his reign to maintain public order and defend the country against foreign invasion. "On one atrocious occasion," David Skal writes in *V is for Vampire*, "20,000 Turkish captives were exterminated in this manner (impaling) and displayed in a mile long semicircle outside Dracula's capital city, Tirgoviste, to ward off oncoming enemy troops. It worked."

THE END . . . AND A NEW BEGINNING

After years of successfully waging war against the Turks, the tide turned in 1462 and Dracula was on the verge of defeat. Desperate, he turned to Matthias Corvinus, the King of Hungary. But rather than help Dracula as he had earlier promised, Corvinus had Dracula arrested and thrown into prison. He languished there for another nine years.

No longer able to torture people, Dracula turned his attention to insects and animals. "Dracula," McNally and Florescu write, "could not cure himself of the evil habit of catching mice and having birds bought at the marketplace so that he could 'punish them' by impalement."

Dracula was finally freed in 1475 when a powerful cousin interceded on his behalf. By November of 1476, Dracula was back on the throne in Wallachia. But this reign was even shorter the second time around. In late December or early January, Dracula died in battle fighting a rival for the Wallachian throne, and his head was sent to the Sultan. According to legend, monks from a nearby monastery found Dracula's body and buried it—without the head—somewhere in their church. The church still stands today, but Dracula's grave has never been found.

TALES OF VLAD THE IMPALER

Dracula's barbarism was extreme even by medieval standards, and tales of his crimes made him a legendary figure across much of Europe within his own lifetime. "His cruelties," McNally and Florescu write, "were committed on such a massive scale that his evil reputation reached beyond the grave to the firesides where generations of grandmothers warned little children, 'Be good, or Dracula will get you!'"

Turn to page 609 for more on Dracula.

* * *

LIFE AFTER DEATH

Deceased: Max Hoffman, a five-year-old boy living in the United States in the 1860s.

News Of His Death: In 1865 a cholera epidemic swept the town where Hoffman lived; he became infected and as far as anyone could tell, died. Soon afterward, he was given a proper funeral and was buried.

Resurrection: For two nights after his funeral, his mother had such incredibly vivid nightmares of him still being alive that she insisted that he dig up the coffin. Perhaps just to ease his wife's fears, Mr. Hoffman did just that, and when he pried open the coffin saw signs of life and was able to revive his son. Five-year-old Max made a full recovery, lived to the age of 90, and kept the handles from the coffin as a keepsake for the rest of his life.

How many stars in the Seven Sisters (also called the Pleiades)? About 250.

SOAP OPERA BLOOPERS

Soaps are relentlessly dire and serious, so soap lovers really treasure those moments when their soap stars blow it and show they're human. Here are a few classic moments.

When soap operas first appeared on TV, there were no videotapes and no teleprompters. All soap operas were broadcast live. Anything could—and did—happen.

- Radio actor Ralph Locke, trying to make the transition to early TV soaps as part of *One Man's Family*, froze on his lines, simply announced he had no more to say, and walked off the set. The scene was taking place on an airplane, so the viewer was left to imagine him falling to his death.

- Apparently, the thought of being seen by an audience thousands of times larger than the biggest theater was just too much for many early TV dramatists. Actor John Raby tells the story of an actress in *A Woman to Remember* who panicked on live TV and tried to run off the set. He grabbed her, pushed her into a chair, and spoke his lines, as well as hers.

- On *Last Year's Nest*, Leonard Valenta was in a love scene with a woman when part of the set fell on her. She did the rest of the scene holding it up.

- Haila Stoddard, playing Pauline on *The Secret Storm* was supposed to say to her mother, "I always thought she was a bit of a witch." Instead, there on live TV, in front of millions, she said, "whit of a bitch." Her astounded mom, instead of going on with her regular lines, responded, "Oh dear, Pauline, you didn't mean to say that!" It took the actors 10 minutes to get back to the script.

- On *Search for Tomorrow*, Jerry Lanning, playing hit man Nick D'Antoni, choked Liza Walton (Sherry Mathis) so hard, she turned blue. They were married in real life a week later.

- On *One Life to Live*, Max Holden (Nicholas Walker) and Gabrielle Medina (Fiona Hutchinson) were supposed to do a

Belgium is about the same size as New Jersey.

candle-lit love scene, then, symbolic of their passion, the place was to go up in flames. The candles set Walker's hair on fire.

- On *The Edge of Night*, John Larkin (Mike Carr) leapt through the door, did a few pirouettes and barked, "Hello, all you folks out there in TV land." Fellow cast members were not laughing, they knew it was live TV. He thought it was a dress rehearsal.

- "I'd like you to make (instead of meet) Anne," said Eileen Fulton as she introduced Anne to a man on *As the World Turns*.

- On *Concerning Miss Marlowe* the prop telephone wasn't a prop. It rang. It wasn't in the script, so thinking fast, actress Val Dufour answered it, said, "It's for you," handed it to a French maid in the scene and walked off. Frantic, the maid faked a scene talking on the phone.

- On *First Love*, it was supposed to be a "Friday cliffhanger." The actress was supposed to say "Chris cracked up his plane." The pilot's wife and another woman were supposed to react with shock and horror, and the audience was supposed to tune in on Monday. But she flubbed it, saying "Chris crapped (pause—horrified tiny voice) up his plane." The show closed on the women screaming with laughter.

- An actor on *The Edge of Night* repeatedly rehearsed a phone conversation by speaking into his hand. He got so used to it that, when the phone rang on live TV, he did his lines into his hand. Part way through, he saw himself on a monitor, talking into his hand like an idiot, but decided there was nothing he could do.

- The toupee of Dean Santoro (Paul Stewart) on *The Edge of Night* fell off during a live scene. What else could he do! He put it back on.

- Nearsighted Ed Zimmerman, playing a surgeon on *The Guiding Light*, had to remember oodles of medical terms for an operation. They became a jumble in his mind, but he knew, if he had to, he could save himself by reading the teleprompter. Suddenly, his contact lens fell out into the patient's "wound." Rattled, he started barking random orders to the nurse. By then, they had departed from the script, and Ed found the teleprompter man running the script backwards, trying to find their place. Doctor Ed forgot to sew up the incision. He sewed up his glove instead.

Mongolia is the only country on earth where horses outnumber people.

WE PANIC IN A PEW

*We always like to include a few clever but simple
palindromes. They're fun and impressive—after all,
it takes a special skill to see when something can be spelled the
same forward and backward. But they seem to be getting
weirder and more complex. Here are some new ones.*

May a moody baby doom a yam?

Do geese see God?

Never odd or even.

Satan, oscillate my metallic sonatas!

Al lets Della call Ed Stella.

Straw? No, too stupid a fad;
I put soot on warts.

Anne, I vote more cars race Rome to Vienna.

Some men interpret nine memos.

Dennis sinned.

No, it never propagates if I set a gap or prevention.

God saw I was dog.

Too bad—I hid a boot.

Campus motto:
Bottoms up, Mac.

'Tis in a DeSoto sedan I sit.

No trace; not one carton.

Oozy rat in a sanitary zoo.

Was it Eliot's toilet I saw?

Lisa Bonet ate no basil.

A relic, Odin! I'm a mini, docile Ra!

"Do nine men interpret?"
"Nine men," I nod.

He did, eh?

Is Don Adams mad?
(A nod.) Si!

Eva, can I stab bats in a cave?

Live not on evil, madam, live not on evil.

No sir! Away! A papaya war is on.

Dogma: I am God.

Oh, no—Don Ho!

So many dynamos.

Are we not drawn onward, we few, drawn onward to new era?

To: Dr., et al. / Re: Grub / Ma had a hamburger / Later, Dot.

We panic in a pew.

Norma is as selfless as I am, Ron.

Sun at noon, tan us.

Lapses? Order red roses, pal.

Motor vehicle with the best safety record in Europe? The moped.

NUDES & PRUDES

It's hard to shock anyone with nudity today. But stupidity is always a shock. These characters demonstrate that whether you're dressed or naked, you can still be dumber than sin.

NUDE . . . "Bernard Defrance, a high school teacher near Paris, told his students that each time they stumped him with a riddle, he'd shed a piece of clothing—starting with his trademark bow tie. As it turns out, the kids were too smart for him. During one round of the game in November, the 51-year-old Defrance was left standing naked before his class. He was later suspended."

PRUDES . . . "In 1934, eight men were fined $1 apiece for bathing 'topless' at Coney Island. 'All of you fellows may be Adonises,' said the presiding magistrate, 'but there are many people who object to seeing so much of the human body exposed.' A year later, a mass arrest of 42 topless males in Atlantic City, New Jersey, fattened the municipal coffers by $84. The city fathers declared: 'We'll have no gorillas on our beaches.'"

NUDE . . . "A 41-year-old Allentown man known to police as 'The Naked Bandit' pleaded guilty to robbing a string of convenience stores while in the nude, authorities said on Thursday. 'His logic was that the last time he did some robberies, he had clothes on and was identified by his clothes,' said Lehigh County District Attorney James Anthony." (Reuters)

PRUDES . . . "Matt Zelen dived into the pool to start the 100-yard butterfly, then remembered something: he'd forgotten to tie his racing suit. When the St. John's University junior felt his suit sliding off, he decided to kick it off and finish the race. Zelen, a contender for the 2000 Olympics, would have won the race by more than two seconds but he was stripped of more than just his suit—he was disqualified for violating a uniform code." (*Parade* magazine)

NUDE . . . "Police in Vinton, Louisiana, were bemused when a Pontiac Grand Am hit a tree and disgorged 20 nude occupants. It

---

Take a million cloud droplets and squish them together. What do you get? A raindrop.

turned out that they were the Rodriguez family, Pentecostalists from Floydada, Texas. Police Chief Douillard commented, 'They were completely nude. All 20 of them. Didn't have a stitch of clothes on. I mean, no socks, no underwear, no nothin.' Five of them were in the trunk. The Lord told them to get rid of all their belongings and go to Louisiana."

PRUDE . . . "The Mayor of North Platte, Nebraska, kept his promise to walk naked down the street. Mayor Jim Whitaker said he'd walk 'naked' if the Paws-itive Partners Humane Society raised $5,000. When his plan drew national attention—and angry calls—Whitaker revealed that he actually planned to walk a dog named 'Naked' instead of walking in the buff himself."

NUDE . . . "A bare-breasted mermaid perched on a rock is causing a stir along Lyse Fjord in Norway. 'One man jumped off a boat and swam over to me,' Line Oexnevad, 37, said of her job as a siren. 'Most people just look and cheer.' Ms. Oexnevad, naked except for a blonde wig and a fish-tail, was hired as a tourist attraction."

PRUDES . . . "At the turn of the century (1900, that is), Boston, Massachusetts, refused to accept shipments of navel oranges from Los Angeles, terming the fruit's name 'indelicate and immodest.'" ("Only in L.A.," the *Los Angeles Times*)

NUDE . . . "Police arriving at the scene of a two-car collision in Los Angeles found a totally nude woman behind the wheel of one car. The 35-year-old L.A. resident reportedly told police that when she began her drive, she thought she was a camel in Morocco, and when she saw the palm trees lining the downtown streets, she was sure of it . . ." (*Bizarre* magazine)

PRUDE . . . "Animal control workers in California recently received a call from a woman who insisted she needed to get a marriage license for a male and a female cat 'before they breed.'" ("Only in L.A.," the *Los Angeles Times*)

A newborn kangaroo could fit in the palm of your hand.

NIETZSCHE KNOWS

Here are some thoughts from the great 19th-century
philosopher Friedrich Nietzsche (1844–1900).

"Insanity in individuals is something rare, but in groups, parties, nations, and epochs it is the rule."

"Love is a state in which a man sees things most decidedly as they are not."

"What does not destroy me, makes me strong."

"He who denies his own vanity usually possesses it in so brutal a form that he instinctively shuts his eyes to avoid the necessity of despising himself."

"Wishing is a symptom of recovery."

"After a quarrel between a man and a woman, the man suffers chiefly from the thought that he has wounded the woman; the woman suffers from the thought that she has not wounded the man enough."

"Perhaps I know why it is man alone who laughs; he alone suffers so deeply that he had to invent laughter."

"The surest way to corrupt a youth is to instruct him to hold in higher esteem those who think alike than those who think differently."

"No one lies so boldly as the man who is indignant."

"The author must keep his mouth shut when his work starts to speak."

"He who fights with monsters might take care lest he thereby become a monster. And if you gaze for long into an abyss, the abyss gazes also into you."

"How did reason come into the world? As is fitting, in an irrational manner, by accident. One will have to guess at it as at a riddle."

"There are no eternal facts, as there are no absolute truths."

"Morality is the best of all devices for leading mankind by the nose."

"My time has not yet come; some are born posthumously."

Eat one lump of sugar, and you've eaten the equivalent of three feet of sugar cane.

ANOTHER POLITICALLY CORRECT QUIZ

As we've always contended, "political correctness" isn't as bad as it's made out to be—after all, there's nothing wrong with becoming more sensitive to people's feelings. On the other hand, people can get pretty outrageous with their ideas of what's "appropriate." Here are eight real-life examples of politically correct—or "incorrect" behavior. How sensitive are you? Can you spot the "correct" one? (Answers on page 750.)

1. In 1994 cellist Anne Conrad-Antoville resigned from the Eureka Symphony Orchestra rather than perform *Peter and the Wolf*. Why?
   a) "The story encourages cruelty to wolves."
   b) "The suggestive overtones of the name 'Peter' should be obvious to everyone."
   c) She wanted the part of Peter to be played by a girl, to show that females are "just as self-sufficient and strong as males."

2. New York Parks department officials became alarmed when they saw a picture of *Man & His Dog*, a life-size bronze statue scheduled to be unveiled in a public park the following month. Why?
   a) The dog was not on a leash.
   b) His hind leg was lifted.
   c) The man "did not appear to be wearing anything beneath his trench coat."

3. In 2000 a British state employment center removed words from its job ads. Which words . . . and why?
   a) "Sober" and "nice smile." It didn't want to be seen as discriminating against substance abusers and people with bad teeth.
   b) "Hard-working" and "energetic." It didn't want to be seen as discriminating against folks who aren't hard-working and energetic.

c) "Clean" and "pleasant." It didn't want to discriminate against people with poor hygiene.

4. In 1995 the board of Walworth County, Wisconsin, changed the language of an antibigotry resolution. In the new language, the Ku Klux Klan was referred to as what?
   a) "White-race enthusiasts" instead of "racists."
   b) An "unhappy group" instead of a "hate group."
   c) "Diversity challenged" instead of "bigoted."

5. In 1995 the Oxford University Press published *The New Testament and Psalms: An Inclusive Version*. How was it different from other versions?
   a) All of the characters in the Bible and Psalms are described as "people of color" because they probably were.
   b) All pets and livestock are referred to as "companion animals," so as not to offend animal rights activists.
   c) All references to the right hand of God are omitted "so as not to offend the left-handed."

6. In the 1960s, the *Pittsburgh Press* refused to include what phrase in its obituaries?
   a) "Died in his / her sleep."
   b) "Please omit flowers."
   c) "Next of kin."

7. Joseph Paul Franklin, who murdered more than a dozen people, objected on principle to the way he was characterized in the media. Which specific phrase did he object to?
   a) "Serial Killer"
   b) "Cold-blooded"
   c) "Sociopath"

8. To avoid offending people, the city council of Longmont, Colorado, voted to change the wording of a street sign. Which one?
   a) "Dead End" ("too macabre") was changed to "No Outlet."
   b) "Stop" ("too rude") changed to "Please Stop . . . Thank You!"
   c) "No Right Turn" and "No Left Turn" ("too political") were changed to "No Turn."

Q. How many times does the word "girl" appear in the Bible? A. Once.

THE HISTORY OF THE IQ TEST, PART III

If you're really intelligent, you've already read Part II
on page 520. Here's the darkest, ugliest part of the story.
It may seem unbelievable . . . but its all true, folks.

SPOILS OF WAR

Not long after the United States entered World War I in 1917, Robert Yerkes, the president of the American Psychological Association (and like many others in the history of the IQ test, a believer in eugenics) proposed that psychologists could contribute to the war effort by administering IQ tests to military draftees. The military approved the plan. Lewis Terman and other eminent psychologists set to work creating a standardized test they called "Alpha," which was then administered to the troops.

"The tests appear to have had little practical effect on the outcome of the war," Leon J. Kamin writes in *The Politics of IQ*. "They were not, in fact, much used for the placement of men. The testing program, however, generated enormous amounts of data, since some two million men were given standardized IQ tests."

There was enough raw data to keep statisticians busy crunching numbers in every conceivable combination for years to come.

BRIGHAM DUMB

One of the number crunchers was a Princeton University professor named Carl Brigham. For some reason, he was completely focused on immigrants. In 1923, he published a book entitled *A Study of American Intelligence*, in which he analyzed the IQs of immigrants who'd been drafted during World War I. Brigham concluded, among other things, that immigrants who'd lived in the United States for 20 years or more tested just as intelligent as native-born Americans, but that immigrants who'd lived in the United States for five years or less scored poorly on IQ tests and were "essentially feeble-minded."

As Brigham saw it, intelligence was directly related to how long the immigrants had lived in the country. Immigrants who'd been in

---

Most popular name for a goldfish in Great Britain: Jaws.

the country for 10 years tested more intelligent than immigrants who'd been in the country for 5 years, but less intelligent than immigrants who'd been in the country for 15 years.

573Brigham used this information to conclude that newer arrivals to the United States were simply dumber. "We are forced to . . . accept the hypothesis," he wrote, "that the curve indicates a gradual deterioration in the class of immigrants examined in the army, who came to this country in each succeeding five-year period since 1902."

ANOTHER LOOK

That was one interpretation of the Alpha Test results. But the fact that the 573test was peppered with multiple-choice questions such as

> The Brooklyn Nationals are called the (1) Giants, (2) Orioles, (3) Superbas, (4) Indians

and

> Revolvers are made by (1) Swift & Co., (2) Smith & Wesson, (3) W. L. Douglas, (4) B. T. Babbit

. . . wouldn't it also be possible to conclude that the test was heavily biased in favor of people who (1) could read English and (2) had lived in the country long enough to know the names of American baseball teams and handgun manufacturers? Was it possible that, instead of measuring innate human intelligence, the test was actually measuring literacy and familiarity with American mainstream culture?

Brigham rejected this possibility—he insisted that failure to answer the questions correctly was direct proof of an inferior IQ. He urged his colleagues to reject "feeble hypotheses that would make these differences [in intelligence] an artifact of the method of examining."

So why were newly arrived immigrants less intelligent than the ones who had been here a while? Brigham had an explanation for this—something he called the "race hypothesis": whereas, before 1890, the bulk of immigrants to the United States had come from England, Germany, and other "Nordic" countries, in recent years immigration patterns had shifted. The huge waves of immigrants from southern and eastern European countries, such as Italy and

Dolly Parton has an insurance policy for her chest.

Russia, had come to be known in academic circles as the "New Immigration."

The Italians, Slavs, and Eastern European Jews who made up the New Immigration, Brigham concluded, must be innately less intelligent than the Dutch, English, and German immigrants who had preceded them. "Our test results," he wrote, "indicate a genuine intellectual superiority of the Nordic group."

AS IF THAT WEREN'T ENOUGH

Brigham also pointed out that, like southern and eastern Europeans, American blacks scored lower on IQ tests than American whites did. Once again, he dismissed the possibility that racism, segregation, lack of equal access to education, or the fact that slavery had ended barely 60 years earlier might have played a role in the low test scores. No—he was convinced that the IQ test proved that blacks were intellectually inferior to whites and warned of what this meant for the future of the United States:

> We must face a possibility of racial admixture here that is infinitely worse than that faced by any European country today, for we are incorporating the Negro into our racial stock, while all of Europe is comparatively free from this taint . . . The decline of American intelligence will be more rapid than the decline of the intelligence of European national groups, owing to the presence here of the Negro.

THE IMMIGRANTS ARE COMING!

Brigham urged the government to take defensive action. But the idea of controlling who was allowed to immigrate to the United States was a relatively new concept. For most of the country's history, there were no federal laws regulating immigration. The first was in 1875, when three "classes" of people—"coolies," convicts, and prostitutes—were denied entry for the first time. Everyone else was admitted.

Then, in 1921, Congress passed a special law establishing "national origin quotas" for each foreign country. The law restricted each nationality to three precent of the number of nationals already living in the United States, with census figures from 1910 used to set the quota for each individual country. If 1 million immigrants from France were counted in the 1910 census, for example, French immigration would be capped at 30,000 people per year. But that law was supposed to be a temporary measure.

THE GOOD OLD DAYS

That was before Brigham and a number of like-minded psychologists brought their "scientific" findings to the U.S. Congress. In 1924, a new bill called the Johnson-Lodge Immigration Act was passed into law.

The act made two major changes in U.S. Immigration policy: it cut the quota for each country from three percent to two percent. And rather than use U.S. population figures from the just-completed 1920 census or even stick with the numbers from the 1910 census, the new law required that national quotas be calculated using numbers taken from the 1890 census. Why? According to Leon J. Kamin in Leon *The Politics of IQ*:

> The use of the 1890 census had only one purpose, acknowledged by the bill's supporters. The 'New Immigration' had begun after 1890, and the law was designed to exclude the biologically inferior peoples of southeastern Europe. The new law made the country safe for Professor Brigham's Nordics . . . [But] the law, for which the science of mental testing may claim substantial credit, also resulted in the deaths of literally hundreds of thousands of victims of the Nazi biological theorists. The victims were denied admission to the United States because the "German quota" was filled.

BACK TO SCHOOL

In the mid-1920s, colleges and universities began to hire Brigham and other IQ experts to administer intelligence tests to college applicants. But because college applicants were, on average, better educated than World War I draftees, their scores were so high that they tested off the Alpha test's charts. So Brigham rewrote the questions to make them harder . . . and while he was at it, he renamed the test. From now on, it would be known as the Scholastic Aptitude Test, or SAT for short.

NOW HOLD ON A MINUTE

The very first SAT was administered for Princeton University, on June 23, 1926, to 8,040 high school students around the country. Soon afterward, the Army decided to use the SAT to test appli-

At its peak, a growing blue whale gains between 200 and 300 pounds a day.

cants at West Point, and in 1930, it was used at the U.S. Naval Academy for the first time. From there, it spread to Harvard, Yale, and then to other colleges in the Ivy League. By the mid-1930s, the SAT was well on its way to becoming a major factor in American college life.

There was one problem—Brigham had begun to question everything he believed about the "science" of intelligence testing.

"At the same time he was promoting the SAT to universities," Nicholas Lehman writes in *The Big Test*, "Brigham was undergoing a momentous intellectual change. He had come to the view that the central tenet held by IQ testers—that the test measured a biologically grounded, genetically inherited quality that was tied to ethnicity—was false."

Well, looks like we're not making IQ tests part of the BRI entrance requirements anymore. So it's okay to turn to page 678 for Part IV.

* * *

ACCORDING TO THE LATEST RESEARCH . . . SUNLIGHT MAKES YOU A BETTER STUDENT

Researchers: An energy consulting firm in Orange County, California

Who They Studied: 21,000 students in California, Colorado, and Washington state.

What They Learned: Kids do better in school when they work in natural light than when they work in artificial light. Specifically, "elementary students in classrooms with more natural illumination scored up to 26 percent higher on standardized tests in reading and up to 20 percent higher in math."

"No one knows for sure why sunlight has such a strong tie to student achievement, but the study's authors have some theories," the *Los Angeles Times* reported. "They believe that the light is a mood lifter for students and teachers alike. Sunlight might also boost overall health, and may make it easier for students to see their books and blackboards."

India has 153,000 post offices, the most of any country on earth.

BOOP-OOP-A-DOOP!

If you're a cartoon fan but have never seen the original Betty Boop cartoons of the late 1920s and early 1930s, do yourself a favor next time you rent a movie: rent some Betty Boop cartoons, too. Here's a look at the origins of one of the earliest and most controversial cartoon "superstars." Boop-oop-a-doop!

BOUNCING ALONG

It was 1928. Grim Natwick had just landed a job at Fleischer Studios, an animation company famous for its "follow-the-bouncing-ball" sing-along cartoons. Founders Max and Dave Fleischer were hard at work trying to find a cartoon character to compete with Mickey Mouse, who had made his screen debut that year in *Steamboat Willie*. The brothers' first attempt, *Bimbo the Dog*, wasn't nearly as popular as Disney's mouse. They knew something was missing.

What if they gave him a girlfriend?

FIRST BOOP

As Natwick would recall years later, Dave Fleischer had an idea:

> One morning [he] came over to my desk and handed me the music to the [popular] song "Boop-Oop-A-Doop," by Helen Kane, and asked me to design a girl character to go with it. At that point, the only character the Fleischers had in their sound cartoons was Bimbo. So without bothering to ask if they wanted a human, I started drawing a little girl dog. I had a song sheet of Helen Kane and the spit curls came from her. I put cute legs on her and long ears. I suppose I used a French poodle for the basic idea of the character.

And drawing from his years of experience, Natwick also gave her something that few female cartoons had ever had before: genuine feminine curves. "Years of art school and night classes, drawing thousands of naked models," Natwick said. "I knew all the sexy angles and shapes, from the turn of the ankle to the shape of the heel of her shoe."

One more influence on the character's look: from their Times Square office, Natwick and the other animators "made careful observation of the exaggerated strutting of that neighborhood's ladies of the night," and incorporated their strut into the character.

In Medieval England, jurors weren't fed until they reached a decision.

RISING STAR

The as-yet unnamed female dog debuted in a cartoon called *Dizzy Dishes*, in a supporting role as a dancer in a nightclub where Bimbo, the main character, was a waiter.

As usual, Bimbo did not light any fires with the audience. But his female costar was another story—audiences loved her . . . and Paramount Pictures, Fleischer Studio's distributor, quickly asked for more cartoons "with that girl in them."

When he realized how popular she was, Max Fleischer had the animators turn her into a human. "Somebody changed those ears into earrings," Natwick recalled nearly 60 years later. "Maybe I did. Everyone thought that as long as she looked like a girl anyway, let's just make her all girl." (Bimbo wasn't so lucky—he stayed a dog.)

And starting with the 1931 cartoon *Betty Coed*, Betty Boop finally had a name.

RISQUE BUSINESS

Betty Boop may have been the Fleischers' answer to Mickey Mouse, but she was a world apart. Disney sought to entertain without offending anyone, creating characters and stories with not a *hint* of adult themes or controversy. In contrast, Natwick explained, "Betty was a suggestion you could spell in three letters: S-E-X. She was all girl."

Freak gusts of wind blew up her skirt, and stray branches tugged at her top. In the 1934 cartoon *Betty Boop's Rise to Fame*, one of Betty's naked breasts is seen on film for a fraction of a second.

WOMAN OF THE WORLD

Betty Boop was one of the most successful cartoon characters of the early 1930s, not just in the United States but also worldwide. She had tremendous appeal for increasingly independent young women growing up in the 1930s. Luminaries such as Jean-Paul Sartre and Gertrude Stein were fans, and her likeness—stamped onto products as diverse as dolls, playing cards, nail polish, and cigarette cases—was one of the most mass-marketed images of the Depression era. Her cartoons also gave important exposure to jazz greats like Cab Calloway and Louis Armstrong, introducing their music to audiences who might never have heard it otherwise.

Armstrong's performance of "I'll Be Glad When You're Dead,

You Rascal You" was one of his first screen appearances ever. However, it was just the musicians' voices that the Fleischers used—they actually made cartoon characters out of the singers, using a device called rotoscope. So next time you see the walrus ghost dancing in *Minnie the Moocher*, (one of Betty's best cartoons), look a little closer—you're actually watching a performance by Cab Calloway.

HEAVENS TO BETTY!

Betty's innocent sexuality was her strongest drawing card, a fact that was unfortunately proven in the mid-1930s, when Paramount Pictures—under pressure from the Hayes office, Hollywood's official censor—told Fleischer Studios to clean up Betty Boop's act. "Naturally," Fleischer historian Leslie Cabarga writes, "Betty was never the same." Betty's short, sleeveless, backless dress was replaced with a much longer dress with sleeves and a collar; her garter belt was never seen again. No longer a nightclub singer pursued by lecherous men, Betty was now portrayed as a schoolteacher, secretary, housewife, or a baby-sitter; about the only man in her life was an elderly, protective professor named Grampy.

Whether or not censorship was to blame, by the end of the '30s the Betty Boop craze had run its course. Fleischer Studios ended the original series with *Yip Yip Yippy*, released in August 1939.

* * *

BOOP-OOP-A-LAWSUIT

One person definitely not a Betty fan was the original "Boop-Oop-a-Doop Girl" herself, singer Helen Kane. She was furious that Betty's success seemed to come at the expense of her own singing career. In April 1934, Kane filed a $250,000 lawsuit against Max Fleischer, alleging that Betty was "a deliberate caricature of me" and had robbed her of both her popularity and her livelihood by imitating her method of singing. Fleischer's strategy was to deny the obvious link between Kane and Betty.

But what decided the case in the Fleischer's favor was a film clip of a Black singer named Baby Esther singing a song containing the phrase "boop oop a doop." Fleischer introduced testimony that Kane had heard Baby Esther sing back in 1928. That was convincing enough, so the judge threw the case out of court.

Eleven percent of Americans have thrown out a dish because they "didn't want to wash it."

MYTH-UNDERSTANDINGS

More cultural "truths" that are really only half-truths.

HIPPOCRATES

Myth: Hippocrates was the father of modern medicine.

The Truth: Thanks to the Hippocratic oath, which is still administered during the graduation ceremonies of many medical schools, the name of the ancient Greek physician has become virtually synonymous with the practice of medicine. He may have tried to heal people, but like all doctors of his era, Hippocrates knew virtually nothing about the workings of the human body. And almost all of what he did believe—for example "that veins carried air, not blood, and illness was caused by vapor secreted by undigested food from unsuitable diets"—was dead wrong.

"WAY DOWN UPON THE SWANEE RIVER . . . "

Myth: The song "The Old Folks at Home" was inspired by the Suwannee River in Florida.

The Truth: Although the Swanee River in the song is the one in Florida, Stephen Foster, who wrote the song, had never seen it. He was writing tunes for a minstrel show and asked his brother Morrison for the name of a Southern river with two syllables. Morrison suggested Yazoo, in Mississippi. Stephen didn't like that, so Morrison ran his finger down a map and came up with the Suwannee. Now it's the Florida state song.

TEDDY ROOSEVELT AND THE TEDDY BEAR

Myth: Teddy Roosevelt liked Teddy Bears. The tale of how the Teddy Bear got its name is legendary: On a hunting trip, President Roosevelt refused to shoot a little bear that had been tied to a tree for him. A political cartoonist named Clifford Berryman depicted the incident in a cartoon, and a toymaker who saw the cartoon began selling stuffed bears as "Teddy's Bears." The cuddly bears became a fad.

The Truth: As the bears grew in popularity, Roosevelt came not

---

A greyhound (the dog, not the bus) can run as fast as 41 miles per hour.

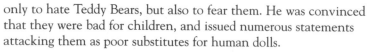

only to hate Teddy Bears, but also to fear them. He was convinced that they were bad for children, and issued numerous statements attacking them as poor substitutes for human dolls.

"Take away the little girl's dolly," he warned in one diatribe, "and you have interfered with the nascent expression of mother-hood. You have planted the race suicide where it will work the most harm—in the very arms of the babies themselves."

THE CIA

Myth: The CIA was meant to be America's top spy agency, policing the world and protecting American interests with elabo-rate clandestine activity.

The Truth: It may be a spy agency today, but, according to Jonathan Vankin in his book *Conspiracies, Coverups and Crimes*, that wasn't the original idea:

> The CIA was never meant to do its own spying. And it certainly wasn't meant to conduct clandestine operations. The origi-nal purpose of the CIA was to summarize and analyze information turned up by the other intelligence operations. It was a report-writing department.
>
> The CIA's one loophole is a fuzzy phrase in the 1947 law [that created the agency]. According to the bill signed by Truman, the Central Intelligence Agency would perform "other functions" at the discretion of the National Security Council. The language of the act is fairly specific. Those "other functions" relate only to intelligence. Nowhere does it mention clandestine operations. Even so, the "the functions" clause has been the rationale for what has become a . . . government-sanctioned, secret society.

MORSE CODE

Myth: The dot-dash code for telegraphs is named after the code's creator, Samuel Morse.

The Truth: The code is named after Morse—actually, he named it after himself. But many historians think his collaborator, Alfred Vail actually created it. Morse's original notes from 1832 suggest that he was planning a code that assigned each word in the dictionary a number. But six years later, someone came up with an alphabet code, using dots and dashes to signify letters. An appren-tice, William Baxter, said it was Vail's innovation. But Morse insisted he'd done it, and history books simply take his word for it.

VIDEO TREASURES

Some more BRI video recommendations.

LOCAL HERO (1983) *Comedy*
Review: "Burt Lancaster plays a Houston oil baron who sends Peter Riegert to the west coast of Scotland to negotiate with the natives for North Sea oil rights. This film is blessed with sparkling little moments of humor, unforgettable characters and a warmly human story." (*Video Movie Guide*) Director: *Bill Forsyth.*

INTO THE NIGHT (1985) *Drama*
Review: "Campy, offbeat thriller about a middle-aged, jilted dead-beat who meets a beautiful woman when she suddenly drops onto the hood of his car (with a relentless gang of Iranians pursuing her) and their search for the one person who can help her out of this mess." (*VideoHound's Golden Movie Retriever*) *Director*: John Landis.

BROADWAY DANNY ROSE (1984) *Comedy*
Review: "A New York talent agent, loyal to a stable of acts that would break your heart, promotes a bloated Sinatra-wannabe and gets mixed up with the Mob and the crooner's screeching mistress. A sweet screwball comedy that revisits the earlier world of Woody's little people." (*Seen That, Now What?*) *Director*: Woody Allen.

RUN, LOLA RUN (1999) *Drama*
Review: "A quick stop for cigarettes derails the normally prompt Lola, and now she has 20 minutes to save her boyfriend Manni. The movie mixes film, video, and animation to show how Lola's journey affects those she encounters during her mad dash. A flaw-less, 81-minute love story perfect for a generation raised on Sega and MTV." (*Roughcut Reviews*) *Director*: Tom Tykwer

THE SNAPPER (1993) *Comedy*
Review: "Wonderful adaptation of Roddy Doyle's novel about a working-class Irish family, and the teenage daughter who finds her-self pregnant—with the circumstances too embarrassing to discuss. Vivid, funny, and believable, sparked by good performances." (*Leonard Maltin's Movie & Video Guide*) *Director*: Stephen Frears.

How do scientists study the moisture in clouds? By studying the dew on spider webs.

POLITICALLY INCORRECT TOOTHPASTE

Next time you go to buy a tube of toothpaste, look at the packaging. See anything besides a pearly-white smile? If you'd been looking for some in the 1920s, you might have seen something dramatically different . . . and offensive. Here's the story of a formerly racist toothpaste.

TOOTHPASTE BLACKENS COLGATE'S REPUTATION

Darlie toothpaste, owned by Colgate-Palmolive, is one of the more popular toothpastes in Asia. But it has a little secret: until recently, it was called "Darkie" toothpaste, and the package was adorned with an offensive logo of a minstrel man in blackface. Apparently the man who created it in the 1920s had come to the United States and seen Al Jolson in his "blackface" show. He was impressed with how white Jolson's teeth looked, and thought that image could sell toothpaste.

Stereotypes of this sort were not unusual in packaging before World War II. What was unusual was that Darkie's racist name and logo were still intact in 1985 when Colgate bought the brand from Hong Kong's Hawley & Hazel Chemical Co.

JUST BUSINESS?

Here's where the story gets a little twisted. Colgate's arch-rival, Procter & Gamble, learned about the sale and immediately used it to their advantage. Both companies were releasing a tartar-control formula that year, and P&G decided to give itself an edge by hiring a public relations firm to surreptitiously leak information to activists and newspapers about Colgate's "racist" Asian brand.

The strategy worked. There was a storm of protest: stories and editorials in major newspapers, threats of boycotts, and even Eddie Murphy expressing his outrage on David Letterman's show. Colgate was perhaps unfairly attacked for a brand it had just purchased, but the attacks became more justified as the toothpaste giant dragged its feet on changing the name, apparently fearing a loss of business. Finally, nearly four years later, Colgate announced that it was

Space dust increases Earth's weight by as much as six tons a day.

changing the name of Darkie to Darlie and making the man on the package an abstraction of indeterminate race.

The name change placated Western critics, who pointed out that the toothpaste actually sold better after the name change. What they didn't know, and apparently still don't, is that only the English was changed. The Cantonese name (*Haak Yahn Nga Gou*) stayed the same, and Chinese-language ads reassured users that, despite the cosmetic change to placate Westerners, "Black Man Toothpaste is still Black Man Toothpaste."

* * *

STRANGERS IN DENTIFRICE

Planning a trip to Asia? If you forget your toothpaste, you can buy a standard American brand like Crest, Colgate, or Pepsodent (they're everywhere). But if you're feeling a little adventurous, try one of the local brands. Many even have ads in English, so you'll know what you're getting . . . sort of.

- **Evafresh Spearmint Toothpaste (China)** "Is made of choice materials with scientific prescription. It does no harm to the animal and prevents the teeth from gum-boil . . . "

- **White Jade (China)** The Shanghai Toothpaste Company claims "Your teeth will be healthy and no usual oral disease can occur . . . It does no harm to animal, it for smokers quite well." They also make Bulb Poll brand for children, saying, "With fresh melon flavour . . . brushing teeth would be of interest for children."

- **Supirivicky Brand (Ceylon)** This herbal toothpaste promises to relieve "obnoxious odours, spongy gums, cough, vomiting, gripe, colic, and paralysis of tongue."

- **Heibao Toothpaste (Hong Kong)** For a mere $96 per tube, Heibao promises an even more profound rejuvenation: "You will find your hair loss to be reduced by up to 90 percent. You will look younger, move younger and feel younger TEN to FIFTEEN years back because your hair becomes darker (as your good old days) and thicker and most important of all, your organic systems will function at their best! . . . Suitable for all ages, sex and race without any bad side effect."

The bite of a King Cobra can kill a fully-grown elephant in less than three hours.

THE BIRTH OF TARZAN, PART II

*Tarzan wasn't only an international superhero—he was
also the cornerstone of an incredibly profitable
business empire. (Part I is on page 510.)*

CHECKS AND BALANCES

Burroughs was just getting started as an author, but his years of business experience, though financially disastrous, had given him a surprising amount of business savvy.

When the $400 check for his first story, *A Princess of Mars*, arrived from *All-Story* magazine in 1911, he noticed that the words "For All Rights" were typed on it. As far as Burroughs was concerned, he'd only sold the magazine the right to publish his story in their *magazine*—and for that matter, only once. "What other rights are there?" he wrote back before cashing the check (which would have implied that he accepted *All-Story*'s terms and was indeed signing over "all rights" to the story.) Few authors—let alone first-time authors with an unbroken, 15-year string of business and career failures—had the sense to ask that question.

OVER A BARREL

All-Story could not publish *A Princess of Mars* without Burroughs's consent, and after a flurry of correspondence, the magazine finally gave in. It sent Burroughs a letter agreeing that he would retain all rights to his characters and story after they published it once.

Refusing to cash that check until he'd won back the rights to his story—and then doing it again when he sold his first *Tarzan* story a few months later—were probably the most important business decisions of his entire career. They would earn him millions of dollars in the years to come. "Had Burroughs's innate genius not guided him at this crucial stage," Gabe Essoe writes in *Tarzan of the Movies*, "he would have had nothing to sell to film makers in later years."

In 1913, Burroughs made another smart move: he registered the name *Tarzan* as a trademark.

Germans once believed a woman could avoid premature birth by carrying her husband's sock.

SHELF LIFE

Burroughs understood that the real money for *Tarzan* was in books, not magazines. Magazines disappeared from newsstands after only a month or two, but books might stay on the shelves for years. Now, armed with piles of fan letters and strong sales of the *Tarzan* issue of *All-Story* magazine, he pitched *Tarzan of the Apes* to book publishers.

They weren't interested. Every publisher Burroughs contacted turned him down, so he put the idea aside and signed up with a newspaper syndicator to publish his stories in newspaper serial form instead. It was a huge success—and convinced A. C. McClurg & Co., one of the publishers that had originally turned Burroughs down, to publish *Tarzan of the Apes* after all.

In the years to come, that first *Tarzan* novel would sell more than three million copies, earning a fortune for both Edgar Rice Burroughs and his publisher. But it was only the beginning: In his lifetime, Burroughs would write 66 more novels, 26 of them *Tarzan* novels. And by the time he died in 1950, he'd sold more than 36 million books in 31 different languages all over the world. This made him the most successful author of the first half of the 20th century.

JACK OF ALL TRADES

Burroughs was more than just the most successful writer of his age: he was a pioneer in the art of marketing a character in every possible medium. After succeeding in magazines, newspapers, hardcover books (paperbacks had not been invented yet), and movies, in 1932 Burroughs formed a radio division of his corporation. He created a 364-episode *Tarzan* radio serial that was sold to radio stations all over the country. (Burroughs's son-in-law, Jack Pierce—who played Tarzan in the 1926 film *Tarzan and the Golden Lion*—and his daughter, Joan Burroughs Pierce, provided the voices of Tarzan and Jane.)

In creating the *Tarzan* radio show, Burroughs actually "introduced the prerecorded radio show," Gabe Essoe writes. "Up to this time, all radio programs had been aired live. *Tarzan's* pioneering success in this field prompted a major trend toward 'canned' broadcasts."

The following year, Burroughs signed a deal with United Features Syndicate to create and distribute a *Tarzan* comic strip to

---

Quartzy is the highest-scoring Scrabble word.

newspapers. At its peak in 1942, the strip appeared in 141 daily papers and 156 Sunday papers around the world. Then in 1936, Burroughs took those same newspaper strips and relaunched them as comic books.

PUT A TARZAN IN YOUR TANK

Meanwhile, as *Tarzan* conquered one mass medium after another, Burroughs was busy licensing his hero's name and image to several hundred different manufacturers. They flooded the nation with hundreds of Tarzan products, including sweatshirts, wristwatches, masks and "chest wigs," candy, peanuts, bubble gum, trading cards, rubber toys, leg garters, bathing suits, and even Tarzan-brand coffee, bread, and gasoline. In Japan, *Tarzan* fitness magazine told people how to stay in shape just like Tarzan.

In 1939, Burroughs even founded the Tarzan Clan of America, which he hoped would one day rival the Boy Scouts. (It didn't.)

Perhaps the most interesting use of the Tarzan name was in 1928, when Burroughs subdivided the Southern California ranch estate he'd bought nine years earlier and began selling off parcels. On July 9, 1928, the U.S. Postal Service granted the former ranch its own post office and official recognition as a town, giving it the same name that Burroughs had bestowed on it when he bought the property in 1919: Tarzana.

KING OF THE JUNGLE

Before Edgar Rice Burroughs came along, no one had ever tried to market a fictional character this way. For that matter, in creating so many different competing forms of the same character, Burroughs had done precisely the opposite of what the brightest business and marketing minds of his day would have recommended. Not just the inventor of one of the most enduring fictional characters of the 20th century, he was also the inventor of an entirely new way of doing business, John Taliaferro writes in *Tarzan Forever*:

> Though marketing experts and syndication agents warned that Tarzan on the radio would compete with Tarzan in the comics or that serial motion pictures would steal audiences from feature motion pictures, Burroughs was convinced that the total would exceed the sum of the parts. As he saw it, there was no such thing as overkill, and well before Walt Disney ever hawked his first mouse ears or Ninja Turtle

The average bowling lane is 3' 6" wide and 60' long.

"action figures" became film stars, Burroughs was already a grand master of a concept that would one day be known as multimedia . . .

In short order, Tarzan became a superhero, the first pop icon to attain global saturation. As such he was the forefather of Superman and more recent real-life marvels such as Michael Jordan. Before Tarzan, nobody understood just how big, how ubiquitous, how marketable a star could be.

Of course, without the successful series of films, Tarzan might never have become the mighty pop force he still is today.

The story of his film career begins on page 690.

* * *

GRAFFITI

Creative writing, from the hallowed walls of
public restrooms across the country.

To kick the bucket is beyond the pail.

If voting could really change things, it would be illegal.

An elephant is a mouse drawn to government specifications.

Who gives a damn about apathy.

Add up the spinal column and get a disc count.

Reality is an illusion caused by lack of alcohol.

Democracy is letting the other fellow have your way.

When all else fails, read the instructions.

I used up all my sick days, so I'm calling in dead.

Democracy . . . three wolves and a sheep voting on what to have for lunch.

My boss has boots so shiny I can see my face in them.

A specialist is someone brought in at the last minute to share the blame.

I wish I were what I was when I was trying to become what I am now.

Between 1873 and 1880, some U.S. doctors gave patients transfusions of milk instead of blood.

ATTACK OF THE MONKEYS!

*Lock your door! Latch your window! Furry little primates
are headed for your town . . . and who knows what they'll
do next?!!! Here are a few reports from the field.*

JAPAN!

"Macaque monkeys are invading Japanese cities to ransack
homes and stores for food. They're blamed for numerous incidents in which they've entered stores and taken candy bars, fruit,
and vegetables right off the shelves. The cities of Hakone and
Odawara built a $2 million preserve for the monkeys outside of the
two cities to deter the urban attacks, but the monkeys apparently
aren't interested."

—*The Oregonian*

NEW YORK!

"A 66-year-old woman was waiting for a ride to church one Sunday
morning when her doorbell rang. She looked out the window to
see two rhesus monkeys standing on the porch, ringing her doorbell, knocking on the door, and trying to turn the doorknob."
Police—who said the pair had escaped from their owner's house—
were called to take them away.

—*Strange Tails*

PUNJAB, INDIA!

"The northern Indian state of Punjab is opening a jail for monkeys.
Wild monkeys—the alleged descendents of escaped laboratory
monkeys—have been mugging women for their handbags and are
terrorizing government officials. Once busted, the monkeys will be
jailed until they are declared fit for release."

—*The Edge*

PENNSYLVANIA!

Becky Kelly found a monkey in a friend's backyard in Hollidaysburg,
Pennsylvania, took it home and put it in a cage. The monkey was
apparently calm until the next day when, let out to play, it looked

---

Plopp is the name of a candy bar sold in Sweden; Moron is the name of a wine sold in Italy.

through a window and saw two men approach the house. "'It went nuts,' said another woman who lived in the house. The monkey grabbed a paring knife from the kitchen and a cigarette lighter and went on a rampage through the home for two hours, running and screaming and trying to flick the lighter on. It bit two women and used the knife to slice open bags of food in the kitchen cupboards, stopping to eat marshmallows, sugar, and bread. Police had to call in animal control officers to snare the animal."

—Strange Tails

TOKYO!

"In Tokyo, monkeys have been swarming into orchards and swiping bushels of apples. The monkeys come well equipped . . . with plastic shopping bags."

—The Edge

AFRICA!

"A troupe of about 60 gorillas invaded the village of Olamze on the border with equatorial Guinea recently, after an infant gorilla was seized earlier in the day by a local hunter. Shortly before midnight the gorillas entered the village in single file, ignoring gunshots fired by villagers to scare them away. The next night they beat on doors and windows until the village chief ordered the hunter to release the baby gorilla. According to the Cameroon newspaper *L'Action*, the gorillas 'returned to the forest with shouts of joy, savouring their victory.'"

—Fortean Times

* * *

WHERE ARE THEY HEADED NEXT?

Wild apes make sophisticated travel plans, says Dr. F. Sue Savage-Rumbaugh of Georgia State University. She studied pygmy chimpanzees, or bonobos, in the Congo and found that the monkeys head to different destinations . . . then meet at the end of the day at a specific spot chosen before they leave.

—This Is True

The largest gold nugget ever found weighed 172 pounds, 13 ounces.

DUMB CROOKS

Here's proof that crime doesn't pay.

CONSUMER PROTECTION AGENCY

"Suspecting that a drug dealer had sold her counterfeit crack cocaine, Rosie Lee Hill complained to Pensacola, Florida, police. Good news: An investigating officer determined the two cocaine rocks were real. Bad news: Hill was arrested. She'd paid $50 for the drugs, she explained, but when she tasted them she thought they were baking soda."

—*Dumb Crooks*

NO BRAINS ALOUD

"A convict broke out of jail in Washington, D.C., then a few days later accompanied his girlfriend to her trial for robbery. At lunch, he went out for a sandwich. She needed to see him, so she had him paged. Police officers recognized his name and arrested him as he returned to the courthouse (in a car he'd stolen during lunch hour)."

—*Bizarre News*

OPEN-DOOR POLICY

"When clerk Lee Johnson of the Li'L Cricket store in Spartanburg, South Carolina, was robbed, he hit the silent alarm. A deputy sheriff responding to the alarm drove up, but apparently the robber didn't notice who it was. So Johnson asked if he could go out and tell the arriving 'customer' the store was closed. 'Sure,' the robber said. Johnson went to the door and let the deputy in to arrest Kim Meredith, 34, who was charged with armed robbery. 'This man needs to be on dumb crook news,' Johnson told reporters."

—*This Is True*

DOES THAT COME WITH A BENEFITS PACKAGE?

"Norman Hardy, Jr., 22, pleaded innocent in a Brattleboro, Vermont, court, to charges of cocaine possession. Then he filled out a form requesting a public defender to represent him. Occupation? 'Selling drugs,' he wrote on the form. The judge granted the request for a public defender."

—*Associated Press*

About 90 percent of time capsules are never recovered.

WHO WANTS TO BE AN IDIOT?

"Ms. Fareena Jabbar, 37, was arrested in Colombo, Sri Lanka, in October and charged with trying to pass a U.S. $1 million bill (a denomination that does not exist). Jabbar supplied a 'certificate of authenticity' signed by officials of the 'International Association of Millionaires.'"

—*News of the Weird*

BLIND JUSTICE

"David Worrell, 25, got a 12-year suspended sentence for his attempted bank robbery in London. Was the judge being soft on crime? No—he just didn't feel Worrell posed a significant threat to society. Worrell, a blind man, had tried to hold up a bank using his cane as a weapon. When he heard the police sirens outside, he panicked and ran smack into a door."

—*Oops!, by Smith and Decter*

SHOULD'VE PLED THE FIFTH

"Michael Carter was arrested for kidnapping and robbery in New Haven, Connecticut, though he insisted that he was innocent. When police officers asked him to return to the scene of the crime so witnesses could see him, Carter responded, 'How can they identify me? I had a mask on.'"

—*The Oregonian*

PAPER TRAIL

"Three men in ski masks robbing a Rolling Hills Estates bank were in need of an empty bag for the money. So one of them emptied his bulging gym bag and filled it with cash. Among the gym bag's contents left behind on the bank floor: two traffic tickets bearing the robber's name and address. It only got worse. When the hold-up men couldn't start their getaway car, they jumped into another and sped away. Left behind in the disabled car were wallets with identification for two of them. Police gathered up the telltale papers and quickly tracked down the trio."

—*Only in L.A.*, by Steve Harvey

The Delaware Indians' name for the North American continent: Turtle Island.

NOT-SO-DUMB JOCKS

Okay, okay. They're not all dumb. Here are some genuinely
clever remarks from America's sports stars.

"I knew it was going to be a long season when, on opening day during the national anthem, one of my players turns to me and says, Every time I hear that song, I have a bad game.'"
> —**Baseball manager Jim Leyland**

"I'm the most loyal player money can buy."
> —**Don Sutton**

"Once you put it down, you can't pick it up."
> —**Pat Williams, NBA executive, on Charles Barkley's autobiography**

"I thought I'd be shot or hung by the time I was 40 anyway, so it's no big deal."
> —**Bill Parcels, on his 53rd birthday**

"It's called an eraser."
> —**Arnold Palmer, on how to take strokes off your golf game**

"You win some, lose some and wreck some."
> —**NASCAR driver Dale Earnhardt**

"It was a cross between a screwball and a change-up—screw-up."
> —**Cubs reliever Bob Patterson, on one that was hit out of the park**

"In 1962, I was voted Minor League Player of the Year. Unfortunately, that was my second year in the majors."
> —**Bob Uecker**

"At first, I said, 'Let's play for taxes.'"
> —**Michael Jordan, on playing golf with President Clinton**

"If he was on fire, he couldn't act as if he were burning."
> —**Shaquille O'Neal, on Dennis Rodman's acting ability**

"[Tommy] Morrison proved that he is an ambidextrous fighter. He can get knocked out with either hand."
> —**Boxing expert Bert Sugar**

"It's been a very good year. Excuse me, it's been a very fine year."
> —**Indy car driver Scott Pruett, whose sponsor was Firestone**

Put 80 people in a room and one bite from a black mamba snake could kill them all.

ENGLISH AS SHE IS SPOKE

This is a great moment for Bathroom Readers—*years ago we heard about a legendary guide to English that was so bad, it was hilarious. Well, we finally found a copy—and we're proud to present this excerpt to you.*

In 1855 Senhor Pedro Carolino wrote and published *The New Guide of the Conversation in Portuguese and English.* Amazingly, Carolino knew *no English*—he did it all using a Portuguese-French phrase-book and a French-English dictionary. That may sound logical, but instead of creating of a usable guide, Carolino ended up butchering the English language—inventing phrases like "I am pinking me with a pin." Even more amazing . . . it was used as a serious textbook in some foreign countries.

The English-speaking world first became aware of the book when a group of Tibetan tourists came to London in 1880 and tried to use *The New Guide* to carry on conversations. It quickly became known as a masterpiece of unintentional humor. Here are some excerpts from Carolino's "great experiment":

Familiar Phrases of English

"No budge you there."

"He laughs at my nose, he jest at me."

"Apply you at the study during that you are young."

"Dress your hairs."

"How do you can it to deny?"

"That are the dishes whose you must be and to abstain."

"Put you con-fidence at my."

"It pinches me enough."

"This girl have a beauty edge."

"I am catched cold in the brain."

"I am pinking me with a pin."

"I dead myself in envy to see her."

"I take a broth all morning."

"I shall not tell you than two woods."

"Do no might one's understand to speak."

"Dress my horse."

"Where are their stockings, their shoes, her shirt and her petlicot?"

"The rose trees begins to button."

"One's find-modest the young men rarely."

"If can't please at every one's."

"Take that boy and whip him to much."

"We are in the canicule."

"Take care to dirt you self."

Clouds don't float—they're actually falling very, very slowly.

English Vocabulary

Of the Man
The brain
The brains
The fat of the leg
The ham
The inferior lip
The superior lip
The entrails
The reins

Defects of the Body
A blind
A lame
A bald
A left handed
An ugly
A squint-eyed
A scurf
A deaf

Properties of the body
Yawn
Good air
Sneesing
Ugliness
Mien
Action

Games
Foot-ball
Bar Gleek
Carousal
Pile
Mall
Even or non even
Keel

Objects of man
The boots
The buckles
The button-holes
The buskins
The lining
The wig
The morning-gown

Woman objects
The sash
The cornet
The pumps
The paint or disguise
The spindle
The patches
The skate

Kitchen Utensils
The skimming-dish
The potlid
The pothanger
The spunge
The spark
The clout
The jack
The draughts

Trades
Starch-maker
Coffeeman
Porkshop-keeper
Tinker, a brasier
Nailer
Chinaman
Founder
Lochsmith

Eatings
Some wigs
A chitterling sausages
A dainty-dishes
A mutton shoulder
A little mine
Hog fat
Some marchpanes
An amelet
A slice, steak
Vegetables boiled to a
  pap

Diseases
The scrofulas
The whitlow
The vomitory
The megrime

Quadruped's beasts
Lamb
Ass
Shi ass
Hind
Dragon
Young rabbit
Leveret
Ram, aries

Military objects
A frame of a cannon
The bait
An arquebuse
A baggage
The firepan
A cuirass
E kettle drum

Q. What's the Australian name for a hurricane? A. "Willy Willy."

Familiar Dialogues clean of *gallicisms* and *despoiled* phrases

With a hair dresser

"'Your razors, are them well?"

"Yes, Sir."

"Comb-me quickly; don't put me so much pomatum. What news tell me? all hairs dresser are news-monger."

"Sir, I have no heared any thing."

For to breakfast

"John bring us some thing for to breakfast."

"Yes, Sir; there is some sausages. Will you than I bring the ham?"

"Yes, bring-him, we will cup a steak put a nappe clothe upon this table."

"I you do not eat?"

"How you like the tea."

"It is excellent."

"Still a not her cup."

To inform one'self of a person

"How is that gentilman who you did speak by and by."

"Is a German."

"Tongh he is German, he speak so much well italyan, french, spanish, and english, that among the Italyans, they believe him Italyan, he speak the frenche as che Frenches himself. The Spanishesmen believe him Spanishing, and the Englishes, Englisman."

"It is difficult to enjoy well so much several langages."

For to ride a horse

"Here is a horse who have a bad looks. Give me another: I will not that. He not sall know to march, he is pursy, he is foundered. Don't you are ashamed to give me a jade as like? he is undshoed, he is with nails up; it want to lead to the farrier."

"Your pistols are its loads?"

"No; I forgot to but gun-powder and balls. Go us more fast never I was seen a so much bad beast; she will not nor to bring forward neither put back."

"Strek him the bridle, hold him I the reins sharters. Pique strongly, make to marsh him."

"I have pricked him enough. But I can't to make march him."

"Go down, I shall make march."

"Take care that he not give you a foot kicks."

"Then he kicks for that I look? Look here if I knew to tame hix."

The French Language

"Do you study?"

"Yes, sir, I attempts to translate of french by portuguese."

"Do you know already the principal grammars rules?"

"I am appleed my self at to learn its by heart."

"Do speak french alwais?"

"Some times; though I flay it yet."

"You jest, you does express you self very well."

King George I of England (1714–1727) was German. He couldn't speak a word of English.

With a furniture tradesman

"It seems no me new."

"Pardon me, it comes workman's hands."

"Which hightness want you its?"

"I want almost four feet six thumbs wide's, over seen of long."

With a banker

"I have the honor to present you a ex-change letter, draw on you and endorsed to my order."

"I can't to accept it seeing that I have not nor the advice neither funds of the drawer."

"It is not yet happened. It is at usance."

"I know again the signature and the flourish of my correspondent; I will accept him to the day of the falling comprehend there the days of grace, if at there to that occasion I shall received there orders."

"In this case, I not want of to do to protest it."

"It can to spare him the expenses of the protest."

"Will you discharge this other trade what there is it? It is payable to the sight."

"Yes I will pay it immediately, I go to count you the sum."

"Would you have so good as to give me some England money by they louis?"

"With too much pleasure."

With a gardener

"What make you hither, Francis?"

"I water this flowers parterre."

"Shall I eat some plums soon?"

"It is not the season yet; but here is some peaches what does ripen at the eye sight."

"It delay me to eat some walnut-kernels; take care not leave to pass this season."

"Be tranquil, I shall throw you any nuts during the shell is green yet."

Idiotisms and Proverbs

"The necessity don't know the low."

"Few, few me bird make her nest."

"He is not valuable to breat that he eat."

"Its are some blu stories."

"There is not any ruler without a exception."

"A horse bared don't look him the tooth."

"Take the occasion for the hairs."

"To do a wink to some body."

"There is not better sauce who the appetite."

"Which like Bertram, love hir dog."

"It want to beat the iron during it is hot."

"He has a good break."

"It is better be single as a bad company."

'The stone as roll not heap up not foam."

"They shurt him the doar in face."

"He turns as a weath turcocl."

"Take out the live coals with the hand of the cat."

As late as 1950, pork was still overwhelmingly the most popular meat in America.

TECHNO-SLANG

Here are a few great "cyber-definitions" we found online.

Alpha Geek: The most knowledgeable, technically proficient person in an office or work group. "Ask Larry, he's the alpha geek around here."

Beepilepsy: The brief seizure people sometimes have when their beeper goes off (especially in vibrator mode). Characterized by physical spasms, goofy facial expressions, and interruptions of speech in midsentence.

Betamaxed: When a technology is overtaken by an inferior, but better-marketed, technology. "Apple was Betamaxed out of the market by Microsoft."

Bit Flip: A 180-degree personality change. "Jim did a major bit flip and became a born-again Christian"

Elvis Year; The peak year of something's (or someone's) popularity. "Barney the dinosaur's Elvis year was 1993."

Food coupons: Twenty-dollar bills from an ATM.

Irritainment: Annoying (but riveting) media spectacles. The O. J. trial was a prime example.

Mouse Potato: The online, wired generation's answer to the couch potato.

Ohnosecond: That miniscule fraction of time in which you realize that you've just made a BIG mistake. Seen in Elizabeth P. Crowe's book *The Electronic Traveler.*

SITCOMs: What yuppie parents turn into. Stands for Single Income, Two Children, Oppressive Mortgage.

Swiped Out: Description of an ATM or credit card that has been rendered useless because the magnetic strip is worn away from extensive use.

Xerox Subsidy: Euphemism for swiping free photocopies from a workplace.

YODA (Young Opinionated Directionless Artiste): Person who sits in coffeehouses voicing strong opinions and perennial wisdom while exhibiting little direction or effort to actually make a difference.

Zen Mail: E-mail messages that arrive in one's mailbox with no text in the message body.

404: Someone who's clueless. "Don't bother asking him; he's 404." From the Web error message "404 Not Found," meaning the requested document couldn't be located.

What's the oldest letter in the alphabet? Experts say "O."

TOO CLOSE FOR COMFORT

What happens when the real world intrudes into the fantasy world of movies and TV? It happens every now and then—some tragedy in the real world is a little too close to something on the screen . . . People get very uncomfortable, and a change is made. For example . . .

TAKE HER, SHE'S MINE (1963)

Background: The film, a romantic comedy starring Sandra Dee, contained one scene in which a character spoke to Jackie Kennedy on the phone...and two scenes in which one of the characters spoke in a voice that sounded like President John F. Kennedy.

Too Close for Comfort: The film opened on November 16, 1963; President Kennedy was assassinated six days later. The studio immediately recalled all of the 350 prints in distribution, cut out the scene with Jackie Kennedy, and dubbed a new voice to replace the one that sounded like President Kennedy.

PROMISED LAND (1999)

Background: In 1999 the TV series, a drama set in Colorado and starring Gerald McRaney and Wendy Phillips, was in its third season. One of the episodes CBS was planning to run featured a shooting at a school.

Too Close for Comfort: Two days before the episode was scheduled to air, two students shot up Columbine High School in Colorado, killing 15 people. CBS pulled the episode.

SMALL SOLDIERS (1998)

Background: The film, about toy soldiers who come to life and start a war in an Ohio town, starred comedian Phil Hartman as the father of the boy who owns one of the soldiers.

Too Close for Comfort: The film was scheduled to open on July 10, 1998; but on May 28, 1998, Phil Hartman was shot and killed by his wife in a murder-suicide. Dreamworks quickly re-edited the film so that none of the soldiers are shown pointing their guns at

---

Canada consumes more Kraft macaroni and cheese than any other nation.

Hartman and removed a scene in which he says, "I think I'm having an aneurysm."

THE GREATEST AMERICAN HERO (1981)

Background: The lead character in the ABC series was named Ralph Hinkley. He finds a superhero suit with magical powers, but can't get it to work properly because he lost the instruction manual.

Too Close for Comfort: On March 30, 1981, 25-year-old John Hinkley, Jr., shot President Ronald Reagan. *Greatest American Hero* was already halfway through the broadcast season, but ABC officials decided to change Ralph Hinkley's name to Ralph Hanley. They didn't explain the change to the audience. They simply dubbed "Hanley" over "Hinkley." Eventually, the character's name was changed back to Hinkley—again with no explanation.

FOR GOODNESS SAKE (1994)

Background: *For Goodness Sake* was a 24-minute-long "corporate and educational training film promoting morality and ethical values" that was produced by a company called Mentor Media in 1994. The film featured a series of cameo appearances by Hollywood stars.

Too Close for Comfort: One of the stars was O.J. Simpson. When he was arrested for murder on June 17, 1994, Mentor Media quickly cut his two-minute scene from the film. But that move was protested by a group called "the Micah Center for Ethical Monotheism," which questioned the morality of removing Simpson, "because that would be like passing judgment on him." So Mentor made both versions of the film available to customers . . . and the one with Simpson sold better than the one without him.

* * *

A GROANER

The flood was over, and Noah told the animals to go forth and multiply. Two snakes remained on the ark, however. "Why aren't you going forth and multiplying?" asked Noah.

One replied, "Because, silly man, we're adders."

Lonely parrots can go insane.

Q & A:
ASK THE EXPERTS

*Here are some more random questions, with answers from
books by some of the nation's top trivia experts.*

HE'S LATE, HE'S LATE . . .
Q: *How does a magician pull a rabbit out of a hat?*
A: "The magician's table is draped with a cloth to prevent
the audience from seeing a small shelf at the back of the table,
upon which the bunny sits, wrapped in a large handkerchief. At
the outset of the trick, the magician removes his hat and displays
the inside—empty. Then he sets it, brim down, near the back of
the table. While waving his wand with his right hand, he grasps
both the brim of the hat and the corners of the handkerchief with
his left. With a swift, graceful—and unseen—move, he turns over
the hat. The bundle drops into the hat and with another wave of
his wand—presto, he raises the rabbit into the air." (From *More
How Do They Do That?*, by Caroline Sutton and Kevin Markey)

VISUAL MATHEMATICS
Q: *When you close one eye, is your sight reduced by half?*
A: "No. There's considerable overlap in the range of vision of each
eye. When an eye is lost, sight is reduced by about 20 percent."
(From *1,000 Facts Someone Screwed Up*, by Deane Jordan)

ORANGE YA GLAD?
Q: *What's the difference between Florida and California oranges?*
A: "They're the same species of orange—*Citrus sinensis*. The differ-
ences are a result of climate, not botany.

"California oranges *look* more like oranges because the
California nights get much cooler than Florida nights. Oranges are
a winter/early spring crop, and need a little nip in the night air to
develop full coloration. They do not ripen once they are picked.

"Because Americans prefer orange oranges, Florida growers
either color their oranges or sell them for juice. Florida oranges are

---

Ninety-nine percent of the pumpkins sold in the United States end up as jack-o-lanterns.

plumper, juicier, and thinner-skinned than California oranges due to the moist subtropical climate. The drier, thicker-skinned California fruits are generally sold as eating oranges. Since there is a greater demand for juice oranges, Florida's production far exceeds California's. Oranges are also grown commercially in Texas and Arizona." (From *Why Does Popcorn Pop?*, by Don Voorhees)

SOLID GOLD

Q: *What is "24-carat" gold?*
A: "A carat is a unit of measurement. In gold, a carat equals one-twenty-fourth part.

"Because pure gold is a very soft metal, it is frequently mixed with other metals, known as alloys, to give it greater strength and durability. Copper and silver are most often used as gold alloys. The amount of alloy added to the gold affects its color as well as its strength, with copper lending a deeper yellow or red hue, and silver giving a lighter appearance.

"If a piece of jewelry is 18 parts gold and 6 parts alloy, we say it is 18-carat gold; if it has 14 parts of gold to 10 parts of another metal, we say it is 14-carat gold. 24-carat is pure gold." (From *A Book of Curiosities*, by Roberta Kramer)

SAY CHEESY

Q: *What's the orange stuff on Cheetos?*
A: "It's a combination of various dyes and seasonings, and it's the only part of Cheetos that has any cheese whatsoever in it. The main part of these snacks is cornmeal, with whey and oil added, mixed into a dough, then squeezed out into a long worm shape by an extruder. When the dough meets the cooler air, it sort of explodes or puffs like popcorn. Blades cut it into bite-sized pieces, which are then fried.

"From there, the pale white morsels are shaken in colored and flavored powder. Real cheese, Yellow No. 6, annatto, and turmeric give the pieces that cheesy effect. A little more salt and vegetable oil are added for sticking power and flavor. Despite rumors, the powder coating is not toxic, but because it's brightly colored and relatively loose, it can be lethal to furniture and clothes." (From *Just Curious, Jeeves*, by Jack Mingo and Erin Barrett)

FOOD SUPERSTITIONS

What can you do with food, besides eat it? Use it to drive evil spirits away, of course. People once believed in these bizarre rituals.

"Sprinkle pepper on a chair to ensure that guests do not overstay their welcome."

"If cooking bacon curls up in the pan, a new lover is about to arrive."

"Eating five almonds will cure drunkenness."

"If the bubbles on the surface of a cup of coffee float toward the drinker, prosperous times lie ahead; if they retreat, hard times are promised."

"Cut a slice from the stalk end of a banana while making a wish. If a Y-shaped mark is revealed, the wish will come true."

"Feed red pistachio nuts to a zombie—it will break his trance and allow him to die."

"When a slice of buttered bread falls butter-side-up, it means a visitor is coming."

"Put a red tomato on the windowsill—it scares away evil spirits."

"If bread dough cracks during baking, a funeral is imminent."

"It's lucky to see two pies, but unlucky to see only one."

"A wish will come true if you make it while burning onions."

"Feeding ground eggshells to children cures bedwetting."

"Stirring a pot of tea stirs up trouble."

"It's bad luck to let milk boil over."

"Bank up used tea leaves at the back of the fire to ward off poverty."

"If you find a pod with nine peas in it, throw it over your shoulder and make a wish. It will come true."

"Finding a chicken egg with no yolk is unlucky."

"If meat shrinks in the pot, your downfall is assured. If it swells, you'll experience prosperity."

"Beans scattered in the corners of a home will drive out evil spirits."

"It is unlucky to say the word 'salt' at sea."

It would take two and a half minutes to fall from the top of Mt. Everest.

JOIN THE CLUB

*You've heard of these organizations—you might even be
a member of a few. Here's how they started.*

THE LEAGUE OF WOMEN VOTERS

Founded by: Carrie Chapman Catt, a leader of the womens' suffragist movement, in 1919.

History: The League of Women Voters is an outgrowth of the National Woman Suffrage Association (NWSA), a 2 million-member women's organization formed in 1890 to push individual states to ratify suffrage amendments. Catt and her cronies believed that if enough states passed their own amendments giving women the right to vote, Congress would be forced to approve a federal amendment.

It worked. After more than 72 years of struggle, the 19th Amendment was added to the U.S. Constitution on August 26, 1920. Catt addressed the final NWSA convention. She suggested that rather than disband, they should alter their mission to educating women about the electoral process and encouraging them to vote. The members agreed, and the League was born.

Today the League is a non-partisan organization with a focus on voter registration and voter education.

THE YOUNG MEN'S CHRISTIAN ASSOCIATION (YMCA)

Founded by: George Williams, a self-described "careless, thoughtless, swearing young fellow" who converted to Christianity while working in the London clothing trade in the 1840s.

History: At a time when there were few recreational opportunities in the cities "other than saloons and brothels," Williams gathered together a group of like-minded religious young men who began meeting regularly for prayer and reflection; in 1844, this group became the first local YMCA.

For the first 45 years of its existence, the YMCA was primarily a missionary group with a focus on "saving souls, with saloon and street corner preaching, lists of Christian boarding houses, lectures, libraries and meeting halls, most of them in rented quarters." (It wasn't until 1889 that the organization began to promote physical fitness.) The YMCA stood out in its time because it ignored the rigid lines that separated class from class, and church from church, in 19th century England. It grew fast. By the 1850s, the group was in seven countries, with 397 branches.

Sidelight: If you read *Uncle John's Absolutely Absorbing Bathroom Reader*, you know the story of how the YMCA invented basketball in 1891. Here's another tidbit: by 1895, it was clear that basketball was too strenuous for some businessmen. So William G. Morgan, physical director of the Holyoke, Massachusetts, YMCA invented a game called "mintonette." Like basketball, it could be played indoors during the cold winter months—but it wasn't as physically demanding. The name of the game was eventually changed when "a professor from Springfield college, noting the volleying nature of play, suggested calling it 'volleyball.'"

THE AMERICAN SOCIETY FOR THE PREVENTION OF CRUELTY TO ANIMALS (ASPCA)

Founded By: Henry Bergh, a philanthropist and diplomat from a wealthy shipbuilding family

Origin: Bergh, aka "The Great Meddler," was known "for using his walking stick to upbraid peddlers who beat their horses on city streets." He wasn't a conventional animal rights proponent—it was cruelty he detested more than anything else. (He later started the Society for the Prevention for Cruelty to Children.) When he founded the ASPCA in 1866, it was the first humane society in America.

Within a year, the ASPCA succeeded in prodding the New York Legislature to pass the country's first anti-cruelty law. The following year, Bergh established an ambulance service for New York City's injured work horses, a full two years before Bellevue Hospital set up the world's first hospital ambulance service for humans. Bergh is also credited with developing and popularizing the clay pigeon in the 1870s to discourage the sport shooting of real pigeons, which was popular at the time.

During his lifetime, 34 states passed animal rights legislation.

THE STORIES BEHIND THE STORIES

Here are the origins of three classic children's books.

PIPPI LONGSTOCKING

Inspiration: A sick child's imagination . . . and a broken ankle

How it Became a Book: In the early 1940s a young girl named Karin Lindgren fell ill with pneumonia and had to spend several days in bed. Her mother, a 38-year-old office worker, took some time off to care for her.

As Astrid Lindgren recounted many years later, her ailing daughter made an unusual request:

> Karen asked me to tell her about Pippi Langstrump [Swedish for Longstocking]. She had invented that name at that very moment, but I didn't ask who this Pippi was. I just started to tell her about a girl with such a funny name. From then on, my daughter kept asking me to tell her everything about Pippi Longstocking.
>
> Shortly afterwards I broke my ankle and had to stay in bed for a few days, so I decided to write down the stories. I showed them to a publisher, and that was how it started.

Since then, more than 15 million *Pippi Longstocking* books have been sold, and they have been translated into 55 languages—making Astrid Lindgren the most successful writer in the history of Swedish literature.

PETER RABBIT

Inspiration: Another sick child; this time it was five-year-old Noël Moore, the son of one of Beatrix Potter's friends.

In 1893, Noël contracted an illness that kept him in bed for months. Beatrix Potter lived too far away to visit very often, so she wrote him elaborate letters instead. When Potter had something interesting to write about, she included it in the letter; when she didn't, she just made up stories. One of the stories, told in a letter dated September 4, 1893, involved Peter, her pet rabbit:

> My Dear Noël, I don't know what to write to you, so I shall tell you

a story about four little rabbits whose names were Flopsy, Mopsy, Cottontail, and Peter.

They lived with their Mother in a sand bank under the root of a big fir tree.

'Now my dears,' said old Mrs. Bunny, 'you may go into the field or down the lane, but don't go into Mr. McGregor's garden . . . '

How it Became a Book: Potter wrote similar letters to other children she knew; they were so well received that it eventually occurred to her that they might make good children's books. In 1900, she wrote to Nöel Moore asking if he still had the "Peter Rabbit" letter she'd written eight years earlier. He did, and he lent it back to her so she could copy it.

Potter submitted *The Tale of Peter Rabbit* to at least six different publishers; each one turned her down . . . so she printed 250 copies using her own savings and sold them to family and friends. She also sent a copy to Frederick Warne & Co. Ltd., one of publishers that had originally turned her down, and they agreed to publish it. (This was no big vote of confidence, though—the company made Potter cover all expenses and take all the financial risks.) That was nearly 100 years ago. Today *Peter Rabbit* still ranks as one of the top 10 best-selling childrens' books of all time.

BABAR THE ELEPHANT

Inspiration: A bedtime story

How it Became a Book: In the summer of 1930, a French woman named Cecile de Brunhoff told her sons a bedtime story about a little elephant named Babar. The story went on night after night; the boys enjoyed it so much that their father, a painter named Jean de Brunhoff, painted some pictures to go along with the story and assembled them into a homemade book. The book was passed from one relative to another among the extended de Brunhoff family that summer. It generated so much enthusiasm among family members that de Brunhoff decided to get it published.

In 1931, his brother-in-law, a fashion magazine editor, arranged to print *L'histoire de Babar, le petit elephant*. Though it was the middle of the Depression, the huge, expensive volume sold well . . . giving birth not only to the Babar series, but to the modern picture book as well.

Coney Island isn't an island, but it used to be.

DRACULA,
"I VANT TO BE A STAR"

Long before Dracula became a pop icon, he was just a character in a not-very-popular novel by novelist Bram Stoker (see page 490) . . . but everyone's got to start somewhere. Here's the story of how Dracula made his way into pop culture through the stage and screen.

IN THE MAIL

Nosferatu—who cannot die!

A million fancies strike you when you hear the name:
Nosferatu!

N O S F E R A T U
does not die!

What do you expect of the first showing of this great work?
Aren't you afraid? Men must die. But legend has it that a vampire, Nosferatu, "the undead," lives on men's blood! You want to see a symphony of horror? You may expect more. Be careful. Nosferatu is not just fun, not something to be taken lightly. Once more: beware.

That was the text of a movie advertisement sent to Bram Stoker's 64-year-old widow from Berlin in April 1922. In the 10 years since her husband's death, Florence Stoker's financial situation had deteriorated. All of Stoker's books had gone out of print, except for *Dracula*, and sales of that were modest even in the best years. Mrs. Stoker, slowly going blind from cataracts, would have been destitute were it not for help from her son, Noel.

Now, to add insult to injury, came this advertisement in the mail. It was for *Nosferatu, A Symphony of Horrors*, a German film which by its own admission was "freely adapted" from Bram Stoker's *Dracula*. All of Stoker's characters were in the film, only under different names: Dracula was renamed Graf Orlok, Jonathan Harker had become Hutter, his fiancée Mina was renamed Emma, and so on.

Mrs. Stoker was furious. She'd never given the filmmakers, Prana-Film, permission to adapt her husband's work. *Nosferatu* was stolen property, and she wanted it destroyed. So she sued.

Q: What animal has the largest brain in proportion to its size? A: The ant.

HONEST MISTAKE?

The makers of *Nosferatu* may not have meant any harm.
Filmmaking was still in its infancy in the early 1920s, and Prana-Film, less than a year old, was owned by two businessmen who'd never made films before. But it turned out they were as impractical about making money as they were in obtaining permissions—and two months after Mrs. Stoker filed her lawsuit, the studio went bankrupt.

All existing prints of the film, including the original negative, scattered to the four winds with Prana-Film's dissolution. With no hope left of collecting any financial damages, most people would probably have left it at that. But Mrs. Stoker spent the next 10 years hunting down every print of *Nosferatu* she could find . . . and had them all destroyed—including the original negative, which is believed to have been burned in 1925.

"Most 'lost' films have vanished through neglect," David Skal writes in *Hollywood Gothic*. "But in the case of *Nosferatu* we have one of the few instances in film history, and perhaps the only one, in which an obliterating capital punishment is sought for a work of cinematic art, strictly on legalistic grounds, by a person with no knowledge of the work's specific contents or artistic merit." Mrs. Stoker had never even seen the film she worked so hard to destroy.

Despite her dedication, though, she was unsuccessful in destroying every print—a handful survived.

FIRST WITH THE MOST

It's fortunate that Mrs. Stoker failed in her attempt to kill *Nosferatu* because the film is not only the first *Dracula* film ever made, it's also considered by many film historians to be the best. "*Nosferatu*," Skal writes, "would go on to be recognized as a landmark of world cinema, elevating the estimation of *Dracula* in a way no other dramatic adaptation ever would, or ever could. It had achieved what Florence Stoker herself would never achieve for the book: artistic legitimacy."

DRACULA ON STAGE

In the mid-1920s, a British actor named Hamilton Deane licensed the stage rights to *Dracula* from Mrs. Stoker and adapted the novel for the stage, creating a play that could be produced on a shoe-

---

John Wayne was related to Johhny Appleseed.

string budget. He also recast the novel's only American character, a Texan named Quincey Morris, as a woman, so that the actresses in his troupe would have more parts.

But the biggest change he made was to clean up Count Dracula. He replaced the vampire's bad breath, hairy palms, and overall bad hygiene with cleanliness, formality, and proper manners. "Gentility and breeding added a new dimension to the character," Skal writes, "and served a theatrical function—he was now able to interact with the characters, rather than merely hang outside their bedroom windows."

COUNT ME OUT

When he set to work adapting *Dracula* for the stage, Deane had himself in mind to play the part of Dracula. But he trimmed the role so much that he decided to play Dr. Van Helsing instead. Perhaps to soothe rocky relations with Mrs. Stoker and her agent, C. A. Bang, Deane cast Bang's brother-in-law, 22-year-old Raymond Huntley, as Dracula. Huntley was paid £8 a week for the part, and was required to provide his own costumes—including lounge suits, full evening tails, a dinner jacket, and a silk hat—all out of his own pocket.

About the only item he didn't have to provide was Dracula's cape, which was considered a stage prop. The cape's huge standup collar completely concealed Huntley's head when he turned his back to the audience, allowing him to "disappear" from the stage by slipping out of the cape and ducking out through a trapdoor in the floor. The trapdoor exit was later removed from the play, but the cape with the standup collar remains a standard part of the Dracula costume to this day.

ON THE ROAD

Hamilton Deane didn't intend his adaptation of *Dracula* to be high art: The play was what was known as a "boob catcher," a play that used gimmickry, sex appeal—and in Dracula's case, death—to draw common people into the theatre. For that reason Deane bypassed the London stage (and London theater critics, who would have savaged the production) and took his show on the road, hitting smaller cities and towns all over Britain.

He stayed on the road for more than two years before finally opening at London's Little Theatre on February 14, 1927. As predicted, it was panned by the London critics. The show was at the end of its run . . . or so Deane thought. But as days turned into weeks, and weeks into months, the crowds didn't get smaller—they got bigger. Despite the bad reviews, *Dracula* was playing to capacity crowds by the end of summer and had to move to a larger theatre called the Duke of York's. "While glittering productions costing thousands of pounds have wilted and died after a week or so in the West End," the *London Evening News* wrote, "*Dracula* has gone on drinking blood nightly."

COMING TO AMERICA

In early 1927, an American theater promoter named Horace Liveright traveled to London to see *Dracula*. He enjoyed it so much that he saw it again three more times. "Although it was badly produced," he recalled later, "I got a kick out of it each time."

Liveright wanted to bring *Dracula* to Broadway. But he didn't think Hamilton Deane's adaptation was written well enough for New York audiences. So he got permission from Mrs. Stoker to write another adaptation, one that retained Deane's theatricality but improved his amateurish dialogue.

Liveright offered to take Raymond Huntley to the United States, too, and Huntley agreed to go . . . providing Liveright agreed to raise his pay to $125 a week. No deal—Huntley stayed in London. The part of Dracula went to a Hungarian expatriate actor named Bela Lugosi.

Lugosi, 46, had established himself in Hungary and Germany by playing romantic parts and an occasional villain. But his American career was burdened by the fact that he could speak barely a word of English, and rather than work on his English, he preferred to memorize his lines phonetically.

The result of Lugosi's inability to speak English, Skal writes, "was the oddly inflected and deliberate style of speech now forever associated with the role of Dracula—and a professional albatross that would forever limit the roles offered to him."

VAMPIRE FEVER

Dracula opened at New York's Fulton Theatre on October 5, 1927.

Country star Lyle Lovett is afraid of cows.

It received better reviews than the London version, thanks in large part to the new script and to Lugosi's acting. Lugosi's experience as a romantic lead made his interpretation of *Dracula* markedly different from Huntley's in London, Skal writes:

> The London Dracula was middle-aged and malignant; Lugosi presented quite a different picture: sexy, continental, with slicked-back patent-leather hair and a weird green cast to his makeup—a Latin lover from beyond the grave, Valentino gone slightly rancid. It was a combination that worked, and audiences—especially female audiences—relished, even wallowed in, the romantic paradoxes.

Dracula was a hit. It played for 31 weeks and 241 performances before closing in 1928. Then, Liveright formed a national touring company, and in the process launched America's first vampire craze. By May of 1929, Liveright had made more than $1 million on *Dracula*, and would make a million more in less than a year.

A SIGN OF THINGS TO COME

Bela Lugosi was not so lucky: he'd joined the touring company for its west coast swing, but when it moved to the east coast he made the mistake of asking for a substantial raise, one that he felt was commensurate with his ability to draw his fans into the theater.

Liveright didn't see it that way, and replaced Lugosi with the man Lugosi had replaced in 1927—Raymond Huntley.

Lugosi, not for the last time in his career, was out in the cold.

For Dracula, "I Vant to Be in Pictures" *turn to page 639.*

* * *

A BRI "FAVORITE ROLE MODEL"

Role Models: The hundreds of thousands of people who gathered in New York City's Central Park on Earth Day 1990 to "express their support for environmental programs, and to display their concern for Mother Earth."

Setting an Example: They left behind more than 154.3 tons of trash, which took 50 park employees until 3 a.m. to clean up.

Dumbest farm animal, according to farmers: the turkey.

POLI-TALKS

Politicians aren't getting much respect these days—but then, it sounds like they don't deserve much, either.

"I think that the free-enterprise system is absolutely too important to be left to the voluntary action of the marketplace."
—**Rep. Richard Kelly (R-Fla.)**

"If a frog had wings, he wouldn't hit his tail on the ground."
—**George Bush, on unemployment benefits**

"I make my decisions horizontally, not vertically."
—**Sen. Bob Kerry (D-Neb.)**

"I hope that history will present me with maybe two words. One is peace. The other is human rights."
—**Jimmy Carter**

"The streets are safe in Philadelphia, it's only the people who make them unsafe."
—**Frank Rizzo, mayor of Philadelphia**

"Rarely is the question asked: Is our children learning?"
—**George W. Bush**

"If we don't watch our respective tails, the people are going to be running the government."
—**State Sen. Bill Craven (R-Ca.), on state initiatives**

"Democracy used to be a good thing, but now it has gotten into the wrong hands."
—**Sen. Jesse Helms**

"I don't see why the legislature should be in the business of artificial intelligence, real intelligence or any intelligence at all."
—**Rep. Hunt Downer (D-La.)**

"A zebra cannot change its spots."
—**Al Gore**

"We, as Republicans, need to start rowing with one oar."
—**Rep. John Kasich (R-Ohio)**

"I haven't committed a crime. What I did was fail to comply with the law."
—**David Dinkins, former New York City mayor**

What do your lungs and a tennis court have in common? They have about the same surface area.

THE ORIGIN OF THE SUPERMARKET

We take it for granted today, but less than 100 years ago, the supermarket seemed like some sort of bizarre fantasy. Wait a minute—that's what it seems like today, too. Well, anyway, here are some historical highlights.

TO MARKET, TO MARKET

At the end of the 19th century, a typical food-shopping trip wasn't as easy as it is today. Buying groceries would have included several steps:

- Stop at the butcher for meat. (You could also choose from a small selection of canned goods and bread.)

- A stop at the fruit store for fresh produce.

- Stopping on the street to buy from milk wagons, and from horse-and-wagon peddlers hawking their specialties—anything from baked goods to fish or ice.

- A final stop at the local grocer, who sold canned goods, potatoes, sugar in 100-pound sacks, molasses, sauerkraut in barrels, bacon in slabs, and butter in tubs. But strolling through the aisles was out of the question. At the counter, customers told the grocer what they wanted and a clerk would fill their order.

THE SELF-SERVE STORE

Then, in 1916 Clarence Saunders opened the Piggly Wiggly Store in Memphis, Tennessee. "Astonished customers," write the Sterns in their *Encyclopedia of Pop Culture*, "were given baskets (shopping carts weren't invented) and sent through the store to pick what they needed—a job formerly reserved for clerks." Although customers were a little bewildered by the dozens of stocked aisles at first, Piggly Wiggly was an immediate success. It grossed $114,000 in the first six months—with expenses of only $3,400. Before long, there were over 1,000 of them in 40 states. The self-serve grocery store began to spread.

ROAD WARRIORS

Amazingly, one of the biggest factors in the growth of the super-

---

How do airports scare birds off their runways? One British airport plays Tina Turner albums.

market was the invention of the automobile ignition switch. Previously, housewives had to limit their shopping to stores within walking distance; it was too difficult and dangerous to turn the starter crank to get a car started. But once there was an easy way to start the car, housewives were set to travel miles to get a bargain.

This led to another significant innovation: the free parking lot. For the first time, parking was available right in front of a store, customers didn't have to look for a space on crowded streets. The attractiveness of this concept was demonstrated when the Kroger Grocery and Bakery Company opened in Indianapolis, surrounded on four sides by free parking lots. The store performed 40 percent above initial predictions, and a whopping 80 percent of customers arrived by car.

PRICE MAULING

When the Depression hit in 1929, families found themselves struggling to buy food. Michael Cullen, manager of a Kroger grocery store, suggested opening a huge self-serve store far from high-rent districts, selling everything a shopper needed under one roof. Kroger executives thought the idea was crazy. So Cullen did it on his own, using his life savings. King Kullen, the Price Wrecker, opened in March 1930 in an abandoned warehouse in Jamaica, Long Island.

Cullen knew the grocery business inside and out, which allowed him to buy drastically reduced merchandise from the surplus stocks of food manufacturers. Plus, his store's size gave him great buying power; he bought massive quantities at lower prices than his competitors could. Success came quickly. Two years later, Cullen was operating seven more stores, and the super-store concept was widely imitated. A few years later, in 1933, Cincinnati's Albers Supermarket became the first store to actually use the term "supermarket."

When Sylvan Goldman invented the shopping cart in 1937, supermarkets had everything they needed for long-term success.

SUPERMARKETS' WEAK SPOT

As chain stores became more powerful, both the media and independent grocers began campaigns against them. Even *Time* magazine referred to them as "cheapies," assuring the American public that these giant disgraces were only due to bad times and would disappear soon. Independent grocers launched campaigns to boycott supermarkets because they used "unfair" methods to overcome their competition—such as staying open at night and selling items at or near cost. But customers were thrilled to be paying significantly less for food and continued to patronize them. In New Jersey, a law making it illegal to sell food at or below cost was passed and then quickly withdrawn when consumers raged that it was making them pay more for no good reason.

A SYMBOL OF DEMOCRACY

But the real explosion in new supermarkets came in the baby boom years. In 1951, *Collier's* magazine reported that more than three supermarkets were opening a day in the United States, a pace that only increased in the 1960s. In 1950, supermarkets accounted for 35 percent of all food sales in America; by 1960, that figure was 70 percent. Small groceries began to thin out.

Now the media reversed itself. Supermarkets were no longer a national disgrace—they were a unique symbol of American ingenuity. Beginning in 1956, the U.S. government even began using supermarkets as a propaganda tool to promote "the American Way." Soviet premier Nikita Kruschev and Queen Elizabeth both paid rapt attention as guides at supermarkets demonstrated how a steak was wrapped in cellophane. The U.S. Information Agency even arranged for the Pope to come and bless an American supermarket.

The government set up demo stores in several European cities, where people were amazed at the variety of food under one roof. Italians in particular were astonished by certain aspects of American supermarkets, such as pet food, which didn't exist in Italy. It drew such a large crowd that the pet food section had to be removed. Another was the concept of self-service. Italians were amazed that they could actually touch food before they bought it. Some even suspected that the United States had devious motives in introducing the supermarket. Left-wing newspapers were full of conspiracy theories.

Supermarkets are widespread in many countries today, but they remain an international symbol of American culture and know-how.

Q. What are bellysinkers, doorknobs, and burl cakes? A. Nicknames for doughnuts.

THE QUOTABLE VAMPIRE

A collection of favorite vampire quotes from books, TV, and film.

"All I know is I haven't had a suntan in one hundred and thirty-six years . . . I'd give anything just to go to the beach for at least fifteen minutes."
—Suzy the vampire,
***Vampire Hookers* (1986)**

"There's no getting around it, kid, vampires drink blood. We suggest pigs' blood—B negative. I think you'll find it surprisingly, um, full-bodied, with a smooth flavor."
—Modoc, *My Best
Friend Is a Vampire* (1988)

"Look. The night. It's so bright it'll blind you."
—The vampire Mae,
***Near Dark* (1987)**

"This part of the seduction is quite simple, really. Just take away everything that she has, then give her everything she needs."
—The vampire Maxmillian,
***Vampire in Brooklyn* (1995)**

"I buried myself for 100 years to get away from you. Can't you take a hint?"
—The vampire Angelique,
***Nightlife* (1989)**

"Fun? How would you like to go around dressed like a head-waiter for seven hundred years? Just once I'd like to go to dinner dressed in a turtle-neck and a sports jacket."
—Dracula to Renfield, *Love
at First Bite* (1979)

"Humans are prey, they are sustenance, cattle. Do you converse with a hamburger before you eat it? Do you converse with a milkshake?"
—Jacob, *To Sleep
with a Vampire* (1992)

"You shall pay, black prince. I shall place a curse of suffering on you that will doom you to a living hell. A hunger, a wild gnawing animal hunger will grow in you, a hunger for human blood."
—Dracula,
***Blacula* (1972)**

"There's only one way you can be with me, but you have to do something you've never done before . . . commit your-self . . . forever."
—The vampire
Louise, *The Girl with
the Hungry Eyes* (1993)

Alfred Hitchcock never won an Academy Award.

"I'll take a lite . . . Blood Lite."
—**Vampire in a vampire bar,**
***Nightlife* (1989)**

"For centuries I have known the magical powers of blood—powers greater even than those of holy water. That fountain of youth that with-stands the ravages of time."
—**Countess Dracula,**
***Mama Dracula* (1980)**

"I think I should warn you I have certain unusual habits. I'm a late riser, very late . . . When I'm sleeping I must never be disturbed . . . And I'm on a liquid diet."
—**The vampire Angelique,**
***Nightlife* (1989)**

"Vampires get such a crummy deal," she complained. "Not only do we have to sleep in worm-eaten old coffins and wear these smelly old clothes,

but we can't even look in the mirror when we want to fix ourselves up a little bit."
—**The vampire Anna to her human friend Tony,** *The Vampire Moves In* **(1985)**

"I may never see the sunrise, but I can take you to worlds beyond your dreams. I can teach you about the stars. We'll dance in their light—for eternity."
—**The vampire Carmilla,**
***Carmilla* (1990)**

"We have lived in this country for four generations. We're Americans— Carpathian-Americans. We work here, we live here, we pay taxes, we're entitled to the protection of the law. I think it's time we came out of the damn coffin."
—**Harry, to his vampire family,** *Blood Ties* **(1991)**

* * *

MONKEY MISCELLANY

"The most intelligent ape is the chimpanzee. At one time western anthropologists thought that the gorilla was smarter, but Africans familiar with both animals say, 'If you throw a spear at the njina [gorilla], he will spring out of its way; but if you throw one at the nchigo [chimpanzee], he will catch it in his hand and throw it back at you."
—***The Guinness Book of Animal Facts and Feats***

Humans have been branding animals for more than 7,000 years.

ANOTHER LOOK AT MOTHER GOOSE

Many historians say nursery rhymes aren't as innocent as they seem—hidden behind the simple verses are political allegories and social commentary. That sounds enticing, but it's not necessarily true. Here's another interpretation.

ROCK-A-BYE BABY, on the tree-top . . ."
Some people believe . . . It's a lesson in humility. In fact, it first appeared in print about 1765, in a volume called *Mother Goose's Melody*, accompanied by the note: "This may serve as a Warning to the Proud and Ambitious, who climb so high that they generally fall at last."

Actually . . . The cradle is probably just a cradle. According to tradition, it was written by a Pilgrim who came to America on the Mayflower. He was "struck by the American Indian practice of hanging birchbark cradles on the branches of trees, where they rocked in the wind." Actually, since people in the Old World also used wind-rocked cradles, "Rock-a-Bye Baby" may even predate the Mayflower.

"HUMPTY DUMPTY sat on a wall . . ."
Some people believe . . . Mr. Dumpty was Richard III, who was killed after he fell from his horse in battle (that's what *we* wrote in *Bathroom Reader #2*) . . . or that he represents a high-born noble in Richard's time who fell from the King's favor.

Actually . . . It's probably just a riddle. Today everyone knows Humpty is an egg, but thousands of years ago—when the rhyme is believed to have first appeared—it would have been a challenge to figure out. Nearly identical riddle-rhymes appeared in Germany ("Humpelken-Pumpelken"), France ("Boule, Boule"), Sweden ("Thille, Lille"), Finland ("Hillerin-Lillerin"), and other European countries. Experts guess that it was during the 18th century, when illustrations of Humpty began to appear, that he became known as a character rather than just a riddle. By the end of the 1700s, the term was so well known that it meant "a short clumsy person of either sex."

According to one study, Winnipeg, Canada, is "the dandruff capital of the world."

"LITTLE MISS MUFFET sat on a tuffet . . ."
Some people believe . . . "Miss Muffet represents Mary Queen of Scots (1542–87), and the unpleasant spider is Presbyterian reformer John Knox, who perpetually berated the Roman Catholic monarch about her religion."

Actually . . . Miss Muffet is more likely to have been Patience Muffet, daughter of a 16th-century English entomologist, Thomas Muffet. He was a big fan of spiders and wrote a natural history called *The Silkwormes and Their Flies.* What's a "tuffet"? Probably "a grassy hillock," not the stool she's often pictured on.

"SING A SONG OF SIXPENCE, a pocket full of rye . . ."
Some people believe . . . The king is Henry VIII; the queen is his first wife, Catherine of Aragon; and the maid is Anne Boleyn, Henry's second wife—whose beheading is predicted in the line, "along came a blackbird and snapped off her nose." The blackbirds are black-robed monks of the monasteries Henry dissolved.

Actually . . . The rhyme probably commemorates a recipe found in a 1549 Italian cookbook, translated into English in 1598 as *Epulario,* or, the Italian Banquet. The recipe gives instructions on how to make pies containing live birds. When the pies were cut, the birds would fly out—"a party favor guaranteed to enliven any feast."

"RING AROUND THE ROSIE, a pocket full of posies . . ."
Some people believe . . . It refers to the Great Plague of London in 1665 or the Black Death of the 14th century. (We repeated that in *Bathroom Reader 2.*) "Ring around the rosie" is the red rash that afflicted plague victims, posies are the herbs carried to ward off infection. "All fall down," of course, is what happens when the plague strikes.

Actually . . . As intriguing as this sounds, most experts now discount it. The oldest known printed version of the rhyme is from 1790, more than 100 years after its supposed origin—and it's American, not English. More likely, the rhyme originated as a dancing game. One American expert, Philip Hiscock, suggests that it may have been invented as a way to avoid the ban on dancing enforced by some Protestant sects in England and America.

The Great Wall of China is long enough to stretch from New York City to Houston.

TRUTH IN ADVERTISING

Did you laugh when you read this title? Well, okay, we agree—it is an oxymoron. And here's some proof.

THE AD SAID: The Coors Brewing Company was launching its "Pure Water 2000 Campaign" in the late 1980s, "because it was the right thing to do." The company's 1990 annual report stated: "Pete Coors [great-grandson of company founder Adolph Coors] personally kicked off the Coors Pure Water 2000 program, a national commitment to help clean up America's rivers, streams, and lakes." TV and print ads showed him "standing streamside, extolling the virtues of clean water."

IN THE REAL WORLD: The *Denver Post* reported that Coors "officially became a toxic criminal on October 12, 1990, when they pleaded guilty to violating state environmental law by illegally pumping industrial solvents into Clear Creek from 1976 to 1989."

- And when a massive Coors beer spill wiped out all of the fish in a 5.2-mile stretch of the creek in 1991, company head Bill Coors told shareholders it was no big deal—the fish were only "junk fish," and Clear Creek "was not a prime fishing stream."

THE ADS SAID: 140 different retailers—including cruise lines, expensive stores, chic gift boutiques, and resort destinations "don't take American Express." So bring your Visa card.

IN THE REAL WORLD: "Some of the featured partners, Carnival Cruise Lines among them, took American Express until just before they appeared in Visa's commercials," The *Wall St. Journal* reported in 1999. "And, after reaping the national publicity at Visa's expense, quietly resumed taking American Express. Others didn't even go that far: 'We never really stopped taking Amex fully,' says Les Otten, chairman of American Skiing Company."

THE AD SAID: In 1999 American Express ran a "reality" TV

First American car race: Chicago, in 1895. Average speed: 7.5 mph.

commercial featuring a man named Robert H. Tompkins, identified as a card member since 1958. "Do you know me?" he asks viewers, then answers, "Probably not." The ad goes on to give viewers a glimpse of his life story: Tompkins moved to Paris 40 years ago to learn about wine, where he fell in love and became a vintner. In a voiceover, he thanks American Express for being there "even in the worst of times," as an air raid siren sounds and black-and-white footage of a tank rolling through the streets fills the screen. "Not to worry," an American Express representative tells him over the phone, "We've found a way to get you out."

IN THE REAL WORLD: "While there really is a Mr. Tompkins, he really is an American Express card holder, and he gave his consent to use his name in the ad, American Express later admitted that . . . none of the events depicted in the commercial had actually happened to him, not even one."

. . . Well, then, what was Mr. Tompkins' life really like? Hard to say—according to news reports, American Express "declined to give any further information about Mr. Tompkins."

AND MORE CLASSIC MOMENTS OF TRUTH . . .

- "Green Giant was ordered to tell consumers its 'American Mixture' variety of frozen vegetables is a product of Mexico."
- "Fabergé Company was fined because its ad campaign promising 'Now: More Brut!' was for a product containing less Brut than previous versions."
- "Allstate Insurance apologized for sending letters praising an agent as a winner of Allstate's 'Quality Agent Award' when the man had just been banned from the business in the largest agent misconduct case in California history."
- The John Hancock insurance company launched an advertising campaign featuring "real people in real situations." When a journalist asked to speak to these real people, a company spokesperson conceded that they were actors and 'in that sense they are not real people.'"
- "A New Jersey company was charged with fraud because its 'secret' hair replacement technique turned out to be sewing toupees to men's scalps."

—*The San Francisco Examiner*

So far, there's no official name for the @.

A 'TOON IS BORN

Here are the stories of how three popular cartoons were created.

THE JETSONS

Background: In 1960, Hanna-Barbera studios broke new ground with America's first prime-time cartoon series, *The Flintstones*. Airing at 7:30 on Friday nights, it became one of the Top 20 programs of the 1960–61 season. It did so well, in fact, that ABC wanted a second prime-time cartoon the following year.

Inspiration: So Hanna-Barbera just reversed the formula. "After *The Flintstones*, it was a pretty natural move," says Joseph Barbera. "The space race was on everybody's mind in the early 1960s . . . so we went from the cave days to the future, the exact opposite direction . . . If *The Flintstones* featured the likes of Stony Curtis, Cary Granite, and Ann Margrock, the Jetson family could go see Dean Martian perform in a Las Venus hotel such as the Sonic Saharia, the Riviera Satellite, or the Flamoongo.

On the Air: *The Jetsons* originally aired at 7:30 PM on Sunday night—traditionally a kids' time slot in the days before cable TV. But against *Walt Disney's Wonderful World of Color* (NBC) and *Dennis the Menace* (CBS), it flopped. *The Jetsons* was canceled after one season; only 24 episodes were made.

The following year (1963), however, ABC scheduled *Jetsons* reruns as a regular Saturday morning cartoon show (pre-cable). That's where it belonged. The show was so popular with kids that for the next 20 years, the same 24 episodes ran over and over again on Saturdays.

REN & STIMPY

Background: Fresh from his success animating *The New Adventures of Mighty Mouse* for television, in 1989 an animator named John Kricfalusi pitched the Nickelodeon channel an idea he had for a cartoon called *"Your Gang."*

Nickelodeon was interested in the show, but it insisted on buying all the rights to the characters, as part of its plan to create a stable of "evergreen" cartoons, like those at Walt Disney and Warner Brothers, that could be broadcast for decades to come.

There are over 7,000 asteroids in the solar system. Only 1 (Vesta) is visible to the naked eye.

Inspiration: Kricfalusi didn't want to sell the rights to his favorite "*Your Gang*" characters. Instead, "he sold Nickelodeon a show about two ancillary '*Your Gang*' characters with whom he was willing to part: a paranoid Chihuahua named Ren (inspired by a postcard of a chihuahua in a sweater), and an excretion-obsessed cat named Stimpy (which originated as a doodle and was named after a college friend)."

On the Air: When *Ren & Stimpy* debuted in August 1991, Nickelodeon had only six completed episodes to broadcast. But the show was such a surprise hit—Nickelodeon's Sunday morning ratings doubled on the strength of "*Ren & Stimpy*" alone—that Nickelodeon aired the six episodes over and over again for about a year until new episodes were ready. The *Los Angeles Times* reported, "*Ren & Stimpy* [has] started a national craze that helped turn Nicktoons into a major force in children's animation."

Meanwhile, however, Kricfalusi and Nickelodeon had a falling-out. The cable station said the cartoonist was too slow with new episodes; Kricfalusi said that Nick was meddling creatively. In 1992, Nick fired *Ren & Stimpy*'s creator and replaced him with a former partner. The show lost its edge and faded away. However, it's still considered the breakthrough series for modern TV animation. "All new shows that have any kind of style have to tip their hat to *Ren & Stimpy*," says animation historian Jerry Beck. *Beavis and Butt-head* actually owes its existence to the show. *Ren & Stimpy*'s success was the reason the channel was willing to pay for its own animated show.

BEAVIS AND BUTT-HEAD

Background: In the early 1990s, a defense industry engineer named Mike Judge grew tired of his job working for a company that made components for the F-18 fighter jet. So he quit and became a musician. After a few months of playing guitar in a bar band, he bought a $200 animation kit and began making cartoons to amuse himself.

Inspiration: "One day in the summer of 1990," *Newsweek* reported, "Judge was trying to draw this kid he remembered from junior high. It didn't much look like the kid, but when he came back to it a week later, it made him laugh, and that was enough. This was the birth of Butt-Head, with his short upper lip and massive gums. 'The guy I tried to draw, he had that laugh: "Huh-huh, huh-huh-

Close Encounters of the Third Kind is a remake of Spielberg's 1964 amateur film *Firelight*.

huh,'" says Judge . . . 'Actually, my hair is really unmanageable, so I may have gotten Butt-head's hair from myself.'"

Judge adds, "There were probably four or five guys who inspired Beavis, just a little Bic-flipping pyro kid. I've noticed that 13-year-old metal heads haven't changed much over the years."

A few years later, Judge decided to make an antisocial cartoon called *Frog Baseball*, featuring Beavis and Butt-Head playing baseball using a live frog for the ball. "I was thinking of when I was a kid and bored," Judge said. "There's nothing to do. That's when kids start blowing up lizards. You're this 14-year-old guy with no car, you just have a bike and testosterone. It's a dangerous situation."

"My mom didn't like *Frog Baseball* at all. I showed it once at this guy's house. He was having this cartoon viewing party, and everything else was very cartoony, standard stuff. When 'Frog Baseball' came on, this girl kept looking at the screen and then at me. She says, 'He isn't actually going to hit the Frog, is he?' And then Butt-head hits the frog, and she says, 'God, you look so normal.'"

On the Air: Judge entered *Frog Baseball* in a *Sick and Twisted* cartoon festival, and a week later a company called Colossal Pictures bought it for the MTV series *Liquid Television*. But before they put it on the air, the channel tested it on a focus group to gauge their reaction. "The focus group was both riveted and hysterical from the moment they saw it," says Gwen Lipsky, MTV's vice president of research and planning. "After the tape was over, they kept asking to see it again. Then, after they had seen it again, several people offered to buy it from me."

MTV put *Beavis and Butt-head* on *Liquid Televison* for two weeks in March 1993. The reaction was so positive that in May it was back full-time. It quickly became MTV's most popular show, with ratings twice as high as any other show on the network.

* * *

AMAZING LUCK

"On February 2, 1931, a horse named Brampton was driving for the wire in a race in Dargaville, New Zealand, comfortably in the lead. But 40 feet from the finish line, the horse stumbled and fell, rolled over several times with his jockey clinging frantically to his back, and crossed the line the winner."

The first canned foods appeared in 1811. But the can opener wasn't invented until 1855.

EMPEROR NORTON

Once he was Emperor of the United States. Now he's
forgotten—swept into the Dustbin of History.

FORGOTTEN FIGURE: Joshua Norton, a wealthy 19th century businessman and speculator who settled in San Francisco.
CLAIM TO FAME: In 1853 Norton bet his fortune on the
rice market and lost it all; by 1856 he was completely bankrupt.
The experience left him mentally deranged, his head filled with
delusions that he was Emperor of California. In 1859 Norton promoted himself to Emperor of the United States, and when the
Civil War seemed inevitable, he issued proclamations abolishing
the U.S. Congress and dissolving the republic and assumed the
powers of the American presidency.

No one listened, of course, but as the years passed,
Californians, San Franciscans especially, began to treat Norton as
if he really were an emperor. Riverboat companies and even the
Central Pacific Railroad gave him lifetime free passes, and the
California State Senate set aside a special seat for him in the
Senate chamber. Theaters admitted him without a ticket, and
audiences showed their deference by standing as the Emperor
entered the hall. He printed 25¢ and 50¢ banknotes that were
accepted by local businesses.

When the San Francisco Police arrested him for lunacy, the
judge dressed down the officers for detaining a man who "had shed
no blood, robbed no one, and despoiled no country, which is more
than can be said for most fellows in the king line." Even City Hall
played along, picking up the tab for Norton's 50¢-a-night "Imperial
Palace" (a room in a boarding house), and buying him a new set of
clothes from the prestigious Bullock and Jones tailors when Norton's
"Imperial Wardrobe," which consisted of old military uniforms combined with a collection of crazy hats, became tattered and worn.

INTO THE DUSTBIN: Although largely forgotten today, when
Emperor Norton died penniless in 1880 at the age of 61, a millionaire's club picked up the tab for his lavish imperial funeral. More
than 3,000 people attended the lying in state, making it one of the
largest funerals ever held in San Francisco.

The game of lacrosse is about 600 years old.

JOIN THE CLUB

Here are more stories about some of
America's most famous organizations.

THE AMERICAN ASSOCIATION OF RETIRED PERSONS (AARP)

Founded by: Two people with entirely different motives:

- *Ethel Percy Andrus*, a retired California school principal, who'd started the National Retired Teachers Association (NRTA) in 1947 to help supply health insurance to retired teachers.
- *Leonard Davis*, an insurance salesman.

History: In the mid-1950s Andrus was looking for private health insurance for her retired teachers, who as a rule lost all their fringe benefits—including health insurance—when they retired. She wasn't having much luck. In those days, insurance companies almost never sold insurance to people over 65, and more than 40 insurance companies had already turned her down, figuring she was a "crank," as Andrus later put it.

Then in 1955 Andrus met Davis, who'd already set up a similar insurance plan for some retired teachers in New York. Together they developed a policy that could be sold through the mail. "The policies sold by the tens of thousands," Charles Morris writes in *The AARP*, "and since the teachers turned out to be good risks, who paid their premiums on time, they were very profitable. Andrus and Davis were quickly besieged by other retired people, who were not teachers but who wanted to buy health coverage."

Sensing a business opportunity, Davis came up with $50,000 to found the AARP, a sort of NRTA for people who weren't teachers. The AARP went on to become perhaps the most powerful lobbying organization in the United States, with more than 32 million members. Davis became a very wealthy man, first by selling insurance to the AARP, then shrewdly starting up his own company, the Colonial Penn Insurance Company—which became the exclusive insurance provider to AARP's members. The AARP provided a number of services to older Americans, including important lobbying efforts with the federal government. Bur beneath the surface, it was driven by a lucrative insurance business.

Tallest mountain on Earth: it's Hawaii's Mauna Kea, 31,800 feet from the ocean floor.

"The AARP was not much more than a front for Davis' insurance company," columnist Andy Rooney wrote in 1996. "The AARP did not even have a list of its own members. That membership was kept under lock and key and in the offices of the Colonial Penn Insurance Company . . . For several years, Colonial Penn was the single most profitable company in the United States, even though the policies it sold AARP and NRTA members were rated poor." The AARP finally became independent from Colonial Penn in 1978, following a 60 Minutes expose that revealed the ties between the insurance company and the AARP.

THE DAUGHTERS OF THE AMERICAN REVOLUTION (DAR)

Founded by: Mary Lockwood (a writer) and six other women living in Washington D.C., in 1890.

History: Celebrating the 100th anniversary of the Declaration of Independence in 1876 led to an increase in patriotic fervor and interest in the American Revolution. A number of patriotic organizations were formed in the years that followed. One was the Sons of the American Revolution (SAR), which limited its membership to the descendants of men "who wintered at Valley Forge, signed the Declaration of Independence, fought in the battles of the American Revolution, served in the Continental Congress, or otherwise supported the cause of American Independence."

One of the first acts of the SAR was to deny membership to female descendants of revolutionary patriots, which offended Mary Lockwood enough to inspire an angry letter to the *Washington Post*, asking why women patriots couldn't be honored as well. That prompted other letters to the *Post*, including those from six women who began to organize the Daughters of the American Revolution. This female-descendants-only group was founded on October 11, 1890, with First Lady Caroline Scott Harrison, the wife of President Benjamin Harrison, serving as its first president.

Historical Footnote: The DAR is best known for its conflict with First Lady (and member) Eleanor Roosevelt. In 1939, the DAR refused to let Marian Anderson sing at its Constitution Hall solely because she was black. Roosevelt then quit the DAR and arranged for Anderson to give an Easter Sunday recital on the steps of the Lincoln Memorial. More than 75,000 people attended; the DAR has never lived the incident down.

Over 18,000 meals are served daily on an aircraft carrier.

ANIMALS FAMOUS FOR 15 MINUTES

When Andy Warhol said, "Everyone will be famous for 15 minutes," he didn't have animals in mind. Yet even they haven't been able to escape relentless publicity.

THE STAR: Number 61, a chimpanzee
THE HEADLINE: *Monkey Has The Right Stuff*
WHAT HAPPENED: On January 31, 1963, NASA launched a Redstone 2 rocket into suborbital flight. The mission's "pilot" was Number 61, a chimpanzee and primate guinea pig for a scientific study on the impact of space flight on humans. He was renamed Ham (an acronym for Holloman Aerospace Medical Center).

His mission was scheduled to last 14 1/2 minutes, but a lot went wrong: A faulty component added 2 minutes to the flight, the oxygen nearly ran out, and as the rocket returned to Earth, Ham pulled 17 G's (17 times the weight of gravity) instead of the 12 G's the scientists had predicted. "Nevertheless," Ruthven Tremain writes in The Animal's Who's Who, "having been trained to respond to flashing lights by working various switches to avoid electric shocks, he performed so well he received only three shocks the entire flight."

THE AFTERMATH: Ham lived out the rest of his life at the National Zoological Park in Washington, D.C., where he was a star.

THE STAR: Hachiko, an Akita dog
THE HEADLINE: *Dog Remains Faithful to the End*
WHAT HAPPENED: For years Hachiko followed his master, Professor Eisaburo Ueno, to the Shibuya railroad station in Tokyo, where the professor caught the train to work; then he waited at the station until the professor returned from work at night. In May 1925, Dr. Ueno dropped dead at the university and never returned home. Hachiko waited at the train station until midnight, and then returned the next day and waited again. He returned to the train station to wait for his master every day until he died in 1934.

Old American weather superstition: If you see a dog eating grass, it will rain.

THE AFTERMATH: Hachiko's loyalty to his master made him famous throughout Japan, and when he died, a statue honoring him was erected in Shibuya station. The station has held an annual memorial service ever since.

THE STAR: Allan F-1, a black stallion born in 1886
THE HEADLINE: *Slow Horse Is Late Bloomer*
WHAT HAPPENED: One of the worst racing horses of his day, every owner who bought Allan F-1 lost money on him and quickly resold him. One owner traded him for a mule, another had to settle for a donkey.

But the horse had one redeeming feature: when he did pace, he looked very pretty doing it. So in 1901 a breeder named James R. Brantley bred the 15-year-old horse to a Tennessee walking horse.
THE AFTERMATH: Allan F-1 wasn't the first walking horse, but he was so beautiful and so successful at transmitting his unique loose gait to his offspring that in 1938, the Tennessee Walking Horse Breeder's Association designated Allan its "foundation sire"—the father of the breed.

THE STAR: Blanco, a white Collie
THE HEADLINE: *First Dog Is Second Rate*
WHAT HAPPENED: When President Lyndon Johnson moved into the White House in 1963, he brought along his Beagles—Him and Her. The dogs made headlines on April 27, 1964, when LBJ picked them up by their ears. A photographer got a shot of Him and Her yelping in pain. The White House was deluged with calls and letters from angry dog lovers.

Her died in November 1964, after swallowing a stone, and Him died in June 1966, run over by a car while chasing a squirrel across the White House lawn. It made national news, and dozens of people wrote the White House offering the president a new dog. LBJ said no, but eventually accepted one. He chose Blanco, a white collie. Bad choice: When Blanco arrived at the White House, she began biting every dog and most of the people she came in contact with.
THE AFTERMATH: Blanco was kept on tranquilizers for the rest of LBJ's presidency, and according to one account, "when Johnson left office, he was finally persuaded to give Blanco away."

A newborn baby's brain weighs only three ounces; the average adult's weighs three pounds.

THE BIRTH OF THE SUBMARINE, PART III

You've probably heard of the Monitor *and the* Merrimack . . . *but have you heard of the CSS Hunley? Here's Part III of our story on the origin of the submarine. (Part II is on page 525.)*

DAMN YANKEES

The situation was desperate. By 1863, the second year of the American Civil War, the U.S. Navy had succeeded in blockading Charleston, South Carolina, ports, halting virtually all Southern shipping. The Confederacy was willing to try just about anything to reopen its ports—including using submarines.

They came up with a class of small, cigar-shaped ironclad subs called *Davids* (From David and Goliath). Fatal design flaw: the *Davids* were steam powered, which meant that they had to run with a hatch open at all times to provide combustion air for the engine. Since the boats floated only a few inches above the water line, they were prone to swamping and sinking in even the calmest waters, which made them deathtraps.

ONE-HIT WONDER

Before the Confederacy abandoned the *Davids*, one managed an attack on the U.S.S. *New Ironsides* as she sat at anchor in Charleston harbor. The *David* closed in and detonated its bomb, but the *New Ironsides* didn't sink. The *David*, on the other hand, took on so much water that the crew had to abandon ship.

"Neither ship suffered serious damage, but the encounter did establish a historical first," Burgess writes. Charles Howard, the ensign who saw the *David* coming and sounded the alarm, was shot by a member of the *David's* crew and "earned the dubious distinction of being the first fatality of submarine warfare."

Another Confederate submarine was the *H. L. Hunley*, named by the inventor, Horace L. Hunley. Realizing the danger of steam power on a submarine, Hunley opted for manpower. Starting with two old boilers welded together to make a 25-foot-long hull,

Hunley added stabilizing fins, diving planes, and a propeller shaft that ran the length of the ship and was powered by eight members of the crew turning hand cranks. Top speed: 4 mph.

DOWN SHE GOES

Confederate General P. G. T. Beauregard was so impressed with the design that he pressed the sub into immediate service. On her first trial, however, the *Hunley* swamped and sank like a stone. Seven crew members drowned. The ship was salvaged and put back in service but again sank, this time killing six of its crew. "It is more dangerous to those who use it than to the enemy," General Beauregard observed.

But Hunley was convinced that human error and bad training were the problem, so he set out to fix them by commanding the ship himself. Big mistake—on its next trip, the *Hunley* sank once more, this time killing everyone on board, including Hunley. "The spectacle was indescribably ghastly," wrote one Confederate general who was present when the *Hunley* was brought to the surface. "The unfortunate men were contorted into all sorts of horrible attitudes, and the blackened faces of all presented the expression of their despair and agony."

IF AT FIRST YOU DON'T SUCCEED . . .

"Since every trip made by this submarine seemed doomed to disaster," Richard Garrett writes in *Submarines*, "it was decided that the time for trials was over. If she was to kill more men, she might as well take a fragment of Yankee shipping with her."

At 8:00 p.m. on February 17, 1864, the *Hunley* attacked the USS *Housatonic*, a 1,400-ton steam-powered Union warship. The *Housatonic's* crew knew that the Confederacy was using submersibiles to attack Union ships, so as soon as they saw the *Hunley* coming they weighed anchor and began steaming away. But it was too late—the *Hunley* closed in on the *Housatonic*, placed a 90-pound explosive charge on her hull, backed away, and detonated the charge. The bomb blew a hole in the *Housatonic's* hull below the waterline, sinking her. It was a huge event in naval history: for the first time, a submarine had sunk an enemy warship in battle, something that would not be repeated until the end of World War I more than 50 years later.

Snails are born with their shells on.

YOU WIN SOME, YOU LOSE SOME

True to form, though, at the moment of her victory the *Hunley's* luck deserted her. The *Housatonic* settled in shallow water. The crew was able to climb up into the rigging and wait for help; in the end, only one officer and four members of the *Housatonic's* 160-man crew died in the attack.

But, as Dan Van Der Vat writes in *Stealth at Sea: The History of the Submarine*,

> The Hunley, having become the first submersible to sink an enemy vessel, promptly became the first such craft to be lost in action. Swamped in the turbulence caused by the unexpectedly violent explosion, the vessel sank with a loss of all nine aboard.

The *Hunley* had sunk one ship and killed five enemy seamen at the cost of the lives of 32 men. But by sinking the *Housatonic*, the *Hunley* proved that submarines could be lethal weapons in wartime, guaranteeing that more subs would be built.

LOST . . . AND FOUND

What happened to the *Hunley*? Workers clearing sunken ships from Charleston Harbor after the war discovered it, then lost it again. P. T. Barnum offered a $100,000 reward to anyone who could find the wreck, but it wasn't found until May 1995, buried beneath 3 feet of silt in 30 feet of water, four miles short of its intended destination. The sub was brought to the surface in August in 2000 and is now being restored.

* * *

BUGS IN THE MOVIES

Tarantulas have a reputation for being dangerous, and all of them look scary on-screen. But, according to Ray Mendez, an "insect wrangler" for film, TV, and commercials, many varieties are harmless.

"The Mexican Red-Knee tarantula and the American Desert tarantula are both passive," he says. "Almost all of the tarantulas on the screen are one of those types." So if James Bond finds a hairy tarantula in his bed, it's really just an innocuous spider? "That's right," Mendez laughs.

An electric eel gives off 400 volts of electricity. (Your refrigerator runs on 110.)

UNCLE JOHN'S
STALL OF FAME

More memorable bathroom achievements.

Honoree: Richard List, a 47-year-old landscaper in Berkeley, California

Notable Achievement: Best artistic use of discarded toilets

True Story: List is the inventor of "plop art." In 1993, he moved 19 old toilets into a vacant lot, painted them Day-Glo orange, pink, and green and declared them the New-Sense (say it fast) Museum. Then, between the commodes, he gradually added decorated television sets . . . disembodied mannequins . . . weird sculptures . . . and a host of other odds and ends. "What can I say?" said a nearby retailer. "Art is whatever you can get away with, I guess. I'd much rather have a nice monumental Picasso or an ice skating rink, but we have the Toilet Museum."

Honoree: The government of Suwon, South Korea

Notable Achievement: Using clean bathrooms as a foreign relations tool

True Story: "In this era of globalization," declared one government official, "it is important to become the leader in the world in the cleanest bathrooms." According to news reports, the city has 580 "plush public restrooms . . . Toilet seats are heated, violin music plays, and tasteful paintings and flower arrangements adorn the rooms . . . There are weekly guided tours and according to officials, some people arrange to meet inside to have tea."

Honoree: Annabel Elliott Outhouse of Nova Scotia

Notable Achievement: Writing the only book about outhouses by someone named Outhouse

True Story: Her book is entitled *Outhouses of the Island*, and although it sounds as though it might be a family genealogy, it really is about outdoor toilets in Long Island, Nova Scotia.

What do a brick and a plate-glass window have in common? They're both made from sand.

Honoree: The Dutch town of Bergen op Zoom

Notable Achievement: Most unusual way of handling dog poop

True Story: On city sidewalks, the town installed flushing toilets for dogs.

Honoree: *Weekly World News*

Notable Achievement: Best supernatural reporting about toilets

True Story: In 1999, a headline in the tabloid read: "PRIEST CALLED IN TO EXORCISE TOILET—AFTER LADY VAN-ISHES!" The story explained that the woman was the fourth victim of "the cursed crapper," which had already claimed three plumbers. "There was something demonic dwelling in that toilet, according to the famed French exorcist who conducted the ceremony. 'It seems clear that those who vanished were sucked straight into Hell,' he said. 'And that, I'm sure, was not a pleasant experience.'"

Honoree: Bob Kelley, radio announcer for the Los Angeles Angels, a minor league baseball team in the 1940s and 1950s

Notable Achievement: Turning a potential bathroom disaster into entertainment

True Story: According to Steve Harvey in *Only in L.A.*, "Kelley re-created road games of the minor league Angels in the studio at KMPC. He obtained the play-by-play from Western Union and called the game as if he were there, using various sound effects. One Sunday . . . Kelley returned from a local bar to call the second game of a double-header . . . And he felt the call of nature—really bad . . . But he couldn't leave because there was no one to take his place. Finally he picked up a metal wastebasket and in a few moments he said, "Uh-oh, folks. It's starting to rain. I think you can hear it coming down on this old tin roof.'"

Honoree: Koko, the gorilla that knows American sign language

Notable Achievement: Being the first member of the ape family to master "potty talk"

True Story: In the late 1990s, Koko participated in a live Internet chat on America Online. According to one account, "When asked about her boyfriend, Koko replied, 'toilet.'"

In 1977, you could have bought a seat on the New York Stock Exchange for $35,000.

WIDE WORLD OF WEIRD SPORTS

Calling all jocks: Tired of baseball, football, etc.? Don't
fret—you've got plenty of options! Here are some
little-known sports that may tickle your fancy.

BOG SNORKELING
Where They Do It: Llanwrtyd Wells, Wales
How It's Played: The idea is to completely immerse yourself
in a bog, breathing through a snorkel. One description: "Snorkelers
plunge into a smelly ditch near the village of Llanwrtyd Wells and
embark on a furious downstream dog paddle. Their aquatic odyssey
presents many daunting challenges: the bog's sludgy consistency,
the disgusting brown backwash that the swimmers generate, and
the determined water scorpions that like to burrow into one's
bathing suit."(*Outside* magazine)

If that's not weird enough, there's also Bike Bog Snorkeling
held in Powys, Wales. As *Bizarre* magazine describes it, "the idiots
who took part in the inaugural mountain-bike bog snorkeling
championship soon realized the error of their ways as they cycled
into the slimy abyss. Visibility was down to a few feet, and despite
the fact that the bikes had been specially prepared by having every
orifice stuffed with lead shot, they did their best to float away . . .
Riders competed against the clock to cycle round a post—with a
special prize for anyone who could cycle back out of the bog—this
proved to be impossible."

CANINE FREESTYLE DANCING

Where They Do It: Everywhere. There are more than 8,000
enthusiasts around the world.

How It's Played: Dancing with your dog for prizes? Not a sport,
exactly, but who can resist? The idea is to move in time with a dog
partner, but you're not allowed to hold the dog's paws, the way you
would in "at-home dog dancing." In fact, you're not supposed to
touch the dog at all. According to the *New York Times*, "costumed
owners and their matching-collared pooches exhibit choreography

---

The first motion picture, copyrighted in the United States, shows a man sneezing (1894).

to such tunes as 'The Yellow Rose of Texas' and 'Get Happy' and compete for prizes. "You will discover," says the national Canine Freestyle Federation, "that your dog likes music! . . . You'll see a new sparkle in his eye, feet stepping higher and a tail wagging harder."

WADLOPING

Where They Do It: In the Waddenzee, a shallow inlet separating the northern Netherlands mainland from the East Frisian Islands

How It's Played: Entrants leap off a dike on Holland's north coast into the knee-deep, sulfurous mud and trudge across the Waddenzee to Simonzand Island, four hours away by foot (when your feet are knee-deep in mud). "Some wadlopers suffer attacks of agoraphobia when they can see no land, just a 360-degree horizon of worm-pocked mud," the *Wall Street Journal* reports. "Veteran wadlopers hike to more distant islands. For the truly obsessed, there's the 'monster walk' to the German island of Borkum, 14 miles away. Borkum, the wadloper's Everest, has been reached by just three men, who waited three years for the lowest possible tide and even then had to walk four miles through neck-high water."

Rules of the Game: "A wrong turn or a change in the wind can put the wadloper in deep water, with no way back to land but to swim. About 15 years ago, a group of wadlopers went astray and had to be rescued by helicopter . . . The Dutch government has since banned freelance wadlopen, requiring wadlopers to travel with trained guides, who carry compasses, maps, two-way radios and rescue equipment."

AND DON'T FORGET . . .

Finnish Wife-Carrying. According to *Parade* magazine, "the goal: carry a woman, preferably someone else's wife, over a 780-foot course through water, on sand, grass, and asphalt, and over two fences. Dropping the woman results in a 15-second penalty. The fastest man earns the big prize: the woman's weight in lemonade."

Welsh Shin-Kicking. Also known as "purring." "Two men face each other, each holding the shoulders of his opponent. They kick each other's shins until one man loses his grip on his opponent. To add to the pain, their shoes are reinforced." (Update: "The sport has failed to catch on in other nations."

Critter rule of thumb: If it's a mammal, it has a tongue (or at least had one at one point).

DRACULA, "I VANT TO BE IN PICTURES"

If Dracula had only made it onto the stage as a play (see Dracula, "I Vant to Be a Star" on p. 609), we probably never would have heard of him. It was the 1931 Universal film, starring Bela Lugosi, that finally made him a household name.

THE SILVER SCREEN

In 1930, impressed by the success of the *Dracula* stage play, Universal Pictures decided to buy it. They paid $40,000 for all rights to the novel *and* the stage plays, so they would have the exclusive film rights to the Dracula character. Unfortunately, none of the play manuscripts proved to be suitable as a movie screenplay. So Universal brought it to Pulitzer Prize-winning novelist Louis Bromfield. And when the lavish sets and scenes called for in his ambitious screenplay threatened to bust the film's budget, two more writers were brought in to "help" him finish the job.

SPLIT PERSONALITY

But before he left Hollywood (never to return), Bromfield made one lasting contribution: he combined the older, nastier Dracula of Bram Stoker's novel with the suave young Count that had become popular on stage. Starved for fresh blood in Transylvania, the old, tired Dracula would regain his youth drinking fresh blood when he arrived in London.

JUNIOR PARTNER

Dracula would be Universal's first horror movie, but it wouldn't come without a fight: Studio head Carl Laemmle, Sr. was vehemently opposed to the idea of making scary movies. "I don't believe in horror pictures," he would later tell an interviewer. "It's morbid. None of our officers are for it. People don't want that sort of thing."

So why did he agree to make the film? Two reasons: first, *Dracula*

In Greece and Bulgaria, nodding up and down means "no."

was a hot property and he didn't want it to go to the competition; and second because, he explained, "Junior wanted it."

"Junior" was Laemmle's son Julius, who changed his name to Carl Jr. when his father made him head of Universal on his 21st birthday. Junior headed Universal until the studio was put up for sale in 1936, and his years at the helm were rocky ones. "His abilities and achievements are still a matter of debate," David Skal writes in *Hollywood Gothic*, "but he made one indelible contribution to American culture: the Hollywood horror movie, an obsessive new genre revolving around threatening, supernaturally powerful male monstrosities."

CASTING CALL

Once they actually decided to make the film, the search for an actor to play Dracula was on.

Silent film star Lon Chaney, Sr., was the top contender for the part . . . until he was diagnosed with terminal throat cancer. At least five other actors were considered for the part, but none of them panned out.

Meanwhile, Bela Lugosi lobbied hard to win the role, trying to ingratiate himself with Universal by printing up publicity photos showing him posing as Dracula, praising the film in print interviews, and offering unsolicited suggestions on how the script could be improved. When the sale of the film rights was still pending, Lugosi had even tried to intercede with Bram Stoker's widow to get Universal a better price.

Lugosi apparently hoped that bowing and scraping would ingratiate him with the studio, but what it really did was make him appear desperate—which he was. Universal finally did offer him the part, of course, but for only $500 a week. The offer was an insult—David Manners, who received third billing as Jonathan Harker, signed for $2,000 a week. But Lugosi took it anyway. He'd already lost the role once by holding out for too much money, and he wasn't about to let it happen again.

ON THE SCREEN

To direct, Universal picked veteran horror filmmaker Ted Browning. Filming *Dracula* took seven weeks. Lugosi delivered a masterful performance, arguably the most memorable and influential ever. It was so convincing that a number of his co-stars wondered if he really was performing . . . or just being himself. "I never thought he was acting," David Manners remembered, "just being the odd man he was . . . I mainly remember Lugosi standing in front of a full-length mirror between scenes, intoning 'I am Dracula.'"

DRACULA MUST DIE!

Dracula is tame by today's standards, but in its day, it was a shocker. When it was shown in previews, people actually demanded that it be banned. "I saw the first fifteen minutes of it," wrote the PTA's previewer, "and felt I could stand no more . . . It should be withdrawn from public showing, as children, the weak-minded, and all classes attend motion pictures indiscriminately." Even Universal head Carl Laemmle, Jr., was put off by scenes that he found to be suggestively homoerotic. "Dracula should only go for women and not men," he dashed off in an angry memo, and the offending scenes were removed.

IT WAS A GRAVEYARD SMASH

The movie opened on February 12, 1931 and despite very mixed reviews, *Dracula* turned out to be a crowd pleaser. The gothic horror film proved to be the kind of escapist fantasy filmgoers were looking for as the country slid deeper into the Great Depression, and the tale of ordinary mortals triumphing over seemingly insurmountable evil must have thrilled a public in the grips of seemingly endless economic troubles.

Dracula went on to be one of the top-grossing films of 1931, and Universal's biggest moneymaker for the year. Thanks to *Dracula*, Universal turned a profit for the first time since 1928, and though its financial problems continued for the rest of the decade, *Dracula* is credited with earning Universal the money it needed to weather the Great Depression.

Just seven weeks after *Dracula* opened in theatres, Universal purchased the film rights to *Frankenstein*, setting it on a course to become Hollywood's reigning horror studio through the 1930s and into the 1940s, thrilling audiences (and its board of directors) with the *Werewolf*, the *Mummy*, and other classic Hollywood monsters.

For more, turn to page 673.

MYTH-SPOKEN

We hate to say it (well, actually, we like to say it), but some of the best-known quotes in history weren't said by the people they're attributed to. Some weren't even said at all!

Line: "That government is best which governs least."
Supposedly Said By: Thomas Jefferson (1743–1826)
Actually: William F. Buckley used this quote in a 1987 newspaper column. He probably took it from Henry David Thoreau, who used it in his 1849 essay "Civil Disobedience." But Thoreau didn't attribute it to anyone in particular. Why did Buckley attribute it to Jefferson? Who knows. Anyway, it was first said by the early American pamphleteer, Thomas Paine.

Line: "Here I stand—warts and all."
Supposedly Said By: Abraham Lincoln (1809–1865)
Actually: Vice President George Bush "quoted" this line in a 1988 campaign speech, but Lincoln never said it. When the *New York Times* called Bush headquarters to question the reference, one of Bush's speechwriters admitted having made up the quote.

Line: "Build a better mousetrap, and the world will beat a path to your door."
Supposedly Said By: Ralph Waldo Emerson (1803–1882), American essayist, philosopher, and poet.

Actually: Sarah Yule, a writer, took it from an Emerson lecture and included it in her 1889 book, *Borrowings*, but she got it wrong. What Emerson actually said, "if a man has good corn, or wood, or boards, or pigs to sell, or can make better chairs, or knives, crucibles or church organs, than anybody else, you will find a broad, hard-beaten road to his house, though it be in the woods."

Line: "I can answer you in two words, 'im-possible.'"
Supposedly Said By: Sam Goldwyn (1882–1974), movie mogul
Actually: This is often quoted as one of his famous "Goldwynisms" (see *Best of Uncle John's Bathroom Reader*, p. 208), but he didn't say it. Charlie Chaplin did.

What two cities combined to form Budapest, the capital of Hungary? Buda and Pest.

Line: "I wish I'd studied Latin at school so I could talk to you in your own language."

Supposedly Said By: Vice President Dan Quayle to a group of schoolchildren, on a tour of Latin American countries

Actually: It was invented by Democratic Congresswoman Pat Schroeder as an attack on Quayle. Even though she publicly apologized to the former vice president for the remark, it lives on as a "genuine quote" in popular mythology.

Line: "What we were striving for was a kind of modified form of communism."

Supposedly Said By: Harold Ickes (1874–1952), secretary of the interior under FDR and a strong supporter of Roosevelt's New Deal

Actually: In 1981, President Ronald Reagan said that Ickes made this statement "in his book," implying that it revealed the true nature of the New Deal. But the White House was "unable to verify the President's reference." Translation: Reagan made it up. Apparently it's just another example of a politician inventing something to make the other side look bad.

Line: "Everyone talks about the weather, but nobody does anything about it."

Supposedly Said By: Mark Twain (1835–1910)

Actually: Twain was so prolific and so clever that a lot of good quotes are mistakenly attributed to him. But journalist Charles Dudley Warner was the real author of this line. To his credit, Twain never claimed it as his own.

Line: "You can't be too rich or too thin."

Supposedly Said By: The Duchess of Windsor, Wallis Simpson (1896–1986)

Actually: Aside from the fact that the king of England abdicated his throne in order to marry her, this is the only thing the duchess is remembered for. Too bad she didn't say it. Truman Capote said it in 1950 on David Susskind's TV talk show.

In an average year, 46 million people from foreign countries visit the United States.

MOVIE BOMB:
WATERWORLD

*Here's another example of a film shoot that turned into a disaster—
and one of the most expensive duds in Hollywood history.*

WATERWORLD

In 1986 a recent Harvard graduate named Peter Rader was working at Venice studios and hoping to get a chance to direct. One day producer Brad Krevoy called. "Listen," he told Rader, "I got some South African money, and they want me to make a *Mad Max* rip-off. If you write one, I'll let you direct it."

Rader had another idea—he wrote a script for a Western set in the future, when global warming has melted the polar ice caps and submerged the entire planet under water. Krevoy rejected it out of hand, "That's ridiculous! That's going to cost us $5 million to make!" Wishful thinking.

Rader's script was shelved. Then, in 1989, Universal Studios found it and signed Kevin Costner, who was at the peak of his career, to star in it. All they needed was a director. Universal knew that shooting a movie on the water would be difficult and expensive, and wanted someone who had experience working on a big-budget films with lots of special effects. They chose Robert Zemekis, who'd directed *Forest Gump* and *Who Framed Roger Rabbit?*

But Costner wouldn't hear of it. He insisted that Universal hire his friend, director Kevin Reynolds, and threatened to quit if they didn't. Universal caved in and signed him to the film. "We call Costner 'Buffalo Head,'" said one studio exec. "He's totally stubborn."

SEASICK

They shot the movie in Hawaii; it was difficult from the beginning. Seasickness plagued the cast and crew, and every time a ship sailed by on the horizon, filming had to halt until it sailed out of the shot. The weather changed from hour to hour, making it nearly impossible to combine footage that had been shot at different times.

But the biggest problem of all was the fact that, as Universal had

---

First person to appear on the cover of *Rolling Stone* magazine: John Lennon.

pointed out from the very beginning, Reynolds and other key players had no experience with a huge and complicated film. They wasted a fortune in some areas, but didn't spend enough in others:

- They built a massive, 1,000-ton floating set, the location of much of the action in the film, using up all the available steel in the Hawaiian Islands , but forgot to put any restrooms on the set . . . or on any of the 30 boats used by the 500 members of the cast and crew. Result: Whenever Costner, Reynolds, or any of the other principals had to use the bathroom, filming had to halt while they were ferried all the way back to a port-o-potty barge anchored near the shore.

- Costner, who received $14 million for starring in the film, was put up in a $4,500-a-night oceanfront villa with a butler, a chef, and his own private swimming pool. At the same time, much of the crew was assigned to un-insulated condominiums subject to temperature swings of as much as 50°.

- The studio didn't spend any money researching weather conditions a quarter-mile off of Hawaii's Kona coast, where the set was anchored. "If they had," Robert Welkos wrote in the *Los Angeles Times*, "they would have learned that the area was subject to sudden 45 mph winds," which repeatedly blew the set out of position, ruining countless shots, and delaying filming for as long as six hours each time as tugboats slowly maneuvered the set back into position.

Thanks to these and other problems, the cost of the film soared from $100 million to $172 million. Costner had personal problems to boot: during filming, his 16-year marriage ended in divorce amid tabloid rumors that he was having an affair with a married hula dancer. Costner also had a falling out with Kevin Reynolds over the direction of the film. "Costner should only appear in pictures he directs himself," Reynolds told *Entertainment Weekly* after he quit. "That way he can always be working with his favorite actor and favorite director."

Word of the film's chronic problems (one crewmember called it "a runaway train under water") found its way back to the mainland. The media was calling it a flop even before it was released. Amazingly, despite the bad press, mixed reviews, and disappointing box office sales, *Waterworld* almost broke even.

Marvel comics put a hyphen in Spider-Man's name so he wouldn't be confused with Superman.

IRONIC DEATHS

*You can't help laughing at some of life's—and death's—
ironies . . . as long as they happen to someone else.
These stories speak for themselves.*

FELIX POWELL, *music composer*
Story: Powell, then a British staff sergeant, wrote the music for "Pack Up Your Troubles in Your Old Kit Bag and Smile, Smile, Smile" in 1915 and entered it in a World War I competition for the best morale-building song. The ditty won first prize and has been called "perhaps the most optimistic song ever written."
Final Irony: Powell committed suicide in 1942.

NIC MARCURA, *a Yugoslavian farmer*
Story: Sensing that his end was near, Marcura set to work digging his own grave.
Final Irony: According to news reports, "in a sudden cloudburst, water began to fill up the hole. Marcura tried to bail it out with a bucket, slipped in, and drowned."

ALBEN BARKLEY, *former U.S. vice president*
Story: On April 30, 1956, Barkley delivered a speech at a mock political convention at Washington and Lee University.
Final Irony: Moments after declaring to his audience, "I would rather sit at the feet of the Lord than dwell in the house of the mighty," Barkley keeled over and died.

FRIEDRICH RIESFELDT, *a zookeeper in Paderborn, Germany*
Story: When his elephant Stefan became constipated, Riesfeldt fed it 22 doses of animal laxative . . . and when that didn't work, he fed it more than a bushel of high-fiber berries, figs, and prunes. Still no luck.
Final Irony: The frustrated zookeeper then gave Stefan an olive-oil enema. That did it. According to one account, the elephant suddenly released approximately 200 pounds of manure, killing Riesfeldt. "The sheer force of the elephant's unexpected defecation knocked Mr. Riesfeldt to the ground, where he struck his head on

Experts say that a belly laugh can help relieve constipation.

a rock and lay unconscious as the elephant continued to evacuate his bowels on top of him," police detective Erik Dern explained. "With no one there to help him, he lay under all that dung for at least an hour and suffocated."

GEORGE STORY, *Life magazine's "Life Baby"*
Story: In 1936, the premiere issue of *Life* magazine featured a picture of newborn baby George Story. The headline: "Life Begins." Over the years, the magazine periodically updated readers on the progress of Story's life as he married twice, had children, and retired.
Final Irony: Less than a week after *Life* announced it was folding, Story died from heart failure. The final issue of *Life* featured one last article on Story. The headline: "A Life Ends."

MYRA DAVIS, *Janet Leigh's body double in the film* Psycho
Story: Davis was Leigh's stand-in, she was one of several people who provided the voice of Norman Bates's mother, and it was her hand that was seen in the famous shower scene in which Leigh's character is stabbed to death.
Final Irony: On July 3, 1988, Davis was found strangled in her Los Angeles home, murdered by a 31-year-old "caretaker and handyman" . . . a man similar to the character Anthony Perkins portrayed in *Psycho*.

BOBBY LEACH, *a professional daredevil*
Story: In 1911, Leach, who made his living risking his life, went over Niagara Falls in a barrel. He survived the attempt.
Final Irony: Fifteen years later, in 1926, Leach slipped on an orange peel and died from injuries sustained in the fall.

JOHANN UNDERWALD, *a Swiss mathematician*
Story: Underwald, one of the brightest stars in his field, was described by his peers as "the next Albert Einstein."
Final Irony: Underwald died in October 1999. Cause of death: mathematical error—Underwald "made a 250-foot bungee jump with a 300-foot bungee cord, and died immediately on impact."

Goldfish were originally green; the Chinese bred them to be many different colors. Gold stuck.

GROANERS

Faithful BRI members keep sending Uncle John their horrible puns.
Of course he loves them—and then insists on sharing them with us.
So why are we inflicting them on you? Have you ever heard the
saying "misery loves company"? Feel free to groan out loud.

A LITTLE GIRL FELL INTO a well, and although she cried for help, her brother stood by and did nothing. Finally the next-door neighbor came over and pulled the girl up.
"Why didn't you help her?" the neighbor asked the boy.
"How," he replied, "could I be her brother and assist her, too?"

A GUY GOES TO a psychiatrist. "Doc, I keep having these alternating recurring dreams. First, I'm a teepee; then I'm a wigwam; then I'm a teepee; then I'm a wigwam. It's driving me crazy. What's wrong with me?"
The doctor replies: "It's very simple. You're two tents."

A DOCTOR MADE it his regular habit to stop off at a bar for a hazelnut daiquiri on his way home, and the bartender would always have the drink waiting at precisely 5:03 p.m.
One afternoon, as the end of the workday approached, the bartender was dismayed to find that he was out of hazelnuts. Thinking quickly, he threw together a daiquiri made with hickory nuts and set it on the bar. The doctor came in at his regular time, took one sip of the drink and exclaimed, "This isn't a hazelnut daiquiri!"
"No," replied the bartender, "It's a hickory daiquiri, doc."

A PSYCHIATRIST'S RECEPTIONIST alerted the doctor:, "a man is out here who says he is invisible."
"Tell him I can't see him right now," said the doctor.

IT IS WELL KNOWN THROUGHOUT Central Europe that members of William Tell's family were early devotees of league bowling. They had sponsors and everything. According to historians, though, the records have been lost, so nobody knows for whom the Tells bowled.

George Washington's shoe size: 13.

A GROUP OF CHESS ENTHUSIASTS checked into a hotel and were standing in the lobby discussing their recent tournament victories. After about an hour, the manager came out of the office and asked them to disperse. "But why?" they asked.

"Because," he said, "I can't stand chess nuts boasting in an open foyer."

TWO ESKIMOS SITTING in a kayak were chilly, but when they lit a fire in the craft, it sank, proving once and for all that you can't have your kayak and heat it, too.

THIS GUY GOES TO A COSTUME party with a girl on his back. "What the heck are you?" asks the host. "I'm a snail," says the guy. "But, you have a girl on your back," replies the host. "Yeah," he says, "that's Michelle."

THERE'S A NUDIST COLONY for communists. Two old men are sitting on the front porch. One turns to the other and says, "I say, old boy, have you read Marx?" And the other says, "Yes . . . I believe it's these wicker chairs."

THERE WAS THIS HOUSE PAINTER who was always looking for a way to save a buck, so he would often thin his paint to make it go further—and he usually got away with it. When a local church decided to do a big restoration, this fellow put in a bid and because his price was so competitive, he got the job.

One day, just as the job was nearly done, he was up on the scaffold, painting away, when suddenly there was a horrendous clap of thunder. The sky opened and the rain poured down, washing the thin paint off the church and knocking the painter down onto the lawn, surrounded by puddles of the thinned and useless paint.

Fearing this was a judgment from the Almighty, he fell down on his knees and cried, "Oh, God! Forgive me! What should I do?" And from the thunder, a mighty voice spoke, "Repaint! Repaint and thin no more!"

A FAMOUS VIKING EXPLORER returned home from a voyage and found his name missing from the town register. His wife insisted on complaining to the local civic official who apologized profusely, saying, "I must have taken Leif off my census."

Not only is Lake Titicaca the highest navigable lake in the world, it's also the most fun to say.

PUT A CORK IN IT!

Here's something you may want to remember next time you go to a fancy restaurant (but only if you're over 21).

WHAT DO YOU DO WHEN HANDED THE CORK?

Quiz time: You're in a restaurant. You've studied the wine list and managed to order something without making a fool of yourself. Just when you've relaxed, thinking that your wine ordeal is over, the waiter pulls the cork from the bottle and hands it to you. Conversation stops, and all eyes turn to you expectantly. What do you do now?

a. Sniff the cork.

b. Lick it.

c. Bite lustily into it.

d. Nibble around the edges of it, leaving enough for your friends.

e. Toss it over your left shoulder for luck.

f. Slip it into your pocket or purse for the next time you go to the ol' fishin' hole.

g. Pass it around the table.

h. Fondle it.

i. See if there's something to read on it.

j. Hand it back.

k. Create a diversion and lose it in the confusion.

The correct answers: **h.** and **i.**

FEEL IT

Fondle it, you ask? In a public place? Well, not exactly fondle it. But feel it. Why? To see if it's wet. Why do you care if it's wet? Because a dry cork means that the bottle was not properly stored on its side. If the cork is dry, can you send the wine back? Well, no, but you can be snotty to the wine steward about it. "Sir," you may say reproachfully, "This bottle has not been properly stored," waving away any apologies and excuses.

France gets **75 percent** of its energy from nuclear power plants.

READ IT

Next, you read the cork. You are not looking for messages like "Help, I'm being held prisoner in the wine cellar," although the smart wine drinker will take heed if such a message is found. No, you are making sure the winery information branded on the cork matches what is on the label.

The little ceremony is a throwback to a century ago, when wine fraud was common. It is meant to assure you that the restaurant hasn't tried to rip you off by changing labels on the bottle. Read the cork, compare it with the label, and lay the cork casually on the table. Later, you can nibble it or put it in your pocket for the next time you go fishin', but for now, you must take part in the second part of the ceremony.

SWIRL IT

The waiter pours a splash of wine into your glass and waits expectantly. It's their little trap, just when you think you're out of the woods. DON'T DRINK IT. Instead, swirl the wine around in your glass and take one long, dramatic sniff. Hold your breath for a second in order to build suspense. Unless it smells like vinegar, you exhale, look the server in the eye, and nod once, significantly.

But what if you get that vinegary smell that evokes memories of salad or Easter egg dye? Luckily, being served wine that has turned into vinegar is a pretty rare occurrence, but if that happens, discreetly tell your server, "I believe this wine has passed its peak" or "turned," or (if you prefer a euphemism) "gone to meet its maker." The server will whisk it away and bring another bottle, beginning the whole process over.

* * *

BUGS IN THE MOVIES

Scorpions are good for building tense moments on the big screen, but they're much safer than they look. If filmmakers are using a deadly scorpion, its stinger is fixed or covered with wax. And there is a less potent scorpion, called a Desert Hairy scorpion (*Hadrurus arizonensis*). It's larger than the lethal ones. Wranglers trap their scorpions by hunting them at night; if an ultraviolet black light is shined at them, "they glow a bright green."

A 7.0 magnitude earthquake is 900 times more powerful than a 5.0 earthquake.

THEY WENT THATAWAY

Malcolm Forbes wrote a fascinating book about the deaths of famous people. Here are some of the weirdest stories he found, along with some from the BRI's own files.

YURI GAGARIN

Claim to Fame: The first man ever sent into space

How He Died: In a plane crash

Postmortem: The details of Gagarin's death were kept secret for more than 20 years and revealed only after the fall of the Soviet Union. On March 27, 1968, Gagarin and his copilot were flying at an altitude of 16,000 feet above a thick layer of clouds about 50 miles northeast of Moscow. They were approaching a runway, preparing to land, when another aircraft passed within 2,000 feet of them. The airstream created by the other plane forced Gagarin's plane to dive into the clouds. Gagarin had been told that the clouds were at an altitude of 3,500 feet . . . but they were actually at less than 2,000, which meant that the ground was 1,500 feet closer than Gagarin thought. By the time he realized what had happened, it was too late to prevent the crash.

HENRY HUDSON

Claim to Fame: A 17-century navigator and explorer; Hudson Bay and the Hudson River are named after him.

How He Died: Mutiny.

Postmortem: Hudson spent the fall of 1611 exploring Hudson Bay, convinced that he was on the verge of finding the mythical Northwest Passage, a direct route to Asia. But he stayed too long, and when cold weather froze the waters, Hudson and his crew were forced to spend the harsh winter on the southern shore of the bay, 500 miles from the settlement of Toronto.

There wasn't enough food for the crew, a condition Hudson made worse by keeping too much of it for himself. When his top officers protested, he fired them. By the end of the winter, Hudson had made enemies of just about everyone on board. When the ice

---

Strange coincidence: Yoko Ono and Linda McCartney both attended Sarah Lawrence College.

melted, the crew seized Hudson, his son, and six other crew members and set them adrift in a small sailboat. Hudson was never seen again.

As for the mutineers, they sailed for Canada, where Indians attacked them. The survivors returned to England, where they were put on trial for mutiny, which was punishable by death. No one knows if they were telling the truth or not, but they blamed the mutiny on the crew members who were killed by natives in Canada. As a result, no one served more than a year in jail.

LOUIS XVII OF FRANCE

Claim to Fame: Son of King Louis XVI and Marie-Antoinette and heir to the throne of France

How He Died: In prison, of tuberculosis.

Postmortem: When the French Monarchy was overthrown in 1793, eight-year-old Louis XVII was thrown into prison. Two years later, the Revolutionary government announced that the boy had died in prison from tuberculosis. He was 10.

That was the official story, but rumor spread that the body of the dead child was too old to have been Louis. A prison guard claimed that he'd heard a boy's muffled screams coming from a covered bathtub as workmen removed it from the prison. Was Louis inside the tub? Did someone sneak him out of jail? For more than 200 years, people have questioned what really happened to Louis XVII. But we now know for sure what happened to Louis XVII. Why? The doctor who performed the autopsy in 1795 stole the dead boy's heart and preserved it in alcohol. When the French monarchy was restored in 1814, he offered to give it back, but the offer was turned down. The pickled heart was then given to the Spanish branch of the Bourbon dynasty, who held on to it until 1975, when it was returned to the royal crypt in France.

In 1999, French historian Philippe Delorme arranged for the DNA in the heart to be compared with the DNA in some surviving locks of Marie Antoinette's hair. "It was Louis XVII" Delorme says. "It was the last little king of France who died in that prison." Will that put an end to the controversy? Not a chance, Delorme says. "There will always be some people who think Louis XVII escaped."

Shortest river: The River D in Oregon. It's 120 feet long.

MORE EXECUTIVE DECISIONS

We don't want to single anyone out—we just want to gloat that even the high and mighty sometimes make embarrassingly bad decisions.

ROSS PEROT

In 1979, Perot employed some of his well-known business acumen and foresaw that Bill Gates was on his way to building Microsoft into a great company. So he offered to buy him out. Gates says Perot offered between $6 million and $15 million; Perot says that Gates wanted $40 million to $60 million. Whatever the numbers were, the two couldn't come to terms, and Perot walked away empty-handed. Today, Microsoft is worth hundreds of billions of dollars.

THE SAN FRANCISCO CHRONICLE

In 1974, the *Washington Post* offered the *Chronicle* the opportunity to syndicate a series of articles that two reporters named Bob Woodward and Carl Bernstein were writing about a break-in at the Democratic headquarters at Washington, D.C.'s, Watergate Hotel. Owner Charles Thieriot said no. "There will be no West Coast interest in the story," he explained. Thus, his rival, the *San Francisco Examiner*, was able to purchase the rights to the hottest news story of the decade for $500.

W. T. GRANT CO.

In the mid-1970s, executives at the W. T. Grant variety store chain, one of the nation's largest retailers, decided that the best way to increase sales was to increase the number of customers . . . by offering credit. It put tremendous "negative incentive" pressure on store managers to issue credit. Employees who didn't meet their credit quotas risked complete humiliation. They had pies thrown in their faces, were forced to push peanuts across the floor with their noses, and were sent through hotel lobbies wearing only diapers. Eager to avoid such total embarrassment, store managers gave credit "to anyone who breathed," including untold thousands of

---

What did actress Dolores Hart do after starring in two movies with Elvis? She became a nun.

customers who were bad risks. W. T. Grant racked up $800 million worth of bad debts before it finally collapsed in 1977.

ABC-TV

In 1984, Bill Cosby gave ABC-TV first shot at buying a sitcom he'd created—and would star in—about an upscale black family. But ABC turned him down, apparently "believing the show lacked bite and that viewers wouldn't watch an unrealistic portrayal of blacks as wealthy, well-educated professionals."

So Cosby sold his show to NBC instead. What happened? Nothing much—*The Cosby Show* remained the #1 show for four straight years, was a ratings winner throughout its eight-year run, lifted NBC from its 10-year status as a last-place network to first place, resurrected TV comedy, and became the most profitable series ever broadcast.

DIGITAL RESEARCH

IBM once hired Microsoft founder Bill Gates to come up with the operating software for a new computer that IBM was rushing to market . . . and Gates turned to a company called Digital Research. He set up a meeting between owner Gary Kildall and IBM . . . but Kildall couldn't make the meeting and sent his wife, Dorothy McEwen, instead. McEwen, who handled contract negotiations for Digital Research, felt that the contract IBM was offering would allow the company to incorporate features from Digital's software into its own proprietary software—which would then compete against Digital. So she turned the contract down. Bill Gates went elsewhere, eventually coming up with a program called DOS, the software that put Microsoft on the map.

* * *

WRANGLING BUGS

You can't train an insect the way you would, say a dog. So how do "insect wranglers" get them to follow a script? "One way," says a wrangler, "is to build the set so it accommodates the natural tendencies of the insects. For example, if an insect is phototropic (goes toward light), you can place the lights where you want the insect to go." Another way: "Have the insect go toward a food source."

What's special about October 6, 1999? The UN says the world's population hit 6 billion.

TOY STORIES

Background info about some toys you may have played with.

CLUE

Inventor: A British law clerk named Anthony Pratt

Origin: Pratt invented the game—which is known as Cluedo in England—during World War II to ease the boredom of long hours spent in London bomb shelters. Pratt loved to read murder mysteries and was fond of playing a parlor game called Murder. "It was a stupid game," he joked years later, "where guests crept up on each other in corridors, and the victim would shriek and fall on the floor." Screaming and falling on the floor was inappropriate in the stressful confines of a bomb shelter, so Pratt decided to create a board game version that could be played more quietly.

The original version had ten characters and nine murder weapons—including an axe, a bomb, and a hypodermic syringe. The original game board, which Pratt's wife Elva drew up on the dining room table, wasn't much different from the one still in use today.

Selling It: Encouraged by a friend, Pratt sold Murder to the British game company Waddington's in 1945. They reduced the number of characters to six, substituted candlesticks and lead pipes for some of the gorier murder weapons, and began selling it under the name Cluedo in 1945. In 1953 Waddington's advised Pratt that sales were beginning to slow. So he signed away the international rights to the game for a final payment of £5,000—the equivalent of about $100,000 today. Bad move: Cluedo went on to sell more than 150 million sets in 23 countries around the world.

MR. POTATO HEAD

Inventor: A professional toy designer named George Lerner

Origin: In 1951, Lerner paid a visit to the Hassenfeld Brothers Company, a manufacturer of pencils and school supplies that was beginning to dabble in the toy business. He wanted to sell them a toy that consisted of tiny body parts made from plastic—eyes, ears, noses, hair, hats, mustaches, a pipe, etc.—that kids were supposed to stick into fresh vegetables to create funny-faced char-

---

The voice of Betty Boop was also Olive Oyl's voice . . . and occasionally Popeye's too.

acters. Any fresh vegetable would do, Lerner told the company's president, Merrill Hassenfeld, but, he added, "potatoes seemed to work the best."

Selling It: Hassenfeld bought the idea for $500 and a 5 percent royalty, and made Mr. Potato Head the first toy ever advertised with TV commercials. (That year he also shortened the company's name to Hasbro.) "Whatever Potato Head's secret," G. Wayne Miller writes in Toy Wars, "the toy struck a chord, with adults as well as children . . . Merrill had been optimistic, but he never dreamed of moving a million units the first year." It was Hasbro's first big hit. They followed with Mrs. Potato Head and the Potato Head Pets. Hasbro, by the way, is now the largest toy company in the world. Coincidence? Or do vegetables really make you grow?

- Going Through Changes: The points on the various pieces had to be sharp for kids to stick into real potatoes, and they were . . . until the early 1960s. That's when Hasbro started worrying about liability, and decided it would be safer to dull the points and provide a plastic potato to stick the parts into.

- This brought protests: "One of the most wonderful things [was] that a child could place the eyes, ears, nose, and mouth anywhere," philosophy professor Stephen Viccio complained in the *New York Times*, "creating potatoes like Salvador Dali would have made if he were God." Even the natural potato's perishability was a plus, Viccio wrote, because it taught kids an important lesson: "the rotting potato skin began to act as a metaphor for the way of all flesh."

- Remember when Mr. Potato Head smoked a pipe? Not anymore, thanks to U.S. Surgeon General C. Everett Koop, who in 1987 complained that "not only is it dangerous to his health, it gives the message to kids that smoking is not a bad thing to do." So Hasbro pulled the pipe. Their reward: Mr. Potato Head became the "official spokes-spud" for the Great American Smokeout.

* * *

Chutes and Ladders was based on the traditional game Snakes and Ladders. Milton Bradley simply substituted "a playground setting for the snakes, which were thought to put kids off," says a company spokesperson.

When Jerry Lewis wanted to make *Catcher in the Rye* into a film, J. D. Salinger said no.

YOU CALL THIS ART?

Have you ever been in an art museum or gallery and seen something that made you wonder, "is this really art?" Maybe you assumed that there was something you didn't understand. Or maybe you just laughed. Well, we don't know what art is, but we know what sounds ridiculous.

ARTIST: Zhang Huan, a San Francisco performance artist
BACKGROUND: Huan's performance, titled "Dream of the Dragon," was part of *Inside Out: New Chinese Art*, an exhibition at San Francisco's Asian Art Museum in 1999. Purpose of the art: "To explore the physical and psychological effects of human violence in modern society."

THIS IS ART? Zhang took off his clothes and lay face down on a tree branch; then an assistant smeared him head-to-toe with pureed hot dogs and sprinkled him with flour. Then, as the grand finale, eight dogs were brought in to take a look. Seven of the dogs were only mildly interested. But one, an Akita named Hercules, mistook the art for food. He took a bite out of Zhang's butt—even drawing a little blood.

Afterthought: "I'm pretty embarrassed." said Lee McCoy, who was dog-sitting Hercules for a friend. "I was afraid Hercules might pee on the tree, but he bit him in the behind instead. Wait until my friend finds out I didn't take the dog to the beach."

ARTIST: Cosimo Cavallore
BACKGROUND: His mother once owned a deli in Canada, and family members made their own cheese to sell there. Cavallore got the idea for using cheese as art one day when he came back from lunch . . . and noticed his father's old armchair in a way that he'd never noticed it before. So he covered it in melted mozzarella cheese. "It was a childish act," Cavallore says. "I was allowing myself to dirty his chair. I guess I finally stood up to him." Then Cavallore got the urge to drape an entire hotel room in melted cheese.

THIS IS ART? He probably wouldn't have been able to live out his fantasy . . . but he crossed paths with Jules Feiler, a gallery owner. Feiler helped him find a hotel that was willing to do it. The

There really is a unit of time called a "jiffy." It's exactly 1/100th of a second.

Washington Jefferson hotel was undergoing renovation anyway and was looking for "something to draw new customers."

In exchange for the standard rate of $100 a night, the hotel let him coat Room 114 and everything in it with more than 1,000 pounds of melted Gruyere, Swiss, and other cheeses. He coated the walls, ceiling, and floor with the stuff; he smeared it all over the furniture; he even draped it over the ceiling fan and overhead lights in long ropes that reached to the floor.

Afterthought: When the exhibition ended on June 20, Feiler arranged for a comic to live in the room for a month, telling jokes to anyone who knocked on the door. He insists that he and Cavallore are serious. "When I first talked to Cavallore," Feiler says, "I thought he was just another in a series of nuts that have entered my life, but that's not the case. I really believe his work is genuine."

MORE "ART"?

Pachyderm Paintings. In March 2000, Christie's Auction House in New York City held an auction for more than 60 "paintings" created by elephants, presumably by holding some kind of paint brush in their trunks. Yale art historian Mia Fineman, who is writing a book about three different styles of Thai elephant art, compared their work to that of Paul Gauguin for its "broad, gentle, curvy brush strokes" and "a depth and maturity."

Garbage Art. Tom Deininger of Providence, Rhode Island, creates sculptures from trash. A network of friends make his work easier by feeding him tips on which dumpsters to raid. At last report, he was working on a self-portrait out of cardboard boxes, "with cheeks made of wads of Pokemon wrappers, teeth of Styrofoam, and a toy soldier forming a nostril."

Celebrity Lint Portraits. Bill Gardner of Calgary, Canada, produces his portraits by placing stencils in his dryer's lint screen. He'll use one stencil and a load of dark laundry to get the darker shades of color; then he'll switch stencils and throw in a load of whites to get the lighter colors he needs. Then he peels the lint off the screen and presses it in between two panes of glass. His portraits of public figures such as O.J. Simpson and the Queen of England have sold for as much as $500.

Paul Newman played Billy the Kid in *The Left Handed Gun*. One problem: Billy was right handed.

WHY DIDN'T WE THINK OF THAT?

Ever see a brilliantly conceived product or service, then slapped your head while you grumbled, "Why didn't I think of that!!?" Well, relax—you don't have to do that with these product ideas.

Entrepreneur: David Anderson, a Minneapolis lawyer
Idea: The Tonya Tapper
Description: A steel club for self-protection. "Named in honor of ice skating's notorious Tonya Harding." Anderson "came up with the idea after hearing about the steel club Harding's henchman whacked rival skater Nancy Kerrigan with." Suggested retail price: $39.95. Anderson dreamed that it might be the start of a whole line of "similar personal security products . . . a whole line of batons, with different colors, holsters, and grips—even one of key chain size."

Entrepreneur: Jun Sato, a 25-year-old man who lost his job in the recession that plagued Japan in the late 1990s
Idea: The Three-minute Beating
Description: Frustrated by his inability to find another job and fig- uring others were as exasperated by the economic downturn as he was, Sato made up his own job: He dressed up in protective padding, and let passersby beat him (with boxing gloves) for three minutes at a time. Price: $1,000 yen, or about $10. "I enjoy being used as a punching bag," he told the Reuters news service. "It's another way to experience life."

Entrepreneurs: Three English advertising executives and a pho- tographer, in the 1960s
Idea: The Really Ugly Modeling Agency
Description: The partners had a hunch that ugly faces would sell products better than pretty faces and perfect profiles. "For example, in the advertisements for second-hand cars," explained one, "we want the salesman to be believable as a second-hand car salesman."

In the Middle Ages, Europeans "cured" muscle pains by drinking powdered gold.

They put an ad in the *Times of London* asking, "Are you ugly"? That got too many ordinary-looking people, so they placed a second ad: "Are you really ugly?'"

Entrepreneur: A Ukranian tourism company called Liko-L

Idea: A tour of Reactor #4 at Chernobyl

Description: Chernobyl was the site of the worst nuclear accident of the atomic age: On April 25, 1986, Unit #4 suffered a partial meltdown, blowing the roof off of the reactor and releasing several times more radioactivity than the Hiroshima and Nagasaki bombs combined. Radiation levels are still more than 1,000 times higher than the accepted safe maximum, and Ukranian citizens are not allowed within a 20-mile radius of the power plant.

But that didn't stop Liko-L. By November 1998, the Ukrainian economy was in such bad shape that the government—hoping to increase tax revenues—granted special permission to the company to begin offering daylong trips to the plant. According to a spokesman, the radiation count around the plant is low and "not dangerous."

OTHER IDEAS

- Hunk Towing. "Dispatches body builders in skimpy 'uniforms' to aid stranded motorists . . . Sometimes calls are received from motorists who haven't actually broken down."

- Belcher Soda. Contains twice the carbonation of regular soft drinks, for "the most 'explosive' belches you'll ever have."

- "A-Bomb" sandals, handbags and accessories, made and marketed in Japan.

- The Lawn Buddy Message Machine. A 5-inch tall mechanical animal "that arises from a flowerpot placed by the front door, announces that the resident is away, and invites the visitor to leave a message."

- Bathtub Spider Ladder. A ladder that helps spiders climb out of bathtubs. "The spider ladder fits neatly around the bath taps and stretches down to the plughole. It comes complete with a poem about saving spiders and the legend: 'Handmade by a mystified craftsman in China.'"

LADIES, BEHAVE YOURSELVES

Ladies, you can follow these antique rules of etiquette . . . or just laugh at them.

"Immoderate laughter is exceedingly unbecoming a lady; she may affect the dimple or the smile, but should carefully avoid any approximation to a horse-laugh."
—*The Perfect Gentleman (1860)*

"Sending out a letter with a crooked, mangled or upside-down stamp is akin to letting your lingerie straps show."
—*Good Housekeeping's Book of Today's Etiquette (1965)*

"Fingernails are another source of feminine excess. The woman who goes about her daily avocations with blood-red finger-nails is merely harking back to the days of savagry, when hands smeared with blood were a sign of successful fighting."
—*Things That Are Not Done (1937)*

"It's a great idea to file your fingernails in the street car, bus, or train. It's certainly making the most of your time. The noise of the filing drowns the unpleasant noise of the wheels. But it is the act of an ill-bred person. Who but an ordinary person would allow her epithelium to fly all over? I think that one might as well scatter ashes after a cremation, around the neighborhood."
—*Manners for Millions (1932)*

"The perfect hostess will see to it that the works of male and female authors be properly separated on her bookshelves. Their proximity, unless they happen to be married, should not be tolerated."
—**Lady Gough's Etiquette (1863)**

"No matter what the fashion may be, the gloves of a well-dressed woman are never so tight that her hands have the appearance of sausages."
—**The New Etiquette (1940)**

"[D]on't affect a lisp or talk baby talk. Somebody will probably kill you some time if you do."
—*Compete! (1935)*

In 1999, there were over 1,800 Web sites devoted to Ricky Martin.

"A lady-punster is a most unpleasing phenomenon, and we would advise no young woman, however skilled she may be, to cultivate this kind of verbal talent."

Collier's Cyclopedia of Commercial and Social Information (1882)

"Girls, never, never turn at a whistle, to see if you are wanted. A whistle is usually to call a dog."

—Good Manners (1934)

"A beautiful eyelash is an important adjunct to the eye. The lashes may be lengthened by trimming them occasionally in childhood. Care should be taken that this trimming is done neatly and evenly, and especially that the points of the scissors do not penetrate the eye."

—Our Deportment (1881)

"If a man must be forcibly detained to listen to you, you are as rude in thus detaining him, as if you had put a pistol to his head and threatened to blow his brains out if he stirred."

—The Gentlemen's Book of Etiquette and Manual of Politeness (1860)

"Still less say of anything which you enjoy at table. 'I love melons,' 'I love peaches,' I adore grapes'—these are school-girl utterances. We love our friends. Love is an emotion of the heart, but not one of the palate. We like, we appreciate grapes, but we do not love them."

—The American Code of Manners (1880)

"Large hats make little women look like mushrooms."

—Everyday Etiquette (1907)

"Never use your knife to convey your food from your plate to your mouth; besides being decidedly vulgar, you run the imminent danger of enlarging the aperture from ear to ear. A lady of fashion used to say that she never saw a person guilty of this ugly habit without a shudder, as every minute she expected to see the head of the unfortunate severed from the body."

—Etiquette for the Ladies (1849)

"Certain daring necklines have a paralyzing effect on the conversation and even on the appetite of the other dinner party guests, who hope to see a little more than is already revealed and would love to change places with the waiter, who has a particularly stimulating view."

—Accent on Elegance (1970)

UNCLE JOHN'S STALL OF FAME

More memorable bathroom achievements.

Honorees: Don and Penny Karch of Pittsfield, Massachusetts
Notable Achievement: Using toilets—lots of toilets—to make a public statement
True Story: According to news reports, the convenience store next to the Karches' home doesn't have a restroom. So when customers have to answer the call of nature, they do so behind the store, "in full view of the Karches' kitchen window." In September 1998, the Karches decided to fight back—by setting up 28 toilets in their backyard in protest. A local newspaper picked up the story; from there, it spread to the wire services, and then to newspapers all over the country. No word on whether the convenience store ever got around to installing a restroom. (Contact us if you know what happened.)

Honoree: Lieutenant Governor Steve Windom of Alabama
Notable Achievement: Strategic use of a chamber pot to wear down his political enemies
True Story: In March 1999, Windom, a Republican, was presiding over the 35-member state legislature composed of 18 Democrats and 17 Republicans. During an important battle over Senate procedures, Windom feared that if he surrendered the gavel and left the chamber for even a minute, the Democrats would take control and his party would lose the fight. So the lieutenant governor decided he wouldn't even go out to the bathroom until the battle was won.

"Anticipating the worst," one reporter wrote, "he brought a pitcher to the chamber and conducted business—both official and personal—from behind a large podium." Two days and two 15-hour marathon sessions later, the Democrats gave in and Windom won the battle. "It takes guts to be an effective lieutenant governor," he told reporters. "It also takes a bladder of steel."

There are two countries named Congo and they're right next to each other.

Honoree: Delaware Water Gap National Recreation Area

Notable Achievement: Creating America's most expensive publicly funded outhouse

True Story: The Recreation Area, which is administered by the National Park Service, needed a new outhouse. The Park Service assembled more than a dozen designers, architects, and engineers and assigned them to the project—which took two years to complete. The final result: A beautiful "two-holer" (one for men, one for women) with a gabled Vermont slate roof, cottage-style porches with Indiana limestone railings, earthquake-proof cobblestone-and-concrete walls, and custom-built composting toilets that cost $24,000 apiece. Total cost for the two-hole privy: at least $333,000, which comes to $166,500 per hole. Portable outhouses used elsewhere in the park cost $500 each.

"We could have built it cheaper, yes," former park superintendent Roger Rector says, "but we wanted someone coming up the trail to encounter a nice restroom facility."

Honoree: Pat Swisher, head of Swisher International, a nationwide bathroom-cleaning service

Notable Achievement: Turning urinals into public service announcements

True Story: Swisher International makes those little rubbery plastic "urinal screens" that sit at the bottom of urinals. Since 1988—at the instruction of Pat Swisher himself—the screens have been imprinted with the message, "Say No To Drugs."

"It's Pat's way of getting the message out," says company spokesman Milt Goldman, "putting it in a place where every guy looks."

Honorees: Officials at the Amsterdam International Airport in the Netherlands

Notable Achievement: Inventing a new "target game"

True Story: It's a simple but brilliant idea. In 1999, airport officials had workers etch the outline of a housefly into each urinal, near the drain. "Men aim at the fly, which limits splashing," says a spokesman. Since the installation, the flies have been credited with reducing "urinal floor spillage" by 80 percent.

When a pole vaulter lands, his thigh bones absorb up to 20,000 pounds of pressure per square inch.

JUST PLANE WEIRD

*Planning a plane trip in the near future? Make copies of
this section and pass them out to the people sitting
around you. They'll appreciate it.*

GOTTA GO

"On a 1999 flight from Sydney to Tokyo, Henry Smithton got so drunk that he thought he was on a bus. Disturbed that he couldn't 'get off at the next stop,' he actually had to be restrained from tugging on the cabin door at 26,000 feet. He was arrested in Tokyo upon landing." (*Bizarre* News)

DO IT YOURSELF

On August 19, 1980, a Saudi Arabian Airlines flight carrying 285 passengers took off from the capital city of Riyadh. Suddenly the cabin was filled with smoke. The cause: according to *Stuff* magazine, it was a pilgrim on the flight who had "decided to brew his own cup of tea in the aisle . . . on a kerosene stove." The pilot immediately returned to the airport and landed safely but did not order an immediate evacuation of the plane. It was a terrible mistake: the fire spread beyond control and killed everyone on board.

NOT JUST ANOTHER CASE OF AIRSICKNESS

In June 1998, a man in his 60s had a heart attack and died on a United Emirates Airways flight from Dubai. A doctor who happened to be on board examined the man and diplomatically declared him "probably dead." To the dismay of other passengers, however, the flight attendants left him in his seat for the remaining three hours of the flight. 'It was quite distressing,' one passenger told the *South China Morning Post*. 'A lot of people were put off their food.'"

THE FOOD HERE IS TERRIBLE

In November 1999, Northwest Airlines Captain Floyd Dean got a look at the meals being loaded onto the flight he was supposed to pilot from Detroit to Las Vegas . . . and decided he wanted something different. So he got off the plane—even though the Boeing 757

Women blink nearly twice as much as men.

was scheduled for takeoff—and looked around the terminal for something better to eat. When he couldn't find anything he liked, he hopped in a cab "and continued his search outside the airport," leaving 150 fuming passengers stranded on the plane for more than 90 minutes until he returned. Northwest fired the 22-year veteran on the spot for "abandoning his plane."

IN THE HOLE

On October 26, 1986, a violent explosion ripped through the rear toilet of Thai Airways flight 602 as it was preparing to land in Osaka, Japan. The plane landed safely . . . at which point investigators found a Japanese "Yakuza" gangster dangling head-first through a hole ripped in the floor by the explosion—his hindquarters badly injured by shrapnel—while two other Yakuza held on to his legs to keep him from falling onto the tarmac. The explosion is believed to have been caused when the Yakuza threw a hand grenade down the restroom trash chute so that it wouldn't be discovered when he went through customs. (*Stuff* magazine)

THE STING

In December 1999, a man on a Mesaba Airlines flight from Detroit to Allentown, Pennsylvania, felt a twinge on his right hand. He looked down and saw a scorpion . . . which had just stung him. The pilot diverted the plane to Cleveland, where the man was taken away for medical treatment. The rest of the passengers were put on other flights; the plane was fumigated.

AIR WARS

In October 1996, Air Europa pilot Jose Carlos Tuccio was scheduled to fly a plane from Seville to Palma. As passengers settled in, he walked up to seat 6-D and said loudly to a flight attendant, "we have paying garbage aboard today." He was referring to the passenger sitting in the seat—a pilot with whom he had been feuding for years. Moments later, Tuccio went on the loudspeaker and welcomed everyone aboard the flight. "Except for the one in 6-D," he said in both English and Spanish. He was suspended for 7 days; a court later fined him $5,000.

New Jersey, the home of Springsteen and Bon Jovi, is the only U.S. state without a state song.

EXECUTIVE DECISION: THE MODEL T

Henry Ford was one of the shrewdest businessmen in American history. But he made one really dumb decision.

SHOULD WE INTRODUCE A NEW CAR?

Executive: Henry Ford, founder of the Ford Motor Company

Background: When Henry Ford first marketed the Model T in 1908, it was a state-of-the-art automobile. "There were cheaper cars on the market," writes Robert Lacey in *Ford: The Men and Their Machine*, "but not one could offer the same combination of innovation and reliability." Over the years, the price went down dramatically . . . and as the first truly affordable quality automobile, the Model T revolutionized American culture.

Decision: The Model T was the only car that the Ford Motor Company made. As the auto industry grew and competition got stiffer, everyone in the company—from Ford's employees to his family—pushed him to update the design. Lacy writes,

> The first serious suggestions that the Model T might benefit from some major updating had been made when the car was only four years old. In 1912 Henry Ford had taken [his family] on their first visit to Europe, and on his return he discovered that his [chief aides] had prepared a surprise for him. [They] had labored to produce a new, low-slung version of the Model T, and the prototype stood in the middle of the factory floor, its, gleaming red lacquer-work polished to a high sheen.
>
> He had his hands in his pockets," remembered one eyewitness, "and he walked around the car three or four times, looking at it very closely . . . .Finally, he got to the left-hand side of the car that was facing me, and he takes his hands out, gets hold of the door, and bang! He ripped the door right off! God! How the man done it, I don't know!"

Ford proceeded to destroy the whole car with his bare hands. It was a message to everyone around him not to mess with his prize creation. Lacey concludes, "the Model T had been the making of Henry Ford, lifting him from being any other Detroit automobile

How many Great Lakes lie entirely within the United States? Just one—Lake Michigan.

maker to becoming carmaker to the world. It had yielded him untold riches and power and pleasure, and it was scarcely surprising that he should feel attached to it. But as the years went by, it became clear that Henry Ford had developed a fixation with his master-piece which was almost unhealthy."

Ford had made his choice clear. In 1925, after more than 15 years on the market, the Model T was pretty much the same car it had been when it debuted. It still had the same noisy, underpowered four-cylinder engine, obsolete "planetary" transmission, and horse-buggy suspension that it had in the very beginning. Sure, Ford had made a few concessions to the changing times, such as balloon tires, an electric starter, and a gas pedal on the floor. And by the early 1920s, the Model T was available in a variety of colors beyond Ford black. But the Model T was still . . . a Model T. "You can paint up a barn," one hurting New York Ford dealer complained, "but it will still be a barn and not a parlor."

IMPACT

While Ford rested on his laurels for a decade and a half, his competitors continued to innovate. Four-cylinder engines gave way to more powerful six-cylinder engines with manual clutch-and-gearshift transmissions. These new cars were powerful enough to travel at the high speeds made possible by the country's new paved highways. Ford's "Tin Lizzie," designed in an era of dirt roads, was not.

Automobile buyers took notice and began trading up; Ford's market share slid from 57 percent of U.S. automobile sales in 1923 down to 45 percent in 1925, and to 34 percent in 1926, as companies like Dodge and General Motors steadily gained ground. By the time Ford finally announced in May 1927 that a replacement for the Model T was in the works, the company had already lost the battle. That year, Chevrolet sold more cars than Ford for the first time. Ford regained first place in 1929 thanks to strong sales of its new Model A, but Chevrolet passed it again the following year and never looked back. "From 1930 onwards," Robert Lacey writes, "the once-proud Ford Motor Company had to be content with second place."

THE CHIMP
THAT SAVED TV

One of the most famous celebrities of TV's early years.
He single-handedly saved the morning talk show.

B ACKGROUND
In 1952, when television was just getting started, few people
thought an early morning news/talk program like the *Today
Show* could succeed . . . and it almost didn't, at first hardly anyone
watched it. But Pat Weaver, the brains behind the show (and
father of Sigourney Weaver), refused to give it up.

In 1953, Weaver added a new cast-member whose popularity
saved *Today*. He was J. Fred Muggs—a chimp. Fred dressed like a
human and acted like an ape, sometimes playing peacefully, sometimes running wild on the set as host (and veteran newscaster)
Dave Garroway watched in amusement—even though he actually
hated sharing the spotlight with an ape. It was an unorthodox way
to do a news show, but America loved it. Fred became TV's first
animal superstar.

TRICKS AND TRAINING

Owner/trainer Buddy Mennella raised Fred like a son. As a result,
the chimp was toilet-trained and enjoyed wearing clothes.

- Fred's more popular routines on the *Today Show* included
  impersonations of celebrities like Jack Penny, Popeye the Sailor,
  and General George Patton. He also did a perfect imitation of
  Groucho Marx's walk.
- Fred's main dislike in clothing: long sleeves, which he voluntarily shed if he had to wear them for too long.
- He was an avid finger-painter, doing over 10,000 paintings in
  his lifetime. Fred's crowning achievement: one of his paintings
  became a *Mad* magazine cover.

INSIDE FACTS

- Fred overslept and missed his first scheduled *Today Show*

Most visited mountain on earth: Mount Fuji, in Japan.

appearance in 1953. When he arrived at NBC, the producers told him "Forget it." So the chimp and his trainer left the studio. Ten minutes later, the producers realized they'd made a mistake—the show needed the chimp. They ran after Fred and found him in a nearby drugstore eating a donut. (Mennella was drinking coffee.) Pushing aside the young man who was playing with Fred, the producers grabbed the chimp and trainer and brought them back to NBC. By the end of the day, Fred had a five-year contract. (They should have grabbed the young man, too. He was James Dean.)

- According to former NBC's Weaver, Fred was directly responsible for over $100 million of NBC's ad revenue.

- Fred's finest hour came in 1953 during the coronation of England's Queen Elizabeth. Because NBC only had access to a radio broadcast of the event, it embellished its television coverage with photographs of the new queen . . . and occasional live shots of Fred playing in the studio. The British were so offended by the NBC coverage that the incident was brought up during a session of the House of Commons, and the London stop on Fred's 1954 World Tour had to be canceled

- Fred let the show in 1957 and went to work in a Florida amusement park. He retired in 1975.

* * *

MOVIE BUGS

You may not realize it, but when you see a butterfly land on someone's shoulder in a movie or TV commercial, you're watching the work of an insect "actor." How do insect wranglers make it happen? Either they drug the insect and throw it toward the actor (on whose shoulder it lands) or—this is cheating—they run the film backward.

"With butterflies or bees," says one wrangler, "at the end of the day's shoot, I take them back and release them. I feel good about that." Where do they come from? "Some I catch, some I raise, some I get from breeders." He adds, "if you don't love doing this, it sounds pretty revolting—but it's actually fun."

Loretta Lynn became country music's first millionairess in 1965.

WIDE WORLD OF WEIRD SPORTS

Here are some more little-known sports that may tickle your fancy.

CANAL JUMPING

Where They Do It: In the Netherlands, where it's known as "fierljeppen"

How It's Played: "Contestants fling themselves into the middle of a canal on a long aluminum pole, like pole vaulting, shimmy to the top of the poles with the aid of bicycle inner tubes strapped to their feet, and then vault off—hopefully (but not always) landing on the opposite bank . . . Victors receive no cash and no lucrative endorsements. 'But to be a Dutch champion,' says contest organizer Wim Vandermeer, 'is always an honor.'"

TOE WRESTLING

Where They Do It: England. The world championships are held each year in a bar in Derbyshire.

How It's Played: Rules are simple: Sit on the floor, with right foot down and left foot suspended in mid-air. Lock halluces (big toes). "Winner must force the top of the other person's foot down, similar to arm-wrestling." Note: Part of each player's bottom must always be touching the ground. "A player may, if the agony becomes too great, surrender by calling out the words 'Toe Much.'"

AND DON'T FORGET . . .

- **Grenade Throwing.** "In 1976, 36 million Russians participated in flinging deactivated grenades in a competition which resulted in the nationwide finals in Tashkent. Valentina Bykova, a 39-year-old woman, threw her pineapple 132.8 feet."

- **Fireball Soccer.** According to *Stuff* magazine: "In Java, Indonesia, martial artists douse a soccer ball in gasoline, set it on fire, and then kick it around—with bare feet. They embark on this madness to help them overcome their fear of fire."

There are more English speakers in China than in the United States.

THE CURSE
OF DRACULA

*In every film about Dracula, there's a curse. But did the curse
extend beyond the screen . . . and actually affect the people
involved with bringing the character to life? Don't dismiss
the idea. Read these stories . . . and then decide.*

Horace Liveright. The stage producer who brought
Dracula—and later *Frankenstein*—to America made a for-
tune doing it. But he was a terrible businessman and spent
money as fast as it came in. He made more than $2 million on
Dracula alone, but was so slow to pay author Bram Stoker's widow,
Florence, the royalties she was due that he lost control of the stage
rights in a dispute over a delinquent payment . . . of a mere
$678.01. He died drunk, broke, and alone in New York in
September 1933.

Helen Chandler. She was only 20 when she signed on to play the
female lead Mina Murray in the 1931 film version of *Dracula*, but
she was already close to the end of her film career. It was tragically
shortened by a bad marriage and addictions to alcohol and sleeping
pills. By the mid-1930s she was no longer able to find work in
Hollywood, and in 1940, she was committed to a sanitarium. Ten
years later, she was severely burned after smoking and drinking in
bed, in what may have been a suicide attempt. She died in 1965.

Dwight Frye. In the 1931 film, Frye played Renfield, the character
who goes insane after meeting Dracula and spends the rest of the
movie as Dracula's slave. He performed so well in that part that he
was offered a similar role in the movie version of *Frankenstein*, as
Dr. Frankenstein's hunchback assistant Ygor.

Unfortunately for him, he took it—and was promptly typecast
as the monster's/mad scientist's assistant for the rest of his career.
He didn't get a chance to play any other type of role until 1944,
when he was cast as the Secretary of War in the film *Wilson*. Not
long after he won the part, Frye had a heart attack on a Los
Angeles bus and died before he was able to appear in the film.

Jimi Hendrix made 26 jumps with 101st Airborn Paratroopers in 1961.

Carl Laemmle, Jr. As president of Universal Pictures, he did more than anyone else to establish Universal as the horror movie studio of the 1930s. He left the studio after it was sold in 1936 and tried to establish himself as an independent producer. He never succeeded. A notorious hypochondriac, Laemmle eventually did come down with a debilitating disease—multiple sclerosis—in the early 1960s. He died in 1979—40 years to the day after the death of his father.

Bela Lugosi. Worn out by years of playing Dracula in New York and on the road, Lugosi was already sick of the vampire character by the time he began work on the film version. The indignity of being paid less than his supporting cast only made things worse. Reporter Lillian Shirley recounted one incident that took place in Lugosi's dressing room between scenes:

> I was with him when a telegram arrived. It was from Henry Duffy, the Pacific Coast theatre impresario, who wanted Mr. Lugosi to play Dracula for sixteen weeks. "No! Not at any price," he yelled. "When I am through with this picture I hope never to hear of Dracula again. I cannot stand it . . . I do not intend that it shall possess me. No one knows what I suffer for this role."

But Lugosi was trapped in his role. *Dracula* was a box-office smash when it premiered in 1931, and Universal, eager to repeat its success, offered Lugosi the part of the monster in *Frankenstein*. It was the first in a series of planned monster movie roles for Lugosi that Universal hoped would turn Lugosi into "the new Lon Chaney," man of a thousand monsters.

Stubborn Kind of Fellow

Foolishly, Lugosi turned down the role of the Frankenstein monster because there was no dialogue—Frankenstein spoke only in grunts—and the makeup would have obscured his features, which he feared would prevent fans from knowing that he was the one under all that makeup.

The role went instead to an unknown actor named William Henry Pratt . . . who changed his name to Boris Karloff and within a year eclipsed Lugosi to become Hollywood's most famous horror star of the 1930s.

"Thereafter," David Skal writes in *V Is for Vampire*, "Lugosi was never able to negotiate a lucrative Hollywood contract. *Dracula* was the height of his Hollywood career, and also the beginning of its end." His last good role was as the monster keeper Ygor in the 1939 film *Son of Frankenstein*, considered to be the finest performance of his entire career.

Count on Him

Lugosi played Count Dracula for a second and final time in the 1948 Universal film *Abbot and Costello Meet Frankenstein*, his last major-studio film. After that he was reduced to appearing in a string of low-budget films, including the Ed Wood film *Bride of the Monster* (1956). Wood also had cast Lugosi in his film *Plan 9 From Outer Space* (1958), but Lugosi died on August 16, 1956 (and was buried in full Dracula costume, cape, and makeup) . . . so Wood recycled some old footage of Lugosi and hired a stand-in, who covered his face with his cape so that viewers would think he was Lugosi. When he died, Lugosi left an estate valued at $2,900.

LAST, BUT NOT LEAST

Florence Stoker. Mrs. Stoker was nearly broke when she sold Universal the movie rights to *Dracula*, a sale that, combined with the royalties from the novel and the London and American plays, enabled her to live in modest comfort for the rest of her life. But she never did get rich off of the property that would bring wealth to so many others. When she died in 1937, she left an estate valued at £6,913.

Then again, Mrs. Stoker may have been luckier than she knew. After her death, it was discovered that when Bram Stoker was issued a copyright for *Dracula* in 1897, he or his agents neglected to turn over two copies of the work to the American copyright office as was required by law. The Stoker estate failed to do so again in the 1920s when the copyright was renewed in the United Kingdom. Since Bram Stoker failed to comply with the requirements of the law, *Dracula* was technically in the public domain, which meant that anyone in the United States could have published the novel or adapted it into plays, movies, or any other form without Mrs. Stoker's permission and without having to pay her a cent in royalties.

For more on Dracula, turn to the next page.

VAMPIRES ON BIKINI BEACH

With the single possible exception of Sherlock Holmes, film historian David Skal writes, "Dracula, has been depicted in film more times than almost any fictional being." Here's a look at some of the more unusual vampire movies that have been made.

Dracula Blows His Cool (1982)
"Three voluptuous models and their photographer restore an ancient castle and open a disco in it. The vampire lurking about the castle welcomes the party with his fangs." (*Video Hound's Golden Movie Retriever* 2001)

Little Red Riding Hood and Tom Thumb vs. the Monsters (1960)
"Little Red Riding Hood and Tom Thumb fight a vampire and a witch in a haunted forest! One of three Hood movies made the same year in Mexico and shipped up here like clockwork in the mid-60s to warp the minds of little kids whose parents wanted to go Christmas shopping." (*The Psychotronic Encyclopedia of Film*)

Planet of the Vampires (1965)
"Some astronauts crash land on a strange planet where the undead kill the living, only to discover that the alien-possessed vampiric survivors are preparing to land on another alien world—Earth!" (*The Essential Monster Movie Guide*)

The Devil Bat (1940)
"Bela Lugosi plays a crazed scientist who trains bats to kill at the scent of a certain perfume." (*Halliwell's Film and Video Guide*)

Haunted Cop Shop (1984)
"When vampires invade a meat-packing plant, the elite Monster Police Squad is brought in to stop them. When the squad botches the job, the Police Commissioner bumps them down to foot patrol until the vampires attack the county hospital. Impressive special effects." (*The Illustrated Vampire Movie Guide*)

The airport in Calcutta, India, is called Dum Dum.

Samson vs. the Vampire Women (1961)

"Sexy vampire women keep muscular male slaves on slabs in their atmospheric crypt. Santo the silver-masked Mexican wrestling hero (called Samson in the dubbed version) defeats them all." (*The Psychotronic Encyclopedia of Film*)

Vampires on Bikini Beach (1988)

"Californians save their beach from undesirable vampires." (Is there some other kind?) (*The Illustrated Vampire Movie Guide*)

Billy the Kid vs. Dracula (1965)

"The title says it all. Dracula travels to the Old West, anxious to put the bite on a pretty lady ranch owner. Her fiancé, the legendary Billy the Kid, steps in to save his girl from becoming a vampire herself. A classic." (*Video Hound's Golden Movie Retriever*)

The Return of the Vampire (1943)

"Bela Lugosi plays Armand Tesla (basically Dracula under another name), who returns to claim a girl after 'marking' her when she was a child. But his assistant, the werewolf-with-a-heart, turns on him and drags him out into the sunlight, where he melts in spectacular fashion." (*Amazon Reviews*)

Atom Age Vampire (1960)

"Badly dubbed Italian timewaster with cheese-ball special effects and a tired premise. A mad professor restores the face of a scarred accident victim." (*Video Movie Guide*)

Haunted Cop Shop II (1986)

"This improved sequel to the 1984 original features non-stop action. The vampire creature is destroyed by the hero relieving himself into a swimming pool and completing an electrical circuit!" (*The Illustrated Vampire Movie Guide*)

Blacula (1972)

"In 1815 in Transylvania, an African prince falls victim to Dracula. A hundred and fifty years later, his body is shipped to L.A. and accidentally revived. Jaded semi-spoof notable chiefly as the first black horror film. The star's performance is as stately as could be wished under the circumstances." (*Halliwell's Film Guide*)

The harvest rat spends 22 hours a day looking for food.

THE HISTORY OF
THE IQ TEST, PART IV

Here's the fourth and final installment of the IQ story.
Part III is on page 573.

Part III is on page 573.

FORGET WHAT I SAID BEFORE

In 1923, Carl Brigham published his book *A Study of Human Intelligence*, an analysis of WWI intelligence test data that laid out his eugenic "race hypothesis," that the assimilation of African Americans and large numbers of eastern and southern European immigrants into the intellectually superior "Nordic" American racial stock would lower the overall intelligence of the American gene pool.

Such racist theories were controversial even in the 1920s, but Brigham was determined to take a public stand. "I am not afraid to say anything that is true," he wrote a friend after finishing the book, "no matter how ugly the facts may be."

It turns out that in spite of all his other faults, Brigham really was committed to speaking what he believed to be the truth. Because when he came to realize just how wrong his racial theories were, he set out to correct his mistake and undo all the damage he'd done. In 1928, he publicly recanted his theories at a meeting of eugenicists, and two years later, he published a formal retraction of his own book, denouncing it as "pretentious" and "without foundation."

Even that wasn't enough—in 1932 he published an entire book called *A Study of Error* that attacked the findings of *A Study of Human Intelligence*.

TEST ANXIETY

Brigham had not given up on the idea of testing; he'd just come to realize that what IQ tests and the SAT really measured was not inborn intelligence. In 1934 he wrote,

> The test movement came to this country some twenty-five or thirty
> years ago accompanied by one of the most glorious fallacies in the
> history of science, namely that the tests measured native intelligence

---

First president to have a "First Cat" at the White House: Abraham Lincoln.

purely and simply without regard to training or schooling. I hope nobody believes this now. The test scores are very definitely a composite including schooling, family background, familiarity with English, and everything else, relevant and irrelevant. The "native intelligence" hypothesis is dead.

CHANGING THE SCORE

Brigham continued to believe that tests had merit as predictors of academic performance and, thus, could be useful for determining which students should be admitted to college.

But "he also began trying to put some distance between the SAT and IQ testing," Nicholas Lehman writes in *The Big Test.* "In the beginning, the SAT score had been a single number, like the intelligence quotient, and Brigham had published a crude scale for converting it to an IQ score. He was persuaded by his assistants, however, to divide the SAT score into two parts, one for verbal and one for mathematical ability, and to drop the conversion scale."

As the years went by, acceptance of the SAT test continued to grow. In 1934, Harvard adopted the test as a means of evaluating applicants for its academic merit scholarship; three years later, Princeton, Columbia, and Yale adopted the test for their scholarship programs. That same year, Harvard president James Bryant Conant proposed establishing a new agency, the Educational Testing Service (ETS), to administer the SAT and other assessment tests that were coming into use so that they could be administered on a nationwide basis.

FILL IN THE DOTS

Just a few years earlier, the idea of giving a test to hundreds of thousands of students all over the country on the same day would have been unthinkable. As difficult as it would have been to organize and administer such a huge test, correcting that many exams, one by one, in a timely fashion by proctors prone to human error, would have been a nightmare.

In 1933, a Michigan high-school science teacher named Reynold Johnson invented the machine that would make nationwide test-taking and correcting possible. The machine was inspired by a childhood prank—he used to scratch pencil marks on the outside of the spark plugs of Model T Fords. Graphite conducts electricity, so Johnson's pencil marks drew the spark away from the plug, and the car wouldn't start. Drawing from this experience, Johnson conceived of a machine that could sense pencil marks electrically and detect whether answers were in the right places. He built a prototype and sold it to IBM. The first IBM Markographs went into service in Rhode Island and New York in 1936.

Now that thousands of exams could be graded at once mechanically and without human error, the last barriers to nationwide testing had fallen. Except one: Carl Brigham himself.

JUST SAY NO

Brigham knew firsthand, from his own painful experience advocating and then renouncing his eugenics theories, just how dangerous a diagnostic tool like the SAT test could be in the hands of well-meaning but wrong-headed or misinformed administrators. And he worried that if a national testing agency were established, it would inevitably become more interested in promoting and defending the tests than it would be in questioning whether the test really was as effective as advertised.

As the father of the SAT, Carl Brigham had a great deal of clout in academia and the aptitude-testing community. He vehemently opposed the creation of the Educational Testing Service (ETS) and was against turning the SAT into a nationwide test. His word alone was enough to prevent either from happening.

So how did the ETS, which now develops and administers more than 11 million tests worldwide each year, come to be established? Simple—on January 24, 1943, Brigham died from heart disease at the age of 52. "The roadblock was removed," Lehman writes in *The Big Test*. "On January 1, 1948, the ETS opened for business."

* * *

IT'S THE LAW!

Boyle's Other Law: "The pull on the cords ALWAYS sends the drapes in the wrong direction."

The Laws of Assembly: "Interchangeable parts, won't."

Fernando Tatis of the Cardinals is the only Major Leaguer to hit two grand slams in one inning.

NEVER SAY NEVER

A few pearls of wisdom from 599 Things You Should Never Do, edited by Ed Morrow.

"Never get in a battle of wits without any ammunition."
—**Anonymous**

"Never ask old people how they are if you have anything else to do that day."
—**Joe Restivo**

"Never underestimate the effectiveness of a straight cash bribe."
—**Claude Cockburn**

"Never kick a mule and turn your back."
—**American adage**

"Never drop your gun to hug a bear."
—**H.E. Palmer**

"Never give black coffee to an intoxicated person. You may wind up with a wide-awake drunk on your hands."
—**Ann Landers**

"Never hate a man enough to give him his diamonds back."
—**Zsa Zsa Gabor**

"Never date a man whose belt buckle is bigger than his head."
—**Brett Butler**

"Never let your schooling interfere with your education."
—**Mark Twain**

"Never buy a fur from a veterinarian."
—**Joan Rivers**

"Never tell anybody to go to hell unless you can make them go."
—**Sam Rayburn**

"Never raise your hand to your children—it leaves your midsection unprotected."
—**Robert Orben**

"Never get deeply in debt to someone who cried at the end of Scarface."
—**Robert S. Wieder**

"Never trust a doctor who sells cemetery plots on the side."
—**Anonymous**

"Never learn how to iron a man's shirt or you'll wind up having to do it."
—**Michele Slung**

"Never choose between two good things; take both."
—**American adage**

Only the female mosquitoes eat blood. Males eat sap.

LIMERICKS

*Limericks have been around since the 1700s. Here are a few
of the more "respectable" ones that our BRI readers have sent us.*

There was a young lady of Ryde,
Who ate some green apples and
    died;
The apples fermented
Inside the lamented,
And made cider inside her inside.

There was a brave girl of
    Connecticut,
Who signaled the train with her
    petticut;
Which the papers defined
As presence of mind,
But deplorable absence of ecticut.

There was a young curate of Kew,
Who kept a tom cat in a pew;
He taught it to speak
Alphabetical Greek,
But it never got further than μû.

There was a young athlete named
    Tribbling,
Whose hobby was basketball
    dribbling;
But he dribbled one day
On a busy freeway—
Now his sister is missing a
    sibling.

A maiden at college named
    Breeze,
Weighted down by B.A.'s and
    M.D.'s,
Collapsed from the strain;
Said her doctor, "It's plain
You are killing yourself by
    degrees!"

There was a hillbilly named
    Shaw
Who envied his maw and his
    paw.
To share in their life
He adopted his wife
And became his own
    father-in-law.

There was a young belle of old
    Natchez
Whose garments were always in
    patchez.
When comment arose
On the state of her clothes,
She drawled, "When Ah itchez,
    Ah scratchez!"

There was a young lady from
    Lynn
Who was sunk in original sin.
When they said, "Do be good,"
She replied, "If I could . . .
But I'd do wrong right over
    again."

There was a young fellow of
    Leeds,
Who swallowed six packets of
    seeds.
In a month, silly ass,
He was covered with grass,
And he couldn't sit down for the
    weeds.

A cat in despondency sighed,
And resolved to commit suicide;
She passed under the wheels
Of eight automobiles,
And after the ninth one she died.

Easy to remember: Alaska's state flower is the forget-me-not.

THE BIRTH OF THE SUBMARINE, PART IV

Believe it or not, it was the invention of the torpedo that transformed the submarine from an underwater deathtrap into a safe, effective killing machine. Here's the last part of our submarine story.

PUSHING AND PULLING

In the final analysis, the main reason governments were interested in developing the submarine was that it had the potential to be an effective instrument of war. If a sub could sneak up on an enemy ship undetected underwater and blow it up, it would be a valuable weapon—but it had to have an effective bomb.

Some early subs mounted a keg of gunpowder on a long pole and tried to ram enemy ships with it. Others dragged barrels of gunpowder behind them until the powder keg (hopefully) bumped into the enemy ship's hull and exploded. Neither method was effective; the kegs seldom hit the target and the attacking submarine was at greater risk than the enemy was.

ABANDON SHIP

In 1867, Captain Giovanni Luppis of the Austrian navy came up with a new, safer method of attacking enemy vessels: rather than improve the sub, Luppis simply eliminated the crew. He tied long ropes to the boat's steering mechanism and controlled it by pulling the ropes from the shore. An explosive charge mounted to the front of the boat was designed to detonate on impact when it hit an enemy ship. It didn't matter if the attacking boat was destroyed or not—it was empty.

Today, historians consider Luppis's invention the world's first self-propelled torpedo, but in 1867, the Austrian navy rejected it out of hand, correctly pointing out that the weapon's range was limited to the length of the ropes. So, working with an English engineer named Robert Whitehead, Luppis spent the next three years working on a new design. By 1870, he'd perfected a 16-foot-long torpedo that was powered by compressed air. Boasting a

76-pound explosive charge and a top speed of more than 9 mph, the Luppis-Whitehead torpedo could sink an enemy warship from more than 400 yards away.

THE ONE THAT GOT AWAY

Rather than keep their awesome new weapon a secret, Austria invited other navies to witness a demonstration. Backfire: The British were so impressed that they talked Whitehead into coming back to England . . . *with* his torpedo. After more than 100 test firings from the deck of a Royal Navy warship, they were convinced that the invention was a winner. "The government, acting with most unusual promptitude, at once came to terms with Mr. Whitehead, and bought the rights of manufacture for £15,000," one naval historian recounted years later. Whitehead torpedoes were soon adopted by the world's leading navies.

CONTEST

With the invention of the torpedo, submarines became an integral part of naval warfare and France, the United States, and several other countries were in a race to build the best one. In 1888, to speed the pace of development, the U.S. Navy held a design competition for a submarine that could travel 8 mph under water, 15 mph on the surface, and fire torpedoes at enemy ships. The best design would win a $200,000 contract to build it.

There were three entries in the competition. George Baker of the Chicago-Detroit Dry Dock Company designed a 40-foot-long egg-shaped sub, made of wood and covered with waterproof cloth. His design was rejected because it couldn't maintain an even depth when traveling underwater. Simon Lake, a Connecticut inventor, submitted a sub that, like an underwater car, had wheels and was designed to be driven along the ocean floor. But Lake must have forgotten that there are no roads on the bottom of the ocean. "The fact that the floor of the ocean might be littered with rocks, that there might be hills and crevices, does not seem to have occurred to him," Richard Garret writes in *Submarines*. "The Navy rejected his submission."

MR. HOLLAND'S OPUS

The third submission came from John P. Holland, an Irish immigrant schoolteacher from Paterson, New Jersey. Not long after

---

More people are killed by donkeys every year than are killed in plane crashes.

arriving in America in 1873, Holland had approached the U.S. Navy with his ideas for a submarine. "The Navy," Roy Davies writes in *Nautilus*, "told him he would do well to drop the matter."

Rejected by the United States, Holland built a submarine, called the *Fenian Ram*, for a group of Irish republicans. They planned to smuggle Holland's sub back to England aboard merchant ships and then use it to attack British warships. But when Holland and his Irish backers had a falling out over money, the backers stole the sub from dry dock in New Jersey and ran it aground in New Haven, Connecticut. Holland refused to have anything more to do with them, but with no further financial backing, he was forced to take a job as a draftsman . . . until the U.S. Navy announced the competition.

Holland had so much experience building subs that he won the competition easily. He based his design "on the model of the Whitehead torpedo," he wrote in the competition notes, "subject to none of its limitations, improving on all of its special qualities, except speed for which it substitutes incomparably greater endurance. It is not, like other small vessels, compelled to select for its antagonist a vessel of about its own or inferior power; the larger and more powerful its mark, the better its opportunity."

DIVE!

Holland began work in 1894 and spent the next three years building the revolutionary porpoise-shaped submarine, which he named the *Plunger*. Holland developed a simpler way to make his *Plunger* dive rapidly, while previous subs had descended slowly by a complicated system of ballasting (making the sub heavy enough to sink by letting sea water enter special compartments in the sub). To comply with the Navy's speed requirements, he had to have two huge steam engines for surface travel, and another innovation—a battery-powered electric motor—for underwater propulsion. But the steam boilers made the inside hull unbearably hot. Holland couldn't fix the problem, so had to scrap the entire design.

By now, Holland was short of cash. To raise enough money to build a submarine that would meet the Navy's specifications, he sold his patent rights to the Electric Storage Battery Company (renamed the Electric Boat Company). The next sub he built,

The average grocery shopper stands in line for eight minutes.

the *Holland IV*, was a success. In addition to Holland's previous innovations, he gave the boat a compressed air system that extended the time it could stay under water to nine weeks. It was also the first submarine capable of recharging its batteries and refilling its compressed air tanks at sea. And it could fire *three* torpedoes.

The *Holland IV* was submitted to extensive sea trials in 1899 and passed with flying colors. "I report my belief that the Holland is a successful and veritable submarine torpedo-boat, capable of making an attack on an enemy unseen and undetectable," the Navy's observer wrote in his report, "and that, therefore, she is an Engine of Warfare of terrible potency which the Government must necessarily adopt in its service."

The Navy followed the advice, paying Electric Boat $120,000 for the sub and ordering five more subs the following year.

SHIPPING OUT

Holland had spent more than 25 years designing and building submarines and had finally designed one that, with a few additional improvements, would serve as the model for virtually all submarines manufactured over the next 50 years. But he would not enjoy his success. In 1900 the Electric Boat Company, which had purchased Holland's submarine patents just a few years earlier, forced him out of the company altogether.

Holland's health failed him, and he abandoned submarine building. He died in Newark, New Jersey, on August 12, 1914, five days after the start of World War I, the first war in which submarines played a major role. Electric Boat became the principal supplier of submarines to the U.S. Navy and is still building them today.

* * *

IT'S THE LAW!

Hartley's First Law: "The probability of someone watching you is proportional to the stupidity of your action."

Maier's Law: "If the facts do not conform to the theory, they must be disposed of."

A roll of pennies, nickels or dimes wrapped in paper is called rouleau.

FINAL THOUGHTS

If you had to pick some last words, what would they be?
Here are a dozen that people are still quoting.

"Don't worry—it's not loaded."
—**Terry Kath,** *leader of the band Chicago, playing Russian roulette*

"I should never have switched from Scorch to Martinis."
—**Humphrey Bogart**

"How about this for a head-line for tomorrow's paper? French fries."
—**James French,** *executed in the Oklahoma electric chair, 1966*

"I'll take a wee drop of that. I don't think there's much fear of me learning to drink now."
—**Dr. James Cross,** *Scottish physicist and lifelong teetotaler*

"I desire to go to hell and not to heaven. In the former place I shall enjoy the company of popes, kings and princes, while the latter are only beggars, monks, and apostles."
—**Niccolo Machiavelli**

"So little done. So much to do!"
—**Alexander Graham Bell**

"Why, of course . . . .That's His line of work."
—**Heinrich Heine,** *German poet, On being told that God would forgive his sins*

"And now, I am officially dead."
—**Abram S. Hewitt,** *industrialist, after removing the oxygen tube from his mouth*

"That was a great game of golf, fellers."
—**Bing Crosby**

"I've had 18 straight whiskeys. I think that's the record."
—**Dylan Thomas,** *poet*

"Am I dying, or is this my birthday?"
—**Lady Astor,** *awaking to find her relatives gathered around her bedside*

"Waiting, are they? Waiting, are they? Well, let 'em wait."
—**General Ethan Allen,** *Revolutionary War hero, on being told that "the Angels are waiting for you."*

Peruvians eat about 65 million guinea pigs each year.

THE EXTENDED SITTING SECTION

A Special Selection of Longer Pieces

Over the years, we've had
numerous requests from BRI members
to include a batch of long articles—
for those leg-numbing experiences.
Well, the BRI aims to please.
So here's another great way
to pass the uh . . . time.

TARZAN OF THE MOVIES, PART I

Elsewhere in this book, we tell the story of Dracula, the creature who couldn't die. In a way, that's Tarzan's story, too. Nothing could kill him—not inept filmmaking . . . or bad scripts . . . or terrible acting. No matter how poor the movie, he kept getting more popular. And ultimately, it was his success in these films that turned him into a pop icon. Here are highlights of his career as a star of the silent screen.

ON SCREEN

At about the same time he signed his first *Tarzan* book deal, Edgar Rice Burroughs became fascinated with the idea of putting Tarzan on the silver screen, too. He hired an agent and tried to sell the idea to several different film studios, but nobody was interested. "The problem with *Tarzan of the Apes* was that it was considered too difficult to film," John Taliaferro writes in *Tarzan Forever*, "No one had ever made a successful movie featuring wild animals. And how to depict a nearly naked man? Even more problematic, how to depict a nearly naked man wrestling and killing a lion? The task was daunting."

LARGER THAN LIFE

Back then, the film industry was brand new, wide open and full of fly-by-night operators out to make a quick buck. When Burroughs finally sold the film rights to *Tarzan of the Apes* in 1916, it was to a Chicago insurance salesman named Bill Parsons, who didn't even have a movie company yet. Parsons scraped together the money to form National Pictures, and then hired an actor to play Tarzan. His choice: a hulk named Elmo Lincoln, a former train engineer whose biggest film attribute (some said it was his only attribute) was his massive barrel chest. He was "everything Burroughs had wished Tarzan *wouldn't* be . . . .His beefy build belied the grace, suppleness, and refinement of the literary Tarzan."

Burroughs was so furious with the choice that he sent a letter to his agent instructing him not to sell the film rights to any more books. In fact, Burroughs was so upset that he boycotted the film's

---

Your brain is only two percent of your body's weight, but uses 20 percent of your energy.

opening at the Broadway Theater on January 27, 1918. He even tried to have his name—and Tarzan's—taken off the film.

SUCCESS!

But even though the first movie Tarzan was little more than a caveman who lived in a tree, audiences loved him. In fact, so many people turned out to see the film that many theaters had to schedule additional screenings, some starting as early as 9:00 a.m.

Film critics were impressed, too. "Remember how you sat up most of the night to finish your first adventure story?" The *Chicago Tribune* asked its readers. "Well, it's better than that! And do you remember your first love story? Well, it's better than that!"

Tarzan of the Apes went on to become one of the most popular movies of the year and one of the first silent movies to gross more than $1 million. The film's popularity introduced the Tarzan character to legions of new fans, and helped drive book and magazine sales to new heights. Burroughs, who was on his way to becoming a national figure, earned a fortune. But success had come at a huge price, Taliferro writes, "in expanding his domain from printed page to motion picture, Burroughs lost custody of Tarzan . . . He could do little more than sit by as the image of Tarzan was appropriated by directors, actors, and the public imagination. In fact as well as fiction, Tarzan was on his own."

THE NEXT FILM

Money notwithstanding, Burroughs hated the film. But at least, he figured, he wouldn't have to deal with Parsons again.

Wrong. One day, Burroughs happened to read in a newspaper gossip column that Parsons was already at work on a sequel—*The Romance of Tarzan*. Burroughs angrily called his lawyer . . . and found out that while he'd sold Parsons the film rights to only one Tarzan novel, there was nothing in the contract that limited Parsons to making only one film.

This time, Parsons expected to cash in. Although *Tarzan of the Apes* cost him $300,000 to make, he spent less than $25,000 on *The Romance of Tarzan*. And it showed. A lot of the action took place in California, not in the jungles of Africa. And Elmo Lincoln wore a tuxedo in much of the film. *Romance* premiered at the Strand Theater on October 14, 1918, and ran for only seven days.

What's Hugh of Provence famous for? He's the first person to wear glasses in a portrait (1352).

Nobody went to see it. Parsons took a financial bath, but it didn't hurt Tarzan.

CHANGE OF HEART

Once again, Burroughs swore he'd never sell the film rights to another story, but a few months later, changed his mind. And who did he choose to pilot Tarzan's comeback? Numa Pictures, a New York film company with a reputation for "shoddy and cheap products."

For *The Return of Tarzan* (later changed to *Revenge of Tarzan*), Numa needed a new star. The smart thing would have been to audition actors. But for some reason, the company's execs decided to visit local firehouses instead.

A 25-year-old fireman named Gene Pollar happened to be working that day. "I slid down the pole," he recounted years later, "and I heard one of the men say, 'That's our man.'" Numa hired him, but Pollar simply could not act.

Numa pictures lived up to its reputation for cheesiness in *Revenge of Tarzan*, but the film still did a decent box office business. If nothing else, this proved that Tarzan would bring in audiences, no matter what the vehicle. Pollar, on the other hand, went back to his old firefighting job and never made another film.

SON OF TARZAN

In September 1919, Burroughs tried again. He sold the film rights to his new book, *The Son of Tarzan*, to the new owners of National Pictures. They turned the novel in to a movie serial with 15 chapters, starring P. Dempsey Tabler as Tarzan. Never heard of him? Of course not. Tabler was a 41-year-old has-been and hoped the serial would revive his career. It didn't. So he gave up acting, moved to San Francisco, and went into the advertising business.

Meanwhile, Numa Pictures had the right to make one more film based on *The Return of Tarzan*. When they saw how profitable *Son of Tarzan* was, they decided to create a 15-part serial called *The Adventures of Tarzan*. They began looking for someone to play the apeman.

Numa may not have made good films, but they knew how to make money. In the three years since his last Tarzan film in 1918, Elmo Lincoln had become a genuine box office star on the

U.S. Government regulations on the sale of cabbage contains 26,911 words . . .

strength of two of his own serials, *Elmo the Mighty* and *Elmo the Fearless*. So when Numa learned he was available again, they signed him up.

Everyone benefitted. Lincoln's final appearance as Tarzan in *Adventures* breathed new life into the franchise, not just in the U.S. but all over the world. "Within three months," Gabe Essoe writes in *Tarzan of the Movies*, "Adventures was completely sold out in the United States, Canada, Australia, Central and Western Europe, Asia, South America, Central America, Mexico, the Indies, Pacific islands and the Philippines."

SON-IN-LAW OF TARZAN

Tarzan's movie career hit a lull, and then in the summer of 1926, Burroughs had a chance to prove that he didn't know to pick the right Tarzan, either. One night he threw a party at his Tarzana ranch. One of the people invited was a former all-American center for Indiana University named Jack "Big Jim" Pierce, who was now coaching high school sports, trying to break into the movie business. As Pierce recalls it, he was minding his own business at the party when he heard a man's voice yell, "There's Tarzan!"

"And then he proceeded to talk me into playing the Apeman," Pierce recalled later. "He said I looked just like what he had always had in mind."

Pierce was already signed to appear as an aviator in the Howard Hughes film *Wings*, but Burroughs talked him out of that role, and Paramount gave it to a young actor named Gary Cooper instead. Pierce signed to star in *Tarzan and the Golden Lion*. During filming Pierce also fell in love with Burroughs' only daughter Joan Burroughs, and they later married.

Tarzan and the Golden Lion premiered in February 1927. It was a moderate success, but it was mauled by the critics. "This wins the hand-embroidered toothpick as being the worst picture of the month,'" *Photoplay* Magazine wrote. Pierce himself became quickly disillusioned. "Because of poor direction, terrible story treatment and putrid acting, the opus was a stinkeroo," he admitted. He went back to coaching high school sports while taking whatever acting jobs he could find. *Wings*, the film he'd backed out of, won the first-ever Academy Award for Best Picture.

. . . The Declaration of Independence: 1,300 words.

TARZAN THE MIGHTY

Burroughs sold *Jungle Tales of Tarzan*, to Universal Studios, the first major motion picture studio to make a Tarzan film. They turned it into a 12-chapter serial called *Tarzan the Mighty*.

    Universal cast a 30-year-old stuntman and weightlifter named Frank Merrill as Tarzan. A former national gymnastic champ, he had the slender, muscular physique that was perfect for Tarzan. Plus, he had the gymnastic skills that made jungle stunts like climbing ropes, swinging through trees, and climbing out of pits and tiger traps a snap. "Wearing an over-the-shoulder leopard skin outfit [and matching headband], he took vine swinging and climbing to a level that shamed all of his predecessors," John Taliaferro writes. "Future Tarzans would scrap Merrill's corny costume, but hereafter each would be expected to live up to his acrobatic standard."

AIII-AHHH---OWWWW

Tarzan the Mighty was a hit (though, as usual, Burroughs hated it), so Universal quickly signed Merrill to a second serial, titled *Tarzan the Tiger*. The last of the silent Tarzan films, it was also the first attempt at making a Tarzan "talkie." Universal distributed a version of the film with a phonograph record, a "soundtrack" that, when played simultaneously with the film, provided a crude musical score and some sound effects that (hopefully) corresponded to the action on the screen. The record also contained the first snippets of lip-synchronized dialog and the very first Tarzan yell ever heard by movie audiences. What did it sound like? As David Fury writes in *Kings of the Jungle*, Merrill's yell "sounded like a man's response to pounding his thumb with a hammer."

    As the 1920s ended, Tarzan was stronger than ever. But once again it was the character, not the actor who played him, who survived. After making a few non-Tarzan films, Merrill gave up acting forever and got a job with the City of Los Angeles teaching athletics to kids. He worked with children for the rest of his life.

Part II of Tarzan of the Movies is on page 719.

THE LOST MASTERPIECE

A few years ago, one of our BRI writers saw the classic 1931 horror film Dracula *for the first time and thought it was terrible. He never knew there was a story behind why the film had so many problems— or even that other people agreed with him that this Hollywood classic was flawed—until he came across this story in a book called* Hollywood Gothic *by David J. Skal, a leading authority on the history of monster movies.*

UNIVERSAL LANGUAGE

One of the nice things about silent films is that everyone can understand them, regardless of what language they speak. Of course they needed title cards to help explain the plot, but it was easy—and cheap—to write new cards for each foreign market.

As a result, American films found their way into countries all over the world, and silent films became a truly universal art form: American studios made half of their revenues from foreign film sales; silent screen stars like Charlie Chaplin and Jackie Coogan became the most recognized human beings on Earth.

SILENT TREATMENT

But the advent of talking pictures changed everything—and not just for silent-screen stars whose thick accents or funny-sounding voices quickly consigned them to the Hollywood scrap heap. Suddenly, American films became incomprehensible to anyone who didn't speak English. American film studios faced the prospect of losing up to half of their business overnight.

Foreign countries that had become used to a steady stream of Hollywood films found themselves left out in the cold. Some threatened to retaliate by slapping tariffs on films with dialogue in English or by boycotting American films entirely.

Making matters worse, sound recording and synchronization technology was still very primitive, and dubbing foreign-language dialogue onto English-language films was all but impossible. Besides, one of the things that attracted audiences to the first "talkies" was the thrill of hearing their favorite actors speak for the very first time. Even if dubbing had been practical, it might not have been popular.

In 1923 Mary Campbell of Columbus, Ohio, became the only woman named Miss America twice.

There was no easy solution to the problem, and as a result many foreign language markets were left out of the early years of the talkie era—except for the Spanish-language market. Spanish was too popular, and Mexico, Central, and South America were too close for Hollywood to ignore.

THE DOPPELGÄNGER ERA

No film crew works 24 hours a day. At some point, everyone goes home, leaving the soundstage and the expensive sets unused until morning. So, reasoned Hollywood studios, why not bring in a second cast and crew at night to film foreign-language versions of the same films that were being made in English during the day?

Because the sets had already been constructed and second-string actors and crews could be hired for much less money than Hollywood stars, a film like *Dracula* that had cost nearly $450,000 to film in English during the day could be remade in Spanish at night for as little as $40,000. By 1930, nearly all of the major studios had begun filming Spanish "doppelgänger" films at night.

GRAVEYARD SHIFT

Universal Pictures was one of the last major studios to adopt the idea, when it filmed Spanish and English versions of the film *The Cat Creeps* in 1930. *Dracula* was slated to be only the studio's second Spanish-language film.

Paul Kohner, Universal's head of foreign production, hired director George Melford, who'd worked with Rudolph Valentino in *The Sheik*, and cinematographer George Robinson. A 38-year-old Spanish stage actor named Carlos Villarias was cast as Dracula, and a multilingual actor named Barry Norton was hired to play the part of Juan Harker (Jonathan in the English version). A 17-year-old Mexican actress named Lupita Tovar was hired to play Harker's fianceé Eva, originally known as Mina.

"The American crew left at 6:00 p.m. and we were ready," Tovar recalled. "We started shooting at eight. At midnight, they would call for dinner . . . .They didn't pay us much, but we didn't complain. We were happy to have some money—most actors were starving."

FIRST RATE

Since they were using a second-rate cast and crew after Hollywood's finest had gone home for the day, the assumption was that a film made at night would be inferior to the original. That may have been true in most cases but not in the case of *Dracula*.

For all of its popularity and accomplishments as Hollywood's first vampire film, on a technical level, the English-language *Dracula* is considered a very poorly made film. A lot of the blame for this goes to director Tod Browning, a hard-drinking recluse with a reputation as a troublemaker. Browning had been fired from at least one studio for his drinking and was blacklisted by the entire industry for two years in the early 1920s. Making matters worse, Browning had directed nine films starring horror superstar Lon Chaney, Sr., when both men had worked at MGM, and he was still reeling from Chaney's recent death from throat cancer.

Browning's myriad personal problems found their way into the finished film. "In scene after scene," Skal writes, "the script demonstrates just how much Browning cut, trimmed, ignored, and generally sabotaged the screenplay's visual potentials, insisting on static camera setups, eliminating reaction shots and special effects, and generally taking the lazy way out at every opportunity." In one scene, a piece of cardboard the crew used to reduce the glare of a lamp takes up nearly a quarter of the entire screen, and in the film's climax, Dracula's death isn't even shown on film; moviegoers had to settle for the sound of Lugosi groaning offscreen.

ON PURPOSE

Legend has it that cinematographer Karl Freund got so exasperated with Browning's slipshod style that he just turned the camera on and let it run unattended. Skal writes,

> Indeed, there is one endless take in the finished film featuring Manners (who played Jonathan Harker), Chandler (Mina Murray), and Van Sloan (Dr. Van Helsing) that runs 251 feet, nearly three minutes without a cut that was clearly meant to be broken up with close-ups and reaction shots. At one point Chandler tells Manners, "Oh, no—don't look at me like that," in an apparent reference to a dramatic change in his expression. The two-shot, however, shows Manners as motionless as a wax dummy—as if oblivious that the camera is even catching his face.

As if that weren't sloppy enough, in the final credits, Universal President Carl Laemmle's title was misspelled as "Presient."

What American author has had the most feature films made of his work? Edgar Allen Poe.

¡EL VAMPIRO!

The film crew on the Spanish *Dracula* was another story. Kohner, who had produced the Spanish version of *The Cat Creeps*, was headstrong and ambitious—and not above second-guessing the English-language unit, trying to improve on their work. On *The Cat Creeps*, he watched the daily footage produced by Rupert Julian, the director of the English version, and found the scenes to be poorly lit and uninspiring. So when filming the same scenes for the Spanish film, Kohner relit every set and filled them with atmosphere-creating candles, cobwebs, and shadows that had been missing in the English version. Universal Pictures head Carl Laemmle, Jr. was so impressed with Kohner's work that he ordered Julian to refilm his own footage, this time using Kohner as his artistic advisor.

Kohner did the same thing during the making of the Spanish version of *Dracula*. Using a movieola machine that was kept on the set, they watched the daily footage, or "dailies," that had been shot for the English-language version, made note of the sloppiness and mistakes, and then made sure that their own scenes were better.

One thing they didn't try to improve on was Bela Lugosi's masterful performance as Count Dracula. Instead, Kohner insisted that Carlos Villarias imitate Lugosi as closely as possible, and he alone among the actors was allowed to watch the English-language dailies to make sure he got it right. They even let him wear Lugosi's hairpiece, though it's unclear whether Lugosi ever knew about it.

NOW YOU SEE HIM, NOW YOU DON'T

Perhaps the most noticeable difference between the two films is in their use—or lack thereof—of special effects. In scenes showing Dracula climbing out of his coffin, for example, the Spanish version uses a double exposure to show a cloud of mist rising out of the coffin and turning into Dracula.

In the English version, the coffin lid starts to tremble, the camera turns away from the coffin and points at a wal. By the time it return,s Bela Lugosi is already out of the coffin.

NUMERO UNO

When completed, the Spanish version of *Dracula* cost just over $66,000 to make and took only 22 nights to film, compared to the

There's enough gold in the ocean to give every human nine pounds.

Years passed. Rumors persisted. In 1919, *The Numismatist* ran an ad in which one Samuel W. Brown of North Tonawanda, New York, offered to pay $500 for any 1913 Liberty nickels. The next month his ad hiked the price to $600. That summer, Brown mysteriously appeared at the annual American Numismatic Convention and exhibited five of them.

As it turns out, in 1913 Brown was curator of the U.S. Mint's "Cabinet Collection." Did he secretly strike the coins, then create a market for them with his ads? No one knows.

In 1924, a Philadelphia coin dealer offered the same five coins, the only 1913 Liberty Nickels known to exist, in a tiny ad in *The Numismatist*. Colonel E. H. R. Green, son of the then-notorious millionaire "Witch of Wall Street," Hetty Green, bought them all. They surfaced again in 1942, when the St. Louis Stamp & Coin Company sold them individually, breaking up the set. Thereafter, the coins were known by numbers 1 through 5.

Where Are They Now?

- **#1** Was purchased by King Farouk of Egypt from Abe Kosoff, the "dean of American numismatics." Later, it was purchased by another numismatist, R. Henry Norweb, whose widow donated it to the Smithsonian.

- **#2** Was part of the fabulously valuable collection of Louis Eliasberg (considered the most complete and highest-grade collection of U.S. coins in existence). The coin brought $1.48 million in 1996.

- **#3** Was "dull, scratched, uncirculated." It was also sold to Farouk, resold in 1972 for $100,000 and again, a few years later, for the then record-setting price of $385,000.

- **#4** Was "uncirculated, but nicked." It has vanished. It was last seen in the possession of George O. Walton, who was killed in a car crash en route to a coin show in North Carolina in the mid-1960s. The American Numismatic Association has a standing $5,000 reward for information on its whereabouts.

- **#5** Was called "uncirculated, but partly rough." When it sold for $46,000 in 1967, this coin had seen a lot of handling. It once belonged to a J. V. McDermott, who would pass it around in his favorite tavern and allow people to admire it, figuring it could never be stolen. Why? No one would be able to sell it. It was too rare.

THE KING

The coin: 1804 Silver Dollar

Number minted: 15

Value today: $4.14 million, which set a record at a 1999 auction

No coin has a more fascinating past than the "King of U.S. Coins." And it's not even an official coin.

This story starts in 1834. To get favorable trade agreements in the Mideast and Far East, the U.S. State Department ordered the Mint to make two cased sets of all domestic coins currently in use—"gifts" for the King of Siam and the Sultan of Muscat (now Oman). But the sets seemed scanty without a silver dollar or gold eagle ($10 gold piece), both of which were discontinued 30 years earlier because bullion dealers were melting them down. What to do? They simply found some old dies in the vault and struck four proof dollars and four proof eagles. And although only four were needed, the Mint struck four more—to trade with serious collectors for rarities missing from the Mint Cabinet Collection. These are the only silver dollars with the 1804 date.

Anna

The Sultan of Muscat's set, in a crimson morocco case, was delivered in 1835. Coins from that set eventually reached a British collector in 1917. The other set, in a yellow morocco case, went to the King of Siam in 1836. The king passed it to his successors, who in turn passed it to the granddaughters of Anna Leon-Owens, known to history as "Anna of Siam," whose exploits as tutor to the royal family were the basis of the hit musical "The King and I."

Two other sets, destined for the Emperor of Cochin-China and the Mikado of Japan, were returned to the Mint when the courier died of dysentery en route.

American collectors knew nothing of the 1804 dollar until 1842, when *A Manual of Gold and Silver Coinage of All Nations* showed an illustration of the coin. Numismatists from all over the country contacted the Mint to find out about it. In 1843, one collector, Matthew Stickney, offered his one-of-a-kind gold colo-

---

If any of the heads on Mt. Rushmore had a body, it would be nearly 500 feet tall.

nial 1785 "Immune Columbia" coin, and the Mint traded an 1804 dollar for it.

Where are they now?

The eight 1804 dollars, according to the September 20, 1998, *Coin World* magazine:

- **#1** From the Mint Collection, now in the Smithsonian.
- **#2** The Stickney dollar, first shown in the 1842 book. It sold in April 1997 for $1.8 million.
- **#3** The King of Siam dollar, a brilliant proof—never scratched, never dropped, never polished—the finest known. It was sold in 1979 for $1 million, then in 1993 for $1.81 million and now is on display at Mandalay Bay Resort and Museum, Las Vegas.
- **#4** The Sultan of Muscat dollar, a blue-toned choice proof. Acquired in 1945 and held in a personal collection for 54 years, it brought $4.14 million at auction in 1999.
- **#5** The Dexter Dollar, so named because one of its many owners, James V. Dexter, stamped his initial "D" on it. It sold in 1989 for $990,000.
- **#6** Bought from the Mint by an "unknown lady" in 1845, this brilliant proof was named the Parmalee Dollar after the Boston baked-bean mogul who bought it in 1874. Now it's on display at the Durham Western Heritage Museum in Omaha, Nebraska.
- **#7** The Mickley Dollar, graded "almost uncirculated." A bank teller found it in a deposit in 1850. It was acquired by the prestigious collector Joseph J. Mickley in 1859. Stack's Auction House sold it for $475,000 in 1993.
- **#8** The Cohen Dollar was received "over the counter" by Edward Cohen of Richmond, Virginia, at his exchange office in 1865. The DuPont family owned it and then lost it in an October 1967 robbery of its Florida estate. It was recovered in Switzerland in 1982 and is now in the museum of the American Numismatic Society in Colorado Springs, Colorado.

A Phony Counterfeit

By 1858, the 1804 dollars had become so famous and valuable that a Mint worker dug up the old 1804 dies and minted some more. Mint nightwatchman Theodore Eckfield fenced these restrikes through a Philadelphia store for $75 each, but the scandal became

---

Most destructive car chase ever filmed: *The Junkman* (1982)—150 cars were destroyed.

public and the Mint demanded their return. (Only one survives, identifiable because it was struck over an 1857 shooting medal from Bern, Switzerland, and parts of the "host coin" are visible.)

In 1859, Eckfield was at it again, this time fencing the dollars through European auction houses to give them a credible pedigree. Only six of these restrikes are known and they sell today in the $200,000 to $400,000 range. Finally, in 1860, the Mint director confiscated the dies and sealed them in a vault. They were destroyed in 1867.

I SCREAM, YOU SCREAM

The coin: 1894-S dime (the "ice cream dime")

Number minted: 24

Value today: $145,000

In 1894, Mint superintendent J. Daggett struck these proof "Barber dimes" for seven banker friends. He gave them three each and kept three for himself. Since these gems would become incredibly valuable very quickly, it's surprising that Daggett gave his three to his young daughter Hallie. "Put them away safely," he told her, "and when you're as old as I am you can sell them for a 'good price." Hallie immediately used one of the dimes to buy a dish of ice cream, inadvertently setting a world record for the amount paid for any dessert. Sixty years later, she sold the other two dimes for large sums.

Where Are They Now?

Today, only 12 of the dimes are accounted for (four are listed below).

- **#1** Passed through seven owners, including Max Mehl, sold in 1980 for $145,000
- **#6** Was sold by Hallie Daggett in 1954, and later resold for $97,000
- **#11** Was found in circulation in 1957 in "good" condition, meaning so worn that it is without detail and only the bust is outlined. This one is likely the "ice cream" specimen. Despite the extreme wear or perhaps due to the charming legend around it, the coin sold in 1980 for $31,000.
- **#12** Offered in a 1942 Stack's auction then withdrawn "for personal reasons" and not seen since

The whereabouts of the other 12 specimens remain a mystery.

Golf was banned in England in 1457, because it was a distraction from archery.

FOOD OF THE GODS

You probably didn't give it much thought the last time you chomped down on a Hershey bar, but the history of chocolate is as rich and as satisfying as the taste of chocolate itself.

SO CLOSE . . . AND YET SO FAR

On May 9, 1502, Christopher Columbus set sail on his fourth—and what turned out to be last—trip from Spain to the New World. He was searching for a direct water route to Asia, plus whatever riches he could find along the way.

In August 1502, he landed at Guanaja Island, 30 miles off the coast of modern-day Honduras. He spied an enormous dugout canoe in the waters nearby and ordered his men to seize it.

The vessel turned out to be a Mayan trading canoe, probably from somewhere on the Yucatán Peninsula, and it was loaded with a full cargo of trading goods—colorful clothing, wooden swords, flint knives, copper hatchets, small copper bells, and other items. As Columbus's son Ferdinand recounted years later, the Maya who had been in the canoe were also carrying a cargo of "almonds"—very valuable almonds, it turned out. Ferdinand wrote:

> The natives seemed to hold these almonds at a great price, for when they were brought on board ship together with their goods, I observed that when any of these almonds fell, they all stooped to pick it up, as if an eye had fallen from their head.

MOVING ON

But Columbus wasn't interested in almonds—he was looking for gold and other riches. "As there was nothing of importance in those Guanaja Islands," Ferdinand Columbus later wrote, "he did not tarry there."

Columbus and his men traveled as far south as modern-day Panama before returning home to Spain, where he died in 1506. He never did find his passage to Asia, and although he was the first European to come in contact with the cacao beans he mistook for almonds, he died without ever tasting chocolate.

The three most common elements in the universe: 1) hydrogen, 2) helium, 3) oxygen.

ORIGINS

The cacao plant is native to Central America. There is evidence
that the Maya established cacao plantations as early as 600 A.D.,
after harvesting and trading the wild cacao beans for hundreds of
years. They used cacao beans to make chocol haa, or "hot water," a
frothy chocolate beverage flavored with vanilla, hot chili powder,
and other spices, including achiotl, a spice similar to allspice that
left the drinker's mouth, lips, and facial hair bright red, "as if they
had been drinking blood." But only Maya royalty were allowed to
drink chocol haa; everyone else had to settle for balche, a fermented beverage made from honey and bark. Cacao beans were
so valuable that by 1000 A.D. they were being used as currency,
which is why Columbus's captives treated them with such
reverence.

The Aztecs acquired a taste for cacao from their contact with
the Maya, and by 1200 A.D. they were collecting tributes of cacao
from the tribes they dominated, including the Maya. The Aztecs
believed that cacao was a gift of the feathered serpent god
Quetzalcoatl, who repeatedly brought a cacao tree to Earth on a
ray of sunlight and taught early people how to make cacahuatl, or
"bitter water," the chocolate beverage that they believed gave
them universal wisdom and knowledge.

FROM ON HIGH

The Aztecs made cacahuatl in much the same way the Maya made
chocol haa: they ground cacao beans into a powder, stirred it into
water, and then gave it a froth by lifting the beverage high in the
air and pouring it into a second container on the ground. But
unlike the Maya, the Aztecs preferred their cacahuatl cold; this
was the beverage that the Spanish conquistador Hernán Cortés
was served by the Aztec emperor Montezuma in an elaborate ceremony in 1519, when he became one of the first Europeans, if not
the very first, to taste chocolate.

There was certainly nothing like cacahuatl in Europe, and it
took a while for the explorers arriving in the New World to
acquire a taste for it. "Chocolate . . . is a crazy thing valued in that
country [Mexico]," Jesuit missionary and historian José de Acosta
wrote in 1590. "It disgusts those who are not used to it, for it has a
foam on top, or a scumlike bubbling."

"It seemed more a drink for pigs, than a drink for humanity," agreed the Italian historian Girolamo Benzoni, one of the first people to describe the experience to readers in Europe:

> I was in [Mexico] for more than a year, and never wanted to taste it, and whenever I passed a settlement, some Indian would offer me a drink of it, and would be amazed when I would not accept. But then, as there was a shortage of wine, so as not to be always drinking water, I did like the others. The taste is somewhat bitter, it satisfies and refreshes the body, but does not inebriate, and it is the best and most expensive merchandise, according to the Indians of that country.

CHANGING TASTES

With time the Spaniards developed a taste for cacahuatl which, like the Maya, they preferred hot, flavored with cinnamon and vanilla, and sweetened with cane sugar, which was unknown to the Aztecs. And rather than froth their cacahuatl by pouring it from a high container into a low one as the Aztecs had, the Spaniards used a wooden swizzle stick or beater called a *molinillo*. Frothing it with a beater became the standard means of preparing chocolate for the next 200 years.

YOU WON'T HEAR THIS ON THE HERSHEY TOUR

By the late 1500s, the Spaniards had abandoned the Aztec name cacahuatl—"bitter water"—and coined a new word, *chocolatl*, possibly a combination of the Maya word for "hot," *chocol*, and adding it to the Aztec word for "water," *atl*.

Why would they do this? Their chocolate was sweetened, not bitter, and they drank it hot like the Maya did. But some historians speculate that there may have been another reason: just as the Spaniards were initially disgusted by the bitter taste and frothy brown appearance of cacahuatl, they may have also been disgusted by its name.

In many Romance languages, including 16th-century Spanish, the sound caca has scatological connotations. "It is hard to believe that the Spaniards were not thoroughly uncomfortable with a noun beginning with caca to describe a thick, dark-brown drink which they had begun to appreciate," anthropologists Sophie and Michael Coe write in The True History of Chocolate. The Spaniards "desperately needed some other word, and we would not be at all surprised if it was the learned friars who came up with *chocolatl* and chocolate."

More than half of all the geysers in the world are in Yellowstone National Park.

CURE-ALL

No one knows for sure when chocolate first arrived in Europe. Cortés may have brought some back to Spain with him on his trips in 1519 or 1528. But the first recorded appearance of chocolate in Europe was in 1544, when some Dominican friars took a delegation of Maya to visit Prince Philip of Spain. Nobody knows if the prince tried the chocolate, and if so, what he thought of it. In any event, it took a few years for the new taste to catch on in Spain.

By 1585, the time the first commercial shipments of cacao beans began arriving in Spain from plantations in Central and South America, the exotic beverage was appreciated mostly for its "medicinal" value. "This drink is the healthiest thing, and the greatest sustenance of anything you could drink in the world," one chocolate advocate wrote in the 1550s, "because he who drinks a cup of this liquid, no matter how far he walks, can go a whole day without eating anything else."

EUROPEAN TOUR

In 1655 England seized the Caribbean island of Jamaica from Spain, including a number of thriving cacao plantations. Up to that point chocolate was practically unheard of outside of Spain. Then, in 1657, London's first chocolate café opened, advertising "an excellent West India drink, called Chocolat." Similar cafés soon opened up in the Netherlands, France, Germany, Switzerland, Austria, and Italy. Hot chocolate quickly established itself as the drink of choice of the European aristocracy (no one else could afford it); by 1690, chocolate was so popular in England that the British Parliament passed a law forbidding its sale without a license, giving King William and Queen Mary a financial stake in the booming trade.

SOMETHING TO CHEW ON

In the late 1600s, chocolate began appearing as a flavoring in food. In France, you could buy chocolate biscuits and pastilles; in Spain, chocolate rolls and cakes. In Italy, you could order chocolate soup, chocolate liver, and chocolate pasta—including chocolate lasagna. And in 1727, an Englishman named Nicholas Sanders became the first person, as far as historians can tell, to make a hot chocolate drink using milk instead of water.

Traditionally, Moroccan brides keep their eyes closed during a wedding to avoid the "evil eye."

But you still couldn't find a chocolate bar—not in Europe, not anywhere in the world. Nobody knew how to make chocolate in solid form in the 17th century—chocolate preparation had hardly advanced at all since the time of Cortés. The beans were ground, usually by hand, and then shaped into wafers or cakes that were dissolved in hot water to make drinking chocolate, which if you wanted, you could pour into your food. That was about it.

A PRESSING MATTER

Things began to change, in 1828, when a Dutch chemist named Coenraad Johannes Van Houten invented a hydraulic press that could remove fatty cocoa butter from the ground cacao beans, leaving behind a solid "cake" that could then be ground into a fine powder—what we know as cocoa powder. Then he treated it with alkaline salts to prevent it from separating when added to hot water.

Drinking chocolate was changed forever. As anthropologists Sophie and Michael Coe write in *The True History of Chocolate*,

> In the year 1828, the age-old, thick and foamy drink was dethroned by easily prepared, more easily digestible cocoa. Van Houten's invention of the defatting and alkalizing processes made possible the large-scale manufacture of cheap chocolate for the masses, in both powdered and solid form.

PASSING THE BAR

The next great change came in 1847, when an English chocolate maker named Francis Fry figured out a way to combine cocoa powder and sugar with melted cocoa butter (instead of the usual warm water) to create a chocolate paste that could be pressed into molds and formed into solid shapes. It was the world's first eating chocolate, which the firm sold under the sophisticated-sounding French name Chocolat Délicieux à Manger, ("Delicious Chocolate for Eating").

Then in 1867, a Swiss chemist named Henri Nestlé discovered how to make powdered milk through evaporation. In 1879, after several years of collaborating with Nestlé, Swiss chocolate maker Daniel Peter finally figured out how to add Nestlé's powdered milk to his chocolate, creating the world's first milk chocolate.

That same year, another Swiss chocolate maker, Rudolphe Lindt, invented a process he called "conching." Until then, chocolate was much coarser and grittier than it is today, kind of like

The highest denomination for a U.S. coin: $100 (It's called the Platinum American Eagle).

granulated sugar. Lindt's conching process crushed chocolate paste beneath huge granite rollers for more than 72 hours, at which point the particles became so tiny and smooth that the resulting chocolate melted in your mouth—the first chocolate to do that. Lindt's invention so vastly improved the texture of chocolate that conching became a universal process and coarse, gritty chocolate became a thing of the past.

CHOCOLATE FOR THE MASSES

The Industrial Revolution helped to make chocolate more afford-able than ever. Now it was possible to grind massive quantities of cacao beans with steam-powered grinders and using hydraulic presses to separate cocoa butter from cocoa powder was much more efficient than making chocolate by hand . . . and the cost savings were passed on to the consumer.

The invention of chocolate that could be eaten created a huge demand for cocoa butter, which caused the price to go through the roof, and made chocolate bars expensive. Anyone could afford to drink chocolate, but if you wanted to eat it, you had to be wealthy.

Then in 1893, Milton Snavely Hershey, owner of the world's largest caramel factory, visited the World's Columbian Exposition in Chicago and saw a demonstration of chocolate-making machin-ery given by Lehmann and Company, a German chocolate maker. Hershey was so impressed by what he saw that when the exhibition closed he bought the machinery and began making chocolate-coated caramels. "Caramels are only a fad," he told anyone who would listen, "chocolate is a permanent thing."

In 1900, he sold his caramel company so that he could focus exclusively on chocolate, and he went about manufacturing it the same way that he'd become the king of caramel—he built the largest chocolate factory in the world.

Hershey then applied the principles of mass production to the manufacture of chocolate—he built his factory on 1,200 acres of Pennsylvania dairyland, and bought up thousands more acres—until he owned enough dairy farms to supply his factory with fresh milk. He built an entire town—Hershey, Pennsylvania—to give his workers someplace to live, as well as another—Hershey, Cuba—near his sugar mill in the Caribbean.

Hershey manufactured his chocolate bars and Hershey's kisses

The scientific name for the dust we kick up when in motion: The "Pigpen effect."

on such an enormous scale—as much as 100,000 pounds of chocolate a day—that he was able to realize huge cost savings, which he passed on to the consumer. He priced his Hershey bars at just a nickel a piece, and they sold at that price until 1969. And rather than settle for selling his chocolate regionally, as other American chocolate companies did at the time, he set his sights on selling his products throughout the United States. He also expanded his sales beyond the traditional outlets of candy stores and drugstores, selling chocolate bars at newsstands, in grocery stores, at bus stations, even in restaurants. Soon, his candy bars were everywhere.

KID STUFF

Hershey didn't think of his products as candy. In fact, he forbade his employees from referring to chocolate as candy. He claimed there was more energy in an ounce of chocolate than there was in a pound of meat. Chocolate wasn't "merely a sweet," he said; it was nutritious food.

Regardless of what Hershey thought, most people considered chocolate candy, more for kids than grown-ups. That began to change during World War I, when the government sent candy and chocolate to soldiers in battle. Why? It was cheap, it didn't spoil, and its high sugar content provided a quick energy boost. American soldiers consumed huge quantities of chocolate during the war, and when the war was over, they continued to indulge their habit at home.

During World War II, virtually the nation's entire candy output was diverted into the war effort. American soldiers brought Hershey bars with them wherever they went; in many places, chocolate became a form of currency. The U.S. Air Force was the largest purchaser of the Mars Company's M&Ms during the war; it bought them by the ton for bomber pilots flying long missions over North Africa and the Pacific. The Army was the #2 customer; it issued M&M's to soldiers in tropical regions where ordinary chocolate melted too easily.

During World War II, the average G.I. consumed 50 pounds of candy and chocolate a year, three times what he had eaten before the war. And he brought his appetite for chocolate home with him. It wasn't just for kids anymore; it was the food that had kept the fighting man strong. The two world wars helped to establish what Hershey had been saying for more than 40 years—chocolate is for everyone.

Q. What sport is played on the largest playing field (300 yards by 200 yards)? A. Polo.

JOIN THE PARTY

Pop quiz: What does the U.S. Constitution say about political parties? Answer: Nothing—there were no political parties immediately after the American Revolution, and the Founding Fathers hoped there never would be. So how did the political parties come to be? Here's how.

PARTY POOPERS

For all the diversity of opinion among the Founding Fathers in the 1770s, there was one thing that virtually everyone agreed upon: political parties were a very bad idea.

In his farewell address as president, George Washington referred to political parties as "the worst enemy" of democratic governments, "potent engines by which cunning, ambitious and unprincipled men will . . . subvert the power of the people." Alexander Hamilton equated political parties with "ambition, avarice, and personal animosity." And Thomas Jefferson could hardly agree more: "If I could go to heaven but with a party," he wrote, "I would not go there at all."

ENGLISH LESSONS

The Founding Fathers' abhorrence of political parties was in response to the partisan politics that characterized England's House of Commons. The Commons was supposed to serve as a check on the power of the monarch, but successive kings had been able to use their vast wealth, power, and control of public offices to create a party of royalists. Thus, it had been reduced to members fighting among themselves instead of working together to advance the common good.

This was what the Founding Fathers were trying to avoid in the United States: warring factions that would pursue selfish interests at the expense of the nation.

But what exactly was the national interest? And if the Founding Fathers couldn't agree on what the national interest was, who among them got to decide? These fundamental questions caused the first factions to form in American political life.

Women got the right to vote in 1920. Native Americans couldn't vote until 1924.

FIRST FEUD: THE ARTICLES OF CONFEDERATION

Bringing the original 13 colonies together to form the United States had not been easy. The Founding Fathers drafted the first U.S. Constitution, the Articles of Confederation, in 1777, but it was flawed. The Americans had just won independence from one central government—England—and they were reluctant to surrender the power of the individual states to a new central government, so they intentionally made that government weak.

But it soon became obvious that the federal government established by the Articles of Confederation was too weak to be effective at all. The most glaring problem was that it had no power to tax the states, which meant that it had no means of raising money to pay for an army to protect its territories from encroachment by Britain and Spain. In 1787, a constitutional convention was held in Philadelphia to draw up an entirely new document.

It was during the debates over the creation and ratification of the new constitution that some of the first and most significant political divisions in American history began to emerge. Those who supported the idea of strengthening the federal government by weakening the states were known as "Federalists," and those who opposed the new constitution became known as the "Anti-Federalists."

The Federalists won the first round: 9 of the 13 states ratified the U.S. Constitution, and Congress set March 4, 1789 as the date it would go into effect. Elections for Congress and the presidency were held in late 1788. George Washington ran unopposed and was elected president.

TROUBLE IN THE CABINET

Washington saw the presidency as an office aloof from partisan divisions and hoped his administration would govern the same way. But by 1792, Washington's cabinet had split into factions over the financial policies of Alexander Hamilton, the secretary of the treasury.

Perhaps because he was born in the British West Indies and thus did not identify strongly with the interests of any particular state, Hamilton was the foremost Federalist of his age. He strongly believed in using the power of the federal government to develop the American economy. In 1790, he proposed having the government assume the remaining unpaid Revolutionary War debts of the states and the Continental Congress. This would help establish the creditworthiness of the new nation, albeit by enriching the speculators who bought up the war debt when most people thought it would never be repaid. Hamilton's plan also meant that states that had already paid off their war debt would now be asked to help pay off the debts of states that hadn't, which added to the controversy.

Secretary of State Thomas Jefferson supported the new Constitution but had Anti-Federalist leanings. He grudgingly agreed to support Hamilton's plan, on one condition: Hamilton had to support Jefferson's plan to locate the new capital city on the banks of the Potomac River. Hamilton agreed.

Hamilton got his debt plan, and Jefferson got Washington, D.C. (Jefferson later regretted the deal, calling it one of the greatest mistakes of his life.)

A BATTLE ROYAL

Then in December 1790, Hamilton proposed having Congress charter a Bank of the United States as a means to regulate U.S. currency. This time, Jefferson thought Hamilton had gone too far. He vehemently opposed the idea, arguing that a national bank would benefit the commercial North more than the agricultural South (Jefferson was a Southerner) and would further enrich the wealthy while doing little to help common people.

Hamilton's financial policies, Jefferson said, were intended to create "an influence of his [Treasury] department over the members of the legislature," creating a "corrupt squadron" of congressmen and senators who would work "to get rid of the limitations imposed by the Constitution [and] prepare the way for a change, from the present republican form of government, to that of a monarchy, of which the English constitution is to be a model."

SPLITTING UP

Like Jefferson, Hamilton deplored political parties. But he and his supporters were also adamant about chartering a national bank and strengthening the powers of the Federal government. Faced with the determined opposition of Jefferson and his allies, they began to organize what became known as the Federalist Party.

Jefferson also began to organize. In May 1791, he and fellow Virginian James Madison made a trip to New York to meet with

State Chancellor Robert Livingston, New York governor George Clinton, and U.S. Senator Aaron Burr.

"The meetings among the New York and Virginia leaders, however informal, were among the most fateful in American history," A. James Reichley writes in The Life of the Parties. "The first links were formed in an alliance that was to last, in one form or another, for almost 150 years and that was to be a major shaping force in national politics from the administration of Jefferson to that of Franklin Roosevelt."

Jefferson, Madison, and the others saw themselves as defenders of the new republic against Hamilton and the "monarchical Federalists." The party they formed became known as the Democratic-Republicans, or Republicans for short. Historians consider them the first opposition party in U.S. history, as well as the direct antecedent of the modern Democratic Party.

ONE SETBACK AFTER ANOTHER

The Democratic-Republicans lost their battle: Hamilton pushed his bank legislation through Congress, and President Washington signed it into law. They lost another major battle in 1792, when Governor Clinton ran against John Adams for vice president and lost. A third defeat came in 1796 when Washington declined to run for a third term as president: Jefferson ran for president against Vice President Adams . . . and lost by only three electoral votes.

THE ALIEN AND SEDITION ACTS

In 1793, France—which was in the throes of its own revolution—declared war against England, giving the Federalists and Democratic-Republicans something new to disagree about. The Jeffersonian Republicans sided with republican France, and the Federalists sided with England; neither side thought the United States should get involved in the war. Partisan emotions intensified in 1796, when the French began an undeclared war on American shipping as part of their war against England and refused to receive President Adams's minister to France.

Angered by the insults, the Federalists began preparing for what they thought was an imminent war with France. They tripled the size of the army, authorized the creation of the U.S. Navy (the Continental Navy had been disbanded in 1784), and

McDonald's originally served hotdogs, not hamburgers.

then in the face of the unanimous opposition of the Democratic-Republicans in Congress, passed what became known as the Alien and Sedition Acts.

The Alien Acts said that aliens (who were assumed to have Democratic-Republican leanings) had to live in the United States for 14 years—up from 5—before they would be eligible to vote. The acts also permitted the detention of citizens of enemy nations and increased the president's power to deport "dangerous" aliens.

The Sedition Act outlawed all associations whose purpose was "to oppose any measure or measures of the government of the United States." It also imposed stiff punishments for writing, printing, or saying anything against the U.S. government.

READING BETWEEN THE LINES

By the time the Alien and Sedition Acts expired or were repealed four years later, only one alien had been deported and only 10 people were convicted of sedition, including a New Jersey man who was fined $100 for publicly "wishing that a wad from the presidential saluting cannon might 'hit Adams in the ass.'"

But no one knew that back in 1798. To Jefferson and his supporters, it was obvious that the Alien Acts, and especially the Sedition Act, were targeted at them. Republicans could now be fined or jailed for speaking out against the Adams administration, and if they weren't U.S. citizens, they could even be deported.

The fact that the Sedition Act expired following the 1800 presidential election seemed to prove their suspicions that the law was intended to curb Anti-Federalist dissent. While the acts were in force, Adams and the Federalists were legally protected from Democratic-Republican criticism, but if they happened to lose the election of 1800, the expiration of the Sedition Act would leave them free to criticize the Democratic-Republicans.

There was more: The Democratic-Republicans also feared that Adams, having tripled the size of the Army, would begin using it against his political opponents. As if to confirm their fears, in 1799, Adams called out Federal troops to put down an anti-tax rebellion led by Pennsylvania farmers opposed to taxes levied for the anticipated war with France.

The Democratic-Republicans were convinced that if the Federalists remained in power, democracy's days were numbered, so

U.S. Army regulation: a standard sandbag holds 40 pounds of sand.

they began mounting their strongest effort yet to capture the White House and the Congress.

A TOUGH CALL

John Adams had mixed feelings about running for reelection. He hated living in Washington, D.C., and he hated being president. The president "has a very hard, laborious, and unhappy life," he warned his son John Quincy Adams. "No man who ever held the office of president would congratulate a friend on obtaining it." And now that he was completely toothless, he was incapable of making public speeches in support of his candidacy for re-election.

The only reason Adams ran at all was that he was determined to prevent Jefferson from getting the job. Adams liked Jefferson personally, but he saw himself and Jefferson as "the North and South poles of the American Revolution." He strongly disagreed with Jefferson's views on government and the Constitution and feared that Jefferson would drag the country into a European war to defend France.

CHANGE OF FORTUNE

The Democratic-Republicans, who believed that freedom was on the line, had no such reluctance—although Jefferson, announcing that he would "stand" for election rather than "run" for it, remained at his Monticello estate during the campaign. The party fought a hard campaign for him.

On election day, Adams carried New England, and Jefferson won most of the South. New York proved to be the swing state, which helped Jefferson, because his running mate was Aaron Burr. As founder and head of the Tammany political machine in New York, Burr was able to deliver the state to Jefferson, allowing him to win the presidency with 73 electoral votes to Adams's 65. The Democratic-Republicans also won control of both houses of Congress.

FEDERALIST FAREWELL

The Federalists had accomplished much in the years following the Revolution: they had succeeded in drafting the U.S. Constitution, which strengthened the power of the Federal government; they had enacted economic programs that strengthened credit and helped the economy grow.

Chinese chopsticks are about 10" long; Japanese chopsticks are 7" (women's) or 8" (men's).

But by 1800, their best days were behind them. "Federalism, as a political movement, was a declining force around the turn of the century," historian Paul Johnson writes in *A History of the American People*, "precisely because it was a party of the elite, without popular roots, at a time when democracy was spreading fast among the states. Adams was the last of the Federalist presidents, and he could not get himself re-elected."

THE LAST STRAW

It got worse for the Federalists. They vehemently opposed the War of 1812, and in the fall of 1814, when things seemed to be going very badly for the United States, Federalist delegates from New England met secretly in Hartford, Connecticut, to draft a series of resolutions listing their grievances with the Federal government, which a negotiating committee would then bring to Washington, D.C. Some of the delegates to the secret convention had even discussed seceding from the Union.

Bad timing: By the time the negotiating committee arrived in Washington to protest the war, it was not only over, it had actually ended on a positive note, thanks to Andrew Jackson's victory in the Battle of New Orleans.

When the rest of the country learned that the Federalists had been holding secret meetings to contemplate splitting off from the rest of the country, the party's image took a pounding. "Republican orators and publicists branded the Hartford convention an act of subversion during wartime," A. James Reichley writes, "ending what was left of Federalism as a political force."

But the die was cast. In spite of themeslves, the Founding Fathers had created what they most feared . . . political factions. The era of the two-party system in the United States had begun.

* * *

"Under democracy one party always devotes its chief energies to trying to prove that the other party is unfit to rule—and both commonly succeed and are right."

—**H. L. Mencken**

Oldest cat ever: Ma, an English tabby, who was 37 when she died in 1957.

TARZAN OF THE MOVIES, PART II: HERE'S JOHNNY!

Besides Edgar Rice Burroughs, the person most associated with the char-
acter of Tarzan is a swimmer-turned-actor named Johnny Weissmuller.
In fact, it wasn't until 1932, when Weissmuller took on the role, that
Tazan developed a stable personality and face the public could get
used to. But to Johnny, it was just a job. Here's the story.

AFRICA SPEAKS

In 1927, MGM bought the film rights to *Trader Horn*, the memoirs of an African adventurer, and assigned director W. S. "Woody" Van Dyke to the picture. The studio originally planned to make it as a silent film, but then decided that *Trader Horn* would be their first talkie.

Making the leap from silent films to sound is considered the biggest technological advance in the history of filmmaking. MGM understood the significance of the coming of sound and wanted its first talkie to be larger than life. Money was no object—*Trader Horn* was going to be the best film possible.

On the Road

Van Dyke persuaded the studio that the only way to do the film justice was to film it on location. So in March 1929, Van Dyke—along with 35 cast and crew members, three sound trucks, and 90 tons of equipment—set sail for Africa. Over the next seven months, they (and 200 African natives) traveled more than 10,000 miles through Africa, shooting more than a million feet of film. Needless to say, the production ran over budget.

"The expense was worth it," John Taliaferro writes. "When *Trader Horn* was released in 1931 it was a huge hit and helped rekindle public interest in the continent of Africa. Even Ernest Hemingway credited *Trader Horn* with giving him his Africa 'bug.'"

MGM had more than just a hit film on its hands: It had thou-

If your car is more than 42 feet long, you can't drive it on U.S. public roads.

sands and thousands of feet of unused African film footage, and the studio began looking for ways to put it to good use. "Inevitably," Taliaferro says, "someone suggested Tarzan."

TOUGH BREAK

By 1931 MGM had bought the rights to *Tarzan the Ape Man* and hired Van Dyke to direct it. For the first time in the history of the Tarzan franchise, a movie studio was simply buying the right to make a movie about Burroughs's character and was free to come up with its own story.

Having Van Dyke direct the film was a good idea from a stylistic point of view: he was considered Hollywood's finest nature filmmaker. But it made casting the film more difficult, because Van Dyke was a perfectionist who wasn't afraid to turn down Tinseltown's biggest stars if he felt they weren't right for the role. Clark Gable was one of the first actors rejected. "He has *no body*," Van Dyke complained. "What I want is a man who is young, strong, well-built, reasonably attractive, but not necessarily handsome, and a competent actor. The most important thing is that he have a good physique. And I can't find him."

STROKE OF LUCK

Meanwhile, screenwriter Cyril Hume was hard at work in his hotel room cranking out the *Tarzan* screenplay. One afternoon he stepped out for a minute and happened to notice a powerfully built young man swimming in the hotel pool. It was 27-year-old Johnny Weissmuller, the greatest amateur swimmer the world had ever seen.

Between 1921 and 1928, Weissmuller had won 52 national titles, held every freestyle record, and broken his own records dozens of times. Weissmuller won three gold medals at the 1924 Olympics and two more at the 1928 games. Not long afterward he gave up his amateur status and signed on as the national spokesman for BVD swimwear and underwear. He was still modelling for BVD when Cyril Hume discovered him.

MR. NATURAL

Hume was so impressed by Weissmuller that he arranged a meeting with Van Dyke. However, rather than give him a formal screen test, they just had him strip to his shorts to get a sense of what he'd look like in a loin cloth. Two things immediately struck them:

World's top-selling author: Barbara Cartland, with over 500 million copies sold.

1) Weissmuller clearly had the right build for the part, and 2) he seemed perfectly at ease stripping down to his underpants in front of two men he hardly knew. He actually appeared comfortable in his skivvies, something almost unheard of in an age where most men still wore two-piece, shirt-and-shorts bathing suits on the beach. In fact, Weissmuller had spent so many years modeling underwear and wearing skimpy one-piece racing trunks that he was completely uninhibited about appearing seminude on film. Even though he was nearly naked, he somehow seemed wholesome.

"Other Tarzan actors, when they wore loincloths and leopard skins, seemed merely undressed," Taliaferro writes. "Weissmuller, by contrast, was clean-limbed in every sense. He gave the impression that he could have sold Bibles door to door wearing nothing but a G-string . . . There was no hint of either embarrassment or braggadocio in his comportment."

Weissmuller won the part hands (and pants) down, and just in case anyone failed to notice his unique abilities, in the publicity leading up to *Tarzan the Ape Man*'s premiere, MGM's publicity agents billed Weissmuller as "the only man in Hollywood who's natural in the flesh and can act without clothes."

A CHANGED MAN

Weissmuller still didn't have much acting experience, but it didn't really matter—rather than change Weissmuller to make him better fit the role, MGM simply adjusted the Tarzan character to fit Weissmuller's strengths and weaknesses: the Tarzan of the Edgar Rice Burroughs novels was a self-educated, cultured gentleman who spoke several languages; the Tarzan of the Weissmuller films was someone who spoke very little and swam surprisingly often for a guy who lived in the middle of a jungle. "The role was right up my alley—it was just like stealing," Weissmuller recounted years later.

Not much of Burroughs's original Tarzan character had ever made it to the screen. But by the time MGM was through, the few remaining vestiges had been swept away. The screenplay made absolutely no mention of Tarzan's noble origins and didn't even bother to explain how he'd ended up in the jungle. Even the sound of Tarzan's name was changed: Burroughs had always pronounced it as TAR-zn, but MGM changed it to TAR-ZAN, and TAR-ZAN it would stay. Burroughs had always resisted changes to his character in the past; this time he just accepted it. "I don't give a damn what they call him," he told a friend, "as long as their checks come regularly."

FINDING HIS VOICE

Because this was the first true Tarzan talkie, the filmmakers had to figure out what Tarzan's jungle yell would sound like. Nobody really knew what to do until Weissmuller came up with the yell on his own. He recalled:

> When I was a kid, I used to read the Tarzan books, and they had kind of a shrill yell for Tarzan. I never thought I'd ever make Tarzan movies, but when I finally got the part, they were trying to do yells like that. And I remembered when I was a kid I used to yodel at the picnics on Sundays, so I said, "I know a yell!"

Nobody gave Weissmuller's yell much thought until after the film opened and MGM realized just how popular the yell was. They quickly invented a story that it was created by sound engineers who blended Weissmuller's voice "with a hyena's howl played backward, a camel's bleat, the pluck of a violin string, and a soprano's high C."

"It was a commentary on the mystique of talkies and the bizarre singularity of the yell itself," John Taliaferro writes in *Tarzan Forever*, "that the public accepted the studio's fib as fact."

LOVE INTEREST

MGM knew pretty quickly what Jane would look like—they cast a contract actress named Maureen O'Sullivan to play her. But it took a while to decide what she should wear. "First," O'Sullivan recalled, "they had the idea of having Jane wearing no bra—no brassiere at all—and she would always be covered with a branch. They tried that, and it didn't work. So they made a costume and it wasn't that bad at all. There was a little leather bra and a loincloth."

THE FILMING

The stage was set. Filming of *Tarzan the Ape Man* began on October 31, 1931, and finished eight weeks later. Total cost, even with the free leftover jungle footage from *Trader Horn*, was just over $650,000. The film had not come cheap, but it turned out to be worth every penny: *Tarzan the Ape Man* opened to

---

Diamonds are up to 90 times harder than corumdum, the next-hardest mineral.

huge crowds and rave reviews in March 1932 and went on to become one of top-10 box-office hits of the year. The movie's success helped increase the popularity of the *Tarzan* novels and comic strips, whose sales had started to suffer in the grip of the Great Depression.

Weissmuller didn't have a lot of dialogue in the film, but his acting was surprisingly authentic. He became the hottest new star of 1932. "However credible or interesting Tarzan may be on the printed page," Thorton Delehanty wrote in the *New York Evening Post*, "I doubt very much if he emerges in such splendor as he does in the person of Johnny Weissmuller. With his flowing hair, magnificently proportioned body, catlike walk, and virtuosity in the water, you could hardly ask anything more in the way of perfection."

Maureen O'Sullivan also won high praise for her performance and, like Weissmuller, set the standard by which all future Janes would be judged; to this day the six movies she made with Weissmuller are considered the best Tarzan films ever made.

THE SEQUEL

When *Tarzan the Ape Man* became a runaway hit, MGM paid Burroughs for the right to make a sequel called *Tarzan and His Mate*. They signed Weissmuller and O'Sullivan for an encore. Influenced by the success of *King Kong* the year before, the makers of *Tarzan and His Mate* spent a lot of money on animal and special effects, including a 20-foot-long, steel-and-rubber mechanical crocodile that Weissmuller wrestles and kills in the film, and a live hippopotamus that was imported from a German zoo so that Weissmuller could ride on its back. Even Cheetah the chimp was given an expanded role to take advantage of the public's newfound fascination with primates.

BIG GAMBLE

The film ultimately cost $1.3 million, nearly double what *Tarzan the Apeman* cost and a huge sum for a Depression-era film. But like its predecessor, it played to packed theaters all over the country— and, when it was released to foreign markets, all over the world. It's considered the best of the Weissmuller Tarzan films and probably the best Tarzan film of all time.

It is also famous for another reason: It features the most nudity of any of Weissmuller's Tarzan films. O'Sullivan wears a skimpy leather top and a loincloth comprised of one flap of leather in front and one in back, leaving her thighs and hips fully exposed. It "started such a furor," O'Sullivan remembered years later. "Thousands of women were objecting to my costume." MGM finally caved in and changed O'Sullivan's costume from "something suitable for the jungle" into "something resembling a suburban housedress," a la Wilma Flintstone. Even Weissmuller had to cover up for the next film in the series: he went from a revealing loincloth to what looked like "leather gym shorts."

BIG BUDGET

In July 1935, MGM began work on *The Capture of Tarzan*, its third Tarzan film. They planned to make it the most elaborate, most expensive, and (they hoped) most profitable one yet.

Set designers built a six-room treehouse for Tarzan and Jane that the Flintstones would have envied, complete with running water, an oven for baking, overhead fans operated by Cheetah, and an elevator powered by an elephant.

The Capture of Tarzan was also supposed to be much more graphic than the earlier films. In one scene, a safari party is captured by the Ganeolis tribe of natives and the captives are spread-eagled on the ground "to be butchered in a two-part ritual: a savage cutting with knives followed by a rock-swing to the head, cracking the skull open," but are rescued by Tarzan just in time. In another scene, the party crosses into a foggy marshland where they're attacked by pygmies, giant lizards, and vampire bats.

Unfortunately, when *The Capture of Tarzan* was shown to preview audiences in 1935, it "terrified children and brought outraged complaints from irate mothers and women's organizations," Gabe Essoe writes. "Afraid that *Capture* would alienate more people than it would attract, studio bosses ordered all gruesome scenes cut out and replaced with re-takes." When director Jim McKay objected to the changes, he was fired and replaced with John Farrow, who was himself later fired. (But not before falling in love with Maureen O'Sullivan, eventually marrying her and fathering seven children—one of whom is actress Mia Farrow.) Next in line for director was Richard Thorpe, who stayed on as director for the rest of the MGM series.

Q: What do the cities of Denver and Orlando have in common?

WATCH OUT FOR THAT TREE!

Thorpe spent months shooting new scenes "as necessary" to make the film "appeal" to young and old alike and changed the name to *Tarzan Escapes*. Thorpe also began the tradition of reusing scenes from older Tarzan films—in this case cutting out the vampire bat attack scene and replacing it with the crocodile fight from *Tarzan and His Mate*—and cheapening what had been considered a top-notch motion picture franchise. "In essence, this film marked a major step in lowering the Tarzan series to the child's level," Essoe writes.

With all of the rewriting, refilming, and reediting, *Tarzan Escapes* took 14 months to finish and cost more than the first two MGM Tarzan films combined. That would have been okay if it was a good film. But when it finally opened in New York in November 1936, it ran into harsh reviews and lousy ticket sales. "The tree-to-tree stuff has worn pretty thin for adult consumption," *Variety* complained, "While at first the sight of Tarzan doing everything but playing pinochle with his beast pals was a novelty, it's all pretty silly now. Derisive laughter greet the picture too often."

JUNGLE FAMILY VALUES

Johnny Weissmuller was content to continue as Tarzan, but Maureen O'Sullivan wasn't. When she learned that a fourth Tarzan film was in the works, she insisted on being written out of it. MGM offered to let her take a leave of absence, but she insisted on leaving permanently. So screenwriter Cyril Hume decided to kill her off with a spear wound at the end of the fourth film.

This created a problem: the female character helped attract women and families to Tarzan pictures, and the studio was afraid that if Tarzan went solo his audience would shrink. So they gave the couple a son—Boy. And to avoid controversy from censorship groups (because MGM's Tarzan and Jane never married), Boy was adopted. Tarzan and Jane find a baby in the jungle following a plane crash and raise him as their own.

MGM ran an ad in the *Hollywood Reporter* asking readers, "Do you have a Tarzan, Jr., in your backyard?" and auditioned more than 300 boys for the part before finally settling on seven-year-old Johnny Sheffield. (Sheffield's stunts were performed by a 32-year-old midget named Harry Monty, who billed himself as the "Midget Strong Man.")

A: Both were named after people—James Denver and Orlando Reeves.

BACK FROM THE DEAD

Edgar Rice Burroughs was furious when he learned MGM wanted to kill off his second-most important character. "MGM reminded Burroughs that while their contract forbade them to kill, mutilate, or undermine the character of Tarzan, it didn't mention Jane," Essoe writes. "MGM was free to rub her out and Burroughs was powerless to stop them."

In the end, though, MGM didn't "rub Jane out." Preview audiences were so upset at the prospect of Jane dying that the studio felt compelled to refilm the ending so that she survives. Not only that, O'Sullivan went on to play Jane in two more films before finally hanging it up for good.

TRAPPED IN THE JUNGLE

O'Sullivan made an average of three other films for every Tarzan she made, but Weissmuller wasn't that lucky. MGM wouldn't let Weissmuller play any other roles, fearing they'd damage his screen image. So although Johnny had been compared to Clark Gable in 1932, by the late 1930s he was hopelessly typecast.

Another thing that irked Weissmuller was that although he'd done so much to bring millions of dollars into MGM's coffers, the studio refused to give him a share of the profits. When MGM used up the last of its Tarzan movie rights making *Tarzan's New York Adventure* (1942) it decided not to buy any more and let Weissmuller's option expire. Weissmuller moved over to RKO Pictures, the new owner of the Tarzan film rights, and made *Tarzan Triumphs*—the first of six RKO Tarzan films. But his deal there was the same as at MGM: no profit-sharing. Weissmuller earned his salary and nothing more.

LARGER THAN LIFE

In the years that followed, the Tarzan film budgets shrank as RKO relied more and more on reusing footage from earlier Tarzan movies, and the films themselves became shorter as they slipped from top billing to second place in double features. About the only thing that grew during the 1940s was Weissmuller's waistline: Now in his early 40s, his svelte swimmer's build had long since given way to the barrel-chested brawn of a middle-aged man who was having trouble staying in shape. Weissmuller gained as much as 30 pounds between Tarzan films, and he wasn't always able to take it all back off.

In 1948, Weissmuller finished *Tarzan and the Mermaids*, his 12th Tarzan film in 17 years. When talk of a 13th film began, Weissmuller again asked for a percentage of the profits. Rather than give it to him, producer Sol Lesser let Weissmuller go.

It wasn't the end of his career, though. Weissmuller wound up with the lead in a new series—*Jungle Jim*, based on a comic strip by the same name. This time he talked and wore clothes. He made 20 Jungle Jim films between 1948 and 1956, and when he finished he began looking around for new roles to play. But no one would have him—after spending 26 years in the jungle, no one could see him playing any other kind of part. "Casting directors wouldn't even talk to him," Essoe writes. "After kicking around Hollywood for awhile, Weissmuller went into a forced retirement."

After more than a quarter century in the movie business, Weissmuller had only one non-jungle film to his credit: the 1946 film *Swamp Fire*. "I played a Navy lieutenant in that one," he joked later, "I took one look and went back to the jungle."

Weissmuller died on January 20, 1984, at the age of 79. At his request, a tape recording of his famous Tarzan yell was played as his coffin was lowered into the ground.

* * *

MONKEY MISCELLANY

- The chimpanzee is also one of the few animals that uses tools. In the forest a stick is used to extract termites or honey from nests, and in captivity to reach objects beyond the reach of its arms.

- According to some reports, chimpanzees have been taught to play tic-tac-toe.

- In September 1971, it was reported that "Washoe," the most advanced of a group of chimpanzees being taught to communicate by signs at the University of Oklahoma, knew 200 words and could construct simple sentences.

France produces 20 million bottles of wine a day.

THE BIRTH OF BIG-TIME SPORTING EVENTS

Ever wonder how they come up with all those tournament championship events that fill the weekend TV schedule? Well, like everything else, they all had a beginning. Here are a few of the biggest.

THE MASTERS

In the 1920s, the world of golf was dominated by a lawyer from Georgia named Bobby Jones. Jones retired from the golf circuit in 1930 at the age of 28, having hit the peak of his career when he won not only the U.S. and British Opens but also the U.S. and British Amateurs, all in the same year. This feat, known as the Grand Slam, has never been repeated.

Throughout his career, Jones maintained amateur status—he never earned a penny playing golf. Then he retired from the game to spend more time with his family and build his law practice. He went on to write golf books and articles, design better clubs, and make instructional movies. But more than anything else, he wanted to design the world's finest golf course near his hometown of Atlanta—a private course where he could play without being mobbed by fans.

Of Course

Jones teamed up with New York banker Clifford Roberts and began to look for property. They wanted land that had a stream, contours, and beauty. As soon as they laid eyes on Fruitlands Nursery, they knew they had found what they were looking for.

Fruitlands was the first commercial nursery in the South, started by a horticulturist named P. J. Berckman. It was a 365-acre farm with trees, flowers, and shrubs imported from all over the world. When Berckman's son, Prosper, died in 1910, the business closed and his heirs began to look for a buyer. The purchase price—at the outset of the Depression—was $70,000. Jones and Roberts bought it.

Work on the golf course began in 1931 and progressed slowly. Each of the holes was named after one of the shrubs or trees that grew there: Pink Dogwood, Juniper, Firethorn, and so on. Jones hit thousands of test shots as the course was being made. He wanted three approaches to each hole: the safe route, the hard route, and the crazy route. It was finally finished in 1933.

The course was so beautiful that the USGA approached Jones with the idea of holding a tournament there, but he declined, feeling that if there were to be a tournament on his course, he should host it. So that's what he did. He held his first tournament in 1934, calling it the Augusta National Invitation Tournament. People came from 38 states to watch golfers compete for a $1,500 purse, and every hotel room in the town of Augusta, population 60,000, was full.

Call Me Master

Roberts wanted to call it "The Masters," but Jones thought that sounded presumptuous. Everyone called it The Masters anyway, so in 1939, Jones relented and the title was officially changed. The Masters remains the only major golf tournament to return to the same site every year.

Bobby Jones played in the first 12 tournaments but never won. His best finish was a tie for 13th place, which was at the very first tournament. He never even broke par but continued to participate because his name was a big draw. He died in 1971 at the age of 69.

THE AMERICA'S CUP

Most people think the America's Cup is American. But it isn't . . . or at least it didn't start out that way. In 1851 Prince Albert hosted the Great London Exhibition in order to pay tribute to the technological advances of the day. In conjunction with the event, Queen Victoria invited all nations of the world to participate in a 53-mile yacht race around the Isle of Wight. The prize was a trophy made of 134 ounces of pure silver.

Over a dozen British vessels entered the race . . . and one American boat, called the *America*. Owner John Cox Stevens was certain he was going to win. And he did—by a wide margin. The trophy, then called the One Hundred Guinea Cup, was awarded to Stevens and his crew. He considered having it melted down and cast into medals, but instead he donated it to the New York Yacht Club in 1857, with the stipulation that it be awarded to

Big blisters are called vesicles, small ones are called bullae.

winners of an international boat race. The trophy and the race were named after the boat, and the America's Cup was born.

The Streak

The race is held approximately once every three years. Americans sailing under the New York Yacht Club flag have won the trophy 25 times in a row over 126 years—the longest winning streak in sports. It wasn't until 1983 that an Australian entry took the trophy away from the United States.

The *America* sailed in 51 subsequent races under various owners but entered only one America's Cup event, where it placed fourth out of 15. In 1921 it was sold to the U.S. Navy and placed in storage in Annapolis, where it suffered years of neglect and decay. In 1942 the roof of the storage shed collapsed under heavy snow, crushing the famous boat. Some of the original wood was salvaged from the ship and used to create a replica, which is now on display at the Naval Academy museum.

WIMBLEDON

Believe it or not, croquet was once considered a serious sport. The All England Croquet Club was founded in 1868, but by 1875 was suffering from a drop in membership because more people were playing a new sport: lawn tennis. So to increase revenue, they removed a croquet lawn and installed a tennis court. Then they changed their name to the All England Lawn Tennis and Croquet Club.

That same year, the club needed to purchase a new roller to care for the lawns, and it was expensive. To raise money, they decided to hold a tournament. An ad placed in the *Times* solicited entries, and *The Field* magazine was persuaded to donate a trophy. Twenty-two people entered the first tournament—men only—and 200 people paid a shilling apiece to watch, more than enough to cover the cost of the lawn roller.

Tennis, Anyone?

The club decided to hold a tournament every year, and every year it grew bigger. Named after the section of London where it was held, Wimbledon quickly became the most important championship event in the world of tennis. By 1884 women were allowed to compete; men's doubles were added that year as well. Mixed doubles were added in 1913.

President Jimmy Carter claims he was once attacked by a rabbit that swam up to his boat.

May Sutten of the United States became the first non-Brit to win, claiming the title in both 1905 and 1907; since then, only two players from Great Britain have won. In 1922 Wimbledon moved to a new site and built a stadium big enough to seat 14,000 with standing room for thousands more. In 1932 the two-week event drew 200,000 fans, despite the worldwide economic depression. During World War II, the grounds were used for military purposes. After the war, when air travel became feasible, international participation soared. However, Wimbledon was open only to amateur players.

Change Brings Change

In 1967 the BBC sponsored a tennis tournament for professional players to publicize its move from black-and-white to color broadcasting. The organizers of Wimbledon watched as many of their champions appeared on national TV, attracting media attention and winning huge purses. The following year, Wimbledon was opened to all players—amateur and professional. Today there are 34 courts located on 42 acres. Attendance approaches half a million, and the prize money given out each year tops $12 million.

THE KENTUCKY DERBY

Edward Smith Stanley, 12th Earl of Derby, was good friends with Sir Charles Bunbury. Both enjoyed breeding horses. Together they founded a new horse race in 1780, a one-mile test of three-year-old thoroughbreds near Derby's country estate in Epsom, England. But before the first race could be held, it had to be named. Which founder should the race be named after—Bunbury or Derby? They flipped a coin, and that's how the word *derby* came to mean a horse race.

In Kentucky, horses flourished on bluegrass pastures that grew from Russian seed brought by immigrants. Because of this, the state became one of the most important thoroughbred breeding centers in the United States, and horse racing became a popular pastime. In 1832 the town fathers of Louisville, Kentucky, bought land from a local family, the Churchills, and built a racetrack.

But the track was too far from town to attract crowds and had to compete against other area tracks that were much more popular. Racing floundered there until the arrival of Meriwether Lewis

---

Acne treatment, circa 350 A.D.: wipe pimples with a cloth while watching a falling star.

Clark Jr. "Lutie" Clark was the grandson of explorer William Clark and a member of the same Churchill family on whose property Louisville's racetrack was located.

After a trip to Europe in 1873, where he studied the layout of the Epsom Downs Derby, Lutie was full of ideas of how to improve racing in Louisville and how to eliminate bookmaking by using the French *pari-mutuel* wagering machines. (Pari-mutuel betting is a system where the winners divide the total amount bet, in proportion to the amount they wagered individually. The odds change according to what people wager, and there is less chance of manipulation than with other systems.)

And . . . They're Off!

With financial backing from his family, Clark leased 80 acres from his Churchill uncles, oversaw construction of a new grandstand and track, sold stock in the venture, and organized the betting. The track—dubbed the Louisville Jockey Club Course—opened on May 17, 1875. Although there were far more important races being run in Kentucky that day, the success of the new track was assured when a horse named Aristides set a new world record for the mile-and-a-half run. The crowd went wild. The Kentucky Derby was born.

In spite of his success, Lutie Clark's quick temper and irascible nature made him quite unpopular. His wife and children left him, and the Churchill family cut him out of the will, leaving him only a few acres of property and a job as overseer of the racetrack. People stopped calling it the Louisville Jockey Club and started calling it Churchill Downs as an insult, to remind Clark who held the purse strings. He committed suicide in 1899.

Back from the Brink

By 1902 the Derby was on the verge of bankruptcy. Then Matt Winn became the manager. Winn had a gift for publicity and promotion, which he used to rebuild the legacy. He hired John Philip Sousa's band to entertain. He had two airplanes shipped in for races—and they made the first recorded flights in the state of Kentucky. During World War I, he pledged 10 percent of track profits to the Red Cross. During the potato shortage of 1918, he turned the entire infield into a huge potato patch. During World War II, he invited the Army to use the infield for public demon-

Russia's Lake Baikal is deep enough to hold four Empire State Buildings stacked atop each other.

strations of the new Sherman tanks. He even invited the State Fair to hold the event in the grounds.

Winn improved the grandstand seating and built a clubhouse. He courted the press. He courted radio broadcasters. He courted movie stars. Business increased, public opinion changed, and revenues skyrocketed. Because of Matt Winn, the Kentucky Derby became an international event. He ran it until his death in 1949.

Today, the Kentucky Derby is one of the world's best-known races. It's been run every May since 1875. Over 100,000 people come to view the race, and millions more watch it on TV.

THE INDIANAPOLIS 500

Around the turn of the 20th century, automobiles were a new and wondrous invention. And Detroit was emerging as the car capital of the world.

Carl Fisher was a businessman in Indianapolis. He made a fortune selling Prest-O-Lite acetylene-powered headlights. In 1909 he sold his business to Union Carbide for millions—just before the invention of car batteries made Prest-O-Lites obsolete.

Fisher wanted to build something with his money, and he decided that what Indianapolis needed was a racetrack for automobiles. In those days, roads were little more than trails and it was difficult to find a place where a driver could really "open 'er up." A racetrack would also give car manufacturers a place to test their new models and pit them against each other. It would put Indianapolis on the map.

Full Speed Ahead

Fisher set up a consortium, elected himself president, and bought 328 acres of countryside for $72,000. He hired an army of 400 workers who moved, on average, 1,500 square yards of dirt every 10 hours to build the two-and-a-half-mile track.

The track itself was made of crushed stone covered by 300,000 gallons of asphalt oil. Turns were banked to handle speeds up to 70 mph. The track was lighted, naturally, with Prest-O-Lite gas. But the best part was that here, the spectators could watch an entire race from start to finish. Fisher called it the Indianapolis Motor Speedway.

The first race on the new track was held August 19–21, 1909.

More words start with the letter *s* than any other letter.

Ten thousand people showed up. On the first day, there was a crash when a tire flew off due to loose lug nuts. The two men in the car were killed. On the second day, everything went well, but the third day, on the final race, a tire blew out and the car spun out of control and crashed into the crowd. The mechanic and two spectators were killed. The race continued, but then another car skidded out of control because the road surface was crumbling under the onslaught. The car slammed into a bridge, injuring the driver. Officials stepped in and stopped the race.

Papers Blast Fisher's Folly

Editorial headlines across the nation blared "Slaughter as a Spectacle" and "Commercial Murder." Protests were mounted. Petitions were circulated. Prohibitions were called for. The Indianapolis Motor Speedway became known as "Fisher's Folly."

But Fisher was not a man to give up easily. First he installed guardrails. Then he decided that the gravel-and-asphalt surface was to blame. He replaced it with bricks—3,200,000 of them—and the Indianapolis Motor Speedway became known as the Brickyard. Still, with other racetracks being built in cities like Chicago and Atlanta, business began to fall off. To promote his Speedway, Fisher announced that in 1911, the best American cars would go up against the best European cars for a purse of $25,000. The race would be 500 miles long and was called the Indianapolis Motor Speedway 500-Mile International Sweepstakes. The Indy 500 was born.

What Comes Around Goes Around

The Indy 500 has been run almost every year since 1911, closed only during the two world wars. It's now the oldest auto race in the world, and the Speedway is the largest spectator-sport facility in the world, with over 250,000 permanent seats. The purse is now around $9 million. In 2000, the Indy 500 placed first among televised motorsports events and generated over $100 million in sponsorship exposure. Besides the Indianapolis 500, the Speedway also hosts the Brickyard 400 and the United States Grand Prix.

Carl Fisher died in Miami in 1939 at the age of 65, but his dream lives on.

* * *

"Without music, life would be a mistake." **—Nietzsche**

Babies are born without kneecaps.

THE HISTORY OF FOOTBALL, PART VI

Here's a football trivia question: After football was invented in 1880, how much time passed before somebody figured out how to throw a spiral pass? Answer: 25 years. Hard to believe, but true. Here's the story.

CLEANING UP THEIR ACT

When the Intercollegiate Athletic Association met in January 1906, it instituted a number of reforms that they hoped would change the way football was played:

- The reforms cut the length of the game from 70 minutes to 60, dividing the game into two 30-minute halves; and they made it illegal for one player to hurdle over another.

- They required a minimum of six men on the offensive line of scrimmage, which made it difficult to use mass formations like the flying wedge.

- They created a "neutral zone" on the line of scrimmage: Instead of the line of scrimmage being drawn through the center of the ball, players now lined up along either side of the ball, and were not allowed to step into the neutral zone in between until the ball went into play. This was intended to reduce the bare-knuckled brawling that routinely broke out when opposing players lined up toe-to-toe; sometimes it took as long as 20 minutes to pull fighting players apart and resume the game.

- They raised the number of yards needed for a first down from 5 to 10.

LOOKING FORWARD

But the most important change of all: In 1906 the Association legalized the forward pass, largely on the suggestion of Georgia Institute of Technology coach John Heisman.

Heisman had witnessed his first forward pass while watching the North Carolina Tar Heels play against the Georgia Tech Yellow Jackets in 1895. The score was tied, 0–0, late in the game,

---

Experts say that most common phobia in the U.S. is arachnophobia—fear of spiders.

and the Tar Heels were losing ground. On the next down, the Carolina fullback ran behind his scrimmage line hoping to find a place to punt. No luck—there was no room to punt, so he just hurled the ball downfield in desperation; one of his teammates happened to catch it and ran 70 yards for a touchdown, winning the game.

The move was illegal, and the Yellow Jackets' coach demanded that the touchdown be tossed out. But the referee let football's first touchdown pass stand—because he hadn't actually seen it.

I'LL PASS

As concerns over increasing football violence mounted in the decade that followed, Heisman saw the forward pass as a means of cleaning up the game. He figured that if players could throw the ball over and past mass formations, defending players would have no choice but to spread themselves out across the football field, and mass plays would become obsolete. But he didn't get his way until 1906, when Yale's Walter Camp was finally shoved aside.

At first the forward pass was restricted: If a quarterback wanted to throw a pass, he had to move at least five yards to the left or right of center before throwing. To make officiating easier, football fields were marked with lengthwise stripes five yards apart, changing their appearance from a gridiron to a checkerboard.

If the ball hit the ground or was touched by an interior lineman before it was caught, possession of the ball went to the other team. If the receiver touched the ball but was not able to catch it, it became a free ball. All the defending team had to do to get possession was knock the receiver down or shove him out of the way so that he couldn't catch a forward pass.

TOSS-UP

Making matters worse was the fact that nobody really knew how to throw a football. Some players threw it sidearm; others threw it underhand like a softball or even with both hands, like a medicine ball. Whichever way they were thrown, underhand passes were inaccurate, and the odds of successfully catching them were slim.

Few football coaches thought forward passes were worth the risk, least of all the established football powers in the Northeast. Mass plays had always worked in the past, and they saw no need to

---

Fill your bathtub with water 20,000 times. That much water falls over Niagara Falls every second.

fix something that wasn't broken, no matter what the reformers thought. As a result, it was the less-established football programs in the Midwest and West—with little or nothing to lose—who were the first to become proficient in the use of the forward pass.

FARM TEAM

One of the first such schools was St. Louis University. In the summer of 1906, coach Eddie Cochems took his team out into the countryside near Lake Beulah, Wisconsin, where they experimented with the move for more than two months.

Back then footballs were nicknamed "blimps"—they were chubbier than they are today—and Cochems had to figure out how best to hold and throw the ball. He instructed his players to grab the ball near the two lacings closest to the end, where it was narrowest, and to throw it overhand with a twist, as if they were pitching a fastball, so that the ball would rotate on its long axis.

Within an hour his players were throwing perfect spirals 40 yards downfield, and in the season that followed, St. Louis won every game it played, scoring a total of 402 points against opponents and yielding only 11. But the Eastern football powers did not take the teams of the West seriously and continued playing football as they always had.

MORE TO COME

Football was growing rapidly, and so were the number of injuries and deaths. In 1909, 33 people died playing football, and 246 more were seriously injured. The NCAA pushed through another round of reforms in 1910:

- They outlawed aiding the ball carrier by pushing or pulling him down the field, and they also banned "interlocked interference"—teammates grabbing onto one another to execute mass plays.

- They increased the number of players on the offensive line of scrimmage from six to seven, further discouraging mass plays.

- Flying tackles were banned, and defensive players were forbidden to interfere with the receiver, other than to catch or block the ball.

- Halves were split into 15-minute quarters, giving tired players a little more time to rest. And for the first time, players who were withdrawn from the game were allowed to return. In the past, players who were taken out had to stay out; as a result, tired players tended to stay in the game rather than take a break, which increased the number of injuries.

- Most importantly, the NCAA lifted some of the restrictions on the forward pass. Now the passer was allowed to throw the ball anytime he was at least 5 yards behind the line of scrimmage (that restriction wasn't removed until 1945), though it was illegal to throw a pass farther than 20 yards. The requirement that he move at least 5 yards left or right of center was removed, and the checkerboard playing field reverted back to the traditional gridiron.

- It was about this time that "head harnesses"—stiff leather caps with ear flaps—began to come into use, as did the first shoulder pads.

ONE MORE ROUND

Two years later, in 1912, the NCAA made some of the last major changes to football. They set the field size at 100 yards long by 53$\frac{1}{3}$ yards wide, moved the kickoff from midfield to the 40-yard line, and created the fourth down.

They also lifted most of the remaining restrictions on forward passes, removing the 20-yard limit and establishing 10-yard "end zones" at either end of the field. For the first time, catching a pass thrown over the goal line counted as a touchdown instead of as a "touchback" that awarded possession of the ball to the defending team on their 20-yard line.

PASS PERFECT

The major football powers remained suspicious of the forward pass even with all of the restrictions removed. That changed in 1913, when Notre Dame coach Jesse Harper wrote a letter to the Army team asking them if they had an opening in their schedule "and if so, would they give us a game." There was an opening on November 1, 1913, so Army invited Notre Dame to come and play at West Point.

Notre Dame's quarterback, Charley Dorais, and left end, Knute Rockne, had spent much of their summer vacation practicing forward passes on the beaches of Lake Erie. "Perfection came to us only through daily, tedious practice," Rockne wrote in 1930.

Notre Dame played three games before meeting Army, racking up 169 points—all from forward passing—and giving up only seven to its opponents. But not many people noticed because the school wasn't a major football power at the time.

No one—least of all the Army team—was prepared for the events at West Point that first day of November. "We went out to play Army like crusaders, believing we represented not only our own school but the whole aspiring Middle West," Rockne remembered. "The Cadet body and most of the other spectators seemed to regard the engagement as a quiet, friendly work-out for the Army."

SNEAK ATTACK

Notre Dame began the first quarter playing a fairly conventional game; its defensive line held against Army, forcing them to kick. When Notre Dame got the ball, Dorais's first attempts at throwing short passes failed; then he told his teammates, "Let's open things up."

The next pass was successful; Dorais only threw it 11 yards, but it so startled Army that they held a huddle to discuss it. Following one particularly rough scrimmage, Rockne started limping as if he'd been hurt, and continued limping through the next three plays, as Notre Dame advanced steadily down to the Army 25-yard line. The normally boisterous crowd was silent as it took in the Midwesterners' new kind of game.

"After that third play," he remembered, "the Army halfback covering me figured I wasn't worth watching. Even as a decoy, he figured I was harmless." On the next play, Dorais signaled that he would throw the next pass to Rockne. Football was about to change forever:

> I started limping down the field, and the Army halfback cover-
> ing me almost yawned in my face, he was that bored. I put on
> full speed and left him standing there flat-footed. I raced across
> the Army goal line as Dorais whipped the ball, and the grand-
> stands roared at the completion of a 40-yard pass. Everybody
> seemed astonished. There had been no hurdling, no tackling, no
> plunging, no crushing of fiber and sinew. At the moment when I
> touched the ball, life for me was complete.

A WHOLE NEW BALL GAME

Notre Dame went on to complete 14 out of 17 passes, gaining 243 yards and scoring five touchdowns in the process, beating Army 35–13. The potential of the forward pass was laid out for everyone to see: A team that few people had heard of had come roaring out of the Midwest to humble a major Eastern football power, master of the old-style game, on their own home field.

"Goliath," Tom Perrin writes in *Football: A College History*, "learned again what a missile can do in the hands of David."

With the arrival of the forward pass, all the major elements of modern football were in place. Very little has changed in the game since then, except for the advent of pro football and the NFL . . . but that's another story.

* * *

THE GOOD OLD DAYS

"There was no bad blood between [Yale and Princeton], but . . . in the very first scrimmage it became apparent that the practice of turning one cheek when the other is smitten is not to be entertained for a moment. As the game progressed, this fact became more potent. The eye of the umpire was the only thing they feared, and when his attention was diverted the surreptitious punches, gouges, and kicks were frequent and damaging . . . The favorite methods of damaging an opponent were to stamp on his feet, to kick his shins, to give him a dainty upper cut, and to gouge his face in tackling."

—*The New York Times,* **describing the national championship game between Yale and Princeton in 1888**

LET'S PLAY MAYA BALL

"Among the Maya the ball game was related to fertility, the sun, warfare, and sacrifice by decapitation. A high-ranking captive might be forced to play a game in which he might lose his head. Courts were often built against staircases. In some well-documented instances, the loser in the game was taken to the top, bound up to form a ball, and rolled down the stairs to his death."

—*The Aztecs, Maya, and Their Predecessors,* **by Muriel Porter Weaver**

An average American 7-year-old watches 20,000 commercials a year—about 55 every day.

THE BACK SIDE

You're not done yet.

Here are the answers to the quizzes and
puzzles found on the preceding pages.

TEST YOUR EGG I.Q.
(answers for page 36)

1. c) Egg shells are porous—as an egg ages, moisture escapes and is replaced by outside air, causing it to become more buoyant over time. Fresh eggs contain the least air and sit right at the bottom of the glass; older eggs are lighter and tend to "stand" at the bottom. Rotten eggs contain so much air that they float right to the top.

2. c) Also known as "chalazae cords," these strands connect the yolk to the ends of the eggshell; the resulting "tug-of-war" helps to reduce movement and keep the yolk centered inside the egg.

3. b) Grade A and AA are the Food and Drug Administration's two highest egg classifications. They have nothing to do with the size, freshness, or vitamin content of the egg—they indicate the quality of the egg white and yolk. Grade AA eggs, slightly higher in quality, have the plumpest yolks and the thickest whites.

4. b) There's a pocket of air in the larger end of the egg and it's the most likely source of contamination from foreign bacteria. Storing the egg with the tapered end pointing down causes the yolk—which is more perishable than the white—to settle toward the tapered end, as far away from the air pocket as possible. When the egg is stored with the tapered end up, the yolk can settle right on top of the pocket, potentially speeding the rate at which the egg will spoil.

5. a) Raw eggs wobble because the white and yolk are still fluid and move around inside the egg when you spin it. Cooked eggs are at least partially solidified and have a much smoother spin.

THE RIDDLER
(answers for page 75)

1. Wet
2. Hi Bud

The smell in your right nostril is more pleasant, but your left side is more accurate.

3. A telephone

4. Holds up the other one

5. A dead bird

6. Post office

7. A glove

8. None. It was Noah who brought them, not Moses.

9. A hole

10. Noise

11. A river

12. The outside

13. The letter T

14. Nine

15. A date

16. Mash them

17. A scale

18. Silence

19. Night and day

BRI BRAINTEASERS

(answers for page 166)

1. One hour. Windup clocks don't have A.M./P.M. settings.

2. He could, but he would be pretty uncomfortable being buried alive.

3. The match.

4. They've got different partners.

5. A 50-cent piece and a nickel. (Only one of them is not a nickel.)

6. The Earth is always under you, so you are eating over dirt?

7. His new computer/word processor is a pencil.

8. Nine.

For only $1,650, you can buy a pen embedded with Abraham Lincoln's "genetic essence."

9. He's the town minister.

10. One hour.

11. One. If he combines all of his haystacks, they all become one big stack.

POLITICALLY CORRECT QUIZ
(answers for page 230)

1. c) Demaret is the mother of David Vetter, a boy who suffered from a disease called "severe combined immunodeficiency" and died in 1984 at the age of 12. "The notion of making a comedy about a life-threatening disease is, in and of itself, a travesty," she writes. "It dishonors the memory of my son David and is an insult to families and children who are born with his disease and died from it."

Counters a Disney spokesman, "The bubble is a setup for a road-trip comedy. It doesn't make fun of immune deficiencies."

2. b) Public servants who gossip face reprimands, sensitivity training, and even dismissal if they refuse to stop. Council member Alcebiades Pereira da Silva says he drafted the law to stop incoming administrations from using gossip to persecute workers from previous administrations.

3. b) "It's a common mistake," says High Priest Kevin Carlyon. "Even the TV series *Bewitched* showed broomsticks being ridden backwards, but this is not correct."

4. a) They want to outlaw the cramped "gestation crates" used to house pregnant pigs. According to Floridians for Humane Farms, "Pigs confined in gestation crates experience chronic stress, frustration, depression, and other psychological disorders."

5. a) Willand also told students that Pocahontas "did handsprings in the nude." But the poster and the Pocahontas trivia "weren't meant to be offensive, they were just meant to perk attention." The school forbade Willand from using "phraseology which does not manifest a clear concern for student

---

Got insomnia? Some experts suggest wearing mittens and socks to bed.

sensibilities." He's suing, alleging that the reprimand was "unjust."

6. b) "The website should be corrected," says Mangal Prabhat Lodha, a state legislator who says the cat's name is an insult. "We are not asking for a renaming. We just want mention of the cat to be removed from the website."

7. c) The group wants to replace "all thy sons" with "all of us" or "all our hearts." Protestor Frances Wright explains, "Parents of children in Canada don't call their girl children 'sons.'"

8. a) After studying corked and capped wines over a period of 24 months, the Institute found that metal screwcaps do a better job of helping white wine retain its sulfur dioxide, which protects against oxidation. "Up to this point, in retaining freshness and overall aroma, a screwcap has performed better," says a spokes-man. The Institute plans to continue the study over 10 years.

THE NAME GAME
(answers for page 291)

1. GEORGE. "Farmer" from the Greek *georgos* "earth worker," which was derived from the elements *ge*, "earth," and *ergon*, "work."

2. AMY. "Beloved" from Old French *aimée*.

3. MICHAEL. From the Hebrew name *Mikha'el*, meaning "who is like God."

4. BARBARA. "Foreign" from the Greek *barbaros*.

5. DANIEL. "God is my judge" from the Hebrew name *Daniyel*.

6. EDWARD. "Rich guard" from the Old English *ead*, "rich, blessed," and *weard*, "guard."

7. AMANDA. "Lovable" from Latin *amanda*. This name was created in the 17th century by the playwright Colley Cibber.

8. HENRY. "Ruler of the Home" from the Germanic *Heimerich*, which came from the elements *heim*, "home," and *ric*, "power" or "ruler."

The Loch Ness monster is a $50 million-a-year business in Scotland.

9. **JOEL.** "YAHWEH is God," from the Hebrew name *Yoel*. Joel was a minor prophet in the Old Testament. YAHWEH is the name of the Hebrew God, represented in Hebrew by the "four letters" *Yod He Waw He*, and written in Roman script as *YHWH*. Because it was considered blasphemous to utter the name of God it was only written and never spoken, so the original pronunciation was lost.

10. **SUSAN.** From the Hebrew word *shoshan*, meaning "lily." In modern Hebrew, it also means "rose."

11. **LINDA.** "Beautiful" from the Spanish *Linda*

12. **MELISSA.** "Bee" from the Greek.

13. **ANN.** "Grace" from the French and German forms of *Hannah*.

14. **ROBERT.** "Bright fame" from Germanic *hrod*, "fame," and *beraht*, "bright."

15. **STEPHEN.** "Crown" from the Greek *stephanos*.

16. **JOHN.** English form of *Johannes*, the Latin form of the Greek name *Ioannes*, itself derived from the Hebrew name *Yochanan*, meaning "YAHWEH is gracious."

THE FOOD QUIZ
(answers for page 317)

1. **a)** Light cream is heavier. "Heavy" and "light" refer to the fat content, not the weight. Heavy cream contains a higher percentage of milk fat (36 percent) than light cream (15 percent to 18 percent), but since fat is lighter than water—the other major component of cream— increasing the percentage of fat reduces the percentage of water, lowering the overall weight.

2. **c)** The air in a jet plane in flight is lower in pressure and less humid than what most people are used to, which affects the way food tastes. The low pressure impairs the passengers' sense of taste by reducing the volatility of the molecules that give food its odor and taste. Low humidity causes people to become dehydrated, especially if they've been drinking alcohol or coffee—both are diuretics that cause your body to eliminate water. So it's not unusual for an airline to add extra

There are 290,000 different beetle species on earth, the most of any animal.

seasoning, with the exception of salt, which would further increase the body's need for water.

3. c) The oils that irritate your eyes when you chop an onion have the same effect on your tastebuds and your sense of smell: they irritate your taste and smell receptors slightly, and in this "raw" state the receptors are more sensitive than they would be otherwise.

4. a) Air is whipped into ice cream as part of the manufacturing process, and it's not uncommon for manufacturers of cheaper brands to whip extra air into their ice cream, reducing the amount of actual ice cream in the container and lowering its weight. So if you want to try a new brand of ice cream but aren't sure how good it is, compare its weight to the same size container of a brand you're familiar with. If the unfamiliar brand weighs as much or more, it's likely to be similar or even better in quality.

5. b) Botanists consider only the "ovary" of a plant—the part that contains the seeds—to be the fruit; so technically speaking, pumpkins, tomatoes, cucumbers, peas, and even corn are all considered fruit. Any other part of a plant that is edible—the leaf, root, stem, and so on—is considered a vegetable.

6. a) It's true—apple seeds contain trace amounts of cyanide, as do apricot and peach seeds. But the amount of cyanide in a single apple seed is so small that it would take hundreds of seeds to amount to a lethal dose. And even if you ate that many seeds you'd probably survive unharmed, because the husk of an apple seed is so hard it's indigestible, even if it's been cooked. The apple seeds—and the cyanide they contain—would pass through your body completely intact.

7. b) Many people incorrectly believe that freezing food more than once makes it unsafe to eat. This myth dates back to the late 1920s, when frozen food pioneer Clarence Birdseye stamped the words "DO NOT FREEZE" on his packages of frozen foods. He feared that if people mishandled his products by repeatedly thawing and refreezing them, they'd blame the resulting poor quality on his company, which might harm sales. Some people mistakenly interpreted Birdseye's warning to mean that refreezing food is dangerous.

State with the most thunderstorms and lightning? The "sunshine state"—Florida.

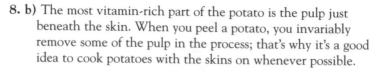

8. b) The most vitamin-rich part of the potato is the pulp just beneath the skin. When you peel a potato, you invariably remove some of the pulp in the process; that's why it's a good idea to cook potatoes with the skins on whenever possible.

9. c) Coffee beans from the port of Mocha in southwestern Yemen had lots of acid but not much flavor; beans from the port of Java in Indonesia had lots of flavor but not much acid. A well-rounded cup of coffee requires both acid *and* flavor, and it even-tually occurred to people that blending the two types of beans would result in a better-tasting cup of coffee than was possible with Mocha or Java beans alone.

10. b) Marinades usually contain acids that tenderize meat. But in the process of tenderizing, they also degrade its ability to retain moisture, which makes the meat drier when cooked. So why bother marinating meat in the first place? It's a tradeoff—the tenderness and the flavor obtained by marinating the meat more than makes up for the loss of moisture . . . at least according to people who like marinades.

WHERE'D THEY GET THAT NAME?

(answers for page 447)

1. b) "The English town Boston has a name that is popularly understood to mean 'Botolphs's stone' on the grounds that the town's main church is dedicated to St. Botolph."

—*Place Names of the World*, Adrian Room

2. a) "In 1721, French travelers explored a section of the Louisiana Territory along the Arkansas River . . . searching for leg-endary treasure. For a long time, the Native Americans had spoken of a 'green rock' that was upstream at the 'point of rocks' along the river. When the French heard about this green rock, they thought it could ony mean emeralds, which is why the expedition began.

The explorers found the point of rocks, which they called Grand Rock. Farther down the stream on the south bank,

Q: What city is next to New Delhi? A: Old Delhi.

they found a smaller rock, which they named Little Rock. About a hundred years later, a permanent settlement grew up at Little Rock."

—*Why Do They Call It Topeka?*, John W. Pursell

3. b) "Idaho is believed to have gotten its name from a Shoshone phrase, Ee-dah-how, translated loosely as 'Look, the sun is coming down the mountain.'

"However, some believe the name was coined by lobbyist George M. Willing, who merely claimed it was a Native American word, which he translated as 'gem of the mountains.'"

—*Why Do They Call It Topeka?*, John W. Pursell

4. a) Hong Kong comes from the Chinese xianggang—xiang (hong) meaning fragrant, gang (kong) meaning harbor. It probably refers to the smell of ships carrying opium or to the incense trade which was important to the development of the port.

5. b) Kalamazoo derives from the Algonquin word kee-ke-la-ma-zoo, which either means "he who smokes," "boiling water," or "beautiful water." It probably refers to the rapids on the Kalamazoo River.

6. b) "French explorer Pierre LeMoyne d'Iberville came upon a red post—a baton rouge in his native language—while mapping the Mississppi Valley in 1699. The post marked the boundry between two Indian nations, the Bayogoulas and the Houmas."

—*A Place Called Peculiar*, Frank K. Gallant

7. a) "The former island in southern Brooklyn, was known as Konihn Eiland, 'rabbit island,' and the present name is a corrupt English form of this."

—*Place Names of the World*, Adrian Room

8. a) "Spanish for 'pelican,' the name was given in 1775 because of the number of such birds there."

—*American Place Names*, John W. Pursell

9. c) "The state capital of Kansas derives its name from a Sioux word said to mean 'good place to grow potatoes.'"

—*Place Names of the World*, Adrian Room

Q: What 5-letter word is pronounced the same when the last four letters are removed? A: Queue.

10. b) "Derives from the Spanish for 'rat's mouth,' referring to the sharply pointed rocks off the coast that were a danger to shipping."

—*Place Names of the World,* Adrian Room

11. c) "The local Indian tribes took their names from the cascades that ran through their region. They called the rapidly flowing stream, 'Walla Walla,' meaning 'little swift river.'"

—*The Naming of America,* Allen Wolk

MORE BRAINTEASERS

(answers for page 489)

1. The four were musicians, hired to play music during dinner.

2. Your name.

3. The French diplomats are husband and wife, both blind from birth.

4. Your right elbow.

5. I-n-c-o-r-r-e-c-t-l-y.

6. A dentist.

7. Nothing!

8. You ask either of them, "If I asked your twin which road to take to get to the hospital, which way would he tell me to go?" And then you would take the other road.

   Why? If the truth-telling twin tells you what his twin would say, it would be a lie, so the direction indicated would be wrong. The lying twin would lie about what his twin would say, which would be the truth, so the lying twin would also indicate the wrong path.

9. A coffin.

More paintings by Pablo Picasso have sold for over $1 million than any other painter—232.

ANOTHER POLITICALLY CORRECT QUIZ

(answers for page 571)

1. a) The conductor offered a compromise: the ending would be changed so that the wolf is released into the wild instead of taken to a zoo, but the cellist refused the offer. "Peter and the Wolf, which teaches children to hate and fear wolves and to applaud a hunter who kills wolves, will be performed despite my protest," Conrad-Antoville wrote in a letter explaining her resignation. "I urge parents to boycott this concert."

2. a) Dogs in the park where the statue was schedule to be unveiled are required to be on a leash at all times. "I've always intended to have a leash," the artist explained after the controversy erupted, "because a man wouldn't sit on a park bench with a dog without having a leash on it. The dog wouldn't stay there. He'd probably be off chasing birds."

3. b) No comment.

4. b) What can we say?

5. c) And the opening line of the Lord's Prayer is changed to "Our Father-Mother in Heaven."

6. b) It was "commercially correct." They didn't want to offend florists who might be buying ads. Their rationale, however, was their own brand of political correctness: Please Omit Flowers "urges a boycott, just like 'don't buy grapes,' and we don't permit that," said a spokesman for the Press.

7. a) "I don't like that term at all," Franklin told the Johnstown, Pa., Tribune-Democrat. I don't consider myself a serial killer. If I'm a serial killer, then King David was a serial killer. So was Samson. I would classify myself as just a killer."

8. a) No details available.

Highest town in the United States: Climax, Colorado, at 11,302 feet above sea level.

THE LAST PAGE

U NCLE JOHN'S CREDO
"Fellow bathroom readers, the fight for good bathroom reading should never be taken loosely—we must do our duty and sit firmly for what we believe in . . . even while the rest of the world is taking pot shots at us."

We'll be brief: Now that we've proven we're not simply a flush-in-the-pan, we invite you to take the plunge. Sit down and be counted! Become a member of the Bathroom Readers' Institute. Log on to *www.bathroomreader.com*, or send a self-addressed, stamped, business-sized envelope to BRI, PO Box 1117, Ashland, Oregon 97520. You'll receive your free membership card, get discounts when ordering directly through the BRI, and earn a permanent spot on the BRI honor roll!

If you like reading our books . . .
VISIT THE BRI'S WEB SITE!
www.bathroomreader.com

- Visit "The Throne Room"—a great place to read!
  - Receive our irregular newsletters via e-mail
    - Order additional *Bathroom Readers*
      - Become a BRI member

Go with the Flow...

Oops! We're all out of space, and when you've gotta go, well, you've just gotta go. Tanks for your support. Hope to hear from you soon. And always remember . . .

Keep on flushin'!